studies in jazz

The Institute of Jazz Studies
Rutgers—The State University of New Jersey
General Editors: Dan Morgenstern and Edward Berger

1. BENNY CARTER: A Life in American Music, *by Morroe Berger, Edward Berger, and James Patrick, 2 vols., 1982*
2. ART TATUM: A Guide to His Recorded Music, *by Arnold Laubich and Ray Spencer, 1982*
3. ERROLL GARNER: The Most Happy Piano, *by James M. Doran, 1985*
4. JAMES P. JOHNSON: A Case of Mistaken Identity, *by Scott E. Brown;* Discography 1917–1950, *by Robert Hilbert, 1986*
5. PEE WEE ERWIN: This Horn for Hire, *as told to Warren W. Vaché Sr., 1987*
6. BENNY GOODMAN: Listen to His Legacy, *by D. Russell Connor, 1988*
7. ELLINGTONIA: The Recorded Music of Duke Ellington and His Sidemen, *by W. E. Timner, 1988; 4th ed., 1996*
8. THE GLENN MILLER ARMY AIR FORCE BAND: Sustineo Alas / I Sustain the Wings, *by Edward F. Polic; Foreword by George T. Simon, 1989*
9. SWING LEGACY, *by Chip Deffaa, 1989*
10. REMINISCING IN TEMPO: The Life and Times of a Jazz Hustler, *by Teddy Reig, with Edward Berger, 1990*
11. IN THE MAINSTREAM: 18 Portraits in Jazz, *by Chip Deffaa, 1992*
12. BUDDY DeFRANCO: A Biographical Portrait and Discography, *by John Kuehn and Arne Astrup, 1993*
13. PEE WEE SPEAKS: A Discography of Pee Wee Russell, *by Robert Hilbert, with David Niven, 1992*
14. SYLVESTER AHOLA: The Gloucester Gabriel, *by Dick Hill, 1993*
15. THE POLICE CARD DISCORD, *by Maxwell T. Cohen, 1993*
16. TRADITIONALISTS AND REVIVALISTS IN JAZZ, *by Chip Deffaa, 1993*
17. BASSICALLY SPEAKING: An Oral History of George Duvivier, *by Edward Berger;* Musical Analysis *by David Chevan, 1993*
18. TRAM: The Frank Trumbauer Story, *by Philip R. Evans and Larry F. Kiner, with William Trumbauer, 1994*
19. TOMMY DORSEY: On the Side, *by Robert L. Stockdale, 1995*
20. JOHN COLTRANE: A Discography and Musical Biography, *by Yasuhiro Fujioka, with Lewis Porter and Yoh-ichi Hamada, 1995*

21. RED HEAD: A Chronological Survey of "Red" Nichols and His Five Pennies, by Stephen M. Stroff, 1996
22. THE RED NICHOLS STORY: After Intermission 1942–1965, by Philip R. Evans, Stanley Hester, Stephen Hester, and Linda Evans, 1997
23. BENNY GOODMAN: Wrappin' It Up, by D. Russell Connor, 1996
24. CHARLIE PARKER AND THEMATIC IMPROVISATION, by Henry Martin, 1996
25. BACK BEATS AND RIM SHOTS: The Johnny Blowers Story, by Warren W. Vaché Sr., 1997
26. DUKE ELLINGTON: A Listener's Guide, by Eddie Lambert, 1998
27. SERGE CHALOFF: A Musical Biography and Discography, by Vladimir Simosko, 1998
28. HOT JAZZ: From Harlem to Storyville, by David Griffiths, 1998
29. ARTIE SHAW: A Musical Biography and Discography, by Vladimir Simosko, 2000
30. JIMMY DORSEY: A Study in Contrasts, by Robert L. Stockdale, 1998
31. STRIDE!: Fats, Jimmy, Lion, Lamb and All the Other Ticklers, by John L. Fell and Terkild Vinding, 1999
32. GIANT STRIDES: The Legacy of Dick Wellstood, by Edward N. Meyer, 1999
33. JAZZ GENTRY: Aristocrats of the Music World, by Warren W. Vaché Sr., 1999
34. THE UNSUNG SONGWRITERS: America's Masters of Melody, by Warren W. Vaché Sr., 2000
35. THE MUSICAL WORLD OF J. J. JOHNSON, by Joshua Berrett and Louis G. Bourgois III, 1999
36. THE LADIES WHO SING WITH THE BAND, by Betty Bennett, 2000
37. AN UNSUNG CAT: The Life and Music of Warne Marsh, by Safford Chamberlain, 2000
38. JAZZ IN NEW ORLEANS: The Postwar Years Through 1970, by Charles Suhor, 2001
39. THE YOUNG LOUIS ARMSTRONG ON RECORDS: A Critical Survey of the Early Recordings, 1923–1928, by Edward Brooks, 2002
40. BENNY CARTER: A Life in American Music, Second Edition, by Morroe Berger, Edward Berger, and James Patrick, 2 vols., 2002
41. CHORD CHANGES ON THE CHALKBOARD: How Public School Teachers Shaped Jazz and the Music of New Orleans, by Al Kennedy, Foreword by Ellis Marsalis Jr., 2002
42. CONTEMPORARY CAT: Terence Blanchard with Special Guests, by Anthony Magro, 2002

43. PAUL WHITEMAN: Pioneer in American Music, Volume I: 1890–1930, by Don Rayno, 2003
44. GOOD VIBES: A Life in Jazz, by Terry Gibbs with Cary Ginell, 2003
45. TOM TALBERT—HIS LIFE AND TIMES: Voices from a Vanished World of Jazz, by Bruce Talbot, 2004
46. SITTIN' IN WITH CHRIS GRIFFIN: A Reminiscence of Radio and Recording's Golden Years, by Warren W. Vaché, 2005
47. FIFTIES JAZZ TALK: An Oral Retrospective, by Gordon Jack, 2004
48. FLORENCE MILLS: Harlem Jazz Queen, by Bill Egan, 2004
49. SWING ERA SCRAPBOOK: The Teenage Diaries and Radio Logs of Bob Inman, 1936–1938, by Ken Vail, 2005
50. FATS WALLER ON THE AIR: The Radio Broadcasts and Discography, by Stephen Taylor, 2006
51. ALL OF ME: The Complete Discography of Louis Armstrong, by Jos Willems, 2006
52. MUSIC AND THE CREATIVE SPIRIT: Innovators in Jazz, Improvisation, and the Avant Garde, by Lloyd Peterson, 2006
53. THE STORY OF FAKE BOOKS: Bootlegging Songs to Musicians, by Barry Kernfeld, 2006
54. ELLINGTONIA: The Recorded Music of Duke Ellington and His Sidemen, 5th edition, by W. E. Timner, 2007
55. JAZZ FICTION: A History and Comprehensive Reader's Guide, by David Rife, 2007
56. MISSION IMPOSSIBLE: My Life In Music, by Lalo Schifrin, edited by Richard H. Palmer, 2008
57. THE CONTRADICTIONS OF JAZZ, by Paul Rinzler, 2008
58. EARLY TWENTIETH-CENTURY BRASS IDIOMS: Art, Jazz, and Other Popular Traditions, edited by Howard T. Weiner, 2008
59. THE MUSIC AND LIFE OF THEODORE "FATS" NAVARRO: Infatuation, by Leif Bo Petersen and Theo Rehak, 2009
60. WHERE THE DARK AND THE LIGHT FOLKS MEET: Race and the Mythology, Politics, and Business of Jazz, by Randall Sandke, 2010
61. JAZZ BOOKS IN THE 1990S: An Annotated Bibliography, by Janice Leslie Hochstat Greenberg, 2010
62. BENNY GOODMAN: A Supplemental Discography, by David Jessup, 2010
63. THE LIFE AND MUSIC OF KENNY DAVERN: Just Four Bars, by Edward N. Meyer, 2010

The Life and Music of Kenny Davern

Just Four Bars

Edward N. Meyer

Studies in Jazz, No. 63

THE SCARECROW PRESS, INC.
Lanham • Toronto • Plymouth, UK
2010

Published by Scarecrow Press, Inc.
A wholly owned subsidiary of The Rowman & Littlefield Publishing Group, Inc.
4501 Forbes Boulevard, Suite 200, Lanham, Maryland 20706
http://www.scarecrowpress.com

Estover Road, Plymouth PL6 7PY, United Kingdom

Copyright © 2010 by Edward N. Meyer

All rights reserved. No part of this book may be reproduced in any form or by any electronic or mechanical means, including information storage and retrieval systems, without written permission from the publisher, except by a reviewer who may quote passages in a review.

British Library Cataloguing in Publication Information Available

Library of Congress Cataloging-in-Publication Data

Meyer, Edward N.
  The life and music of Kenny Davern : just four bars / Edward N. Meyer.
    p. cm. — (Studies in jazz ; no. 63)
  Includes bibliographical references and index.
  ISBN 978-0-8108-7692-7 (cloth : alk. paper) — ISBN 978-0-8108-7693-4 (ebook)
  1. Davern, Kenny. 2. Jazz musicians--United States—Biography. I. Title.
  ML419.D386M49 2010
  788.6'2165092—dc22
  [B]
                                                               2010008520

∞ ™ The paper used in this publication meets the minimum requirements of American National Standard for Information Sciences—Permanence of Paper for Printed Library Materials, ANSI/NISO Z39.48-1992.

Printed in the United States of America

Contents

	Series Editor's Foreword	ix
	Introduction and Acknowledgments	xi
Chapter 1	Difficult Beginnings	1
Chapter 2	Apprenticeship	21
Chapter 3	The Band at Nick's	49
Chapter 4	Elsa, Dick, and a Musical Voice	69
Chapter 5	Reversal of Fortune	85
Chapter 6	In the Big Leagues	105
Chapter 7	Soprano Summit	127
Chapter 8	Changes	145
Chapter 9	Out Front	165
Chapter 10	Public Person, Private Man	185
Chapter 11	Too Good to Last	199
Chapter 12	Rebuilding	227
Chapter 13	Summit Reunion	245
Chapter 14	The Arbors Years	271

Chapter 15	Recognition	291
Chapter 16	Change of Place, Change of Pace	313
Chapter 17	Journey's End	327
	The Issued Recordings of Kenny Davern	343
	Selected Bibliography	421
	Index	431
	About the Author	441

Series Editor's Foreword

Two of my closest friends among the many musicians I've had the good fortune to know were Dick Wellstood and Kenny Davern, themselves at times inseparable musical and personal companions. Both left us too soon and without warning, and both are sorely missed. It was Edward Meyer who decided that there should be a biography of Wellstood, and as he stated in his foreword to *Giant Strides* (Volume 32 in this series), he "could not have succeeded . . . without the assistance of Kenny Davern." The two men became friends, and Ed was eager to do Kenny's biography. But characteristically, Kenny was not—he'd opened up about his relationship with Dick, but that was as far as he was prepared to go, at this point in his life. As a friend and fan, Ed was, of course, able to experience and document public events, and he was prepared to bide his time.

Then, suddenly, Kenny was gone. As you will learn from Ed's foreword, it was Elsa Davern, for so many years Kenny's devoted wife and now his widow, who provided the essential information that makes this a book about the man, as well as the artist. Things in his life that Kenny had only hinted at come into focus here and will make his many fans, who were sometimes puzzled by his comments and actions, which could be acerbic, understand him better.

But this is no exposé—Ed is always tactful, and the primary subject is the music. It is rewarding to share how Kenny discovered that vital brand of jazz to the legacy of which he remained so faithful—yet always open to new ways, if they made aesthetic sense to him. He was always absolutely honest in his reactions to music and his playing of it—and to people. I loved to discuss music with Kenny, or rather, listen to what he had to say. We shared certain loves, foremost among them Pee Wee Russell, the musician and the man, but also an affinity for classical music, which Wellstood also had. Kenny and Dick got me so hooked on different versions of a certain passage in the last movement of Mozart's Piano Concerto No. 20, the D Minor masterpiece—the violent orchestral outburst that tests a conductor's sense of drama and time—that by now I own more than twenty. And it was great fun to go classical CD shopping with Kenny, after a concert in Manhattan, when record stores were still fully stocked and open late.

Of course, he convinced me to get something by Wilhelm Furtwangler, his favorite conductor. When I discovered that great love of his (and it was truly that), I presented Kenny with a handwritten postcard from the great man to my maternal grandfather, and it pleased him so much that I was almost embarrassed. He sent me a photo with a warm inscription that I framed and put on my wall. When I came home on the day that Mat Domber, Kenny's dedicated record producer, had called me with the tragic news, there was Kenny smiling at me. He's still there, and this fine book helps to ease the loss of a unique and vital man and artist. Thank you, Ed Meyer. (And after you read about Kenny, listen to his music!)

Without permission, because I couldn't say it better, I'm selfishly transmuting Kenny's epigraph to the Wellstood book: I loved him and still miss him, and am proud to have been his friend.

Dan Morgenstern

Introduction and Acknowledgments

When I interviewed Kenny Davern for my book about Dick Wellstood, I knew that someday I would write Kenny's biography. He was fascinating, far more complex than he appeared at first blush, and too interesting to pass up. I had a lot of useful material about him from my interviews, to which I added information from my collections of books and magazines. The only impediment to the project was Kenny, who steadfastly refused to participate, first because I think that he believed that it was unseemly and second, because it might open some doors that he had closed many years before.

Periodically, I raised the issue with him and, with varying degrees of good humor, he brushed the question aside. There the matter lay until he died. Some time afterward, I was talking to Elsa Davern about the fact that I had wanted to write a biography of Kenny and had even started to work on it. She told me that, after he read the book about Wellstood, Kenny had told her that if anyone were to write a book about him, I could do it. (He never said that to me.) We agreed that she would think about it. I started work, and this is the result.

I could not have done this without Elsa's kindness, help, and support. She gave graciously of her time and memories, and patiently answered my sometimes impertinent questions, even when doing so caused her pain. She opened her home, and allowed me unfettered access to Kenny's voluminous letters and files. She dug through documents and suggested paths of inquiry when I was stymied. I am in her debt.

A number of people whose assistance and friendship was invaluable disrupted their lives to help me. In (reverse) alphabetical order they are: Don Wolff, who was one of Kenny's closest friends. A practicing attorney, jazz historian, radio broadcaster, and fan, Don has the largest collection of video and audio recordings by Kenny, and he shared many of them—and also some fresh and still-painful memories of Kenny—with me at a time when he had far more pressing concerns with which he had to deal.

Al White, whose skill in photographing musicians is unmatched, allowed me to use some of his best. R. Claire Weintraub was untiring in her efforts to track down and read the darkening microfiche copies of the *Long-Islander* newspaper to find articles concerning events in the life of Kenny's father that occurred more than seventy years ago. Mark Weber provided invaluable information on Kenny's years in New Mexico, and allowed me to use the comprehensive and informative interviews that he conducted of Kenny on his radio show. Jack Stine was a trove of facts, often wrapped in well-told, humorous stories. Christian Plattner prepared several short papers dealing with specific areas of Kenny's life, and gave me access to the letters that Kenny wrote to him.

Brian Peerless, who helped me on the Wellstood book, was a friend of Kenny's, promoted his tours of the United Kingdom, wrote liner notes for several of Kenny's CDs, and chronicled Davern's life when he was honored by Arbors Records in 2004. Brian was a mine of information and anecdotes, especially on Kenny's visits to England. Sabine Nagel-Heyer sent me detailed and helpful information about her late husband, Hans Nagel-Heyer, and the start of their record company.

Dan Morgenstern knows more facts about more people, places, and events in music than anyone I know. If I had a question, Dan always had the answer. I cannot adequately thank him for all of his help. Frank Laidlaw patiently helped me to understand the mysteries of the clarinet and the manner in which it could be played. Mat Domber not only shared his memories with me, but also gave me access to recordings and other material that were not available to the public.

Loretta and Joe DiBenedetto have been my good friends for almost forty years: Joe was also my law partner for most of that time. Joe always had the unique ability to find solutions to legal problems that seemed to be insurmountable. I thank him for applying that talent to some of the issues that arose during the writing of this book and, in the process, discovering facts that seemed to be lost to the passage of time.

Finally, Joseph Veltre and Tom Arata were able to locate documents and people when all other efforts had failed.

A number of people allowed me to interview them. I spoke to some before they had fully assimilated the horrifying fact of Kenny's death and were still trying to come to terms with their loss. Talking with me was a burden that they did not need; yet, they gave generously of their time and recollections. Although their names are listed in the bibliography at the back of this book, I should like to publicly thank all of them for their courtesy and help: Howard Alden, Red Balaban, Ron Brady, Romy Britel, John Bunch, James Chirillo, Evan Christopher, Greg Cohen, Vinnie Corrao, Mat Domber, Sylvia Fogarty, Dave Frishberg, Nat Garratano, Marty Grosz, Dennis Gruenling, Tom Guralnick, Ed Hubble, Nancy Hubble, Thomas P. Hustad, Dick Hyman, Conrad Janis, Jon-Erik Kellso, Frank Laidlaw, Mark Lass, John Luckenbill, Jon Manasse, Dan Morgenstern, John Norris, Hank O'Neal, Leroy "Sam" Parkins, Brian Peerless, Ken Peplowski, James "Jimmy" Pirone, Bucky Pizzarelli, Ed Polcer, Randy Reinhart, Monk Rowe, Roswell Rudd, Cynthia Sayer, Jack Six, Jack Stine, John Trentacosta, Allan Vache, Warren Vache, Jr., Johnny Varro, Al Vogl, Mark Weber, George Wein, Claire Weintraub, David Weintraub, Don Wolff, and Deborah Wuensch.

Thanks also to Renée Camus of Scarecrow Press. Her patience, good humor, and unflagging dedication to the pursuit of excellence eased my tasks and benefited this book.

Although many people helped me to assemble information, the final product was mine alone. Therefore, the responsibility for mistakes, omissions, and other errors is also mine alone.

Finally, there is my wife Sharon, who has inspired me to do things that I never would have attempted and has made my life a place of joy. I couldn't have a better friend, helpmate, companion, and cheerleader. If I could have conjured up the wife of my dreams, it would have been her.

A Note about the Endnotes

I conducted a number of in-person and telephonic interviews in the preparation of this book. I received oral permission to record the conversation before I started the tape and confirmed that with a written consent. References to those discussions have the name of the person interviewed followed by "interview by the author."

There were instances when I did not record a conversation, but made note of some remark or statement. Those discussions are referred to with the name of the person, followed by "conversation with the author."

Hank O'Neal allowed me to interview him. He also digitally recorded some of his recollections and sent them to me. They are referred to as

"Hank O'Neal, interview by the author," and "Hank O'Neal recorded recollections."

Dick Hyman spoke with me and subsequently prepared and sent me a short article that I have referred to as: Dick Hyman, *Remembering Kenny Davern*, Unpublished, Venice, FL, 2008.

Christian Plattner prepared and sent me several memoranda concerning his recollections of Kenny Davern.

Davern kept all of his date books, beginning with the year 1971. These books furnish an invaluable record as to where, and with whom he was working, and shall be referred to throughout the balance of this book as "Date Book."

CHAPTER ONE

Difficult Beginnings

It was nine o'clock and time to start, but the music had not begun. The customers in the club continued to talk among themselves, as did the musicians on the stage. The leader of the band had his back to the audience. He was a compactly built man, standing 5'9" tall and weighing about 160 pounds. He wore a blue blazer, gray slacks, a dress shirt, and tie. His clothes were pressed and his shoes were shined. His bushy mustache was neatly trimmed: his graying hair was closely cropped.

From time to time, he would play a glissando, climaxed by a high-pitched cry on his clarinet and then return to his conversation. Finally, he turned to the audience, squared his shoulders, counted off the time and, taking a deep breath, began to play. As the sound of music filled the room, the conversations came to a halt. They had come for this.

"I always wanted to develop my own voice" Kenny Davern said, "one that people would recognize in just four bars."[1]

> When you can make your own noise out of your instrument and people say "I know who that is" no matter how many millions there are in the world playing the same instrument or the same medium, that's a rare thing to be able to do that, and I think I'm to the point where I'm fairly recognizable.[2]

He was more than fairly recognizable. Whether he was soaring in the upper range of the clarinet, or purring in its lower register, the musical voice of Kenny Davern was unmistakable.

"You could pick Kenny out on a record after two or three notes, like a hot knife going through butter," said his longtime friend, cornetist Warren Vache, Jr. Clarinetist Ken Peplowski was one of the many others who agreed. "He had a sound that was his own. It wasn't a classical sound, it wasn't a New Orleans sound. It was really identifiable in a couple of notes as *his* sound."[3]

The unique *timbre* of Kenny Davern's musical voice was a lifetime in the making. It was something that he worked at every day, honing and refining it until it was distinct and unmistakable. Davern's voice was more than just sound: it was emotion and feeling, with music as the vehicle for its expression. But, it did not come easily. It came only after years of turmoil that had their origins in an event that occurred several years before he was born.

The first of Kenny Davern's ancestors to come to this country was his paternal grandfather, John Joseph Davern ("John Joseph"), who was born in Ireland in about 1872. When he was about nineteen years of age, he emigrated, leaving from Queenstown, Ireland, and arriving in New York on June 13, 1891. He was naturalized in 1893. His wife, Elizabet O'Connell (known as "Bessie") was born in Ireland in June 1871, and arrived in the United States in about 1890, at age nineteen.

John Joseph and Bessie were married in about 1900. They set up residence at 546 Hart Street, Brooklyn, and between 1900 and 1913, had four children: Mary (known as Mae, born 1903), John Joseph (Kenny's father, who was nicknamed "Buster," born November 10, 1906), William (born 1909), and Stanley (born 1911). By 1920, the family had moved to rural Long Island and were living at 100 Carley Avenue in Huntington.[4]

John Joseph had been a foreman for the telephone company. In the early 1920s, he was injured by a fall from a telephone pole, which left him subject to seizures during which he became angry and aggressive. His conduct became increasingly erratic, and the local health officer sought to commit him to an insane asylum. Bessie interceded on her husband's behalf and dissuaded the official, promising to care for her husband if he was not institutionalized.[5]

On April 26, 1925, John Joseph, who was then employed as a night watchman at the Marshall Field estate in Lloyd's Neck, Long Island, came home and shot and killed his wife while their four children were away. On the following day, he was committed to the Kings Park Hospital for the Insane.[6]

Kenny's maternal grandfather was Fritz Alfred Rooth, who was born in Vienna, Austria, on April 26, 1882. Prior to emigrating from Austria, he was a colonel in the Austro-Hungarian cavalry, the highest position to which a Jew could rise in that era. He arrived in the United States in around 1906, at the age of twenty-four. On July 12, 1908, he married Charlotte Tilly Dall, known as Lottie, the daughter of Jacob and Rebecca Dall. She was born on September 28, 1888, in Johauiskel, Russia, and had immigrated to the United States in 1905, at the age of seventeen. After their marriage, Fritz Americanized his name to Frederick A. Roth.[7]

Fritz and Lottie set up housekeeping in Brooklyn, New York, and on December 28, 1910, she gave birth to their only child, Josephine. The Roths lived in several apartments in Brooklyn until, in the mid1920s, they moved to 34 Highview Court in Huntington.[8]

Josephine, who grew up to be a strong-willed and independent young woman, became involved with Buster Davern. He was four years older than her, an Irish Catholic, and seemed to be a dashing sort of ruffian. Although Josephine was dazzled by him, her parents, who were Orthodox Jews, were not. They disapproved of Buster and attempted, unsuccessfully, to convince their daughter to end her relationship with him. Josephine refused and, when she was only nineteen years of age, she and Buster eloped. The young couple moved into the house at 17 Fairview Avenue in Huntington to live with Buster's sister, Mae, who had married Robert Goudie.[9] During this period, Buster worked for the telephone company.

The events that would so drastically affect the life of the yet-unborn Kenny Davern began on September 24, 1932, when Buster and several associates attempted to rob the Huntington movie theater. Constable George Probeck of the Town of Huntington was watching the movie with his wife and daughter. When Probeck tried to stop the robbery, he was shot and killed: the theater's night watchman was also wounded. The robbers were unable to open the safe in the office and left empty-handed.[10] Within a day, the police arrested Danny Di Minno as the shooter. He confessed and named several of his accomplices, including Buster Davern.

When the police came to arrest Davern, he was gone, having fled to Baltimore with Wilbur Kennedy, one of the others who had been identified by Di Minno. Davern and Kennedy were apprehended on October 9. They consented to being extradited to New York and were returned to Huntington in the following week. Basing his case on Di Minno's confession and the anticipated testimony of another witness, Anthony Scalza, who was prepared to link Davern to the crime, the district attorney charged Di Minno, Davern, and Kennedy with murder.

At the trial, which began later that month, Scalza changed his story. He claimed that he was unable to identify Davern as a participant in the crime, and the prosecution's case collapsed. On November 4, 1932, the jury convicted Di Minno, and returned verdicts of not guilty against Davern and Kennedy.[11]

Shortly thereafter, Scalza was indicted by a grand jury on charges of perjury and, when he was unable to make bail, incarcerated. He apparently rethought the wisdom of protecting Davern and Kennedy and disclosed that shortly before the trial, he had been visited by one of Davern's brothers and threatened. As a result of that visit, Scalza said, he was afraid to testify against Buster at the murder trial.[12]

Although double jeopardy protected Davern and Kennedy from being retried for their involvement in the death of Constable Probeck, they were not entirely home free. At the end of March 1933, the case was presented to a grand jury in Suffolk County. Scalza testified, and Davern, along with Kennedy, was indicted for attempted robbery in the first degree arising out of the events at the theater.[13]

Kennedy was promptly taken into custody, but Davern went into hiding. He eluded arrest until July 10, 1933, when he was picked up as he was about to enter a beer garden in Brooklyn. On the following day, he was brought to the Suffolk County seat in Riverhead and arraigned.[14]

The trial began on April 1, 1934. Several witnesses testified, including Scalza, who admitted that he had lied at the earlier trial. The evidence showed that Buster Davern was one of the men who first conceived of the robbery. Davern also acted as the lookout and furnished the getaway car.[15]

The trial took four days: the jury deliberated for only two hours and fifteen minutes before finding Davern and his co-defendants guilty of first-degree attempted robbery. On April 9, 1934, they were sentenced to serve not less than five years, nor more than fifteen, in New York's notorious Sing Sing prison. It was the maximum sentence.[16]

Shortly after Buster was convicted, Josephine discovered that she was pregnant. She returned to her family home, where she stayed until, on January 7, 1935, she gave birth to her only child, whom she named John Kenneth Davern. After being released from the hospital, she and Kenny moved in with her parents, where they remained for about a year.

As her conduct over the years indicates, Josephine apparently decided to expunge all evidence of the existence of Buster and his family from her son's life.[17] Early in 1937, she commenced a proceeding in the Supreme Court of the State of New York seeking to have her marriage to Buster annulled on the grounds of fraud. He did not oppose the petition and, on September 18, her request was granted and the court entered a judgment declaring that the marriage was annulled. In that same document, the court granted custody of Kenny to his grandmother, Charlotte "Lottie" Roth—which Josephine had also requested.[18]

When Kenny was about one year old, Josephine moved to Washington, D.C., taking her young son with her. Her reasons for relocating are not clear. However, on several occasions, Josephine told her friend Celia Weintraub that she was afraid of Buster and his family. Her concerns may have been justified, for other members of his family were involved in criminal conduct.[19]

Josephine supported herself by working as a secretary, and she put Kenny in a series of foster homes and boarding schools during the workweek. In the four years that they lived in Washington, he was in nine such institutions, and his lasting memory of them was that they were strict and regimented, where acts of casual cruelty by the teachers, and in one case, the nuns, were not uncommon.[20]

Life assumed a pattern for the young boy. On Friday night or Saturday morning, Josephine would pick him up and, perhaps to compensate for leaving him all week, lavish him with attention and buy him gifts. But, every Sunday night, she would take him back to a life that was cold, Spartan, and harsh. It was a traumatic time for Kenny. He never forgot the feeling of abandonment when his mother returned him to the control of the authority figures who told him what he had to do and when he had to do it.[21]

For at least one summer, Josephine and her son escaped the heat and humidity of the nation's capital. Photographs show that they spent June and July of 1940 at Tacaro Farm, a horse-breeding enterprise in Anne Arundel County, Maryland. From August through November 1940, he was enrolled at Countryside School in Silver Spring, Maryland.

Shortly after Josephine and Kenny left for Washington, D.C., Fred and Lottie Roth moved from Huntington to Woodhaven, Queens. Fred opened a delicatessen and candy store at 88-02 91st Avenue, and he lived with Lottie in an apartment over the store. Near the end of 1940, Josephine and her son moved back to New York and established a residence with her parents, so that Kenny could be enrolled in elementary school. He began the first grade at Public School 58 in January 1941.[22]

Josephine allowed her parents to take the principal role in raising their grandson. Kenny once said: "She gave me to her folks."[23] Life in the Roth apartment was far from tranquil. The Roths were Orthodox Jews who spoke Yiddish when they were in their apartment, maintained a kosher home, and went to Sabbath services. Josephine led a less traditional life. She and her mother were both strong-willed, and their dinner-table arguments were vociferous and frequent.

Of his grandparents, Lottie was the disciplinarian who strictly enforced the rules of her home. Grandfather Fred had a more relaxed view of life.

He liked to have fun, and enjoyed the comradeship of his grandson. Kenny fondly remembered that the two of them would occasionally sneak out of the apartment for a ham sandwich or some other treat. It was their secret: his grandmother could never know.

Although Josephine had attempted to distance herself from her parents' religious practices, they saw to it that their grandson received the training and schooling that a young Jewish boy was expected to have.[24] Kenny attended Hebrew school and, on January 17, 1948, when he was thirteen years old, he was bar mitzvah at Congregation Beth Israel on Atlantic Avenue in Woodhaven. The invitations to the bar mitzvah ceremony read "Mr. & Mrs. Frederick A. Roth request the honor of your presence at the Bar Mitzvah of their grandson, Kenneth." Josephine had apparently absented herself from this part of her son's childhood.

She was, however, involved in other aspects of his upbringing. He was a bright and inquisitive child, and his mother encouraged him in his academic and other pursuits. For a time, he wrote poetry, but abandoned it when a thoughtless teacher made fun of him. He studied butterflies, then went on to learn about amphibians. He later collected stamps. In all of these endeavors, Josephine went out of her way to buy tools, books, and supplies so that he could pursue his hobbies.[25]

The Roths, like many immigrants of their generation, listened to classical music, which in New York City was broadcast over radio station WQXR. This was Davern's first exposure to any type of music, and he developed a lifelong love of the work of composers such as Bach, Beethoven, and Mozart. His mother once took him to a concert at Carnegie Hall. The program was Schubert, and the memory of it stayed with him throughout his life.[26]

When he was old enough to make his own musical choices, he became interested in the music of the gospel services that were broadcast on Saturday nights and Sunday mornings from churches in Brooklyn and Jersey City.

> They used to come on very late. I had my own little room where I used to put my radio under the covers so nobody else could hear it. And, that was very thrilling to me. I loved the kind of feeling that was going on there. It wasn't commercialized like it is now with gowns and lights and all kinds of crap. Then it was fairly raw music, and I was very taken by it.[27]

It was the era of the big bands and radio programs featuring live performances, and recordings were on the air, day and night. Two of the giants of the period played the clarinet. Benny Goodman had reigned as the King of

Swing for about a decade, and Artie Shaw had a love-hate affair with his fans since he burst on the scene in 1938.

At first, neither of them made much of an impression on Davern, who was initially attracted by the sound of the trumpet. When he was about ten years old, he heard Artie Shaw's rendition of *Concerto for Clarinet*. "I was lying in bed. As a kid, I always loved music and one day I heard this recording of Artie Shaw playing the Clarinet Concerto. I heard this instrument—the whole orchestra came in and the clarinet just soared above it. Sort of like a bird that was free and able to fly. I liked the texture of it."[28]

He asked his mother to buy a clarinet for him. It took some time and pleading and, when she eventually yielded, she bought him an Albert system C clarinet. At that time, most clarinetists were using the simpler Boehm system, and there were few teachers in her neighborhood who knew the older fingering system. Several months passed before Josephine located Louis Bruno, a teacher who taught both the Albert and Boehm systems. The young boy took lessons and practiced for about four hours every day. But, he did not think about making music his career.[29]

The event that transformed Davern's life and launched him on the road to becoming a jazz musician occurred in his grandparents' kitchen on a Saturday morning. He was listening to Ted Husing's *Bandstand*, a local radio show. At the end of every program, Husing devoted a short segment to "dixieland." On this day, he played *Memphis Blues* by Muggsy Spanier's Ragtimers, which featured a solo by Pee Wee Russell. Pee Wee's approach to the clarinet was unlike that of Goodman, Shaw, or any of the other clarinetists of the time. It was not smooth or fluid: instead, it was gritty, emotional, and driven by a unique musical conception. Davern told interviewer Mark Weber: "It was filthy. It was the way I felt about things. There was something very raw and something in me that wanted out and that would come out like that—as opposed to the lily-white existence that I had been living up to that time."[30] At another time, he said: "I heard all these grunts and groans and sounds of spittle—I had no idea even what horn he was playing, but I said to myself, 'This is what I wanna do with my life.'"[31]

It wasn't that Kenny was captivated by Russell's sound and sought to copy it. Rather, as he told the BBC's Martin Gayford, it was that Russell "used the instrument as a medium of expression, rather than just playing it. And that's when Artie Shaw went out of the window. He pointed the way as to what could be done with a musical instrument as opposed to being a pyro-technician."[32]

For his bar mitzvah present, Josephine bought him a B♭ Boehm-system clarinet. The Russell record had turned him on to jazz, and he devoted himself to learning to play his instrument. Although he clearly spent a great deal of time practicing, he seems not to have neglected his academic studies. When he graduated from Public School 58 on January 26, 1949, he received three prizes, one in history and civics, another in school service, and a third one for his service in the school orchestra. At the graduation ceremony, he played the *Twelfth Street Rag* and carried the flag in the transfer of colors.[33]

His musical talent enabled him to attend Newtown High School, which was outside of his school district, but was one of only two schools that offered an academic music diploma. Music had become his consuming interest: in high school he was an average student, and his only extracurricular activities related to music. In addition to learning the clarinet, he had been taking lessons on the baritone saxophone and became a member of the Newtown High School Band and also the school's orchestra. The band wore black and red woolen uniforms with waist-length capes, and pants made of heavy white duck. It played Sousa marches, and both musical organizations played works such as the *William Tell Overture*, light classical pieces by composers such as Victor Herbert, and selections from Broadway shows like *Brigadoon*.[34]

Although George Schoette, the school official who directed the Newtown High School Band and also its orchestra, was stern and demanding, he was liked by his pupils. Schoette apparently recognized that Davern was a cut above the average student, for he treated him with respect and reinforced the young man's already formidable work ethic. Davern was awarded the first clarinet chair in both the band and the orchestra and occasionally doubled on baritone saxophone. He was elected band manager.[35]

As a music major, Davern came in contact with several youngsters who were also interested in jazz—one of whom was Bobby Grauso. His father, Joe Grauso, was a working musician who had played drums on several of the Muggsy Spanier recordings. Because Davern's home was far from school, he started eating lunch at Grauso's apartment.

> And there was Joe Grauso, just getting up out of bed at twelve noon. He worked till four in the morning and probably didn't get to bed until about six or seven. He comes out in the silk robe with a long cigarette holder—"Whaddya say, kids? How're you doing? blah, blah, blah" He was working with Bobby Hackett at Lou Terassi's, which was on Forty Seventh, off of Eighth.
>
> He would take us down to the original Eddie Condon's on West 3rd Street and take us in the back way. You'd be able to hear these guys like Wild Bill Davison, and Pee Wee, and Eddie Condon—all these wonderful players who were there at that time—Lou McGarity and Bud Freeman. It was just a thrill to hear these guys in person.

They were my heros, plain and simple. The whole Condon gang, which I'm very proud to say I became a member of, even if it was in the latter part of his life. It was to me a highlight. It was the kind of music that I liked and I've stayed with it.[36]

During the years that Davern was in high school, jazz was still in vogue and there were a large number of clubs featuring live, small-group music. In downtown Manhattan, at 178 7th Avenue South, was Max Gordon's Village Vanguard. One block south, at West 10th Street, Nick's was still thriving under the management of Grace Rongetti, who took over when her husband, Nick, died. Diagonally across the avenue from Nick's was the Riviera Club. Barney Josephson's Café Society Downtown was situated on Sheridan Square, slightly to the South and East. Condon's and the Cinderella Club were both located on West 3rd Street. Finally, on 2nd Avenue on the East Side of Manhattan were buildings that housed catering halls for bar mitzvah receptions during the week. On the weekends, one hall was converted to become the Central Plaza and, across the street, another became the Stuyvesant Casino. Both venues featured live jazz.

In midtown, there were a number of clubs on and near 52nd Street. Some of these venues featured the music and musicians of the early generations of jazz. However, there were a larger number of establishments where the younger musicians, such as Charlie Parker and Bud Powell, held forth. Although Davern visited those places and listened to these voices, it was still the music of the earlier generations that attracted him. He recognized that "I was at odds with my own contemporaries. I thought the real jazz was Louis Armstrong—and I still do."[37]

At Lou Terassi's Hickory Log and similar places, Davern could watch musicians like Bobby Hackett and Ernie Caceres, who was his favorite baritone saxophone player, and, occasionally, the young man got to play with some of them. "After a while, I became a face there, and I used to be able to sit in for Buster Bailey when he was with Jimmy McPartland. We'd just walk in and: 'Hey, my man. Come on up and sit in'. I didn't realize why Buster got off the stand so readily: because he would go into a corner booth and sleep."[38] Occasions like this gave Davern a reason to continue practicing and trying to improve. "I'd met Rex Stewart, he was the first cat to encourage me. 'Keep playing,' he said."[39]

Davern and Bobby Grauso, together with trumpet player John Hurstius, who went on to own the Cork 'N' Bib restaurant, and Larry O'Brien, who led the Glenn Miller ghost band for decades, formed a band. Davern's friends had their own musical favorites, and each of the youngsters began to expose the others to new musical voices.

> Little by little, we began to hold Sunday afternoon sessions, first at Jack Sohmer's apartment in Queens, with all these guys who liked Bix Beiderbecke and Frank Teschmacher—the Chicagoans in general—and they turned me on to this music. I was listening to Jelly Roll Morton. I had discovered Pee Wee Russell on the radio prior to that and my instincts told me that was the real music. . . . What little money I had went to buying Teschmacher, Beiderbecke, and Jelly Roll Morton recordings, especially the LPs that had just started to come out—the ten-inch LPs. My money went to that.[40]

Davern was about to begin playing professionally and was required to have working papers. To get them, he needed his birth certificate—a document that he had never before seen. Josephine and her parents had told him that his name was Kenny Roth. He had entered grade school and high school under that name and interacted with friends as Kenny Roth. Until he saw his birth certificate, he was not aware that his father was named John Joseph Davern and that his full name was John Kenneth Davern. His mother had never mentioned anything about his father and, if Kenny had ever asked her about him when he was younger, he had no recollection of it. When Kenny confronted her with his birth certificate, she told him that his father was dead and refused to discuss the matter any further. In fact, he was alive. But, Kenny did not learn that fact for about fifteen years and by that time, his father had died.[41]

He learned the truth by accident. Celia Weintraub had been Josephine Roth's closest friend for most of their adult lives. She had watched as Kenny grew up, and shared Josephine's pride as he became a successful professional musician. She also shared some of Josephine's secrets. In the early 1960s, Josephine moved to upstate New York, but Kenny maintained the relationship with Celia and, on occasion, went out to her home in Huntington to visit with her.

On one of those visits, Celia casually let it slip that she had seen one of Kenny's uncles in town. This came as a shock, for Josephine had never even hinted that Kenny had any living relatives. In response to Kenny's question, Celia said that the uncle's name was Stanley Davern, his father's youngest brother. Eventually, Kenny located his uncle, called to introduce himself, and arranged to go to his house to meet him.

Over the course of that conversation, and several other meetings with Stanley and William, another of his uncles, Kenny learned that his father had been imprisoned for participating in the robbery of the Huntington Theater. He also learned that Buster had been alive until 1954, and that he could have spoken with him at the time when he found his birth certificate. At some point, one of the uncles gave Kenny several pictures of his father: he was certain that he recognized the man in the pictures as someone who had been standing across the street from the synagogue when he was bar mitzvah.

When Kenny confronted his mother with what he had learned, she refused to talk about it. She never explained the reasons for her deception to Kenny, never responded to any of his questions about his father, and, as before, simply would not discuss him. The relationship with his father's family did not prosper. Although he met with one or both of his uncles sporadically over the years, they were unable or unwilling to satisfy Kenny's curiosity about his father's life before Kenny was born or after Buster was released from prison. These conversations were extremely frustrating and painful, and eventually, Kenny broke off all contact with the Davern family and abandoned his efforts to find out anything about his father.[42]

Throughout his teen years, Davern continued to perfect the skill and art of playing music. On January 13, 1950, he took part in a concert given by the Music Department of Newtown High School at Dillingham Hall, 48-01 90th Street in Elmhurst. He had a job on December 22–23, 1950, playing clarinet and baritone saxophone in a quartet at the Silhouette, a bar and restaurant in Elmont, Long Island. Kenny apparently was toying with the idea of adopting a professional name: the table card that bears the handwritten names of the musicians identifies him as "Kenny Verne." In 1951, he was playing with his own trio at the A-1 Club in Astoria, and for the school year ending June 29, 1951, he received a Certificate of Merit for outstanding scholarship in orchestra and a similar certificate for his scholarship in band.[43]

Although he was barely sixteen years old, he continued to get called for work. He took on Friday night jobs at fraternity houses playing in trios and quartets for three or four dollars. "[T]hen—somewhere around fifteen or sixteen, I was playing in strip joints from midnight to four in the morning. They used to have two trios—one went from midnight to four and that's like—one five-minute break on the hour."[44] In his response to a questionnaire that he completed several years later for Leonard Feather's *Jazz Encyclopedia*, he said that he had played on a *Studio One* television program that was broadcast on CBS during 1951 and, in that same year, had played on the *Let's Dance* radio program that emanated from the Hotel New Yorker.

The American Federation of Musicians was still a force in music in the 1950s, and Davern had to join. He had been taking clarinet lessons from

Leon Russianoff and saxophone lessons from Joe Napoleon, the younger brother of Phil. Joe told him: "'Sonny, you'll never get any work if you're listed in the 802 directory as just a clarinet player.' So I auditioned on baritone sax to a panel of cigar-smoking nonmusician officials who asked, 'What is that thing called? What kind of parts do you read?'"[45]

With increasing frequency, he was spending his weeknights and weekends hanging around in the bars and clubs that were frequented by the established stars of the jazz world. He listened to the older musicians and learned from them and, over time, they got to know him.

Among the musicians whom Davern met in those years was Adrian Rollini. Trained as a classical pianist, Rollini had become interested in jazz and learned to play the bass saxophone. He had been featured with the California Ramblers, a successful band in the 1920s, and had recorded with Bix Beiderbecke and Frank Trumbauer, Joe Venuti and Eddie Lang, as well as with Red Nichols and Miff Mole. Both Harry Carney and Budd Johnson cited him as an influence. Late in 1927, Rollini left for England to join the band of Fred Elizade, returning five years later.

The bass saxophone, like the tuba, had been used as a rhythm instrument in bands of the 1920s. By the time that Rollini returned from England, it, as well as the tuba, had gone out of style: the combination of better amplification and musicians like Pops Foster and Wellman Braud made the more supple string bass the preferred instrument in rhythm sections. Rollini taught himself to play the vibraphone and was one of the pioneers on that instrument. In the mid1930s, he opened his own club, Adrian's Tap Room, where he led a racially mixed band for many years.

Davern had gone to see his clarinet repairman and noticed a bass saxophone hanging on the wall. The repairman told him that it had once belonged to Rollini, who had sold it. The buyer had brought the instrument in for repair and to have the pads replaced. Davern asked him:

> "Are those the original pads?" He said "Yeah." I said "What are you going to do with them?" "Throw them away." So I said, "Give me the middle G. . . ." So he took the Bunsen burner and burned out the pad for me. It had the original brown shellac, the white kid leather pad.[46]

Davern went to see Rollini, who was then playing at the Hotel New Yorker. He talked his way past the "gorilla" at the door ("I think he was the hatcheck girl. To quote Rodney Dangerfield 'The joint was so tough, the hatcheck girl's name was Vito'") and sat down at a table to wait for Rollini to finish his set. When Rollini stepped off the stage, Davern pulled the keypad from his pocket and approached the older man.

> I said "Do you know what this is," and I held out my paw with this big white saxophone pad in my hand. He looked at it, picked it up. "Where'd you get this?" So I told him the story of how I'd been in New York earlier. . . . He said "Whaddya want this for?" I said, "I was a big fan of your bass saxophone playing, specially the Bix Beiderbecke recordings that you made with him." And he grabbed the edge of the chair and tears came to his eyes and he said, "I didn't think anyone cared anymore," which moved me to the quick. He said, "What do you want me to do with this?" And I said "Would you autograph it to me?" And he wrote, "To Kenny, sincerely, Adrian."[47]

Sixty years later, the pad still hung in Davern's study, one of his prized possessions.

No doubt, there was an element of hero worship in Davern's decision to buy the pad and approach Rollini with it. But he kept and displayed it because the pad and Rollini were part of a tradition that he cherished and wanted to preserve and propagate.

Davern's career took a giant leap forward when trumpeter Henry "Red" Allen called him for a job. Red's father, Henry Allen, Sr., was the leader of Allen's Brass Band, one of the premier marching bands in New Orleans. As a teenager, Red, who was born in 1908, played with his father's band, learned to read music, and to improvise. By the early 1920s, he was a veteran musician.

Red left New Orleans in April 1927 to join King Oliver in New York, and returned to New Orleans when the job ended. He went back to New York in the late spring of 1929, to join Luis Russell's band. It is generally an exaggeration to say that someone takes a locale "by storm," but in the case of Red's arrival in New York City, the overstatement is not a great one. There is no doubt that, like every other musician, Allen was influenced by Louis Armstrong and adopted some of the older musician's devices. But, his own ideas—what Gunther Schuller defined as his stock-in-trade—were emerging: an odd turn of phrase, double-time flurries mixed with long-held notes, fast single-note trills, quick octave jumps.[48]

The Russell band had two successful years at the Saratoga Club before the Depression took hold and work became hard to find. Allen left and joined the Fletcher Henderson band, where he remained until it broke up at the end of 1934. After a two-year stint with the Mills Blue Rhythm Band, Allen rejoined Russell, who was then the Musical Director of Louis Armstrong's orchestra. He remained there until 1940, then took a small group into Barney Josephson's Café Society. From then on, he led a number of small groups, usually appearing at clubs and venues such as Metropole, the Central Plaza, and the Stuyvesant Casino.[49]

> I don't know how he got my name, but somehow I get this call: "Kenny, my man. Red Allen here. We got a gig on Queens Boulevard in an American Legion Hall." I go there. I don't remember anything: I was so terrified. But the place was packed out. Red Allen was, I think, the most dynamic leader I ever worked with in my life. He could have an audience of hardened criminals eating out of the palm of his hand within seconds of his arrival into a club.[50]

Over the years, he and Red became close friends (they were both born on January 7), and he would always give the older man credit for teaching him the art of attracting and holding an audience. Although Davern became Allen's musical equal over the years, he never forgot the excitement of playing with Allen on that first date, and it permeated every telling of the story.

The musical voice that attracted Red Allen's interest has been preserved on record. On July 24, 1951, Davern and several friends rented a studio at the Nola Recording Studios in New York City and recorded several tunes. Davern was joined by Tone Kwas on trumpet, Larry O'Brien on trombone, Ray Vitale playing piano, Tony Evans on bass, and John Nardossa playing drums. They called themselves *Kenny Davern's Dixiecats* and recorded one take of *Basin Street Blues* and two versions of *At the Jazz Band Ball*. The surprising aspect of these recordings is not the difference between the boy of sixteen and the mature Kenny Davern. It is that notwithstanding his interest in Pee Wee Russell, Frank Teschemacher, and the other clarinet players to whom he was attracted at the time, when he decided to record a tune associated with the New Orleans Rhythm Kings, he first listened to and absorbed the sound and concepts of Leon Rappolo, the band's clarinetist.[51]

Kenny's next recording was made with Dick Sutton on cornet, Robert Lovett on clarinet, Dick Wellstood on piano, and Davern on baritone saxophone—probably late in 1951. This unissued recording was intended as a demo tape. Of the four participants, only Wellstood has his own voice. Sutton is in a Bobby Hackett mood, Davern's baritone sounds much like Ernie Caceres, and Lovett is an unabashed Pee Wee Russell clone. (Lovett would ultimately give up playing jazz. He became a professional film editor and, among his other accomplishments, he received credit for his work on Francis Ford Coppola's extravaganza, *The Cotton Club*.) Four tunes were recorded; *Please Don't Talk About Me When I'm Gone, Singin' the Blues, Jazz Me Blues,* and *Little Coquette*. Davern has ample solo space on all but the second tune and, while his work is artfully constructed, it is far different from the unique musical voice that ultimately emerged.

One of the triumphs of Davern's years at Newtown High came on April 23, 1952, when he produced a program at a local hall titled "Kenny Davern Presents a Night of Jazz at Newtown for the Benefit of the General Organization." He appeared with a group titled Gene Shannon's Dixieland All-Stars that included Shannon, Davern, pianist Ray Vitale, and Larry O'Brien on trombone. They played the *Tin Roof Blues* and *The Saints Go Marchin' In*.[52]

Throughout his life, Davern spoke of that evening with pride. It was the first occasion that a jazz concert had been held to benefit a New York City School. He even went so far as to write the script for the master of ceremonies. It began: "How do you do, Ladies and Gentlemen. I'm . . . , your host for the evening. It gives me great pleasure to present for the first time in this high school, a full-scale jazz concert, which is being brought to you under the direction of Kenny Davern."

Playing jazz was not Davern's only source of income. In the early 1950s, Latin music had become popular, and there was a demand for musicians who could play in that idiom. The work was not steady: for the most part it consisted of sporadic weekend jobs played with bands that were assembled on an ad hoc basis.

With his baritone saxophone, Davern quickly created a niche for himself. He was in the bands of Tony Novo, Jimmy Romo, and Juanucho Lopez. He was seventeen years old when, as a member of Alfredito's Mambo Orchestra, he made his first recordings: two sides of a 78-rpm record on the Rainbow label titled *Goofus Mambo*, and *Round the World Mambo*.[53] Half a century later, Davern could recall the price that he had to pay to work for Alfredito.

> His real name was Alfred Levy. He was from Forest Hills, Queens, and he had all the Jewish dances sewed up, playing tymbales. And he had a very good Spanish Mambo band. He was sort of the Mambo Band King of Queens. And I remember that date was $41.25, which was union scale, and we had to kick back another $15.00 to him. It made everybody in the band very mad.[54]

Shortly before Davern was due to graduate from high school, he was offered a job with the band of Shep Fields. The band featured five clarinets, of which Davern would have been the fifth. However, he would have had to quit school. His family, as well as Joe Napoleon, urged him to finish out the semester and get his diploma and, although he was tempted to accept the offer, he decided to stay in school.[55]

He graduated from Newtown High School in January 1953. The list of honors earned by the graduates included the "Music Department Award for Advancement of Music in Newtown High School to Kenneth Davern." He was awarded a Certificate of Merit for "Outstanding Scholarship in Band."[56]

Notes

1. Kenny Davern, conversation with the author.

2. Kenny Davern, interview by Terry Gross on *Fresh Air*, a program broadcast on WHYY, the National Public Radio Station in Philadelphia (date unknown) (hereinafter "Fresh Air Interview").

3. Warren Vache, Jr., quoted in Dennis Hevesi, "Kenny Davern, 71, Clarinetist Who Loved Traditional Jazz," *New York Times*, 14 December 2006. Ken Peplowski, interview by the author. In interviews with the author, Conrad Janis and Jon-Erik Kellso said the same thing.

4. The information in the foregoing paragraphs comes from copies of pages in the Twelfth, Thirteenth, and Fourteenth Censuses of the United States (1900, 1910, 1920) and the New York Passenger Lists. 1820–1957, printed on www.Ancestry.com.

5. *New York Times*, 27 April 1925.

6. *New York Times*, 17 and 28 April 1925.

7. This information comes from the Fourteenth Census, from an Affidavit for License to Marry dated July 1, 1908, Document No. 15105, and Certificate of Marriage for Fritz Alfred Rooth and Charlotte Tilly Dall. The information as to Fritz Alfred Rooth's status in the Austro-Hungarian cavalry comes from Brian Peerless, "Kenny Davern, My Personal Observations on His Life in Jazz," printed in the program for *Arbors Records, The Final March of Jazz Celebrates the Birthdays of Kenny Davern, 69; Skitch Henderson, 86; Stanley Kay, 80*; Clearwater Beach, FL, March 19–21, 2004 (hereinafter "Peerless, Program Notes"), p. 5.

8. Certificates of Citizenship of Frederick A. Roth dated November 9, 1922, and Lottie Roth dated June 30, 1936; Fifteenth Census of the United States (1930), printed on www.Ancestry.com.

9. Fifteenth Census of the United States (1930), printed on www.Ancestry.com.

10. Brief of Respondent, the People of the State of New York in *People of the State of New York v. John Davern, Wilbur Kennedy, Daniel DiMinno, et. al.* 243 App. Div 551, 276 N.Y. Supp. 89. (2nd Dept., 1935) (hereinafter "Respondent's Brief."), p. 4; Brief of Appellant John Davern in *People of the State of New York v. John Davern, Wilbur Kennedy, Daniel DiMinno, et. al.* 243 App. Div 551, 276 N.Y. Supp. 89. (2nd Dept., 1935) (hereinafter "Davern's Brief"), p. 29.

11. *The Long-Islander*, articles published on 30 September 1932, sec. 1, p. 1, sec 2, p. 6; also 7 October, 14 October, and 4 November 1932; *New York Times*, 26 September 1932, 27 and 29 October 1932. It is interesting to note how quickly the criminal

justice system worked in those days. The time that elapsed between the commission of the crime and the jury verdict was only thirty-nine days.

12. Respondent's Brief, pp. 21–22, 36. This was revealed in deliberately obscure terms during the second trial. The name of Buster's brother was not disclosed.

13. *The Long-Islander*, 21 March 1933; Davern's Brief, p. 15.

14. *The Long-Islander*, 21 March, 31 March, 14 July 1933.

15. Respondent's Brief, pp. 4–9, Davern's Brief, pp. 6, 12.

16. *The Long-Islander*, 6 April 1934; Respondent's Brief, p. 2; Brief of Appellant Wilbur Kennedy in *People of the State of New York v. John Davern, Wilbur Kennedy, Daniel DiMinno, et. al.* 243 App. Div 551, 276 N.Y. Supp. 89 (2nd Dept., 1935), p. 2. The convictions were subsequently affirmed on appeal.

17. Father and son never met or even spoke with each other. As indicated, *infra*, it is possible that Kenny saw him once, on the occasion of his bar mitzvah.

18. The petition filed by Josephine that specified the nature of the fraud that had been practiced upon her is no longer available. It is unclear why Josephine granted custody of Kenny to her mother. Notwithstanding, the boy always resided with Josephine.

19. R. Claire Weintraub, interview by the author. See also, *The Long-Islander*, 5 January and 12 January 1934 and footnote 13, *supra*.

20. Kenny Davern, conversations with the author; Elsa Davern, interview by the author.

21. Kenny Davern, conversations with the author; Elsa Davern, interview by the author. During his lifetime, Davern gave numerous interviews to writers of books and magazine articles, discussed the events of his life on countless radio programs, and spoke about them with his friends. However, he always avoided talking about the first six years of his life and, even when he did, he would only mention that he spent some time moving among several unpleasant foster homes and institutions and then would quickly change the subject.

22. At some later time, the Roths moved to an apartment at 90-20 97th Street in Ozone Park, Queens, only a few blocks away from the store. Elsa Davern, conversation with the author; Kenny Davern's Selective Service card dated 13 January 1953.

23. Peter Vacher, "Straight Talk from Kenny Davern," *Mississippi Rag*, xxv, no. 5 (May 1997), 32 (hereinafter "Vacher, Davern").

24. Kenny Davern, conversation with the author; Elsa Davern, interview by the author.

25. Elsa Davern, interview by the author.

26. E-mail from Christian Plattner, *Kenny Davern and the Clarinet*, 15 September 2008.

27. Kenny Davern, interviewed by Mark Weber, recorded for the *Jazz of Enchantment* series in the studios of KUNM, Albuquerque, New Mexico, on 17 January 2006; Paul Ingles, producer (hereinafter "Kenny Davern, interview by Mark Weber,

17 January 2006"). The interview is available on line at www.newmexicojazz.org. In addition, Weber had Davern as his guest on the radio show that he hosted on radio station KUNM. Davern's comments on those shows will be cited as "Kenny Davern, interview by Mark Weber," followed by the date of the broadcast.

28. Kenny Davern, interviewed by Martin Gayford on *Meridian, The Jazz Clarinet*, recorded 14 August 1990, and broadcast on BBC World Service on 4 September 1990 (hereinafter "BBC Interview"). See also: Kenny Davern, interviewed by Monk Rowe, Joe Williams Director of Hamilton College Jazz Archive, 16 March 2001 (hereinafter "Rowe Interview").

29. Leroy Dirk, "Kenny Davern Interviewed," transcribed and edited by Richard Cowie, *Jazz Journal International*, 33, no. 9 (September 1980): 6–7 (hereinafter "Dirk interview"); Rowe interview; Fresh Air Interview.

30. Kenny Davern, interview by Mark Weber, 17 January 2006.

31. Davern, quoted in Will Friedwald, "A Traditionalist Who Makes Every Note Count," *New York Sun*, 29 November 2005.

32. BBC Interview.

33. Graduation Ceremony Program.

34. Al Vogl, interview by the author.

35. Jimmy Pirone, Al Vogl, interviews by the author.

36. Kenny Davern, interview by Mark Weber, 17 January 2006.

37. Dan Morgenstern, "Kenny Davern, Overdue," *DownBeat*, (16 May 1968): 23, 39 (hereinafter "Morgenstern-*DownBeat*").

38. Kenny Davern, interview by the author.

39. Morgenstern-*DownBeat*, 23.

40. Kenny Davern, interview by the author.

41. Kenny Davern, conversations with the author; Elsa Davern, interview by the author. Kenny's father died on 27 April 1954, at the age of forty-seven years and five months. His death certificate stated that the cause of death was a coronary occlusion.

42. Kenny Davern, conversations with the author; Elsa Davern, Claire Weintraub, David Weintraub, interviews by the author. Kenny was accompanied to the first meeting at his uncle's house by his then-fiancé, Sylvia. Although her recollection of how it came about and what transpired while they were there varies in some respects from the version told by Kenny, she corroborates the fact that he was unable to establish a connection with his father's family. Sylvia Fogarty, interview by the author.

43. Newtown High School event program; table card from the Silhouette; Peerless Program Notes, p. 28.

44. Shirley Klett, "Kenny Davern, Interview," *Cadence*, 3, no. 12 (December 1978): 18 (hereinafter "Klett interview").

45. Peerless Program Notes, p. 7; see also: Kenny Davern's responses to Feather's *Jazz Encyclopedia* Questionnaire completed in about 1955–56.

46. Kenny Davern interview by Mark Weber, January 17, 2006.

47. *Ibid.* A short comprehensive discussion of Rollini's career appears in Richard M. Sudhalter, *Lost Chords, White Musicians and Their Contribution to Jazz, 1915–1945* (New York, Oxford, 1999), 159–180 (hereinafter "Sudhalter").

48. Gunther Schuller, *The Swing Era, The Development of Jazz, 1930–1945* (New York, Oxford, 1999), 618–619.

49. See, generally, John Chilton, *Ride Red Ride, The Life of Henry "Red" Allen* (London, Cassell, 1999).

50. Kenny Davern interview by David Holt, broadcast on Jim Cullum's NPR radio show, *Jazz from the Landing* on 13 May 2004: program titled *Jazz Memories with Kenny Davern* (hereinafter "Holt Interview").

51. Davern told interviewer Leroy Dirk that he had bought some of the New Orleans Rhythm Kings stock arrangements with Rappolo's parts written out. Dirk interview, 6.

52. Event program.

53. In a questionnaire that Kenny completed for Leonard Feather's *Jazz Encyclopedia*, in about 1955–56, he said that the titles of the tunes that he recorded with Alfredito were *Round the World Mambo* and *Goofus Mambo* and that they were recorded at Nola Studios in 1953. Many years later, he told historian Phil Schaap that the titles of his first commercially issued recordings were *Round the World Mambo, Parts 1 & 2* and that they were made in 1952. Phil Schaap, liner notes to *the Kenny Davern Quartet at the Mill Hill Playhouse Celebrating Fifty Years of Records*, Arbors ARCD 19296, September, 2003; e-mail from Phil Schaap to the author. In all likelihood, Davern's recollection was sharper when he filled out the Feather Questionnaire.

54. Kenny Davern, interview by Mark Weber, 11 July 2002. See also: Feather Questionnaire, picture courtesy of Charles Klaif.

55. Rowe Interview.

56. Document titled *Honors Won by Newtown Graduates*, January, 1953; Certificate of Merit.

CHAPTER TWO

Apprenticeship

The months following graduation were difficult for the eighteen-year-old. He had occasional jobs playing in Latin bands or pickup groups, but most of his time was spent frequenting places where work might be found or talking with other musicians who were also looking for jobs. On one such day, he was hanging around Nola Studios, where musicians frequently rehearsed. There was a sign advertising that the Ralph Flanagan band needed baritone saxophone and bass clarinet players and that auditions would be held on the following Monday.[1]

Although the golden years of the great swing bands had ended in the late 1940s, there were several newly formed orchestras led by musicians, including Ray Anthony, Ralph Marterie, and the Elgart brothers, that had met with some success. In 1949, pianist Ralph Flanagan, who had arranged for Boyd Rayburn and Tony Pastor, formed his own band. Built on arrangements that emulated the sound of the late Glenn Miller, the Ralph Flanagan Orchestra became quite popular and had a number of hits, the best remembered of them being *Hot Toddy*.

Davern got his horns and, at the appointed time, arrived at the audition. "When I got there, there were about ten guys ahead of me, but I went up to the manager and said 'Let me play, I gotta be somewhere. I have an appointment.' They gave me the 5th part book—that band had very close harmony—and I had to play it solo. It had no rhyme or reason by itself, and I had to play sixteen bars in one breath at one spot. Then Flanagan went over to the piano, and we played two choruses of *Muskrat Ramble* and that was it."[2]

The manager told Davern that they would call him, so he went back to a friend's house to have dinner and hang out. At about nine o'clock that night, his mother called and told him to come home and pack because he was leaving on a road trip with the band at noon on the following day. "Away I went," said Davern.[3]

Once the tour got under way, the excitement of joining one of the most popular bands of the time quickly wore off. The Flanagan band maintained a rigorous regime of one-night stands. The 1953 summer tour began with a recording session in New York on June 8. They played in Fort Belvoir, Virginia, on June 9, had a day to travel and then played in Augusta, Georgia, on the 11th. Over the next ten days, they played in South Carolina and North Carolina, spent three days in three cities in Virginia, one day in Maryland, then back to Virginia, North Carolina, and Delaware. For the rest of the month, they played dates in Pennsylvania, Crystal Beach in Ontario, Canada, Detroit, Cincinnati, and Russell's Point, Ohio, ending on June 29 in Kentucky. In July, the band played twenty-seven different cities, being off or traveling on the other four days. August was a little easier: they were in Denver until the 11th. But, for the remainder of the hottest month of the year, they wended their way through Kansas, Oklahoma, Texas, Louisiana, Arkansas, and Missouri, playing every night from the 13th to the end of the month.[4]

Kenny remembered the torture of those trips vividly. The chains of roadside restaurants like McDonald's or Bennigan's did not exist: the musicians would stop for an occasional hot dog or hamburger at a ramshackle stand, wash down their food with a soda, get back in their sweltering cars, and keep on driving. Eventually, they would get to the ballroom at which they were to perform.

> To shave, you had to plug in: there was one outlet by the bandstand. You'd plug in, each guy would take a turn with his electric shaver shaving. And then there was one sink in back of the bandstand with cold water only, and a naked light bulb hanging down, and a cracked piece of a mirror. That's where you washed up.
>
> It was the summertime. . . . Nylon shirts had just come out; short sleeve nylon shirts, because you needed something you could wash out right away and hang up and dry and cotton shirts just weren't in then. I mean you could do that but it wasn't really practical. And so you know these shirts were hot, I'm telling you. You closed up that collar and you put on a black bow tie, which you had to make yourself in those days, and then you put a wool jacket on over you, and your tuxedo pants. You were roasting. And then you did four sets, four-hour sets, and then you packed up the horn and folded up the book and

put it on the pile and packed up your horns and they put them on the truck and you got in the car. . . .⁵

The cars did not have air-conditioning. Five men would be crowded into each vehicle, and one of them had to sit on the hump in the backseat with his knees tucked under his chin. They would drive through the night, trying to get to the next town as quickly as possible, often over poorly maintained two- or three-lane roads. (Construction of the interstate highways system did not begin until 1957.)

> Maybe about 6:30, 7 o'clock in the morning you've rolled into the other great town which boasted of a . . . hotel at $3.75 or $2.75 a night, I forget which, and you couldn't check in, you see. So . . . the bell captain would take your luggage. These were very cheap hotels. And then you'd walk around town. You'd have breakfast in one of those Dew Drop Inn places, maybe visit the local music store to see what kind of instruments they have, because good horns were still relatively easy to find, premium horns. Of course, none of us had any money, but if we needed it we would borrow or whatever.
>
> Then when you checked in maybe at 11, 12 or 1, you may have gotten a haircut, whatever. Anything to kill some time. You slept 'til about five o'clock, and that's when you had your wake-up call. You got dressed, you shaved and showered, and you went down to the local buffet . . . well, cafeteria style. . . . You had spaghetti or whatever, depending on what part of the world you're in. And then you went to the gig, and that night you were able to stay over but you left at nine o'clock the next day because again, you had 350 miles to go.⁶

The physical drudgery of the tour was compounded by the fact that Davern was playing alto saxophone, occasionally varying the routine by switching to baritone. He played the same tunes in the same way, night after night, never rising to his feet for a solo. The only relief came occasionally at the end of a show when Flanagan would call a few musicians down to the front of the stage.

> Really, one of the first thrills of my life was when Ralph would get bored playing with the big band . . . you know, tired of the Miller sound, and point to me and say, "just a quartet." It was me and the rhythm section. We would play something like *That's a Plenty* or *I Found a New Baby*, and all the people would stop dancing, and you could see them twenty deep at Crystal Beach. . . . You know how huge that place was. To get that feeling going was really a ball for me because I really joined the band for the last fifteen minutes when, quote, "the hot music occurred." As far as the rest of it was concerned, it was a matter of everything by rote; once you learned it, that was the end of it.⁷

These interludes were not enough to satisfy Davern. At the end of August, he gave his two-weeks' notice and left the band in the middle of September. "I quit in Texas . . . I couldn't take it anymore. That band was the last of the money-making big bands—it took in $90,000 for 60 one-nighters—but I didn't want to play sax in a dance band. I wanted to play red hot clarinet."[8]

When he returned home, Davern was a hero of sorts. Of all of his friends, he was the one who had made the major leagues, and they envied him his success. From time to time, one of them would sidle up to him and ask "How was it?" The response was not what they expected. "'It was the f—ing worst' I said, 'Plain and simple. It was the f—ing worst. . . .' They all wanted to do that. And I had done it. So I didn't see any romance to that whatsoever."[9]

The job market had not changed in the time since he had left New York. There were extended periods when he could not find steady work. He took occasional gigs, or sat in at the Cinderella Club, the Central Plaza, the Stuyvesant Casino, and other jazz venues, sometimes playing clarinet, occasionally baritone saxophone. There were sporadic jobs in the Latin band of Jimmy Romo. In November, he worked in the Johnny Long band. He had managed to save some money while traveling with Flanagan, and it kept him alive financially.[10]

More important to Davern was the ability to play with and learn from the great older musicians. These men were his heroes and, at nineteen years of age he was onstage with them. They liked him and encouraged him: he often spoke about the experience. "To be on the bandstand with a Roy Eldridge or a Buck Clayton is an honor and a privilege not granted to everyone. Making harmonious music with such people in your formative years, you come away with something in your head."[11] Davern told Brian Peerless, "They let you sit in, and you listened to them, and you wanted to go home, practice, and get better."[12]

One of the musicians who hung around with Davern and sometimes competed with him for work was Steve Lacy. In December 1953, Lacy put together a dixieland-type band to play at the Savoy Ballroom in Boston. Dick Schwartz (later Dick Sutton) was on cornet and Elmer Schoebel, who had been one of the original New Orleans Rhythm Kings in 1922, played piano. Lacy played clarinet and soprano saxophone, Davern was on baritone saxophone, and the rhythm section consisted of Schoebel, Bill Goodall on bass, and Eddie Phyfe on drums.

> We rehearsed at the old Condon's for one day and drove up to Boston, where we got shut out after a week because I was playing the saxophone. The woman that owned the place, Mrs. Donahoe, hated the saxophone, my saxophone,

because it didn't belong in a traditional jazz band. We hung around to see who would take our place, and who did they bring up, but Hot Lips Page with Paul Quinichette, a tenor player. She took one look at his tenor and locked it in the basement.[14]

Davern returned to New York and, for the next several months, struggled for work. Red Allen sporadically called him, and there were occasional gigs in places that Kenny referred to as "sailor bars" (Neary's, at the corner of 47th Street and 8th Avenue, was one of them.) But, there was a great deal of time during which he was not earning money. And so, in May 1954, he rejoined the Flanagan band.

The band's 1954 itinerary was no less arduous than the previous year's tour. But, this year they avoided traveling through the South in the summer. They criss-crossed Missouri, Iowa, Indiana, Illinois, Wisconsin, and Minnesota during the month of May. The band had two dates in the beginning of June, and then went on vacation until June 15. When they came back to work, they played in Maine, Massachusetts, New Hampshire, and Connecticut, until they arrived in New York for a record date for RCA Victor on June 28. Davern played alto saxophone on the four tunes that were recorded that day: however, he was only a member of the reed section and had no solos.

Then it was back on the road. They did seven days at the Steel Pier in Atlantic City at the beginning of July, followed by a series of one-nighters in Pennsylvania, Ohio, Canada, and Indiana, ending with a two-week stint at the Aragon Ballroom in Chicago from July 16 to August 1. Then it was back to the one-night stands, crossing and recrossing Michigan, Wisconsin, Iowa, Indiana, Ohio, and West Virginia. In September, they wended their way back east and in the following month they were in New York City where, on October 13 and 15, the Flanagan band recorded a total of seven songs. Davern also made some movie shorts with the band.[14]

His departure from the Flanagan band resulted from an unforeseen event. He and Joe Lanza, Flanagan's lead alto saxophone player, had not spoken to each other for about two weeks. One day, Lanza turned to Davern and asked if he wanted to go with Jack Teagarden. It turned out that Hank D'Amico, who had been Teagarden's clarinetist, had left, and the trombonist was looking to replace him. Davern told Flanagan that he was going to audition for the job and went to the tryout at Frank Dailey's Meadow Brook, in Cedar Grove, New Jersey, where Teagarden was then working.

> So, I went out there and played a couple of numbers and nobody said anything to me—not a word. And I was sitting behind the stage. When the set was over,

everybody went their own separate ways, probably to the bar. I noticed that Jack was up in the bleachers and talking with his wife Addie. I was sitting there looking, and I said to myself "What am I doing just sitting in a chair behind the stage like an orphan. Let me go and see what's happening. . . ." I walked over to Jack and I said, "What's happening, Jack?" He said, "Where you been all my life, Kenny?" And that was it: that was heaven.[15]

"I came back to the New Yorker that night. Ralph sees me and he mouths the words "How did you do?" I said, "I made it," and he said "Do they need a piano player?"[16]

Jack Teagarden was then forty-nine years old and had been an established star since 1927, when he came to New York and revolutionized the trombone as a jazz instrument. In the decades that followed, Teagarden had appeared and recorded with Ben Pollack, Benny Goodman, Paul Whiteman, various Eddie Condon groups, the Mound City Blue Blowers, Jimmy McPartland, and Max Kaminsky. He had led his own band, been named to the Metronome All-Star Band, and, with Barney Bigard and Sid Catlett, had been part of Louis Armstrong's original All-Stars. After leaving Armstrong, Teagarden began touring with a sextet. At nineteen, Davern was the youngest member of the band: Fred Greenleaf, who was forty years old, was next.

Three days after joining Teagarden, the band had a recording session, and Davern played his first recorded solos. The band, with Kenny, Fred Greenleaf on trumpet, Jack, his sister Norma Teagarden on piano, Kass Malone on bass, and Ray Bauduc on drums, cut four titles that were released on a 10-inch Period label LP titled *Meet Me Where They Play the Blues*. Kenny had just begun to learn the band's arrangements and, on *King Porter Stomp*, it is clear that he was not quite comfortable. His solos on *Mis'ry and the Blues*, *Milenberg Joys*, and *Riverboat Shuffle* were far better constructed and revealed a facile and inventive musical mind. However, there was virtually nothing in Davern's playing to presage his unique tone and color.

Nat Hentoff, writing in *DownBeat*, gave the album three stars: Davern was not mentioned in the review.[17] In responding to a questionnaire for *the Encyclopedia of Jazz*, Davern said that his chorus on *Riverboat Shuffle* was his best on record. But then, he added "Hell, I'm still young yet."

Davern had joined while the band was at the Meadowbrook. It then played a three-week gig at the Savoy Cafe in Boston that started on November 15, followed by a stint at the Bali-Kea in Pittsburgh beginning on December 8. Davern liked working with Teagarden. "He was the greatest: he was just a marvelous, marvelous, guy. He was very laid back, the least likely candidate to become a bandleader."[18]

Kenny only remained with Jack for a few months. After the Pittsburgh job, Teagarden had booked an engagement on the West Coast, and union regulations would have limited Davern to only working one night a week for a period of six months. Instead, Davern gave notice and joined Phil Napoleon's band, which had a steady job at Nick's, a restaurant in Manhattan.[19]

Nick Rongetti had operated several speakeasies in the Greenwich Village section of New York. With the repeal of Prohibition, speakeasies were quickly transformed into restaurants and, in 1936, Rongetti opened a new place located at 7th Avenue and 10th Street, called Nick's, the Home of Sizzling Steaks. He decided to feature jazz at his new establishment. Davern remembered: "The band room was in the back and so was the liquor room. It was always kept under lock and key. With the likes of Miff Mole, Muggsy Spanier, and people like that, you'd have to keep it under lock and key."[20]

Eddie Condon and Pee Wee Russell quickly became fixtures at Nick's and, over the next decade, many well-known jazz musicians appeared there, including Max Kaminsky and Muggsy Spanier, Brad Gowans, Sidney Bechet, Bud Freeman, and Zutty Singleton. The music took on a distinct flavor and became known as "Nicksieland." Condon left in 1946, to open his own club on West 3rd Street, also in Greenwich Village and, in that same year, Nick Rongetti died. His widow, Grace, took over the management of the restaurant and, although she tried to continue as before, the music began to stagnate. By the time that Davern arrived in 1955, it had become "kind of a bloodless dixieland, commercial and uninspired."[21]

Phil Napoleon (born Filippo Napoli in 1901) had come to prominence in the early 1920s as the leader of the Original Memphis Five. When it first caught the public's eye, the OM5 was a progressive force in music, having refined the approach of the Original Dixieland Jazz Band and eliminated many of its comedic aspects. The group's stay at center stage was short for, as the music matured and changed in the late 1920s, Napoleon did not. During the early 1930s, Napoleon went into studio work, playing with several dance bands. In the late 1930s, he had his own big band, but then went back into studio work. In 1949, he formed a small group that appeared regularly at Nick's: he called it the Memphis Five.

The arrangements for the Napoleon group, for the most part, reflected Phil's musical origins. In his early years, he had played in speakeasies, where the music was expected to excite and entertain the customers. The arrangements reflected this, and there was a vaudevillian air to them. Tempos were halved or doubled in mid-song. There were rim shots, stop-time effects, and a host of gimmicky commercial tricks. Davern detested them. "It was a very structured band. A lot of people tend to like that kind of structure. I thought it was strictured—it was fun if you knew how to play very, very cleanly. I was always trying to schmutz it up a little bit and try to get as funky as I could. But really, I was a kid and wasn't that much in control of my situation, so to speak."[22]

Napoleon had set routines on many of his tunes and could not understand why Davern wanted to create something new each time that he played. Napoleon would ask him, "Kenny, why don't you play the same chorus on the same tune nightly?" I'd say "I can't do that."[23] Johnny Varro, who played piano in Napoleon's band, recalled the conflicts between the two men.

> Kenny and Phil were on totally different pages, musically. Kenny was young and aggressive and was very interested in playing like no one else. He didn't want to play like Benny, he didn't want to play like Peanuts or anyone else. He had his own ideas of how to play. He loved people like Jimmie Noone and . . . Omer Simeon. So, Kenny came in to play with Phil Napoleon, and they didn't hit it off. Kenny would come up with some funny phrases, or have some idiosyncrasies in his playing that Phil didn't quite understand. He wanted Sal Franzella or Gail Curtis. They just didn't hit it off well at all.[24]

One of the customers at Nick's was actor-comedian Jackie Gleason, then approaching the zenith of his career in television. Gleason liked dixieland jazz as played by Conrad Janis, Max Kaminsky, and Phil Napoleon, and he used Napoleon's band to warm up the audience for his Saturday night shows on CBS and to play for the audiences during scene changes on his *Honeymooners* television show. Gleason also had them perform at some of his parties. Davern was often part of the band at these events, as was Johnny Varro.[25]

> He also used him for the Jackie Gleason shows that we did in New York, the original half-hour shows that were so great. We sat in on all of those things. It was quite a treat. Gleason would come into Nick's and listen. He grew to like Phil, grew to like the band, and appreciated the music. The music was good. It was really an easy band to understand. Gleason was a conservative, and so he decided to use us. We played at some of his parties.[26]

Bands worked for six months at Nick's, and Napoleon's stint ended in the winter of 1955–56. During the off months, the musicians scuffled: some could get jobs in other venues or with other groups. Others, including Davern, lived from hand-to-mouth, collecting unemployment, and picking up an occasional odd job at places like the Cinderella Club, the Central Plaza, or the Stuyvesant Casino. Sam Parkins recalled playing at the Cinderella. "I met everybody there. I met Wellstood, I met Kenny, Abdul Ahmed-Malik, Billy Watrous. It was a helluva cast. It was a Friday and Saturday night place. A cornet player named Jack Fein had the band there. It was peanuts: $15 per night. But Jack had the urge to lead the jazz life."[27] For Davern, there were other aspects of working at the Cinderella that compensated for the low pay. "We all worked for about $17 or $18 a night and all you could drink. They wouldn't even feed us, but it was all the whiskey you could drink. Don't worry, we wiped them out."[28]

Tony Spargo (Sbabaro), the original drummer with the Original Dixieland Jazz Band, had worked at Nick's with Phil Napoleon while Davern was with him. When he heard that trumpeter Pee Wee Erwin was looking to put a new group together, Spargo recommended Davern, and Erwin hired him. In late March 1956, they started at the Melody Lounge in Woodside, Queens. From there, they went to the Windsor Park Hotel in Washington, D.C., where Spargo replaced Donaldson.

They opened at the Preview Lounge in Chicago on April 23, and stayed for three weeks. From there, they went to Mike Fletch's Grandview Inn in Columbus, Ohio, where they were scheduled to work through the end of the month. May 30 was Pee Wee's birthday. He had been struggling with alcohol for years: on this occasion, he fell off the wagon and went on an extended bender. By the time he sobered up, Davern and Spargo had left the band and returned to New York.[29]

Davern took occasional gigs in the big bands of Billy Butterfield and Johnny Long. He was touring army camps with Tommy Tucker's orchestra when he decided finally to quit playing in big bands.[30] In the meantime, Erwin had recovered and was working again. He had some bookings and, when he began to form another band, Kenny joined him. They played a week in Philadelphia, then opened at the Metropole on Broadway between 47th and 48th Streets in November 1956. Davern was with Erwin for several months, then left in early February to join Tony Spair.[31]

Spair was a trumpet player who liked Phil Napoleon, to the point of adopting his style and his arrangements. Tony had the job at the Rendezvous, a club in Trenton, New Jersey, and put together a group that was called the Empire City Six. The members were Harry DeVito, Davern, Varro, Pete Rodgers, and Phil Failla—in effect, Phil Napoleon's Memphis Five without Phil Napoleon. They opened at the Rendezvous on February 8, 1957, playing Fridays, Saturdays, and Mondays, and remained there through the end of June.[32]

Phil Napoleon had moved to Florida in 1956, and had taken up permanent residence there. In the late spring of 1957, Pee Wee Erwin was working steadily at several jobs, and Nick's was looking for a band to play for the last half of the year. Recognizing that their annual six-month gig was at risk, Davern, Varro, and DeVito approached Grace Rongetti and suggested that she hire the Empire City Six. To their relief, she agreed.[33]

The Empire City Six opened at Nick's on July 8, 1957. Mrs. Rongetti and the management at the restaurant were pleased with the group: it sounded very much like the Napoleon outfit. Customers liked them as well. During their term at Nick's, the band made two recordings that are of markedly different musical quality. Johnny Varro was instrumental in arranging the songs for the first album, titled *Empire City Six Salutes the Colleges*.

> At one point someone came in from ABC Paramount and liked the band. He wanted us to do an album, and we had a session with the people at ABC Paramount. They wanted an album of college songs—college fight songs. . . . I went into the library with blank sheet music and copied every one that I thought would be a feasible tune to play in our style. And, sure enough, a lot of them had little interludes that would lead us into the chorus. I did all of the arrangements, and I was very pleased with it. . . . It came off good, and it really sold. We'd get a report from ABC Paramount, and they were making up the money that they had spent for it. And, little by little, they made up all that money and, as soon as they did, sales stopped—according to ABC Paramount. We never heard from them again.[34]

The album, recorded on September 19, 1957, is surprisingly likeable, despite the fact that no tune runs more than two minutes, fifty seconds. The repertoire is unusual, the solos are fresh, and Varro's arrangements are tight, especially on the *Whiffenpoof Song* and *Harvardiana*. Davern and Varro have a great deal of solo space, and the group turns what could have been a boring exercise in commercialism into something quite dynamic. The only discordant note was that Davern's name was misspelled on the jacket as Kenny Laverne, which upset him greatly.[35] (His name was spelled correctly when four of the tunes were pressed on an HMV 45-rpm disk and released in England.) Sinclair Traill said that the band played with "style and agility." He also said that "the clarinetist plays with great fluency and has a very warm tone."[36]

The second album, the *Empire City Six Plays Dixie*, is far less adventuresome. It is a collection of often-played standards using arrangements that had been created for Phil Napoleon when he played at Nick's. The sound is commercial, and there are some Napoleon-style gimmicks, such as on *Tin Roof Blues* and *Black and Blue*, where the tempo is doubled for a short time, just as Napoleon had played it.

The job at Nick's ended in the winter of 1957, and Davern was again without steady income. The building at 111 2nd Avenue in Manhattan housed several catering halls that were usually hired for bar mitzvah receptions. On Friday and Saturday evenings, one room became the Central Plaza where Jack Crystal, the manager of the Commodore Record Shop by day, managed the activities of two bands that furnished continuous music. (He was the brother-in-law of Commodore owner Milt Gabler and the father of comedian Billy Crystal.) Across the street on 2nd Avenue was the Stuyvesant Casino, a similar operation.

The memory of the atmosphere at the Central Plaza stayed with Davern over the years.

> Jack Crystal ran sessions at the Central Plaza . . . and the greatest musicians in New York played there. . . . You name them: they all played there. I worked for Jack for many years on the weekends: they ran on Friday and Saturday nights. They generally catered to longshoremen and their wives who were out to have a good time. The inevitable fight would break out, with guys crashing pitchers of beer on each others' heads. Those were those heavy glass pitchers that they would buy for a buck-and-a-half. They would stack them, one on top of the other until they began looking like the Tower of Pisa. Of course, some wise guy would come along and push the whole kit and kaboodle onto the floor and a fight would ensue. They had three or four bouncers, and these guys were huge. We'd have to play *The Saints Go Marching In* until they cleared the floor and threw these guys down the flights of steps and out on 2nd Avenue—which happened a lot.[37]

Conrad Janis played trombone and led one of the house bands at the Central Plaza. His father, Sidney Janis, owned a successful art gallery in Manhattan and his mother, Harriet Janis, was the co-author, with Rudi Blesh, of the acclaimed history, *They All Played Ragtime*. When he wasn't playing trombone in his raucous, tailgate style, Janis was acting in plays. In this period, Conrad's band was working eight jobs each week. Although Gene Sedric was Janis's regular clarinet player, there were times when he could not make a gig, and Conrad would call upon Davern.[38]

At the Central Plaza, Davern frequently worked with the band that was opposite Janis.

> When I worked there, I generally worked with Roy Eldridge or Buck Clayton or Maxie Kaminsky, and occasionally with Red Allen and Joe Thomas. Louis Metcalf also played trumpet there. I played with Louie when we used to play those sailor joints on 8th Avenue. He had a little quartet. That's when there

was music all night long. I used to come in and sit with him. Trombone players ranged anywhere from Dickie Wells to Chief Moore. Clarinet players would vary from Eddie Barefield, Tony Parenti, or Gene Sedric. Willie "The Lion" Smith was one of the piano players, and the drummers could be Jo Jones, Arthur Trappier, or Manzie Johnson. There were no basses; they never used a bass.[39]

Davern worked less frequently at the Stuyvesant Casino, where he occasionally sat in and played baritone saxophone.[40]

These were tough times for a young musician. To make ends meet, Kenny took a job as a sales assistant at the Record Hunter, an upscale music store on 5th Avenue between 42nd and 43rd Streets, which specialized in selling recordings of classical music. Davern would upset the manager, Fritz Stahl, by refusing to push the records that the store was promoting, especially if he thought that there were better versions available. Yet, he kept his job. After two months, Davern got an offer from Buck Clayton to play the Rustic Lodge in New Brunswick, New Jersey, a gig that would have required him to leave fifteen minutes early in order to make the train. When Stahl refused to give Kenny the time off, he quit. Stahl must have liked Davern because he hired him again to work at the Record Hunter outlet on East 54th Street.[41]

Even though he was just out of his teens, there was something engaging about Kenny Davern. He read relentlessly and wanted to learn, not only about music, history, and the traditional education disciplines, but also about philosophy, existentialism, and a variety of abstract concepts. He was intelligent and quick, with an infectious sense of humor, and he had strong opinions on a number of subjects that he advanced vigorously.

He was subject to different moods; sometimes ebullient, on other occasions sad and withdrawn. He angered easily, often at things that others found trivial. His quick temper could be frightening, even to his friends, and he sometimes said things in the heat of anger that he would later regret. He was drinking and experimenting with substances that affected his state of mind and his reactions.

Davern desperately wanted to be noticed. For a time, he wore a long black cloak when he went out. He grew a beard at a time when musicians who were playing dixieland were clean shaven. He would wait outside the restaurant until the very last minute, then rush in and onto the bandstand as the band was about to start. He had little pieces of "business" designed to draw attention to himself while the others were playing. He would disassemble his clarinet and peer through it as if something was wrong, or change reeds in mid-song and throw the discarded one over his shoulder into the piano. He usually achieved his goal of attracting attention, often annoying the other musicians in the process.

But, he was clearly talented. Moreover, he had an appeal that transcended what appeared on the surface. He may have angered and bewildered Phil Napoleon, but the older man liked him and continued to hire him. He developed lifelong friendships with Pee Wee Erwin, Pee Wee Russell, and a host of other members of older generations. The friendship and respect that they gave to the young man, who was more than twenty years their junior, bespoke an intelligence and personality that were not often found.

It drew people to him. While still in his twenties, Davern began personal relationships that lasted for more than fifty years. Sam Parkins, whose friendship with Kenny dated from about 1956, called him a "very attractive person" and said that there was a "sweetness about him." Conrad Janis was attracted by Davern's independence and his refusal to pander to anyone.[42] Johnny Varro, who was also a friend for over a half-century, said:

> I liked him because he was different. He was his own man, his own personality. In the beginning, I couldn't understand him; I don't think anyone could understand Kenny. He was hard to understand. But, when you got to know him—when you sat down and drank with him and talked with him—even at that early age, he was a very intelligent guy. He was very well read, very bright, very opinionated. He would challenge society in many different ways—the government, churches. He was always challenging something. But, when you sat down and had a conversation with him, he was very bright, very intelligent.[43]

After a while, the music that Davern was playing at Nick's ceased to challenge him. In the mid 1950s, he fell under the spell of the New Orleans clarinetists like George Lewis and Albert Burbank. Davern had come upon an album titled *A Night at Artesian Hall with Wooden Joe Nicholas and Albert Burbank*, and the music struck a responsive chord with him. He told Peter Clayton:

> But, around that time I was playing what you might call New York Nicksieland style. This had much more emotion to me, much more appeal. Of course, I was twenty-three years old and very impressionable. I decided that this was a *cause celebre*, so to speak, and that was it. You know "you guys are all wrong. This is the way it's supposed to be. Listen! This is it. . . ." It was my protest against the New York studio-dixieland jazz band, which was really puerile, as far as I was concerned—not much substance.[44]

Kenny was at Nola Recording Studios on a day when the members of the Red Onion Jazz Band were making a record. The Red Onion played in the New Orleans ensemble (or polyphonic) style, and Davern stopped to listen. When the session was over, he struck up a conversation and mentioned that he wanted to form a New Orleans–style band in the style of George Lewis.[45] The other musicians wanted to be a part of the venture.

The group that Davern assembled consisted of Frank Laidlaw on cornet, Steve Knight on trombone, Carl Lunsford on banjo, Arnold Hyman on bass, and Vince Hickey on drums. With the exception of Davern, all of them were earning the bulk of their income from nonmusical sources. Laidlaw was working at a Madison Avenue firm, Knight was studying experimental psychology at Columbia University, and Hyman was a schoolteacher in Philadelphia. Lunsford was then pursuing a career in acting. Hickey held several jobs: he would later appear on recordings with Turk Murphy and other members of the West Coast revival movement.[46]

They rented space at Carl Fisher Hall and, on October 15, 1957, recorded several tunes on a demo tape that Davern sent off to Elektra Records. While they were waiting for a response, the band had a number of engagements. They put on a program of George Lewis–type material, playing spirituals, blues, rags, and stomps at a country club in Englewood, New Jersey. Carmine DeSapio, then one of the most powerful political bosses in the history of New York, hired them during his re-election campaign to play while riding around the Chelsea district on the back of a flatbed truck. The band played a number of parties around Greenwich Village, in lofts, at the Village Gate, and at a few colleges in Pennsylvania and New Jersey.[47]

Although Kenny was playing with the Empire City Six or in Pee Wee Erwin's band, and the other musicians were playing with the Red Onion Jazz Band, everyone liked the music and made an effort to be available when the band got a gig. When they weren't working, they still got together to play for their own enjoyment.

After a while, Davern's interest in playing in the ensemble style waned, as did that of Laidlaw and several other members of the band. Davern told interviewer Terry Gross that, for a time, he had "waved the New Orleans banner." He abandoned the style because it was "crippling, like playing with one hand behind my back. I wasn't giving expression to what my full potential could be."[48]

In May 1958, Davern learned that Elektra had decided to proceed with the recording. He reassembled the group, except for Hickey, who was not in the City. To play drums, Davern hired Bob Thompson, who was the leader of the Red Onion Jazz Band and who also taught psychology at Columbia

University. In June, they recorded *In the Gloryland* for Elektra Records under the name *Ken Davern and His Salty Dogs*. It was Davern's debut recording as a leader.⁴⁹

There are only eight relatively short tunes on this album. Several of the songs, *In the Gloryland, Just a Closer Walk with Thee, Precious Lord*, and *The Old Rugged Cross* were derived from the gospel tradition and the remainder, *Tiger Rag, The Streets of the City, Shake It and Break It*, and *Willie the Weeper* were staples of the New Orleans style. All of the numbers were played in the New Orleans polyphonic style, which bassist Pops Foster once described by saying: "In the early days, when you had a solo, the other instruments were always doing something behind the solo. None of the guys took their horns down for a chorus to let another guy play a solo. . . . The music was written so that you couldn't take down your horn."⁵⁰ Davern had a number of solos throughout the album, most of which featured Laidlaw or Knight playing phrases underneath him. At other times, Davern occupied the traditional clarinet player's role of playing obbligatos and counter melodies to support the brass.

Kenny and the others were not pleased with the result, preferring the session from the previous fall. They had little enthusiasm for playing in a musical idiom that most of them had abandoned some time before, and felt that the recording reflected their lack of interest. Elektra was then experimenting with stereo recordings, and Davern said that it sounded as if the date had been recorded in a telephone booth.⁵¹

Pee Wee Erwin, who had led a band at Nick's several years before, went back for a six-month stint beginning in June 1958. With him were some of his regulars: DeVito, Davern, and Varro, along with Charlie Traeger on bass and Mousie Alexander on drums. The personnel changed from time to time: Whitey Mitchell or Irv Manning sometimes played bass, and Andy Russo took the trombone chair. Varro and the other musicians liked working with Pee Wee.

> It was a fun band. The house wasn't always happy because we'd swing too hard. It wasn't a two-beat band: this was a straight-ahead, four-beat band, and it swung. They didn't like it because we swung too much. They wanted us to play more dixieland, Phil Napoleon style. The following season, when we came back with the same band, they didn't want Mousie (Alexander) on drums because it swung too hard. They wanted Tony Sbabaro (Tony Spargo): that was a change we made. Now, Tony was a good drummer and had good time, but he was a two-beat drummer, and it didn't swing as hard and it affected his [Davern's] playing.⁵²

On October 24, 1958, Pee Wee and Kenny recorded the first of six albums that they would make together over the next four years: *Pee Wee Erwin's Dixieland Eight, Oh Play That Thing*. Erwin later wrote that "Kenny Davern, whose musical judgment I have always appreciated and trusted, did most of the groundwork."[53] The title notwithstanding, most of the selections are not of the dixieland warhorse variety. There are four Jelly Roll Morton pieces, plus Morton's arrangement of *The Chant*, a Mel Stizel composition. In addition, the album includes a Joe Oliver tune, two Pee Wee Erwin originals, and several rarely heard songs.

Erwin and Davern were the only musicians from the band at Nick's on this date. Lou McGarity was on trombone, Dick Hyman played piano and organ, Tony Gattuso played banjo and guitar, Jack Lesberg was on bass, Harvey Phillips was on tuba, and Cliff Leeman played drums. Although the musicians echoed the original recordings in many instances, they did not slavishly copy them. Two numbers, *Black Bottom Stomp* and *The Chant*, had been recorded in 1926 by Jelly Roll Morton and his Red Hot Peppers, with George Mitchell on trumpet and Omer Simeon on clarinet. The opening notes of Davern's solo on both numbers paid homage to Simeon, and then he proceeded to transform Simeon's concepts into his own. Erwin's solo on *Black Bottom* gave similar treatment to George Mitchell's solo.

The song from whence the title of the album was derived, *Dippermouth Blues*, was recorded in 1923 by King Oliver's Creole Jazz Band, with Louis Armstrong, who was then playing cornet, and Johnny Dodds on clarinet. Davern began his solo like Dodds', but soon restructured it into his own creation. Erwin, like most other trumpeters who have essayed this tune, incorporated much of Oliver's work into his solo. And, like almost every version since that time, this one contains the shouted break "Oh, play that thing!" originally called out by banjoist Bill Johnson.

In his autobiography, Pee Wee wrote: "At Nick's, [Kenny] had perfected an unbelievably successful solo on *Over the Waves*, using a straight, heavy, four-four beat behind it. The pitch and intensity he built up would literally drive the audience into a frenzy, and to this day I consider it to be the most consistently sensational solo ever heard on a bandstand."[54] The song was retitled *Big Pond Rag* for this album and was a Davern showcase. But, in Pee Wee's opinion, cutting the length of the tune to comply with the limitations of recording destroyed the effect of Kenny's work.[55] As will be seen, it did not make it any less memorable.

Sinclair Traill reviewed the *Play That Thing* album in *Jazz Journal*, and was not overwhelmed by it. However, he noted, "The band boasts a most interesting newcomer, clarinetist Kenny Davern. . . . He uses a lovely fat tone, and in his feature piece, *Big Pond Rag*, he shows a complete mastery over his instrument."[56]

The Erwin band's tenure at Nick's came to an end in December. Davern landed a job with trumpeter Herman Autrey, playing at Henry's, a restaurant in Brooklyn. At times, Davern also appeared on the *Tonight Show*, the *Jimmy Dean Show*, the *Today* show, and the *Jackie Gleason Show*.[57]

Davern recorded frequently during 1958–62 and, early in this period, he participated in one of his more unusual musical adventures, the making of *Hans Conreid Narrates Peter Meets the Wolf in Dixieland*. The recording was the creation of co-producers Fred Hertz and Joel Herron: Herron abridged the original score by Sergei Prokofiev, sandwiched the remnants into a dixieland format, and wrote some original themes as fillers. Hertz wrote the narrative.

Pee Wee Erwin, Davern, Lou McGarity, and Cliff Leeman were the nucleus of the band, along with Boomie Richman on tenor, Billy Maxted on piano, George Barnes and Tony Gattuso playing guitar and banjo, and Trigger Alpert on bass. Hans Conreid, who had enjoyed a long and successful acting career on the stage and screen, as well as in radio and television, read the narrative.

Side one of the record ran less than fifteen minutes in length, with Conreid telling the story in comic fashion, and the musicians playing short, heavily arranged, interludes. The reverse side consisted of six tracks, none more than two and one half minutes in length, where the musicians improvised on the various musical themes of Prokofiev's score. Davern's reaction to the project may be judged by the fact that, when his copy of the record fell down behind a radiator, he left it there and never sought to replace it.[58]

Erwin made a second recording for United Artists early in 1959. He reassembled McGarity, Davern, and Hyman, together with Lee Blair on banjo, Milt Hinton on bass, and Osie Johnson on drums, to make what was expected to be an album of gospel songs. Kenny had introduced a blues and spirituals singer named Chet Ely to Erwin, and Pee Wee decided to feature him on a recording on which he would be backed by the Hall-Johnson Singers. Tunes were selected, arrangements scripted, musicians engaged, and rehearsals with Ely and the Hall-Johnson Singers were held. But on the day of the recording session, Ely turned up with a sore throat and was unable to sing. United Artists paid off Ely and the singers, and the band recorded an all-instrumental album titled *Pee Wee Erwin and the Dixie Strutters, Down by the Riverside*.[59]

The result was somewhat disappointing. Almost all of the tunes were of the gospel genre and included *Down by the Riverside, Careless Love, Swing Low Sweet Chariot, Just a Closer Walk with Thee*, and *Lead Me On*. Tunes were short, solos did not stray far from the melody and, with the exception of Hyman's efforts on *When the Saints Go Marchin' In* and *Give Me the Good Word*, the individual work seemed bland. Only *Marching into Glory Land* and *Everybody Needs a Helping Hand* had the drive that the group was capable of generating. Kenny soloed throughout. Don DeMicheal reviewed the release in *DownBeat* and called it a "nice album." He went on to call Davern ". . . especially adroit in this style. His ability puts me in mind of George Lewis, while his solos take on an Irving Fazola hue. Some of his work is marred, however, by a tendency to play a little flat."[60]

At the end of July 1959, the Pee Wee Erwin band returned to Nick's with DeVito, Davern, Varro, Traeger, and Spargo, where they remained until February 1960. To Davern, it seemed to be part of the pattern of life.

> I used to do that for six months a year. Johnny Varro and I played with Pee Wee Erwin's band. . . . We'd be off for six months: I'd be playing the Central Plaza or the Cinderella Club on West 3rd Street and, when we got back and hit the stand, I'd look over at Johnny after the third tune and he'd look at me and this recognition would come: "Jesus Christ, it's like we never left."[61]

A certain amount of subterfuge surrounded Erwin's next recording, which was titled *The Dixie Rebels Strike Back with True Dixieland Sound*. Pee Wee had agreed to record for Enoch Light on his Command label, but, at the time, he was still under contract to United Artists. To circumvent this restriction, the anonymously written liner notes identified the trumpet player as "Big Jeb Dooley" and wove a fanciful story about how "Dooley" had made this record because he was indignant about the misidentification of Chicago-style playing with "True Dixie." Perhaps out of an excess of caution, none of the other musicians on the date were identified on the record jacket. In fact, the band consisted of Erwin and Davern, with Lou McGarity, Gene Schroeder on piano, Milt Hinton, and either Cliff Leeman or Panama Francis on drums.

This album includes twelve dixieland standards and, although each of the musicians had played them many times, neither the tunes nor the musicians sound tired or bored. McGarity is featured on *St. James Infirmary*, where he evokes memories of Jack Teagarden. Davern takes slow mournful solos on *Basin Street Blues* and *Tin Roof Blues* and an up-tempo chalumeau stroll on *South Rampart Street Parade*. On the remainder of the album, which includes *Original Dixieland One Step*, *Hindustan*, *Clarinet Marmalade*, and *When the Saints Go Marchin' In*, all of the horn players have full one-chorus solos. Schroeder only solos on *Panama*, *That's a Plenty*, and *Fidgety Feet*, and then for very short periods.

Stereophonic sound was still in its infancy at the time of this recording, and Light was enamored with its possibilities. On this record, he went to great lengths to aurally separate the instruments, and Davern recalled that, during the recording session, Light was far more interested in the sound of the music than in the music itself.[62]

George Hoefer reviewed the album in *DownBeat* and gave it three stars. A knowledgeable and sophisticated writer, Hoefer must have been in on the joke, for he described the fictional Jeb Dooley as a "well-known trumpet player who led his own band around New York." *Hi Fidelity* magazine said that the performances were "lusty and spirited," and singled out the "consistently impressive clarinet playing of Kenny Davern."[63]

In October 1959, Kenny made the first of three albums with Phil Napoleon (which are discussed below). In that same month, he also made a recording that became one of his favorites. Dick Cary had written arrangements of a number of songs that were in the public domain, and assembled an eclectic group of musicians to play them. Lee Blair and Tommy Benford, both of whom had played with Jelly Roll Morton, were on banjo and drums, and Tommy Potter, a long-standing member of Charlie Parker's groups, played bass. Leroy "Sam" Parkins, who was leading a group called the Yazoo River Jazz Band, played clarinet, tenor saxophone, and bass saxophone. In addition to Davern on clarinet and Cary on trumpet, the rest of the group consisted of Harry DeVito on trombone, Dick Wellstood on piano, either Harvey Phillips or Phil Cadway on tuba, and Cliff Leeman, who had played drums with Artie Shaw, Tommy Dorsey, Charlie Barnet, and Woody Herman. Davern called the assemblage a "mish-mosh."[64]

The album was called *Dick Cary and His Dixieland Doodlers*. On three days in late October, the group recorded twelve titles, including *Nobody Knows the Trouble I've Seen, I've Been Working on the Railroad, There's a Tavern in the Town,* and *Swing Low, Sweet Chariot*. There are no extended performances here: the longest tune is three minutes, eighteen seconds and the shortest is two minutes, four seconds. With the exception of Davern's outings on *I've Been Working on the Railroad* and *In the Good Old Summertime*, none of the solos were more than one-half chorus. Kenny had substantially more musical freedom than the others, and he played gracefully underneath the many ensemble passages, particularly on *There Is a Tavern in the Town* and *Camptown Races*. On *Jeannie with the Light Brown Hair*, he duetted with Potter on the opening and closing choruses, and gave the tune a languid and reflective air that contrasted pleasantly with the remainder of the album. Davern thought that it was his best album up to that time.[65]

During the period that Davern was entranced by the New Orleans style of music, he had returned to playing an Albert system clarinet, feeling that it gave him a more authentic sound. He continued using it until he finished the *Dixieland Doodlers* recording, then gave it up. He told Dan Morgenstern:

> The reason that I went back to Boehm is because you could not tell the difference. People I played both systems for could not hear any real difference between me playing Albert or Boehm systems. They claim, whoever "they" are, that there is a real big, serious difference. I think that Jimmie Noone or Johnny Dodds or any of those guys, including Irving Fazola, would have sounded the same—no matter which instrument they chose. So strong were their personalities that it would have shown true. I think that there's quite a myth going on.[66]

At either the end of 1959 or the beginning of 1960, Erwin recorded his second album for Enoch Light, this one titled *The Dixie Rebels Starring "Big Jeb Dooley," True Dixieland Sound*. The anonymously written liner notes again related a tale about the views held by this legendary, but fictitious, trumpeter. However, the notes did identify the sidemen as McGarity, Davern, Hinton, Leeman, and pianist Johnny Varro, then sometimes playing under the name of John Mortillero.

Like its predecessor, this album was composed of standards on which all of the horn players and Varro take solos. Davern takes the obbligato in the chalumeau register under the ensemble's refrain of *Tiger Rag* and constructs some unusual solos on *Wang Wang Blues* and *Livery Stable Blues*. The arrangement of *Limehouse Blues* is basically the same as the one that Phil Napoleon used, but the tempo and Erwin's musical personality change the sound and feel of the piece.

Napoleon had been invited to play at the Newport Jazz Festival in July and, on the way up from Florida, stopped in New York to hire Davern and Varro to go with him. In October 1959, Napoleon returned to New York and, using DeVito, Davern, Varro, Pete Rodgers, and drummer Sonny Igoe, cut the first of three albums for Capitol records, *Phil Napoleon and His Memphis Five*. He had the same personnel when, on January 26 and 27, 1960, he recorded *Phil Napoleon in the Land of Dixie*, and shortly thereafter when they started making *Tenderloin in Dixieland*.[67] Varro understood why Napoleon had called Davern. "He grew to understand that Kenny was *the* player of the time. He used him at Newport. At this point, Kenny had modified himself, had gotten more into a flowing style, had straightened out all of these idiosyncrasies, and it came together so well. Kenny created an excitement that Phil appreciated, even if he didn't understand it."[68]

Although some of the tunes and arrangements are the same as on the Erwin records, there is a vast difference between them. There is a relaxed feel to the music of the Pee Wee Erwin albums, regardless of the tempo at which it is played. But, on the Napoleon albums, there is a sense of being rushed. Virtually every tune is taken at a faster than usual pace, and *Creole Rag, Wang Wang Blues, Shake It and Break It, Just Hot, Shim-Me-Sha-Wabble,* and *Sensation Rag* are unduly quick.

All of the tunes were heavily arranged, especially *Milenberg Joys* and *Come Back to Sorrento,* on the *Memphis Five* album and *Tin Roof Blues, Dardenella,* and *Ciri-Biri-Bin* on the *Land of Dixie* record. Tempos were doubled or halved, and there were clearly scripted rim-shots and breaks that coincided with high notes by Napoleon. All in all, there was a contrived and vaudevillian feeling to these albums.

Napoleon only gave his sidemen a half-chorus solo on each tune; an exception being on *After You've Gone* on the *Memphis Five* album, where Kenny had two full choruses, the first of which was almost in a Goodmanesque vein. He was heard in the chalumeau range on *South* and *Creole Rag* and, on the remainder of the cuts, he played obbligatos underneath Napoleon or soared over the rest of the ensemble.

Davern was not pleased with Napoleon or the recordings. "But the music was too slick and commercial. I hated it. On our Capitol sides, where we had Sonny Igoe on drums . . . we did thirteen takes on one tune before Phil got his set chorus the way he liked it sounding, without him flubbing."[69]

Don De Micheal reviewed the *Memphis Five* album in *DownBeat* and gave it only two stars. He said that the New York style of jazz in the 1920s was "noted for its sterility, pretentiousness, stiffness, and contrived routines," and that Napoleon was one of the creators of that style. After savaging the album, De Micheal noted that Davern and DeVito "played with some fire."[70]

Tenderloin was the title of a play that ran for 216 performances on Broadway. The music for the show had been written by Jerry Bock and Sheldon Harnick, and, although one of the tunes, *Artificial Flowers,* had become a hit for singer Bobby Darin, the remainder of the music was less than memorable. Nonetheless, management at Capitol records thought that it was a suitable vehicle for Phil Napoleon and so, after finishing the *Land of Dixie* album, Napoleon and the other musicians returned to the studio to begin recording *Tenderloin in Dixieland.*

The music did not improve when presented in a dixieland format. Davern said: "There was a show on Broadway called *Tenderloin,* and it was one of the biggest flops of all time. But, just the same, someone got the bright idea that we should record the hit tunes from the show—of which there were none—and consequently the record was just as bad as the show."[71]

The recording process was arduous and was made even more so by Napoleon's focus on his own solos, which necessitated numerous retakes. Davern, already unhappy with the effort involved in making the earlier albums, became increasingly upset as the session progressed. In later years, Davern liked to say that he and Varro got fed up and walked out. Johnny had a different recollection:

> We didn't walk out: actually, we were fired. We wanted to play our own stuff, to play some jazz. They had all of these arrangements made for all of these strange show tunes, like *Artificial Flowers*, and a lot of those tunes didn't swing. There wasn't too much to them. So, Kenny and I spoofed on them and laughed at them. We were very bush-league, very amateurish. We had some Wild Duck wine, too. Next thing we know, we got a call "Don't come back for the rest of the date." Peanuts [Hucko] took over Kenny's role and Buddy Weed took over my role.[72]

At about this time, Davern became involved in a project that was far different from anything he had done to date. Although he had always been associated with earlier styles of music, his interests were more far-ranging. When Ornette Coleman started to become a musical force, Davern listened to him. Kenny told interviewer Shirley Klett that Coleman's concepts "knocked me out."[73]

Davern was friendly with trombonist Roswell Rudd, who had begun his professional career playing the same genre of music as Davern. By the end of the 1950s, Rudd was writing and arranging in an avant-garde style. Both Rudd and Davern were close to Steve Lacy, who had led the ill-fated band that played at the Savoy in Boston. Like Rudd, Lacy had moved away from the older style of music and was then playing Free Jazz. It was Rudd's idea to put a rehearsal band together, a project that the others enthusiastically endorsed. The personnel varied, depending on who was available when the group was scheduled to rehearse. The concept was for everyone to regularly get together and play—strictly for their own enjoyment. Getting a paying gig was not the purpose of the project, although occasionally one came along.

Davern liked the way that the band started out:

> Our motto was "From Bunk to Monk," with Ellington as the common ground. Roz wrote some great charts, and we'd play things like *Ko Ko* and *Harlem Airshaft*. Then it was decided to expand the band, and Roz added Charles Davis on baritone and Archie Shepp on tenor. Carla Bley and Cecil Taylor brought

in charts, and both played piano occasionally with different drummers and bass players.[74]

From time to time, Kenny would come over Roswell's place, and the two of them would play together. Rudd found it exhilarating:

> The thing I remember is that Kenny would come by and we would just play. And he was one of the few people who was good at this. To me, he was a free player. He could go in any kind of a direction. It was possible to get together in a space with him and just see what happens. I think that's the way that I best remember him.
>
> We would just see what happened and blow for about an hour and see what comes out. He was really good at this. Great ears, good sensitivity, great inventiveness. He could really do the call-and-response thing. He was really grounded in the collective counterpoint. He really knew his part. He learned it from the old music; Johnny Dodds, Jimmie Noone, those great cats who were masters of collective improvisation.[75]

However, the new players who came on board eventually caused the project to fall apart. Davern never attempted to substitute technique for content and always resisted the notion that playing for long periods of time was, of itself, the making of a meaningful musical statement. He told Dan Morgenstern, in one of his most pithy and frequently quoted comments:

> The expansion was the beginning of the end. We'd start a thing like *In a Mellotone*, and Roz would take a modest five or six choruses and I three or four or five. And then Archie would do forty-five minutes! This was at rehearsal: we were going to do some public school concert.
>
> I didn't know that I was in on the beginnings of energy playing—which doesn't necessarily mean *content* playing. Louis Armstrong can say something with one note, but there are others who take an hour to rev up, and wind up with a fart in a bathtub. . . . The band broke up.[76]

As the 1950s ended, Davern could look back on his accomplishments with more than a modicum of pride. At the age of eighteen, he had been hired by one of the most popular bandleaders in the country. One year later, he was working for Jack Teagarden and, shortly thereafter, he was playing at one of the most prestigious jazz spots in New York, hired first by Phil Napoleon and then by Pee Wee Erwin. He was accepted as an equal by his peers, who recognized that he was a gifted artist. Indeed, almost half a century after the event, pianist Dick Hyman would remember his initial encounter with Davern: "The first time I played with Kenny was on the Pee Wee Erwin album, *Oh, Play That Thing*. Kenny had a featured track on the old waltz, *Over the Waves*—the label calls it *Big Pond Rag*—which he played in a George Lewis style, and I thought it was wonderful."[77] It should have been a satisfying time for him.

It was not. Although he had switched from the Boehm system to the Albert system and then back to Boehm, and experimented with any number of clarinets, mouthpieces, and reeds, he still had not found a way to satisfactorily express his emotions on his horn. He had spent time following the muse of George Lewis, only to find himself confined and restricted to a primitive and narrow musical spectrum. Dodds, Teschemacher, Noone, and Fazola offered alternatives, but did not provide a solution. And, while he was searching for a way to find his own unique musical identity, he was playing nightly at Nick's, where the customers and the management wanted the same old tunes played in the same old way.

There were other problems. Several relationships with women had failed to develop, and at least one had ended badly. He had not come to terms with his relationship with his mother. She was involved in several aspects of his life, and he would sometimes verbally lash out at her.

The combination of professional frustration and personal distress resulted in emotional anguish. Davern was depressed and distraught at what he perceived to be his own lack of creativity and skills, and by his inability to express himself musically. He was lonely and withdrawn, angry at himself, his audiences, and the world, and willing to strike out at everyone. Even though he sought professional help, these problems continued to plague him.[78] So he did the only thing that he knew how to do to survive: he continued to play music wherever he could.

Davern had been living in Riverdale, in the same apartment building as Ruby Braff who, in the spring of 1960, put together a small group. Davern played clarinet and, for the only time outside of a big band, also played alto saxophone. The other members were Bobby Pratt on piano and trombone, Russell George on bass, and Buzzy Drootin on drums. The band had only one gig before they broke up, at the Roundtable in Toledo, Ohio. Kenny went back to New York and, in August, was back with Pee Wee Erwin at Nick's.[79]

Notes

1. Morgenstern-*DownBeat*; Rowe interview.
2. Morgenstern-*DownBeat*; Rowe interview.
3. Rowe interview.

4. Flanagan band itinerary.
5. Rowe interview.
6. Rowe interview.
7. Dirk interview, p. 6. The vocal group with the band was called the Singing Winds: Davern renamed them the Passing Winds. Will Friedwald, "A Chat with the Clarinetist, A Traditionalist Who Makes Every Note Count," *New York Sun*, 29 November 2005.
8. Morgenstern-*DownBeat*.
9. Rowe interview.
10. Kenny Davern, interview by the author; Peerless Program Notes, p. 8.
11. Morgenstern-*DownBeat*.
12. Peerless Program Notes, p. 8.
13. Vacher, Davern, pp. 32–33. See also: Kenny Davern recorded on the *Jazzspeak* track on *Summit Reunion*, Chiaroscuro CRD 311.
14. Flanagan Band itinerary.
15. Kenny Davern, interview by Mark Weber, 17 January 2006.
16. Kenny Davern, interview by Mark Weber, 17 January 2006. See also: Kenny Davern, interview by Peter Clayton, broadcast on *The Sounds of Jazz* on BBC Radio 2 on 22 April 1984.
17. Nat Hentoff, "Jack Teagarden," *DownBeat*, 22, no. 4 (23 February 1955): 14.
18. Kenny Davern, interview by Mark Weber, 11 July 2002.
19. Advertisements for both engagements; Kenny Davern, interview by Mark Weber, 17 January 2006.
20. Kenny Davern, interview by Mark Weber, 5 September 2002.
21. Dan Morgenstern, interview by the author, 16 May 2007; Warren Vache, Sr., *This Horn for Hire, The Life and Career of Pee Wee Erwin* (Metuchen, N.J., Scarecrow Press and the Institute of Jazz Studies, Rutgers, University, 1987), 253 (hereinafter "Vache, Erwin").
22. "Kenny Davern, interview by Bob Rusch" on 15 October 1987, published in part in *Cadence* 15, no. 5 (May 1989): 11 (hereinafter "Rusch interview part 1") and in *Cadence* 15, no. 6 (June 1989) (hereinafter "Rusch interview part 2"). The cited material can be found in Rusch interview part 1 at 14.
23. Kenny Davern, quoted in Rusch interview part 1, 18.
24. Johnny Varro, interview by the author.
25. Varro interview; Rusch interview part 1, 14; Kenny Davern, interview by Mark Weber, 17 January 2006.
26. Johnny Varro, interview by the author.
27. Leroy "Sam" Parkins, interview by the author.
28. Kenny Davern, interview by Mark Weber, 28 November 2002.
29. Kenny Davern, interview by Mark Weber, 15 January 2004; Vache, Erwin, 256–258.
30. Kenny Davern on Fresh Air Interview.

31. Kenny Davern resume, Vache, Erwin, 266–267.

32. "Duffy's Doubletalk," the *Trentonian*, 8 March 1957; advertisements in the *Trentonian*.

33. Warren Vache, Sr., "A Visit with Johnny Varro," *Mississippi Rag*, xxii, no. 9 (September 1994): 1, 4; Johnny Varro, interview by the author.

34. Johnny Varro, interview by the author.

35. The record jacket also incorrectly spelled the name of the trumpet player as Tony Spars. This error was repeated on the other Empire City Six album, which is doubly unfortunate since he never made another recording.

36. Sinclair Traill, "The Empire City Six," *Jazz Journal*, 11, no. 10 (October 1958).

37. Kenny Davern, interview by Mark Weber, 17 January 2006.

38. Conrad Janis, interview by the author.

39. Kenny Davern, interview by the author.

40. Kenny Davern, interview by the author.

41. Peerless Program Notes, 11.

42. Leroy "Sam" Parkins, Conrad Janis, interview by the author.

43. Johnny Varro, interview by the author.

44. Kenny Davern, interview by Peter Clayton, 22 April 1984. See also: Kenny Davern with Bob Porter, "Before and After, Kenny Davern," *Jazz Times*, December, 1997, 119–120.

45. Frank Laidlaw, interview by the author.

46. Anonymous, liner notes to *Ken Davern and His Salty Dogs, In the Gloryland*, Electra 201-X.

47. Frank Laidlaw, interview by the author; Frank Laidlaw, e-mail to the author.

48. Kenny Davern, interview on Second Fresh Air Interview; Frank Laidlaw, interview by the author.

49. Frank Laidlaw, interview by the author.

50. Pops Foster, as told to Tom Stoddard, *The Autobiography of Pops Foster, New Orleans Jazzman* (Berkeley, University of California Press, 1971), 75.

51. Frank Laidlaw, interview by the author.

52. Johnny Varro, interview by the author. See also: Vache, Erwin, 262–263; Peerless Program Notes, 10.

53. Vache, Erwin, 282–283.

54. Vache, Erwin, 283.

55. Vache, Erwin, 283.

56. Sinclair Trail, "Pee Wee Erwin's Dixieland Eight, Oh Play That Thing," *Jazz Journal*, 12, no. 5 (May 1959): 16.

57. *Jazz Journal*, 12, no. 3 (March 1959): 33; Leonard Feather, *The Encyclopedia of Jazz* (New York, Horizon Press, 1960), p. 175; Small newspaper advertisement in Davern's files.

58. Kenny Davern, conversation with the author.

59. Vache, Erwin, 285–286.
60. Don DeMicheal, *DownBeat*, 27, no. 6 (17 March 1960): 36.
61. Kenny Davern, interview by the author.
62. Kenny Davern, conversation with the author.
63. George Hoefer, "The Dixie Rebels," *DownBeat Jazz Record Reviews*, vol. iv (1959): 58; Anonymous, *The Dixie Rebels*, Hi Fidelity, 9, no. 12 (December 1959): 135.
64. In July 1990, Dan Morgenstern interviewed Kenny Davern for the radio show that he hosted on station WBGO titled *Jazz from the Archives*. The first hour of the interview was broadcast on 11 August 1990 and will hereinafter be referred "Davern-Morgenstern interview 1." The second hour was broadcast on 26 August 1990 and will hereinafter be referred to as "Davern-Morgenstern interview 2." The material referred to in the text came from Davern-Morgenstern interview 2.
65. Davern-Morgenstern interview 1. *Mardi Gras* was a movie released in 1958, by Twentieth-Century Fox. An album of songs from the movie was issued on the Waldorf Music Hall label. Most of the music was performed by Enoch Light Orchestra, with a vocal chorus. However, on one cut, *When the Saints Go Marching In*, the band consisted of Erwin, McGarity, Davern, Hinton, Panama Francis, and an unidentified pianist and guitarist. Grant Elliot states that the Erwin septet and the Enoch Light Orchestra with a vocal chorus were on *Mardi Gras March* and *Bigger Than Texas*. Grant Elliot, *Swingin' Americans, No. 3, Kenny Davern Discography* (Zwolle, NL, Gerard Bieldeman, 2001), p. 9 (hereinafter "Elliott Discography"). The aural evidence does not support this, and the arrangements, as well as the performances, suggest that they were played by studio musicians.
66. Davern-Morgenstern interview 2.
67. The date of the *Land of Dixie* recording comes from pay stubs issued by Capitol Records.
68. Johnny Varro, interview by the author.
69. Vacher, Davern, 33.
70. Don De Micheal, "Phil Napoleon," *DownBeat, Jazz Record Reviews*, vol. v (1960): 145.
71. Allan Vache, "Jersey Jazzmen of Note, Kenny Davern," *Jersey Jazz*, 1. no. 1 (February 1974): 7 (hereinafter "Vache, Davern").
72. Johnny Varro, interview by the author; Kenny Davern, interview by the author. Late in the 1990s, Davern listened to the album and was only able to identify himself on *Good Clean Fun*. Varro was unable to recall any of the songs that had been finished before he left. Elliot Discography 9: Johnny Varro, telephone conversation with the author.
73. Klett interview, 22.
74. Morgenstern, *DownBeat*, 24–25.
75. Roswell Rudd, interview by the author.
76. Morgenstern, *DownBeat*, 24–25.

77. Dick Hyman, *Thinking About Kenny Davern*, unpublished article.

78. Letters sent to Davern over several years by Charles Ansell, M.D. and Donald Kaplan, M.D.

79. Peerless Program Notes, 11, Vache, Davern; *Melody Maker*, 36, no. 12 (19 March 1960): 14.

CHAPTER THREE

The Band at Nick's

The Hustler was a movie starring Paul Newman, Jackie Gleason, George C. Scott, and Piper Laurie in the story of a self-destructive pool hustler, played by Newman, who gets involved with Laurie, an alcoholic cripple. George C. Scott portrayed the cruel and devious manager of a pool shark named Minnesota Fats, played by Jackie Gleason.

One of the scenes takes place at a party in Louisville, Kentucky. Director Robert Rossen hired trumpeter Dan Terry to put together a dixieland band and to write a piece of music for them to play. Terry hired Roswell Rudd on trombone, Davern, Phil Woods on alto saxophone, guitarist Billy Bauer, and drummer Bunny Shawker. The tune he wrote was titled *Louisville*, and they shot the scene about a year before the movie was released in the fall of 1961. It was Kenny's only appearance on the silver screen.

Davern and the other musicians are visible as Piper Laurie limps slowly down a long staircase holding a drink in her hand, past the band, and into another room: they continue to play unseen as Laurie has a short scene with Scott. Rossen shot the scene numerous times from every conceivable angle and, as Kenny recalled the process, it consumed two eight-hour days. (Rudd said it was only one day and well into the evening.) But, both remembered that they kept repeating the same fragment of music for hours on end as the actors walked through the scene over and over again.[1]

The movie received an Oscar nomination for Best Picture of the Year. Newman was nominated for an Oscar for Best Actor, Laurie received a nomination for Best Actress, and both Scott and Gleason received nominations for Best Supporting Actor.

Davern had gone back into Nick's with Pee Wee Erwin in the summer of 1960. The music may not have been as stimulating as the musicians would have wanted. But, they liked each other and, when they weren't working, they were having fun. "We were a hard-drinking band at that point," said Johnny Varro. However, because management did not approve of drinking, and because drinks and food were cheaper at Julius's, which was down the street, the band did much of its between-sets relaxing there.[2] Drinking and having fun was an integral part of Davern's life at that time.

> I figured I started drinking about that period, in the '50s. I drank about two shots of booze with a beer chaser every set. So that's seven intermissions, which means fourteen shots of booze and seven bottles of beer. Then, after the night was over at 4:00 a.m., (trumpeter Johnny) Windhurst and I would go back to Hymie's, which was at 55 Christopher Street, and drink there until all hours. The detectives would come in at about 6 or 7 a.m. Hymie was the owner of the joint. He lived where I lived up in Riverdale with Ruby Braff. He would take me by cab up to where he lived, and I would walk the rest of the way. I would get home about 9 or 10 with a bag of rolls and a quart of milk and orange juice, and I would sleep to 5 p.m. I had a 9 to 5 job: 9 p.m. to 5 a.m., and the rest of it was fun and games.[3]

Erwin's band was replaced in November, but Davern was back at the beginning of 1961, in a band led by trombonist Harry DeVito that was sometimes called the Empire City Six and also the Empire State Six. Its members were Jimmy Sedlar playing trumpet, DeVito, Davern, Johnny Varro, Whitey Mitchell on bass, and Phil Failla playing drums.

Beginning in mid-1960, Pee Wee Erwin had begun to take an increasing number of studio jobs that interfered with his ability to perform nightly at Nick's. Eventually, he told Grace Rongetti that he would not be returning in the spring of 1961, and he turned the job over to Davern. Kenny took the opportunity to create a band that had his personal stamp upon it.

When Kenny Davern and his Washington Squares opened at Nick's on May 23, 1961, he was the youngest man in the group. Trumpeter Johnny Windhurst, born in 1926, had been an established performer for over a decade. He had played with Sidney Bechet, Red Allen, Ruby Braff, Jack Teagarden, James P. Johnson, Eddie Condon, and Lee Wiley. Windhurst had appeared at Town Hall and was a regular at Eddie Condon's club. Davern once called him "the most talented natural musician of . . . my generation."[4] He and Davern were also personal friends.

Trombonist Cutty Cutshall, born in 1911, had worked in several of Benny Goodman's big bands and became a regular at Condon's club when it opened shortly after the end of World War II. Buzzy Drootin, who was the drummer, was the oldest member of the group, having been born in 1910. He was a regular at Condon's and had performed with most of the jazz greats of the 1940s and 1950s, including Billy Butterfield, Bobby Hackett, and Pee Wee Russell.

> The first drummer was Buzzy Drootin and I said, "Who do you want on piano?" and he said, "Have you heard this guy Davey Frishberg?" I said, "No," and he said, "You've got to hear him." So, I hired Dave Frishberg. Then I said to Dave, "Who do you want on bass?" And he said, "Have you heard this guy, Jack Six?" On the strength of that, I thought that here's the basis for a rhythm section. Because all these guys are happy together. And, you can hear how well they played together.[5]

About a month after the band opened, Drootin left and was replaced by Cliff Leeman.

Jack Six, born in Illinois in 1930, had grown up studying trumpet, but switched to bass. He had played in the bands of Claude Thornhill, Woody Herman, and the Tommy Dorsey ghost band. Six's musical interest lay in bebop, and he had little experience with the repertoire that Davern intended to play. Dave Frishberg was born in 1933, and had played with Kai Winding, Carmen McRae, and Gene Krupa. Like Six, he was interested in more modern music and had little familiarity with the tunes that Davern would call.

Davern was determined to avoid the structured sets that he had played over the past five years at Nick's. "You could tell what time it was by what tune you were playing," he once said.[6] Although his band was compelled to play some of the dixieland warhorses that their audiences had come to expect, they were far from the bulk of an evening's performances. Davern would put together an "Ellington Set," with tunes like *Azure, Shout 'Em Aunt Tillie,* or *Black and Tan Fantasy.* There was a "Louis Armstrong Set" with obscurities like *It's the Last Time Honey Babe* and *I'm Not Rough.* Frishberg lived across the street from Nick's and, sometimes during the thirty-minute breaks between sets, he and Davern would go back to Dave's apartment, have a few beers, listen to some records, and, if they found something new, they would teach it to the others.[7]

Davern was always proud of that band and thought it was one of the best he ever played with—a feeling shared by the other musicians. Dave Frishberg said:

> It was a very good band: they were really wonderful, inspired ensemble players. Windhurst was a real stylist, an uncommonly good trumpet player. He

was like Hackett, only hotter. It's hard to imagine the band without Kenny. He flavored the band: it was mainly Kenny that you walked away with after you heard the band. . . . The band was so good, and the audience loved it. But, it intimidated Grace Rongetti and the management because it wasn't what they were used to. It was more the management of Nick's that was disappointed with Kenny's band, not the people. Everybody thought it was the hottest band they ever heard. Kenny loved that band and loved the way they played *his* music.[8]

Dan Morgenstern wrote in *Metronome* that it was the best band to have appeared at Nick's in ten years. In his *Dream Street* column in the *News*, Robert Sylvester mentioned the Davern band favorably on several occasions. In May, he called the band "one of the liveliest of the new combos," and in July, he said that the band played "music that sounds like music."[9]

But, Grace Rongetti, the owner of Nick's was not pleased by the music or by Davern's attitude. As Dan Morgenstern remembered, the situation was fraught with tension. "Kenny was, even then, a rebel. I think that what happened was that she wanted the band to play all of the warhorses, and they wanted to play what they wanted to play. They certainly allowed for stuff like *Royal Garden Blues* and *That's a Plenty*, but they didn't want to be confined to that. She thought the band was too modern."[10]

Frishberg also roused the ire of the restaurant's management. Because he lived across the street, he could time his arrival so that he reached the stand at precisely 9:00 p.m., after the rest of the band was already on stage. The other members of the band mingled with the crowd before the music began. Although he knew that management wanted him to arrive in time to talk to the customers, Frishberg refused to do it, and Mrs. Rongetti was miffed.[11]

For at least one night, Nick's was not the only venue where Davern played. The New York *Post* reported that, at about 9:00 a.m. on the morning of July 27, two policemen spotted two men on a plank raft, floating down the Harlem River. One had a trumpet, the other a clarinet, and they were playing a dixieland tune together. It was Davern and Dick Sutton (Schwartz) and, when asked, Davern told the policemen that they had been standing on the bank of the river at about 250th Street when a raft floated by. "It seemed like a nice day for a ride," Davern said. The policemen told them to dock the raft at 225th Street, where they had been sighted, and to go home.[12]

About three months after the gig at Nick's began, it ended in spectacular fashion. The band had begun its Ellington set and, although memories differ about the name of the tune they were playing (Frishberg remembered it as *Black and Tan Fantasy*; Davern thought it was *C Jam Blues*), everyone agrees that, at some point in the song, Frishberg would hold down some of the keys on the piano with his left hand, stand up and lean into the piano, and pluck the strings with his right. For some reason, it upset Jack Russell, the manager at Nick's, and, in the middle of the song, he rushed over to Davern. As Kenny recalled the event, Russell yelled: "He's ruining the piano, he's ruining the piano. Tell him to stop it." I took the horn out of my mouth and I said: "Can you tell me after the set?" "No, tell him now, tell him now. He's ruining the piano." I said: "Get the f— out of my face, you asshole."[13]

Enraged, Davern halted the music and ordered the band off the stage. He then turned back to Russell, who had not only rudely shouted orders to him, but had done so in front of all of the customers while the band was performing. Davern verbally attacked Russell, who responded with equal vigor and vituperation and, in full view of the astonished patrons of the restaurant, the volume of the exchange and the quality of the profanities escalated. Eventually, Russell retreated to a place of safety behind the cash register, the hubbub died down, and the band returned to the stage and finished out the evening.[14]

Grace Rongetti liked Davern, and he probably could have kept his job if he had apologized to her. But he did not and she fired him and also Frishberg. On the following evening, the band at Nick's included Windhurst, Cutshall, Six, and Leeman, all of whom had been there on the prior night. Joe Barufaldi and Dick Wellstood replaced Davern and Frishberg, and the group was now called Johnny Windhurst and His Sheridan Squares.[15]

The debacle at Nick's was a harbinger of things to come. Davern had an unyielding resentment of authority that was coupled with a quick temper and an often self-destructive refusal to keep his mouth shut. His friend, Sam Parkins, called it Kenny's "self-defeating integrity."[16] It cost him the job at Nick's, and it cost him work throughout his life.

Davern believed that musicians (and himself in particular) knew—better than recording supervisors, promoters, club owners, and other non-musicians who were in a position to hire and fire performers—what music should be played, how it should be played, what would make the music sound best, and which musicians should be assembled to play it. These propositions seem almost beyond dispute, and many producers who agreed with them gave their performers a great deal of leeway in putting their performances together.

Among them was Hank O'Neal, President of Chiaroscuro Records, who recorded Davern frequently and brought him on his annual jazz cruises for more than fifteen years.

> Somebody who is highly intelligent can see flaws that ordinary folks can't. And so they get more upset about things than ordinary folks do. I learned a

long time ago that you're going to deal with creative artists like that. They are really creative artists on a high level and not some poopy-doopy artists that you don't take any guff from. Somebody like a Ruby Braff or Kenny, people who are unique at what they do and are deadly serious and not an act—this is something that you just put up with. Because, generally speaking, what you wind up with is going to be pretty good.[17]

Mat Domber, founder and owner of Arbors Records, invited Davern to perform at his annual jazz parties for a decade and recorded him over a dozen times. He had a similar point of view:

My philosophy of recording was, and still is, that you pick a leader who you think has the ability to lead and who has, musically, something to impart. By and large, I allowed the leader to choose the sidemen and the tunes. Because I always felt: do I know more about music than Kenny Davern? I certainly don't. So, if I have confidence that Kenny is that kind of player, let him do his thing.[18]

Not everyone had this attitude. The people who employ musicians often have an idea of what they want to hear, and that expectation might not coincide with the musician's vision of what he wants to play. Many musicians would yield and give the employer what he wants. Davern often did not.

Add to this a hair-trigger temper, especially when he believed that his musical integrity was being challenged, and one has a recipe for disaster. In most cases, the affront was not as overt as on that summer evening at Nick's, and Kenny's reaction was not as violent. But, he would bitch and grumble about things, even when he knew that the argument was unwinnable. If he thought that an audience or some of its members were being disrespectful, he would lecture them. He would bristle when asked to perform in circumstances that were not to his liking. He would get upset when asked to perform with musicians whom he felt were not competent, or whose playing he did not like. Once the mood overtook him, Davern took irascibility to a new level.

When he was upset, he would say things that were unkind or hurtful. He was not oblivious to what he was doing and knew that such conduct would have adverse repercussions. But, he seemed to be almost incapable of keeping the anger inside of himself. As his friend Allan Vache remarked: "He came with a set of instructions: open mouth, insert foot. Because he would say things and be very honest about it, and it would piss a lot of people off. It cost him a lot of work. I was talking to Elsa one time and she said that she would do everything to get him to keep his mouth shut and then he wouldn't."[19]

Many of the people who knew Kenny Davern accepted the grumbling, grousing, and occasional outbursts of temper as part of the overall package that comprised the man. They were not the entirety of his personality, and they did not affect the beauty of his music. But, there were others who decided that they did not have to put up with the *sturm und drang* that Davern brought with him and hired other clarinetists who did not cause them as much aggravation.[20]

In the early 1960s, Davern made *The Charleston City All-Stars Go Dixieland* album. It was the eighth recording that he had made with Erwin and McGarity in less than four years, and there are many similarities between their performances here and those on their prior albums. As with their earlier collaborations, the songs were of the "warhorse" variety and were well arranged. Everyone had opportunities to solo, and Kenny did well on *Sweet Georgia Brown* and *Shine*.

There was some significance to the way that Davern played on this album. It provided evidence that he was beginning to change his concept of musical construction. On three tunes, *When You're Smiling, Somebody Stole My Gal*, and *Ballin' the Jack*, he used far fewer whole-note, major-tone runs and began to employ the bent notes, half-tones, and flatted notes that became hallmarks of his later style. This transition in style would take years to be complete, but it was clearly under way.

One of the more important events that occurred during this period was when Kenny met Pee Wee Russell. Although Russell had played a significant role in Davern's decision to become a professional musician, the two had never come into contact.

Pee Wee was born Charles Ellsworth Russell in a suburb of St. Louis on March 27, 1906. When he was twelve, his father took him to see Alcide "Yellow" Nunez, the clarinet player then leading the Louisiana Five, and Russell was taken by the music and the instrument. His parents bought him a clarinet and found a teacher to instruct him. Like many others of his time, he listened to and learned from the first recordings of the Original Dixieland Jazz Band and particularly from the clarinet of Larry Shields.

He was sixteen years old when he left home to play professionally. Over the next few years, he worked Peck's Bad Boys, the Houston-based group led by pianist Peck Kelley, as well as with the band that Frank Trumbauer had put together that included Bix Beiderbecke.[21] A telegram from Red Nichols brought Pee Wee Russell to New York on August 14, 1927. His recordings at this time reveal a proficient clarinet and tenor sax player who sounded like most of his contemporaries. But, the work began to dry up and Russell returned to St. Louis at the beginning of 1929. After a few months, Pee Wee returned to New York and, on June 11–12, 1929, he recorded as part of the Louisiana Rhythm Kings, a group put together by Nichols. Russell's biographer, Robert Hilbert, wrote:

> In these first recordings made after a year's recording silence, we hear a very different voice. All traces of traditional clarinet convention are gone. Pee Wee employs many different sounds: at times, his tone is rough or shrill, precariously sliding on and off pitch; at other times, the sound is soft and warm, whispering, or full. His improvisations are punctuated with rasps or growls. He constructs new melodic lines, based on the chords of tunes. They are constructed with unusual choices of notes, including the frequent use of flatted fifths, which were not commonly used in jazz improvisations until the bop innovations of the mid-forties.[22]

This was Pee Wee's voice—one that was instantly associated with him. It was not the sound that listeners of Benny Goodman and Artie Shaw associated with the clarinet. To their fans, Russell's sound was disturbing; to his admirers—among whom were a large number of musicians—he was unique.

Russell worked steadily, but when the Depression took hold he had to scratch to stay afloat. There were occasional jobs and, most notably, a series of recordings that began in April 1932, with Henry "Red" Allen, as part of a group known as the Rhythmakers. In October 1934, he joined Louis Prima's band, where he stayed until early 1937 and, after remaining in Chicago for eight months, returned to New York to appear at Nick's.[23]

Over the next fifteen years, Russell, along with Bobby Hackett, Bud Freeman, and Eddie Condon, became fixtures on the bandstand at Nick's and later, at the place that Eddie Condon opened on West 3rd Street in Greenwich Village. Although Russell was intelligent and articulate among his friends, the public never saw this side of him. He was ill-at-ease among fans and hated small talk: his public conversations were often incomprehensible, filled with stammered mutterings. On the bandstand, he usually leaned against the piano while he played: his deeply lined face would contort and his body would twist and bend as he played, filling the air with the creaks and groans that characterized his playing. He drank steadily, although it did not seem to affect his performances. He was the quintessential oddball, a depressed artist making beautiful music.

For years, it was common knowledge that Russell was not taking care of himself. A gastric illness that went undetected for years rendered him unable to eat solid foods. He existed on milk, canned tomatoes, and increasingly more substantial amounts of liquor.

On New Years Eve, 1950, he collapsed while onstage in Sacramento, California. He was rushed to a hospital and admitted to a charity ward. He weighed only seventy-three pounds and was not expected to survive. The story was picked up on the wire services, and the jazz community responded. Louis Armstrong and Jack Teagarden, along with a number of other musicians, held a benefit in San Francisco that raised $1,500—enough to move Pee Wee out of the charity ward. There was a story in *Life* magazine, and more benefit concerts raised more money. At the end of February, he was released from the hospital in California and flew home to New York.[24]

Russell had married Mary Chaloff in 1943. Their marriage had been a stormy one, exacerbated by the fact that she was also a heavy drinker. At the time that Pee Wee fell ill, they were separated. After his return to New York, they reconciled, and Mary took charge of his recovery, severely limiting his alcohol intake, seeing that he ate and took vitamins, and helping him get his strength back. By July 1951, he was playing again in public, sober and emotionally stronger than he ever had been. He met up with producer George Wein and, when Wein began to produce the Newport Jazz Festivals, Pee Wee was featured prominently.

Kenny wrote about the unusual circumstances surrounding the first time they got together. It started with a call from Mary Russell, Pee Wee's wife:

> I was living in a squalid railroad flat on East 11th, between Avenues B and C; a six floor walk-up replete with cockroaches and frozen pipes in the down-the-hall toilet during winter. I wasn't as happy as a pig in shit, so to speak, but I existed working at Nick's six months a year and collecting unemployment the rest.
>
> One Sunday, the phone rang. Mary had heard from Ruby Braff that I had some of Pee Wee's records with Louis Prima, made in 1935 for Brunswick. According to her, it was one of the better times during Pee Wee's up-and-down career. and he often mused about whatever happened to those sides that he cut. I had them. . . .[25]

Mary asked if they could arrange to get together to hear the records, and Davern offered to walk over to their apartment, even though Manhattan was then in the midst of a blizzard.

> I marched through the snow with the dozen-or-so sides, holding on to them as if I were delivering the "grail" to the Pope. When I arrived at the apartment door marked 3D and buzzed the buzzer. . . . The door opened and Mary looked at me as if I was an absolute loon for having come out in the snow, mad enough to carry heavy 78s without falling on my ass on the ice. Pee Wee sat in a red

leatherette chair in this rather small but cozy apartment and stood up to greet me. At least they had heat, and I could hardly wait to grab for my handkerchief to relieve my nostrils of their usual unpleasantness.[26]

It was the start of a friendship that lasted to the end of Russell's life.

In the year following his departure from Nick's, Davern scuffled for a living. There were intermittent gigs at the Cinderella Club, the Riviera, and other venues. He had a job at the Colonial Tavern in Toronto near the end of 1961, and returned in the spring of the following year. Later, he joined the band that Ted Lewis was fronting at Roseland for a month. There were substantial periods when he did nothing and survived by collecting unemployment.

Kenny met Sylvia White in the winter of 1961, while he was at the Colonial Tavern in Toronto. Born Sylvia Hendry in Toronto in 1931, she was then separated from her husband, Mike White, with whom she had run a jazz club. She was quick-witted and clever, and stood about 5 feet 7½ inches tall with blue eyes and brown hair. Davern was attracted to her, and she was to him. They spoke on the telephone several times, and Davern saw her again when he returned to Toronto. The friendship grew, and Davern began to importune her to move to New York. About three months after they met, she agreed, and moved in with Davern in his apartment in Riverdale.

The transition was difficult for Sylvia. As he was throughout his life, Kenny spent most of his waking hours absorbed with the clarinet. For a while, Sylvia's closest friend was Kenny's mother. "Josephine was just like a girl friend. When I came here I was terribly lonely. . . . Josephine found that out and she just made herself available whenever she possibly could to me. She would phone me up and take me out to lunch, go shopping for clothes. . . . I was a just a poor lost soul at that point."[27] Sylvia needed someone to lean on, and Kenny took on the task. He listened to her, encouraged her and, when he thought that therapy would be helpful, brought her to the psychiatrist who he had been seeing for several years. "And, that's just the kind of guy he was—he would pick up a dog or a lost soul—and take care of it. He just wanted to take care of me. . . . He was just a very good guy."[28] The program worked: over time Sylvia began to regain her physical and emotional strength.

Kenny introduced Sylvia to Pee Wee and Mary Russell, who were then living at 37 King Street, and Sylvia became a close friend to Mary. When the Russells had the opportunity to move to a newer building, they offered their old place to Kenny and Sylvia. However, the new building had a prohibition against pets, and Pee Wee and Mary had a dog, Winky. The solution was a simple one: they left Winky behind, along with all of their old furniture. A few days later, Pee Wee came back to see if there was anything that he wanted to take with him. Davern told Russell biographer Bob Hilbert:

> While he was looking, I accidentally tipped over his recliner. Under it, we saw something that looked like it had been alive at some time. It was a formless shape, covered in dust and grime—Mary never cleaned. We poked it with a stick and finally I picked it up and wiped off years of accumulated dirt. It was a clarinet case, and in it was a Conn. Pee Wee looked at it and said, "So, that's where it went!" He had lost it eight years before. He insisted I keep it, and I have it to this day.[29]

These were especially hard times. Davern no longer had the security of working for six months each year at Nick's. The resurgence of interest in dixieland that had generated a number of recording dates for small labels and supported a number of short-lived nightclubs was on the wane. To complicate matters, Kenny, whose monetary needs were usually minimal, suddenly had a need for a large amount of money. Sylvia had become ill, was hospitalized, and underwent surgery. She had no insurance, no income, and no assets: however, she had a hefty hospital bill to pay. Kenny was determined to help her through this financial problem. To generate income, he signed a contract in November 1962, agreeing to play with the Dukes of Dixieland for one year. It was unthinkable to Kenny that he leave Sylvia behind: part of his arrangement with the band was that she could travel and stay with him.[30]

The Dukes were founded in 1949, by New Orleans–based brothers Frank and Freddie Assunto. Their father, Jac, joined them in 1955. Frank played trumpet, Freddie was on trombone, and Papa Jac played both trombone and banjo. Over the years, the group's personnel included clarinetist Jerry Fuller, who had been with Jack Teagarden, pianist Gene Schroeder from the Eddie Condon aggregation, and guitarists Herb Ellis and Jim Hall. The Dukes of Dixieland were very successful for over a decade, performing steadily and recording prolifically with a variety of artists, including an album with Louis Armstrong.

Although the Assunto family had homes in Las Vegas, the Dukes were on the road for the better part of every year. The band's itinerary shows that they began 1963 with a New Year's Eve performance at the Shamrock Hotel in Houston. They remained there until January 9, then went on to San Antonio, Waco, Dallas, and Baton Rouge before arriving in New Orleans for two weeks at the Roosevelt Hotel. They then did two weeks at the beginning of February in Chicago at the Palmer House, and a couple of one-nighters in Ohio and Massachusetts, before arriving in New York City to play a four-week engagement at the Metropole beginning on February 22.

In the middle of that appearance, Kenny and Sylvia were married at Manhattan's City Hall on March 11, 1963. Pee Wee Russell was Kenny's best man.[31] Kenny's mother, Josephine, had supported the idea. As independent as she may have been in her own personal life, the idea that her son and his lady friend were unmarried and living together disturbed her. Of more significance to Kenny was the impact that the decision would have upon Kenny's grandmother, Lottie. Then approaching her seventy-fifth birthday, Josephine's mother lived alone in her apartment in Queens, still faithful to the tenets of Orthodox Judaism by which she had lived her life.

Kenny understood that his "Bubbie" would be deeply hurt if she knew that he had married outside of his faith. ("Bubbie" is the Yiddish word for grandmother and was the term by which Kenny addressed her.) Sylvia was not Jewish. To explain her presence in Kenny's life, they had concocted a story that Sylvia was his cleaning lady and occasionally cooked for him.[32] The tale was obviously false and did not deceive the older woman. Yet, she played along with the ruse. ". . . [S]he had the strength to know that Kenny and I were together—and probably to know that we were married—but let us play that game that I was the cleaning lady. She didn't blink an eyelash about it. She would give me things: she gave me a few pieces of China. She would show me how to make potato *latkes*."[33]

The couple did not have a honeymoon. They left New York with the Dukes of Dixieland and did five nights at the Grandview Inn in Columbus, Ohio, a one-nighter in Joliet, Illinois, and then drove to Las Vegas, where they played at the Thunderbird Hotel. That gig was interrupted so that the band could travel to New York, where Davern made his only recording with the Dukes; a date with the famous Clara Ward Singers that was arranged by John Hammond.[34] The resultant album was released on the Columbia label under the title *We Gotta Shout—The Dukes of Dixieland with the Clara Ward Singers*. The Singers were a gospel group, and they are the featured artists here with the Dukes providing backup. The tunes include *Lord, Let the Train Run Easy*; *I'm Too Close to Heaven*; *In the Morning*; *Just a Closer Walk with Thee*; and *Just a Little While to Stay Here*—all sung in a traditionalist vein.

Davern was no stranger to this genre of music: both the *Down by the Riverside* album, with Pee Wee Erwin and his own *In the Gloryland* LP were from this repertoire. This was one of the few occasions on which he played an E♭ clarinet. The shorter and higher-pitched instrument had a more piercing tone that ensured that he would be audible, if only as a member of the supporting players. Dan Morgenstern, writing in *Jazz* magazine, gave the album a good review and said that organist Alton Williams, Buzzy Drootin, Davern, and Frank Assunto were "outstanding" in the background.[35]

On May 6, four days after the job at the Thunderbird ended, the Dukes were in Atlanta for a five-day engagement, followed by five days in Memphis, and one-nighters in Norfolk and Richmond, Virginia. They were in New York on May 24 for three weeks at the Metropole, then crossed the country, stopping at Harrisburg, Pennsylvania, Baltimore, Washington, D.C., and Chicago. There was a three-week engagement at Harrah's starting in June, followed by a string of eighteen one-night engagements that began in Erie, Pennsylvania, and covered Ohio, New Jersey, New York, Virginia, Maryland, Iowa, Massachusetts, Indiana, and Nebraska. The Dukes played five days in Denver, then returned to the Thunderbird.[36]

> I was with the Dukes of Dixieland for a year, from November 1962 to November 1963. I came off the road with them the day after Kennedy's assassination, that was my last day. When I got back, I called up all the people that I used to work for, as one does. I called up Conrad Janis and his first words were: "Motherf—er, I wished I had known that you were going to be back because we got this Broadway show. We just set the final thing." Then he says: "Wait, wait. Get off the phone and let me see what I can do."[37]

Janis was referring to *Marathon 33*, a somber play, set against the backdrop of the Depression. It told the story of the marathon dancers who sought to make a few dollars by dancing continuously for days and occasionally weeks. The band, which was onstage throughout the entire performance, consisted of Johnny Windhurst and Johnny Letman on trumpets, Janis, Davern playing clarinet and occasionally doubling on soprano saxophone, Eddie Barefield on tenor, Dick Wellstood, Ahmed Abdul-Malik on bass, and Panama Francis on drums. The musicians were on dressed in "old time" suits. Davern was not happy with the one that was given to him and mentioned it to Mary Russell, Pee Wee's wife. She rummaged around in her husband's wardrobe and picked one out for Kenny, who had it altered and wore it throughout the run of the play.[38]

The cast included several rising stars: among them were Ralph Waite, Joe Don Baker, and Julie Harris. Lonnie Chapman was also a member of the cast, as was Gabriel Dell, who had become known as one of the Dead End Kids. *Marathon 33* ran from November 1963 through January 1964 and received mixed reviews from the critics.

Wild Bill Davison took Kenny with him when he went up to Toronto in March 1964 for a gig at the Colonial Tavern. A few weeks later, Davern joined up with Davison at the Metropole, alternating first with the Woody Herman band and later with the Dukes of Dixieland. For the balance of the year, Kenny worked at odd jobs around the city, occasionally appearing with Wild Bill Davison at Jimmy Ryan's. He played with Shorty Baker and Bud Freeman, who had put their own group together. Conrad Janis called him early in 1965 to join a band that he was forming to go into the Metropole for a few weeks.[39]

Entrepreneur George Mauro had purchased a working ferryboat and had sailed it into an inlet in Brielle, New Jersey, where he converted it into a restaurant called the Ferryboat. Mauro, who was an enthusiastic, but inept, trumpet player, decided to feature jazz at the venue. He hired Davern to begin playing on the Memorial Day weekend of 1965, along with Don Coates on piano, and Charlie Traeger on bass. The band included a local trombone player and the son of the police chief on drums. Davern remembered the first time that he heard the trumpet player.

> We did have the beginnings of a band until this guy comes up and starts to play like you've never heard; so loud. I couldn't play with anyone who was—not so much terrible—but just callous, indifferent to everything that was going on around him. He got a sound that was great, and he had chops of iron, but he was like a musical illiterate. He had no range, and he just didn't know what to do with the sound.[40]

The trumpet player who had offended Davern was George Mauro, who usually spent the greater part of the evening mingling with the customers at his restaurant. But, for the last set, he frequently joined the professional musicians on the bandstand. Ed Hubble, who spent 1967 and part of 1968 there, recalled:

> Musically, he didn't have a lot of sensitivity. He was straight ahead, blow, blow, blow. George had a habit of dropping meter, or jumping it once in a while. Not consistently: it wasn't like he did it all the time. All of a sudden, Bam! He was in another gear. So, we would be with him. But, if George was being a pain in the ass, we'd jump meter. And George would think he did it. He also had a habit of putting in a different bridge. And when he did, we would put a different tune on the end. So, he wouldn't know where the hell he was.[41]

Mauro's playing became an irritant to Davern and, after a few days, he addressed the problem in characteristic fashion:

> I gave the boss an ultimatum. Either he watches the store and greets the people like Grover Whelan in his white dinner jacket, but not play the trumpet, or I

wouldn't work for the guy. I told him: "I'll be the leader." I had nothing to lose: I didn't want to stay at the Jersey Shore. So, I left.[42]

For once, Davern had a backup plan: he had been approached to work with Phil Napoleon. During the years that they had worked together, they were frequently at loggerheads, each being critical of the other's style. But, even though their last job together (on the *Tenderloin* album) had ended badly, it did not affect Napoleon's personal feeling about Kenny: Phil liked him.

Johnny Varro had been working with Napoleon in Miami in the early months of 1965. That gig ended when the tourist season did, and Varro returned to New York. Napoleon then entered into a long-term arrangement with the management at the Roney Plaza Hotel in Miami Beach to work in a venue that would be called Napoleon's Retreat. In June, Napoleon called and offered Johnny the piano chair in the band he was forming. Phil also offered a job to Davern. Both Kenny and Varro accepted.

At about the same time, comedian Jackie Gleason had decided to move his CBS television network show to Miami. Never one to miss the opportunity for a good time, Gleason had chartered an entire train to take him and his friends to Florida. He called upon Napoleon to put a band together to play on the train, and Davern and Varro were among the musicians who were hired. The group left on August 1 and, as Varro remembered the event, the celebration never stopped.

> It was a twenty-four-hour party. We met at Toots Shor's, and we played a set there to get the party underway. Then they put us on buses and we went to Penn Station, got on a train, got our bunks and our places, and eventually we got the call to play. They had a piano that was bolted down, and we played. Gleason would sit right across from us. He loved the music. . . . Kenny was on that trip. . . . So was Eddie Hubble. We got on the train, we didn't play that much. It was a fun bash. We arrived in Florida about twenty-four hours later. We made some whistle-stops, and Gleason would go out to greet the people. They were all waiting for this train to go by. You'd think it was the presidential train. But, it was Jackie Gleason: he was more important.[43]

Davern was more succinct. "We played up until Jackie passed out between two blondes."[44]

As soon as the band reached Florida, they began working and, on the very first night, the musical differences between Napoleon and Davern surfaced.

> So we land in Florida and the gig starts. The first night, we start playing *At the Jazz Band Ball*. Phil turns the first chorus over to Kenny, and Kenny starts with

some of his quirky little sayings. After his chorus, Kenny puts his clarinet over his shoulder like it was a rifle and Phil turns and looks at him as if to say "What the f— are you doing?" And Kenny says "just playing my chorus." Phil shakes his head and they go on. A couple of songs later, Phil's looking at Kenny and watching him, and Kenny's playing some new things that Phil never heard before. He's playing his ass off. Kenny always swung. He could hold one note and it would swing. Phil didn't quite understand that. He was from the old school. After the set, Kenny comes over to me and says, "this isn't going to work." Phil gave him two weeks' notice: Kenny did his two weeks, and then left.[45]

Within a few weeks, he had joined up with Wild Bill Davison and returned to the Colonial Tavern. But then work again became scarce. He gigged around Manhattan, appearing occasionally at Ryan's and at the Gaslight Club where he subbed for Clarence Hutchenrider in George Wettling's trio. When Wettling went on the road, Kenny went with him.[46]

Wettling called his group the Manhattan Trio and, on March 19, 1966, he, Davern, and Charlie Queener on piano opened at Mike Fletch's Grandview Inn in Columbus, Ohio, for a three-week stay. The *Star*, a local newspaper, ran a lengthy article on Davern, in which he discussed the history of the clarinet and some of the technical aspects of playing it well.[47] While he was there, a chance encounter with Wild Bill Davison resulted in his next recording.

Born on January 5, 1906, in Defiance, Ohio, Davison had begun playing trumpet professionally in about 1922. He remained relatively unknown outside of the Midwest until about 1941, when he traveled to New York and landed a job at Nick's. His big brassy tone attracted attention: he soon became a fixture there, and subsequently at Condon's. Davison's personal life was as primitive as his tone. He was unrelentingly boisterous, frequently crude, attracted and attractive to women, and a drinker of immense proportions.

In early April 1966, Davison was driving from Toronto to his home in Santa Barbara and saw the sign outside the club advertising the Manhattan Trio. He stopped, walked into the club, and asked if he could sit in. Davern suspected that the trumpeter might try to cut himself in on the job, and it turned out that his concerns were justified. By the next night, Wild Bill had spoken to Fletch and convinced him to convert the trio into a quartet.[48]

Davison had a tape recorder with him and, over the next few days, recorded many of the numbers played by the group, assuring Davern and the others that it was only for his own enjoyment. However, several weeks later, Davison called to say that he had sold the tape to George Buck, owner of Jazzology Records, for $400 and that Kenny would receive a check for $100.

But, when the check came, Anne, Davison's wife, told him that he, Wettling, and Queener would only receive $80. Wild Bill kept the extra $60 for himself. Although Davern continued to work with Davison over the years, he never forgave Wild Bill.[49]

The album, titled *After Hours with Wild Bill Davison*, is a typical collection of the cornetist's work. Among the thirteen titles on the CD are *I Never Knew, Tin Roof Blues, Wolverine Blues, Beale Street Blues, Ballin' the Jack, Song of the Wanderer,* and *Easter Parade*. All of the tunes are a medium tempo or faster, and Davison takes the lion's share of space.

Kenny's homecoming to New York was not a happy event. During the years that Kenny and Sylvia were together, she had slowly recovered her emotional and physical health, in large part due to Kenny's efforts and his support. Before moving to New York, she had worked as a commercial animator in Canada. After several years, she was able to resume her career. She had a series of jobs, opened her own firm, and then merged it with another entity. As time passed, her work consumed increasing amounts of her time. She made new friends, with whom she socialized while Kenny was working or away, and she no longer needed Davern's constant and nurturing presence as she once had. "I just drifted right out of his life," she said. "He knew it and he hated it." They argued with increasing frequency and intensity, and the situation grew progressively more intolerable. Finally, before he left to go on tour with Wettling, she told him that she would not be there when he returned. When he came home, she was gone.[50]

Notes

1. Kenny Davern on Fresh Air interview; Roswell Rudd, interview by the author.
2. Johnny Varro, interview by the author.
3. Kenny Davern, interview by the author.
4. Rusch interview part 2, p. 11. See also: Vache, Erwin, 290. The opening date is from a Table Card at Nick's.
5. Kenny Davern on Davern-Morgenstern interview 2.
6. Kenny Davern, quoted in Rusch interview part 2, p. 12.
7. Dave Frishberg, interview by the author.
8. Dave Frishberg, interview by the author; See also: Jack Six, interview by the author.
9. Kenny Davern, quoted in Ross Firestone, liner notes to *Bob Wilber and Kenny Davern, Reunion at Arbors*, Arbors Records, 1998, Arbors ARCD 19183; Robert Sylvester, "Dream Street," *The News*, 27 May 1961; Robert Sylvester, "Dream Street," *The News*, 29 July 1961. During the stay at Nick's, Frishberg recorded part of one

night's proceedings and made a cassette for Davern. In later years, Kenny would play it for his friends, smiling at what he and his cohorts had accomplished. Because he was so proud of the group that he had assembled, he kept all of the canceled paychecks that he wrote bearing the endorsements of the members of the band.

10. Dan Morgenstern, interview by the author, 16 May 2007.
11. Dave Frishberg, interview by the author.
12. Anonymous, "Ol' Man River—at 225th Street," *New York Post*, 17 July 1961, 3.
13. Kenny Davern and Mark Weber, recorded conversation, in about September 2003. Cassette titled *Penultimate Link*.
14. Kenny Davern, Jack Six, Dave Frishberg, interviews by the author; Rusch interview part 2, at p. 12. As Frishberg remembered the event, Russell was yelling at him.
15. Jack Six, interview by the author.
16. Leroy "Sam" Parkins, interview by the author.
17. Hank O'Neal, interview by the author.
18. Mat Domber, President of Arbors Records, interview by the author.
19. Allan Vache, interview by the author.
20. Evan Christopher said: "As much as everybody says they loved Kenny, there were quite a few people to whom it wasn't worth it. Kenny lacked a certain diplomacy. . . . He didn't necessarily have the amount of patience." Evan Christopher, interview by the author.
21. Robert Hilbert, *Pee Wee Russell, The Life of a Jazzman* (New York, Oxford, 1993), 1–23 (hereinafter "Hilbert"); John McDonough, *Pee Wee Russell, Biography and Notes on the Music*, Time Life Records, TL-J17, 1–8.
22. Hilbert, 59–60.
23. Hilbert, 91–103.
24. Hilbert, 188–193.
25. Kenny Davern, unpublished writing.
26. Kenny Davern, unpublished writing.
27. Sylvia Fogarty, interview by the author.
28. Sylvia Fogarty, interview by the author.
29. Kenny Davern, quoted in Hilbert, 246.
30. Sylvia Fogarty, interview by the author. Sylvia thought that it was "beneath him" for Kenny to join the Dukes, but that he did it to make money.
31. Dukes of Dixieland itinerary; information about the date and place of marriage from the marriage license.
32. Sylvia Fogarty, interview by the author.
33. Sylvia Fogarty, interview by the author.
34. Peerless Program Notes, 13.
35. Dan Morgenstern, "Jazz Capsules, Jazz, Clara Ward Singers, We Gotta Shout," *Jazz*, 30, no. 1 (January–February 1964): 20.
36. Dukes of Dixieland itinerary.

37. Kenny Davern, interview by the author.

38. Robert Sylvester, "Dream Street, Music Notes," *The News* 23 December 1963.

39. Letter to Kenny Davern from Bill Ritchie; *DownBeat*, 31, no. 13 (4 June 1964): 41; Davern, Vache; *DownBeat*, 32, no. 5 (25 February 1965): 41; *DownBeat*, 32, no. 7 (25 March 1965): 40.

40. Kenny Davern, interview by the author.

41. Ed Hubble, interview by the author.

42. Kenny Davern, interview by the author.

43. Johnny Varro, interview by the author.

44. Kenny Davern, interview by Mark Weber, 17 January 2006.

45. Johnny Varro, interview by the author; letter dated 29 June 1965 from Phil Napoleon to Kenny Davern.

46. *Down Beat*, 32, no. 16 (29 July 1965): 42; Vache, Davern.

47. Neville Hatfield, "Woodwind Whiz," *The Star*, 19 March 1966, 10.

48. Hal Willard, *The Wildest One, The Life of Wild Bill Davison* (Monkton, Md., Avondale Press, 1996), 329 (hereinafter "Willard, Davison"); Kenny Davern, interview by the author; Kenny Davern, interview by Mark Weber, 13 January 2005.

49. Willard, Davison; 329–330; Kenny Davern, interview by the author. In the 1990s, the album was rereleased on CD with some additional tunes from the date.

50. Sylvia Fogarty, interview by the author.

CHAPTER FOUR

Elsa, Dick, and a Musical Voice

The breakup with Sylvia left Kenny feeling furious and, at the same time, relieved. Within a few days, he consulted a lawyer who drew up a formal separation agreement.[1] Shortly afterward, Kenny moved to the Jersey Shore, where he lived and worked for the next thirty-five years. "I went down there in April, just after my marriage fell apart," Davern said. "One of the nice people down there rented me a station wagon, and I went up to New York during the day, and I took half of everything: half the china, half the silver, half the bed, half of everything. I put it into a f—in' station wagon and rented a place."[2]

He found work, thanks to Dick Wellstood, who was then playing piano at the Ferryboat in Brielle. Richard McQueen Wellstood was born in Greenwich, Connecticut, on November 25, 1927. His father died when Dick was three, and his mother May, who never remarried, raised her son alone. Wellstood showed evidence of a superior intelligence at a young age, but also displayed an emotional dependence on his mother. In an effort to develop his self-reliance, she periodically sent him away for extended periods. He spent several summers at camp: ultimately he became a boarder at the Wooster School, a private institution that he attended for four years on a partial scholarship.

May had given her son piano lessons and, while he was at Wooster, he began to hone his skills. By the time that he graduated, in June 1945, he had become an accomplished pianist. One of his friends, Charlie Traeger, who played trombone (and later bass), introduced him to Bob Wilber, who was then at the center of a group of young musicians known as the Scarsdale High Gang.

Within a year, Wellstood was the group's pianist. Then known as Wilber's Wildcats, they made several recordings with, among others, Sidney Bechet, before breaking up at the end of 1947. Over the next few years, Wellstood's reputation as a soloist and a band pianist grew. He married and had the first of four daughters.

Wellstood had a far-ranging intellect, and playing the piano did not satisfy it. He was also concerned about his ability to support his family on the earnings of an itinerant musician. In 1954, he enrolled as a freshman at New York University. By working nights and going to school full-time during the day, he amassed enough credits to enter New York Law School in 1956, and, by adhering to that same grueling regimen, he graduated in June 1958—completing in four years a course that normally took seven. After he passed the bar examination, thereby earning the right to practice as an attorney, he abandoned the law and went back to playing the piano.

Davern had met Wellstood in 1951, when both recorded a demo tape with Dick Sutton and Robert Lovett. Although they ran into each other over the years after that time, it was not until they were performing together in *Marathon 33* that their friendship jelled. Wellstood's marriage had fallen apart several years before Davern called him in 1966.

When Davern returned from Ohio, he had called Wellstood to see if he knew of any jobs that might be available. Dick mentioned Davern's call to George Mauro, who clearly recalled his earlier encounter with Kenny. "'Mauro won't have you,'" Wellstood said. "'You really told him off and he's pissed off at you. But, it would be great if you were down here, we'd really have a great trio.'"[3] Mauro eventually relented, and Davern began working at the Ferryboat. He took an apartment at 197 Parker Avenue in Manasquan through the summer of 1966, then rented a house at 332 Cedar Avenue, also in Manasquan.[4]

Initially, the band at the Ferryboat consisted of Davern with Wellstood, drummer Al McManus and, occasionally, Blaze Turi, a local trombone player. After a time, they persuaded Mauro to add bassist Jack Six, who had been part of Davern's band at Nick's. At the beginning of 1967, trombonist Ed Hubble became a member of the group. It was a good time in Davern's life.

> Next thing you know, we literally had a family of guys. We all loved each other. We used to stay up to 7:00 or 8:00 in the morning, blind drunk. All the cops knew us, and they would drive us home if we were too drunk to drive. It was very nice down here at that time.

We used to go to Wellstood's house sometime when we were all loaded after work and he would chop up garlic—maybe five or six cloves, which he would chop up in chunks—and put them on great pieces of romaine lettuce with olive oil and pass them out. We would munch this stuff down as if it were candy.[5]

Davern always said that his years at the Ferryboat were "the most creative time of his life."[6]

Mauro usually stayed off the bandstand, confining himself to mingling with the customers and, if he played at all, participating only in the last set. The bulk of the band's repertoire were familiar tunes, some dixieland mixed with a bit of Ellington, a few swing-era tunes, and an occasional never-ending ballad medley for the dancers.

It was also a time of experimentation. Music was changing, and Davern and his colleagues were listening. Jack Six, who was into more "free" types of music, brought a copy of Albert Ayler's *Spiritual Unity* album over to Wellstood's house after work. Six recalled the effect that it had.

It absolutely turned everybody around. We used to go over to Dick's and drink after a job. One night, he put on a record and I said, "what the hell is that?" It was the Beatles—one of those electronic things they were doing. Dick and I especially got into that Sargent Pepper era—Kenny didn't. With that and Albert Ayler—Kenny really got into that. He used to start playing like that at the Ferryboat. He started getting into that screech and scrawling thing that he used to do. It really turned us all around. Roswell [Rudd] came down for one weekend and turned the whole band around.[7]

Two privately issued albums document the sound of the Ferryboat band. One evening in 1966, at a time when Tim Jordan held down the trombone chair, Mauro recorded them at the restaurant and released the album on his own Gamco label titled *A Night at the Ferryboat*. The record opens with a polka, *The Ferryboat Theme*, during which George introduces the musicians, plugs the restaurant, and then segues into *Dixie*. The remaining tunes include a schmaltzy *Birth of the Blues*, two danceable, extended medleys, and two flagwavers, *Nobody's Sweetheart* and *Battle Hymn of the Republic*. There's more fun on this album than great music. Davern, Wellstood, Six, and McManus labor mightily at times, but Mauro frequently borders on dreadful.

Early in 1967, the band, with Ed Hubble replacing Tim Jordan, journeyed to a studio in Philadelphia to make its second record for the Gamco label, called *The Ferryboat Dixieland Band*. This is also a happy album: it begins with a rousing *I Found a New Baby*. The second cut is a medium-tempo *St. James*

Infirmary that has a nice solo by Hubble and several choruses by Davern in the clarinet's upper register. Wellstood solos on *Russian Rag*, which is followed by a tightly arranged *Aggravatin' Papa*. *When the Saints Go Marchin' In* closes the first side.

To begin the second side, Mauro sings the lyrics to *Pink Elephants*, a simple ditty, reminiscent of the novelty tunes of the 1920s. Mauro believed that it could be a hit: he sang it at the restaurant and plugged it whenever the band had a radio spot. It never got off the ground. One of the band's interminable dance medleys, consisting of *Apple Blossom Time*, *Georgia on My Mind*, *Danny Boy*, *The Days of Wine and Roses*, and *I Don't Know Why I Love You Like I Do*, is followed by a Mauro feature *Wonderland by Night*, and the album closes with another medley, *Secret Love*, *I Can't Give You Anything but Love*, *Bei Mir Bist Du Schon*, *Puttin on the Ritz*, and *Crazy Rhythm*, which features Kenny Davern's first recorded vocal. (There were only two.)

The formal atmosphere of a recording studio may have had a salutary effect on Mauro. Although he was far from the equal of the other band members (Hubble, Davern, Wellstood, Six, and McManus), he was far less distracting in the ensemble parts than before. Dan Morgenstern gave the *Night at the Ferry Boat* album three stars in *DownBeat* saying: "Davern is without doubt the finest clarinetist of his generation."[8]

Listening to the *Ferryboat* albums reveals that Davern had finally found the unique musical voice that would mark his playing for the rest of his life. To some extent, he had been identifiable on the albums that he recorded in the 1957–63 period with Pee Wee Erwin, the Empire City Six, and Dick Cary: the sound of his horn was different from that made by other clarinetists. But, he was limited in what he could play by the setting in which he performed. No matter how the group in which he was playing was characterized, it was a dixieland band, and he was a sideman, confined to playing the role that a clarinetist always played in a dixieland band.[9]

At the Ferryboat, he was the *de facto* leader and free to incorporate his own concepts and his personal passion into his music. He had strengthened his embouchure and had developed the ability to "bend" notes; that is, to alter the pitch slightly and thereby achieve a different, and often, a more emotional sound. He taught himself to extend the upper range of his clarinet by developing alternative fingerings (sometimes called false fingerings) that enabled him to reach notes that were generally considered to be beyond the instrument's reach.

The normal range of a B♭ clarinet extends up to G above high C. Many clarinet players can play up to double high C, but not with any facility and often by attempting to turn a partially controlled squeak into a note. Davern could play those notes in the center of the pitch with relative ease and, on occasion, could reach F above double high C. The fingerings that he used were not something that could be found in a book. Some were the result of combining fingerings from the Boehm and Albert systems. However, most alternative fingerings were found by trial-and-error and occasionally, by mistake, and it took years for Davern to discover them.

To guitarist James Chirillo, Davern's command of that difficult instrument was amazing.

> He always had, no matter what the instrument, . . . complete command over all those notes. And some of those notes you ain't gonna hear any other clarinet players do—period. I've seen and heard a couple of guys crash and burn trying to grab a couple of those notes. But, he always had a big, full, fat, dark, sound—whether he was playing that low E on the clarinet or way up to that altissimo E-flat or whatever. Even when he got way up that high, it never was shrill, and it was always in tune. That's the amazing thing that boggles my mind; how well in tune he played.[10]

Kenny taught some of these unique fingerings to Allan Vache who said:

> He developed things on the clarinet that nobody had done before. Benny hadn't done it: nobody had done it. It came from understanding the early guys, as well as the later guys. He started on the Albert system clarinet, and then switched over to the Boehm system. So he could play both systems. Because of that, he was able to come up with these upper-register fingerings that nobody else knew about. He used some things that he knew from playing the Albert system clarinet. Nobody else has done that since. . . . It's unfortunate that he did not get wider recognition as being an innovator—a guy who developed things that nobody knew about.[11]

Vache continued:

> What was very recognizable about Kenny's sound was his ability to bend the notes. When he was playing with Pee Wee Erwin on those Dixie Rebels albums, he'd hit a note way up above the other two horns, and it was very recognizable as Kenny Davern. As he moved into doing different things, he expanded his harmonic depth. He tried using some different ideas in expanding the notes that he played because it expanded the harmonies. Instead of playing a third, or a fifth, above the melody, he was expanding to use a ninth or a thirteenth—to give it a more interesting sound.[12]

As his contemporaries acknowledged, the result of his efforts was a sound and a technique that were unmatched. Other clarinetists, who knew, better than anyone else, the limitations of their instrument, were frequently awed by what he could accomplish. Ken Peplowski was of the opinion that: "He did a lot of things that were avant-garde for the instrument, bending notes, slurring notes, fingering. . . . He was an individual."[13] And Frank Laidlaw described it as follows: "Kenny had his way of getting at the truth and the beauty. He had the equipment, he had the technique, he had everything a person needs."[14]

Because the sound of his musical voice was so important to him, he refused, whenever possible, to perform with a microphone. Working at the Ferryboat, where diners talked and dishes clanked while musicians played, required him to develop an ability to cut through the ambient noise without external amplification. It was a skill that Ken Peplowski admired.

> Actually, he had one of the biggest sounds on the clarinet that I've ever heard—a huge sound. He really was a room filler with the clarinet. So, he could get away with that more than most of us. I don't have a loud sound, so I'm grateful for a microphone. But, Kenny could really fill up a room. He had a big fat sound. There's a difference between having a big sound and just playing loud. Kenny had a big sound. He could project to the back wall, and it was just amazing. So, a lot of times, he didn't need a microphone and everybody else did.[15]

The last element to be added was a clarinet that would enable him to duplicate on a horn the sound that he heard in his head. He had tried a number of Selmers, Buffets, LeBlancs, and Yamahas, but they were unsuitable.

> I needed a more stable instrument. And that included the pads too. I wanted waterproof pads, so I wouldn't get off a plane which had less than 2% humidity and find that the rings fell off the clarinet, the keys bound up between the posts, or the pads swelled up, or whatever. . . . Sure enough, I found a Pan American instrument which was made in the mid '30s that hadn't been used. It was a student-line instrument, used generally outdoors in parades and snowstorms and stuff like that. Somehow or other, it had the flexibility . . . that reproduces the sound that you hear in your head. And this one worked for me. This is the one that lasted thirty three years.[16]

By the end of his stay at the Ferryboat, all of the elements of Davern's musical voice were in place and made him instantly identifiable. He had a vibrato that was wide and slow. His tone in the chalumeau register was warm, soft, and woody: it caressed the notes even on faster tunes. His construction of his solos, the use of bent, slurred, and "blue" notes, resulted in a sound that only he could produce. He could play notes at the top of the clarinet's range and hold them: the sound would soar over the rest of the band, and either end sharply or slowly fade away. Sometimes, he would reach the high register by a great, upward-sweeping glissando that was staggering in the smoothness of its execution. He had the power to be heard whenever he chose, regardless of the number of instruments that were playing at the time. These were the things that his audiences came to hear: they became his unique musical signature.

From time to time, Davern would acknowledge the musicians who had influenced him. Jimmie Noone's downhill ride-out in *Apex Blues* found its way into some of his solos. Occasionally, he would play a series of staccato notes or the *wooop, wooop* figure that Frank Teschemacher used on his recordings with the Chicago Rhythm Kings and the Jungle Kings. Now and then, a Pee Wee Russell–like grunt or squawk could be heard. But, these were just ornaments: the basic voice was that of Kenny Davern. As Ken Peplowski said: "You listen to Kenny, and you don't hear any influences. You could try hard and say 'here's a little bit of this, or a little bit of that.' But, really, in a couple of notes it's him."[17]

Having struggled to find a musical voice to serve as his vehicle for expression and to set him apart from everyone else, Davern was also concerned about acoustics, amplification, and about how his clarinet would sound in performance. His friend, Christian Plattner, who saw him frequently on his trips to Europe, remembered how consumed he was.

> He was very proud of the sound he could produce on the clarinet (although he very rarely said so to strangers). In every dressing room he ever entered before playing a concert—be it the small, greasy, olfactory and visually disgusting chamber left to the musicians in the Jazz Club; be it the grand, polished, well-smelling, and architecturally satisfying surroundings of a big Concert Hall dressing-room—he was happy when the sound of his instrument was to his liking, and he was sad and/or angry if not.[18]

Although Davern was unquestionably the leader of the Ferryboat band, one problem that he encountered was that, when Mauro was not playing, the band needed a stronger lead voice than the clarinet could provide. To forestall the possibility that Mauro might hire another trumpet player, or, worse, take a more active role in playing with the band, the other band members began to pressure Davern to take up the soprano. "I was playing soprano saxophone because, as Eddie Hubble put it: 'If you don't play it, we all stand a chance to lose the job because of you. We don't have a trumpet all the time, and we need a strong lead in the center. A clarinet and a trombone are too far apart.'"[19] Kenny bought a curved Buescher for $40 that Ed Hubble nicknamed Mighty Mite. After a while, he decided that he didn't like the way it looked and bought a straight Martin.[20]

Although Davern had listened to Dodds, Noone, Simeon, and all of the other great clarinet players during his early years, he hadn't spent much time listening to Sidney Bechet playing soprano saxophone, and what he had heard had not impressed him. Consequently, he had no preconception of how the soprano should sound and was able to develop a distinctive voice on that instrument. He told interviewer Sinclair Traill:

> I never took any lessons on soprano. I merely transferred what I knew about clarinet to the other instrument. Maybe it was the wrong method, but I love the soprano's strong voice.
>
> The instrument should be tuned by ear, like a violin with no frets, and should be blown with as broad a tone as possible—it should make a big noise like an opera singer filling a whole big theater. Breadth in jazz is often what is needed—too many sax players sound like snake charmers, playing under the basket, along with the snake.[21]

In the midst of his stay at the Ferryboat, Davern was invited to join Louis Armstrong's All-Stars. He received a call asking him to come up to Joe Glaser's office at Associated Booking Corporation. There he was interviewed by Ira Mangel and, as part of the process, he had to roll up his sleeve to show that he wasn't a junkie.[22] They offered him the job—but although the prospect of working with Armstrong was tempting, there were other factors to be considered.

> At that time, I'd just met my wife-to-be. Her marriage had just broken up, and she had moved to Manasquan. I used to see her at the Laundromat, and she used to come into the Ferryboat and stuff like that. I had that going. I also had a band that was terrific.
>
> We were working 365 days a year, when the place was packed and when it wasn't packed. George Mauro loved music so much that he kept the band on even when there were seven people in the joint. So, I had a good thing going here. I was making $130 a week, out of which I was saving money, paying rent, being responsible, and all this kind of stuff. I had my own car, I was renting a house for $90 a month, and I was eating well. If I showed up drunk, the boss would just say: "Come on, have another drink." We'd end up getting juiced

while the rest of the band played. George was really very loose. You couldn't do that with Louis Armstrong.[23]

Davern turned the offer down and never regretted it: Joe Muranyi took the job.

Kenny's "wife-to-be" was Elsa Green, born in 1941. She and her twin sister, Elaine, grew up in Avon, New Jersey, a small town on the New Jersey shore. She intended to pursue a career in nursing and, after graduating from high school, was accepted into a three-year nursing program. In her senior year of high school, she had begun to date Ernest Donald ("Don") Lass, who was then attending Lafayette College. They decided to marry one year after Don graduated from college and, because the nursing school prohibited enrollees from marrying, she left the program to take a course in business.

They were married on August 6, 1960, when Elsa was nineteen years old. Don enrolled at Columbia University in the School of Journalism, and Elsa worked for several professors at the Business School. After he graduated, they set up housekeeping in Deal, a small town on the Jersey Shore, where they had two children: Deborah, who was born on September 18, 1961, and Mark, who was born on December 11, 1962. Although Elsa thrived as a mother, she felt that she needed to develop some outside interests.

She went to Monmouth College and took some courses, including several that dealt with painting. It turned out that she had an innate talent for it. "I always got a lot of feedback wherever I went," she recalled. "I was a natural painter." In about 1968, she began to attend classes at Kean College in Newark, New Jersey, majoring in art and art history, and driving about seventy miles each way, two days a week, to get to class. Her mother (and later, Kenny) baby sat for the children when they were young. It would take her twelve years to complete her studies: she graduated summa cum laude and received a bachelor of fine arts degree in 1980.[24]

Don Lass liked to listen to jazz and occasionally visited the Ferryboat, taking his wife with him. Elsa was, and is, strikingly attractive, and when she entered the club, heads turned, including Kenny's. The band was on a break, and Davern was sitting on a table, talking with the musicians. When he saw her, he jumped off and exclaimed: "Oh boy." Elsa was not impressed. "I thought: 'another one.'" But, he turned out to be clever and funny. And, when she heard him play, she came to view him in another light. "I was so moved, musically. . . . I couldn't believe how he could play the clarinet."[25] Don's father was the editor of the *Asbury Park Press*, and Don often reported on music-related events. Don and Elsa became friends with some of the musicians that they heard and saw.

Eventually, Elsa's marriage to Don disintegrated, and she moved out, taking the children with her. She rented an apartment in Manasquan, deciding to live near her mother, so that she could watch the children while Elsa went to school. There was no washing machine or dryer where she lived, and she was compelled to take her laundry to a nearby Laundromat. As it turned out, Kenny used the same facility to do his clothes, and they met one evening, wholly by happenstance.[26]

Within a short time, they became emotionally involved. Elsa found that, in addition to the humor and intelligence that Kenny exhibited in public, in private he was kind, tender, and generous. "Every book that he ever read that he loved, he would beg me to read. Everything that he loved to eat, he would beg me to eat. He was the ultimate 'sharer.'"[27] He also turned out to be a romantic.

> There was this Laundromat in Manasquan where we used to talk when we first met. I was doing some laundry one time after we had a fight, and he rode into the Laundromat on his bicycle, carrying a bouquet of flowers. He dismounted, bowed, presented me with the bouquet and, without saying a word, remounted the bike and rode out the other door. The people in the place stood there with their mouths open, and then they started to applaud. He was my knight in shining armor, except that he was riding a bicycle.[28]

Elsa had just begun taking classes at Kean College. Kenny not only encouraged her to pursue her interest in art, but also offered to act as babysitter for her children—a daunting endeavor for someone with his lack of exposure to youngsters. But, it was important to him that Elsa have the freedom to realize her potential. She said:

> I knew that I had talents, and my mother encouraged Elaine and me. I just knew that my life quest was: when I died, whoever met me at whatever gate there might be would say "And, were you Elsa?" That was always in my brain. So, I spent much of my life trying to find out who I was. Kenny was very instrumental in that because he was a free person, and he believed that you needed to go and see and do what you needed to do to find that person.[29]

Davern's musical career received a boost when *DownBeat* magazine devoted its May 16, 1968, issue to young reed players. Davern and four others were pictured on the cover, and Dan Morgenstern wrote a long and favorable article titled *Kenny Davern, Overdue*. Shortly after that, Kenny was fired after two years at the Ferryboat. "I ended up leaving the Ferryboat in June of 1968, just as the height of the season was about to begin. I was let go for telling

George Mauro for the umpteenth time to go f— himself; that the best thing he could do was to stick the horn up his ass."[30]

Although that job ended, the relationship between Kenny Davern and Dick Wellstood, which matured and deepened during their years at the Ferryboat, endured until Wellstood's death almost twenty years later.[31] They were an unlikely pair: the shambling, seemingly inarticulate white, Anglo-Saxon, Protestant from Greenwich, Connecticut, and the sharply dressed, quick and caustic, Viennese-Russian, Irish Catholic–Jewish kid from Queens, New York. Wellstood had gone through college and held a law degree: Davern had only graduated from high school.

The similarities between them were far less obvious. Neither knew his father: Harold Wellstood had died when Dick was three; Buster Davern was either in jail or simply absent. Both had been raised by a strong-willed maternal figure who had periodically sent her son away to be badly cared for by others. Both were voracious readers who were self-educated on a number of subjects, some of which were wholly unrelated to music. Davern and Wellstood were not only well-versed in the musical history of jazz, but were also conversant with the works of many classical composers and musicians.

They worked together in a number of settings over the next two decades and, when they were playing in different places, dined or drank with each other frequently and spoke several times during the week. Wellstood was Davern's accompanist of choice: of all of the pianists and guitarists that Kenny played with during those years, Dick inspired, excited, amused, supported, and, at the same time, aggravated and annoyed him more than any other. On a personal and professional level, each loved the other.

Davern might not have been working at the Ferryboat, but he continued to play with the members of the band. He, together with Hubble, Wellstood, Six, and McManus, had formed a group that they sometimes called *The Jersey Ramblers*, and, at other times, referred to as *Can O'Worms*. Although the term was not then in vogue, the Ramblers were one of the first crossover groups, playing a repertoire that consisted of traditional dixieland material and arrangements of tunes made popular by the Beatles. It was the idea of Jack Six.

> It was that period and people would always ask us to play rock and roll music. . . . We had already been into the Albert Ayler free kind of thing. Then all of a sudden, I heard the strange sound of the Beatles thing, all of that electronic thing. So, I wrote out some things for us to play, quasi-rock sort of things, because people were always asking us to play some rock things. Then I started listening on the radio, and I did *Sonny*. Then I got the Beatles' book and started

orchestrating them the way that the Beatles sang them. They came out good. *Day in the Life* was done electronically, and we did it acoustically. *Day Tripper* was the first thing I did. Kenny enjoyed playing it: he was the lead.[32]

The band had made a demo tape at Nola Studios in New York City in May and sent it to several club owners in an effort to get work. In October–November, they had a gig at the Theatrical Lounge in Cleveland, followed by a date at the Colonial Tavern in Toronto. Over the next few years, the group would make isolated appearances, one at a program honoring Pee Wee Russell (discussed *infra*) and another at the Wooster School, where Wellstood had spent several years.

But, the band never caught on. The public furor that the Beatles had generated upon their arrival in this country had distracted parents and others of their generation from the beauty and originality of their music. They did not want to hear Kenny Davern, Ed Hubble, and Dick Wellstood play songs by a bunch of youngsters from England: they wanted to hear *St. Louis Blues*. Conversely, the young people who were listening to the music of the Beatles wanted to hear the Beatles—or their contemporaries—play it. They had no interest in hearing the older generation play their music and surely did not want to hear the older generation's music—like *St Louis Blues*. Within a few years, the Jersey Ramblers ceased to exist.

The late 1960s were a difficult period for musicians such as Davern. Musical tastes were changing, clubs were going out of business or adopting a new musical orientation, recording dates were declining, and work was drying up. Traditionally, the venues at the Jersey Shore closed for the winter months—the Ferryboat being an exception—which resulted in increasingly large vacant blocks in Davern's date book. To add to the miasma, Pee Wee Russell died on February 15, 1969.

In the last years of his life, Pee Wee had become one of Davern's closest friends. During one of the slow periods in Russell's life, his wife Mary had given him some paints and brushes and suggested that he learn to paint to pass the time. He turned out to be quite talented: his work was bold and startling, evoking memories of Juan Miro in his use of colors. Within a short span of time, Pee Wee was being recognized for his talent as a painter as well as a musician.

The good times came to an end for Russell in 1967. For several years, Mary had complained of stomach pain. Various ailments were diagnosed and cures prescribed, but the condition kept worsening. Finally, she was admitted to St. Vincent's Hospital in New York City in May 1967 where she was found to have stomach cancer. She died on June 7.[33]

For all purposes, it was also the end of Pee Wee. He was grief stricken and inconsolable. He stopped painting and sat for hours in his apartment drinking from a large tumbler of vodka. He kept working, but he became steadily more depressed. He stopped taking care of himself and, although Kenny and Elsa, and Pee Wee's other friends, tried to take care of him, his health deteriorated. Finally, while he was in Washington, D.C., he was taken to a hospital where he died soon afterward.

Russell bequeathed two Buffett clarinets to Kenny. Davern gave one to the Institute of Jazz Studies and lent the other to publisher Eddie Cook. He kept the clarinet that he found under the couch.[34] Plans were made to establish a scholarship in Russell's name, and Davern became an integral part of the project.

Professionally, things continued to spiral downward for Davern through the spring and summer of 1969. A new club called the Shipwheel opened several hundred feet from the site of the now-closed Ferryboat. Al McManus had the job, and he hired Davern and Wellstood to play as the Kenny Davern Trio. There were guest stars such as Roy Eldridge and Jimmy Hamilton, who appeared with his big band, Wild Bill Davison, Ed Hubble, and Gene Ramey.[35] But, the income that Davern was able to generate was not enough to keep him afloat and so, for the second—and last—time in his life, Kenny Davern took a job that was not related to playing music.

In an act of desperation, he obtained a license as a bus driver and went to work for the school system in nearby Eatontown, New Jersey. They assigned him the task of driving mentally and physically handicapped students to and from class, twice a day. Elsa tried to support him during this bleak time.

> He had to pick them up at a quarter to seven and bring them home and then, go back again in the late afternoon and bring them back because there were a couple of sessions. I had an apartment then and, by the fourth day, he would sit in the chair and I didn't recognize who he was. He was declining into deep depression: even the hours were against him. "What is this? Where is there any kind of life fulfillment in this?" And, of course, the paycheck would not do it. Never. . . . It was pitiful. He aged twenty years. And then, Wild Bill called. In a heartbeat, he left.[36]

Davison had a three-week job playing at Economy Hall in the Royal Sonesta Hotel in New Orleans. Ed Hubble was part of the band, doubling on trombone and baritone horn. Davern doubled on clarinet and soprano saxophone, and the rhythm section consisted of Chuck Folds, Johnny Giufredda, and Smokey Stover.[37] Kenny was back in the world of music.

Notes

1. Bill dated 25 April 1966, from Julius Gantman, Esq. See also: Mark Weber, interview by the author.
2. Kenny Davern, interview by the author.
3. Kenny Davern, interview by the author.
4. A 2 September 1966 bill from Davern's lawyer is addressed to Davern at 197 Parker Avenue in Manasquan; lease for 332 Cedar Avenue, Manasquan.
5. Kenny Davern, interview by the author.
6. Kenny Davern, interview by the author; Davern-Morgenstern interview 1.
7. Jack Six, interview by the author.
8. Dan Morgenstern, "George Mauro, The Ferryboat Dixieland Band," *Down-Beat*, 34, no. 7 (6 April 1967): 34. The review is of the first album even though the title is the same as the second.
9. Regardless of the style of music played, the combination of trumpet, trombone, clarinet, piano, bass, and drums is referred to as a dixieland band.
10. James Chirillo, interview by the author.
11. Allan Vache, interview by the author.
12. Allan Vache, interview by the author.
13. Ken Peplowski, interview by the author.
14. Frank Laidlaw, interview by the author.
15. Ken Peplowski, interview by the author.
16. Kenny Davern, interviewed by Mark Weber, 9 November 2006. When that clarinet gave out, he could never find another just like it and eventually settled upon a plastic Conn.
17. Ken Peplowski, interview by the author.
18. Christian Plattner, *Kenny Davern and the Clarinet*, Unpublished, Altenmarkt, Austria, 15 September 2008.
19. Kenny Davern, interview by the author. See also, Rusch interview part 1, p. 22.
20. Peerless Program Notes, 15.
21. Kenny Davern, quoted in Sinclair Traill, "Two of a Kind," *Jazz Journal*, 27, no. 10 (October 1974) 8 (hereinafter "Davern, Traill"). See also: Rusch interview part 1, pp. 22–23.
22. Rusch interview part 2, pp. 6–7.
23. Kenny Davern, interview by the author.
24. Elsa Davern, interview by the author.
25. Elsa Davern, interview by the author.
26. Kenny Davern, conversation with the author; Elsa Davern, interview by the author.
27. Elsa Davern, interview by the author.
28. Elsa Davern, quoted in Zan Stewart, "Kenny Davern, Craftsman on Clarinet," *Star Ledger*, 15 December 2006.

29. Elsa Davern, interview by the author.

30. Kenny Davern, interview by the author. The Ferryboat closed at the end of that summer.

31. See also *Giant Strides*, 81–82.

32. Jack Six, interview by the author.

33. Hilbert, 278–279.

34. Hilbert, 293.

35. *Asbury Park Evening Press*, 2 September 1969; Willard, Davison, 358–359.

36. Elsa Davern, interview by the author.

37. Willard, Davison, 358–359.

CHAPTER FIVE

Reversal of Fortune

Davern's life turned around in the 1970s. At the beginning of the decade, he was living alone in an apartment above a shoe store. Except for making the second record with the Ferryboat band, he hadn't been in a recording studio since 1963. He was primarily a sideman who was well known among musicians in the New York–New Jersey area and had some popularity among a small group of knowledgeable fans in those states. But, he was virtually unknown when he ventured outside of his home base.

By the end of the decade, everything had changed. He was married, living in a home, and helping to raise two children. He had made a number of studio recordings throughout the '70s, and his live performances were recorded frequently. No longer just a sideman, he often appeared as a leader at venues throughout the United States, as well as in Canada, England, Europe, and South Africa.

For Davern, the first major event of the 1970s resulted from his close friendship with Pee Wee Russell. Lee Goodman was Mary Russell's nephew and Pee Wee's only surviving relative. Shortly after Russell passed away, Davern was at Goodman's house, helping him sort through Pee Wee's effects. Jack Stine, a good friend and fan, was also there. He had previously told Goodman that he wanted to hold a concert to raise money to establish a scholarship fund in the late clarinetist's name, and Goodman mentioned the project to Davern. Kenny said that he wanted to participate.[1]

It took almost a year to put the program together. The event was called the First Annual Pee Wee Russell Memorial Concert, and it was held on

February 15, 1970, at the Martinsville Inn in Martinsville, New Jersey. About 800 people turned out to honor Russell and hear *Can O' Worms*, with Davern, Hubble, Wellstood, Jack Six, and Al McManus. Chuck Slate's Traditional Jazz Band, with vocalist Natalie Lamb, also performed. The program raised $1,500, which was turned over to the Institute of Jazz Studies at Rutgers University, and a scholarship was established in Russell's name at Rutgers University. The Pee Wee Russell Memorial Stomp and the award of a scholarship became an annual event that continues to this day.[2] When the New Jersey Jazz Society was formed, it took over the task of producing the Stomp. Davern was a frequent and popular performer.

The Allaire Hotel in Spring Lake was one of a number of hotels that were scattered throughout the small towns of New Jersey on or near the Atlantic Ocean. They catered to vacationers from New York and Philadelphia and flourished during the summer months. From Memorial Day through the end of June, Davern led a band at the Allaire on weekends and, from June 28 through Labor Day, he spent five nights per week there. The group was called Kenny Davern and His Clamdiggers, and its members were usually Wellstood, Nabil Totah on bass, and Phil Failla on drums.

Most of the audience at the Allaire was elderly, and the band frequently played long medleys of slow ballads so that the aged dancers could sway in rhythm on the dance floor. Kenny called it the Spring Lake Shuffle. "It was like we were playing for defrocked nuns and priests. They were like crows on a high tension wire where they would move over, one at a time, and move over again, and they would be hitting on each other."[3]

He had some other jobs. From time to time, Wellstood called him for work at the Harbor Island Spa in West Branch, New Jersey. "These were regular Catskill mountain–type shows with the mambo dancers, the black tap dancers, the pseudo-opera singers, the Broadway show people. It was awful. The rest of the time, we played for dancing."[4] He played at Charlie O's in Spring Lake and the Union House in Red Bank. "I used to bring Conrad down there and Wellstood and anyone else who was available for these Wednesday night soirees."[5]

About this time, Davern recorded two unusual albums for the Music Minus One label, *Little Jazz Duets* and *Little Jazz Duets in the Round*. These were "play along" disks, designed as instructional aids for clarinet students with one or two years of experience. On each of the original tunes that were written by Norman S. Farnsworth and William F. Minor, Jr., Davern, aided by bassist George Duvivier and drummers Bobby Donaldson or John Cresci, played both the melody and, through dubbing, the harmony parts, so that the student could hear how the duet should sound. Then the tune was repeated twice: first, with Davern playing the melody so that the student could play harmony, and then with Davern playing only the harmony part. There was no jazz here. Davern played only one scripted chorus of the tunes, each of which lasted only about a minute. No effort was made to mass-market these albums.

In the fall, Davern began to work on Saturday nights with Leonard "Red" Balaban at the Town House in Rutherford, New Jersey. Red had come to New York from Florida, where he owned a ranch and played banjo or string bass with some local bands. He put together a group of musicians, which changed from time to time, and called his band Balaban and Cats. The name owed its origins to Red's father, Barney Balaban, who, with his partners Sam and Morris Katz, owned a string of theaters that operated during the 1920s, when vaudeville was in its heyday, under the name of Balaban and Katz. In the 1930s, Balaban became the president of Paramount Pictures.

Davern was not in the regular band at the Town House which consisted of Ed Polcer on cornet, Dick Rath on trombone, Herb Hall on clarinet, Gim Burton on banjo, Balaban on bass, and Marquis Foster on drums. However, Balaban made some changes for a one-time engagement in October 1970, and recorded the evening's performance. Davern replaced Hall, Ed Hubble replaced Rath, Balaban switched to banjo, and Howard Johnson joined on tuba. On another evening, in late January 1971, he substituted Davern for Hall and again recorded the Town House band. Balaban packaged six tunes from that date, plus two from the October session, into an album titled *Bits and Pieces*.

The record is pleasant enough. Almost all of the tunes are taken at a medium-to-fast tempo and the clanking banjo, whether in the hands of Burton or Balaban, keeps the rhythm pounding. Polcer is the featured instrumentalist, but everyone has some solo space.[6]

There was another connection between Davern and Balaban. In New York, a club called Your Father's Moustache (YFM) had opened on the site once occupied by Nick's. YFM featured sing-along entertainment six nights per week. But, at the beginning of November, it began to offer a program of jazz on Sunday afternoons. Red Balaban was the contractor on the job and, he usually hired the men from his Town House band. Periodically, Balaban brought in guest musicians; among them were Al Cohn, Roswell Rudd, and a fifteen-year-old Warren Vache, Jr. Davern was frequently, but not always, the clarinet player.

The most significant event of 1970, if not in all of Kenny's adult life, concerned his relationship with Elsa Lass. Her divorce from Don had become final in 1969 and, with part of the settlement proceeds, she had purchased a house at 85 Virginia Avenue in Manasquan. Although Kenny had begun divorce proceedings from Sylvia in 1968, she was not served with process until April 1970. On October 30, Kenny's petition was granted, and he and Sylvia were divorced.[7]

John Kenneth Davern and Elsa Green Lass were married on November 9, 1970, in the living room of the Virginia Avenue home. Dick Wellstood, dressed in a tuxedo and sneakers, was Kenny's best man: Sharon Wellstood was Elsa's matron of honor. Elsa's children, Debbie and Mark, were there, and the other guests included Kenny's mother, Josephine; Elsa's mother, Elsa Conover and her husband, Frank; Elsa's brother, Don Green, together with his wife, Rue, and their children, Terri and Dawn; and Nancy Hubble. The ceremony began at 6:15 p.m. and, when it was over, there were some refreshments and a wedding cake with which the bride and groom pelted each other. The festivities ended early because the bride had an examination in one of her courses at school the following day.[8]

They did not have a honeymoon at that time—or at any time afterward. In the beginning, the children were young, money was scarce, and both of them had commitments that they could not break. In later years, they occasionally tacked a few private days onto an engagement away from home. But, like many men in other occupations, Davern was uncomfortable when he wasn't working. Playing the clarinet was what he did, and he was unable to relax when he wasn't.[9]

Although he had more opportunities to play in 1971, there were almost no opportunities for Davern to advance his career, which now seemed to be firmly stalled in New Jersey, with only an occasional foray into New York. During the first two months of the year, he had a steady Friday–Saturday night job at the Harbor Island Spa, and played on Sunday afternoons at YFM. In March, he added Tuesday nights to his appearances at Harbor Island and got a job on Wednesdays at the Orange Lantern in Paramus, New Jersey. In addition, he did one-nighters at some clubs and restaurants, played some private parties, subbed for others when their schedules demanded, and occasionally gave lessons. He often worked six and sometimes seven days per week.[10]

From time to time, Davern and Wellstood would spend an evening in New York, and Kenny made a point of staying in contact with the musicians who played or hung out at Eddie Condon's. At the end of April, Condon called Davern to play a one-night stand at a high school outside of Syracuse, New York. Along with Condon on guitar and Davern on both clarinet and soprano saxophone, the All-Stars, as they were billed, consisted of Bernie Privin on trumpet; Lou McGarity on trombone; Dill Jones, the Welsh-born pianist who had settled in the United States; Jack Lesberg on bass; and Cliff Leeman.

The program was a typical Eddie Condon–style ad hoc affair, beginning with *At the Jazz Band Ball*. The next tune was *Rosetta*, which was quickly stopped by Condon and restarted at a slower pace. Some of the other selections were *Royal Garden Blues*, *Rose of Washington Square*, *China Boy*, *Muskrat Ramble*, and *St. Louis Blues*. The activities were recorded by Leo Rayhill, who had a local radio program. Rayhill filed the tapes in his basement and apparently forgot about them. In 1999, Davern learned of their existence. He arranged for them to be sent to Mat Domber of Arbors Records, who issued them on a CD titled *Kenny Davern, A Night with Eddie Condon*.[11]

The reviews were quite favorable. Scott Yanow said that the CD was "an unexpected treasure from the past." David Franklin gave the album good marks, noting that the band seemed to be having a good time. He singled out several players for praise, including Davern who, he said, "solos with emotion and an easy sense of swing."[12]

Back in New Jersey, Davern's life quickly resumed its old course. Although the season at the Jersey Shore did not officially begin until Memorial Day, many hotels offered entertainment earlier. At the beginning of May, he returned to the Allaire, where he played on Friday and Saturday nights. After a week-long appearance at Blues Alley in Washington, D.C., Davern returned to New Jersey and added a two-night-per-week engagement at the newly openly Beau Rivage in Wildwood Crest to his schedule. Sunday afternoons were spent at YFM. At the end of June, his schedule at the Allaire expanded to five nights weekly, which, with Sundays at YFM, accounted for almost the entirety of the summer.[13]

When Davern was in New York City, he frequently stopped by the studio of David Weber for an hour of study, or conversation, or both. Weber, who had played in the New York Philharmonic Orchestra, the Metropolitan Opera Orchestra, the CBS Symphony, and the Symphony of the Air, was then the principal clarinet in the New York Ballet Orchestra.

When he was a teenager, Davern had studied clarinet with Leon Russianoff, who taught at the Juilliard School of Music, the Manhattan School of Music, Queens College, and several other institutions.[14] Later, he began studying with Weber.

> He taught a great foundation for the clarinet itself. If you wanted to learn how to tongue, if you wanted to learn how to articulate on the instrument and just get a sound, you had to go through this basic thing that he would teach you. To this day, I still practice what he taught. He was a real master clarinet player.

> I used to pass by his studio en route to my saxophone teacher. . . . I used to get off at the second floor instead of the third floor where I belonged, on the pretext of buying reeds at the music store that was in the building, just to hear him warm up to practice. Finally, I got enough nerve to ask him, "Will you teach me?"[15]

Weber was known for the beauty of his tone—a skill that was of paramount importance to Davern in his own playing. Jon Manasse, presently the principal clarinet with the Metropolitan Opera Orchestra and the American Ballet Theater Orchestra, among others, was a friend of Kenny's and a student of Weber's. He shared Davern's respect for the older man.

> You know the stories that he [Davern] would hide outside of Dave Weber's studio at Carnegie Hall just to hear him practice. Remember, Weber was not a jazz clarinet player—he was a legit player, and Kenny became completely enamored—sort of as I did. I didn't love the sound of the clarinet until I heard Dave Weber play it. It has a particular bell-like sweetness and warmth, the proper balance of mellow and ring at its best.[16]

Kenny told author Sue Terry: "He can produce a sound so superb, anyone would want to emulate it. And he can impart that knowledge. Studying with David, you get results."[17]

The relationship with Weber evolved into more than that of teacher and pupil. The two shared many opinions about how the clarinet should be played and how it should sound. But, Weber was also a valued source of knowledge. At this point, Davern did not need formal lessons. But, from time to time, he needed to talk with someone about technical or other problems he was experiencing. As Jon Manasse put it: "It's basically mentoring—having a very warm trusted set of ears that have your best interest at heart. And, if you have questions or concerns, you can go to this person—in this case it was Dave Weber—for a checkup or an opinion."[18]

Davern always admired the older man and the reverse must have been true, for the relationship between them lasted until Kenny's death. When Weber died in 2007, only three of his many students were mentioned by name in his *New York Times* obituary: Kenny Davern was one of them.[19]

In the last four months of the year, he worked sporadically at the Allaire, had a week in October at Blues Alley, followed by several dates at the Hillside Lounge in Chester, and a weekly engagement at the Union House. He was at YFM almost every Sunday afternoon. At the beginning of December, he joined Wild Bill Davison, pianist Claude Hopkins, and drummer Cliff Leeman for a two-days-per-week gig at the Gaslight Club in New York City.[20]

The Gaslight, located at 124 East 56th Street, was not a jazz room. It was a key club that featured scantily clad hostesses who would periodically run up onstage and do a Charleston while the band played the tune of the same name or *Black Bottom*. Customers were prone to shout out requests for *When You and I Were Young Maggie Blues* or *My Wild Irish Rose*. But, the pay was good and the tips were better, especially during the holidays. The band must have been popular for, by the end of the year, they were playing six days per week with Sundays off. The job, originally scheduled to last two weeks, was periodically extended and ended over six months later on May 19, 1972.[21]

Sundays were not necessarily days of rest. During this period, Davern had jobs at the Shipwheel, Harry's Place in Somerville, and the Union House. On Sunday, February 13, 1972, he, Wellstood, and drummer Freddie Kohlman recorded a demo tape that was never released.

Davern did not work at the Gaslight on Monday, April 3, 1972. Hank O'Neal, who had recently founded Chiaroscuro Records, was teaching a course at the New School of Social Research in New York City. It consisted of four two-hour lectures at which musicians would play for the first half of the program and then, after a short intermission, return to answer questions. With a budget of $80 per man, O'Neal built a band around Eddie Condon and Gene Krupa, who had first played together in Chicago in 1927 as part of McKenzie and Condon's Chicagoans. Condon hadn't been taking many dates, and Krupa was ill with leukemia, but both wanted to play. O'Neal hired Davern, Dick Wellstood, and Wild Bill Davison to fill out the band.[22]

The first concert was held on April 3 and, although 150 people had signed up for the course, 500 packed into the auditorium to hear the music. Davern played soprano saxophone, and his wide sweeping sound was an effective counterfoil to Davison's ebullient tone. He was featured in a trio setting on *Shim-Me-Sha-Wabble* and on *The Mooche*, which has a different feeling from his later versions with Soprano Summit. Davern took extended solos throughout the program and was particularly impressive on *I Want to Be Happy* and *I Can't Believe That You're in Love with Me*.[23]

The concert was recorded by students at the school and was subsequently released by O'Neal on his Chiaroscuro label titled *Jazz at the New School*. O'Neal recalled:

> I remember that when the record came out, Gene was in the hospital with the leukemia that finally got him. I told him that it was a five-star record and

everybody was thrilled with it, and he was too. He was absolutely determined to make another one, but it never came about. But, of all players on this record, Kenny Davern was the one who was the most exciting, followed by Gene. It was a remarkable evening.[24]

After a hiatus of about five years, Davern returned to the recording studio on May 1. *Dick Wellstood and His Hot Potatoes, Featuring Kenny Davern*, recorded in the penthouse studio at Steinway Hall in New York City, is an odd album. Several of the cuts, *Atlanta Blues, Suppertime*, and *George Sanders* (a blues dedicated to the actor who had recently committed suicide) show Davern at his ballad-playing, lyrical best.[25] *Shout 'Em Aunt Tillie* (with an introduction by Wellstood that echoes the opening of Ellington's 1940 recording of *Ko-Ko*), is driving and compelling. *That Shakespearian Rag* is really *Diga Diga Do* in disguise, and it also swings.

In a Mello Role was Davern and Wellstood's satire on the too-often-played *In a Mellotone*: Davern's contribution is a series of whimsical, almost-discordant variations on the themes of the tune. *Naughty Sweetie Blues* seems to be an effort to bring the some of the concepts of Free Jazz into a traditional setting. Davern's solos contain unconnected shrieks and wails that do not follow the melodic or harmonic lines, and there is little of the lyricism that marks most of his efforts.

Davern was upset with the recording engineer who, he said, took the growl and spittle out of his playing, thereby "taking out the unique aspects of my playing." He called the album a "magnificent failure."[26] Author Nat Hentoff had a different opinion. Writing in the *New York Times*, he said that album was "one of the most deeply pleasurable jazz (I still use that word) recordings that he had heard in recent years," and described Davern as "the most accomplished and certainly the most lyrical soprano saxophonist extant." Sinclair Traill took a middle ground, finding that some of the tracks "lack that certain spark." Nonetheless, he praised the efforts of Wellstood and Davern, particularly, the soprano saxophone on *Naughty Sweetie Blues* and *Shout 'Em Aunt Tillie*."[27]

The job at the Gaslight had ended as the summer season began and in May, Davern went back to the Allaire on a two-nights-per-week basis. There was work at the South Street Seaport on Manhattan's East Side and Fairleigh Dickinson University in Madison, New Jersey, in May, a date at Harry's in Somerville, and a job with Conrad Janis at the Cosmopolitan Club in New York City in June. He was still playing frequently at YFM on Sundays.

At the end of June, Davern's appearances at the Allaire increased to five days per week and those dates, along with the Sunday dates at YFM, again accounted for the greater part of his summer work. However, on a Monday in July, he squeezed in one more recording. In the 1940s, Irving Kratka was a drummer and one of a group of youngsters, including Dick Wellstood, Eph Resnick, and Joe Muranyi, who hung around Nola Studios, trying to find their musical way. In the following decades, Kratka became a record producer, and, under the catchy title of Music Minus One had produced a series of albums, designed as teaching aids for students and professional musicians. At the recording session, each musician had a separate microphone. The albums were released with one instrument silenced: hence *Music Minus One—Trombone* or *Music Minus One—Trumpet*. In addition to allowing the purchaser to play in the ensemble, each tune had a section in which the horns dropped out and only the rhythm section played, thus allowing the novice musician to play a solo. Some of the albums included sheet music and a suggested form of solo.

Davern's participation in this series came on July 10, 1972, when, along with Doc Cheatham on trumpet, Vic Dickenson on trombone, Wellstood, George Duvivier on bass, and Gus Johnson, Jr., on drums, he recorded eight tunes that were released under the title *From Dixie to Swing*.[28] On *Royal Garden Blues*, *Sunny Side of the Street*, and *I Want a Little Girl*, he weaves in and out of the opening and closing statements, playing counterpoint to Cheatham's trumpet lead. He takes short, but inventive, solos on *Second Hand Rose*, *Rose of Washington Square*, *Royal Garden Blues*, and *Exactly Like You* and, with Wellstood, states the verse of *On the Sunny Side of the Street* on soprano before switching to clarinet.

A number of versions of the album, with different instruments muted, were released on Kratka's Music Minus One label. However, the musicians were apparently unaware that Kratka intended to also release it on his Classic Jazz label as a straight, commercial recording. Although the Classic Jazz issue retained Dick Wellstood's liner notes from the teaching edition, a paragraph that indicated that the record was intended as a play-along teaching aid for home musicians was omitted, and purchasers found themselves listening to songs where, without explanation, musicians were playing supporting riffs and patterns, but no one was soloing or playing the melody. Davern and several of the musicians who had played on earlier releases were upset: "That kind of stuff was not kosher," he said.[29] The album received mixed reviews.

Davern subsequently made one more album for the Music Minus One label. Along with Ed Hubble, Wellstood, Jack Six, drummer Joe Cocuzzo, and a four-piece string section led by violinist Manny Senerchia, Kenny recorded five titles for an album titled *Bacharach Revisited*. This was not a jazz date: it was intended for sing-alongs. The musicians only played soft, flowing, harmonic backgrounds, leaving a great deal of space in which the purchaser could sing the melody. On one side of the LP, the tracks have a vocal added: on the reverse they do not. Decades later, the album was re-released on CD with several new tracks of songs by Hal David added, titled *Sing Along with Bacharach and David* and marketed to appeal to the karaoke trade.

At the end of the summer, Davern headed off to Colorado and the annual Labor Day party thrown by Dick and Maddie Gibson. That engagement changed his life. Dick Gibson grew up in Alabama: his wife, Maddie, was born in Canada. After working in advertising and on Wall Street, Dick and Maddie moved to Denver, where Dick made the acquaintance of a dentist who had a novel device for cleaning teeth. Gibson put together a group of investors to market this product, which they called the *Waterpik*. Eventually, Gibson and his colleagues sold the *Waterpik* to Teledyne and emerged with a substantial amount of money.

Although the Gibsons liked their lives in Colorado, the one thing that they missed was listening to good, live, jazz. Because they were unable to find it in Denver, they decided to import it. In 1963, they hired ten musicians from New York and put on a party for about one hundred paying guests at the Jerome Hotel in Aspen over the Labor Day weekend. The event was a success, and the Gibsons decided to make it an annual affair. In the ensuing years, the number of attendees grew as the Gibsons invited more musicians and also, their wives and girlfriends.

By 1972, playing at the Gibsons' Labor Day weekend party had become a badge of honor for musicians. For guests, an invitation was something to be prized. In addition to the formal sessions, the weekend also included pre- and post–jazz party events at the Gibsons' home for the musicians and selected friends, where the "real" partying took place.[30]

The 1972 party was held at the Broadmoor Hotel in Colorado Springs over the weekend of September 2–4, and, for the first time, Kenny Davern was invited. Playing for Gibson was a significant event for him. Although he had performed with some of the greats of jazz over the years, this was, for many of them, their first extended exposure to him. Playing both clarinet and soprano saxophone, Davern appeared in sets with trumpeters Ruby Braff, Pee Wee Erwin, Clark Terry, Joe Wilder, and Snooky Young. Buster Cooper, Urbie Green, Benny Morton, and Frank Rosolino were among the trombone players, and the reed players included Barney Bigard, Budd Johnson, James Moody, and Flip Phillips. The rhythm sections were drawn from Hank Jones, Roger Kellaway, Dick Hyman Teddy Wilson (pianos), Les Paul and Bucky Pizzarelli (guitars), George Duvivier, Milt Hinton, and Slam Stewart (basses), and drummers Cliff Leeman and Bobby Rosengarden.

Bob Wilber was in the cast of musicians that Dick Gibson had invited. Born in 1928, in the upper-middle-class New York City suburb of Scarsdale, he had become attracted to the music of Sidney Bechet and his contemporaries at an early age. He learned to play clarinet and, by the time that he was in high school, he was at the center of a group of youngsters, including Dick Wellstood, who became known as the Scarsdale High Gang. Wilber met Bechet and persuaded the older man to give him lessons, eventually adopting a style that was very similar to that of his teacher. In 1946, the Scarsdale Jazz Band made their first recording (which was not released until several years later) and in 1947, the group, now named Bob Wilber and His Wildcats, made a number of personal appearances, as well as several records.

Wilber broke up the Wildcats in the summer of 1948, when he appeared at the festival in Nice, France, produced by Hughes Panassie. It was the first of the post–World War II international jazz festivals: the guests included Louis Armstrong. When Wilber returned, he went into the Savoy Café in Boston, where he remained until April 1950.

By then, the association with Bechet, which had been so beneficial to Wilber when he was getting started, was becoming a burden. He was becoming typecast as a Bechet play-alike. So, over the next two decades, Wilber meticulously remade his musical style, abandoning the prominent vibrato that identified him with Bechet, and substituting a technically impressive, melodious sound that evoked musical images of Benny Goodman. During these years, he worked in a number of settings, playing at Eddie Condon's, appearing at the Voyager Room in the Henry Hudson Hotel with Bobby Hackett, and eventually being a charter member of the World's Greatest Jazz Band—an unfortunate name that was imposed upon the band by Dick Gibson, who financially supported it. By 1972, the reinvention of Bob Wilber was complete.

Wilber and Davern had encountered each other at several events. But, the only occasions on which they played together were in June 1972, when Red Balaban booked them both to play at YFM on two consecutive Sundays. In later years, both Bob and Kenny recalled those afternoons as just another job—with nothing to distinguish them. Ed Hubble, who was in the band on one of those dates, and his wife Nancy, who was present, remembered that the rapport between the two and the music that they generated was extraordinary.[31]

As with all Gibson parties, the music was virtually nonstop, beginning on Friday night at 7:00 p.m. and ending at 2:00 on Saturday morning. It resumed at 11:00 a.m. and, with a dinner break, continued until 2:00 a.m. on the following day. The same schedule was followed on Sunday and, by the time that the music resumed on Monday, excitement had turned to exhaustion.

Davern remembered the end of the weekend.

> By the fourth day, people were beginning to stick to their chairs, getting a little brain dead. So Gibson says: "Kenny and Bob, why don't you get together and do something—two soprano saxophones." The only thing worse than one soprano saxophone is two. But, Bob could play the instrument well, and I was doing okay myself. So we decided to do *The Mooche* by Duke Ellington and, like I say, there we were, the last tune of the last set of the Labor Day Weekend with Dick Gibson. We get up on the stage, and we play this thing and fortunately, we had Dick Hyman on the piano, Bucky Pizzarelli on the guitar, Bobby Rosengarden on drums, and Milt Hinton on bass. Now, it's a dollar-and-a-half band, at least.[32]
>
> After we played the number, 650 people gave us a standing ovation. I could not believe it; tears came to my eyes. . . . At the bar, Dick Gibson said to a promoter: "You ought to record these guys. . . ."[33]

On that note, the weekend came to a close.

The weekend at the Gibsons' gave Davern exposure to musical constituencies that had not heard him before. The performers included a number of musicians who were at the top of the musical pyramid. The audience was sophisticated, knowledgeable, and influential: some were involved in hiring musicians for jazz events, while others reported on them for newspapers, magazines, and jazz-oriented publications. Kenny started to get more work at the better jazz parties and festivals and, with increasing frequency, he began working with members of the upper level of the jazz hierarchy. When Soprano Summit, as it came to be known, began to tour and record, a new audience came to attend his performances, buy his records, and become fans and friends. In the short span of four days, Davern's career had turned around.

However, all of that was in the future. More than one year elapsed between the birth of Soprano Summit and the date on which the musicians gathered in the studio to make their first recording. In the meantime, Kenny returned home to resume his professional life.

For the next two months, he was working at many of his usual venues. There were Saturdays at the Town House and Sundays at YFM. He had gigs at the Orange Lantern, Harry's, O'Connor's Beef and Ale House in Watchung, New Jersey, the Landmark in Paterson, and he performed on three Mondays in October at Michael's Pub in New York City. He played some private parties and participated in a benefit concert for the widow of Jimmy Rushing. From November 6 to 11, 1972, he was at the Town Tavern in Toronto.[34]

On November 13, Kenny and Elsa left for Durban, South Africa, where Kenny was scheduled to play for a month. Shortly before the Daverns arrived, cornetist Jimmy McPartland had played there. He had been well received and, when asked to recommend someone else to invite, McPartland had suggested Davern.

The trip was well and favorably publicized in the Durban newspapers. There were two articles about him on the day after his arrival, *Top Clarinet Player Blows in for Season*, and *Sax-Man Blows a Treat for Jazz Fans*, followed by another article on November 17, *Exquisite Jazz from a Young Performer*, and a fourth article titled *The Man Who Said "No" to Armstrong*, on the 26th. Elsa was profiled by someone identified only as "Daily News Woman Reporter," in a piece titled *Fascinated by Her Husband's Jazz*.

Davern played Fridays and Saturday evenings at the Queens Tavern in Durban, where he was backed by a quartet named Steve Gale and His Dixielanders. He made some trips to play engagements in Uvongo, Himeville, and Empangeni; played Saturday lunches at the Congelia Hotel and at a dinner dance for the South Africa Air Force Association. Elsa, who returned home on December 2, said it was a "great experience."[35] Kenny remained there until the 17th.

In those days, international travel was still an adventure for him. There were new people to meet, new places to explore, new music to hear, and new stores to visit. But, when the evening's work came to an end and he had to spend a night alone, often in a primitively equipped room, he was lonely. He missed his wife and the children, and he wanted to be with them. It was just another aspect of the changes that were occurring in his life.

When Kenny married Elsa, he became stepfather to her daughter, Debbie, who was nine years old, and her son Mark, who was just a month short of his eighth birthday. Parenting was a role for which he had no training or experience. His father had never been part of his life, and he did not know that his uncles existed when he was growing up. He had no brothers or sisters with whom to interact, and no nieces or nephews to observe. In all of his thirty-five years, Davern had never been around young children.

Debbie and Mark were normal, active, youngsters who fought, yelled, and made noise as a routine part of their lives. They had no understanding of a man who worked at night, wanted to sleep during part of the day, and was used to reading, listening to music, or practicing his clarinet in a silent house. Moreover, this particular man had very little patience and a quick temper.

In the beginning, the adjustment was difficult for Kenny. Outbursts were frequent, and Elsa had to intercede as the stabilizing influence. She remembered how taxing it was for all of them:

> The very first couple of years were probably the hardest because they were so young. Kenny didn't get it. He had absolutely no idea of how to be a father.

> But, he knew how to be a friend. When he went off the rails, I would step in and say, "If you can't do this right, you have to step back and think about this." I would never let him go very far when I was around. I think that through all the years that he was with the kids, he was a good friend. I think that they forgave him his craziness when he went off the rails because they loved him.[36]

It was also a trying time for the children. Davern was not like other parents, and it took some time for the children to understand him. Years later, Debbie looked back on Kenny's experience with understanding.

> My brother and I were your typical kids: we fought and we were loud. We weren't the perfect, well-behaved, your "sit in the corner" children. We were kids. And, it was a lot for him to learn to deal with that. It's funny, because he was so proud of us: we always felt very loved even though—discipline-wise—he didn't know. . . . He had to feel his way through our childhood, and it was quite a ride, it really was.
>
> When I think of how he was as a dad, he wasn't your typical dad. Kids eluded him. He had an impatience about him—which he had with many people. But, you could see that he loved children, and he wanted to understand children. It's just that they perplexed him and they fascinated him.[37]

Although the process of parenting may have been difficult for Davern, the children were at the core of the home life that he cherished, and he was determined to make sure that they were never in doubt about how he felt about them. When he was away, he wrote a letter every day to each of them—and sometimes more than one. His letters to Elsa always mentioned that he loved and missed the kids.

As the children grew and matured, he found that he had interests in common with them. When Mark was about nine years old, he became captivated by horror movies. These were the days before cable television and twenty-four-hour movie channels, and pictures of this genre were hard to find in Southern New Jersey. So, father and son took a trip to New York to see a triple feature.

> We saw *Dracula*, and *Frankenstein*, and I think there was another movie, *Creature from the Black Lagoon*. I thought that this was the coolest thing—to go to New York City to go and see horror movies. Because we both loved horror movies. He got me onto reading Bram Stoker and *Dracula*, and all of that stuff. It was really the first young memory—bonding experience—that I remember having with him. Until the day that he passed away, he would go through these genres of horror movies.[38]

Occasionally, Davern took a page from his grandfather's book of child rearing and indulged the children in "forbidden" pleasures. Mark said: "As a kid, if there was a movie or a show on, I'd go to bed early and he'd wake me up at midnight or one o'clock and say 'Okay, here it is.' We'd go downstairs and watch these shows and movies, and then we'd go back to bed. I don't know if my mother ever knew."[39]

If Kenny was interested in a subject, he would share his enthusiasm with the children. He turned Mark onto collecting stamps and, when the youngster showed an interest in them, Kenny gave him the collection that he had started as a child. They went to stores together to pick out additions to the collection. As the children grew older, he began to give them books that he had read. He shared his library of material on the Mafia with Mark and, later, his collection of books about the West. "He'd go through these themes as life went on. We always shared that, which was kind of interesting."[40]

Debbie had the same experience.

> It was very interesting growing up. You know what kind of a mind he had. He was brilliant. And he wanted to talk about wonderful intelligent things, and we would just look at him like, "What is he talking about?" It was very funny sometimes when he'd get into conversations, and the things that he wanted to talk about. So, I did come away with a lot of understandings of not just music—because he was interested in so many things—but, I came away with so much more culture and intellect and that wonderful curiosity about all kinds of things. He always wanted to try to get us to read some book, or listen to some music. It wasn't just jazz in our house. And, God forbid we ever listened to Aerosmith and Led Zeppelin in his presence. As I said, it wasn't just jazz in our house. He loved gospel and classical music: there was always classical music in our house.[41]

To be sure, there were times when living under the same roof with Kenny was taxing for the children. He could be strict, arbitrary, bad-tempered, and simply unpleasant. But, those weren't the emotions that left their mark. Debbie said: "It must have been so hard: it must have been very hard for him. But, I always felt that he just loved us. And so it really didn't matter if he wasn't the perfect father. He just loved us, and I always felt that. That's a nice thing to have."[42] And Mark echoed the sentiment.

> He was kind, caring, and gentle. When he traveled, he always sent letters. I go back and read them, and he would tell me everything he was doing. I don't remember reading them as a kid. Reading them now, my God, the guy really

loved us. He was thinking about us all the time, he was telling us everything he was doing, that he couldn't wait to get home. It was hard.[43]

Davern started the year 1973 with some degree of financial stability. He had signed a year-long contract to work in the Fifth Avenue Room at Jack Sullivan's Spring Lake Lodge in Spring Lake, New Jersey. His group, called the Fifth Avenue Four, consisted of the rhythm section from the Ferryboat Band: Wellstood plus Jack Six on bass, and Al McManus on drums. From January through July 4, they worked four nights per week.

There were other dates, including a concert in New York for Jack Kleinsinger on February 5 and another in Keene, New Hampshire, on the 20th. He did some dates with Red Balaban in February and March and, beginning on February 26, he worked Mondays at Michael's Pub through March and April.[44]

Over the years, a number of bars and restaurants in New Jersey had regularly hired jazz musicians who lived in New Jersey or New York, or who were otherwise available. As some closed, others opened: among the better-known venues were the Martinsville Inn in Martinsville, O'Connor's Beef and Ale House in Watchung, the Town House in Rutherford, Gullivers in Paterson and later in Lincoln Park, the Watchung View Inn in Pluckemin, the Chester Inn in Chester, and the Cornerstone in Metuchen.

These venues were supported by a small but dedicated group of fans: among them were Warren and Madeline Vache, Bert and Jack McSeveny, Hubie and Dossie (Dorothy) Scott, Dick and Judy Neeld, Jack and Audrey Stine (Jack conceived of and organized the first Pee Wee Russell Memorial Stomp), and Red and Carrie Squires. At the beginning of 1974, they organized the New Jersey Jazz Society, which was dedicated to the performance, promotion, and preservation of jazz. The Society's first concert was held on April 8, 1973, at the Watchung View Inn, Pluckemin, New Jersey, with Pee Wee Erwin, Davern, and Wellstood among the musicians. Davern would be one of the most frequent performers at the Society's events.

Davern was in Denver on April 25 for the opening of the Spaghetti Factory. In May, he had a Monday date at Michael's Pub, flew back to Denver for a Gibson party, and returned home the following day. He was at the Eastern Branch of the Monmouth County Library in Shrewsbury leading the Kenny Davern Quintet, with Roswell Rudd, Wellstood, bassist Gene Ramey and Cliff Leeman on drums. On June 18, he had an appearance for Jack Kleinsinger and, on the following day, he played in the Promenade Café at Rockefeller Center. His date book for that event bore the handwritten notation "Ugh."[45]

Davern's schedule at the Spring Lake Lodge increased to six days per week on July 4. Shortly thereafter, the Lodge attempted to renegotiate the terms and duration of the contract. Davern hired an attorney and ultimately the parties agreed that, after Labor Day, the Quartet would continue to play four days per week until November 12 and, in exchange therefore, Davern would receive a lump-sum cash payment.[46] Subsequently, they agreed to end Davern's engagement at an even earlier date.

Davern was in a New York recording studio at the request of Earl Hines at 10:00 a.m., on Monday, August 6, to add his soprano saxophone to several cuts on an album released on the Thimble label, titled *This Is Marva Josie*. Josie, who was Hines's band vocalist, sang a varied group of tunes, including *Jelly, Jelly, Jelly* (the Hines–Billy Eckstine collaboration); *Why Was I Born*, by Oscar Hammerstein II and Jerome Kern; the traditional *Scarborough Fair*; and, in a more modern vein, *Understanding* and *You're Not Mine Anymore*. Although she changed her approach to fit the style of each tune, the result was marred by multiple tracking and other engineering gimmickry that sometimes made it sound as if the musicians were leaving the studio. Kenny had generous solos on *Jelly* and *Love, Love, Love*, and could be heard on several other tunes. Shortly after this session, Hines told Sinclair Traill, the founder and then editor of *Jazz Journal*, that Davern was the best clarinet player he'd heard since Jimmie Noone.[47]

Eddie Condon died on August 4. His funeral was held on August 8, and Hank O'Neal put together a band consisting of Wild Bill Davison, Johnny Windhurst, Vic Dickenson, Davern, Earl Hines, Al Hall, and Cliff Leeman to play at the chapel. Kenny remembered the occasion.

> We'd played one tune and then—the place was packed out and Gene Krupa had just come off the dais saying, "So long, Slick," with tears in his eyes. It was a memorial service. Someone said, "C'mon band, play something." We were just about to play something when Wild Bill says, "Hold it fellas, here she comes." It was Lee Wiley, and she had become very fat and bloated from alcohol.

Wiley was Condon's favorite singer. After leaving the music business for some time, she had returned to appear with a Condon-led band at Newport in 1972 and to make a recording for Monmouth-Evergreen. Wiley was then quite ill. "She comes waddling over to the dais where we are. 'Gimme a hand, fellas.' So, we help her up onto the stage. And she says, 'This is for Eddie. Lay out.'" She began to sing *Back Home Again in Indiana* as a ballad—very slowly.[48]

> And the hackles on my neck stood up, just like a porcupine. I never heard anything so beautiful in my life. She did it a cappella. When she finished, she got off the stage, and that was the end of that. I never heard or saw that song

that way again. I heard it in a totally different light. So I started playing it as a ballad.[49]

Through the balance of August, he continued working at the Spring Lake Lodge, with dates at the Pines Manor in Edison, New Jersey, and O'Connor's. At the beginning of September, he returned to Colorado for the Gibsons' annual Labor Day party, where he performed with an all-star cast that included Bobby Hackett, Clark Terry, and Benny Carter. When he returned home, he had some Thursday night engagements at Brews in New York, and a gig in Morristown, New Jersey. On September 29, he played his last date at the Spring Lake Lodge.[50]

Notes

1. Jack Stine, interview by the author.
2. Willo Roach, "800 Pay Honor to Pee Wee's Memory," *Somerset Messenger Gazette*, 19 February 1970, 33; John S. Wilson *New York Times*, 26 February 1970.
3. Kenny Davern, interview by the author, quoted in *Giant Strides*, 95.
4. Kenny Davern, interview by the author.
5. Kenny Davern, interview by the author.
6. Red Balaban, interview by the author. In his discography, Grant Elliott reversed the titles of this album and *A Night at the Townhouse* and placed both of them in 1968 (*Swingin' Americans, No. 3, Kenny Davern Discography* (Zwolle, NL, Gerard Bieldeman, 2001). A physical examination of the disks and jackets reveals that the proper title of this LP is *Bits and Pieces*. Moreover, in a telephone interview with the author, Red Balaban was certain that these cuts were made in October 1970 and January 1971, and not at the earlier date. Finally, information that appears on the record jacket, as well as on a printed insert, is consistent with the 1970–71 recording dates. In addition to the eight titles recorded at the Town House, Balaban included three other cuts that were made in a barn on his farm in Florida by a group consisting of Hubble, Balaban, and trumpeter Johnny Windhurst.

With respect to the *Night at the Town House* album, the only tune on which Davern plays is *Your Father's Moustache*. Balaban was certain that he did not begin playing at that club until October 1970, and I have therefore concluded that this cut was recorded in the same period as Davern's other recordings with Balaban. Red Balaban, interview by the author.

7. Elsa Davern, interview by the author; *Davern v. Davern*, Judgment of Divorce.
8. Elsa Davern, Nancy Hubble, interviews by the author. The fact that Kenny married Elsa did not seem to affect Don Lass's opinion of him as a musician. He continued to favorably review Kenny's performances in the *Asbury Park Press* and even wrote the liner notes for one of Kenny's Soprano Summit albums.
9. Elsa Davern, interview by the author.

10. Davern kept all of his date books beginning with the year 1971. These books are an invaluable record as to where, and with whom, he was working and shall be referred to throughout the balance of this book as "Date Book." The Date Books have also been helpful in pinning down a number of recording dates that were heretofore unknown.

11. Brian Peerless, liner notes to *Kenny Davern, A Night with Eddie Condon*, Arbors ARCD 19238, December 2000.

12. Scott Yanow, "Kenny Davern, A Night with Eddie Condon," *Cadence*, 28, no. 2 (February 2002); David Franklin, "Kenny Davern, A Night with Eddie Condon," *Jazz Times*, March 2002, 72.

13. Date Book.

14. Davern response to Feather Questionnaire.

15. Kenny Davern, interview by Mark Weber, 13 January 2005; see also: Sue Terry, "Personal Sound, a Portrait of David Weber at 90," *Allegro*, April 2004, 14.

16. Jon Manasse, interview by the author.

17. Terry, *supra*, at p. 15.

18. Jon Manasse, interview by the author.

19. *New York Times*, 9 July 2007. The other students mentioned in the article were Jon Manasse and Benny Goodman. As to Goodman, the article reported that he took lessons but never paid for them and, Weber once said, took his best reeds.

20. Date Book; Willard, Davison, 381–382.

21. Willard, Davison, 381–382; Date Book.

22. Hank O'Neal, recorded recollections; Patricia O'Haire, "Night Owl Reporter, Rambling Along," *Daily News*, 5 April 1972, 6.

23. Hank O'Neal, recorded recollections. The exact date of this concert comes from Davern's date book.

24. Hank O'Neal, recorded recollections.

25. The liner notes say that the recording took place a few days after George Sanders committed suicide; i.e., 25 April 1972. Davern's date book refers to a recording date at the Nola Studio at Steinway Hall on May 1. Although no other information is provided, the Hot Potatoes disk is the only unaccounted-for recording during this period.

26. Kenny Davern, in Rusch interview part 1, at 24; Kenny Davern, interview by the author.

27. Nat Hentoff, "Pop: Piano That Sings," *New York Times*, 29 July 1973; Sinclair Traill, "Dick Wellstood and His Hot Potatoes Featuring Kenny Davern," *Jazz Journal International*, 32, no. 11 (November 1979): 43.

28. Date Book.

29. Kenny Davern, quoted in Rusch interview part 1, p. 19. The problems that some musicians encountered when they were issued to the general public are detailed in *Giant Strides*, 61–62.

30. Whitney Balliett, "Ecstasy at the Onion," reprinted in *Ecstasy at the Onion, Thirty-One Pieces on Jazz* (New York, Bobbs Merrill, 1971), 184–185; e-mail from Dan Morgenstern to the author.

31. See, e.g., Kenny Davern and Bob Wilber, recorded on *Jazzspeak* on *Summit Reunion*, Chiaroscuro CRD 311; Ed Hubble and Nancy Hubble, interviews by the author.

32. Kenny Davern, interviewed by David Holt, broadcast on Jim Cullum's NPR radio show, *Jazz from the Landing* on 13 May 2004: this program, titled *Jazz Memories with Kenny Davern* ("Holt Interview").

33. Dirk interview, p. 7; See also: Wilber/Webster, p. 127 and the Gibson party Schedule of Events.

The story, as Davern often related it, has a certain excitement to it ("the last tune of the last set of the Labor Day Weekend"), and it probably only stretches the truth a little. The last set of the party was usually a free-for-all. It is highly unlikely that Gibson would have put Wilber and Davern into that spot. Moreover, the schedule of events states that Davern was to play soprano saxophone in the fifth set of the day, along with Budd Johnson and Howard Johnson, both playing baritone saxophones, with a rhythm section of Hyman, Hinton, and Rosengarden. It is more likely that Wilber replaced the two Johnsons in that spot to play with Davern, Hyman, Hinton, and Rosengarden, plus Bucky Pizzarelli. Regardless of where in the schedule they appeared, there is unanimity among everyone who has written of the event that their performance provoked intense excitement and a long, standing ovation.

34. Date Book; *DownBeat*, 39, no. 18 (9 November 1972): 11; *New Yorker*, 28 October 1972, p. 6; Thomas P. Hustad, interview by the author.

35. Anonymous, "Top Clarinet Player Blows in for Season," *Daily News* (Durban), 15 November 1972; R. S. "Sax-Man Blows a Treat for Jazz Fans," *Daily News* (Durban) 15 November 1972; M. M., "Exquisite Jazz from a Young Performer," *Daily News* (Durban), 17 November 1972; Anonymous (Daily News Woman Reporter), "Fascinated by Her Husband's Jazz," *Daily News* (Durban), 26 November 1972; Elsa Davern, interview by the author.

36. Elsa Davern, interview by the author.

37. Deborah Wuensch, interview by the author.

38. Mark Lass, interview by the author.

39. Mark Lass, interview.

40. Mark Lass, interview.

41. Deborah Wuensch, interview by the author.

42. Deborah Wuensch, interview.

43. Mark Lass, interview.

44. Contract signed by Kenny Davern; Date Book.

45. Vache, Erwin, 315; contract from Davern's files; Date Book; John S. Wilson, "Library Books Jazz Band for Concert," *New York Times*, 29 April 1973.

46. Agreement between Kenny Davern and Shamrock, Inc.

47. Sinclair Traill, *Liner Notes to Soprano Summit II*, World Jazz WJLP, S-13. The recording date of August 6 appears in Davern's date book.

48. Condon had been born in Indiana.

49. Kenny Davern, interview by Mark Weber, 17 January 2006.

50. Date Book; Gibson party invitation letter.

CHAPTER SIX

In the Big Leagues

The last quarter of 1973 began on an auspicious note. On October 9, after a weekend gig at the Town House, Davern, together with Wellstood and Cliff Leeman, opened a six-week engagement at the prestigious Michael's Pub. Reviews of their performances were good. Nat Hentoff, writing in the *Village Voice*, called Davern "the preeminent master of the jazz soprano saxophone." The critic for the *Daily News* said that the trio was "inspired."[1] Davern was invited to perform at the *Private Jazz Party at the Waldorf*, an all-day and evening event at the Waldorf Astoria Hotel held on October 21, 1973. Others on the program included Pee Wee Erwin, Urbie Green, Milt Hinton, Major Holley, Bucky Pizzarelli, Zoot Sims, Clark Terry, and Teddy Wilson.

In November, Davern played some Sunday dates at the Spring Lake Lodge and participated in a Tribute to Eddie Condon produced by Jack Kleinsinger.[2] When the Michael's Pub job came to an end, he and Wellstood turned their attention to a record that they had been thinking about for some time, one on which they would be the only musicians.

The album was to be released by Hank O'Neal, on his Chiaroscuro label, and it was recorded under unusual circumstances. Dick and Kenny were working during the week, so the sessions could only be held on Sundays. However, O'Neal's studio was in an industrial building where the heat was turned off on weekends. The November cold adversely affected Wellstood's fingers and the keys on Davern's soprano saxophone. They tried using several space heaters to blow hot air and raise the temperature, but the heaters emitted a hum that interfered with the recording process.

The solution was primitive. When the heaters warmed the studio to the point where it became habitable, they would be turned off and the musicians would begin to play. The temperature would start to drop and, when the chill began to work on Davern's horn, the musicians would stop and the heaters would be turned on again. The process was arduous, and it went on for an extended period of time. Both Davern and Wellstood were perfectionists, and they insisted, as Hank O'Neal recalled, on "zillions and zillions of takes." When one or both of them became fed up with the process, they would end the session and adjourn to Jack Delaney's for a roast beef dinner and a number of drinks.[3]

They called the album *Dick Wellstood and His Famous Orchestra Featuring Kenny Davern*, and it was startling. The opening tune was *Fast as a Bastard*—in reality, an up-tempo rendition of Ellington's *Jubilee Stomp* that featured some technically excellent, flank-speed piano and powerful straight-ahead saxophone. The pace slowed down for Jelly Roll Morton's *Winin' Boy* and then Davern launched into one of his features on the soprano, a dynamic *Wild Man Blues*. *Georgia on My Mind* was followed by Davern's *a capella* treatment of his own composition, *Cashmir and Togas*, that was based on the chord pattern of *Lover Come Back To Me*. (The title, which is transliterated roughly from Yiddish, means "kiss my ass.")

The second side began with a leisurely version of *Smiles*, followed by another Jelly Roll Morton composition, *Sweet Substitute*. *Once in a While* (the tune recorded by Armstrong's Hot Five) came next, then the Eddie Condon composition, *Liza*. Cole Porter's *So in Love* was then one of Wellstood's solo features, and he used it as the closer for the album. When the LP was reissued on CD, *Cashmir and Togas* and *So in Love* were, unfortunately, omitted.

Although he almost always found some flaw in his recordings, Davern thought this was one of his best. He told Sinclair Traill: "Of my soprano albums, I think I like best the one I did alone with Dick Wellstood. The one on Chiaroscuro, which Dick satirically titled *Dick Wellstood & His Famous Orchestra*—it goes along nicely, and Dick of course played some wonderful piano."[4] Although most critics praised the album, not all the reviews were glowing. Jon Balleras, *DownBeat's* critic, seemed to like the album, but criticized Wellstood's occasional lapses of taste and "predictable" licks. He deemed Wellstood to be a "basically retrogressive stride pianist." Balleras found Davern "easier to take seriously" and approved of his playing, which was "idiomatically correct and frequently quite exciting."[5]

Recording of the *Famous Orchestra* album was still in progress when Kenny traveled to Manassas, Virginia, to perform at Johnson "Fat Cat" McCree's All-Star Festival. McCree was one of the first promoters of the traditional jazz festivals. (At festivals, the musicians perform in several different venues, usually outdoors: jazz parties are held indoors and have only one stage; the cost of attending a jazz festival is generally substantially less than that for a jazz party.) McCree would assemble a large group of musicians, consisting of a few major attractions mixed with some local talent, and, over the course of a three-day weekend, mix-and-match them in bands of various sizes. In many cases, players of varying skills and experience, some of whom were unknown to their colleagues, were thrust together. Because no time was allotted for rehearsals, the usual result was a series of often-played tunes that could be performed by the least experienced or least talented member of the group.[6] These proceedings were recorded by McCree, sometimes without the knowledge or informed consent of the musicians, and released on his Fat Cat Jazz label.

Davern made his first appearance at McCree's Manassas Jazz Festival over the weekend of November 30–December 2, 1973. He can be heard on all or parts of six LPs—*1973 Eighth Annual Manassas All-Star Jazz Festival, Swingin' The Soprano, The Mighty Driving Horn at Manassas, Doc Evans Is Back, Natalie Lamb Wails the Blues,* and *The Golden Horn Speaks Jazz*—that were subsequently released by Fat Cat. These sessions were not memorable, and Kenny was distressed to find out that they had been released commercially.[7]

On the Monday of his return from Virginia, and again on December 11, Davern was in the recording studio, this time for a Dick Hyman–led project. Hyman assembled an orchestra composed of some of the best musicians then working in the New York area to record his arrangements of a group of Jelly Roll Morton compositions. The album was titled *Some Rags, Some Stomps, and a Little Blues, Ferdinand Jelly Roll Morton*. Jazz repertory was in favor during the mid-1970s, perhaps as a result of the use of Scott Joplin's compositions in the movie *The Sting*. Hyman not only recorded a five-LP solo album of all of Joplin's compositions, but led large groups in performing the works of Morton, James P. Johnson, and, a year later, Louis Armstrong. He did the arrangements for many of these concerts, and those that he did for this event were among his best.

Although Morton's music and Hyman's arrangements were the centerpieces of this recording, it abounded with excellent musicianship. Pee Wee Erwin, Joe Wilder, Vic Dickenson, Davern, and Hyman were spotlighted throughout. Kenny was featured on *Grandpa's Spells* and *Black Bottom Stomp*, where he reprised Omer Simeon's clarinet solo. He switched to soprano saxophone for *Fickle Fay Creep*, gave an unusually breathy treatment of *Buddy Bolden's Blues*, and it was on that instrument that he performed the as-composed, four-strain version of *King Porter Stomp*.

Ralph Laing reviewed the album in *Jazz Journal*, calling it one of the "major landmarks in jazz recording." It was voted one of *Jazz Journal*'s top twenty albums for 1974. New York *Times* critic John S. Wilson praised the concept and the execution, saying that Davern was the "solo star of the set" for his work on both clarinet and soprano saxophone.[8]

In the middle of December, over fifteen months after Davern and Wilber had brought the crowd at the Gibsons' 1972 Labor Day party to its feet, Bob, Kenny, and the other musicians who performed at the party that day got together to record an album that they called *Soprano Summit*. Part of the delay in making the recording was due to a lack of money: Dick Gibson was unable to support the project financially, and it remained in limbo until railroad heir Barker Hickox, who had also acquired the World's Greatest Jazz Band from Gibson, agreed to produce it on his World Jazz label. The other problem was in coordinating the schedules of all of the musicians, especially Dick Hyman, Bucky Pizzarelli, and Milt Hinton, who were busy with live performances and recording sessions. Even when the players were able to find three free dates in December 1973, Hinton was only available on the last of them. George Duvivier had to take the bass chair on the first two.

One person who was not invited to be a member of Soprano Summit was Dick Wellstood. Although he had played with Wilber and Davern, and was a friend of both, his name was quickly ruled out.

> When Soprano Summit was formed, we were picking the sidemen to make the recording with us, Wellstood's name came up and it was dropped, unanimously, by both Wilber and myself because we had too much past history with him. We got Dick Hyman. What we wanted to do was have a fresh view of what we were doing, with no past ties.[9]

Listening to this album—and to those that Wilber and Davern made together over the next few years—reveals what drove the Gibson-party crowd to such heights. Bob and Kenny each inspire the other, and there is a unity of concept between these two artists that results in glorious harmonic passages, interspersed with exciting chase sequences. When they are apart, the differences between them are readily apparent. Davern's soprano is a broadsword: it cuts through the crowd, swaggering and overcoming all obstacles as it exudes emotion and drive. Wilber is more mannered and well-tempered, almost polite: his emotions seem to be intellectually filtered before he lets them escape. On ballads, Wilber is lush and rhapsodic; Davern glows soft, yet strong. Together, they were, in Dan Morgenstern's words, a "stimulating partnership."[10]

All of the tunes were selected and arranged by Wilber, and there were no warhorses or oft-played titles among them. The instrumentation varied. On several, including *Swing Parade*, *The Mooche*, and *Song of Songs*, they used two sopranos. Wilber and Davern both played clarinet on *Egyptian Fantasy*, *Please Clarify*, and *Stealin' Away*; and on *Oh Sister, Ain't That Hot* and *Penny Rag*, they used one soprano and one clarinet. *Johnny Was There* showed Wilber paying tribute to Johnny Hodges. Davern soloed on *Where Are We*, which he composed with bassist Jack Six. When Davern met up with Dick Gibson, shortly after the recording was over, Gibson said that the session was a "bitch," and that it came off better than he thought it would.[11]

The album was a success. Over the years, *Song of Songs*, a lush, romantic European popular song from 1914 played by the two sopranos, was the most requested tune. Various iterations of Soprano Summit played *Song of Songs*, countless times over the next five years, and versions of it appeared on several of the band's recordings.

Many critics liked the group. Burnett James, writing in *Jazz Journal* called it a ". . . lightly swinging, inventive and continuously pleasure-giving set . . . ," and said: "This is one of the most purely enjoyable records to come my way for a long time, reminding us that once upon a time jazz was actually a music to be enjoyed." The album was voted one of *Jazz Journal*'s top twenty albums for 1974.[12]

The reaction to Soprano Summit was not uniformly favorable. Many listeners found it to be over-arranged and overly stylized. Others were put off by the seeming lack of spontaneity on some of the numbers. Not everyone was entranced by the playing of Wilber and Davern, or by the harmonies created by the two reeds. John Litwiler, writing in *DownBeat*, was particularly unimpressed. He thought that Wilber and Davern lacked the "pure ego, the expressive vitality" that was necessary to recreate Bechet and Hodges. He found their attempts to evoke Noone and Goodman to be "rather unhappy," and said that their improvising was not "stylistically original." In Litweiler's opinion, Hyman was the "wrong pianist" for the group, and he wished that they had found "a more lively drummer."[13]

However, the participants in the making of the album knew better. Even before it was released, they knew that they had a hit. And so, in May 1974, Davern, Wilber, Hyman, Pizzarelli, Hinton, and Rosengarden returned to the studio to begin recording *Soprano Summit II*.[14] However, they were able only to record four tracks. One of them was a truncated version of Scott Joplin's tango, *Solace*, featuring the entire group: there was also an extended take of the same tune on which Pizzarelli's banjo playing was showcased. The two other tunes that they were able to complete were Joplin's *Sun Flower*

Slow Drag, plus *Tango a'la Caprice* by Willie "The Lion" Smith. When they adjourned, the musicians expected to reconvene shortly afterward to finish the album. As events turned out, they did not return to a studio for over three years.

From the outset, it was clear that if Soprano Summit was going to travel and perform at festivals and parties, Hyman, Pizzarelli, and Hinton might not be able to participate. They all had active careers in the clubs and studios of Manhattan: none had the time for tours or festival and party appearances. Moreover, they could earn far more money by staying close to home than from going on the road as part of a sextet. Thus, when the first album was released, and demand for personal appearances began to grow, they were unable to make more than a few dates. On the other side of the equation, few promoters and producers had the funds to pay for six musicians of the quality of the original group. And, the problem of out-of-tune pianos, the bane of every horn-player, would have been exacerbated in Soprano Summit's setting, which featured closely harmonized playing.

The solution was to eliminate the piano and use Marty Grosz in place of Bucky Pizzarelli. Grosz was the son of painter George Grosz, whose scathing political satire had earned him the enmity of the Nazis. When Hitler took power in 1933, Grosz emigrated to the United States, bringing his three-year-old son, Marty, with him. He began his musical career in New York, but moved to Chicago in about 1954, where he remained for almost two decades. A talented guitarist, arranger, vocalist, and raconteur, Grosz remembered that, at the time that Wilber called him, he had fallen upon hard times:

> I was at my wits end at that point in my life. I had already sent to the Post Office for a federal civil service job. It's absolutely true that I played in a propeller beanie with a big bow tie playing *Down by the Riverside* for Riverside Savings down on the Chicago River. And every time the Special Events Manager came around, we had to go into it.[15]

As Marty told the story, Wilber called him to say that he and Davern were putting together a group and wanted Grosz to play with them. Marty asked Bob where he was, and Bob replied that he was sitting in his kitchen. Marty told him to look out of his window and said: "Do you see that tiny dot way off in the distance? Keep looking at it, and you'll see it gradually increasing in size. That's me, heading to your house in New York."[16]

Davern was not averse to using Marty, but had never heard him. An on-the-job tryout was not feasible, because Soprano Summit didn't have any work booked for several months. When Grosz came to visit with Wilber, Bob called Kenny to resolve the issue and put Grosz on the phone. "Kenny had an up-and-coming job at the Dinkler Hotel in Syracuse, with Mickey Golizio on bass and Cliff Leeman on drums. He hadn't gotten a guitar player yet, and he asked me on the phone, 'Do you know *Oh Peter?*' And I said 'yes,' and he said, 'okay, you're hired. . . .'"[17]

Grosz, one of the last great guitarists to play an acoustic instrument, was a perfect choice. He was well-versed in the music that Soprano Summit would play, his rhythm guitar (or banjo) gave the group a solid musical foundation, and his vocals and humorous stories provided a break from the tight-knit sound of the two reeds. He joined Soprano Summit at the beginning of 1975, and stayed until it disbanded.

It was this group, centered around Davern, Wilber, and Grosz, with a variety of bassists (including George Duvivier, Milt Hinton, Ray Brown, and Monty Budwig) and drummers (some of whom were Bobby Rosengarden, Fred Stoll, Connie Kay, and Jake Hanna) that most audiences saw. The band made more than fifteen records or cassettes; all but three of them were made by the piano-less entity.

Soprano Summit's success was sufficient to impel Wilber and Davern to formalize their arrangement. They signed an agreement that, effective January 1, 1976, created a partnership known as Soprano Summit. Notwithstanding its effective date, the agreement was not signed until December 28, 1976. At some point, they also formed a corporation named Soprano Summit, Inc., with Wilber as president and Davern as vice president.

Although Bobby Rosengarden was not a full-time member of Soprano Summit, he often appeared with Davern and Wilber in that group and in many other settings. Born in 1924, he began to study drums at age of twelve and graduated from the University of Michigan with a degree in music. After serving in the army, he joined the band of Henry Busse in 1945. Rosengarden spent twenty years with the NBC Studio orchestra, toured with Benny Goodman, and led the band for the Dick Cavett television show until it moved to California in 1974. He recorded prolifically, appearing frequently with musicians of every style, ranging from Frank Sinatra to Tito Puente and including Miles Davis and Duke Ellington. He was energetic and aggressive in seeking to land jobs and that, coupled with his engaging personality on the bandstand, made him frequently in demand.

A number of factors contributed to the uniqueness of Soprano Summit. First, although they played a variety of familiar tunes, their performances often included a number of little-played titles, such as *Swing 39*, *Wake Up Chillun*, *Prince of Wails*, and *Netcha's Dream*. In addition, Wilber composed a number of original songs that kept the performers and the performances fresh. Third, Wilber wrote the arrangements for many of the songs, and the band played them as written. This allowed them to avoid having to play a program of warhorses when they encountered a bassist or drummer who was unfamiliar with their repertoire. As Grosz put it,

> I liked the idea of a little group that had variety and everybody could contribute to. I thought "Finally, we had a band that doesn't have to play *Tin Roof Blues* or *Perdido*." They were great, they put it across. What other band did you come across that would go all the way from *Swing 39* to Jelly Roll Morton's *Sidewalk Blues* or *Kansas City Stomp*? The nice thing about the group was that they played it right, and they played it musically. They didn't slop through it and treat it like joke music. They were fun things to play and we all enjoyed them.[18]

In the years to come, Soprano Summit attracted a devoted following that survived long beyond the group's dissolution. Davern and Wilber were not the first musicians to play clarinet duets or to combine the clarinet and the saxophone. Johnny Dodds and Junie Cobb had recorded two sides for Paramount in 1926, with both of them playing the clarinet. Jimmie Noone and Joe Poston had combined the clarinet with the alto saxophone at the Apex Club in 1928 and on many recordings. Sidney Bechet and Albert Nicholas had played soprano saxophone and clarinet on several sides made for Blue Note.

But, the emotion and the sound that Kenny and Bob generated together were unique. Davern thought that "It had a magic. The magic was Wilber and myself."[19] At another time, he said:

> I always say . . . that when the two of us play two notes, you'll hear a third note—a harmonic that suddenly appears. There's a richness. You could take any two players on the same instruments, anywhere in the world, and you're not going to get the same *timbre*: the harmonics are not going to leap out like when he and I get together. It's a phenomenal thing.[20]

Davern also attributed part of the appeal of Soprano Summit to its unique approach to the music.

> We play in an idiom, but we don't use the traditional method. . . . When you attempt to recreate the original energy of an artist, you defeat the purpose of the original work. The great groups in jazz didn't have what the revivalists or traditionalists wanted, and with Soprano Summit we feel we have avoided the stereotype too.[21]

Davern also admitted that pride and competitiveness played a large part in the success of Soprano Summit. "Bob's playing is a challenge to me . . . I have to find ways to counteract his great abilities so as to provide a musical counterbalance. That allows a contrast, which is essential to our concept. And when it comes to a ballad, Bob is just about the best there is."[22]

When Davern and Wilber were onstage, they were clearly competing with each other. The duels were not as overt as the fabled cutting contests of earlier years, and no winner was crowned at the end of the evening. However, the audience could sense that both men were striving to win the musical combat between them. As Don Wolff, who followed the careers of both men, recalled:

> I saw two horns battling it out with each other, and we got the best of both of them because they were trying to best one another. That's what made the sound. You can see it in their eyes watching each other, and one's respecting what the other one is doing, but saying to themselves, "but I'm going to do better." You got that sense: it was a battle.[23]

Finally, there was the visual contrast between them: Wilber, so bookish and self-contained, and Davern, dapper and urbane, joking with the audience between numbers. As Sinclair Traill wrote: "Bob still retains the looks of a youthful college boy, who hardly knows the facts of life. Kenny, with the sardonic mien of a high-ranking Tsarist officer, looks as if he might have had a hand in inventing them."[24]

For Kenny and Elsa, this was a period of hope and excitement. Shortly after the Gibsons' Labor Day party in 1972, Bob Wilber and his then-wife, Ricky, visited the Daverns in Manasquan. Over dinner and afterward they talked about Soprano Summit and how best to proceed toward the bright future that all of them foresaw. Kenny had put on the record that he had made with the Clara Ward Singers and the Dukes of Dixieland and, such was the mood that, one-by-one, all of them got up and began to dance. "It was a spontaneous life experience," Elsa said, "never to be lost."[25]

The excitement of performing and recording that marked closing months of 1973 gave way to an extended period of mundane work in 1974. Davern, Wellstood, and Cliff Leeman played weekends in January and February at a restaurant called Chicago, in White Horse, New Jersey. There were some Sunday concerts in New Jersey and two days at Brews. When the job at Chicago ended in early March, the trio began working on Fridays at the Town House, with vocalist Nancy Nelson. As March turned into April, Davern had some gigs with Warren Vache, Jr., and Claude Hopkins, and dates at

Brews, the Town House, the New York Jazz Museum, and the Fashion Institute of Technology.

On May 5, Kenny, Wilber, Hyman, Pizzarelli, Hinton, and Rosengarden began recording the album that was eventually released as *Soprano Summit II*. As noted earlier, they adjourned after only four tracks were finished and did not resume for three and a half years. For Davern, there were jobs at Gulliver's and the Bayhead Yacht Club, and six days in Texas at the Odessa Jazz Party. During June, he was in Princeton, at the Equitable Building in New York for a lunchtime concert with Hyman, at Freehold Raceway, and at the Atlantic Beach Club.

Although Davern had a substantial number of local jobs in the balance of 1974, there were some more significant appearances. On June 29, he was at Carnegie Hall as part of the Newport Jazz Festival. There were some local concerts, and then he left for France.[26]

George Wein, the guiding force behind the Newport Jazz Festival, had decided to organize a week-long jazz festival in Nice, France, on the French Riviera. The first of these programs was held in 1974. Wein called it the *Grande Parade du Jazz*, and, from July 15 to 21, he presented music on four outdoor stages simultaneously, beginning at 5:00 p.m. and lasting until midnight. Davern and Wilber put on a tribute to Sidney Bechet, and Davern was also onstage with Jimmy McPartland, Vic Dickenson, and Bud Freeman.[27]

When Davern returned to the United States, he appeared with Wilber on the steps of Federal Hall in New York City for a noontime concert, and had a gig playing weekends at O'Connor's during August. He did three weeks at Michael's Pub in September and, at the end of the month, traveled to Denver for the Gibsons' annual party. There were some local gigs in October, then spent October 14–November 2 in Virginia Beach at the Sheraton Beach Hotel.

On November 3, he led the Kenny Davern Trio, consisting of pianist John Eaton and Cliff Leeman, at the Hall of Musical Instruments in the Kennedy Center at the Smithsonian Institution. The program featured the music of Scott Joplin, James P. Johnson, Jelly Roll Morton, and Fats Waller. Martin Williams, Director of the Jazz Program for the Division of Performing Arts, acted as moderator.[28]

The New York Jazz Repertory Company had been formed by George Wein. Its Board of Directors consisted of notables from the world of music, including Ahmet Ertegun, Stanley Dance, Dick Hyman, Charles McWhorter, and Bob Wilber, mixed with influential private citizens and several persons involved in public works. The board decided upon the programs that the orchestra would perform and, depending on the subject of the program, a musical director for the event would be chosen. Over the course of its existence, the New York Jazz Repertory Orchestra (NYJO) was led by Dick Hyman, George Russell, Gil Evans, Paul Jeffrey, Budd Johnson, and Sy Oliver. The director would then select the musicians to perform from a pool of about one hundred artists of varying musical persuasions.[29]

Under Hyman's direction, the NYJO appeared at Carnegie Hall on November 8, 1974, to perform *Satchmo Remembered, A Salute to Louis Armstrong*. The band was stocked with an all-star lineup that included Ruby Braff, Pee Wee Erwin, Mel Davis, Ray Nance, and Joe Newman on trumpets; Vic Dickenson and Eph Resnick, on trombone; Davern on clarinet and soprano sax; and a rhythm section of Hyman, Carmen Mastren on guitar, Hinton, and Rosengarden. Combining film and sound clips of Louis with intricate and exciting transcriptions and arrangements by Hyman, the program traced the music that Armstrong heard and played from his childhood through 1927. In the words of one reviewer, the program was "a model of imaginative, entertaining, informative, and rewarding jazz programming."[30]

Here, as with the Jelly Roll Morton program that Davern had recorded with Hyman eleven months earlier, the star of the evening was the music. Hyman had transcribed Armstrong's solos on *Chimes Blues, Cake Walking Babies from Home, Potato Head Blues, Willie the Weeper*, and *S.O.L. Blues* into three-part harmony for trumpets that was performed by Davis, Erwin, and Newman. Davern was given substantial solo space: playing the soprano saxophone, he soloed on *Big Butter and Egg Man* and *S.O.L Blues*, and took the Sidney Bechet part on *Cake Walkin' Babies from Home*. He switched to clarinet for his outings on *Potato Head Blues* and *Willie the Weeper*. The album was given good marks by Sinclair Traill, who said: "Davern on both clarinet and soprano chips in with splendid solos perfectly molded to the music." At the end of 1976, the album was voted one of *Jazz Journal*'s best for that year.[31]

On December 3, after a two-week stint at the Tobacco Valley Inn in Windsor, Connecticut, Davern left for Iceland to begin a tour with the Kings of Jazz. The Kings had their origin in the spring of 1974, when Pee Wee Erwin was in England as part of the Tommy Dorsey Orchestra, then under the direction of Warren Covington. Kennedy Masters Limited were the agents who were booking the tour, and Eddie Kennedy suggested to Erwin that he put together a group of musicians for a winter tour.

Erwin's choices were all excellent musicians, in addition to being his longtime friends and associates. Bernie Privin shared the trumpet duties with Pee Wee. Ed Hubble was on trombone, Dick Hyman had the piano chair, and the rest of the rhythm section consisted of bassist Major Holley and Cliff Leeman. Johnny Mince, who had played with the bands of Joe Haymes, Ray

Noble, and Tommy Dorsey in the 1930s, followed by a two-decade stint with Arthur Godfrey, was the primary clarinet player. Davern was featured on soprano saxophone.[32]

The Kings of Jazz never appeared in the United States. They began their tour from Rekjavik, Iceland, where they gave their first concert on December 3, 1974. Their stay there was extended when several venues in England and Europe canceled, and the promoters found it less expensive to keep the band there, rather than housing them on the Continent. They moved on to the Atlantic Club in Stockholm, followed by a concert in Hanover, then in West Germany. The Kings then traveled to Edinburgh, London, Croyden, back to London, then Nottingham, Edinburgh, and Manchester before their final performance in Hampstead on December 23. From there, the Kings returned to the United States and disbanded.[33]

Although they never appeared in a studio, several of their concerts were recorded and, almost three decades later, a CD titled *The Kings of Jazz Featuring Kenny Davern in Concert, 1974* was released on the Arbors label. Everyone in the band had at least one solo spot, and Davern's features—*Wild Man Blues* and *Black and Tan Fantasy*—showed him at his best. He switched to clarinet and Mince picked up the alto, for a duet on *Oh Sister! Ain't That Hot*. When the album was released in 2003, Eddie Cook gave it an excellent review in *Jazz Journal International*. Writing in the *Mississippi Rag*, Jim Adashek said that he liked the Davern–Mince duet on *Oh Sister, Ain't That Hot* and Kenny's solo on *Black and Tan Fantasy*. In the *IAJRC Journal*, Russ Chase wrote: "Waiting thirty years for Kenny Davern's playing of *Wild Man Blues* on soprano saxophone, as heard on this CD, was worth it for me."[34]

Grosz came to New York at the beginning of January 1975, to rehearse the Soprano Summit repertoire. Davern had a date at the New York Jazz Museum on January 5, and then he and Grosz left for Syracuse, where they played at Dinklers from the 6th through the 24th. In February, Davern was in Indianapolis; Mundelein, Illinois; and Vail, Colorado; and, from the 24th through March 1, he and Wilber were at the Colonial Tavern in Toronto as Soprano Summit.[35]

The highlight of March came on the 20th, when he appeared with the New York Jazz Repertory Orchestra at Carnegie Hall for a concert of music composed by Jelly Roll Morton. The first half of the program featured Dick Hyman leading a nineteen-piece orchestra as it played his arrangements. The music was interspersed with slides and excerpts from the spoken portions of the recordings that Alan Lomax had made of Morton for the Library of Congress in 1938. Davern and Wilber were part of the large orchestra and also appeared in the second half of the program as Soprano Summit.

Later that evening, Soprano Summit appeared at the Downbeat on 42nd Street and Lexington Avenue. The engagement was scheduled to last through April: on weekdays, the group would consist of Wilber, Davern, Grosz, and Duvivier. Rosengarden was added on the weekends.[36] Pianist Dave Frishberg was at the Downbeat after the concert at Carnegie Hall and wrote to Davern:

> What a pleasure and an inspiration to hear you and Bob play. It was the best music I've experienced in years. . . . I think you and I (and Wilber too), despite our differences in tactics and musical material, share a common point of view about melody and rhythm and especially the emotional content of jazz music—and I think it's remarkable that we've clung to our convictions the way we have. I hope we play together again. To me you're a rare artist—so personal, so unique.[37]

Within a few days, Davern began to rehearse for a program of the music of Bix Beiderbecke that the NYJO was planning. The concert, which was previewed on television on NBC-TV's *Sunday Show* on March 30, took place at Carnegie Hall on April 3. Bob Wilber was the musical director, and Dick Sudhalter, the author of *Bix, Man and Legend*, the definitive biography of the short-lived cornet player, commented and shared the musical role of Bix with Warren Vache, Jr.

Davern appeared in several parts of the program. In the segment devoted to the Bix and His Gang, Davern played the bass saxophone and took the part of Adrian Rollini. When the program turned to the Jean Goldkette Orchestra, Davern played tenor saxophone, sitting alongside Chauncey Morehouse, Spiegel Willcox, Paul Mertz, and Bill Rank, all of whom had played with Bix. John S. Wilson reviewed the concert favorably in the *New York Times*, noting that Davern "wrestled in a masterly way with a huge bass saxophone."[38]

Soprano Summit had three engagements during the week of April 20. The first of them had its origins when Red Squires, chairman of the Music Committee of the New Jersey Jazz Society, heard the group at one of the Gibson parties. When he returned home, he began to lobby for the Society to hire the group, which resulted in its appearance at the Martinsville Inn on Sunday, April 20.[39]

This was one of the rare—if not the only—occasions when the pianoless version played on the same stage as the originally instrumented group. The afternoon began with Wilber, Davern, Grosz, Duvivier, and Connie Kay performing *Swing Parade* at a slightly faster than usual pace. Next came *The*

Mooche, on which Kenny's biting soprano saxophone and Grosz's banjo were heard to good advantage. *Oh Sister Ain't That Hot*, which was normally a Davern feature, had a long and excellent solo on soprano by Wilber.

The leaders switched horns on *Steal Away*: the two clarinets played the first chorus in unison before bursting into the second chorus in glorious harmony. *Linger Awhile* was almost eleven minutes of straight blowing; Wilber turned in an extended and dynamic solo, literally flying over chorus after chorus. When it was Kenny's turn, he eschewed his usual legato playing and concentrated on sound and effect—dipping his musical toe into a pool of Free Jazz without really getting wet.

The opening choruses of *Panama* featured Bob and Kenny playing in classic New Orleans ensemble style, in which one played the melody and the other played obbligato, then they switched. Each then took a solo without the other, but they returned to the ensemble style at the end. *Song of Songs* was not yet the "closer" on Soprano Summit performances, and here it was not as saccharine as it would later become. *Swing 39* and *Egyptian Fantasy* followed and, after just over an hour of music, the set closed with *The Fish Vendor*.

In the second part of the program, Dick Hyman joined the group and they reprised part of the Jelly Roll Morton program that they had performed at Carnegie Hall one month earlier. Although much of the earlier set was arranged, there was a light and spontaneous feeling there that was lacking on some of the tunes in this set. Only *Shreveport Stomp*, a trio outing featuring Wilber, Hyman, and Rosengarden, and *Sidewalk Blues*, in which the musicians recreated the verbal byplay that marked the beginning of the 1926 Morton recording, had some sparkle.

The performance was recorded by the New Jersey Jazz Society (NJJS), who gave the tapes of this and a number of other performances to the Institute of Jazz Studies at Rutgers University, to be preserved in a protective environment. In about 2006, Mat Domber of Arbors Records learned of the existence of the tapes and expressed an interest in them. After an agreement was reached with NJJS, Domber asked Dan Morgenstern, the director of the Institute of Jazz Studies, to select material that might be appropriate for release. His choices were forwarded to Domber for approval, then given to Doug Pomeroy, an engineer, for restoration. The result was the issuance, in 2007, of a two-CD set of this performance, along with a date by Davern, Wellstood, and Bobby Rosengarden, and a performance by Wilber with Ruby Braff.[40]

On the following day, Soprano Summit appeared in Jack Kleinsinger's *Highlights in Jazz*. Tuesday, April 22, was an off-day, then the quintet spent three days in the Vanguard studio recording an album titled *Soprano Summit III*.[41] As was true of all of their releases, this one contained an eclectic selection of tunes. *Frog-i-More Rag*, *Milenburg Joys*, and *Panama* (titled *Panama Rag*) all came out of the New Orleans tradition. *Japansy*, a little heard, lyrical piece that was recorded by Jimmie Noone in 1937, begins as a waltz with Wilber on clarinet and Davern on soprano playing very rich harmonies over Duvivier's bowed bass, before they switch into straight 4/4 time.

Marty Grosz vividly recalled the next number that was to be recorded:

> We recorded a tune that Wilber must have recorded three or four times in his career, *Swing 39* by Django Reinhardt. I said, "Oh Boy, Django Reinhardt." It stays on a plateau for a while; doesn't change chords for long periods. And I said, "What am I going to do with it? Well, Bob's really going to go to town with this. It's his number." And Kenny was saying, "You better play this Bob." And then Bob says, "Okay, you take a guitar chorus," and then turning to George Duvivier says, "And you take one on bass."
>
> We looked at each other and George, he'd been everywhere and done everything—he was the bass virtuoso—he said: "Listen, we're going to come back in a couple of days, right? Record it then." And in the meantime, he went and wrote out his solo. I struggled with it too. The conception that I had didn't match the tune. It's more like a modal thing.[42]

Soprano Summit III also included a dynamic rendition of *Once in a While*, with Bob on clarinet and Kenny on soprano saxophone. There were vocals by Grosz on *Rose of the Rio Grande* and *How Can You Face Me*. The recording also contained *Oriental Strut* and *I Had It But It's All Gone Now*, the last a tune long associated with Sidney Bechet, which featured soaring harmonies by Wilber and Davern.

Any possibility that the public might be confused by the release of *Soprano Summit III*, which was completed long before *Soprano Summit II* was finished, was eliminated by producer Barker Hickox. Apparently, he did not like the sound of the pianoless group, and held the final version of the recording for ten years before releasing it, and then only on cassette.[43]

From then through mid-July, Davern worked at O'Connor's, traveled to Washington, D.C., for a performance of the Louis Armstrong retrospective at the Kennedy Center for the Performing Arts, then flew to Texas for the Odessa Jazz Party. There was a week with Soprano Summit at Dinkler's in Syracuse and, on June 23, a recording session with Red Norvo.[44]

Red came to prominence in the 1930s, playing the xylophone. He had led a big band from 1936 to 1943 that featured his wife, singer Mildred Bailey, with whom he was billed as Mr. & Mrs. Swing. In the early 1940s, he began leading a small group and, at about the same time, switched to the vibraphone. Norvo performed with artists as diverse as Benny Goodman and Woody Herman, and led a trio with Charles Mingus and Tal Farlow. Norvo had been at the Odessa party, and had been teamed with Davern for a set. The collaboration pleased the Texas crowd and impelled producer Harry Lim, the impresario of Famous Door records, to record them together when Norvo traveled to New York to appear at Michael's Pub in June.[45]

The album was titled *The Second Time Around, The Red Norvo Combo*. Aided by Dave McKenna on piano, and Milt Hinton and Mousie Alexander on drums, the quintet recorded four tunes, *Lover Come Back to Me, A Long One for Santa Monica, When You're Smiling,* and *Exactly Like You*. Because the songs lasted only about twenty minutes, Lim convened the group, without Davern, at a later date and recorded three more titles to increase the length of the album to about thirty-four minutes. Although that play time was minimally acceptable for an LP, it would have been far too short for a compact disc. So, when the CD was issued on the Progressive label, Gus Statiras included two alternate takes each of *Lover Come Back to Me* and *Santa Monica Blues* (the retitled name for *A Long One for Santa Monica*). All of these songs are taken at a medium-to-fast pace, and the combination of vibraphone and piano provide a solid propulsive background for Davern's vibrant soprano saxophone, which soars throughout.

Kenny continued to play local jobs, except for a trip to Vail, Colorado, over the July 4th holiday, until the middle of July, when he and Elsa, together with Wilber and Grosz, left for Nice to appear in George Wein's *Grande Parade du Jazz*. He performed with Soprano Summit, and was also in a Fats Waller program. When the festival ended on July 27, Kenny and Elsa took a few days for themselves. At the beginning of August, she went home. Davern, Wilber, and Grosz flew to South Africa for a three-week tour as Soprano Summit.[46]

The trio arrived in Durban on August 3 and, using a local bass player and drummer, performed that night at the Elangeni Hotel. They played in Capetown on the next three days, and then had a day off before returning to Durban. On the 8th and 9th, they played at the Wagonwheels Hotel for lunch and at the Jazzclub at night. On Sunday, there was a concert at Durban's City Hall and, on the following day, a performance at the Pietemaritzburg City Hall. Although racial segregation was still rigidly enforced in South Africa, the band's promoter obtained a permit to perform the concert before a mixed audience of whites, blacks, and Indians—one of the first such performances in that country.

They played two lunchtime concerts at the University in Durban, traveled back to Pietemaritzburg for a nighttime concert at Natal University, then continued south to play the Port Elizabeth Jazz Festival on August 16–17. All of them were off for two days and then, on the 20th, Davern visited the studios of the South African Broadcasting Company where, accompanied by the John Drake trio and alto saxophonist Basil Metaxas, he taped a radio program to be broadcast later. Another off day was followed by a program at Witswatersrand University in Johannesburg, a concert before an all-black audience in Jabulani Stadium, and a final appearance before the Johannesburg Jazz Club. They left for home on August 24.[47]

Although Soprano Summit performed as a quintet, the newspaper clippings and advertisements often called them an American Trio. Marty Grosz preferred not to remember anything about the local musicians.

> In South Africa it was murder. We had a drummer who didn't know when the tune ended; he just kept going. It was brutal. . . . He didn't know when to start a tune or when to stop it. He didn't know what a chorus was. We had a guy who played bass with the local symphony—a very fine player—but he couldn't play *Indiana*. He couldn't play blues: he didn't know what a blues was.[48]

Davern arrived home on August 25 and, four days later, was in Denver, playing a fund-raiser. On the next weekend, he played the Gibsons' party in Colorado Springs. In September and October, he performed at the Monmouth County Library, spent two days in Pine Bluff, Arkansas; he was at Condon's, the Chicago Restaurant, the Chester Inn, and O'Connor's.[49]

Although O'Connor's was a hospitable venue for musicians, its primary business was to seat and serve its customers. As Jack Stine remembered, these aspects of its operation occasionally conflicted and, one evening Davern furnished his own solution to the problem.

> In the 1970s, one of the places where live jazz could regularly be heard was O'Connor's Steak House in Watchung, New Jersey. Good music, coupled with excellent food and plentiful drinks ensured that the place was always crowded.
>
> There was a PA system that was controlled at the main desk, from which calls such as "The Grommicks, your table is ready," would issue, followed by similar pages for the Browns and the Watsons, and on and on. The bandstand had its own amplification system. But when the PA system was activated, the band's mikes were killed, with the result that a soloist often ended up playing to a dead mike.

One evening when the place was unusually busy and the activity from the main desk seemed to break in every three or four minutes, Kenny, in exasperation, grabbed the mike and said "Judas Iscariot, table for twelve. . . . "

You could have heard a pin drop.[50]

There were three days of rehearsals before Davern left, on October 23, for a month-long tour of Europe for George Wein, performing the *Satchmo Remembered* Carnegie Hall Program. The schedule was a grueling one: it began in Umea, Sweden, then went on to Warsaw—then to Gothenburg, Sweden; Aarhaus, Denmark; Stockholm, and then Brussels on October 31. From there, they played Rotterdam; Ostend, Belgium; Paris; Kamen, Germany; Baden, Switzerland; West Berlin; Lausanne; Belgrade and Zagreb in Yugoslavia; Bologna; and Barcelona, and Marseilles on November 11.[51]

The orchestra was composed of seasoned veterans including Ruby Braff, Davern, Hyman, Marty Grosz, and Bobby Rosengarden. They were all professionals, accustomed to the rigors and exhaustion of traveling. But, sometimes a penchant for pranks emerged. Grosz recalled:

> [Rosengarden] used to do a thing during a performance of this Louis Armstrong thing on *Mack the Knife* that morphed into a bongo solo. What that had to do with anything was anybody's guess. But it was an accommodation to feature Rosengarden's bongos. About a week into the trip, the bongos disappeared. It wasn't me, I don't think it was Kenny, I can't speak for Ruby.[52]

As usual, Kenny wrote numerous letters to Elsa and the children while he was away. One of the persistent themes in his writings to Elsa was that he was lonely and that this trip was the last one that he would take without her. In one letter, he told her that he was thinking of changing careers and opening a music store near their home in Manasquan. Elsa, the practical one, wrote back, painting a vivid picture of what would happen to Kenny and to customers if he had to stand behind a counter for eight hours every day and deal with the retail trade. The project died, then and there.

The stops in Germany upset Davern, who had been raised in a Jewish household during World War II, where the revelations of Nazi atrocities had a greater impact. He wrote to Elsa that he felt a coldness there and a sense of discomfort; almost as if the Nazis still walked the streets. In later years, he came to terms with these feelings, but, on his first visit, they were powerful and very distressing.[53]

The tour was scheduled to end in Portugal. However, there were stories of an impending revolution in that country, and Wein gave the musicians the option of leaving the tour if they were concerned. Davern and Grosz departed. The rest of the musicians stayed and finished the tour; the revolution did not occur.[54]

When he returned home, Davern was concerned that his decision might adversely affect his relationship with Wein and cost him work. It did not. Wein continued to hire Davern whenever he could and made him a regular part of the Newport (and later the Kool and JVC) Jazz Festivals. Over thirty years later, Wein recalled:

> It was a joy to have him around. There was a warmth that came from his personality as well as his music. There was a warmth and a love: it was obvious that the man loved what he was playing. He wasn't trying to impress anybody with technique. He was trying to play songs where he knew the meaning of the song. He knew the lyrics to the songs, and he knew what the message was of the songs. He conveyed it because he played with a lot of emotion....
>
> He personified the purity of jazz in its most romantic and idealized way. That's what he did: he played jazz. He didn't care about other things. He picked up his horn, and every time he played he wanted to play something that he enjoyed and that was a little different from the last time he played it. He personified the attitude: he was not concerned with being a commercial figure. He wanted to play jazz.[55]

For the rest of 1975, Davern played sporadic one-nighters at Condon's, O'Connor's, and some other venues in New Jersey and Connecticut. His last date was a New Year's Eve dance in Chester, New Jersey, thrown by the NJJS. Warren Vache, Jr., Ed Hubble, John Bunch, Warren Vache, Sr., on bass, and drummer Jackie Williams constituted the remainder of the band. The music was recorded and released on a NJJS LP titled *Jersey Jazz at Midnight*. As would be expected, all of the tunes were played at ballad or businessman's-bounce tempos, and the result is enjoyable, if not exceptional. Eddie Cook called it "fine" and "happy swinging music," and said that "Kenny Davern's liquid clarinet sparkles throughout, swooping and soaring in typical style...."[56]

Notes

1. Nat Hentoff, "Riffs," *Village Voice*, 25 October 1973, 8; Patricia O'Haire, "Inspired Jazz Combo," *Daily News*, 16 October 1973, 52.

2. Invitation to the Private Jazz Party; Date Book.

3. Kenny Davern, interview by the author; Hank O'Neal, interview by the author.

4. Kenny Davern, interview by the author; Kenny Davern, quoted in Davern, Traill, p. 8.

5. Jon Balleras, "Dick Wellstood and His Famous Orchestra Featuring Kenny Davern," *DownBeat*, 42, no. 1 (16 January 1975): 27. But, cf., Don Lass, "Record Previews," *Asbury Park Press*, 25 August 1974, D22; Russ Chase, "Dick Wellstood and His All-Star Orchestra Featuring Kenny Davern," *IAJRC Journal*, 25, no. 4 (Fall 1992): 90.

6. MacCree sometimes sang with the groups, which did not increase the quality of their performances.

7. Kenny Davern, conversation with the author.

8. Ralph Laing, "Some Rags, Some Stomps, and a Little Blues, Ferdinand Jelly Roll Morton," *Jazz Journal*, 30, no. 7 (July 1977): 43; *Jazz Journal*, 27, no. 12 (December 1974): 6; John S. Wilson, "Rediscovering the Classic Swing of Jelly Roll Morton," *New York Times*, 15 October 1974.

9. Kenny Davern, interview by the author. Wellstood was offended by their decision, and Davern thought that it adversely affected their friendship for a while. Occasionally, Wellstood would agree to play intermission piano when Soprano Summit performed at a venue in New Jersey. But, he was adamant in refusing to play with the band when they were looking to use a pianist. As it turned out, Soprano Summit rarely used a pianist after Grosz joined. Kenny Davern, Marty Grosz, interviews by the author.

10. Dan Morgenstern, liner notes to *Soprano Summit*, World Jazz WJLP-S-5.

11. Letter from Dick Gibson to Kenny Davern, dated 11 February 1974.

12. Burnett James, *Soprano Summit*, *Jazz Journal*, 27, no. 10 (October 1974): 46.

13. John Litweiler, "Bob Wilber/Kenny Davern, Soprano Summit," *DownBeat*, 41, no. 21 (19 December 1974): 33.

14. The liner notes place this session in April 1974. The correct date is May 5, 1974. Tom Lord, *The Jazz Discography*, Version 9.0 (West Vancouver, B.C., 2008) (hereinafter "Lord Discography").

15. Marty Grosz, interview by the author.

16. Marty Grosz, "The Tweetie Birds," *Liner Notes to Soprano Summit, 1975 and More*, Arbors ARCD 19328, December, 2007.

17. Marty Grosz, interview by the author.

18. Grosz interview.

19. Rusch interview part 1, p. 20.

20. Kenny Davern, recorded on *Jazzspeak* on *Summit Reunion*, Chiaroscuro CRD 311.

21. Kenny Davern, quoted in Don Lass, liner notes to *Soprano Summit: Chalumeau Blue*, Chiaroscuro, CR 148.

22. Lass liner notes.

23. Don Wolff, interview by the author.

24. Sinclair Traill, "Soprano Summit," *Jazz Journal*, 29, no. 12 (December 1976): 41.

25. Elsa Davern, interview by the author.

26. *Jazz Journal*, 27, no. 8 (August, 1974): 11.

27. George Wein, with Nate Chinen, *Myself Among Others, a Life in Music* (New York, DaCapo, 2003). 475 *et. seq* (hereinafter "Wein,"); *Jazz Journal*, 27, no. 9 (September 1974): 3–5.

28. Date Book; *Jersey Jazz*, 2, no. 8 (October 1974): 9; event program.

29. Wein, *supra*, 392 *et. seq*; Wilber/Webster, 121.

30. John S. Wilson, Jazz, "A Lively Mixture of Armstrong," *New York Times*, 10 November 1974. In 2010, video clips from the concert were posted on YouTube.

31. Sinclair Traill, *Jazz Journal*, 29, no. 3 (March 1976): 38; *Jazz Journal*, 29, no. 12 (December 1976): 4.

32. Vache, Erwin, 320; Brian Peerless, liner notes to *The Kings of Jazz Featuring Kenny Davern, Live in Concert, 1974*, Arbors ARCD 19267, April 2003.

33. Peerless liner notes; *Jersey Jazz*, 2, no. 10 (December 1974): 15, 47; Vache, Erwin, 320.

34. Eddie Cook, "The Kings of Jazz Featuring Kenny Davern, Live in Concert," *Jazz Journal International* 56, no. 12 (December, 2003): 33–34; Jim Adashek, "The Kings of Jazz Featuring Kenny Davern, Live in Concert," *Mississippi Rag*, xxxiii, no. 2 (February 2005); Russ Chase, "The Kings of Jazz Featuring Kenny Davern, Live in Concert," *IAJRC Journal*. 27, no. 2 (Spring 2004): 71.

35. Marty Grosz, interview by the author; Date Book; contract.

36. John S. Wilson, "Jelly Roll Theme for Jazz Repertory," *New York Times*, 22 March 1975; John S. Wilson, "Jazz Pianist to Slow Pace," *New York Times*, 23 March 1975.

37. Letter From Dave Frishberg to Kenny Davern, 26 March 1975.

38. John S. Wilson, "A Warm Salute for Beiderbecke," *New York Times*, 5 April 1975. See also Vache, Erwin, 322–323; *Jazz Journal*, 28, no. 5 (May 1975): 13, *Jersey Jazz*, 3, no. 4 (May 1975): 4; Date Book

39. Jack Stine, liner notes to *Soprano Summit, 1975, and More*, Arbors ARCD 19328, October 2007.

40. E-mail from Dan Morgenstern to the author.

41. The Lord and Elliott Discographies place the recording date in late 1974. In an interview with the author, Grosz was certain that he did not join the group until the beginning of 1975. Grosz also said that they recorded for three days at Vanguard Studio in New York. There are entries in Davern's Date Book for April 23, 24, and 25, 1975, that say "Record Vanguard." Finally, by scheduling the recording for two days after their live appearances, they could use the concerts as *de facto* rehearsal sessions, as they and many other musicians often did.

42. Marty Grosz, interview by the author.

43. Wilber/Webster, 131.

44. Date Book, Contract, Marty Grosz, interview by the author.

45. Harry Lim, liner notes to *The Second Time Around, The Red Norvo Combo*, Progressive PCD 7121, 1976. The date of the recording session with Davern appears in the liner notes to the CD: no information is supplied as to the date of the continued session.

46. *Jazz Journal*, 28, no. 9 (September 1975): 6–7, Elsa Davern, Marty Grosz, interviews by the author.

47. The primary source is a typed note on the stationery of John Waters. See also: Wilber/Webster, 129–130; Date Book. The material on the August 20 South African Broadcasting Company taping comes from a newspaper clipping, with no identification as to source. See also, *Jazz Journal*, 28, no. 10 (October 1975): 19; *Jersey Jazz*, 3, no. 5 (June 1975): 3; and 3, no. 7 (August 1975): 4.

48. Marty Grosz, interview by the author.

49. Document in the possession of Elsa Davern; Date Book.

50. Jack Stine, *Classic Stine, Jersey Jazz*, 33, no. 5 (June 2005): 4.

51. Vache, Erwin, 329–333, *Jersey Jazz*, 3, no. 11 (November 1975): 15. Date Book.

52. Marty Grosz, interview by the author.

53. Letters from Kenny Davern to Elsa Davern; conversation with Elsa Davern.

54. Vache, Erwin, 329–333; conversation with Elsa Davern.

55. George Wein, interview by the author.

56. Eddie Cook, "Jersey Jazz at Midnight," *Jazz Journal International*, 34, no. 8 (August 1981): 45.

CHAPTER SEVEN

Soprano Summit

Although the greater part of Davern's recording activity for the next few years revolved around Soprano Summit, many of his personal appearances did not. He had struck up a friendship with cornetist Warren Vache, Jr., and began 1976 by playing one or two days a week with him, Ed Hubble, and Marty Grosz at the Watchung View Inn. At some point during the year, Grosz was hired to provide a band to play the opening theme in a Sean Connery movie titled *The Next Man*. He chose Davern, Vache, Hyman, and trombonist Jack Gale. Davern also played for parties at several local country clubs; among them the Creek Club in Locust Valley, New York, as well as at gigs in Richmond, Virginia, and Cherry Hill, New Jersey.[1]

He was working several nights a week at Condon's in February, until he started at the Gaslight Club on the 23rd. On February 29, Davern, Wilber, and Grosz, along with bassist George Duvivier and drummer Fred Stoll, gathered at Condon's to make a Soprano Summit album for Chiaroscuro. It was a Sunday night and there were only a few people in the audience. The musicians were able to record five acceptable titles, *Lover Come Back to Me*; a red-hot version of *Nagasaki*; *Everybody Loves My Baby*, on which Grosz takes a cue from Eddie Lang at the beginning; *Georgia Cabin*; and *Song of the Wanderer*. A continuation of the session was never scheduled, and the titles were not issued until 1994, when they were included in a reissue of two other Soprano Summit albums.[2] In mid-March, Soprano Summit went into the Down Beat, a venue on Lexington Avenue and 42nd Street in Manhattan.

The music that was composed in the period prior to World War II was Davern's consuming passion, and he played it throughout his life. However, he listened to all forms of music, and some of them appealed to him. Trombonist Roswell Rudd had been one of the organizers of the rehearsal band that Davern had played with in the early 1960s. In the years that followed, Rudd had made occasional appearances with Davern at the Ferryboat and some of the other venues on the Jersey Shore. But, his interests were far from the type of music that he played on those jobs. He gravitated toward and composed in the style of music that was known as Free Jazz, and performed with musicians that included Don Cherry, Mike Mantler, Steve Lacy, and Paul Motian.

Free Jazz also interested Davern. "[W]hen Ornette Coleman hit town, I suddenly went, 'Isn't this a breath of fresh air?' See, it transcended bebop: I could hear the older influences, but not in the form I was used to. I do think it was a very valid statement."[3] While Davern was at the Ferryboat, he occasionally incorporated elements of Free Jazz into his solos—to the consternation of the regular patrons.[4] There were elements of that idiom in the Beatles tunes that Jack Six arranged for Can O' Worms, and there were parts of Kenny's solos on the *Hot Potatoes* album that bordered on Free Jazz.

Rudd had written a four-movement suite titled *Blown Bone* and believed that Davern could apply his grounding in traditional forms of jazz to the concepts that the composition demanded.[5] Davern was pleased to play a part in the project and, on March 27, he joined Rudd, with Steve Lacy on soprano saxophone, Tyrone Washington on tenor saxophone, and a rhythm section that consisted of Patti Bown, Wilbur Little, and Paul Motian to record Rudd's composition.

Some of this is far from Davern's usual musical fare. The title tune is taken at a fast pace and, although there are some arranged passages, large sections of the piece are given over to unstructured solos. The second title is *Cement Blues*, a traditional twelve-bar blues on which guitarist-vocalist Louisiana Red is featured and Davern takes a solo. The tune runs almost nine minutes and, although there are some dissonant arranged backgrounds and solos using electronic instruments, the song never loses its basic link with the blues.

Street Walking is a slow feature for the ensemble that couples musically modern concepts to a 1940s big-band sound. *Bethesda Fountain* is the final tune and uses a repeated Latin figure as the base on which several individual performances and arranged figures are built. Davern has an extended—and often unstructured—clarinet solo that begins in the chalumeau range and climbs into the middle and higher registers.

Almost no one besides the musicians ever heard the finished product, which was titled *Blown Bone*. The album was issued on Phillips (Japan) and never offered for sale in the United States. Upon its release, it plummeted silently into obscurity.

After a one-day hiatus, followed by a concert at Rockland College, Davern went into a studio on March 30 with Soprano Summit to record an album titled *Chalumeau Blue*. Although it was not the first album to be recorded by the pianoless version of Soprano Summit (*Soprano Summit III* was), *Chalumeau Blue* was the first on the market. With George Duvivier on bass and Fred Stoll on drums, it introduced the working quintet to the public and, in doing so, made it clear that this was no ordinary band.

Clearly, the choice of songs was unusual. Four of the twelve titles were originals, *Chalumeau Blue*, *Grenadilla Stomp*, and *Debut* were written by Wilber, and *Slightly Under the Weather* was written by Grosz and Wilber. Of the remaining titles, *Black and Tan Fantasy* was an Ellington favorite and *Wake Up Chillen* was not often played.

It took three days to complete the album. Davern and Wilber played soprano saxophone on the opening tune, *Nagasaki*. The next selection was the unusually structured title tune, on which both leaders switched to clarinet. Grosz played banjo, and Bob and Kenny played soprano saxophone on *Black and Tan Fantasy*, which was arranged by Davern. *Grenadilla Stomp*, a happy piece for two clarinets with an intermittent habanera rhythm, was followed by a short rendition of *Danny Boy*, which Kenny played straight, accompanied only by a bowed bass.

Everybody Loves My Baby and *Linger Awhile* preceded *Slightly Under the Weather*, a melancholy-sounding piece that carried out the theme of its title. *Wake Up Chillen* was next, followed by W.C. Handy's *Ole Miss*. The next title was *Debut*, and Wilber made an appearance on alto saxophone. After an opening a cappella chorus by Davern, *Some of These Days* took off at a medium-fast tempo and turned into a powerhouse.

Ralph Laing reviewed the album in *Jazz Journal*, and concluded: "Grosz's playing is magic." He then said: "Frankly, I think it is one of the best albums I've ever heard since Edison invented the phonograph. . . . It embodies fifty-five years of jazz heritage with the technical instrument mastery and musical experience of 1976. No serious record collection should be without it."[6] The album was voted one of *Jazz Journal*'s 20 best for 1976, and, when it was re-released as part of a two-CD package in 1995, was voted one of *Jazz Journal International*'s best reissues for that year.

There were dates at O'Connor's and Condon's. Davern made an appearance on April 7, in the Clarinet Clinic at the First New York City Regional

Meeting of the International Clarinet Society held at Carnegie Recital Hall before he left the country on a three-week tour. From April 23 through May 14, Soprano Summit performed at venues in Europe and England, with a final appearance in Dublin before returning home on May 15. The trip was not as successful as Davern had anticipated. A number of American musicians were in England at the same time, and some of Soprano Summit's engagements were canceled so that other musicians who were more well known could be hired.[7]

In the last two weeks of the month, Davern played at Monmouth College and at Condon's, had a date with Pee Wee Erwin, and appeared at the Odessa Jazz Party. Over the weekend of May 30–31, 1976, Wilber, Davern, and Grosz, along with Milt Hinton and Fred Stoll, returned to the Big Horn Jazzfest at Mundelein, Illinois, for a Soprano Summit performance that was recorded. There were especially swinging renditions of *Swing Parade* and *Grenadilla Stomp*. *Ole Miss* was a barn-burner; *Porter's Love Song to a Chambermaid* and *Swing That Music* both featured Grosz on vocal and guitar, as well as the leaders. Wilber was glowing on *Black and Tan Fantasy*. As usual, *Song of Songs* was the crowd pleaser, and Wilber gave it an especially rococo treatment.

Pee Wee Erwin had gotten a job playing Monday nights on the *Binghamton*, a converted ferryboat that was moored in the Hudson River at Edgewater, New Jersey, and Kenny played there on several occasions. There were concerts with Soprano Summit at the Jersey City and Plainfield public libraries, and an appearance in Doylestown, Pennsylvania. He played both baritone and soprano saxophones when, on June 13, the Duke Ellington Society put on its annual concert at the New School for Social Research.[8] Late in the month, Kenny went into Reno Sweeney's on West 12th Street in Manhattan as member of the band in the *Rag 'N Roll Revue*.

Cathy Chamberlain, who composed, sang, and played concertina and jug, had created the *Rag 'N Roll Revue*, a vaudeville act that mixed traditional, jazz, and popular standards with country and western and some of her own compositions. From the early 1970s, the Revue played a number of clubs in New York City and, as Chamberlain's popularity increased, she added more, and better, musicians to the show's band.

By mid-1976, when her troupe appeared at Reno Sweeney's, either Warren Vache, Jr., or Ed Polcer was playing cornet, Davern or Joe Muranyi was on clarinet, and Howard Johnson or Bob Stewart was accompanying Ms. Chamberlain on tuba. The drums were handled by Freddie Moore, the oldest member of the group. Warren Vache, Jr., remembered the job well.

In the world of the freelancer, when a job comes, you take it. It's a bag of groceries. Cathy Chamberlain and her *Rag 'N Roll Revue* were a thorn in both Kenny's and my sides. It paid fairly well, it was a dixieland—sort of—oriented, a pop-ish little cult group that got some attention and had a record company behind it. It was not very good music. It was one of these things where we did it because we were working.[9]

George Wein's annual Newport Jazz Festival opened at the end of June. Wein had decided to hold some of the events outside of New York City. He approached Jack Stine of the New Jersey Jazz Society (NJJS) to ask if the Society was interested in the idea and, if so, for suggestions as to a possible site. Stine looked at several places and eventually recommended Waterloo Village, a restored Revolutionary War town located near Stanhope, in Sussex County, in a beautiful, parklike setting. For the Society, the weekend Picnic at Waterloo Village became an annual event, lasting until the Village closed for the 1995 season. The association with the Newport Jazz Festival (and its successors, the Kool and JVC Jazz Festivals) lasted for over fifteen years.[10]

Soprano Summit appeared on the *Today* show on the NBC television network. The group was on stage at Waterloo on June 27, and Davern also appeared with Warren Vache, Jr., John Bunch, Wayne Wright, and Cliff Leeman. Two days later, he played with the New York Jazz Repertory Orchestra at Carnegie Hall, in a retrospective titled the *Ellington Epoch*.[11] July saw Davern in Toronto, playing a week with the Climax Jazz Band. He returned to play two days with Cathy Chamberlain at Reno Sweeney's and then, on July 16 flew to Nice for George Wein's *Grande Parade du Jazz*. Davern, Wilber, and Grosz recrossed the Atlantic, spent a few days at home, then headed west to appear on July 30 at the Concord, California, Jazz Festival. Their appearance, with Ray Brown on bass and Jake Hanna on drums, was recorded and released as *Soprano Summit, In Concert*.

The band performed three titles written by the artists: *The Grapes Are Ready*, which was credited to Wilber, Davern, and Grosz; *The Golden Rooster*, a slow and unusual Wilber composition that is his showpiece number; and *Moxie*, which Grosz authored and on which he is featured. A one-minute Davern–Grosz comic routine introduces *Doin' the New Lowdown*, which has extended solos by everyone. Davern's featured number is *Brother, Can You Spare a Dime*, on which he plays soprano saxophone, accompanied only by Brown on bass. Other titles include *Stompy Jones*; a laid-back version of *All by Myself*, on which Wilber sounded quite Goodmanesque; and *Swing That Music*.

The album got good reviews. Sinclair Traill said, "Bob and Kenny, in that order, exemplify all that is best in jazz clarinet playing." Kevin Jones said it was "the group's best live recording." In a similar vein, David Badham remarked, "This was one of the finest small groups of the last 40 years and this was their best live session. . . . Bob and Kenny seemed always to bring out the best in each other. . . . Quite the best thing, however, is Kenny's superlative soprano feature *Brother, Can You Spare a Dime*, which threatens to bring tears to the eye!"[12]

Martin Williams, director of the Jazz Program for the Division of Performing Arts at the Smithsonian Institution, was an enthusiastic supporter of Davern's. In the mid 1970s, Williams attempted to interest colleges and high schools in booking Davern for performances. The Smithsonian mailed out brochures, and Williams and one of his colleagues made some personal visits to schools that they thought would be interested in the program.

But there were no takers, and Williams wrote to Davern to say that his efforts were "a bomb, a bust, a failure." He went on to say: "I still harbor the conviction—perhaps the delusion—that music of the high caliber that you make could be reasonably promoted to the right kind of colleges and even some high schools by someone who ignores current 'name' and 'hit' value, but keeps his aesthetic standards high."[13]

Davern was back in Colorado for the Gibsons' annual party over the Labor Day weekend, followed by a job at the Hit Factory in New York. He played for five days in Annapolis, had a lunchtime gig with Cathy Chamberlain and, on September 22, left for a three-week engagement in Paris, followed by a three-week tour of England. From September 23 to October 13, he played with Wilber and a local rhythm section at the Hotel Meridian. Their contract required them to play four sets per night, seven nights per week, from 10:00 p.m. to 2:00 a.m.[14]

Davern's interest in the clarinet went beyond knowing how to play it well. He was expert about its history, both in classical and jazz, and in the technical aspects of its construction and operation. He could make emergency repairs if his instrument was damaged while he was on the road. He knew how to reface his mouthpieces—a precise and exacting process, with tolerances in micromillimeters. He had reed-cutters, measuring tools, pads, cork, razors, and barrels of different lengths.

There was a time, before he began playing a Pan American rubber clarinet, that he used several instruments that were made of wood. However, in humid weather, wood instruments absorb moisture and swell; in dry climates, they tend to contract. Either change affects the performance of the instrument. As he told Frank Laidlaw, "'I'd like to wind up the night playing the same clarinet I started with.'"[15] To deal with this problem, he had a bore gauge and a lathe at home so that he could machine the barrel of his horns.

While he was in Paris, Davern made several visits to the Van Doren company, whose mouthpieces he occasionally used. Tired of modifying commercially made mouthpieces so that they met his individual specifications, he had designed one for his own use that had a very wide opening. It gave a "bigger" sound, although it was harder to control. He offered the design to the Van Doren Company for purchase and manufacture and, after testing Davern's prototype, the company's executives finally agreed to manufacture it. The Model 5JB remains in the Van Doren catalog today.[16]

The job at the Meridian ended on October 13. Wilber and Davern took a few days to rest and then, on October 17 began an arduous two-week, fourteen-performance tour as Soprano Summit with guitarist Dave Cliff, either Bernie Cash or Peter Ind on bass, and Lennie Hastings on drums. The performance on October 26 took place at Thatchers in Surrey and was recorded.[17] Of all of the recordings made by the pianoless version of Soprano Summit, this is the only one on which Marty Grosz did not appear, and the difference in the music was manifest.

Dave Cliff, born in 1944, was fourteen years younger than Grosz. His musical roots were embedded in the 1940s, not in the years favored by Soprano Summit's leaders. He played electric, not acoustic guitar, and did not play banjo. With Peter Ind playing straight four-to-the-bar accompaniment on many of the songs, there was a far more modern sound to the event. Of the ten tunes, only one was less than four minutes in length, and five ran for more than seven minutes, with *Old Stack O'Lee Blues* coming in at just over twelve.

During an intermission, Davern had learned of the recent death of Albert Burbank, one of his favorites among the first generation of New Orleans clarinet players. He and Wilber dedicated their performances on *Old Stack O'Lee Blues* as a tribute to Burbank, and the four-chorus solos taken by both are among their finest.[18] As noted earlier, *Swing 39* had troubled Marty Grosz and George Duvivier when it was first presented to them. If it gave concern to Cliff and Ind when they first saw it at the start of the tour, they were adept at coping with its unusual structure by the time they reached Thatchers, for their solos were both well constructed. Everyone seems to have had fun on *Oriental Strut*, which swings, as do *Stealin' Away; Oh Sister, Ain't That Hot;* and *I Had It, But It's All Gone Now.*

The performance was not released until 1992, when it was issued in England as *Soprano Summit, Live at Thatchers,* on the J&M label. Several years later, it came out in the United States on Jazzology, titled *Soprano Summit,*

Live in England. It was well reviewed by Eddie Cook and was voted one of *Jazz Journal International*'s top 10 new albums for 1992.[19]

Davern and Wilber returned to the United States on Wednesday, November 3. On the following weekend, they performed as Soprano Summit in Chicago before the Iliana Jazz Club with Grosz, Eddie de Haas on bass, and Bob Cousins on drums. By then, their touring-performance repertoire had become standardized with *Song of Songs, Stompy Jones, Grenadilla Stomp, Chalumeau Blue* (mistitled *Chalumeau Blues*), *Black and Tan Fantasy*, and two songs associated with Sidney Bechet, *Egyptian Fantasy* and *I Had It But It's All Gone Now*. Nonetheless, the three mainstays made it all sound fresh, especially on *Chalumeau Blue* where Grosz's solo brought laughter from Davern.

When the *Rag 'N Roll Revue* appeared in live performance, the band, together with the ensemble, was the star of the show and Cathy Chamberlain provided "atmospheric dressing with her blond brassiness."[20] Unfortunately, the elan of these live performances did not carry over to the long-playing record that was released on Warner Bros. records, titled *Cathy Chamberlain: Rag 'N Roll Revue*. All but one of the tunes featured Ms. Chamberlain's singing, and the band played heavily arranged background parts with hardly any individual expression.

Absent any visual stimulation, the lack of depth of Ms. Chamberlain's voice became apparent and, when it was coupled with the trite, music-hall-style, original melodies, any charm that the stage show had simply disappeared. In the view of John S. Wilson of the *New York Times*, making Ms. Chamberlain the star of the recording and relegating the band to a background role, reversed the merits of the *Rag 'N Roll Revue* and exposed Ms. Chamberlain's singing as "thin and forced."[21]

One week after finishing that recording, Davern was back in the studio for another project. Although Warren Vache, Jr., had been playing cornet professionally since he was in his teens, it was not until he was twenty-five years of age that he made his debut recording as a leader. The title of the album was, appropriately, *First Time Out*, and it was released on the Monmouth-Evergreen label.

Vache was recorded in two settings. In one, he appeared with Davern on soprano saxophone, Bucky Pizzarelli and Wayne Wright on guitars, Michael Moore on bass, and Connie Kay on drums. The only ballad by that group is *I Surrender Dear*; the other tunes, *Oh Baby* and *Song of the Wanderer*, are compelling foot-tappers. On the final selection, *All of Me*, the rhythm section stays out of the first chorus, allowing Vache and Davern to weave counter-melodies back and forth. When the other four members join in, the tune becomes a dazzling romp. In the other setting, Vache and Bucky

Pizzarelli duetted on five tunes, ranging from Ellington's *Black Butterfly*, to Strayhorn's *Chelsea Bridge*, and then on to Clifford Brown's *Joy Spring*.[22] Nevil Skrimshire gave the album a good review and said "Kenny is great," even though he thought the side "seems to get more frantic as it progresses."[23]

On November 19, Davern had started a Friday and Saturday night engagement at the Town House that lasted until the middle of January. Through the end of the year, he was at Town Hall in Newark, at the Smithsonian Institution for an Ellington concert, played two dates at Reno Sweeneys, and a Sunday date with Soprano Summit at Condon's.

As 1976 came to an end, it was clear that the changes in Davern's career that had begun at the Gibsons' party in the fall of 1972 were well under way. Soprano Summit had made two international tours in 1976, its concerts were always well attended, and its records had sold well. On an individual basis, Davern was getting more work at better venues with superior musicians. As his wife Elsa viewed Kenny's career,

> I think Gibsons' impacted lives too: it firmly impacted Kenny's. It was where Kenny met all of those players. He would be standing on the bandstand with these guys. He was amazed; he was awed. And then, he got a lot more work afterwards. A lot of people didn't know who Kenny was because he was in that milieu of "Oh, a dixielander"—which he never beat. But then they realized that there was a lot more to him than just a dixielander.
>
> His career certainly took a turn for the better for a long time. These were very happy days, very hopeful and exciting. Because we all looked forward, and we were surrounded by good things.[24]

As the new year began, Davern was working steadily. He had jobs at Condon's, the Town House, and the Root Cellar in Doylestown (Pennsylvania); the Nassau Inn in Princeton; and at a party in Billings, Montana, hosted by Joe Sample, where he played with Ralph Sutton, Jack Lesberg, and Gus Johnson, Jr. On the first of February, he was part of the band put together by Bobby Rosengarden for a six-week engagement, playing for dining and dancing at the Rainbow Room on the sixty-fifth floor at Rockefeller Center in New York City. He took some days off from that job to play a concert at Allegheny College in Meadville, Pennsylvania, with Soprano Summit; a benefit at the New York Jazz Museum; and a date for the Connecticut Traditional Jazz Club.[25] After a few dates with Pee Wee Erwin in March, Davern had a weekend engagement in Toronto and, from March 25 to 27, was in Great Gorge, New Jersey, for the *Strides of March*, hosted by the NJJS.[26] On the night that the festival ended, Davern flew to Stockholm, where Soprano Summit with singer Carrie Smith appeared at the Atlantic Club from March 28 through April 9.

Singer-guitarist Jose Feliciano was the headline act at the Bottom Line club from April 12 to 16, and the *Rag 'N Roll Revue* opened for him. After that ended, Davern worked at Condon's, had a four-day gig in Philadelphia, and a one-nighter on the *Binghampton*.[27] He also visited at the California home of pianist Dave Frishberg, where the two played together casually. They were sufficiently pleased by the result to consider making an album of duets. Frishberg was then recording for Concord Records, and he broached the idea to Carl Jefferson, its president. Jefferson seemed initially receptive to the idea, but later told Dave that he didn't feel that the duet concept was strong enough. The project was never pursued further.[28]

The next three months were filled with work that kept Davern away from home. In May, he performed in Boca Raton, did a one-nighter in Providence, then traveled to the Odessa Jazz Party. From there, he played in Annapolis; Philadelphia, with the *Rag 'N Roll Revue*; traveled to the Cheyenne Mountain Country Club in Denver; returned home for a Soprano Summit concert at the New York Jazz Museum; spent eleven days at Condon's; and performed at the Newport Jazz Festival at Waterloo Village. In July, he was in Nice, for George Wein in the middle of the month, and spent the end of July at Sandy's Jazz Revival in Beverly, Massachusetts.

Soprano Summit was at Colorado College in Colorado Springs, and then at Zenos in Denver before returning, on August 5, to the Concord Jazz Festival. This year, Monty Budwig was on bass, alongside Jake Hanna on drums and, as in the previous year, the performance was recorded by Concord Records. The album was called *Soprano Summit, Concord '77*, and it opened with a rousing *Strike Up the Band*. Wilber saluted his then wife-to-be Joanne (Pug) Horton with *Puggles*, and Davern essayed *Elsa's Dream* for his spouse. *How Can You Face Me*, *Tracks in the Snow* (an instrumental composed by Grosz), and *The Panic Is On* were all features for Marty that were separated by *Dreaming Butterfly*, one of Wilber's prettiest compositions, with Bob on alto saxophone. *Lament* was a Davern composition that featured Kenny on soprano saxophone and Grosz on banjo. A light and swinging *Panama*, driven by Grosz and Budwig, was the closing tune.[29]

By the time that Davern and Wilber went into the studio to record for Chiaroscuro on September 12, 1977, they had played their highly arranged library of songs countless times, and the routine was becoming increasingly less challenging and steadily more stultifying with each performance. Therein may lie the explanation for *Crazy Rhythm*, an album that bore little resemblance to the previous offerings of Soprano Summit.

The most startling difference from all of the quintet's other recordings was that Davern played C-melody saxophone on four of the titles: *Netcha's*

Dream, When My Dreamboat Comes Home, If You Were the Only Girl in the World, and *Crazy Rhythm*. The C-melody saxophone, the range of which lies between an alto and a tenor, had fallen out of favor over thirty years before. Its most famous exponent, Frank Trumbauer, played it more like an alto, and his tone had been an influence on many reedmen, including Lester Young. But Davern emphasized the instrument's lower range and closeness to the tenor, and created a heartier sound on the instrument. To add to the variety of texture, Wilber played alto on several charts.

There were none of the group's tried-and-true crowd-pleasers. *When My Dreamboat Comes Home* and *Crazy Rhythm* really cooked. *If You Were the Only Girl in the World* was lush without being saccharine, and for those who would have liked still another performance of *Song of Songs*, the group's overly rococo rendition of *When Day Is Done* was a more-than-acceptable substitute. There were two Wilber originals, and a duet with Grosz, who played banjo. Davern, backed only by bass and drum, was featured on his tribute to Pee Wee Russell, *I'd Climb the Highest Mountain*.

Davern was not pleased by the use of the alto and C-melody saxophones. He thought that they compromised the musical integrity of Soprano Summit, and told interviewer Bob Rusch that he thought that "the sound of the group was being phased out by gimmickry." He also said that he thought that the recording date marked the beginning of the end of Soprano Summit.[30]

Kenny's next job enabled him to play with two men who had been among his idols since he was a child. Trumpeter Yank Lawson had met bassist Bob Haggart in the 1930s while both of them were members of the Bob Crosby Orchestra. Haggart had composed a number of tunes that became associated with the Crosby band, including *My Inspiration* and *What's New*.

After the Crosby band broke up, Bob and Yank became busy New York studio musicians. They often got together to co-lead a recording (and occasionally performing) group called the Lawson-Haggart Jazz Band, the personnel of which remained fairly stable for a decade and included Lou McGarity and Bud Freeman. In 1966, at the behest of Dick Gibson, they got together to lead a band that played at the Elitch Gardens in Denver for three weekends. They returned in 1967 and, in the following year, Gibson offered to back the group as a formal venture.[31]

Gibson gave them the grandiose name of the World's Greatest Jazz Band (WGJB), but the caliber of the personnel and the quality of the arrangements fairly justified the title. On its first recording, made at the end of 1968, the group consisted of Lawson and Billy Butterfield on trumpet and Lou McGarity and Carl Fontana playing trombone. Bob Wilber doubled on clarinet and soprano saxophone, and Bud Freeman played tenor saxophone. The rhythm section consisted of Ralph Sutton (piano), Clancy Hayes (banjo and vocals), Haggart, and Morey Feld on drums. Soon afterward, Gus Johnson, Jr., replaced Feld; when Hayes dropped out, he was not replaced.

A substantial factor in the band's success was Haggart's arrangements. The repertoire included such contemporary tunes as *Sunny, Mrs. Robinson, Ode to Billy Joe, Love Is Blue,* and *The 59th Street Bridge Song*—all played in a dynamic, jazz-oriented style. There were Haggart's compositions, such as *I'm Praying Humble, Dogtown Blues,* and *South Rampart Street Parade,* and some by Wilber, who contributed *Century Plaza, A Long Way from Home,* and *Dreaming Butterfly.* Even the old warhorses like *Beale Street Blues* and *Panama* were bright and crisp, played in the instantly recognizable style of the WGJB.

For almost five years, the only changes in personnel were in the trombone section, where Vic Dickenson and Ed Hubble replaced the original members. However, the musical focus of the band began to shift: there were no new contemporary songs being played, and more of the too-often-played tunes were creeping into its repertoire.[32] By the end of 1974, Butterfield, Dickenson, Hubble, and Freeman were gone; Wilber and Sutton left in the following year. High-paying engagements began to dry up.

Lawson and Haggart kept the band alive by downsizing to one trumpet and one trombone and reconstituting the band on an ad hoc basis as jobs materialized, using players from an informal pool. Although the performances of the WGJB were always crisp and professional—Haggart's distinctive charts being more than sufficient to unify any group of musicians—the downsized WGJB was only a shadow of its original self.

Davern's first engagement with the WGJB was on September 25, 1977, for a one-night stand at the Watchung View Inn in Pluckemin, New Jersey. Lawson played trumpet, George Masso was on trombone, Al Klink played tenor saxophone, Jimmy Andrews was on piano, Haggart had the bass chair, and Cliff Leeman was on drums.[33] Over the next decade and a half, Davern made a number of appearances with the band and also recorded with it.

During September and October, Davern worked at Condon's, as well as at O'Connor's, and had some one-night jobs in Providence and Doylestown. He also made his second studio recording of the year—and his first with tenor saxophonist Flip Phillips. Phillips, born in 1915, had become prominent as a member of the 1944–46 Woody Herman band. He had toured with Jazz at the Philharmonic, played with Benny Goodman, and, after a period of semi-retirement in the 1960s, returned to playing full time in the 1970s. Phillips was a regular on the jazz festival–jazz party circuit, where he was a favorite among fans and writers.

Davern and Phillips had developed a personal friendship, as well as a professional relationship. Their first recording together was made on October 23, 1977, when, along with a rhythm section that included George Duvivier, Bobby Rosengarden, and Dave McKenna on piano, they recorded seven tunes that were released on an album titled *John and Joe*. (Their names at birth were John Kenneth Davern and Joseph Edward Filipelli.) "All of that was done literally in one take. It was a flawless afternoon," remembered producer Hank O'Neal. "We did it on a Sunday afternoon, literally in two-and-a-half or three hours at my studio and afterward, all the guys went their separate ways. They didn't even want to hear a playback: they knew it was down. They knew it had happened."[34]

There were some unusual aspects to this recording. Davern, who switched from clarinet to soprano saxophone throughout the session, played the C-melody saxophone for his feature on *Sweet Lorraine*. Flip played both tenor saxophone and soprano, but used the bass clarinet on *Mood Indigo*. Most of the other tunes were taken at a fast tempo, and the powerhouse feeling that the leaders achieved owed much to Duvivier's dynamic, straight four-to-the-bar bass. *Elsa's Dream*, written by the two leaders, was the opener, and, after the two features, *If Dreams Come True*, with some exciting, unaccompanied four-bar exchanges between Kenny and Flip, closed the first side. The second side began with Fats Waller's *Squeeze Me*, which was taken at a pleasant, loping, tempo with both leaders on soprano saxophone. It was followed by Flip's feature, *Candy*, played as a ballad. The album closed with a driving rendition of Duke Ellington's *Cottontail*.

Davern always liked this record. When it was released, the reaction was generally favorable. Clement Meadmore, writing in *Jazz*, said that the collaboration had some "wonderful moments," among them, the unaccompanied duet between Davern and Phillips on *Elsa's Dream*, and the clarinet and bass clarinet collaboration on *Mood Indigo*.[35]

For the balance of October, Kenny played at Condon's, had a job with Pee Wee Erwin, and played a party for the Delaware Jazz Fraternity. Davern was on the front cover of *Jersey Jazz* in November and, during that month, guested with the Scott Hamilton Quartet at Condon's, and traveled to Midland, Texas, for its first annual jazz party.[36]

Davern, Wilber, and Grosz were at the Maryland Inn from November 22 through December 3, after which they appeared at Johnson "Fat Cat" McCree's annual festival. That evening, and on the following night, they were teamed with bassist Steve Novosel and drummer Tommy Benford to perform as Soprano Summit. The performances were recorded and released on the Fat Cat Jazz label as parts of three albums: one was titled *Soprano Summit: The Meridian*, and included seven tunes from the two nights. The other recordings, which were titled *Song of Songs* and *Oh Sister, Ain't That Hot* were held for a year, and when they were released they included some songs from this engagement and some from the group's appearance at the 1978 festival.

The greater part of the *Meridian* album consisted of Soprano Summit's staples. However, on two numbers, Jacques Kerrien joined on soprano saxophone and Mason "Country" Thomas took the stage to provide another clarinet voice. In addition, Dick Wellstood came in on piano, Van Perry took over the bass, and Skip Tomlinson played drums. Although Kerrien and Thomas were capable players, neither was of the caliber of Davern or Wilber, and the possibility of a train wreck among four reed players who were feeling their way while playing before a live audience loomed large. It never happened. A tasteful and heartfelt *Buddy Bolden's Blues* came off without a hitch. *Sweet Georgia Brown* was a blowout, marked by sparkling solos that were backed by swinging and complex riffs from the other three reeds.

Less than a week after leaving Manassas, Davern and Wilber were in a recording studio with Dick Hyman, Bucky Pizzarelli, and Milt Hinton to complete the album titled *Soprano Summit II*, the album that they had begun in 1974. However, even after three years of trying to match schedules, one member of the original group was missing: Bobby Rosengarden was not able to make the date, and Tommy Benford took his place. Benford, born in 1905, was the oldest member of the group, having played drums with Jelly Roll Morton in the 1920s.

Two of the tunes recorded that day, *Frog-I-More Rag* and *Sidewalk Blues*, had been composed by Morton. There were three compositions by Wilber—*If You Went Away*, *Lincoln Garden Stomp*, and *Creole Nights*—that fit the tenor of the album perfectly. The recording concluded with George Gershwin's *Rialto Ripples*. The technical credits reflect, in wry fashion, that Davern's preoccupation with sound and balance must have been especially acute throughout the session. One of the entries reads "Sound Engineer, Jeff Zaraya. Assisted Nobly by Kenny Davern."

John S. Wilson thought that the side recorded in 1974 was "Soprano Summit at its best," while the second side, which featured more of Dick Hyman's playing was "scarcely Soprano Summit at all."[37] The record did not reach the reviewer for *Jazz Journal International* until more than a year after Soprano Summit had disbanded. He felt quite differently. "[T]this is likely to be the last Soprano Summit album we see. And that is an absolute tragedy.

. . . The consummate musical ability, the creative invention, the superb arrangements—indeed the whole concept—is quite unique. . . ."[38]

On Christmas Eve, Davern left New York and, after stopping in Honolulu, Sydney, and Melbourne, arrived in Hobart, in Tasmania, off the coast of Australia, to perform at the Thirty-second Annual Australian Jazz Convention. The job, which started on December 26, ended on December 31, and Kenny flew home on the January 2, 1978. He did not enjoy the tour. He wrote Elsa that he had to play with "no-lip trumpeters, washboard players, electric bass, and amplified guitars."[39]

The month of January 1978 was especially grim. Except for playing Tuesdays at Condon's, Kenny had very little work. February was substantially better. He worked for two weeks at the Rainbow Room with Bobby Rosengarden, interrupting his stay for dates in Pine Bluff, Arkansas, and Jackson, Mississippi. Before the month ended, he worked an evening at Condon's. March saw Davern at the Paradise Valley Jazz Party in Scottsdale, Arizona, and at the end of the month, he was at the NJJS's concert at Great Gorge, New Jersey. Davern played the King of France Tavern in Annapolis on April 4–9, then performed in New Orleans. There was a date at Condon's with Scott Hamilton; one in Darien, Connecticut, with Lou Stein; and then a week in Toronto. He played a job with Pee Wee Erwin on the island of Bimini on May 5, and then, in a herculean effort, he left the island and, stopping in Miami and again in Dallas, flew to Phoenix, where he played two dates with the WGJB on May 6–7. After jobs in Big Horn and Ames, Iowa, he flew to Odessa for its annual Jazz Party on May 16, 1978, where he and Wilber formalized a change in their relationship.[40]

Notes

1. *Jersey Jazz*, 4, no. 1 (February 1976): 7; Chip Defaa, "Marty Grosz, Listen to the Rhythm King," printed in *Traditionalists and Revivalists in Jazz* (Metuchen, N.J., Scarecrow Press and the Institute of Jazz Studies, 1993), 144; Date Book.

2. Hank O'Neal, producer's notes to *Soprano Summit*, Chiaroscuro CR (D) 148.

3. Kenny Davern, quoted in Vacher, Davern, 32.

4. Jack Six, interview by the author.

5. Roswell Rudd, interview by the author.

6. Ralph Laing, "Chalumeau Blue," *Jazz Journal*, 30, no. 1 (January 1977): 37.

7. Letter from Kenny Davern to Elsa Davern dated 6 May 1976; *Jersey Jazz*, 29, no.4 (May 1976): 7; Date Book.

8. Vache, Erwin, 336; Date Book; John S. Wilson, "Concert Salutes Ellington Groups," *New York Times*, 15 June 1976; *Jazz Journal*, 29, no. 8 (August 1976): 12.

9. Warren Vache, Jr., interview by the author.

10. Wein, pp. 406–407; e-mail from Jack Stine to the author.

11. *Jersey Jazz*, 4, no. 5 (June 1976): 5; *Jersey Jazz*, 5, no. 7 (August 1976): 13; Carnegie Hall Event Program.

12. Sinclair Traill, "Soprano Summit, In Concert," *Jazz Journal*, 30, no. 4 (April 1977): 36: Kevin Jones, "Soprano Can Still Scale the Heights," *The Australian*, 2 January 1992; David Badham, "Soprano Summit, In Concert," *Jazz Journal International*, 34, no. 6 (June 1981): 42.

13. Letter from Martin Williams to Kenny Davern dated 23 August 1976.

14. Contract dated 12 July 1976, between Bob Wilber and the Hotel. Letter from Kenny Davern to Elsa Davern dated 28 September 1976. See also: Wilber/Webster, 134.

15. Kenny Davern, quoted in Frank Laidlaw, interview by the author.

16. Letters from Kenny Davern to Elsa Davern. The letters JB in the designation of the mouthpiece stand for Jazz Band. Davern thought that it should be called the Model 5 KD. Davern had also designed a mouthpiece for Bob Wilber that had a smaller opening. He offered that design, which Davern called a Model 3 BW, but Van Doren declined. Frank Laidlaw, interview by the author; Christian Plattner, conversation with the author.

17. *Jazz Journal*, 29, no. 10 (October 1976): 3, document in the possession of Elsa Davern. The discography of the recorded performances of Soprano Summit published by Derek Coller and Bert Whyatt states that this recording was made on 26 October 1976. "Soprano Summit Discography, Part One, 1973–May 1977," *Jazz Journal International*, 30, no. 4 (April 1982): 22–23, and "Part Two, August 1977–December 1978," *Jazz Journal International*, 30, no. 5 (May 1982): 43 (hereinafter the "Coller-Whyatt discography"). Although the CD jacket says that the date was 12 October 1976, Soprano Summit was still working at the Meridian on that date: the tour of England did not start until the 17th. The 26 October date would therefore seem to be correct.

18. Alun Morgan, liner notes to *Soprano Summit, Live at Thatchers*, J&M CD 501, July 1992.

19. Eddie Cook, "Soprano Summit, Live at Thatchers," *Jazz Journal International*, 45, no. 12 (December 1992): 46; *Jazz Journal International*, 46, no. 2 (February 1993): 6.

20. John S. Wilson, "A New Kind of Song in the Cabarets," *New York Times*, 22 May 1977; see also John S. Wilson, "A Rag-Rock Star to Watch," *New York Times*, 10 December 1976.

21. John S. Wilson, "A New Kind of Song in the Cabarets," *New York Times*, 22 May 1977. The recording was made on 19 November 1976.

22. The album was recorded in two sessions, on 22 November and 6 December.

23. Nevil Shrimshire, "First Time Out," *Jazz Journal International*, 34, no. 2 (February 1981): 37.

24. Elsa Davern, interview by the author.

25. James D. Schacter, *Loose Shoes, the Story of Ralph Sutton* (Chicago, Jaynar Press, 1994), 227–228 (hereinafter "Schacter, Sutton"); *Jersey Jazz*, 4, no. 11 (January 1977): 14, 15; letter from New York Jazz Museum to Kenny Davern dated 25 February 1977; Date Book.

26. The Connecticut Traditional Jazz Club issued an LP recorded on 12 March 1977. Although several discographies say that Davern was present on three tunes (*Chicago Stomps*, *Rock My Soul*, and *Ghost of a Chance*), listening to the recording reveals that he is not. The first two songs are solos by Stein, and the third features Warren Vache, Jr., with a rhythm section.

27. Robert Palmer, "Feliciano Mesmerizes, But Songs Lack Bite," *New York Times*, 18 April 1977; Date Book; Vache, Erwin, 341.

28. Letters from Frishberg to Davern dated 9 June 1977 and 27 August 1977.

29. Date Book; letters from Kenny Davern to Elsa Davern postmarked 10 May, 16 May, and 7 July 1977; Peerless Program Notes, p. 42.

30. Rusch interview part 1, p. 21.

31. Wilber/Webster, 110–111.

32. In September 1972, they made one of the best-ever albums of Christmas songs titled *Hark, the Herald Angels Swing*, World Jazz, WJLP S-2.

33. *Jersey Jazz*, 5, no. 8 (October 1977): 23, and 5, no. 9 (November 1977): 11.

34. Hank O'Neal, interview by the author.

35. Clement Meadmore, "Kenny Davern/Flip Phillips," *Jazz*, Fall, 1978, 60.

36. Date Book; Vache, Erwin, 345–346.

37. John S. Wilson, "Bob Wilber, A Jazzman Comes into His Own," *New York Times* 5 August 1979.

38. Ralph Laing, "Soprano Summit II," *Jazz Journal International*, 8, no. 9 (September 1980): 39.

39. Letter from Kenny Davern to Elsa Davern dated 26 December 1977; see also contract dated 7 November 1977; letter from Peter Hicks to Kenny Davern dated 31 October 1977.

40. Date Book.

CHAPTER EIGHT

Changes

By the spring of 1978, Davern and Wilber had been co-leading Soprano Summit for over three years. They had spent long periods of time together, sharing lengthy rides in uncomfortable cars, bad meals, cheap and dirty hotels, and sleepless nights. The strain was beginning to show.

Each of them chafed at the other's personality. Davern was volatile and impulsive; Wilber was quiet and reflective. Davern would curse and argue; Wilber would nod, agree, and then do what he wanted. Virtually every decision—from what tune to play to what tempo to select—involved some conflict. Each wanted their fair share of time at the microphone in front of the audience—and both felt they weren't getting it.[1]

From Wilber's standpoint, there were a number of other problems. He believed that he was the one charged with the responsibility of selecting the programs, writing the arrangements, and managing the band. But he was only getting half of the credit and half of the money. In addition, Soprano Summit was not getting as much money as he thought it should, and the fees that he received were less than he could command as a solo act. Wilber had always looked for new musical horizons, and he was coming to the belief that Soprano Summit had run its course.[2]

From Davern's position, the profitability of Soprano Summit was far from satisfactory. The fees that Soprano Summit was able to command were not extravagant and, when the salaries of the other three musicians were deducted, along with travel, lodging, and other costs, the net amount that remained to be divided between Wilber and Davern was relatively small.

Equally troubling was the lack of work being offered to Soprano Summit. Davern believed that Wilber could have done more to get jobs for the group, but that he chose to spend more time getting work for himself. Finally, Davern never liked repertory. He always preferred to improvise in live performances, rather than play from written arrangements. Playing the same songs in the same way, week after week, was becoming tiresome.[3] Like his musical partner, Davern was ready to move on.

Finally, there were changes in the personal relationships of the co-leaders that caused friction between them and had an adverse effect on their friendship, as well as on their ability to work together.

They agreed to part. The business partnership named Soprano Summit was formally dissolved by an agreement signed in Odessa, Texas, on May 17, 1978, effective June 30, 1978: Soprano Summit, Inc. was also dissolved in that year. Kenny and Bob had undertaken to perform as Soprano Summit through the end of the year, and the documents allowed them to do so. Finally, they agreed that the name Soprano Summit would only be used in endeavors in which both of them were participants.

In the years to come, Davern remained steadfast in his refusal to publicly discuss the details of the breakup, saying, in essence. "He wanted to go his way, and I wanted to go mine." Wilber usually pointed to the factors mentioned earlier, or said that he had explored all of Soprano Summit's musical possibilities and wanted to move on.[4]

In truth, the reasons for the breakup were not as important as the fact that, for whatever reasons, Soprano Summit had ceased to exist. Musicians and the public mourned its passing. Bucky Pizzarelli, who had been with Davern and Wilber at the beginning, said: "When you hear a group like that play spontaneously, and all of a sudden it starts to be magical, everything starts to pop. I think that was a lucky day for both of them. . . . It was very exciting: both guys played beautifully. Too bad that . . . they split up and never played the two sopranos again." Author Chris Sheridan said: "Soprano Summit was a precarious balancing act that avoided falling into anachronism by virtue of the electricity that Wilber and Davern generated within each other."[5]

For many years after the dissolution of Soprano Summit, Davern and Wilber did not play together, even though they were frequently at the same parties and festivals. Efforts by their fans, promoters, and friends to reunite them were invariably unsuccessful; one or the other would beg off on some pretext. And, although many in their audiences remembered and longed to hear again their glorious collaboration on tunes like *Song of Songs*, it became clear that both of the principals had moved to new stages in their careers.

The success of Soprano Summit changed Davern's life. Before then, he was well known among musicians, but, except for people who had seen him in New York or at the Ferryboat, he was largely unknown to the general public. With one exception, his recording career had consisted of appearances as a sideman in bands led by others. Davern's playing as the co-leader of an innovative and dynamic band riveted new audiences to their chairs; his quick wit, sardonic humor, and roguish charm brought them back, again and again.

The same thing was true for Wilber. Although he had been a professional musician for almost a decade longer than Davern, his career had been languishing since the early 1950s. The success of Soprano Summit restored his flagging fortunes. Soprano Summit also revived the career of its third permanent member, Marty Grosz, whose unparalleled mastery of the acoustic guitar, encyclopedic memory of the lyrics of hundreds of long-forgotten songs, and penchant for tall and humorous tales made him a star in the jazz firmament.

At about the time that Soprano Summit broke up, Davern decided to abandon the soprano saxophone and concentrate all of his efforts on the clarinet. He told interviewers that doubling on soprano affected his clarinet playing.

> I think to come to terms with any instrument you have to stay with it. If you don't, by the end of the second set you can pick up any of the other mistresses and, how shall I say it, BS your way through the rest of the evening. But once you are confronted with only one instrument and you cannot in any way switch, you're really stuck, and you better come to terms with it.[6]

Giving up the soprano may also have been the result of his view of his own place in the tradition of music. The clarinet had a long-established chair in classical orchestras. It had a wide range, spanning almost four octaves, and was often referred to as the violin of the woodwinds. Mozart, Brahms, and Debussy, among others, composed extended pieces for the clarinet, and it was an established member of the family of "legitimate" musical instruments.

The clarinet had been a part of jazz since its beginning, and the history of this music was filled with names like Tio, Nelson, Lewis, Bechet, Dodds, Burbank, Nicholas, Bigard, Simeon, Noone, Teschemacher, Fazola, Russell, DeFranco, Goodman, and Shaw. These musicians had set standards that very few could approach, no less equal. Playing the clarinet in a classical or jazz setting was recognized as a challenging task. Only a few could do it well.

Davern had chosen, when still in his teens, to make the clarinet his means of expression and to become a part of a long and proud family of musicians. Over the years, he amassed an extensive library of books on music that included several treatises on the clarinet and its history. He had thousands of LPs and CDs, many of which featured the clarinet in a classical or jazz setting. There was a history and a structure to the place of the clarinet in music, and Davern believed that he was properly a part of it. He told interviewer Michael Woods: "I grew up loving the instrument, that's all I can say. And whatever doubling I did on the way up was always with the clarinet being the instrument that I was going to focus on, from then on, you know, for the rest of my life—whether I made money or not."[7]

The soprano saxophone (both curved and straight) had no similar niche in musical history. It was barely a century old. No great sonatas or concerti had been written for it, and there was no chair for it in the great classical orchestras. It had a limited range of about two and a half octaves, and was difficult to play in tune. In Davern's eyes, it was little more than a gimmick.

Sidney Bechet had used it in order to assume the lead voice in a small jazz ensemble and eliminate the need for a trumpet. Davern had started playing the soprano at the Ferryboat for many of the same reasons as Bechet. But, as he told John S. Wilson, he began to "wince" at the "false bravura sense" that Bechet "milked" from the instrument and came to think of Bechet as the "crown prince of Mittel European, turn-of-the-century, 1920s Richard Tauber stuff."[8] Although the soprano saxophone subsequently became a part of contemporary jazz in the mid 1960s, played by musicians like Wayne Shorter, Steve Lacy, and John Coltrane, it was a different voice in a different setting.

Finally, with the demise of Soprano Summit, Davern assumed the role of the leader of a small group, most often a clarinet-piano-drum trio. For about the next decade, he most frequently appeared with pianist Dick Wellstood and a variety of drummers including Bobby Rosengarden (the Blue Three), Cliff Leeman (the Free Swinging Trio), and also with Chuck Riggs and Freddie Kohlman. He formed the Hot Three with pianist Art Hodes and drummer Don DeMicheal (occasionally Wellstood and DeMicheal), and toured and recorded with Ralph Sutton and drummer Gus Johnson, Jr. He had no need for the strident voice of the soprano saxophone in these groups. And so, he put it away.

Many of his colleagues regretted his decision, believing that he had a unique talent on the various saxophones. Hyman, Wilber, and Dick Sudhalter continued to call him to participate in repertory recreations where he would play one or more saxophones. Wilber once told him:

I've always felt that you're absolutely a natural saxophone player and, for instance, when we've done recreations of Ellington in the past, Kenny has played the baritone part of Harry Carney, and he gets closer to the sound that Carney got than anyone I've ever heard. And, also, when we did the Bix Beiderbecke recreations, Kenny played the bass saxophone, incredibly like Adrian Rollini. You have a real feel for the saxophone.[9]

In the years that followed, Davern would occasionally pick up a new soprano, play it for a short while, and then return to the clarinet. Eventually, even those occasions passed. By the mid 1990s, the clarinet was Kenny Davern's only instrument.

When Davern left the Odessa party near the end of May 1978, he returned to his usual haunts, playing at Condon's, taking a one-night gig with the World's Greatest Jazz Band, and a job in Rhode Island. On the 30th, he recorded an album that was properly titled *Unexpected*.

Although critics and audiences had, for ease of description, if not ease of thought, categorized Davern's music as "dixieland" or "mainstream," his interests were not limited to those fields. He read biographies of musicians in other areas of music and spent time listening to their works. He was fascinated by the different sounds that various conductors could get from their orchestras, particularly Wilhelm Furtwangler, conductor of the Berlin Philharmonic Orchestra. He listened closely to, and became expert about, their works.

In the field of jazz, he listened to and appreciated musicians from far beyond the areas that people usually associated with him. He told interviewer Shirley Klett:

> When Ornette Coleman came to town—really—his music, it knocked me out. I couldn't wait to get back every night. The original quartet with Don Cherry, Charlie Haden and . . . Billy Higgins. . . . Those guys had the guts of their convictions. And, like most middle class boys, I was of my generation—we wanted to please. You know, bebop is very structured—you can get very free with bebop—Phil Woods certainly shows that. But, I mean, this other thing was such a highly personalized form of expression that it reminded me sometimes of field songs and hollers and shouts.[10]

Even before he recorded the *Blown Bone* album with Roswell Rudd, Davern had been talking about making an entire LP in the Free Jazz idiom. But, it took three years for him to assemble the musicians that he wanted. The album that was recorded on May 30, 1978, featured Davern on clarinet and soprano saxophone, Steve Lacy on soprano saxophone, with Steve Swallow on bass and Paul Motian on drums.

Kenny had known Steve Lacy, born Steven Lackritz, since the time that both of them were in their teens, competing for jobs at the Stuyvesant Casino and the Central Plaza. Davern had played baritone saxophone, and Lacy was on the clarinet and soprano saxophone in the band that they took to Boston, in 1951, for a short-lived engagement at the Savoy.

In the mid 1950s, Lacy had abandoned that style of music and began working with avant-garde pianist Cecil Taylor in a quartet. He recorded with Gil Evans in 1957 and, three years later, started playing with Thelonious Monk. Lacy worked with Roswell Rudd from 1961 to 1964 in a quartet that featured Monk's compositions. He emigrated to Europe in 1967, settling first in Rome and then moving to Paris in 1970, where he established his permanent residence.[11]

Kenny had been looking to expand his musical horizons, if only to see if he could perform competently in a wholly modern idiom, and he wanted Lacy for the album that he envisioned. However, Lacy, who came to the United States in 1976 to make the *Blown Bone* album, had returned to Paris, and Davern would not proceed without him. When Lacy announced that he would come back to New York to make the date, Kenny called the other musicians whom he wanted. More problems arose. Motian, who had previously said that he would do the job, sought to back out because he only wanted to record his own material. Davern told him to come and said that, even if he didn't play, he would get paid. Motian came and played.[12]

There are eight songs on this album, with composer credit for two given to each of the musicians. Davern wrote the opening title, *Swirls*, and also the last tune on the album, *Unexpected*, which ran twelve minutes, thirty-one seconds. There is no discernible melodic or harmonic structure to any of the songs and very few parts that appear to be arranged. Rather, the musicians play phrases, notes, and sounds that seem to strike them at the moment: Swallow and Motian are less a rhythm section than two players of counterpoint. Each musician has the lion's share of space on his own compositions.

Elsa Davern accurately described the proceedings in the note that she wrote anonymously on the album jacket. In its entirety it reads: "The music herein being, for the most part, spontaneous responses by the players to unforeseen circumstances and unexpected predicaments."

The album was aptly named. Nothing in Davern's performance or recorded repertoire had prepared his audience for the music that they would find on *Unexpected*. It presented difficulties for reviewers, who did not know how to describe the record in terms that would be accurate, yet meaningful to their readers. The review published in *Jersey Jazz* said that the music "defies description."

> To the average listener, it sounds as though the players, without any discernible pattern of rhythm or melody, are fashioning and emitting notes and sounds, which to them and their fellow players have some meaning and presumably in turn inspire some creative response from the others. The music is not harsh and indeed the tones and shadings are provocative and, I am sure, extremely interesting to those who enjoy their jazz on the cerebral side. While this is not mainstream jazz in any sense of the word, it is experimental rather than progressive. Summing it up, *Unexpected* is decidedly unusual.
>
> We recommend this record to (1) collectors of the "complete" Kenny Davern, (2) those interested in truly different jazz sounds, and (3) anyone who curiosity has been hereby aroused. Dixielanders, stay away.[13]

Whitney Balliett said that the album consisted of "eight surprisingly witless concoctions."[14]

Other columnists were more sympathetic toward Davern's efforts to break out of the "dixieland-mainstream" box into which he had been thrust. In a lengthy review, Dan Morgenstern analyzed the music and concluded:

> It's a pity there is so much prejudice against this kind of music, much of it stemming from the mistaken notion that it is somehow hostile or threatening in intent. Perhaps Davern's name on the record will lead to some unexpected discoveries among the uninitiated; conversely, the presence of the other players may cause followers of this branch of jazz to discover Davern. I, for one, am glad he made this record. To hell with categorization.[15]

Years later, Morgenstern said, "Kenny was not a one-trick pony. There were many sides to him."[16] Barry McRae seemed to understand what Davern was attempting to do. "It is all a long way from Soprano Summit, and I have no doubt that Davern will not always want to play quite as freely. It represents the greatest test he has yet set himself, and he has come through it successfully."[17]

The *Unexpected* album may have been, as Barry McRae suggested, a self-imposed test for Davern; one that he believed he passed with high marks. When asked about the recordings that he liked most, he always mentioned this one. However, he never again recorded in this idiom, and, with one notable exception that occurred twenty-eight years later, he never again publicly played Free Jazz.[18]

A certain inevitability attended Davern's becoming the leader of the groups in which he played. There is a common musical language that all musicians know: it defines the role that each instrument plays within an ensemble and within each tune that the ensemble plays. It allows total strangers to play together, secure in the knowledge that each of their cohorts knows the language and will play their part throughout the song.

However, defining the role of an instrument within an ensemble limits the person who plays it. Within the "usual" band (trumpet, trombone, clarinet, piano or guitar, bass, and drum), the role of a clarinet as a supporting instrument is firmly established. Even when it is the clarinet's turn to solo, the notes and chords that the others play restrict the clarinetist's choice of notes and their placement and timing.

It was a role that restricted Davern unduly. As Warren Vache, Jr., said:

> In many ways, Kenny was a solo voice and being limited by the constraints of what a dixieland band clarinetist was supposed to do seemed to him, at the time, to be limited—shall we say in a kind way. . . . If you listen, his most satisfying work and the stuff that made him the happiest is the stuff that he did on his own. He was a soloist. He was one of the premier soloists on the clarinet.[19]

Ed Polcer agreed: "Kenny had strong feelings about how he wanted to play music, so he gravitated toward being a leader from way back."[20] Davern wanted no restrictions on the way that he played, as well as on the tunes, the keys in which to play them, and the tempos at which to proceed. He said, ". . . I prefer to work . . . in as small a group as possible—a trio, quartet, or quintet where a guitar is added or whatever. Because then I can control the situation. And, I think it's a need to control and not be controlled."[21]

As was often the case with Davern, having the right to control the situation was not something that he always wished to do. Although he carried an extensive list of tunes with him, he rarely thought through the program for an evening, believing that selecting a tune on the spot would increase spontaneity. That led to a situation that all of the musicians who played with him came to expect. Davern would turn to the band and ask, "What do you want to play?" There would be a short silence, then someone would suggest a song title, which would be met with, "I don't want to play that," or "I hate that tune." The process would continue with other titles being offered by the band and rejected by Davern until he decided on what song he wanted to play.

Warren Vache, Jr., had a plan to short-cut the process. Warren made some copies of Kenny's tune list.

> I gave one to each of the members of the ensemble with instructions that, when Kenny comes in and says "What are we gonna play?" nobody pick a song. Force him into picking the first song. Because, no matter what tune you picked, his response was "I hate that f—ing tune." And then you'd have to pick another one. So, we made him pick the first song, and everybody in the band said in unison "I hate that f—ing tune." Then, we went into our wallets, pulled out his song list, and we started pulling tunes off his song list—none of which he liked. He finally figured what was going on. I don't think he was displeased.[22]

At various times during the summer of 1978, Davern toured with Wild Bill Davison. They were together at the Big Horn Festival at the end of May, reunited at Condon's for two weeks in the middle of the next month, then were at the Newport Jazz Festival—New Jersey Jazz Society Picnic at Waterloo Village on June 25. They had separate jobs during July and early August, then reunited for a week at the Maryland Inn in Annapolis, with a rhythm section that consisted of Larry Eanet, Carlos Laguana, and Eddie Phyfe on piano, bass, and drums.

Their performance on August 20 was recorded and released by Johnson "Fat Cat" McRee on his Fat Cat Jazz label as *Wild Bill Davison and Kenny Davern at the King of France Tavern*. There were some interesting moments: *Our Love Is Here to Stay* was lyrical, and *If I Had You* was marred only by some momentary confusion as to who would play melody and who would play harmony. The remaining tunes, *Song of the Wanderer*, *Rosetta*, *On the Alamo*, *My Monday Date*, *Sunny Side of the Street*, and *I Never Knew*, were all standards for both Wild Bill and Kenny, and they played them in their usual exemplary manner.

Dick and Maddie Gibson invited Davern to their annual Labor Day weekend party at the beginning of September. He and Wilber fulfilled a contractual obligation on the ninth of that month, appearing in Lafayette, Pennsylvania. Davern then left for the first of two back-to-back tours of Europe and the United Kingdom.

On the first trip, Kenny performed as a solo artist, backed by rhythm sections made up of local musicians. From mid-September, he appeared in Vienna, Bern, Switzerland, Zurich, and Holland. He crossed the English Channel for appearances in Harfield, London, Leicester, and Manchester, plus some gigs in the south of England, before coming home on October 6 to have some dental work done. Then he flew to Billings, Montana, for a private party and recrossed the Atlantic to join the World's Greatest Jazz Band for its Tenth Anniversary Tour. They began a six-day tour of Britain on October 21, flew to Hamburg on the 27th, and played in Muenster, Dusseldorf, Basel, and Stuttgart, before flying home on November 3. Within a few days, he was off to the Jazz Party in Midland, Texas, then came home to play a series of local dates.[23]

Before the breakup of Soprano Summit, Wilber and Davern had agreed to return to Fat Cat McCree's 1978 festival. Davern and Wilber may have been at odds personally, but no one in the audience had cause to complain about the performances that they heard. Soprano Summit went out in style, performing *Song of Songs*, *Changes*, and *Meet Me Tonight in Dreamland*, among others, with the grace and verve that had always been a hallmark of their performances.

As noted previously, the two albums that resulted from this date, *Song of Songs* and *Oh Sister, Ain't That Hot*, contained some performances from the year before. Trumpeter Billy Butterfield was featured on the first night of the festival, leading a band that included Davern, Wellstood, Grosz, Di Nicola, Spiegel Willcox on trombone, Spencer Clark on bass sax, and Van Perry on bass. Five numbers from their performance were released on an album titled *Swinging at the Elks'—Billy Butterfield and His World Class Jazz Band*.

One of the better albums to come out of Fat Cat McCree's festivals was *The Free Swinging Trio in the Jazz Tradition*, which had Davern and Wellstood teamed with Cliff Leeman. The LP consisted of seven tunes, of which five were from this festival, with the balance recorded in 1979. *Maple Leaf Rag* was played in a stately manner. There was an exuberant *That's a Plenty*, followed by *Yellow Dog Blues*, played without the shouted audience break that festival crowds seem to love. The trio also essayed a mournful *Sweet Substitute*, which Davern introduced as "the story of a boy and his dog." The most exciting piece was *Fidgety Feet*, which began in a lightly swinging fashion and built steadily to a driving conclusion. The album also included two selections from the trio's appearance in the following year, *Wild Cat Blues* and *Eccentric Rag*, the latter being one of Wellstood's features during this period.

During the first three months of 1979, Davern returned to his schedule of short stands at his usual venues. Elsa went with him to the Paradise Valley Jazz Party in Scottsdale in the middle of January and, when the gig was over, the two of them enjoyed a short vacation in Mexico City. Back in New York City, Kenny performed with Flip Phillips at a Sunday concert at the Church of the Heavenly Rest on 5th Avenue and East 90th Street.

From time to time, the church was the site of Sunday afternoon jazz concerts, and over the years, many great musicians performed there. Constructed in 1929 in a gothic design, the church was a relatively narrow structure, built primarily of stone, with a vaulted ceiling about two stories high. Unfortunately, within the cavern-like interior, sound tended to bounce off the hard stone surfaces and, for those more than eight rows away from the musicians, the echoes that reverberated through the structure made it difficult to hear the music emanating from the stage with any degree of clarity.

Late in January, Davern was working with Bobby Rosengarden. Every professional musician understands that it is necessary to get work. Some musicians are content to wait to be called; others concentrate on finding jobs, if for no other reason than it is generally accepted that the person who is called to put a group together gets more money than the men that he books. Bobby Rosengarden fell into the latter category. He had made it his business to know, and to be known by, the people who hired musicians, and when he got called, he often turned to Davern. Rosengarden had been asked to put together a band to appear at the Rainbow Room, and Davern was there for a week beginning on January 28.

The job at the Rainbow Room, and several similar types of gigs that Rosengarden got over the years, called for musicians who could sight read music. Davern could read; but he didn't like to do it, and he didn't do it well. Yet, Rosengarden continued to hire him for as long as he was active in the business, partially because they were personal friends, but also because Davern's innate musicianship overcame any difficulties caused by his lack of reading skills.

Davern was in Annapolis from February 13 to 17, and, in the balance of the month, played a concert with Dick Wellstood and Don DeMicheal in Marlton, New Jersey, some dates at Condon's, and a gig at Trenton State College. He opened March in Minneapolis for a five-day stand with Art Hodes at the Emporium. While there, he probably recorded a segment with Hodes for his short-lived television program titled *Art's Place*.[24] After he left Minnesota, Davern performed at a benefit concert for the Somerset Hills Symphony, made appearances with the World's Greatest Jazz Band, and had several gigs at Condon's.

The New Jersey Jazz Society held its annual *Strides of March* concert in Somerset, New Jersey, over the weekend of March 23–25, and Davern was teamed with Dick Wellstood and Bobby Rosengarden for a twenty-minute set. Although they were not yet billing themselves as the Blue Three, Davern and Wellstood had played together countless times, and both of them had been on the bandstand with Rosengarden in various settings. There was clearly a chemistry among them. Davern built to a stirring climax on C. C. Rider, and ended the piece at the top of the clarinet's range. *Fidgety Feet* was marked by Wellstood's unusual chordings. Kenny used the full range of his horn on *Sweet Substitute*, beginning with a mournful chalumeau-register statement and ending with a powerful upper-range chorus. Everyone seemed to enjoy *Shim-Me-Sha-Wabble*, which ended with some four-bar exchanges. When the Blue Three became a working trio, these selections became mainstays of its repertoire.

The Society recorded almost all of its performances for reference-archival purposes. Under an agreement with Arbors Records, the music from this and several other concerts was released in 2008, as part of a two-CD package titled *Soprano Summit, 1975, and More* on the Arbors label.

The April edition of the *Mississippi Rag* had a picture of Davern on the front cover and an interview by Ron Johnson titled *Goodbye Soprano, Hello Clarinet*.[25] Also, at the end of March, Wellstood and drummer Freddie Kohlman joined Davern for a week-long stand at the King of France Tavern in Annapolis. The performances were recorded and subsequently released on two cassettes on the Fat Cat Jazz label, titled *Dick Wellstood and His Famous Orchestra*, and *Kenny Davern and His Famous Orchestra*.[26]

This was the third recorded live appearance by Wellstood and Davern in a trio setting within a twelve-month period. Each of them featured a different drummer. Of Kohlman, Leeman, and Rosengarden, Kohlman, who had spent his musical life playing in the New Orleans idiom, had far less playing time with Kenny and Dick. Yet, the lines of communication between Kenny and Dick were so strong that Kohlman's musical idiosyncrasies had no effect on their ability to anticipate and react to each other.

The *Kenny Davern and His Famous Orchestra* cassette opens with a medium-fast *Shake It and Break It* followed by *Black and Blue*, with a vocal by Kohlman that unfortunately rewrites a part of the original lyric and destroys the symmetry of the rhyme. An ebullient *Shout 'Em Aunt Tillie* precedes *Mood Indigo*, played very slowly and with an exceptionally woody-sounding opening statement by Davern. *Lullaby of the Leaves* is next, Kohlman has a vocal on *Birth of the Blues*, and, for his solo feature, Wellstood plays his then-standard medley of Ellington tunes (*Lush Life*, *Prelude to a Kiss*, *Sophisticated Lady*, *Perdido*, and *Caravan*). The cassette concludes with *Beale Street Blues*.

The *Dick Wellstood and His Famous Orchestra* tape begins with *My Daddy Rocks Me*. The next cut is titled *Wellstood Wanderings*, a curious solo excursion in which Dick seems to patch together little otherwise-unconnected snippets that he has played throughout the years. *Tin Roof Blues* is followed by a rollicking *Three Little Words*. An up-tempo *That Da Da Strain* precedes a stately *C. C. Rider*, on which Kohlman takes a vocal. Davern dances along on *My Blue Heaven* propelled by Kohlman's infectious drumming. Wellstood solos on the Fats Waller showpiece *Handful of Keys*, and the set closes with *I Would Do Anything for You*.

After some local jobs, Davern left for Europe. For about the next decade, Kenny would make a spring tour of Europe, stopping frequently in Sweden, where he had made the acquaintance of clarinetist and alto saxophonist Tomas Ornberg. Ornberg was then leading a group called the Blue Five and, on April 24, he and Davern were in Jarfalla, Sweden, where they recorded with Bent Persson on trumpet, Ulf Lindberg on piano, Holger Gross on banjo, and Bo Juhlin playing tuba. On the next day, they traveled to Stockholm to appear at the Stampen Jazz Club. That performance was also recorded, but neither date was ever released. Davern appeared at the Bern Festival in Switzerland in early May and then spent May 8–13 on tour in Italy.[27]

In some respects, Lino Patruno could be called the Eddie Condon of Italy. Like Condon, he played the guitar and banjo, and his musical repertoire included songs from the New Orleans–Chicago school. He also produced concerts and recordings and, in the 1970s had a one-hour-long television show emanating from Milan that featured jazz. Many American musicians made guest appearances on the show.

Davern was featured on May 10. Backed by Patruno and a cast of local musicians that varied in size from four to seven, Kenny played three up-tempo tunes, *Cake Walking Babies from Home*, *Lullaby of the Leaves*, and *Sweet Georgia Brown*, and three slower numbers, *Mood Indigo*, *C. C. Rider*, and *Some of These Days*. He then traveled to Genoa and appeared at the Louisiana Jazz Club, playing with a group of local musicians.

Davern returned home and, on May 15, flew to Texas for the jazz party in Odessa. In the weeks to come, he played a gig with Lou Stein, a date with Wellstood, and the New Jersey Jazz Society—Newport Jazz Festival Weekend at Waterloo Village. From June 26 to July 1, he was at the King of France Tavern in Annapolis with Art Hodes and Don DeMicheal and, during that stay, recorded an album titled *Kenny Davern, The Hot Three*.[28]

Art Hodes, who was born in the Ukraine in 1904, was then almost seventy-five years old. His parents had immigrated to the United States and landed in Chicago, where Hodes grew up. As a young man, he hung out in the cafes of the South Side, where he listened to many of the great African American musicians. In the 1920s and '30s, he appeared with the Wolverines, Wingy Manone, Joe Marsala, and Mezz Mezzrow. From 1943 through 1947, he edited and published a magazine, *Jazz Record*, which, along with *The Record Changer*, was a voice of the traditional jazz faction during the wars with the advocates of bebop. He had developed a unique and basic style of playing the piano, in which his interpretations were heavily laden with the blues. He and Davern had played together from time to time and, when they added drummer Don DeMicheal to the mix, they became The Hot Three. They performed together for several years until DeMicheal's death in 1982.[29]

This recording was made in the Great Hall at St. John's University in Annapolis, Maryland, a wooden structure built in the 1700s. Davern loved the venue and the way that the music reverberated throughout the hall. The album was released on the Monmouth-Evergreen label, and the cover bore a photograph of Hodes, DeMicheal, and Davern.

There is a spark to the playing on this recording, even though many of the songs, including *Fidgety Feet, Shim-Me-Sha-Wabble, Ballin' the Jack,* and *C. C. Rider,* were part of the everyday performance repertoire of both Hodes and Davern. The seldom-played *Chimes Blues* is excellent, with both Davern and Hodes taking lyrical solos on this composition that Lil Hardin had written for the Creole Jazz Band. Kenny said of Hodes, "He's got King Oliver's band in his head when he's playing it."[30] Kenny takes an extended solo on *It Don't Mean a Thing If It Ain't Got That Swing* accompanied only by DeMicheal. *Tennessee Waltz* is a Hodes feature. Throughout the recording, Davern tailors all of his performances to Hodes' style, and the result is what would be expected from two artists who enjoyed the luxury of playing the music that they loved with someone who shared their musical views.

Sinclair Traill said that it was "one of the best clarinet records (or maybe I should say trio records), to be issued for a very long time." Jack Sohmer gave the release four and a half stars in *DownBeat* saying of Davern that "his own inviolable streak of irreverency, his own affectionate disturbances of long unstirred shores, will ultimately mark him as one of the most unique players of this genre of jazz."[31]

DeMicheal had apparently raised some questions about the placement of Kenny's name in the title of the album, and word of his inquiry reached Davern. Kenny asked Hodes about it and Art responded in a letter:

> My feelings then and now are these: if you hadn't gotten us the date in Annapolis, there'd have been no Hot Three. And we've been there four times! If you hadn't engineered the date, there'd have been no record date (and all this I'm saying I pointed out to Don). Finally, if you hadn't sold Monmouth on the date, if you hadn't talked it up in the right circles, truly, we'd have had to go to a smaller label or forget it.

Let's put this on the table clearly. I have a tremendous good feeling for Kenny Davern—period—and that stands if we never do another record again. Hopefully, we'll play music again and again. I don't know how anybody could have been more fair and above board with us.[32]

The flare-up faded away.

Over the years, Davern and Hodes played together on many occasions. Hodes had a fundamental and basic style, and rarely ventured far into advanced chord extensions. For Kenny, playing with Art meant that he had to fit into the older man's conceptions. Davern once said: "Hodes is very ethereal, he's spiritual, on his own religious trip. . . . With Art every nuance, every note counts more." There were other limitations. "With Art Hodes, you had to go his way and be flexible enough to figure out something to do without inhibiting him from going his way. Hodes had a great deal of depth. But, he had no mischief in him."[33]

There was a reward to playing with Hodes that Davern rarely discussed. Art Hodes was one of the pioneers of jazz. He had known and played with all of Davern's idols, the great musicians of the early days in New Orleans and Chicago. Now, Kenny Davern, raised in Queens, New York, and barely half of Hodes's age, was standing in the same place that Oliver, Armstrong, Dodds, Noone, Teschemacher, and all of the other pioneers had stood. It was the same rush that he felt when, at age sixteen, he stood on the bandstand with Red Allen in that American Legion Hall.

It was the same when he played with Yank Lawson and Bob Haggart, Pee Wee Erwin, Pee Wee Russell, Jack Teagarden, Bud Freeman, Eddie Condon, and all of those earlier-generation musicians. They were his heroes, and now they had accepted him as an equal. For someone who was never convinced that he was as good as others said he was, this was heady stuff. And, although he would receive awards and accolades attesting to his greatness, the thrill of walking the same path as his idols continued until the end of his life.[34]

Directly after the recording date with Hodes, Davern opened at Condon's for a week, played a Sunday gig at Liberty State Park, returned for another week at Condon's, and then worked some short local jobs. He returned to the recording studio on July 26, 1979.[35] Pianist Lou Stein, along with Milt Hinton and Connie Kay, participated in several recording sessions to complete an album that was released on World Jazz under the title *Lou Stein and Friends*. Four tunes were recorded in a trio setting, four more with Bucky Pizzarelli on guitar, and still another four with Davern. Stein was the featured performer on all of them, which have a relaxed air, as if the musicians were casually sitting around and playing. The music is pleasant, but far from exciting. On *What Is This Thing Called Love, Let's Face the Music and Dance,* and *The Sweetest Sound,* Davern plays less than a chorus, never straying far from the melody or generating any heat. He has two solos on *A Fine Romance.* Also in mid-July, he began an eight-week series of Monday-night appearances at Mary's Husband's Pub in South Belmar, New Jersey. Jazz was not the only attraction at the venue: An article in a local newspaper mentioned that the pub featured turtle races at noon on Mondays.[36]

Gus Statiras, the producer of Progressive Records, staged a two-day jazz festival at Waterloo Village at the beginning of August, and Davern was one of the featured musicians. He was at O'Connor's, played a gig with Maxine Sullivan in Katonah, New York, traveled to Colorado for the Gibsons' annual Labor Day party, played a wedding with Pee Wee Erwin, and left on his fall trip to England and the Continent.

After a layover in London, he arrived in Vienna for a three-day gig on September 13. He returned to England for some one-night stands outside of London, had two days in the capital at Pizza Express in Dean Street, then performed in Glasgow and Edinburgh before returning home on October 2.[37] He immediately went back on the road, playing a party in Corpus Christi, Texas, followed by a week in Billings, Montana, with Ralph Sutton and Gus Johnson, Jr. Then it was on to Annapolis for a week. He was home for most of November, opened December at Fat Cat McCree's festival in Manassas, Virginia, then went on to Northampton, New Hampshire, to record at Charlie Baron's home.[38]

Baron had been present at the Gibsons' 1979 Labor Day party where pianist Ralph Sutton had been paired in a two-piano setting with Jay McShann. A longtime fan of Sutton's, he thought that the duet should be recorded, and the principals agreed. Once Baron set the wheels in motion, he decided to record Sutton in several different musical settings. He created a record label, *Chaz Jazz,* and brought Sutton and cornetist Ruby Braff into a studio in New York City for an album of duets, which was followed by a quartet album.

In December 1979, Sutton flew from his home in Colorado to Northampton, where Baron had built a recording studio under his house. On the 10th and 11th, he recorded an album of piano solos and, as the second day was coming to an end, Davern and Gus Johnson, Jr., arrived. The three musicians got along well. Kenny would make a batch of Bloody Marys in the morning, Gus would cook up ham hocks and beans, and Ralph would make his hot sauce. Occasionally, they would go downstairs to record a few tracks, but would soon return to the food and drink. The result was two long-playing albums, issued on the Chaz Jazz label as the *Ralph Sutton and Kenny Davern, Trio, Volumes 1 and 2*.[39]

Volume 1 begins with a powerhouse rendition of *That's a Plenty*, one of the few up-tempo numbers in the batch. The second track of the long-playing record is an infectious, calypso-grounded *Jazz Me Blues*, followed by a three-minute selection cleverly titled *Gus Que Raf* that features Sutton and Johnson playing several choruses of rhythmic variations on *Jazz Me Blues*. (When the two LPs were combined on a single CD, this track was omitted.) The other tunes include *Take Me to the Land of Jazz*, which features Davern's second (and last) recorded vocal, *My Honey's Lovin' Arms*, and *I Would Do Anything for You*.

Volume 2 begins with Sutton providing his patented, rolling, express-train background as Davern powers through *St. Louis Blues*. Both of them excel on *Am I Blue*, which has some exceptionally expressive moments, as does the Irving Berlin composition, *All by Myself*. Among the other songs they recorded are *Tain't Nobody's Business If I Do* (which is Sutton's vocal feature) and a bluesy *My Daddy Rocks Me*. There was an unexpected bonus for Davern. Baron had used an RCA Model 44 microphone at the recording sessions, and Kenny liked the way it captured the sound of his horn. Baron eventually gave it to him, and Davern frequently brought it with him and insisted that it be used to record him.

After a few local appearances, and a week-long date in Annapolis with Charlie Byrd, Davern, along with Yank Lawson, George Masso, Eddie Miller, Lou Stein, Bob Haggart, and Bobby Rosengarden left New York and flew to Perth, Australia, where they performed as the World's Greatest Jazz Band. They played on Christmas day in Sydney, then went on to Perth where they spent the 26th through the 31st. For the first two days of the new year, they were in Adelaide, then on to Melbourne for two days, finishing up on January 5, 1980, in Sydney.[40]

Their programs on December 28–30 were recorded, and portions of them were released. Unfortunately, on some of the sessions the balance was off: several of the performers were over-amplified, while others could barely be heard. Davern was featured on *My Baby Rocks Me* and on *Everybody Loves My Baby*, where he was accompanied only by Lawson and Rosengarden.

Thus, the decade of the 1970s came to an end. For Davern, they were a tumultuous time. In a period of ten years, he had transformed himself from a rootless and restless man in his thirties to a husband and father with a stable and loving home life. The sideman who was known primarily to musicians and fans in the New York–New Jersey area was now a leader who was recognized and respected throughout the United States and overseas.

Notes

1. Wilber/Webster, 131–132; conversation with Elsa Davern.
2. Bob Wilber, Letter to the Editor, *Jazz Journal International*, 32, no. 10 (October 1979), 5; Wilber/Webster, 131–132.
3. Conversation with Elsa Davern; Rusch interview part 1, pp. 21–22; Marty Grosz, interview by the author.
4. Davern on Fresh Air Interview; Bob Wilber, Letter to the Editor, *Jazz Journal International*, 32, no. 10 (October 1979): 5; Wilber/Webster, 131–132. However, in an interview in 1989, Davern said that he did not want Soprano Summit to end, placed the blame on Wilber, and hinted at other factors that precipitated the breakup. Rusch interview part 1, pp. 20–22.
5. Bucky Pizzarelli, interview by the author. Chris Sheridan, "Arne Domnerous/Bob Wilber, Rapturous Reeds," *Jazz Journal International*, 32, no. 11 (November 1979): 31.
6. Davern, Dirks, 6.
7. Michael Woods interview.
8. Quoted in John S. Wilson, "A First for Two Clarinetists at Heavenly Jazz Session," *New York Times*, 11 December 1981.
9. Bob Wilber, *Jazzspeak, Summit Reunion*, Chiaroscuro CRD 311.
10. Kenny Davern, quoted in Davern, Klett, 22.
11. Barry McRae, "Steve Lacy," *Jazz Journal International*, 57, no. 8 (August 2004): 16–17.
12. Kenny Davern, on Davern-Morgenstern, Interview 1.
13. D.M., *Jersey Jazz*, 8, no. 3 (April 1980): 11. The identity of the reviewer is lost in time. However, as the material in text demonstrates, and Dan Morgenstern insists, it is clearly not him.
14. Whitney Balliett, "Unexpected," *New Yorker*, 30 September 1979: 124.
15. Dan Morgenstern, "Kenny Davern, Unexpected," *Jazz [U.S.A.]* Winter 1979, 74–75.
16. Dan Morgenstern, interview by the author.
17. Barry McRae, "Kenny Davern, Unexpected," *Jazz Journal International*, 33, no. 4 (April 1980): 39.
18. However, it was one of the very few albums made by Kenny that his wife did not like, and he never played it in her presence. Elsa Davern, conversation with the author.
19. Warren Vache, interview by the author.
20. Ed Polcer, interview by the author.
21. Kenny Davern, in the Michael Woods interview.
22. Warren Vache, Jr., interview by the author.
23. Date Book; letters from Kenny Davern to Elsa Davern; letter to Kenny Davern from Judaine Music, dated 6 September 1978; *Mississippi Rag*, vi, no. 12

(December 1978): 6; World's Greatest Jazz Band Tour Itinerary; Vache, Erwin, 361–362; Date Book.

24. In 2009, George Buck released a DVD on his Jazzology label titled *After Hours at Art's Place* that included a segment featuring Davern and Hodes performing on a sound stage made up to look like a club. The liner notes say only that the performance dates from 1979. However, the screen credits at the end of the segment say that it was produced in Minneapolis. The only time that Davern was in Minnesota in 1979 was on this date with Hodes at the Emporium. Peerless Program Notes, 44; *Jersey Jazz*, 6, no. 11 (January 1979): 23; *New York Times*, 26 January 1979, C19; Date Book; event contract; *Jersey Jazz*, 7, no. 4 (May 1979): 9.

25. Ron D. Johnson, "Goodbye Soprano, Hello Clarinet," *Mississippi Rag*, vii, no. 4 (April 1979): 1.

26. In *Giant Strides*, I said that both of these recordings were made at the Manassas Jazz Festival on 30 November–2 December 1973. See pp. 106, 219–220. I thought that the insert to FCJ 240, which dated that recording on 30 March–1 April 1979 was incorrect. In fact, I was incorrect. Davern's Date Book confirms that he, Wellstood, and Kohlman were at the King of France Tavern in Annapolis 30 March–1 April 1979. Although Davern and Wellstood were at Manassas in 1973, there is no evidence that Kohlman was there. Also, recordings issued on Fat Cat Jazz (FCJ) from late 1973 bear catalog numbers ranging from 155 through 178. By 1979, Fat Cat Jazz's releases were numbered in a range over 200. Although the numbering on FCJ releases was not always chronological, it is more likely that these recordings, numbered FCJ 239 and 240, were issued in 1979. Accordingly, I have concluded that these cassettes were recorded on 30 March–1 April 1979 at the King of France Tavern in the Maryland Inn in Annapolis.

27. Date Book; letter from Kenny Davern to Elsa Davern dated 25 April 1979; Lord Discography; Festival Event Program.

28. Date Book; *Jersey Jazz*, 7, no. 5 (June 1979): 5.

29. See Art Hodes and Chadwick Hansen, *Hot Man, The Life of Art Hodes* (Urbana, IL, University of Illinois Press, 1992), 20–42.

30. BBC interview.

31. Sinclair Traill, "Kenny Davern, The Hot Three," *Jazz Journal International*, 33, no. 12 (December 1980): 33; Jack Sohmer, "The Hot Three," *DownBeat*, 42, no. 2 (February 1981): 31.

32. Letter from Art Hodes to Kenny Davern, dated 11 June 1980.

33. Kenny Davern, interview by the author; BBC interview.

34. Kenny Davern, Elsa Davern, conversations with the author.

35. Most discographies date this recording from around 1980. The entry in Davern's Date Book for 26 July 1979, says "Record Lou Stein, National Studios, Edison Hotel, 2–5." This is the only recording that Davern made where Stein was the leader. There are no other entries in Davern's 1979 or 1980 Date Books that could refer to this recording.

36. Gretchen Schmidhauser, "Dixieland Thrives in South Belmar," *Asbury Park Press*, 22 (August 1979): B7.

37. Date Book; Raymond B. Cushing, "Jazzpeople Roll Out a Musical Magic Carpet for a Marriage," *The Advocate*, 14 September 1979, 17; *Jazz Journal International*, 32, no. 9 (September 1979): 4; *Jazz Journal International*, 32, no. 12 (December 1979): 13.

38. *Jersey Jazz*, 7, no. 9 (November 1979): 14; Date Book.

39. Schacter, Sutton, 243 *et. seq.* Kenny Davern on the Fresh Air Interview.

40. Date Book; letter dated 5 December 1979 from John Healty to Kenny Davern, and itinerary dated 7 December 1979.

CHAPTER NINE

Out Front

The first two months of every year were usually the slowest for Davern. Paying for the excesses of the Christmas season consumed everyone's disposable cash, and there were few club jobs or private parties. He returned from Australia on January 5, 1980, and was idle until the 13th, when he had a job with Tony DeNicola, then did not work for two more weeks.

The situation improved in February. He was at Jimmy Weston's on the 1st and 2nd. Bobby Rosengarden again had the contract for the band at the Rainbow Grill, and he again hired Davern. After ten days, Kenny left to work with Art Hodes and Don DeMicheal. He played the Pee Wee Russell Memorial Stomp, rejoined Rosengarden for two days, then did two more days with Art Hodes, and an evening at the Chicago Restaurant in White House, New Jersey.[1]

President and Mrs. Jimmy Carter hosted a formal dinner for West German Chancellor Helmut Schmidt on March 5, 1980. Music for the occasion was furnished by a nine-piece band consisting of Davern along with Pee Wee Erwin, Jimmy Maxwell, Joe Newman, Vic Dickenson, Budd Johnson, Lou Stein, Milt Hinton, and Bobby Rosengarden. On the following evening, David Rockefeller, chairman of the board of the Chase Manhattan Bank, gave a dinner for Schmidt. Derek Smith played for the cocktail hour: his repertoire included *Brother, Can You Spare a Dime*. The Bobby Rosengarden Jazz Band, comprised of Warren Vache, Jr., George Masso, Davern, Smith, bassist Michael Moore, and Rosengarden, played for dancing.[2]

From then, Davern was on the road. He traveled to Scottsdale for a party, followed by an engagement in Billings. He spent the first week of April at the Maryland Inn, performed at Jack Kleinsinger's Highlights in Jazz Concert, and then went to New Orleans for three weeks. He had a week at home, and then a two-day gig in San Antonio, followed by the Odessa Jazz Party.[3]

After finishing up in Texas, Davern and Pee Wee Erwin traveled to Hollywood. There they joined trombonist Bob Havens, Eddie Miller, pianist Dick Cary, Ray Leatherwood on bass, and drummer Nick Fatool in recording nine tunes that were released on the Qualtro label in an album titled *Pee Wee Erwin, Classic Jazz in Hollywood*. The repertoire was standard dixieland. Kenny took the opening statement on *Naughty Sweetie Blues*, which he played in the chalumeau range, then provided counter-melodies throughout the tune as it built to its climax. When they were touring together in the World's Greatest Jazz Band, Davern and Eddie Miller used *Hindustan* as a vehicle for challenging each other in eight-bar, and then four-bar, phrases, and they reprised that routine. Miller and Davern also had some interesting exchanges on *Rose Room*. Kenny was at his best on *Old Fashioned Love*.

One of the hallmarks of a Davern performance was a harmonic trill that he played on two notes, a third apart. He used it on *Bye, Bye, Blues*. Eddie Cook, who almost always gave Davern's recordings good reviews, called it "Kenny Davern's well-known yodeling clarinet."[4]

In June 1980, Elsa graduated summa cum laude from Kean College, with a Bachelor of Fine Arts degree. One of the teachers at school had organized a three-week tour of Greece. Because the Daverns had no money to pay for the trip, Kenny sold one of his soprano saxophones so that Elsa could have a graduation present of a twenty-one-day holiday.[5]

The late 1970s and the 1980s were halcyon years for Davern. Work was plentiful. He was busy playing club dates, concerts, jazz parties and festivals, and private jobs. At least annually, he went overseas, touring throughout Great Britain or on the Continent. The audiences were large and enthusiastic, the reviews were favorable.

At the same time, a disturbing trend began to emerge. The audience for Davern's kind of jazz was living in the suburbs, getting older, and less willing to travel to listen to music. The jazz clubs of 52nd Street had all closed in the 1960s and 1970s, as had Nick's and many of the venues downtown. Jimmy Ryan's would close in 1983, the last Eddie Condon's would close in 1985, and Jimmy Weston's would shutter its doors in 1989. Neighborhood restaurants that featured jazz abandoned the policy as costs rose and patronage changed. Although some new places featured live music, the number of openings was far smaller than the closings. Private parties and business affairs were still an important source of income. But, as time passed, there simply was less work in and around New York and the other big cities.[6]

Being hired to play at jazz festivals and jazz parties assumed a greater significance. These events were usually promoted by clubs or individuals whose membership or patron lists provided some assurance that they would have an audience sufficient to cover expenses. Most of them remained in existence throughout the decade. However, the finances of these ventures were usually thin, and one bad weekend might imperil their viability. Like the restaurants and the clubs, their audiences were also getting older and, over time, becoming smaller.

There was a large and enthusiastic audience for jazz in Great Britain and Europe. In addition to attending the summer festivals, the citizens of the United Kingdom, Denmark, Sweden, Germany, Austria, Italy, and the Netherlands came out in large numbers to hear touring American musicians in concerts and in clubs. There was also work in Australia and Japan, but the jobs were fewer and the travel time greater. Working overseas became a vital key to survival.

One of the side effects of this trend was that musicians spent progressively more time on the road. Playing a weekend festival or party in the United States usually meant that a musician was away from home for four days; going overseas extended the time by at least a day. And, if a musician had committed the time to travel to an event in Germany, Italy, or England, it made sense to book other jobs throughout Europe. Musicians began to use local promoters to arrange their tours, paying for the airfare overseas out of their own pockets or using frequent-flyer miles. By the end of the decade, Davern was booking tours overseas for between thirty and sixty days at a time, and was on the road for nearly half of the nights of every year.

Davern made his first foreign tour of the decade at the end of May. He was in Stockholm from May 28 to June 7, spent three days in Copenhagen, followed by three days in Vienna, five days in Rome, and two days in Stuttgart. He traveled to England on June 23, toured for the next three days, finished up his visit with a two-day engagement at London's Pizza Express, and returned home on June 29.

When Davern arrived in Sweden, he was met by Gosta Hagglof, who had produced the still-unreleased recordings in the previous year. He wanted Davern to continue the session, and arranged for Persson, Ornberg, Lundberg, Gross, and Juhlin to get together with him on June 7.[7]

The resulting album was called *Kenny Davern, El Rado Scuffle, a Tribute to Jimmie Noone*. It was a testament to Davern's knowledge of the obscure that, although there were a number of tunes that were clearly associated with

Noone, the title tune was one that Noone did not record until February 3, 1930, probably as a salute to the El Rado Club, where he worked after the Apex Club had closed. Were that not sufficient, Noone was the only person to ever record the tune, and he only recorded it once.

Persson's arrangements capture much of the New Orleans ensemble-style of playing and, on this and the next tune, *Apex Blues*, Davern and Ornberg faithfully reprise (although they do not attempt to sound like) the Noone and Poston roles. A frantic *You Rascal You*, with a two-chorus solo by Davern and one in half-time by Persson, is followed by a stately *Tight Like That*. Although Noone had recorded *Monday Date* in 1928, Persson's arrangement and solo on this version owes more to Louis Armstrong's recording with his Hot Five. Davern's tasteful solo is marred slightly when he seems to have turned away from the microphone. The clanking banjo underneath Davern's chalumeau opening statement on *My Daddy Rocks Me* gives the tune an almost-Ellingtonian air.

The recording of *Shine* that Noone made in 1934 was not one of his better-known efforts. But, it is one of the best tunes on this album. The group returns to the ensemble style at the beginning, and Davern plays attractive counter-melodies underneath Ornberg and then Persson. *Oh Sister, Ain't That Hot* is nothing less than torrid. It does not appear that Noone ever recorded *Trouble in Mind*, a gospel tune that is artfully executed here. Noone did record A *Porter's Love Song to a Chambermaid* in 1934, but Davern's solo here is filled with almost-staccato, cleanly articulated notes that owe much to Frank Teschemacher. The closing tune is *Blues My Naughty Sweetie Gave to Me*. Noone used to play it at a slow and stately pace, and Davern does here. Kenny rarely played it at this tempo, and his solo is mournful and very different from his other versions.

The album was not released in the United States. However, in England, *Jazz Journal International*'s reviewer called Davern's performance "excellent" and said, "His sizzling and expressive clarinet, with its molten liquid tone dominates these tracks."[8]

Immediately upon his arrival home, Davern began rehearsing for an upcoming concert. *Blues Is a Woman* was a production at Avery Fisher Hall on July 2 that was put on by George Wein's Newport Jazz Festival. It starred a number of singers, including eighty-three-year-old Sippie Wallace, and music was provided by the Classic Jazz Band, which was composed of Doc Cheatham, Vic Dickenson, Davern, Dick Hyman, Major Holley, and Connie Kay. After a festival appearance in Saratoga, New York, Davern returned to Manhattan and, for the rest of the month, he appeared in the off-Broadway production of *One Mo' Time*.

The play was written by Vernel Bagnaris and depicted a black vaudeville show in 1926 that was being performed at the Lyric Theater in New Orleans. A five-piece band was onstage throughout the production to play for the singers, dancers, and other acts. *One Mo' Time* had opened at the Village Gate in 1979, to critical acclaim. It would run in that venue and on the road for three years.[9]

August saw Davern at the Maryland Inn in Annapolis, and then back on the stage in *One Mo' Time* for a week. On August 24, he was at the Downtown Athletic Club in Manhattan for a benefit to aid an ailing Pee Wee Erwin, then recovering from surgery. He flew to Denver at the end of the month for the Gibsons' annual Labor Day party. The remainder of September consisted of one-nighters in Taos and Albuquerque, New Mexico; Boston; Wilmington, North Carolina; Chicago; and Indianapolis, interrupted by an evening in Philadelphia in *One Mo' Time*. On October 1, he left for a two-week tour of Australia.

Davern returned to the United States on October 16, 1980, and stopped in San Antonio to spend two days with Jim Cullum's Happy Jazz Band at the Landing. A Sunday date in St. Louis preceded an appearance at the Midland Jazz Party. Then Davern returned to New Jersey.[10]

November 7 marked Kenny and Elsa's tenth wedding anniversary. A number of changes had taken place in Kenny's personality during that decade. He was no longer the angry, self-doubting, possibly self-destructive person that he had been before they met. Davern would always be volatile and quick to react—it was his nature. But, he wasn't as frighteningly aggressive as he had been.

Part of the change was due to the process of aging and maturation: he had grown up. Part was due to the emotional peace that he felt having found his musical voice: his efforts were now directed at refining and improving it. But, most of it was due to the security of knowing that he had a wife whom he loved without reservation and who loved him as much, no matter how he behaved or taxed her. Together, they had a family and a home where he could go to find quiet, beauty, and security.

Elsa's life with Kenny was not always a bed of roses. He could be argumentative, would harass, pressure, and annoy her, and would know, at the time, that he was wrong for doing it. He routinely consumed alcohol and sometimes drank to excess. There were times when he used drugs that affected his behavior. He once told Frank Laidlaw: "God, I'm such a miserable husband. Elsa would have left me except I think that she's just too tired to do it."[11] But, Elsa wasn't leaving.

"One of Kenny's immeasurable gifts to me was how he played," she said. "The honesty and grace that pass from him through his horn was who I perceived Kenny to be. It sustained me during our life together—and now."[12]

He made her laugh, loved her deeply, and showed it in unexpected ways. At one of the programs at the 92nd Street Y, "the musicians had to come down the aisle playing. Kenny stopped and he kissed me—a long kiss on the lips—and he held the whole thing up. I was shocked. It was lovely."[13]

The children, Debbie and Mark, were in their teens and off at school, and Elsa began to travel with Kenny with increasing frequency. Her presence alleviated some of the aggravation and obviated the loneliness of being on the road. Kenny and Elsa spent their days together visiting museums and shopping and, when work was done, she was waiting for him at the end of an evening.

For Elsa, traveling with Kenny presented its own set of problems. She did not stay to the end of every one of Kenny's performances, and there were long stretches when she was alone. She needed something to occupy her time, and bringing brushes, paints, and canvas on extended trips was impractical. However, she had been to a museum in Santa Fe and had seen an Indian necklace made of red beads. It interested her, and she found some red and amber beads and made a necklace for herself.

> People wanted to buy it off my neck. So, I thought that this would be a good way for me to travel with Kenny and make some money, and yet be able to do my own thing when I was on the road. I wasn't going to sit in a club until two o'clock, six nights a week. So, I used to go out at five or six o'clock in the morning and go places where I'd probably get killed now—to markets—and buy beads and better pieces. Then, when I got home, I would make necklaces and sell them. . . .
>
> And there were great things to buy, especially in England. I would buy things and take them home and sell them. It was word-of-mouth. I was in a couple of galleries. I sold everything I made.[14]

November saw Davern in Washington, D.C., from the 4th through the 8th. He had a one-night stand at Bechet's, a newly opened club on the Upper East Side of New York, and then was on the road with Bobby Rosengarden. At the end of the month, he played a private party at the fashionable St. Regis Hotel. He flew to Denver for a job on December 6, then went on to spend a week in Billings.[15] He went back to Bechet's for five days with Dick Wellstood and Don DeMicheal as the Hot Three. Dan Morgenstern wrote about them: ". . . Davern isn't shy. He plays the hell out of his instrument from top to bottom. He hit some notes the other night that I hadn't heard before. Not that Davern is a show-off, he plays music. But he has achieved the mastery that allows him to take risks, and when he does, the other two are right there with him."[16]

Soprano Summit II and the two albums that Kenny cut with Ralph Sutton on the Chaz Jazz label were voted among *Jazz Journal International*'s top 20 for 1980.[17]

Beginning in the 1970s, Time-Life Records issued a series of 28 boxed sets of long-playing records under the name of *Giants of Jazz*. The series began with Louis Armstrong and included Jelly Roll Morton, Duke Ellington, Jack Teagarden, Bix Beiderbecke, James P. Johnson, Benny Goodman, and Frank Teschemacher. Each set consisted of three LPs that spanned the artist's career and a booklet that was divided into a biographical section and a section with detailed notes on the recordings. A number of well-known musicians and authors contributed to the series.

When Time-Life turned its attention to Pee Wee Russell, it asked Davern to write the section of Notes on the Records.[18] Although he apparently attempted to do so, he was unable to discipline himself to bring the project to completion. Time-Life ultimately turned to John K. McDonough for both the biography and the notes. The last page of the booklet said that the Editors gave a "special thanks" to Jeff Atterton and Kenny Davern "for their help in the preparation of the biography and the Notes on the Music."

The hectic pace of the last months of 1980 gave way to the doldrums of early 1981. From January 8 through 10, Davern, Hodes, and DeMicheal were in Annapolis, performing as the Hot Three. The were some dates with Pee Wee Erwin and Tony DeNicola, but the balance of the month was marked by open spaces in Davern's date book. Things began to get better in February, and Davern had one of his most unusual gigs. *Ryan's Hope* was the title of a daytime drama on the ABC television network. One of the plot lines called for a background of jazz, and Davern spent parts of two days at the ABC studios as part of a group that furnished it.[19]

Also in February, Reed McKenzie hosted a party at the Lafayette Country Club outside of Minneapolis. He had asked Ralph Sutton to assemble a band for the occasion, and Sutton chose Ruby Braff, George Masso, Davern, Bud Freeman, Milt Hinton, and Gus Johnson, Jr. McKenzie recorded the event and gave the tape to Charlie Baron, who released four of the tunes on his Chaz Jazz label, titled *Ralph Sutton and the Jazzband*.[20] This was a straight blowing session by seasoned professionals who were completely comfortable. The selections were all familiar warhorses—*Struttin' with Some Barbecue*, *Keepin' Out of Mischief Now*, *Ain't Misbehavin'*, and *Muskrat Ramble*. *Mischief* was the longest tunes at about thirteen and a half minutes, and *Muskrat* was the shortest at just over nine.

On February 15, the New Jersey Jazz Society (NJJS) honored Kenny as its Outstanding Musician. The award was presented at the Society's annual Pee Wee Russell Memorial Stomp, which was held at the Martinsville Inn. Davern wrote to Jack Stine, the Society's president, to express his thanks.

> When you phoned to inform me of the award-reward, I was truly flabbergasted, shocked, elated and, as many times as I can count on one hand in my life—speechless.
>
> I'm truly honored to be the recipient. Thanks to you who have chosen me. Thanks to the NJJS. Thanks to my contemporaries and peers. Thanks to my friends. Thanks to my enemies.
>
> Thank you all. I deserve it.[21]

Dick Cavett interviewed Kenny for PBS on March 3. In the middle of the month, Kenny spent ten days with Bobby Rosengarden's band at the Rainbow Room. There were appearances in Windsor, Canada, at the Theatrical Lounge in Cleveland, and the Paradise Jazz Party in Scottsdale, along with dates with Wellstood and Lou Stein.[22]

Hanratty's was a bar and restaurant that opened in 1979 on 2nd Avenue between 91st and 92nd Streets. Originally, Don Coates was the pianist-in-residence, but when he and the owner, Bradford Swett, got into a disagreement, Wellstood got the job. Dick persuaded Swett to refurbish the back room and to install a 5-foot, 9-inch Kawai grand piano for him that was always kept tuned.

Wellstood was usually there. But for the periods when he was away, he hired a number of great pianists, including Art Hodes, Tommy Flanagan, Johnny Guarnieri, Ralph Sutton, Dick Hyman, and John Eaton to cover for him. Although the place quickly became known as a room where good solo piano could be heard by appreciative audiences, there were occasions when other musicians could be heard. Davern performed there in 1979 and 1980.[23]

Davern, Wellstood, and Rosengarden had played together numerous times over the past three years. They made their only "studio" recording, *The Blue Three Live at Hanrattys*, over a three-day period in mid-April.[24] Although the restaurant was officially closed for the occasion, selected guests were invited to hear the trio perform a repertoire that spanned the lifetime of jazz.

The opening song was the first jazz piece ever recorded, *Original Dixieland One Step*, which had been performed by the Original Dixieland Jazz Band in 1917. On this outing, it was thoroughly modernized, a sprightly piece that was full of humor. Jelly Roll Morton's *Don't You Leave Me Here* came next, beginning with a breathy and plaintive-sounding clarinet, accompanied only by the drums. In nineteenth-century New Orleans, people danced the quadrille to the song that became known as *Tiger Rag*. The Blue Three played it as a medium-tempo march, restoring the original stately and dignified mien that had been lost over the years by countless performances at breakneck tempos.

Although *Back Home in Indiana* had a wistful lyric, it had become an up-tempo vehicle for dixieland bands. Ever since Davern had heard Lee Wiley sing it at Eddie Condon's funeral, he had played it slowly and with great warmth, as he did on this album. *Sweet Georgia Brown* got the usual rollicking treatment. Then Davern and Wellstood turned to one of their favorites from the modern era, *Blue Monk*, a straight-ahead, medium-tempo blues.

Joshua Fit the Battle of Jericho began and ended with Rosengarden playing tom toms underneath Kenny. Sidney Bechet had recorded the tune in 1949 for Blue Note, with Wild Bill Davidson and Art Hodes. This version, however, was clearly the inspiration of a more modern mind-set. *Please Don't Talk about Me When I'm Gone* came next, and the last tune was *Oh Peter*, composed by and a speciality for Rudy Wiedoft. It was put on the jazz map by Billy Banks' Rhythmakers, featuring Red Allen and Pee Wee Russell in 1932.

Please Don't Talk about Me When I'm Gone was another tune that Davern liked to play as a ballad, whereas others did not. When Peter Clayton interviewed him for BBC Radio 2, he asked how that came about.

> Barbra Streisand would take a normally fast tune, like *Happy Days Are Here Again* and make a beautiful ballad out of it. And somehow or other, this banal, puerile, tune of the '20s or the teens, *Please Don't Talk about Me When I'm Gone*, was also played as a slapstick, banjo, comedy routine kind of tune, or sing-along with the garter-belt, straw-hat brigade, and I just thought it would make a nice ballad.[25]

The *Blue Three* album was recorded by Charles Baron and released on his Chaz Jazz label. Audiences liked it, and the trio began to appear as the Blue Three. The name was a sufficient drawing card for Davern and Wellstood that they used it when Rosengarden could not appear and even after the three of them were no longer performing together.

The album received uniformly excellent reviews. Reviewing this album and the *Dick Wellstood, Live at Hanratty's* album, Jack Sohmer said:

> A skilled ensemble player as well, Wellstood also makes a perfect partner for the equally anointed Davern. Together, the two are capable of virtually anything within the realm of classic jazz and on this trio date they prove it without

question. . . . Space, unfortunately, does not permit a rundown of his many attributes and excellences, but suffice it to say that Kenny Davern is the most "complete" of any historically minded clarinetist now alive.[26]

The LP was voted one of *Jazz Journal International*'s top 20 for 1982.[27]

On April 19, Davern set out on a tour that would last almost two months and cover several countries in Europe, as well as the United Kingdom. Although traveling was less burdensome then than it has become recently, there were aspects of touring that irritated Davern. He listed some of them:

- Traveling anywhere with a Burt Reynolds movie.
- Arriving at the destination with little or no sleep in spite of the dozen or more "drimmels," plus tranquilizers, and going through customs (hoping they don't find your two extra cartons of American cigarettes), waiting for baggage, discovering that the temperature is 80 degrees and humid, and your promoter hasn't arrived, and, when he does, it's two hours to the hotel where you're staying.
- Making the mistake of striking up a conversation with a neighbor after the second martini and discovering that she is a (a) neo-Nazi, (b) Jesuit in drag, (c) John Bucher, (d) communist, (e) imperialist that has a brother-in-law who played saxophone in the Catskill Mountains twenty years ago and currently is an officer in the U.S. Government's drug control enforcement agency.[28]

The first stop on the tour was Stockholm, where Davern appeared with Tomas Ornberg's band. The job ended on April 24 and, because he was scheduled to travel on the next day, Davern celebrated heavily. The next morning, Ornberg phoned Davern's room at 8:00 a.m. and asked Kenny to join him along with Hilger Gross on banjo and Bo Juhlin playing tuba on a recording date. One of the tunes that Ornberg had selected was *Too Busy* and, when Davern heard the recording, he thought that, for the only time, he sounded like "early Benny Goodman, when he was with Ben Pollack. It was a period of his playing that I particularly admired and respected. No one has ever articulated or played the clarinet like that before, with the exception of Jimmie Noone."[29]

They did another take of *Too Busy* and also recorded *Tain't Nobody's Business If I Do*, *Let's Sow a Wild Oat*, and a particularly musical rendition of *Bienville Blues*, with Davern soloing on all of the numbers in an atypical, short-phrases style that meshes well with the ambiance of the date. He was not on the balance of the record, which was completed later with a different group.

The album was titled *Tomas Ornberg's Blue Five Featuring Kenny Davern* and, when it was released, it won the Svenska Grammophon Priset for 1982. The reviewer for *Jazz Journal International* called it "A truly delightful record for those who like classic jazz.... Kenny Davern plays the clarinet in his own exciting style, as ever completely devoid of the slightest hint of cliche...." It was also one of *Jazz Journal International*'s top 20 new records for 1982.[30]

From Stockholm, Davern went to Bern, Switzerland, and then to Italy. He spent the beginning of May in London, went back to Bern for an appearance with the World's Greatest Jazz Band, then returned to London. He was in Stuttgart, West Germany, for a week, starting on May 19, then played at Nuremberg and Frankfurt before journeying to Holland on the 28th.

The Eleventh International Jazz Festival was held at Breda, where Davern appeared with Pee Wee Erwin. Pee Wee had been ill for some time; he had undergone two abdominal surgeries and was tired and in pain.[31] Kenny appeared with him on both the 28th and 29th. The performances were recorded and were posthumously released as *Pee Wee Erwin—Memorial, A Giant among Giants*. As with all of Davern's appearances with Pee Wee, the leader gave him ample space to stretch out, and he took a long, lyrical solo on *I Can't Believe That You're in Love with Me*, which included work at the very upper limits of his horn. Other tunes were *Savoy Blues*, *I Want to Be Happy*, and *Indiana*, where Davern ended his solo in the clarinet's highest reaches. From Breda, it was back to London for three days at Pizza on the Park and then, on June 4, after seven weeks on the road, Kenny flew home.

He took a week off before playing a one-night stand at the Yankee Clipper, a restaurant in Sea Girt, New Jersey. From June 18 to 21, he was at the Maryland Inn with Dill Jones and Don DeMicheal and, on the following Tuesday, he was at St. Peter's Church in Manhattan, to participate in a memorial for Pee Wee Erwin who had died on June 20. For the rest of the week, he was working at Bechet's at night and attending rehearsals during the day for a program on the 27th at Avery Fisher Hall that was part of the Kool Jazz Festival. Two days later, Davern was one of fifty-five musicians who gathered at Carnegie Hall for a benefit to establish a fund for needy musicians. The reviewer for the *New York Times* wrote:

> A performance of *Am I Blue* by Kenny Davern, clarinet, and Dick Wellstood, piano, dedicated to the late Pee Wee Erwin in which Mr. Wellstood wove a remarkable tapestry of borrowed blues and Mr. Davern with his vivid low register, his unusual leaps and plaintive wails, and his intensely dramatic use of rhythm, showed once again that he is one of the great masters of the jazz clarinet.[32]

The Kool Jazz Festival moved up to Purchase, New York, for July 4 and 5, where Davern participated in George Wein's tribute to drummer Sonny Greer. On the 8th, he was at the Changing Times Country Club in Darien, Connecticut. (One tune from the Darien date, *When You're Smiling*, has been issued on a Jump label CD.) Near the end of the month, he appeared in Cincinnati, with the Kool Jazz Festival. In between, he played two nights at Condon's, filled in for an evening with *One Mo' Time*, and had a number of dates at the Jersey Shore.[33]

Elsa's mother's family was of Hungarian ancestry. Every summer, they held a family picnic, marked by food, laughter, stories about the generations that came before, and songs. These gatherings were especially enjoyable for Kenny, who loved to listen to the tales of life in the "old country," and the haunting and beautiful melodies that had their origins in Eastern Europe. The title of his favorite song, loosely translated, was *Yonish Is Sad Because the Rats Have Eaten the Soles of His Boots*.

One year, the event was held at the home of Elsa's brother, Don, whose house was nestled away in a forest-like setting. In the middle of the festivities, Kenny abruptly left, saying he had forgotten something. Shortly thereafter, the sound of a soprano saxophone could be heard as Kenny returned, striding through the woods, wailing a Hungarian melody. "Some of the relatives laughed, and others cried. It was Kenny's way of giving the family a beautiful gift—one that they would remember."[34]

On August 1, Davern flew down to Florida for a two-week engagement at Disney World. Elsa went with him, and management put them up in a condominium. Warren Vache, Jr., was also in the band, along with a local rhythm section. As both Warren and Elsa recalled, Kenny's gift for the unpredictable reached new heights. According to Warren,

> They used to have the Village Lounge in Disney World, where they would hire jazz acts. Kenny and I went down to do this, and it was Mickey Mouse's birthday—what number birthday, I don't know. Big celebration. There's a long codicil in the contract that if there's any offensive material in your act, Disneyland has the right to tell you to take it out. No foul language—all the rest of that stuff.
>
> So, Kenny took umbrage at this, and one night—Kenny loved to talk on the microphone—he said: "We understand it's Mickey Mouse's birthday. Happy Birthday, you little f—ing rat." And, the entire room went silent. For the rest of the run, the guys in the band all thought they were going to get fired. . . . I'm not sure that we ever worked there again.[35]

After finishing at Disney, Davern stopped in San Antonio for a night before returning home, where he spent the rest of August playing at the Yankee Clipper or at the Union House. He was at the Gibsons' annual Labor Day weekend bash in Colorado Springs, which was followed by some local dates, an appearance in North Carolina, and a performance at New York University in a Jack Kleinsinger–produced program. Then it was off to the United Kingdom and Europe for five weeks of performing as the Blue Three.[36]

The Chaz Jazz release had sold well, and the trio wanted to take advantage of the public's favorable reception. However, Rosengarden had commitments that he could not break and so, until October 27, British drummer Kenny Clare filled in for him. There was little time for the musicians to see the sights of Great Britain. Their tour itinerary shows that when the musicians weren't playing, they were in a car or on a train or a plane. They played twenty-two cities in England, Scotland, and Ireland from October 6 to November 8, then flew to Sweden where they stayed from November 11 through the 22nd. They were scheduled to continue for a week in West Germany, but that part of the tour was canceled. Instead, they came home.[37]

The remainder of 1981 consisted of one-night jobs at schools, restaurants, and clubs including Trenton State College, Somerset State College, the Cornerstone, Hanratty's, and Condon's, ending on New Year's Eve at the Yankee Clipper. There were two dates that did not fall into this pattern.

On December 10, Davern participated in a recording date with Freddie Moore. By the end of 1981, Moore, who was born in 1900, had been playing drums for almost seventy years. He began playing at the age of twelve, and made his first recording with King Oliver in 1930. Moore was pianist Art Hodes' favorite drummer in New York, and they recorded together frequently. Banjoist Eddy Davis, the driving force behind the New York Hot Jazz Orchestra, arranged for Moore to spend two days recording with two different groups, during which time Moore played drums and washboard, sang, and told stories.

At the first session, Moore was supported by Warren Vache, Jr., Joel Helleny on trombone, Davern, Joe Muranyi playing clarinet and soprano saxophone, pianist Dill Jones, Davis, Lew Micallef on guitar, and Milt Hinton on bass. This was a living tribute to Moore and, for the most part, Kenny was a member of the ensemble that supported him. His only audible performance was on *Blue Turning Grey over You*, where he and Muranyi had solos. Kenny was not a member of the band that performed with Moore on the following day. Three days later, Davern was at the Church of the Heavenly Rest in a two-clarinet program with Phil Bodner, accompanied by Derek Smith, Bucky Pizzarelli, Milt Hinton, and Bobby Rosengarden.[38]

If there was a pattern to Davern's working life, it was not followed in 1982. He did not have a winter tour of Sweden and continental Europe, or a spring trip through the United Kingdom. He made no studio recordings at all, and none of his live performances was released on records. On the other side of the coin, the month of January, usually a time of little activity, was relatively busy.

Near the end of the prior year, the Cornerstone Restaurant in Metuchen, New Jersey, adopted a policy of featuring jazz on Wednesdays, Fridays, and Saturday. The house band was led by bassist Warren Vache, Sr., and when Davern appeared there on several occasions late in 1981, the audience reacted favorably. In early 1982, he was a frequent guest there, performing on seven evenings in January and ten in February.

In between, he had jobs at the Empire State Ballroom in the Grand Hyatt Hotel in Manhattan and the Grand Ballroom in the Waldorf Astoria. Davern, Hodes, and DeMicheal returned to the King of France Tavern on January 7–10, 1982, and, from the 13th through the 17th, Kenny was in Toronto.[39]

Don DeMicheal died of cancer at age fifty-three on February 4, 1982: it marked the end of the Hot Three. Kenny remembered: "We worked together, Art, Don and myself until Don's passing. We never found another drummer quite like that—for that context. It's really barrelhouse-Chicago style. It's something that you read about and you hear about. But, when it comes to performing, you can't just get anybody off the street."[40]

Davern did not have much work in February: aside from playing at the Cornerstone, there were only a few local jobs. March was decidedly better, beginning with two Tuesday-through-Saturday jobs at the Rainbow Room. In the middle of the month, he worked at the Short Hills Country Club with Dick Hyman and Bobby Rosengarden, and also played at the Boston Globe Jazz Festival for George Wein.

On March 20, Davern appeared at the Private Jazz Party (PJP) held at the Downtown Athletic Club in lower Manhattan. Produced by many of the same individuals who were active in the New Jersey Jazz Society, the PJP ran from about 11:00 a.m. to about 5:30 p.m. on Saturday and Sunday. It was open to the public for a modest admission price and, because it was timed not to conflict with anyone's high-paying, Saturday night job, the Party was able to attract the cream of the crop of musicians playing in the New York–New Jersey–Connecticut area. In the week following that job, Kenny performed at the Starlight Room of the Waldorf Astoria, did a gig at the Monmouth County Library, and then flew to Minneapolis at the end of March for a week.[41]

Although they had not yet formally organized the Minneapolis Jazz Party, Reed McKenzie and John Stevens put together a week of music with Davern, Al Grey, Flip Phillips, Ralph Sutton, Milt Hinton, and Gus Johnson, Jr. Afterward, Kenny returned to New Jersey, played some local gigs, made a one-day trip to Chicago, was at the Empire State Theater in Lincoln Center, and played the Officers' Club on Governor's Island in New York Harbor.[42]

Davern, Wellstood, and Vic Dickenson returned to the Chateau Laurier in Ottawa on May 10. Kenny then flew to Texas for the Odessa Jazz Party and, at the end of the month, he performed in the Kool Jazz Festival at the Kennedy Center in Washington, D.C. The New York Jazz Repertory Orchestra reprised its Louis Armstrong program at St. Peters Church on Lexington Avenue at East 54th Street in Manhattan on June 5. At the end of the month, Kenny spent two days at Waterloo Village for the New Jersey Jazz Society's annual picnic. Many of the intervening dates were spent at the Cornerstone and at other venues in New Jersey and New York.[43] For a short time during this period, Kenny turned columnist.

Off Beat Jazz was the bimonthly publication of the Overseas Jazz Club, an organization headquartered in Scarsdale, New York. Beginning with the paper's first issue for July–August 1982, Kenny wrote a short humorous column titled *Davern's Tavern*, that dealt with such diverse subjects as playing at jazz festivals ("Sometimes it sounds like a pet shop on fire"), dealing with audiences and festival directors, a list of "technical" information about Kenny's clarinet (Mr. Davern endorses the "'Truss' ligature"), and Kenny's encounters with Barney Bigard and Joe Venuti. A total of six of his articles were published in the paper.

Davern worked several venues on the Jersey Shore around the July 4th holiday. He appeared at the *Grande Parade du Jazz* in Nice, during the week of July 12. On the way, he stopped for a one-night stand at Sandy's in Beverly, Massachusetts, before flying on to France, where he performed with Sippie Wallace and the Classic Jazz Band. He left the Festival and appeared at the Hague on July 17, did one night in London on the 18th, and then flew home.[44]

Davern made a number of appearances at the Cornerstone during the remainder of July. He also played the first of many of what were known as "MPTF jobs." Kenny was a member of two locals in the American Federation of Musicians. He belonged to Local 802, which had jurisdiction over Greater New York and Long Island. He also had joined Local 399, headquartered in Asbury Park with jurisdiction over almost all of the Jersey Shore.

The American Federation of Musicians had established a Music Performance Trust Fund (MPTF) that was used by some local chapters to provide free concerts for communities within their jurisdiction. Local 399 had a program of such concerts, called MPTF jobs, using the Fund to pay part of the cost of the musicians, with the balance being paid by the local town. The performances were usually held during the day and lasted about two hours. Although the pay was modest, Kenny took them whenever he was available, usually appearing with guitarist Vinnie Corrao, bassist Mickey Golizio, and a local drummer.[45]

Corrao, who lives in Point Pleasant, New Jersey, had grown up listening to Miles Davis. Over the years, he had played with Ella Fitzgerald and, in the summer of 1975, had joined the Ruby Braff–George Barnes Quartet upon the recommendation of its bassist, Michael Moore. He met Kenny Davern at the festival in Nice that year and, upon returning to the United States, shared a ride home with him from the airport (Point Pleasant is not far from Manasquan). When they began to play together, Corrao was not completely familiar with the music that Kenny liked to play. He learned by spending time at Davern's home, listening to recordings and analyzing them.[46]

Davern began the month of August at Waterloo Village in Stanhope, New Jersey, in a version of the Blue Three that consisted of Wellstood and Tony DeNicola. He had a job at Pier 6 in Baltimore, played some local jobs, and appeared at the Second Annual Jersey Shore All American Jazz Concert in Ocean Grove.

As usual, he was at the annual Gibsons' Labor Day party, held at Denver's Fairmont Hotel on September 4–6. He sandwiched in a job at the Hotel Pierre in New York City with Bobby Rosengarden and some dates at the Cornerstone until, from September 17–19, he played the Third Annual North Carolina Jazz Festival in Wilmington. Kenny's date book records that from the 20th to the end of the month, he was on vacation.[47]

When he came off his holiday, he traveled to Denver for two days, starting on October 1. Davern had several dates with Bobby Rosengarden, and did one night at the Soundstage on West 52nd Street in Manhattan with his old friend, Roswell Rudd. The Midland Jazz Party occupied his time starting on the 13th, and he had five dates at the Cornerstone before October ended.

Davern's second trip abroad occurred during the first two weeks of November, when he appeared at the Pizza Express in Dean Street, in London's Soho district. There were some dates at the Cornerstone, and between them, he drove to Vienna, Virginia, to appear at Wolf Trap with Wellstood and Rosengarden as the Blue Three. The trio also performed at Somerset College in New Jersey, and were on the program at Loeb Auditorium on the campus of New York University for a salute to Doc Cheatham. Kenny and Wellstood were at Hanratty's on the 21st, and Davern had jobs with Rosengarden at the Grand Hyatt and Pierre Hotels in New York; the Hilton in Danbury, Connecticut; and, on New Year's Eve in Hot Springs, Virginia. At the end of the year, *Jazz Journal International*'s Readers Poll named Davern as the best clarinet player for 1982. Bob Wilber was voted best on soprano saxophone, and Davern, who had not played a soprano saxophone in public for almost four years, came in fourth.[48]

As the new year began, things were going well for the members of the Blue Three. Davern and Rosengarden worked at the Grand Hyatt on January 3rd, then the trio played at the Maryland Inn for five days. Kenny flew to Topeka, Kansas, for a one-night date with Al Cohn on the 16th, and then went back to the Chateau Laurier Hotel in Ottawa for a week. He played a job with Rosengarden on the 23rd, and went into Hanratty's with Wellstood on the following day. On February 8, 1983, Wellstood, Rosengarden, and Davern traveled to Lexington, Massachusetts, to cut a demo tape at the studio of Dick Burwen. The selection of tunes was eclectic, ranging from well-known pieces such as *Sweet Lorraine, Sweet and Lovely, How Come You Do Me Like You Do,* and *If Dreams Come True,* to a romantic *Blue and Sentimental,* an infectious calypso-beat *St. Thomas,* and Luis Russell's *Jersey Lightning.* One week later, the trio left for England for a three-week tour.

They played at the Canteen in London, then visited Oldham, Yalding in Kent, Leicester, Eastleigh, and the Isle of Man. They had dates in Switzerland and Glasgow. At the beginning of March, they were back in London and, on March 6, they flew home.[49]

The Blue Three was a casualty of the trip. Davern recalled how it happened.

> We had three very strong individuals with very singular drinking habits, and there was a bit of friction going on. Wellstood might not like some of the things that Rosengarden or I did; so he might sulk. Or Rosengarden might have had a nip too many, so he wouldn't like Dick's attitude on the bandstand. And then, one day, for some flukey accident, Rosengarden and I had a to-do and we didn't speak for the rest of the tour.[50]

The "flukey accident" to which Davern referred occurred onstage during one of Rosengarden's solos, when Kenny pulled the plug on Bobby's microphone out of the amplifier. Rosengarden got upset and, after he and Davern exchanged insults, Rosengarden stalked off the stage into the bar. When Wellstood tried to get the drummer to return to the stage, he was met with a shouted "F— you," whereupon, Dick announced, "Ladies and gentlemen, Dick Wellstood and His Famous Orchestra featuring Kenny Davern will now perform for you."[51] It was only one of several such incidents that occurred among Davern, Wellstood, and Rosengarden, but it turned out to be the last.

It took some time for the principals to calm down and resume a civilized discourse. They limped along for several months, fulfilling engagements that they had made as the Blue Three. But the damage was done and, after they performed in Europe in the summer, Davern, Wellstood, and Rosengarden stopped appearing together.

The breakup of the trio did not affect the friendships between Davern and Wellstood and Davern and Rosengarden: to the contrary, Kenny continued to work and to socialize with both of them. All three musicians continued to make efforts to interest record producers in issuing the demo tape that they had made in Dick Burwen's studio. There were no takers.

Notes

1. Date Book; *Jersey Jazz*, 7, no. 11 (January 1980): 3, and 8: *Wilmington Star News*, 17 February 1980, 4-D.

2. Vache, Erwin, 364–365; Peerless Program Notes, 40; letter dated 27 February 1980 to Davern on White House Stationery; dinner program; *Jersey Jazz*, 8, no. 3 (April 1980): 9.

3. Vache, Erwin, 365, 378; Date Book; *New York Times*, 13 April 1980.

4. Eddie Cook, "Pee Wee Erwin, Classic Jazz in Hollywood," *Jazz Journal International*, 35, no. 3 (March 1982): 27.

5. Elsa Davern, interview by the author.

6. There were always a number of places like the Cajun in Manhattan and the Cornerstone in New Jersey that hired well-known musicians during the week. But the pay was relatively miniscule. Musicians took those jobs because they paid something and were better than sitting at home.

7. Gosta Hagglof, liner notes to *Kenny Davern, El Rado Scuffle, a Tribute to Jimmie Noone*, Kenneth KS 2050, October 1980. The band recorded thirteen tunes that day, which were sufficient to complete an album. The cuts from 1979 were never commercially released.

8. Eddie Cook, "Kenny Davern, El Rado Scuffle, a Tribute to Jimmie Noone," *Jazz Journal International*, 34, no. 6 (June 1981): 34.

9. Date Book; July 2, 1981 program; Peerless Program Notes, 20.

10. *Jersey Jazz*, 8, no. 9 (November 1980): 12; Date Book; Vache, Erwin, 382.

11. Frank Laidlaw, interview by the author.

12. Elsa Davern, interview by the author.

13. Elsa Davern, interview by the author.
14. Elsa Davern, interview by the author.
15. Date Book; Schacter, Sutton, 230.
16. Dan Morgenstern, "Hot Three Are Sizzling," *New York Post*, 19 December 1980.
17. *Jazz Journal International*, 34, no. 1 (January 1981): 23, (musician) and 34, no. 2 (February 1981): 5 (album).
18. He was also a consultant on Time-Life's Teschemacher set, as were Artie Shaw and Frank Chace.
19. Date Book.
20. Charles Baron, *Liner Notes to Ralph Sutton and the JazzBand*, Chaz Jazz CJ 113.
21. Kenny Davern, Letters to the Editor, *Jersey Jazz*, 9, no. 3 (April 1981): 8, reprinted in *Jersey Jazz*, 20, no. 8 (October 1992): 43.
22. John S. Wilson, "Jazz, Bobby Rosengarden Leads His All-Stars at the Rainbow Room," *New York Times*, 16 March 1981; Date Book.
23. Meyer, *Giant Strides*, 136 *et. seq.*
24. For 14–16 April, Davern's Date Book reads "record w/D.W. + Rosengarden. Hanratty's record afternoon only."
25. Kenny Davern, interviewed by Peter Clayton, 22 April 1984 and broadcast on *The Sounds of Jazz* on BBC Radio 2.
26. Jack Sohmer, "The Blue Three at Hanratty's," *Cadence*, 8, no. 4 (April 1982): 49.
27. *Jazz Journal International*, 36, no. 2 (February 1983): 6.
28. Kenny Davern, unpublished writing.
29. Davern Morgenstern interview 2.
30. David Badham, "Tomas Ornberg's Blue Five Featuring Kenny Davern," *Jazz Journal International*, 35, no. 3 (March 1982): 37, 38; *Jazz Journal International*, 36, no. 2 (February 1983): 6.
31. Vache, Erwin, 387–394.
32. John S. Wilson, "A Night to Benefit Colleagues," *New York Times*, 1 July 1981.
33. Document in the possession of Elsa Davern; *New York Times*, 26 June 1981; Date Book.
34. Elsa Davern, interview by the author.
35. Warren Vache, Jr., interview by the author.
36. Date Book.
37. United Kingdom tour itinerary; Date Book.
38. Date Book; John S. Wilson, "A First for Two Clarinetists at Heavenly Jazz Session," *New York Times*, 11 December 1981.
39. Date Book.
40. Kenny Davern, interviewed by Peter Clayton, recorded and broadcast on *The Sounds of Jazz* on BBC Radio 2 on 22 April 1984.

41. Date Book; *Jersey Jazz*, 10, no. 2 (March 1982): 12, and 10, no. 5 (June 1982): 22.

42. Elsa Davern, interview by the author; Date Book.

43. Date Book; document in the possession of Elsa Davern; Kennedy Center event program; *Jersey Jazz*, 10, no. 5 (June 1982): 4, and 10, no. 6 (July–August 1982): 15.

44. Document in the possession of Elsa Davern; Date Book.

45. E-mails to the author from Dorian Parreott and John Luckenbill of Local 399; Elsa Davern, interview by the author.

46. Vinnie Corrao, interview by the author.

47. Gibson party lineup; Date Book; *Jersey Jazz*, 10, no. 7 (September 1982): 6.

48. *Jersey Jazz*, 10, no. 8 (October 1982): 5; Date Book; *Jazz Journal International*, 36, no. 2 (February 1983): 13.

49. Date Book; *Jazz Journal International* 36, no. 2 (February 1983): 3.

50. Kenny Davern, interview by the author.

51. Meyer, *Giant Strides*, 148; Kenny Davern, interview by the author.

CHAPTER TEN

Public Person, Private Man

Audiences liked Kenny Davern: he engaged them. He talked about the music, kibbitzed with the other musicians, and joked with the customers—all the time with a wicked twinkle in his eye, as if he and they were party to some naughty secret. It was not accidental.

One of the secrets to Davern's popularity was that he understood that there was more to performing than just playing music. He told an interviewer: "You must relate to your audience, you must communicate with them, you must know what their pulse is, what they feel. They're there to see you and hear you, and it's the least you can do, to involve them. It's very important to create a relaxation, a tension, and a rapport."[1] At another time he said: "The music that we play has been relegated to a sanctified role, where everybody is supposed to sit there and not talk. You're supposed to deliver some kind of emotional message to them. It's garbage. You're supposed to dance, have a good time, talk. Get up, flirt, whatever."[2]

He worked at maintaining that rapport throughout a performance. Between songs, he would tell anecdotes about the music or the musicians. If the mood was upon him, he would tell long jokes and stories. He was a skilled raconteur, with a gift for the sound of language and could easily transform himself into an Irish priest or an Italian doctor. Without missing a beat, he could assume the role of an English barrister, an Arab beggar, a Jewish businessman, or an Indian fakir. It was all calculated to create a warm and comfortable atmosphere for the audience, as well as for the musicians.

It was a talent that endeared him to some producers. For over twenty years, Dick Hyman was the Musical Director of the *Jazz in July* series at the 92nd Street YMHA. in New York, and he chose Kenny to play for at least one concert every year. "Kenny was a regular at the Y because of the emotion and confidence of his playing. He communicated directly with the audience. Now and then he'd say something shocking and funny in his announcements. . . . The audience loved him, and so did Hadassah Markson, the series' producer."[3]

Brian Peerless was his friend and promoter. When Davern traveled to England, it was Peerless who drove him to and from his nightly performances and watched as audiences reacted to him.

> He had charisma, is what he had. From the moment he was up there, he would have the audience in the palm of his hand. In the years that I knew him, he would tell very long jokes that went on forever. But it didn't make any difference. People liked it. They didn't seem to mind what he did. He had that thing, that magic—a presence. People used to say "When's Kenny coming over?" Once he got to them, they were fans for life. . . . It was magic, wasn't it?[4]

But, when the chatter ended and the music began, Kenny Davern was all business. Randy Reinhart remembered: "One thing Kenny did, every time he stepped on the stand is, he came to play." As James Chirillo said: "As soon as he put that clarinet in his mouth, it was one hundred percent. He never gave it any less, whether he was playing at some festival in Europe or the Cornerstone." John Trentacosta, who played with him in Albuquerque echoed that opinion.

> No matter where he was playing—in the Baja Grill, this little fast food burrito joint in Santa Fe—the level of his playing was always at the top. No matter what, no matter who the audience was, no matter how many people were there, he would go for it. He went for the best and he expected that from everybody in the band.[5]

For Davern, there was more to making music than trying to think of an appealing sequence of notes and then playing them. Kenny said: "It's a means of trying to put the frustration, joy, pain, and beauty that one can feel through the instrument."[6]

Playing the clarinet was an emotional experience in which Kenny sought to become at one with the music. In every respect, it was the antithesis of planning and conscious thought. He once said, "The idea is to get in touch with your subconscious immediately if not sooner and evaporate from your situation and your physical environment immediately. Don't pass go, don't collect $200, just get out, tune in, and dance with the music. . . . It's a dance basically."[7] Kenny amplified on that in an interview with Mark Weber early in 2006.

> All I'm trying to do is to get to my subconscious as fast as I can, just to get away from myself. Then, whatever happens, happens. I plan nothing. I'm a creature of what goes on around me, what I have to play and who I have to play off of, or with, and what my audience is about. That determines my performance. It doesn't matter if I play *Three Blind Mice* or *Lady Be Good*. The thing that's going to happen—if it does happen—is that I've stepped out of myself and I'm watching myself dance with whatever's going on.[8]

Watching Davern in performance confirmed that he was no longer focused on his surroundings. He would stand with his neck slightly bent, clarinet pointed toward the floor. Once he launched into his solo, his eyelids would be squeezed tightly shut, occasionally fluttering open, but seeing nothing. His eyebrows seemed to be independent forces. They moved in response to impulses that only he understood—sometimes together, usually separately. His cheeks would fill with large quantities of air, and the swelling of his face, now turned dark red, would extend over his jaw line and into his neck. He seemed to frown with intensity at some phrases.

Sometimes he stood stock still, with his legs spread apart; at other times, he rocked back and forth in time to the music, and there were times that he swayed gently from side to side. Occasionally, during a medium-tempo passage, he might unconsciously lapse into a momentary shimmy, sinuously moving his hips and shoulders, before reverting back into immobility. As his solo came to an end, he would open his eyes, take stock of his surroundings, and then pass the spotlight to one of his cohorts.

Reaching that place—achieving that state of mind—was a goal that he did not always attain. But, on those rare occasions when he did, the experience was indescribable. Kenny said:

> You work for that. If it happened once a year when I was a kid, just that one time would keep me practicing for the rest of the year. And soon, it might happen twice a year, and then maybe three times a year. And soon, my goodness gracious, you look for it around the corner every time you take your horn out of the case. And this, of course, is an absurdity. It will not happen all the time. But you get to a certain kind of professional expertise, you get to that point where you can emulate it. But it's better when you're really feeling it. It's a

dance that you don't even want to describe to anyone. That's how wonderful it is. That's what's kept me in music for fifty some-odd years, through thick and thin.[9]

Playing with Davern when he was able to reach that state was a joy to behold and to hear. But, when he was unable to get there, it affected him. He admitted: "I become outraged. I become angry. I'll mumble, or grumble, and start swearing. I become very scatological."[10] Sometimes the problem lay within him: he was not in the right frame of mind, or was weary, or didn't feel well. Whatever the cause, he just could not get where he wanted to go. On those occasions, the horn became his enemy, he treated it like a living thing that was standing between him and the place he wanted to be. And he hated it! He would rip the clarinet from his mouth in the middle of a solo, glare at it and curse it aloud, jam it back between his teeth, and continue playing without missing a beat.

There were other times when the fault lay with the musicians with whom he was playing.

"He had the highest possible standards," said Jon-Erik Kellso. "And I loved that about him. Kenny did not suffer fools gladly. If other musicians onstage didn't take their parts seriously, or serve their functions in the band according to Davern's expectations, he'd shoot them a look, or worse—letting them know in no uncertain terms he was not happy with them."[11]

There was a reason why Davern would not tolerate slacking off on a gig. As Mat Domber observed, "To him, it wasn't just a job, it was a life. . . . It was more than a job, more than coming to a recording session, more than playing an instrument."[12] His heart and soul were in it. Warren Vache, Jr., put it as follows: "Sometimes he was happy—very often he was not—with the way that another person played. Kenny had a very specific idea of what was supposed to happen when you got on a bandstand. And, if it didn't happen his way, he could throw a hissy fit."[13]

Greg Cohen was Davern's bassist of choice for about the last fifteen years of his life. He played with Kenny in the best of times and when things were not as Davern wanted them to be.

> When, in the height of what he was doing, it was not about Kenny Davern, who had just been grumpy, or Kenny Davern, a big mensch and close friend. It was about Kenny Davern, a guy who had reached that plateau in the realm of music where he leaves the everyday world. He's crossed over into the world of pure music. And, if he wasn't allowed to get there, for whatever reason, whether it be his own body's faults—being tired, or in a bad mood, or one thing

or another—he would get pissed at himself and often grumpy with others. And with a musician he knew to be capable, but who was just not able to free up the space in his mind for the music to have the air and breathe—he would get crazy, and he would lose some of his "social skills." This was the biggest insult to him, because he really was a man in love with music. He expected that of his peers.[14]

Not everyone found Davern's idiosyncratic behavior to be charming, or even acceptable. As noted earlier, many club owners, and festival and jazz party producers who had been on the receiving end of Kenny's unkind remarks chose not to rehire him. Davern usually knew when he had crossed the line and talked himself out of a job. But, he was loath to admit what he had done. His wife Elsa remembered: "The funny thing is that he wouldn't always tell me. I'd ask him 'How come you don't do this party or that party anymore?' He'd come up with some excuse of why he wasn't invited. Two or three years afterward, he'd tell me the truth. He insulted somebody or he did this or that. What could I say?"[15]

There were friends who parted company with him over a thoughtless comment. Others, like Frank Laidlaw, a friend for over fifty years, stayed the course. "To be his friend, you had to put up with a lot of shit sometimes. We all did. But, it was well worth it. [His death] leaves such a big hole—not only artistically, because there's no one who could even lift his clarinet—but also personally."[16]

Much of it was part of his onstage personality. No entertainer allows his audience to see every aspect of his life. Entertainers create a public persona that may be wholly different from their "real" or private personality, and they only allow a few friends to see behind the facade that they have erected. In the case of Kenny Davern, his private persona was not substantially different from the one that he showed to the public: it was that there were dimensions to it that few people ever perceived, no less saw.

He read voraciously—his stepson Mark called him a "book sponge"—and became knowledgeable, if not expert, in a number of subjects, wholly apart from music.[17] He was fascinated by gangland figures of the first half of the twentieth century and had an extensive collection of books about Lucky Luciano, Meyer Lansky, Al Capone, and Dutch Schultz. There was a separate group of volumes dealing with Nazi Germany, including William L. Shirer's seminal work, *The Rise and Fall of the Third Reich*, and the writings of Albert Speer.

Less extensive, but still the subject of several books each, were his interests in the Civil War, Mark Twain, Anton Chekhov, Fyodor Dostoyevsky, and

W.C. Fields. He read science fiction (of the *Frankenstein* and *Dracula* genre), had single volumes dealing with Charlie Chaplin and H.L. Mencken, and a large number of works of fiction, including several written by Pete Hamill and Carl Hiassen, the award-winning reporter for the Miami Herald.

However, his overriding interest was in music—and not only jazz. He was particularly interested in, and had large numbers of recordings of, the works of Bach, Beethoven, Mozart, Schubert, and Brahms. His library included CDs of Richard Strauss, Antonin Dvorak, and Sergei Prokofiev. He liked opera, and had several collections, including one by Maria Callas.

As would be expected, he collected recordings of classical works for the clarinet, including Mozart's *Quintet for Clarinet and Strings*, Debussy's *Premier Rhapsody for Clarinet and Orchestra*, Handel's *Overture*, Beethoven's *Duet No. 3 in B-Flat*, as well as compositions by Brahms, Dvorak, and Carl Maria Von Weber. Although Davern's method of playing the clarinet was different from the technique employed by classical musicians, he had a number of recordings by a variety of contemporary classical clarinet players including Jon Manasse, Keith Puddy, and Gary Brodie, plus a CD by four early twentieth-century French clarinet players: Louis Cahuzac, Auguste Perier, Prospere Minart, and Gaston Hamelin. His interest in other clarinet players had other facets to it: he had several recordings of Klezmer music featuring Naftule Brandwein and Dave Terras. He had become intrigued by the *biguines* of the island of Martinique, and had some recordings by Alexandre Stellio, a West Indian clarinetist.

He was interested in conductors and the way in which they interpreted particular pieces of music that he liked. Davern also paid particular attention to the sound that they coaxed from the orchestras that they led.

Of all of them, his passion was the life and work of Wilhelm Furtwangler. Born in Berlin in 1886, Furtwangler rose to become the conductor of the prestigious Berlin Philharmonic Orchestra. He never joined the Nazi party, and there is substantial evidence that shows that he was not a sympathizer, and that he helped some Jewish musicians flee Germany. Still, Furtwangler was well-treated by the Nazis, and he accommodated them; he remained as conductor of the Berlin Philharmonic throughout World War II, leaving only at the beginning of 1945, when he fled to Switzerland. During that time, he conducted at the Wagner festivals in Bayreuth that were beloved by Hitler and let himself be used as a symbol of cultural prestige by the Nazis. After the war, two schools of thought emerged about Furtwangler's conduct, those who condemned him as a Nazi collaborator and those who did not.

Davern was one of Furtwangler's champions. There was something about the dilemma that confronted him—wanting to continue to conduct the orchestra that he loved while detesting the regime that sponsored it—that struck a responsive chord. The main attraction, however, was the sound that Furtwangler could get from the orchestras he conducted. To Kenny, it was as if he could pick out the sound of each instrument in the orchestra, even as they were all playing together.[18] One of Davern's most prized possessions was a postcard that Dan Morgenstern gave to him that was written by Furtwangler to Morgenstern's maternal grandparents.

Furtwangler's performances of the pieces in his repertoire were not always the same: James Chirillo thought that it was a concept that appealed to Davern.

> It parallels the way that Kenny does it—how an arrangement develops on the bandstand. He would always do it a little differently. It wouldn't always be clarinet play the melody, clarinet play the first chorus, guitar take the next chorus, bass solo, drum solo, get out of there. He would always be mixing it up, and Furtwangler was the same way. It was a symbiotic thing between him and the players. If he was feeling a little differently—maybe the tempo had to go a little bit slower that night—he didn't try to force guys to play faster or go slower. With Furtwangler, each performance would develop a life of its own. Maybe he would feel it has to go faster and kick the tempo up from what it was the night before. It isn't true of all conductors. A lot of guys will rehearse things and say "This is the tempo for this part."
>
> There are different ways, and both approaches can be valid. But, that's the way Furtwangler liked to do things. So, you can hear different recordings of the same piece by him, and conceptually they are totally different. And that's exactly the way Kenny liked to call a tune on the bandstand.[19]

Davern had every Furtwangler recording that he could find—whether made in the studio or recorded off the air. He had every reissued and remastered release of Furtwangler's works and delighted in playing the best "Fifth," or the best "Ninth." Although almost all of them were made long before hi-fidelity was invented, and many of the air-checks were of relatively primitive quality, they were the recordings to which he listened, over and over again.[20]

He not only listened to these composers and conductors, he read about them and about the technique and art of conducting. He had numerous biographies and books about Furtwangler, and several biographies of each of Johannes Brahms, Ludwig van Beethoven, Wolfgang Amadeus Mozart, Igor Stravinsky, Herbert von Karajan, and Alban Berg. There were single volumes dealing with the lives of Bruno Walter, Dimitri Mitropoulos, Arturo Toscanini, Kurt Weill, Richard Strauss, Richard Wagner, Leopold

Stokowski, Artur Rubenstein, Arthur Schnabel, Emmanuel Feuerman, Yehudi Menuhin, Niccolo Paganini, Enrico Caruso, Cole Porter, and Adolphe Sax. In addition, there were books about the history of the clarinet, and about conductors and conducting, pianists, and opera. Most of the people with whom he discussed classical music were impressed by the breadth and depth of his knowledge.

He had an extensive collection of jazz recordings, commencing with the Original Dixieland Jazz Band, with a heavy concentration on small groups and clarinet players including Sidney Bechet, Leon Rappolo, Albert Burbank, Albert Nicholas, Johnny Dodds, Jimmie Noone, Frank Teschmacher, Omer Simeon, Benny Goodman, Artie Shaw, Irving Fazola, George Lewis, and Pee Wee Russell. There were a number of recordings by Jelly Roll Morton, McKinney's Cotton Pickers, King Oliver, Louis Armstrong, Coleman Hawkins, the Condon groups, and Mildred Bailey, and a lesser number by Duke Ellington and Tommy Dorsey. His library of books on jazz included a number of biographies.

Kenny was always excited about the things he enjoyed, and he wanted to share them with others. Many of his friends told essentially identical stories about Kenny's enthusiasm and his generosity. Howard Alden recalled visits to Davern's home in Manasquan, where Kenny would pull out recordings of performances of the same composition by various artists and play them so that Alden could hear the difference. If Alden liked what he heard, Davern would lend him the recordings.[21] Warren Vache, Jr., had several similar experiences.

> He would sit around all night long, comparing conductor after conductor after conductor—and pianist after pianist—and soprano after soprano. I came up with a recording of the *St. Matthew Passion* with Sophie von Otter, a relatively new recording. Next thing I know, in the mail are two more copies of the *St. Matthew Passion*—one of course by Furtwangler with another soloist and another where he liked the soprano best. . . .
>
> I found these late Brahms piano pieces. So, in very typical Kenny fashion "Oh, you've gotta get Backhaus. He's the guy, he studied with Brahms. That's as close to Brahms playing it as it's ever going to be." So, don't you know, in the mail, a couple of weeks later, I got three cassettes of everything that Kenny had of Wilhelm Backhaus playing Brahms. And, he's right, they're glorious recordings. Another couple of weeks go by and his technology had improved. He could burn CDs. So, he burned me CDs of Backhaus playing Brahms, so I could play them in the car.[22]

If Davern liked a recording or a book, he wanted you to enjoy it also. And, he was insistent that his friends should at least listen to or read it—if only to have the experience. Dave Frishberg was sometimes on the receiving end of Kenny's exuberance.

> I loved him from the minute I met him. I thought he was such a terrific guy. I loved his enthusiasm. He was fiercely enthusiastic about what he was reading at the time, and he would force me to read what he was reading. "Take this home and read it." Stuff that I wasn't interested in. He shoved these things at me and I would take them, not that I would always read them. . . .
>
> He got me interested in music that I didn't know about. He showed me Igor Stravinsky: all I knew was the *Firebird*. Kenny took hold of me, made me listen to all kinds of stuff, and I became a Stravinsky fan. I think it was Kenny who showed me early Duke Ellington. I knew about him as a bandleader and about him later on. But, I didn't know about the early Duke Ellington. He played me this recording—it was on Camden—of Duke's band from the Cotton Club days. Wow, that record just turned me around.[23]

Allan Vache would periodically drive down to Manasquan for a lesson from Davern. Vache would play a few tunes, and Kenny would show him some exercises and then, after an hour, Kenny would say. "Okay, it's time for a drink." He would mix up some vodka martinis and begin playing records. Sometimes, they were by jazz artists like Jimmie Noone, or Johnny Dodds, Tony Parenti, or Pee Wee Russell, and Davern would critique the performances. "This is a great thing here. But, listen to that thing. Why would he do that? What kind of harmony is that?"[24] Often, he played classical material for Vache. "He just wanted me to hear it. The whole idea was to become as well versed in music in general as possible. He was a great teacher. Because he wasn't trying to tell me 'I think you should do this or that.' What he was telling me was 'Here are your options.'"[25]

There were few ambiguities in Davern's life: he tended to see things in black and white. If he did not like someone, then that person was forever excluded from his personal group, and there was virtually nothing that could be said or done to change his opinion. If he liked someone, then he was both generous and intensely loyal. Ken Peplowski observed:

> He could be very generous with praise. He was the first person to defend his friends. If someone bad-mouthed someone, or treated him badly, he'd be the first person up to the plate. . . . He was very funny and, if you take him away from the stage—and I think he liked that persona of a crotchety guy, the turd in the punch bowl, "what are we doing here? This place looks like it used to be used for Nuremberg rallies." But, if you could get him away from that, and

in a private setting, he was actually a very warm, giving, guy—very quick with praise and, as I say, very generous with compliments and support.[26]

Jack Six, who first met Davern in the 1961 band at Nick's and remained friendly with Davern for the remainder of his life, said, "As a friend, you knew he was your friend. Or your enemy. If he was, he was your friend: there were no grays. He didn't kinda like you or kinda not like you. He would do anything for you, give you anything. He would stand up for you. He was a loyal, honest guy."[27]

He wanted to share the things that he liked with his friends. Brian Peerless believed:

> I think that a lot of people don't realize what a kind person he was. He was incredibly kind and generous. He was very generous with presents. If he found something when he was on the road, he thought you'd like, he'd get it. He was kind that way. But, he was kind with his time. If he thought people were genuine and were interested, he'd spend hours talking with them. . . . He was a very patient guy if he thought somebody was really interested.[28]

Few members of his audiences saw these facets of Davern's personality. To most of them, he was a musician who could also be very funny when he chose. They came to have him entertain them and, when the performance was over, they applauded and went home. They liked the man who they heard and saw and, if their picture of him was incomplete, it was because that was all that he let them see and, for the most part, it was all that they wanted to see.

For performers who work in the world that Kenny Davern inhabited, there was no other way to live. Entertainment is the only profession in which an individual is publicly critiqued on his performance at work every day. For most people, a mistake at work may be the subject of a comment by his boss or a reprimand in his file—an admonition usually delivered in private. For an entertainer, audience approval or condemnation is a public event. It comes in the form of applause—or lack thereof—and it comes with every performance.

Without repeating at length a subject that I covered in *Giant Strides*, there is a difference between what the musician plays and the audience hears.[29] Musicians are often confounded by vigorous audience applause to a performance that they thought was unexceptional and by audience apathy to something with which they were very pleased. The mechanism by which they deal with this disconnect is dismissal: the audience really doesn't know or understand what it just heard and therefore, its approval or disapproval is without artistic significance.

Sometimes, the criticism appears in a newspaper or magazine. Musicians may dismiss the opinions of critics and claim they do not read them. But, if they don't, they always learn what has been written about them. And, being criticized in print is, regardless of what musicians say about critics, hurtful and often wounding. Davern professed to be indifferent to and disinterested in what critics wrote about him. But, he had folders that were filled with thousands of reviews of his records and live performances.

Customers who patronize the venues where Davern played adopt a degree of familiarity with the musicians that would be unknown and unacceptable in most other fields. The fact that a performer has planned an evening's performance does not deter a customer from asking "Say, would you play *Sweet Lorraine?*" Customers gratuitously express their opinions without ever considering the impact of "That was an okay rendition of *Summertime*. But, I liked the way you played it last week better." The unspoken rules of acceptable audience behavior that protect performers in other disciplines are often absent from jazz performances.

To deal with this strife every day compels a musician to create a shell, a barrier that allows him to preserve intact his sense of self, while appearing to share it with his audiences. So, audiences saw Kenny the musician, the raconteur, and the entertainer. Sometimes, they saw the intemperate Davern, the man who sought perfection and found it just beyond his grasp. They saw little more, because he gave them little else to see.

Only his very close friends got to see the man inside the shell. Don Wolff was one of them.

> The real Kenny Davern was very protected: he was very private, and he protected his feelings. He was not a person who really showed his feelings, except the sound or the perfection he required when performing. There you saw him show a lot of feelings as it related toward anger if it wasn't perfect. But, you never saw his sadness, you never saw his love. Those kinds of things he kept rather private. . . . Once he trusted you, he was an entirely different person as a friend than he was as a "personality."
>
> People ought to know what a loving human being, what a generous, sharing, kind, considerate, warm, person he was. Unfortunately, most people will never get to know that now, and most people didn't get to know that when he was alive. But, the truth of the matter is that he was all of those things I just said, and the Kenny Davern that you got to know on a personal level was an entirely different person than you got to know on a professional level. And

because he was so private and somewhat protective, he didn't let a lot of that be seen or shown. The word that describes the reason is vulnerability. When you know Kenny's background as a child, when you know his background as a musician, you understand why he was so private and protective and so vulnerable and not willing to share some of those sensitive parts of Kenny Davern. If he was never known for anything else, he should be known for being a loving, devoted, loyal, husband, father and friend.[30]

Warren Vache, Jr., succinctly summed up his friend of over thirty years.

He was a pain in the ass, he was your best friend. He was dependable and erratic—all at the same time. . . . It's all part of the way he was and, if you look at the giving, instead of the demanding, he's a helluva guy.[31]

Notes

1. Kenny Davern, interviewer unknown, interviewed on 14 November 1985 at Heresford, UK, broadcast on the BBC Radio Hereford (hereinafter "Hereford interview").
2. Hereford interview.
3. Dick Hyman, *Thinking About Kenny Davern*, unpublished.
4. Brian Peerless, interview by the author.
5. Randy Reinhart, James Chirillo, John Trentacosta, interviews by the author.
6. Kenny Davern, quoted in Zan Stewart, "Clarinet's Range Lets Davern Express His Feelings," *The Star Ledger*, 16 May 2003: ticket section, 17.
7. Kenny Davern, interviewed by Martin Gayford, on *Meridian, The Jazz Clarinet*, recorded 14 August 1990 and broadcast on BBC World Service on 4 September 1990 (hereinafter "BBC Interview").
8. Kenny Davern, interview by Mark Weber, 17 January 2006.
9. Davern-Weber interview, 17 January 2006.
10. Davern-Weber interview, 17 January 2006.
11. Jon-Erik Kellso, interview by the author.
12. Mat Domber, president of Arbors Records, interview by the author.
13. Warren Vache, Jr., interview by the author.
14. Greg Cohen, interview by the author.
15. Elsa Davern, interview by the author.
16. Frank Laidlaw, interview by the author.
17. Mark Lass, interview by the author.
18. Kenny told Warren Vache, Jr., that Furtwangler recorded with one microphone behind his left ear and another behind his right, so that the audience could hear the music exactly as he did. Warren Vache, Jr., interview by the author.
19. James Chirillo, interview by the author.

20. Kenny Davern, conversation with the author; Dan Morgenstern, interview by the author.
21. Howard Alden, interview by the author.
22. Warren Vache, Jr., interview by the author. Conrad Janis recalled that Davern only played classical music during these sessions, pointing out what he liked and disliked. Conrad Janis, interview by the author.
23. Dave Frishberg, interview by the author.
24. Quoted in Allan Vache, interview by the author.
25. Quoted in Allan Vache interview.
26. Ken Peplowski, interview by the author.
27. Jack Six, interview by the author.
28. Brian Peerless, interview by the author.
29. Meyer, *Giant Strides*, 39–42.
30. Don Wolff, interview by the author.
31. Warren Vache Jr., interview by the author.

CHAPTER ELEVEN

Too Good to Last

Davern returned from England in the beginning of March 1983. One of his first stops was at the office of his chiropractor, Dr. Edwin C. Doe. He suffered from chronic lower back pain, and the discomfort of traveling for long periods of time in uncomfortable plane, train, or bus seats, and lugging a large, heavily loaded suitcase, exacerbated the condition. He visited Dr. Doe at about two-week intervals to receive an adjustment that minimized the pain and allowed him to continue working.

He saw several other health professionals as part of a prophylactic program. One of the greatest concerns for every horn player is the health of his teeth and gums. Davern periodically saw a dentist, and with more frequency visited a periodontist, Dr. Ron Odrich, who happened to also play the clarinet.

Because he suffered from hypertension, Davern saw a cardiologist, Dr. Harold Chafkin, on a regular basis. He took medication to control his blood pressure, made sure that he had enough sleep, watched his diet, and kept his weight at a relatively constant level.

But, there were deficiencies in Davern's health maintenance regimen. He did not want or like to exercise and, although he occasionally began a program of walking-striding along the boardwalk on the beach at Manasquan, he quickly abandoned it. More important, regardless of what his medical advisers told him, and what he knew, he refused to stop smoking between one and two packs of unfiltered Camel cigarettes every day.

Part of Davern's concern for his health was motivated by a desire to maintain and preserve his ability to play music. Part of it was motivated by a fear of having to be hospitalized—a thought that almost paralyzed him. Except for an occasional test that was administered on an out-patient basis, Davern was never admitted to a hospital. He hated to visit friends who were hospitalized, and the few times that he went were when friends like Pee Wee Erwin and George Duvivier, or his mother—the people who he "had" to see—were ill.

Davern did not tolerate illness well. He fretted over every pain and possible symptom of some possibly severe illness and discussed them endlessly with anyone who would listen. Elsa remembered:

> I saw him when he got the flu. It was dreadful. He really was unhinged when he was ill. He could not cope with it very well. I had to watch my power because I really could have looked at him at any time, even if he was perfectly healthy, and say "Are you okay?" And I could have led him down the merry path to feeling ill. He was very suggestible that way.[1]

On March 10, 1983, Davern played the first of a series of Thursday-night jobs with guitarist Vinnie Corrao and bassist Mickey Golizio at Posillippo's, a restaurant in Asbury Park. Posillippo's was one of several restaurants on the Jersey Shore, including the Yankee Clipper in Sea Girt and the Union House in Red Bank, that featured a trio or quartet playing jazz one or more nights per week. The pay was relatively nominal and, if the music did not attract customers, employers often canceled the program without notice—regardless of how long they had said the job would continue. Conversely, it was generally understood that a musician was free to occasionally take a higher-paying job, provided that he found a substitute.

Davern was invited to return to the Paradise Valley Jazz Party on March 11–13. Over the next ninety days, he played at the Downtown Athletic Club in New York, in Minneapolis, and at the Mid-America Jazz Festival in St. Louis. After that engagement, he flew to Madrid, Spain, to connect with a flight to the isle of Majorca, where he performed for a week.

He was home on the weekend of May 10 and, over the balance of that month, appeared at the Sarasota Jazz Festival, was in Las Vegas for a night at Caesar's Palace, came home, and then appeared at the Odessa Jazz Party. There were some small local jobs until, near the end of the month, he and Dick Wellstood were at the Maryland Inn.[2] On May 30, Davern left the country for an almost two-month tour of Europe and England.

He played a week in Italy and a week in West Germany. He flew to England on June 12 and played some out-of-London one-night stands and two two-night stands at the Pizza Express in London. On July 8–9, he performed with the Classic Jazz Band at the North Sea Festival, held at the Hague. Starting on July 10, he appeared in the *Grande Parade du Jazz* at Nice. Davern, Wellstood, and Rosengarden performed as the Blue Three at Nice, and also at Interlaken, where they made their last scheduled appearance together as a trio. Davern came home on July 23.[3]

He and Elsa spent a week in California from July 29 through August 4. The remainder of the summer consisted of odd jobs and appearances at the Long Island Jazz Festival with Jay McShann, and at Liberty State Park in New Jersey. There were dates at several local Elks clubs, two nights at Hanratty's, and a job in Rhinebeck, New York. He finished out the month at Waterloo Village with Wellstood, Zoot Sims, and Bucky Pizzarelli.[4]

As he had since 1972, Davern spent Labor Day weekend playing the Gibson party in Colorado. Through the beginning of October, he played several local dates and some one-night stands in New Jersey, Pennsylvania, Florida, New Hampshire, and North Carolina. He appeared in Midland, Texas, then flew to Dallas, and on to John F. Kennedy International Airport in New York where, at 8:15 p.m., he boarded an overnight flight to Italy. He was in Milan through the 16th, and appeared on Lino Patruno's television show. When he returned, Kenny resumed his usual grind of appearances. In mid-November, he joined Ruby Braff, Billy Butterfield, Carl Fontana, and Allan Vache at the Great Colorado Springs Invitational Jazz Party.[5] His picture was on the front cover of *Jazz Journal International* in November.

Joe Amiel, the owner of the Old Mill restaurant in Spring Lake, was involved in raising money for various causes. He decided to hold a fund-raiser at his restaurant to fight cancer and, because he was a devotee of the movie *Casablanca*, to turn the Old Mill into Rick's Place—the establishment owned by Humphrey Bogart's character in the movie. Davern was Amiel's friend, and he asked Kenny to put something special together for the event.

Kenny's first thought was to form what he called a Brass Choir; four trumpets, four trombones, a four-piece rhythm section (piano, guitar, bass and drums), and only one reed—Davern's clarinet. Once the project got under way, Kenny expanded it, adding three or four French horns. Then he expanded it again, to add about twelve string players.

A number of local musicians were enlisted in the cause, including John Luckenbill playing trumpet, Joe Turi on trombone, Ruth Olshansky on French horn, Manny Senerchia on strings, Vinnie Corrao playing guitar, Mickey Golizio on bass, and Nat Garratano on drums. Larry Cassara, who arranged professionally under the name of Sonny Lawrence, did some of the charts and played trombone. The band rehearsed once weekly for several weeks.

On the night of the concert, Amiel arranged for a camel and several donkeys to be tethered in front of the restaurant. The parking lot attendants were dressed in period costumes, and a neon sign proclaimed that the name of the venue was *Rick's Place*. Amiel also arranged for the event to be broadcast live on a local radio station.[6] Nat Garratano remembered another aspect of the evening.

> The secret ambition of Joe Amiel was that he always wanted to conduct a band or an orchestra. So, one of the tunes was designed so that Joe, with some tutelage, would have the capability of leading the band. All he did was wave a stick. But it came off quite well. We raised a lot of money: it was over $40,000. In those days that was a bunch.[7]

The orchestra only made one other public appearance: at the Monmouth County Library, Eastern Branch, in Shrewsbury on November 20, 1983, where it played a one-hour set.[8]

After the Blue Three's successful appearance at Wolf Trap Farms in November 1982, they had been asked to return in the following year. When the trio appeared on December 10, 1983, Rosengarden was absent. His place was taken by Chuck Riggs.[9] The trio then went on to a week-long job, starting on the following day, at the King of France Tavern in the Maryland Inn. On December 18, the last night of the engagement, their performance was recorded. It yielded two albums: *Live Hot Jazz*, which was issued as an LP on the Statiras label and later as a CD on Jazzology, and *Stretchin' Out*, which was released as a CD on Jazzology.

The event signaled the end of a recording drought of over two years. Except for his appearance in December 1981, on the Freddie Moore album, and his participation in the Pee Wee Erwin sets at Breda in May of that year, Davern's last recordings had been made in April 1981, when he recorded the Blue Three album and the LP with Tomas Ornberg.

The two albums that were recorded at the Maryland Inn contain, with one exception, no new selections. Nonetheless, there is much to listen to. On the *Live Hot Jazz* album, *Rosetta* and *Beale Street Blues* feature some unusual clarinet–piano voicings. *Rose Room* has Dick and Kenny trading oddly constructed phrases, and Kenny's solos on *Travelin' All Alone* and *Lady Be Good* have some ideas that were not present in his previous recordings of these tunes. Davern ends *Travelin'* on a concert C above double C.[10] The only slow number is *Then You've Never Been Blue*, with an especially plaintive opening by Davern. Throughout this recording, Wellstood interjects snatches of other tunes into his playing: *The Christmas Song* appears in *Wrap*

Your Troubles, *The Mooche* pops up in *Beale Street*, and *Say It Isn't So* can be heard in *Rose Room*.

There was more of the same on the second release. *The Man I Love*, taken at a relatively fast pace, opens with a Davern statement that lasts over four minutes, *Lover Come Back to Me* is another barn burner. *Chicago Rhythm* features a solid walking bass by Wellstood, followed by some up-tempo stride in which a reference to *Johnson Rag* can be heard. This was one of Jimmie Noone's specialties, and Kenny told Dan Morgenstern that this recording was the only occasion on which he consciously tried to sound like the older man.[11] *Love Me or Leave Me* and *There Is No Greater Love* are both medium-tempo outings.

The highlight of the *Stretchin' Out* album was Davern's first recording of George Gershwin's *Summertime*. Over the next two decades, he would record it on ten other occasions, often slowing the tempo down, so that he could use the song as a vehicle to delve increasingly deeper into his own emotions. This version runs almost seven minutes and ends with one of Davern's specialties; three on-pitch, but beyond-the-upper-register notes that would be unplayable by almost anybody else.

The reviewers gave *Live Hot Jazz* high marks. Jack Sohmer awarded it five stars in *DownBeat* and said it was the best record Davern had made. Scott Yanow said that Davern was "often in miraculous form."[12] When the *Stretchin' Out* CD was released several years later, it also received excellent reviews. Russ Chase liked the album, as did Jack Sohmer who said: "*Stretchin' Out* is so cohesive a showcase that it would be impossible to cite a favorite track."[13]

Tom and Elisabeth Brownell were the owners of the Thunderbird Lodge in Taos, New Mexico. Tom was a fan of Ralph Sutton's, and invited him to play at the Lodge for two weeks at the beginning of 1983. During their stay, the Brownells became friends with Ralph and Sunnie Sutton and invited them to return in the following year. They came and, in January 1984, so did Kenny and Elsa Davern, Milt Hinton, and Gus Johnson, Jr.

For over a decade, the Daverns and the Suttons spent the first weeks of January at the Thunderbird Lodge, and it was here that Kenny frequently celebrated his birthday. The roster of musicians who joined them was impressive, including Warren Vache, Jr., Conte Candoli, Jim Galloway, Flip Phillips, Howard Alden, Ross Tompkins, Bob Haggart, and Jake Hanna.[14] In 2009, a two-disc package of recordings made by Davern, Sutton, Hinton, and Johnson came on the market.[15] The balance of the first quarter of 1984 consisted of one-night stands, interrupted by an occasional appearance away from home. In addition, Davern and Wellstood appeared as featured guests on Dick Sudhalter's radio show.

Sudhalter, an accomplished musician and acclaimed writer, was the producer and moderator of a program titled *Live at the Vineyard Theater* that was recorded before a live audience and broadcast at a later date on National Public Radio. It was his practice to invite one or more prominent jazz musicians who would perform and, between numbers, would converse with Sudhalter about their lives and different facets of the music business. Davern and Wellstood were on the program on January 15, 1984. A decade later, a CD recorded from the broadcast was issued as a tribute to Wellstood, titled *Never in a Million Years*.

Kenny and Dick had been playing together for over twenty years, and there is a relaxed air to their performance. *Lady Be Good* swings powerfully, but lightly, as do *Don't Get Around Much Anymore*, *If Dreams Come True*, *On the Sunny Side of the Street*, and *Rosetta*. Davern played *Please Don't Talk About Me When I'm Gone* as a ballad, befitting the mournful lyrics. Equally moving were the duets on *Travelin' All Alone* and *Summertime*. Davern performed *Mood Indigo* without piano accompaniment.

The discussion that took place between the songs will forever remain a mystery. The liner notes disclose that the audience enjoyed the humorously scatological, if not obscene, conversation among Wellstood, Davern, and Sudhalter. However, no part of it was considered suitable for radio broadcast. Instead, the three principals met in a studio several weeks later, and Davern and Wellstood recorded some inoffensive remarks about their early musical experiences.[16]

John S. Wilson was present at the theater performance, and called Davern and Wellstood "the only ongoing, viable comedy team in jazz." He found the music to be "warm and sparkling and inventive, particularly in Mr. Davern's sudden changes of direction and his use of the bottom reaches of the clarinet. . . ."[17]

At the beginning and at the end of March, Davern joined the big band that Bob Haggart was leading at the Rainbow Room. He was at Rick's Cabaret in Philadelphia on March 4, then returned on March 9–11. In connection with the latter engagement, Kenny was interviewed by Terry Gross on her National Public Radio Show, *Fresh Air*.

Kenny played the Paradise Jazz Party in Scottsdale, Arizona, on the weekend of the 17th, and performed with Wellstood and Chuck Riggs at the New School in Manhattan and at the Summit Art Center. Over the weekend of March 30–April 1, he flew to St. Louis for the Mid America Jazz Festival where he, Wellstood, and Rosengarden were reunited. Wellstood and Marty Grosz traveled with Davern from Missouri for one-night stands in Pine Bluff, Arkansas, and Jackson, Mississippi. From there, Kenny went back into the

Rainbow Room for three days and, after a few days of rest, he was off on his spring tour of England.[18]

Brian Peerless started teaching in 1963, and ultimately became a senior lecturer in mechanical engineering at Middlesex Polytechnic, later to become Middlesex University. He was also a jazz fan and a frequent visitor to London's jazz clubs and record shops. In 1962, through his friendship with the staff at Dobell's Record Shop, he started working there as a "Saturday man." The flexibility in his teaching schedule allowed him to sometimes work at Dobell's on staff holidays, and he remained there on a part-time basis until it closed its doors in 1992. Dobell's was famous worldwide for the stock it carried, both new releases and extensive out-of-print and secondhand records. Davern was one of the many visiting American musicians who made an effort to visit the shop and examine the stock. He and Peerless met in December 1974.

At the time, Davern's tours in Great Britain were being handled by Robert Masters, one of the large bookers of jazz musicians. From time to time, Masters would call Peerless and ask him to drive musicians to dates. Davern often rode with Peerless.

One evening in June 1983, he and Peerless stopped for a few drinks after a job. Davern was not satisfied with the way that he was being treated by his current management, and he broached the subject of having Peerless arrange a tour for him. By the next morning, Peerless had forgotten the conversation, but Davern had not. On a Sunday morning some eight months later, he called Peerless, who recalled the conversation. "Kenny said, 'Hey, about this tour.' And I thought that he was passing through Heathrow, because he often would phone for a chat. 'I'm going to come over between . . . ' whenever it was. And he said, 'don't you remember, we talked about it.'" In fact, Davern was calling from Colorado. When Peerless started to protest that he didn't know anything about the mechanics of booking a foreign artist, that they had become friends, and that he wanted it to stay that way, Kenny cut him off. "'Don't worry: we're mates now. It'll be all right. I'll phone you in a couple of weeks to see how you're getting on.' And that was the start of it."[19]

Because of his work at Dobell's, Peerless did know a number of people in the music business. But, putting a tour together was still a complicated process that involved arranging venues, hiring musicians, negotiating wages, and obtaining work permits. The reciprocal Musician's Union arrangement required Peerless to organize exchange dates for British musicians to work in the United States. Notwithstanding his reservations, Peerless agreed to take on the job.

The tours were done primarily by car, with Peerless driving. On most occasions, they returned to London after the job was finished. Occasionally, when Davern was booked in towns such as Hereford and Dorchester, which were about 130–140 miles away, they would stay over. Kenny flew to dates in Scotland and Ireland.

There were different rhythm sections almost every night.

> It was always a question of cost. Sometimes, like at Tunbridge Wells, we could have what we wanted, and it might be Brian Lemon, or Colin Purbrook, Dave Green, or Len Skeat, and Allan Ganley or Bobby Worth. At the Pizza Express, it was the same guys or sometimes Jack Parnell. On the London dates, we were usually all right.

Sometimes Davern would be saddled with musicians of a lesser-caliber, and those dates did not always go smoothly. Peerless remembered an evening in Wales when Elsa was with them. "The rhythm section was a bit grim and suddenly, he threw his clarinet in the air and screamed 'Aaaaaaah, Help!' and Elsa said 'I'm off. I've got to phone Elaine [her sister].' And I said 'Don't leave me here.' The audience, of course, thought it had something to do with the clarinet."[20]

On some of the early trips, Davern rented a hotel room for the duration of his visit. That became prohibitively expensive, especially when Elsa began to join him on these tours. For a time, they rented an apartment for a month in Earl's Court. Later, they stayed in an apartment in the Notting Hill Gate area. On one of her flights, Elsa met Joan Maxwell, who was an antiques dealer. Elsa purchased some material from her, and the relationship ripened into a friendship. Maxwell had Elsa to her apartment for dinner and later went to see Kenny play. Eventually, Maxwell insisted that the Daverns stay with her when either or both of them came to England, and made her flat available to them if she was out of town.[21]

On this trip, Davern reversed his usual pattern, beginning his tour in Edinburgh, Scotland, on April 13. He moved on to Glasgow on the 15th, and arrived in London two days later. At the beginning of May, he played in venues through England, including two appearances in London. In all, he had twenty-one performances in thirty-one days, plus a recording session.

The City of Milton Keynes, which lies about thirty miles northwest of London, was once described by Davern as an "awful kind of architectural monstrosity" and "absolutely grim."[22] However, tucked away on the outskirts of the city was the Stables at Wavedon, a theater that was run by Johnny Dankworth and his wife, Cleo Laine. Peerless had left May 7 as an open date on the tour so that Davern could stop at the Stables for a recording session with Britain's premier rhythm section, Brian Lemon on piano, Len Skeat on bass, and Allan Ganley on drums. The result was an exceptional album called *Kenny Davern and the Brian Lemon Trio, the Very Thought of You*.

The title tune leads off the album, played slowly and softly with great emotion. Lemon and Skeat generate a strolling feel to *Don't Get Around Much Anymore*, and Davern saunters along on top of it. *Melancholy Baby*, at medium tempo comes next, followed by a very laid-back version of *Cherry*. The first side of the LP closes with an original tune titled *Milton Swing*, for which the entire group takes composer credit.

Kenny's approach to *Love Me or Leave Me* is reflective, markedly different from his other recordings of the tune. Brian Lemon plays counter-melodies underneath Kenny on Bob Haggart's *What's New*, giving Davern an opening to formulate a different concept of the song. Until this point, most of the tunes show Davern in an almost-contemplative mood—a feeling that disappears on *There Is No Greater Love*, on which Kenny is driving, increasing the volume as he increases the heat. Another ballad, *I Surrender Dear*, precedes the closer, an original credited to the entire band, titled *Keyne on You*.

One thing that was different on this album was that Davern rarely raised his musical voice. There is a reflective quality that permeates most of the numbers: even on the faster ones, the volume did not increase substantially, although the intensity did. The result was a series of interpretations that often bore little resemblance to what Davern did—before or afterward—with the same tunes.

The LP got a good review from Kevin Henriques in *The Financial Times*. Eddie Cook wrote that the musicians were "in top form," their rapport was "exceptional," and that the album "should be in every jazz lovers' collection." It won first place in the Music Trades Association Records Awards for 1984.[23] Unfortunately, this was the first release on the Milton Keynes label, and it was not widely distributed in the United States.

Davern came home on May 14, and two days later left for the Odessa Jazz Party. He returned to open on May 22 at the prestigious Village Gate in Greenwich Village for ten days, then appear at the Maryland Inn from June 6 to 10. From there, he flew to Ottawa for a week.

The advent of warm weather heralded the beginning of the summer jazz festivals and an increase in the volume of work. He played the Kool Jazz Night in Pennsauken, New Jersey, had a lunchtime gig at Grace Plaza in Manhattan, and performed at the New Jersey Jazz Society Piano Spectacular, with Wellstood and drummer Ron Zito. He played a date at the Tavistock

Country Club on June 24, then headed to Toronto for the Molson International Jazz Festival.[24]

Throughout July, there were local dates at the Cornerstone and nearby venues. Over the last weekend of July, Kenny appeared at the Peninsula Jazz Party at Palo Alto. He and Elsa took the occasion to spend a few days in San Francisco and visit the Napa Valley. For the balance of August, he played a number of local jobs and participated in making a movie.

Warren Vache, Jr., was subbing for Billy Butterfield at Condon's. Between sets, he was sitting at the bar nursing a drink when someone tapped him on the shoulder. "I turn around and it's a little white-haired man who says, 'Have you ever done any acting?' I took a drink and said, 'Do I get to keep my clothes on?' He laughs and says, 'I'm serious. Have you ever done any acting?' I said, 'No, but I'll give it a try. What have you got in mind?'"[25] The little white-haired man turned out to be Frank Gilroy. He had written a screenplay that he titled *The Gig*, and he thought that Vache might be right for one of the parts.

The Gig told the story of six amateur musicians who meet every week to play some dixieland music for their own enjoyment. One of them, a used-car salesman played by Wayne Rogers, gets them a two-week job at Paradise Manor, a typical "Borscht-Belt" Catskill Mountain resort run by Abe Mitgang (played by Joe Silver). Each of the men has a reason why he can't take the time to play the job, but in the end all but one of them makes the trip.

Their first week is spent adjusting to the staid musical tastes of the resort's elderly clientele, who are turned off by the group's "biff-boom-bang" style. However, the job is cut short when an out-of-favor pop singer, seeking to make a comeback, arrives at the resort. His mobster managers quickly see that the band is not good enough to play the singer's arrangements, and they are soon replaced and sent home.[26]

After their initial encounter at Condon's, Gilroy again met with Vache to discuss Vache's role in the project. Ultimately, Gilroy named Vache the film's musical director and gave him an on-screen role.

> What do you do when you're in a situation where you don't know shit from shinola? You hire people that do. So I hired the best people I could find, which was Kenny, and Dick Wellstood, Milt Hinton, and Reggie Johnson, and the one guy that had hired me to do a couple of movie soundtracks, because he knew the inside of the business and the paperwork. He was the drummer, Herb Harris. As a result it all got done.[27]

The film was shot over a four-week period at Sacks Resort in Saugerties, New York. The band came up to the resort to shoot an extended dance sequence, in which Davern's hands can be seen playing the clarinet and Wellstood's hands are on the piano. But, all of the segments of the tunes that were allegedly played by the band were recorded in one session on August 28, 1984. Vache remembered the date with some chagrin.

> The interesting story about this is when the big day comes to pre-record all the music for the film. I had just come back from England, and I got sick. I went to the studio with a fever, and we sat down and we did all of the corny stuff—the *Hava Negilas* and the waltzes. We did all of that first. I sat down, and somebody took my temperature, and it was 104, and Gilroy said "you're going home." They began a mad scramble to find somebody to play the cornet for the rest of the date.
>
> Just to show you how irreplaceable I was, it turned out that Bob Barnard from Australia was not only visiting, but he was upstairs in the studio looking down. So, no sooner had I left the building than Bob Barnard had his cornet out, and he played all the jazz. The whole reason for having me in the picture in the first place was so they could put the camera on my fingers and sell everybody as a jazz musician and, when it got time to do the filming, it wasn't me playing. I had to try to figure out what Bob Barnard's solo was and get the fingering as close as possible.[28]

Although the picture was not widely distributed, it was acknowledged as an unsentimental portrait of the music business.

The day after he recorded the music for the *Gig*, Davern flew to Pittsburgh to appear with the World's Greatest Jazz Band as part of the Pittsburgh Jazz Festival. Labor Day weekend fell on September 1–3, and Davern again worked the Gibson party at the Fairmont Hotel. On the 19th, he was at Brandeis University. Davern played the Cornerstone and Rick's in Philadelphia, as well as a few other venues before leaving for a short tour of West Germany on October 17. On the 21st, he and Ralph Sutton stopped in Ludwigsburg, where they recorded two tunes with the Flat Foot Stompers, a band of German musicians that occasionally invited touring Americans to play with them. Davern may not have been happy doing this recording. He turned in a workmanlike performance on *Eccentric Rag* and on *Wolverine Blues* he hardly played at all.

When he came home, he left for Florida to spend a week aboard the S.S. *Norway*. Hank O'Neal, who founded Chiaroscuro Records, had come up with a novel concept for a jazz festival. The cruise ship business was undergoing difficult times, and O'Neal convinced the management of Norwegian Cruise Lines that their bookings would increase if they provided passengers with some form of added value. O'Neal hired some musicians, invested in some advertising, and the first Floating Jazz Festival was held on the S.S. *Norway* in late 1983. It lasted for a week and was a success.

Although Kenny had not been on the first cruise, he was invited for the 1984 event. He appeared with a group led by Wild Bill Davison, and also led a trio with Dave McKenna on piano and Bobby Rosengarden. Davern attended all but one of the subsequent festivals, including the last one which was held on the *Queen Elizabeth II* in 2002. O'Neal liked Kenny on a personal level and was gracious and generous to him, covering the cost of bringing Elsa on the cruises whenever she chose to come.[29]

On the weekend of November 3–4, Kenny flew to attend the Colorado Springs Jazz Party with Wellstood, Urbie Green, Vache, Hyman, Grosz, and Rosengarden. Then it was back to Manhattan for a concert at noon on Wednesday at St. Peters Church. The weekend saw Davern in Sacramento, then he came home to pack before leaving on a four-week tour of England.[30]

The trip was designed to coincide with the release of *The Very Thought of You* CD that Davern had recorded during his spring tour. He was in London at the 100 Club on November 21, and at Pizza Express on the next day. After an appearance out of the city, he was back at Pizza Express, where he performed with the Brian Lemon Trio and also with guitarist Al Casey. From then, he alternated engagements in small towns with dates in London. He also managed to squeeze in a recording date with British trumpeter Humphrey Lyttelton.[31]

Lyttelton, born in 1921, was educated at Eton College, where his father was a housemaster. During World War II, he served as an officer in the Grenadier Guards. A disciple of Louis Armstrong, Lyttelton played trumpet with George Webb before forming his first band in 1948. Over the years, he reformed his band several times, at first playing a traditional songbook, and later a more mainstream library. By the 1980s, he was England's premier jazz figure, having recorded prolifically, played with every visiting musician of note, and fostered the careers of numerous British musicians, among them, Wally Fawkes, Tony Coe, and Joe Temperley.

Lyttelton also wrote several well-received books on jazz and hosted a long-running radio show, *the Best of Jazz*, on BBC Radio 2. He was the master of ceremonies of an award-winning comedy show, *I Haven't a Clue*, and authored articles on various non-musical subjects.[32]

Guitarist Al Casey, who had been a fixture on the jazz scene since he was a member of Fats Waller and His Rhythm, was also in Britain, and his booker, Dave Bennett, arranged for Casey, Davern, and Lyttelton to perform for the Swindon Jazz Society. On that occasion, they were accompanied by pianist

Stan Greig, along with Paul Sealey on banjo, bassist Paul Bridge, and drummer Adrian MacIntosh, and it was this group that recorded *Scatterbrains, The Humphrey Lyttelton Rhythmakers with Kenny Davern and Al Casey*, on December 2, 1984.[33]

Davern is out for the title tune, which is the first cut on the album. For the balance of the session, he and Lyttelton display an uncommon musical bond: they frequently share the opening and closing melodic statements and, throughout the date, each complements and supports the other by playing counter-melodies and obbligatos. On *Oh Baby*, Davern is the featured performer: Lyttelton has only a minor role in the opening and closing statements. Davern has the opening on *Yellow Dog Blues*, then plays thirds underneath the trumpeter at the start of the second strain. He drops out as Lyttelton takes a muted solo, then returns for a dynamic ending. Davern acquits himself well on *Bugle Call Rag*, a tune that was not part of his usual list of songs.

I Would Do Anything for You opens the second side of the album, followed by a medium-tempo *Old Fashioned Love*, a piece that was one of Kenny's features at the time. *Fidgety Feet*, written by several members of the Original Dixieland Jazz Band, is the third tune on this side and, on the band's repetition of the second strain, Davern tosses in some humorous Larry Shields-style, bleating clarinet figures. The album closes with *Shim-Me-Sha-Wabble*.

There is a joy to this album, in large part due to the formidable combination of Al Casey on guitar and Paul Sealey on banjo. Before the session began, Casey was apprehensive about playing acoustic guitar. But, as listening to this release makes clear, he was quickly at home on the instrument.

The January 1985 edition of *Jazz Journal International* featured a photograph of Davern sitting on a stool with his legs crossed and his hands clasped over his knees looking slightly unhappy. The caption read: "Would you buy a used clarinet from this man?" That bright spot aside, the first months of the new year were marked by large open spaces in Davern's date book. He had a date at the Grand Hyatt hotel in Manhattan with Bobby Rosengarden before he and Elsa flew to New Mexico, to spend a week at the Thunderbird Lodge in Taos with Ralph Sutton, Milt Hinton, Gus Johnson, Jr., and Buddy Tate. They spent another week on vacation with Elaine and Fred Corbalis, Elsa's sister and brother-in-law, before heading home.

He had two stints at the Rainbow Room in February, interrupted by an appearance at the North Carolina Jazz Festival. In early March, he played jobs at the Short Hills Country Club, the Rainbow Room, and at Condon's, before appearing at the Paradise Valley Jazz Party on March 9–10. Then it was off to West Germany for a tour that included Heidelberg, Dortmund,

Stuttgart, Emden, Bremen, and Frankfurt, before he flew home on March 24. At the end of the month, he was at the Zimmerle Art Museum on the campus of Rutgers University in New Brunswick.[34]

Things began to get better in the middle of April, when Davern went up to Toronto for a short gig with the Climax Jazz Band. Climax was composed of mostly British-born musicians who played in the British trad-band style. The band had been together since 1971, and had developed a wide-ranging repertoire that included pieces from the New Orleans, Ellington, Latin, and traditional songbooks. Davern had played with them on some of his earlier visits to Canada. He and the band performed for live audiences on April 19–20, and spent Sunday, April 21, at the studio of Comfort Sound, where they recorded *The Climax Jazz Band with Kenny Davern*.[35]

The disc opens with *Ole Miss*—titled *Ole Miss Rag* on the liner notes—which runs almost five minutes. *Oh Baby* features a two-clarinet outing with Davern and Lewis sharing melodic statements and solos before they jointly bring the piece to a close. Kenny is out for *Jeep's Blues*. The rhythm section of Jack Vincken on banjo, Daniels, and Pete McCormick on drums drives *Bobby Shaftoe* at a very fast calypso pace. Davern is right at home playing obbligatos and weaving counter-melodies underneath Mick Lewis's alto saxophone. *Muskrat Ramble* is taken at a medium tempo and has a hint of a Latin influence. The band takes *Mood Indigo* at a quick tempo, and Kenny takes a warm solo in the chalumeau range while Lewis plays counterpoint underneath him. *I Want a Girl (Just Like the Girl That Married Dear Old Dad)* is next, followed by Ellington's infrequently played *Big House Blues*. The album closes with *Get Out of Here*.

At the end of the month, Davern worked two days at Condon's that were separated by a job at the Canoe Brook Country Club in Short Hills and followed by a date at the Museum of Modern Art. At the beginning of May, he was at the Cornerstone and then worked with Loren Schoenberg at St. John the Divine Cathedral in Manhattan before he was off to England and the Continent on May 10. Kenny, Wellstood, and drummer Jake Hanna were there for a week, where they were billed as the Blue Three. They played at Davern's usual stops in London and the countryside before crossing the Channel for an appearance at the Breda Festival in Holland on May 18. On the following day, they flew back to the United States.[36]

Cornetist Ed Polcer was an admirer of Eddie Condon and the swinging style of music that Condon promoted. He put together a group called the Eddie Condon Memorial Band that included Tom Artin on trombone, Davern, pianist Keith Ingram, Jack Lesberg on bass, and drummer Oliver Jackson, and arranged a two-week tour for them. On June 11–14, the band played dates in London and the surrounding communities. They flew to Switzerland for the Jazz Festival in Lugano on June 15–16, then came back to play a week in England, interrupted by a one-day trip to perform in Northern Ireland. The last performance of the tour was at the 100 Club in London on June 23. Dave Gelly was there, and wrote that Davern's version of *Summertime* "made everybody sit up and listen."[37]

The Kool Jazz Festival was in full swing when Davern returned to New York, and he was a part of it at Carnegie Hall on June 27. After dates at Michael's Pub, and some local work, Kenny made his first appearance in the *Jazz in July* program at the 92nd Street YMHA, where he appeared with Yank Lawson and Bob Haggart as part of the Lawson–Haggart Jazz Band.

Davern played the Peninsula Jazz Party in Palo Alto on July 27–28. In August, he had engagements at Hanratty's, the Bayhead Yacht Club, the Cornerstone, and several MPTF jobs. The Eddie Condon Memorial Band was at the Action Park Dixieland Festival on August 17 and in Stanhope on the following day, playing at Waterloo Village. After some more local jobs, Davern flew to Denver for the Gibsons' annual Labor Day party.[38]

He had a new gig on Thursdays in September, playing at a restaurant in Long Branch, New Jersey, called Ishkabibble. (It does not appear that the venue had any connection with Merwyn Bogue, the novelty singer of the same name, who appeared with bandleader Kay Kyser and His Kollege of Musical Knowledge in the 1940s.) In mid-month, Davern was at the Minneapolis Jazz Party. Then, after some odd jobs and an appearance at the Midland Jazz Party, he was on the S.S. *Norway* with Hank O'Neal's Floating Jazz Festival.[39]

He had some performances in a group led by Doc Cheatham and appeared as leader of his own quartet. O'Neal had a project which, unfortunately, never came to pass.

> What I had tried to do that week at sea was to try and hook him up with Gerry Mulligan. Now, Gerry had always wanted to do a project with Kenny, and Kenny was always reluctant to undertake a project, primarily because he was a little shy or insecure about it. Mulligan always kicked himself that he hadn't made any serious recordings with Pee Wee Russell. He felt that Kenny was the next best thing, and tried to do something about it. I tried to put the two of them together in as many circumstances as I possibly could. Unfortunately, it just didn't take, and nothing happened that week at sea—but not for the want of trying.[40]

The *Norway* docked in Florida, and Davern came home to play a tribute to his friend, Pee Wee Erwin, at Union College in Cranford, New Jersey.

Then it was off to the United Kingdom for a month of one-nighters. Along with the live performances, three recording dates were scheduled, and four albums resulted from them.[41]

Brian Peerless, who booked the tour for Davern, had arranged for him to play some of the dates with a group led by drummer Jon Petters that included Martin Litton on piano, Roger Nobes on vibes, and Keith Donald on bass. By the time that they reached the Square Jazz Club in Harlow, Essex, on November 10, everyone had become comfortable with each other, and their show, which was broadcast on Essex Radio, showed it.

One of Davern's lifelong concerns was being compared with Benny Goodman. He went out of his way to avoid participating in tributes to, or recreations of, Goodman's work, and generally stayed away from situations in which he could be matched against or identified with Benny. The association with Petters' band brought that issue to the fore. Petters liked Gene Krupa's style of drumming, and the older man's influence on him was readily apparent. Even more striking was the similarity between the work of pianist Litton and that of Teddy Wilson, who was one of his most powerful influences. Finally, the addition of a vibraphone brought the group perilously close to a place where Davern did not want to go.

There the problem ended. Davern placed his own imprimatur on each of the selections, and all of the sideman did the same, thus avoiding any direct Goodmanesque musical references. The group played a varied selection, including *Royal Garden Blues*, *Jazz Me Blues*, and *That's a Plenty*, through *Love Me or Leave Me*, *The Man I Love*, *Deed I Do*, and including *Blue Monk*. Only two songs were played slowly, *Georgia on My Mind*, which was relatively short and featured Davern at the end playing high above the normal reach of the clarinet, and *Blue Monk*. Throughout the evening, Roger Nobes proved to be an intelligent and perceptive player, backing Davern with well-constructed chords and fills, then soloing with verve and elan.

Afterward, Petters obtained a set of the broadcast tapes and sought Davern's consent to issue some of the tunes on compact disc. Because of the possibility that some critic might make the comparison with Goodman, Davern was at first reluctant to give it. But, Petters said that he intended to release the CD on his own label, which would never be circulated in the United States, and Davern ultimately agreed.[42]

Of the ten available tunes, six were pressed on the CMJ label, titled *Live and Swinging, Kenny Davern and John Petters Swing Band*. Petters held on to the remaining four songs and eventually added them to a recording that he made with Yank Lawson on May 28, 1986. That CD was issued on the Rose label and was titled *Makin' Whoopee, Yank Lawson with John Petters and His Dixielanders*. Most of these recordings were sold by Petters at his performances.

The performance drew conflicting reviews. Derek Coller was at the Square Jazz Club on November 10 and saw the group. In his view, Davern "had no problems steering clear of the Goodman sound." Eddie Cook thought that this was the problem, saying that Davern did not "gell" with the vibes because he was not a Goodman type.[43] Martin Richards listened to the *Live and Swinging* album and called Davern "superlative." He liked Nobes, and said that he was convinced that a good vibraphonist was the best possible front-line partner for Davern. Richards went on to say, "Kenny Davern is at the top of the clarinet tree and, with musicians like Litton and Nobes behind him, can do no wrong."[44]

Davern continued with the tour, traveling out from the London area to play a gig, then returning in the early hours of the morning. After two weeks of these one-nighters, he arrived at the Pizza Express in London. The restaurant was closed for the afternoon, so that Kenny could record an album with Litton and Petters, titled *Playing for Kicks, The Kenny Davern Trio*. On this occasion, Litton sounded very much like Teddy Wilson, and Petters' reverence for Krupa was clearly on display. The clarinet-piano-drums format was the setting in which Goodman had excelled, and all of these things combined to awaken Kenny's Goodman-related concerns.

But, Davern was clearly himself and he turned in solid performances, especially on *You're Lucky to Me, Black and Blue, Lullaby of the Leaves*, and *New Orleans*. Unfortunately, the sense of excitement that permeated the November 10 performance was not recaptured here, and there were stretches that seemed to go flat. Because the recording was intended to expose Litton's talents, there were two numbers on which Davern sat out.

At the time that he agreed to make this recording, Davern believed that it would only be released on cassette in the United Kingdom and used by Litton as a promotional vehicle. However, the recording found its way to the United States, where it was issued by George Buck on his Jazzology label as *Kenny Davern's Big Three, Playing For Kicks*—much to Kenny's distress.[45] The press gave it mixed reviews. Eddie Cook praised Kenny, but Jack Sohmer was far less enthusiastic, especially in his treatment of Litton and Petters.[46]

There were two more weeks of touring that ended on December 9. Both Davern and Humphrey Lyttelton had been pleased with their earlier recording and arranged to make another. The result was an album that was different in style and feel from their earlier collaboration, but no less excellent or enjoyable.

The title was *This Old Gang of Mine* and, in addition to Humph and Kenny, the musicians consisted of John Barnes, playing soprano, alto, and baritone saxophones; Martin Litton; Mick Hutton on bass; and Colin Bowden on drums. *Mood Hollywood*, a Lyttelton composition, opens the album, followed by Mel Stizel's *Jackass Blues*, with solos by all three horns. On *That Old Gang of Mine*, Kenny noodles his way through a chorus, then continues to meander alongside Lyttelton. When Barnes solos on *Of All the Wrongs You've Done to Me*, Kenny plays some attractive counter-melodies, and takes a propulsive solo on *Who's Sorry Now*.

The second side of the LP opens with a swinging version of *Porter's Love Song to a Chambermaid*, which features both Lyttelton and Davern. Kenny claimed composer credit for *My Mama Socks Me* (in realty, *My Mama Rocks Me*) and, on this recording, his performance is moving and innovative, ending at the upper limit of the clarinet. Litton is featured on *Undecided*, and then the group essays Lyttelton's tribute to Sidney Bechet, *Sidney My Man*. Everyone is lyrical here: Barnes solos expressively on soprano saxophone, followed by Davern and the leader. The closer is an original by the three horn men, titled *Time to Jump*. Eddie Cook wrote: "This is probably the finest record I have heard this year. . . ." and concluded: "What more can I say? Get this LP!" It was voted one of *Jazz Journal International*'s 20 best for 1986.[47]

Kenny came home on December 15 and, for the rest of the year worked around New Jersey. He had no tours during the first months of the new year and, with a few exceptions, spent most of his time working near home. At the beginning of January, he traveled to the Thunderbird Lodge. When he returned to the Northeast, he had jobs at the Loeb Student Center on the campus of New York University and at the Church of the Heavenly Rest. On the last day of January, he played the North Carolina Jazz Festival, and he was in Sarasota on February 9–10. Davern played at the New School for Social Research before traveling to Topeka for the weekend of February 15–17. In between these gigs, he worked at the Cornerstone, some local country clubs, and some of his other fill-in jobs.[48] He had gigs in Arizona and Annapolis and, from May 15 to 17, Davern was in Florida with Dick Hyman, Brian Torff, Chuck Wayne, Bob Wilber, Ricky Ford, and Bobby Rosengarden for concerts at Van Wetzel Hall in Sarasota. He remained for the Sarasota Jazz Festival on the 18th. From Florida, he went on to the Odessa Jazz Party before returning to New Jersey.[49]

On June 10–13, he appeared at Michael's Pub, as part of the Condon Gang First Anniversary Reunion put together by Ed Polcer. In 1975, after Eddie Condon died, Red Balaban had, with the permission of Condon's widow, Phyllis, opened a third Eddie Condon's club at 144 West 54th Street. Polcer became the manager of the club and ultimately purchased an interest in it from Balaban. The club had a life of about ten years, closing in July 1985, and the program at Michael's celebrated the anniversary of that event.[50]

Michael's Pub, located at 211 East 55th Street in New York City, had opened in 1972 and, over the years, presented a diverse group of jazz musicians, among them, Davern, Wellstood, Dave McKenna, Benny Carter, and Ruby Braff, and singers, including Mel Torme and Anita O'Day. The New Orleans Funeral and Ragtime Band played there regularly on Mondays, and Woody Allen would occasionally drop in to play clarinet with them. The owner of Michael's Pub was Gil Weist, who was not known for being a genial host. He had a reputation for being rude, if not cruel, to musicians and for treating them badly. Guests at the club often fared no better. The club prospered, seemingly in spite of him.

The New Jersey Jazz Society's Piano Spectacular was the kickoff event for George Wein's annual jazz festival, and Davern was there on June 21. On the next day, Wein presented a concert at Town Hall in New York City, dedicated to the music of Chicago in the 1920s. Some parts of the event were recorded and released on the Atlantic label titled *Chicago Jazz Summit*. Davern appeared in two settings that evening. He was first heard with trumpeter Yank Lawson and Vince Giordano's Nighthawks in a recreation of Louis Armstrong's *Potato Head Blues*. The arrangement was furnished by Dick Hyman and is the same one that was used in the 1974 *Satchmo Remembered* concert at Carnegie Hall.[51]

Later that evening, Kenny performed two numbers, *Blue Turning Grey Over You* and *When You're Smiling* with, among others, eighty-year-old Wild Bill Davison on cornet, eighty-three-year-old Art Hodes on piano, and seventy-four-year-old Franz Jackson on tenor sax. As always, Hodes played a blues-tinged style of piano, bereft of unusual harmonics and flashy histrionics, yet filled with drive and depth. "Here's a record you gotta love," said reviewer Ernie Labovich.[52]

This was the first of only two of Davern's performances in 1986, live or in a studio, to be recorded. It was not an aberration—the one thing that was noticeably absent from Davern's work schedule in the 1980s was recording time. The resurgence of interest in dixieland that had generated the demand for records by Phil Napoleon and Pee Wee Erwin in the 1950s and early 1960s had long ago petered out, as had the interest of the major recording labels in this genre of music.

A number of independent labels appeared in the 1970s. Almost all of Davern's recordings during that decade were for companies such as Chiaroscuro (six releases), Music Minus One (four), Chaz Jazz (two), Jazzology (two), Monmouth-Evergreen (two), Seeds, Thimble, Concord, and Kharma (one each). A substantial number of recordings came from live performances: Fat Cat Jazz, which was owned by Johnson "Fat Cat" McCree, released twelve LPs and cassettes, with songs that Davern had played at the various Manassas festivals. There were also over six releases featuring Soprano Summit. In all, over forty albums with performances by Davern were issued during the 1970s, all by small independents.[53]

In the 1980s, the number dropped substantially. Many of the independents simply disappeared. There were no recordings for Music Minus One, and no appearances at Fat Cat McCree's festivals that generated releases on the Fat Cat Jazz label. Hank O'Neal was concentrating on the Floating Jazz Festival and his other interests, and was producing far less output on his Chiaroscuro label.

The recording industry in the United States was in such a state of decline that a substantial proportion of Kenny's recordings in the 1980s were made outside of the country. Of the twenty-seven LPs, cassettes, and CDs that were recorded and released during the 1980s, seven were made in England, two in Sweden, and one in each of Norway, Holland, West Germany, Canada, and Australia. All of these recordings were made while Davern was on tour in those countries.[54]

On the day after the Town Hall concert, Kenny was back at Waterloo working for the New Jersey Jazz Society. On June 30, 1986, he participated in a memorial concert for drummer Cliff Leeman, who had died in April. Then, it was back to Michael's Pub on July 1 for a continuation of the Eddie Condon celebration. On this visit, Davern led a group consisting of George Kelly, Dick Wellstood, Milt Hinton, and Gus Johnson, Jr. There were several local jobs before Kenny returned to the 92nd Street Y. One of the programs in the *Jazz in July* series was titled *Licorice Shticks*, and Kenny performed with fellow clarinettists Peanuts Hucko and Eddie Daniels. The month ended with an appearance at the Peninsula Jazz Party in Palo Alto.[55]

In its August 1986 issue, the readers of *DownBeat* magazine voted Kenny first place in the category of most deserving of wider recognition on clarinet. With that under his belt, Davern headed off for a whirlwind tour of New Zealand and Australia.[56]

He landed in Auckland on August 3, and appeared at the Mandalay in Newmarket. On the next day, he flew to Australia and made appearances in Perth, Coffs Harbor, Brisbane, Hobart, Adelaide, Melbourne, and Sydney. He returned to the States, and stopped in Denver for two days with Ralph Sutton, before landing at Newark on August 17.[57]

There were a couple of local jobs before Davern flew back to Colorado for the Gibson bash. Two weeks later, he was in Minneapolis and, on September

15, he, along with Conrad Janis, Dick Wellstood, and Bobby Rosengarden, were at the Museum of Modern Art in New York City to celebrate the ninetieth birthday of Conrad's father, renowned art dealer Sidney Janis. Before the month was out, Kenny appeared at Brandeis University, the Waldorf Astoria, and the Church of the Heavenly Rest, and he also performed at Gulliver's in Lincoln Park.[58]

Davern stopped in Chicago for a one-night stand at the Palmer House on the way to Texas for the Midland Jazz Classic. There was a job in Pittsburgh, and then Kenny flew down to Florida to leave on Hank O'Neal's annual Floating Jazz Festival aboard the S.S. *Norway*. A anthology CD was released that features a number of the performers on the cruise. It has one selection in which Davern appears with Vache, Masso, pianist Eddie Higgins, guitarist Chris Flory, Jack Lesberg, and drummer Mel Lewis. Of greater significance, the second track has Davern playing with Bob Wilber.

Eight years had passed since Soprano Summit had split apart and, during that time, a number of promoters and producers had unsuccessfully tried to get Wilber and Davern onstage together. By 1986, the events that had led to their separation were in the past, and both of them recalled the enjoyment that playing with the other yielded. So, they allowed O'Neal to present them together. The CD contains one cut of *Moonglow*, performed by Davern, Wilber, Howard Alden, Phil Flanigan, and Chuck Riggs.

When the *Norway* docked, Davern got off the ship and flew to England for what turned out to be his last winter tour of the United Kingdom. He stopped at all of his regular venues, meeting up with Dick Wellstood at some and with Bob Wilber at others, and flew home on November 30. For the remainder of the year, Davern had a gig at Windows on the World at the top of the World Trade Center, played three days with Ralph Sutton in Colorado Springs, and had two jobs at Ishkabibble. On New Year's Eve, he played for the New Jersey Jazz Society.[59]

As had become their habit, Davern and Elsa spent a week at the Thunderbird Lodge in Taos, renewing their friendship with Ralph Sutton, his wife Sunnie, and with Tom and Elizabeth Brownell, owners of the Lodge. They returned to New Jersey to find that Elsa's successful jewelry-making enterprise was the subject of an article in the January 14, 1987, edition of the *New York Times*. In all, the business lasted about ten years before Elsa finally gave it up.

> It got too hard. It also got too difficult to find good things. The bottom fell out of the antiques market, and the things that I loved the most got too expensive. I would have had to sell necklaces for one or two thousand dollars, and it wasn't worth it anymore. But, I stayed a collector. Whenever I see something

unusual, I still buy it, and I still make them, and I give them away as gifts. But, I've got tons.[60]

Kenny, Wellstood, and Tony DeNicola were at the King of France Tavern on the weekend of January 16–18. Davern had a weekend gig for the Gibsons in Denver on the last days of the month. He opened February at William Patterson College in Wayne, played with guitarist Howard Alden at St. Peter's Church, then headed to the North Carolina Jazz Festival. In between, he appeared at Ishkabibble and other local venues.[61]

Activity picked up in March. On the first three days of the month, he had a job with Tony DeNicola at the Short Hills Country Club, worked with Ed Polcer at Pier 17 in Brooklyn, and played at the New York Hilton. On the 7th, he took a day trip to Toronto, returned for a job at the Manasquan River Golf Club, and played a date with Tony DeNicola. He sandwiched in some appearances at the Cornerstone before flying to the Paradise Valley Jazz Party.

A pattern had developed to Davern's tours and festival appearances. In March–April or April–May, he would tour Britain. At the end of June, he would appear at George Wein's Kool (or Newport or JVC) Jazz Festival; in July, he would be at the Jazz in July program held at the 92nd Street Y in New York. The summer would be spent at the festivals in the United Kingdom and Europe, usually the North Sea, Edinburgh, Nairn, Brecon, and Oslo Jazz Festivals. On Labor Day, he would perform at the Gibsons' jazz party, which was succeeded by Ralph and Sunnie Sutton's Rocky Mountain party. His last tour of the year would take place in October, when he would be at the jazz festival aboard the S.S. *Norway*.[62]

The 1987 spring tour of Britain began on March 19 in Kingston. He played in Cambridge, Inverness, and at venues in Hampstead, Woking, and Tunbridge Wells, before reaching the Pizza Express on Dean Street in London. From there, he played at Rotherham, returned to the Pizza Express, and also appeared in Epsom, Rotherhilde, Eastbourne, and Yalding before traveling home on April 14.[63]

During Davern's stay in England, Humphrey Lyttleton invited him to substitute as the host of his weekly radio program on the BBC, *The Best of Jazz*. Kenny played what he described as the "classic jazz recordings made by American Jazz clarinetists." He closed the show by promising that next week, they would play recordings by great Albanian jazz clarinetists.

Back in the United States, he had some dates at the Cornerstone and spent one day in Toronto before attending the Jazz Club of Sarasota's Seventh Annual Jazz Festival. He had a job in Wilkes-Barre, Pennsylvania, on May 1, and then left for a week-long tour of Iceland. During the rest of the month, Kenny worked in Stamford, Connecticut, played at Princeton, flew to Denver to perform at a wedding, was at Waterloo Village, and performed at the New York Academy of Art.

Ed Polcer had been invited to play at the reunion of the Princeton University class of 1957 on June 6, and hired Kenny for the job. The two of them also worked together on the 19th in Charlotte, North Carolina. In between, Kenny was at the Cornerstone and played on the weekend of the 12th through the 14th at the King of France Tavern with Dick Wellstood and Tony DeNicola.[64]

Pianist George Shearing was the headliner at Town Hall on June 22, and Davern was in the band for a program that included a dixieland and a bebop segment. Shortly afterward, Kenny left for a weekend in Stockholm, where he appeared with Wild Bill Davison at the Jazz and Blues Festival. On the July 4th weekend, he was in Indianapolis at Jam '87. There was a date in Princeton on July 12, then he and Elsa left for a week in California that ended with Kenny's appearance at the Peninsula Jazz Party in Palo Alto on July 24–26.

Dick Wellstood was also at the party and, on the first night, he and Davern were scheduled to play together in the second set. Wellstood did not show up and, because he had also missed the sponsor's party, Victor Horvitz, a friend of many of the musicians, went up to his room to check on him. He came down and, when the set was over, took Davern aside and told him that Wellstood was dead. Kenny and Elsa, along with Mona Hinton and Denisa Hanna, went upstairs to formally identify Dick's body. Then, Kenny and Elsa called Hank O'Neal in New York to arrange for Hank and Shelly Shier to visit Dick's wife, Diane, who had not made the trip, to break the news.[65]

Wellstood had been suffering from hypertension and bouts of cardiac arrhythmia for some time. He had a heart attack in 1986, and his doctors had advised him to limit his physical exertion, stop drinking, and to modify his diet. Wellstood did stop exercising, but did little else to retard the progress of the disease. He told no one how sick he was, and his death came as a complete shock to Kenny—and everyone else.

Wellstood was Kenny's closest personal and professional friend. For almost half of Davern's life, he and Wellstood had spoken several times weekly and had seen each other often when both were at home. They recorded together and toured together, laughed and talked, argued often about any subject that came to mind, and loved each other deeply. Kenny said:

> We used to fight bitterly. We had arguments all the time: he'd slam the phone down on me, and I'd slam the phone down on him. Five minutes later, call

up again; it was like a lovers' quarrel. We made some very good music for the better part of twenty-five years. . . . Some of the best recordings I ever made were with him.[66]

The loss to Davern was beyond comprehension. He told his friend, Dick Sudhalter:

Joe Venuti used to say that when Eddie Lang died, 50 percent of him died too. I think I know what he meant: for twenty-five years Wellstood and I would carry on a conversation, on the bandstand and off the bandstand, for better or worse. Then, all of a sudden, he's gone. No more conversation. Everything stops. How do you *think* that feels?[67]

Years later, he spoke of Wellstood and said, "He's probably the most remarkable musician and person I'd ever met in my life. If I could bandy the term 'genius,' it would have to be applied to him. There was nobody quite like him, and there never will be anyone like him. We were friends for twenty-five years."[68]

Davern never had time to grieve for the loss of his friend. There were jobs to be played, and Kenny had to play them. Even when he was not working, events intruded upon him. Wellstood's widow proved to be exceptionally needy, and thrust her grief on Kenny and Elsa, as well as on other close friends of Dick. Caring for her needs prevented the Daverns from attending to their own. For several years, Kenny was incapable of listening to any recordings that Wellstood had made. And, when he was interviewed for *Giant Strides*, almost six years after Dick's death, he had to interrupt the session several times in order to compose himself.

Before Wellstood died, he and Davern tore a dollar bill in two and each kept a segment in his wallet. The idea was that the one who survived the other would have the torn bill to remind him of his friend and that, if there was an afterlife—which neither of them believed—they would be able to put the bill back together again some day. Although he kept the half-bill in his wallet until the day he died, Davern did not need the reminder: he thought of Wellstood almost every day for the rest of his life.[69]

Notes

1. Elsa Davern, interview by the author.
2. Date Book, *Jersey Jazz*, 11, no. 1 (February 1983): 5; 11, no. 4 (May 1983): 19; event program.

3. Date Book; *Jazz Journal International*, 38, no. 6 (June 1983): 3, and 38, no. 9 (September 1983): 22.

4. *Jersey Jazz*, 11, no. 7 (September 1983): 4, and 11, no. 9 (November 1983): 17; Date Book.

5. Date Book; *Jersey Jazz*, 11, no. 11 (January 1984): 15; document from Elsa Davern; Thomas P. Hustad, interview by the author.

6. Nat Garratano, John Luckenbill, Vinnie Corrao, interviews by the author.

7. Nat Garratano, interview by the author.

8. *Jersey Jazz*, 11, no. 11 (January 1984): 10, 12.

9. Letter agreement between Wolf Trap and Davern.

10. Kenny Davern, interviewed by Mark Weber, 11 July 2002.

11. Davern-Morgenstern interview 2.

12. Scott Yanow, Kenny Davern: "Live Hot Jazz," *Cadence*, 9, no. 8 (August 1983): 77; Jack Sohmer, "Live Hot Jazz," *DownBeat*, 50, no. 8 (August 1983): 34–35.

13. Russ Chase, "Stretchin' Out," *IAJRC Journal*, Spring 1990, p. 51; Jack Sohmer, "Stretchin Out," *Mississippi Rag*, xviii, no. 4 (April 1990).

14. Schacter, Sutton, 258–260; Date Book.

15. *Ralph Sutton and Kenny Davern, Live at the Thunderbird Lodge; To Elsa and Sunnie with Love*. Victoria VC 4377. The liner notes state that the recordings were made in 1983 and 1984. However, Davern's date books, and the information in Schacter/Sutton, establish that Davern did not make his first appearance at the Thunderbird Lodge until January 1984. While it is possible that Sutton's solo performance dates from 1983, it is certain that Kenny's performances took place later. See also e-mail from Don Wolff to the author.

16. Richard M. Sudhalter, liner notes to *Never in a Million Years*, Challenge CHR 70019.

17. John S. Wilson, "Jazz: Wellstood and Davern," *New York Times*, 25 January 1984.

18. Date Book; John S. Wilson, *New York Times*, 8 April 1984; Jazz Festival event program.

19. Brian Peerless, interview by the author.

20. Peerless interview.

21. Elsa Davern, interview by the author; Brian Peerless, e-mail to the author.

22. Davern-Morgenstern 2.

23. Kevin Henriques, *Financial Times*, 17 August 1985; Eddie Cook, *Jazz Journal International*, 38, no. 1 (January 1985): 3; Peerless Program Notes, 21; copy of award.

24. *Jersey Jazz*, 12, no. 3 (April 1984): 7; and 12, no. 7 (September 1984): 13; Date Book.

25. Warren Vache, interview by the author.

26. For a thorough discussion of the sociological themes that pervade the picture, see William J. Schafer, "Learning from the Gig," *Mississippi Rag*, xxxv, no. 11 (November 2007): 33.

27. Warren Vache, interview by the author.
28. Warren Vache interview. The date comes from a date book entry that reads, "Hold for Vache day recording."
29. Hank O'Neal, Elsa Davern, interviews by the author.
30. Document from Elsa Davern; Date Book; *New York Times*, 27 September 1984.
31. *Jazz Journal International*, 37, no. 11 (November 1984): 3, and 37, no. 12 (December 1984): 4; e-mail from Brian Peerless; Peerless Program Notes, 21.
32. See www.HumphreyLyttelton.com.
33. Steve Voce, liner notes to *Scatterbrains, The Humphrey Lyttelton Rhythmakers Featuring Kenny Davern and Al Casey*, Stomp Off, S.O.S. 1111; e-mail from Brian Peerless.
34. *Jazz Journal International*, 38, no. 1 (January 1985): 2; Thunderbird Lodge event program; Date Book; *Jersey Jazz*, 13, no. 1 (February 1985): 5.
35. The recording was released on a Tormax cassette and sold by the band at its appearances. In 2008, it was released on a compact disc.
36. Date Book; MOMA event program; *Jazz Journal International*, 38, no. 5 (May 1985): 4. Wellstood prepared a specimen publicity release for the appearance at Wavedon, in which he referred to Kenny as Kenny LaVerne (as Davern's name was misspelled on the *Empire City Six Salutes the Colleges* LP in 1957), and created a less-than-flattering biography of his friend. It took Davern a few moments to realize that Wellstood was toying with him. See *Giant Strides*, 148.
37. Dave Gelly, "Dixie Dean," *The Observer*, 23 June 1985; Date Book; *Jazz Journal International*, 38, no. 6 (June 1985): 5.
38. Date Book; *San Francisco Examiner*, 30 July 1985; *Jersey Jazz*, 13, no. 7 (September 1985): 4, 6.
39. Date Book; Elsa Davern, interview by the author; program from Minneapolis Jazz Party.
40. Hank O'Neal recorded recollections.
41. *Jersey Jazz*, 13, no. 9 (November 1985): 5; *Jazz Journal International*, 38, no. 11 (November 1985): 5.
42. Brian Peerless, interview by the author.
43. Derek Coller, "Jazz in England," *Mississippi Rag*, xiv, no. 2 (February 1986): Eddie Cook, *Jazz Journal International*, 39, no. 1 (January 1986): 19.
44. Martin Richards, "Live and Swinging," *Jazz Journal International*, 42, no. 3 (March 1989): 23.
45. Brian Peerless, e-mail to the author; Kenny Davern, conversation with the author.
46. Eddie Cook, "Kenny Davern's Big Three, Playing for Kicks," *Jazz Journal International*, 39, no. 11 (November 1986): 24; Jack Sohmer, "Kenny Davern's Big Three, Playing for Kicks," *Mississippi Rag*.
47. Eddie Cook, "This Old Gang of Mine," *Jazz Journal International*, 39, no. 12 (December 1986): 22; *Jazz Journal International*, 40, no. 2 (February 1987): 10.

48. Date Book; *Jersey Jazz*, 13, no. 10 (December 1985): 10, and 13, no. 11 (January 1986): 32.

49. Date Book; *Jersey Jazz*, 14, no. 2 (March 1986): 7, and 14, no. 3 (April 1986): 5; Sarasota events program; *Jazz Journal International*, 39, no. 8 (August 1986): 5.

50. Date Book, *Jersey Jazz*, 14, no. 5 (June 1986): 18; Red Balaban, Ed Polcer, interviews by the author.

51. E-mail from Dan Morgenstern to the author.

52. Ernie Labovich, "Chicago Summit," *IAJRC Journal*, 22, no. 4 (Fall 1989): 66–67.

53. This discussion excludes recordings that were made in the 1970s, but not released until later, such as those on the Arbors label, *Soprano Summit III*, and *Stretchin Out*.

54. These figures do not include recordings that were made in the 1980s, but not released until some later time.

55. Date Book; *Jersey Jazz*, 14, no. 5 (June 1986): 3, 18.

56. *Jersey Jazz*, 14, no. 6 (July 1986): 5; *New York Times*, 22 July 1986.

57. Tour itinerary. See also Peerless Program Notes, 22; Date Book.

58. Date Book; Conrad Janis, interview by the author.

59. *Jazz Journal International*, 39, no. 11 (November 1986): 3; Date Book; *Jersey Jazz*, 14, no. 8 (October 1986): 4.

60. Elsa Davern, interview by the author.

61. Date Book; *Jersey Jazz*, 15, no. 1 (February 1987): 4.

62. Date Book; Peerless Program Notes, p. 22.

63. *Jazz Journal International*, 40, no. 3 (March 1987): 3.

64. *Jersey Jazz*, 15, no. 3 (April 1987): 5; Date Book; Sarasota Jazz Festival event program.

65. Kenny Davern, interview by the author. See also, *Giant Strides* at 189 et seq.; Rusch interview part 1, p. 8.

66. Mark Weber, recorded conversation in about September 2003.

67. Kenny Davern, quoted in Richard M. Sudhalter, liner notes to *Never in a Million Years*, Challenge CHR 70019.

68. Kenny Davern, interview by Mark Weber, 17 January 2006.

69. Elsa Davern, interview by the author. There were three half-bills in Davern's wallet when he died. Elsa said that he did the same thing with Tony DeNicola and with pianist Norman Simmons, who, as of March 2010, is still alive.

With Grandfather Fred Roth at about six months.
Courtesy of Elsa Davern

About five years old.
Courtesy of Elsa Davern

His mother, Josephine Roth Davern, circa 1941. Courtesy of Elsa Davern

His father, John Joseph Davern, circa 1953. Courtesy of Elsa Davern

Mr. and Mrs. Frederick A. Roth
request the honor of your presence
at the Bar Mitzvah of their grandson
Kenneth
on Saturday morning, January 17, 1948
at nine-thirty o'clock
Congregation Bnai Israel of Woodhaven
8907 Atlantic Avenue
Woodhaven, Long Island

Today, I am a man.
Courtesy of Elsa Davern

With his trio at the A-1 Club in Astoria, 1951; unknown piano and drums.
Courtesy of Elsa Davern

At his mother's cabin in Woodstock, New York, 1953. Courtesy of Elsa Davern

On the road with the Ralph Flanagan Orchestra. Courtesy of Elsa Davern

Ray Bauduc, KD, Norma Teagarden, Jack Teagarden, circa 1954.
Photo by Ella B. O'Neill; Courtesy of Elsa Davern

At Nick's, circa 1958–1959: Harry DiVito, KD, Pee Wee Erwin, Cliff Leeman, Whitey Mitchell.
Courtesy of Elsa Davern

At the Central Plaza with Lee Blair, Henry "Red" Allen, KD, and Jimmy Buxton, circa 1961.
Courtesy of Elsa Davern

With Pee Wee Russell, circa 1962.
Courtesy of Elsa Davern

The Ferryboat Band: Wellstood, Jack Six, KD, George Mauro, Al McManus, Ed Hubble.
Courtesy of Elsa Davern

At home with son Mark, Elsa, and daughter Debbie. Courtesy of Elsa Davern

The 1972 Dick Gibson Party: KD, Flip Phillips, Ruby Braff, Roy Haynes, George Barnes.
Photo by Al White

Dick Wellstood and His Famous Orchestra, featuring Kenny Davern.
Photo by Hank O'Neal

Soprano Summit: Connie Kay, George Duvivier, KD, Bob Wilber, Marty Grosz, and friend Robert Nixon. Arkansas, 1975. Photograph by Al White

On the Lam? circa 1977.
Courtesy of Elsa Davern

That's the Guy.
Courtesy of Elsa Davern

Soprano Summit: KD, George Duvivier, Marty Grosz, Bob Wilber, Bobby Rosengarden.
Courtesy of Elsa Davern

Al White's party, 1979.
Photo by Al White; courtesy of Elsa Davern

The Hot Three: KD, Don DeMicheal, Art Hodes, circa 1980.
Courtesy of Elsa Davern

With Elsa at home in Manasquan, 1977.
Courtesy of Elsa Davern

Ralph Sutton, Gus Johnson, Jr., KD, at Pine Bluff, Arkansas, April 1979.
Photo by Al White)

At the White House, March 1980: Chancellor Helmut Schmidt, Rosalind Carter, Budd Johnson, Carrie Smith, President Jimmy Carter, Frau Loki Schmidt, Bobby Rosengarden, KD, Pee Wee Erwin, Jimmy Maxwell. Courtesy of Elsa Davern

Kenny captioned this picture "Waiting for Lansky," with Warren Vache, Jr., and Michael Moore.
Courtesy of Elsa Davern

At Don Wolff's home: KD, Don, and Glenn Connors, 1984.
Courtesy of Elsa Davern

With Elsa, September 1980.
Courtesy of Elsa Davern

With Mel Powell, mid 1980s.
Courtesy of Elsa Davern

With Brian Peerless, circa 1989.
Courtesy of Elsa Davern

The Quartet: James Chirillo, unknown, Greg Cohen, Tony DeNicola, KD. At Bumble Bee Bob Weil's in Santa Fe. Photo by Mat Domber

Inducted in the American Jazz Hall of Fame by Dan Morgenstern, Waterloo Village, June 1997. Courtesy of Elsa Davern

Kenny and Elsa, Waterloo Village, June 1997.
Photo by Sharon Meyer

With Johnny Varro at Waterloo Village, June 1997.
Photo by Al White

With Tony DeNicola, Bill Holaday, and John Bunch at the Cornerstone in 2002.
Courtesy of Elsa Davern

Doctor of Music Kenny Davern, with Milton Filius, Hamilton College, May 21, 2000.
Courtesy of Elsa Davern

The Quartet: Greg Cohen, Tony DeNicola, KD, James Chirillo, Denver, October 2004.
Photo by Al White

Photo by Nancy Miller Elliott, Courtesy of the Institute of Jazz Studies, Rutgers University

CHAPTER TWELVE

Rebuilding

Although Davern was devastated by Wellstood's death, he still had commitments to fulfill. At the beginning of August, he played a job in Princeton, then traveled to Scandinavia to appear at the Oslo Jazz Festival. As was the practice at jazz festivals, Davern was occasionally thrust into groups of musicians with whom he had no musical affinity. "'I just got back from Scandinavia,' Kenny Davern told Alan Morgun, 'I played with one of those progressive young groups. You know. They sound like a pet shop on fire.'"[1]

Not all of his appearances were as painful. On August 9, he was teamed with Flip Phillips and Norwegian tenor saxophone player, Bjarne Nerem, plus a Scandinavian rhythm section to record a CD titled *Mood Indigo*. The combination of two tenor saxophones and a clarinet gave the group a deep and powerful sonority that was beautifully displayed on the title tune. *Crazy Rhythm*, taken at its usual quick pace, was followed by an almost stately version of *Just Squeeze Me*. The leaders stretched out on a lazy nine-and-one-half minute version of *Tin Roof Blues*, and then took an up-tempo excursion on *Jeff's Blues*, a retitled *Sweet Georgia Brown*. Kenny had a warm opening statement on *Embraceable You*, then everyone jumped in on a frantic version of Flip's composition, *Great Scott*. The closing title was a medium-tempo *If I Had You*.

The disc was issued on the Norwegian Gemini label and received little play in the United States. The reviewers who did get a copy of the recording were pleased with it. Shirley Klett wrote "This one's a keeper."[2]

Davern returned to New Jersey and, beginning on August 14, worked on four successive days at the Cornerstone, in Blooming Grove, Pennsylvania, on Long Island, and at Grace Plaza in Manhattan. In addition, along with Derek Smith, Warren Vache, Jr., Milt Hinton, and Butch Miles, Davern played at Margaretville High School in Margaretville, New York, in a tribute to Erroll Garner. In the last week of the month, Kenny was in California.

He began September in Colorado, at the Gibsons' party, stayed a few extra days to work with Ralph Sutton, then flew to Minnesota to appear at the Minneapolis Jazz Party.[3] He had some local appearances before he went to Texas to play the Midland Jazz Classic. There was a memorial service at St. Peters Church on October 6 for Dick Wellstood: Kenny was one of the speakers and afterward joined the Vince Giordano band for an emotional performance of *Travelin' All Alone*. After a weekend in Raleigh, North Carolina, and some dates at the Cornerstone, Kenny and Elsa left for a month at sea on the Norwegian Cruise Line.

For the first week, they were on the S.S. *Norway*, where Kenny was teamed with Flip Phillips and was also in a group with Wild Bill Davison. They transferred to the S.S. *Starward* for a week, then transferred again for a final week on the S.S. *Skyward*.

The ships stopped in Mexico, and Elsa was able to take some land tours and buy some jewelry. But, four weeks at sea was too much. "We were two weeks on the *Norway*, then we went to the *Starward*, then we went to the *Skyward*. We did a month, and we never did that again. Flip was with us the whole time. We all went nuts."[4] However, there were some unusual moments, such as when Hank O'Neal invited some local musicians to perform on board the ship.

> It was a small band on board the ship that played nothing but flutes and carved wooden whistles and things, and Kenny sat in with them. It was absolutely wonderful because he was astounded how the musicians from Ecuador or Peru or something, could play things on their little wooden whistles that he could barely play on the clarinet. He had all these keys to work with and these guys just simply had a few holes in a piece of bamboo or whatever it was they made those whistles out of.[5]

Back on land, there was work at the Cornerstone and in Colorado Springs and Manassas, Virginia. In Manhattan, he played a lunch-time performance at St. Peter's Church and an evening job at Gallagher's Steak House. On December 6, he joined Dick Hyman, Howard Alden, and Phil Flanigan at the Church of the Heavenly Rest in a tribute to Dick Wellstood.[6]

Wellstood's death had forced Davern to reevaluate the musical setting in which he wanted to perform. Previously, he preferred to play with a piano and drums behind him. Although there were a number of excellent pianists around—including Dick Hyman, John Bunch, and Marty Napoleon—none of them had the extensive points of reference that he and Wellstood shared. None of them gave him the musical and emotional support that Wellstood did. And so, although he continued to work with piano-led rhythm sections, his preferred environment came to be with a guitar, bass, and drums.

Davern had several explanations for his choice. He told one interviewer that he didn't want to be "battened down to the tempered scale which was horrendously out of tune."[7] On another occasion, he said: "The piano nails you down with the tempered scale. I like open spaces. I despise chord changes—chords muddy things up, bleed over. And I like to feel the pulse all the time from a rhythm section."[8]

All of these explanations were partially true. However, the underlying motivation for the change was that there was no one who could replace Dick Wellstood, and playing in front of a piano was a constant reminder of that fact.

Howard Alden, who was born in California in 1958, first met Davern when he visited the East Coast in 1979 with vibraphonist Red Norvo. Alden returned to New York in 1981 and made a point of finding Kenny.

> When I moved here about a year later, I'd run into him about town, and I'd look him up. Eventually, he started calling me for little gigs whenever he had the chance to book a band. That evolved into trying to do more. At that point, Kenny had very specific types of groups that he wanted to work with. He either wanted to work with a piano and a drummer—no bass—or else bass, guitar, and drums—no piano. So I started working in a quartet setting with him.[9]

Davern and Alden played together with increasing frequency over the years and when, in December 1987, Kenny had a recording date for Musicmasters, he called Howard. The bass player on the job was Phil Flanigan, with whom he had been playing for several years. Born in 1960, Flanigan had come to New York with Scott Hamilton and performed with Bob Wilber and Warren Vache, Jr. He and Davern were also together at one of Hank O'Neal's festivals. The fourth member of the quartet that Davern assembled was drummer Giampaolo Biagi. (Biagi suffers from having his first name misspelled in a variety of ways. This is the spelling from the Musicmasters CD.) Born in Florence, Italy, in 1945, he came to New York in the late 1960s. He had played with Chet Baker and Hazel Scott, and had appeared at the Red Garter.

Davern had a large repertoire of songs that he wanted to play. Fortunately, Musicmasters had contracted for two eight-hour sessions in the studio, beginning at 6:00 p.m. on Monday, December 7, and continuing until 2:00 on the next morning. A similar session was scheduled for Tuesday night.[10] Although it was unplanned, the result was enough music for two CDs: *One Hour Tonight*, which was issued in 1988, and *I'll See You in My Dreams*, which went on the market one year later.

Davern's old friend, Leroy "Sam" Parkins, was the producer on these recordings. He remembered what happened before the microphones were turned on.

> The first night of those Musicmasters sessions, he brought three clarinets. There was his old plastic Conn, a wooden Conn, and a Buffet. He played them all. But, with the hard rubber Conn, there was no contest. In his warmup, he played huge chunks of the Von Weber First Clarinet Concerto—which he played brilliantly. What he had, that Louis had, was complete mastery of the instrument. He never showed off his technique. He had the facility but he had no need to show it off.[11]

The *One Hour Tonight* CD begins with *Elsa's Dream*, a tune that Kenny co-wrote with Flip Phillips and often played with a tenor sax accompanying him. With Alden as his partner, this version is bright and floating, without losing any of its musical insistence. *Pretty Baby*, which Davern did as a ballad is next, followed by a medium-tempo *Comes Love*. The seldom-heard *Love Is the Thing* is next, and then *No One Else but You*, which had been recorded in 1928 by Louis Armstrong.

Kenny liked to play *Pee Wee's Blues*, and this version features some exchanges with Alden. Howard plays some unusual counterpoint under the next tune, the infrequently played *On with the Dance*. *Old Folks* and *Oh Baby* follow, and the CD closes with the title tune. Over the next few years (*If I Could Be With You*) *One Hour Tonight* became one of Davern's showpiece ballads, played with a soft and wistful tone.

The second disc was titled *I'll See You in My Dreams*. The opening tune is a crackling version of Edgar Sampson's *Blue Lou* that is followed by a soft and haunting rendition of *Sweet and Lovely*. The next song is the Eddie Condon composition, *Liza*, which is followed by *Pee Wee's Blues II*, a version that is slightly shorter but faster than the version on *One Hour Tonight*.

According to George Kanzler's liner notes, Davern wanted to use some tunes associated with Bix Beiderbecke, and Hoagy Carmichael's *Riverboat Shuffle* was the first of them.[12] It was followed by *Oh, Miss Hannah*, a buoyantly played piece from the Bing Crosby–Paul Whiteman songbook. *Melancholy Baby* is a vehicle for a Davern–Flanagan duet that exorcizes all traces of the weary saloon aura from this ballad. *Royal Garden Blues*, another song associated with Beiderbecke is given a fresh and light treatment by the quartet. *Solitude* follows, and the CD closes with a swinging, medium-tempo version of *I'll See You in My Dreams*.

Both albums received excellent reviews from a wide variety of sources. When *One Hour Tonight* was released in 1988, Shirley Klett "highly recommended" it and called the disc "a recording of singular merit." Russ Chase wrote, "It happens to have been my opinion for some time that Kenny Davern is the world's best jazz clarinetist. . . . This record, however, can be regarded as the best one he has ever made, here or abroad."[13]

I'll See You in My Dreams garnered similar praise. When Will Friedwald listened to both albums, he concluded, "Mr. Davern is probably the finest clarinetist playing today . . . a rare performer who transcends style and instrument." *Time* magazine's Critics Voices cited this as one of two outstanding jazz albums and said that Davern gave a "dazzling performance." Randy Salman, writing in *The Clarinet*, called Davern "a fine clarinetist, possessing command of tone, intonation, and technique," and highly recommended the release.[14]

For the next several years, Alden would be Davern's first call on guitar. Kenny usually wanted his guitar players to play rhythmic chords while he embroidered the melody. But, Alden did more, and Davern liked it.

> He enjoyed the chordal support and another melodic voice . . . I felt that I got into a nice musical conversation with him, just to support things he was doing by playing another melodic voice, almost like two horns. He used to mention that "I like to have Howard as my sparring partner," not really sparring—just someone to converse with. It was so easy to do because he was so definite rhythmically and so solid, that I knew that if he was going to play something, he really meant it. So, I could play a big note underneath him and know that he was going to be there.[15]

On the weekend after the recording date, Davern traveled to Naples, Florida. He came home and played a few local jobs before he flew south again, landing in Sarasota on December 29. He was in Baltimore on the following day, and in Brielle for New Years Eve. He noted in his date book that he had spent 163 days on the road in 1987.

He celebrated his birthday in Manasquan, then flew to Taos for the following week, where he played with Sutton at the Thunderbird Lodge. He was home for a date in Bloomfield, before spending a weekend in Raleigh. A date at the Cornerstone preceded an engagement at the Central Illinois Jazz Festival on January 29–31. He stopped for a day in Indianapolis, and then, after a short stop at home, performed at the North Carolina Jazz Festival.

His next stop was in Pine Bluff, Arkansas, to help Al White mark the occasion of his sixtieth birthday. White not only promoted jazz parties, he also photographed them, and he had been successful at both for many years. After joining Sutton, Bob Haggart, and Gus Johnson, Jr., at White's party, he went to Denver, followed by a weekend in California. He played the New York–New Jersey area through mid-March, when he was in Scottsdale. On the weekend of March 18–20, he played the Mid America Jazz Festival in St. Louis, then was off to Europe for nine weeks—the longest tour he ever made.

From March 22, he was in Switzerland, playing with Yank Lawson. On April 11, Elsa flew from the United States, and Kenny traveled from Switzerland to meet her in London. He played three dates in England before he and Elsa left for Zurich, where Kenny played at the Widder Bar on April 18–24. Then it was back to the United Kingdom for twenty-nine days of one-night stands in England, Scotland, and Wales, with groups that changed from night to night. The venues were as varied as the musicians, including pubs, theaters, restaurants, an adult education center, a school, an art gallery, and several festivals.

On May 14, Davern met up with Art Hodes, who was on a separate tour, and drummer Colin Bowden at the Pizza Express in London to record a CD. There were fourteen songs on the disc, which was titled *The Kenny Davern Trio Featuring Art Hodes, The Last Reunion*. *Buddy Bolden's Blues* and *Save It Pretty Mama* were slow and moving, displaying the emotion, depth, and range that Davern could summon. Hodes soloed on *Love for Sale*, displaying his unique tremolos and chorded runs and giving the piece his signature blues-drenched sound. On a slower-than-usual *There'll Be Some Changes Made*, and a medium-tempo *Sometimes I'm Happy*, Hodes provided Davern with some unusual harmonies that moved him in different directions.

Kenny frequently played *After You've Gone* slowly, giving the song the doleful feeling that its lyrics demanded. Here, he took the tune from a meditative beginning to a striking close, crying out the closing notes at the top of the clarinet's range. Other tunes included *I Would Do Anything for You, New Orleans, All of Me*, and *Exactly Like You*, which begins sounding like

Armstrong's *Monday Date*. The release was well received. Frank Rubolino said that the result of reuniting Davern and Hodes was "an album of solid hot jazz performed in the traditional style of swing...."[16]

On May 25, Kenny and Elsa flew home. Coincidentally, during the months of April and May, Swissair was featuring music by Dick Wellstood on its transatlantic flights. There was a channel devoted to his albums, and two of the selections were from the *Dixie to Swing* and *Blue Three* albums that featured Davern.[17]

Kenny played at the Cornerstone on the last weekend in May and on two dates in June. The Cajun was a restaurant and bar located on 8th Avenue, between 17th and 18th Streets in Manhattan that hired good musicians for nominal pay on off-nights. Davern played there on four Mondays in June. The annual Jazz Festival, run by the Wein Organization, was now called the JVC Jazz Festival and, on June 24, it presented a program at Carnegie Hall called *For the Love of Louis*. Les Jeske, writing in the *New York Post* said: "Best soloist in the bands was Kenny Davern whose soulful clarinet playing is a succinct summation of the great traditional clarinetists of yore."[18] On the following day, Davern was at the picnic at Waterloo Village sponsored by the New Jersey Jazz Society. Then it was out to Indianapolis for four days, ending on the Fourth of July.

Kenny had been drinking alcohol since he was in high school.[19] At first, it was a rite of passage: all musicians drank and, since he was a musician, he drank too. Later, it was simply part of the environment in which he worked: the customers drank and they bought him drinks.

He wasn't an alcoholic. He drank for the same reason that most people did; because it relaxed him and induced a feeling of well-being. For a time, he dabbled with cocaine and sometimes smoked marijuana. They were part of the culture of post-war musicians, and using them allowed Davern to feel as if he fit in with that crowd. However, drugs were expensive and Davern could not sustain a habit without diverting money from the payment of household and other expenses. It got to the point at which he had to choose: he could continue living at home with Elsa or he could continue to do drugs. He chose to continue his life with Elsa.

However, he continued to drink. Alcohol releases the inhibitors that allow people to regulate their behavior. Kenny was witty when he was drinking, even if he had a tendency to be more sarcastic and caustic. However, every musician interviewed for this book who discussed the subject said that Kenny never drank enough while he was working to affect his playing.

When he was not drinking, he was able to control his temper—although he sometimes chose not to do so. When he drank, he was prone to say unkind and offensive things that he would later regret. And, when Kenny was on a tear, everyone—musicians, promoters, audiences, friends, and family—were targets. Drinking cost him work—and friends.

On July 9, 1988, Kenny and Elsa's daughter, Debbie, married Rob Wuensch at Joe Amiel's Old Mill Inn. Kenny drank to excess at the reception and behaved badly. The next morning, he did not remember what he had done and, when Elsa told him, he was mortified. He stopped drinking "cold turkey" and never took a drink again. He did it without any help from any external sources, refusing to go to an Alcoholic Anonymous meeting because the idea of public confession and self-abasement repelled him.[20]

Kenny had developed an interest in West Indian clarinet playing. He had discovered Alexandre Stellio, a clarinet player from Martinique, where the music combines French and African influences, much as the musicians in New Orleans did at the beginning of the twentieth century. Although Stellio did not play jazz, Davern had found stylistic similarities between Stellio's improvisations and those of the early New Orleans clarinetists, such as Albert Burbank and George Lewis. He played several recordings by Stellio for Dick Hyman, and the result was a program at the 92nd Street Y on July 26 during the *Jazz in July* festival.[21]

It was called *A Day in New Orleans, A Night in Martinique* and, for an evening, Davern and Hyman, along with Dan Barrett, Howard Alden, Major Holley, and Oliver Jackson became the St. Pierre Six. They dressed up in tropical hats and shirts and, as the *New York Times* reported, a few days later, they

> played lightly swinging tunes that floated gracefully over calypso and rhumba-like rhythms. Mr. Davern, a master soloist, let loose crying solos, filled with loping lines, and bent, bluesy, and insinuating notes. Mr. Davern and Mr. Barrett would play languid melodies in unison, tangle things up with New Orleans (or Martinique) styled polyphony, then break into solos.[22]

Directly after the program, Davern left for California to play the Peninsula Jazz Party in Palo Alto. Just over a week later, he and Ralph Sutton began a three-week tour of Australia and New Zealand. On August 22, they stopped at Bridgewater Mill in South Australia to record an album that they called *Revelations*.

The album opens with *Shine*, a tune that Sutton liked but that Davern did not play frequently. Kenny rides along the melodic line, propelled by Ralph's rolling bass. Kenny begins *Indiana* without accompaniment, in a contemplative vein, until Sutton joins in to provide a warm foundation for the remainder of the piece. The next track features Sutton alone in an extended medley of Ellington tunes. Kenny's feature is *New Orleans*, and he inflects the tune with a mournful air. There is a happy sound to *Three Little Words*, which is followed by *Sugar*. An up-tempo *Should I* and a relaxed *Dinah* are the other two tunes on this disk. On some tunes, Davern and Sutton played without accompaniment; however, on three of them, drummer Bill Polain was added.

The album was originally issued on cassette, and limitations of space allowed for only seven tunes to be included. When the CD version came out, it contained all of the songs and, because there was far more time available than tunes to fill it, alternate takes of the Ellington medley and *New Orleans* were included. Michael Steinman gave the CD a good review in the *Mississippi Rag*, as did Eddie Cook in *Jazz Journal International*.[23]

On the way home from Australia, Davern stopped in Colorado for the Gibsons' Labor Day party. After ten days in Manasquan, he performed at the Third Minneapolis Jazz Party that included Scott Hamilton and Marshall Royal. There were more dates at home until, on the weekend of September 30, he participated in the North Carolina Jazz Party for benefit of Multiple Sclerosis in Raleigh, an event that subsequently was renamed the Triangle Jazz Party. Early in October, he performed at the Midland Jazz Classic. After some jobs in the Northeast, Davern headed off for two weeks with the Floating Jazz Festival.

For the third consecutive year, Hank O'Neal invited pianist Mel Powell to appear. Born in 1923, Powell was an established talent before the end of his teen years. At the age of eighteen, he recorded with Wingy Manone. He then joined Benny Goodman, for whom he also composed and arranged. He was featured with the big band as well as in Goodman's small groups. Powell was inducted into the military in 1942, and he became a key member of Glenn Miller's Army Air Force Band. After the war, Powell played with Django Reinhardt in Paris. He rejoined Goodman for a time, freelanced and moved to Los Angeles, made some superb recordings for the Vanguard label with Ruby Braff and Paul Quinichette, and returned to New York to rejoin Goodman for a nightclub engagement in 1954.

Powell had received classical instruction as a child and, in the mid 1940s, his interest in non-jazz forms of music was rekindled. He enrolled at Yale University, where he studied composition under Paul Hindemith. In 1955, he left the field of jazz. For a time, he taught at Yale University, then went to California, where he helped found the California Institute for the Arts in Los Angeles in 1969. He taught there through 1988 and, from 1970 to 1988, also served as dean of its school of music. He became a major classical composer, winning the Pulitzer Prize for composition in 1990.

By 1986, Powell was suffering from muscular dystrophy and was unable to get around without a wheelchair. He had not been involved in jazz for about thirty years. Nonetheless, when Hank O'Neal invited him to be part of his Floating Jazz Festival, he accepted. Powell, whose talents as a speaker and raconteur rivaled his abilities as a pianist, captivated the audience and his fellow musicians. He returned in 1987 (a CD of his performance was released on the Chiaroscuro label, titled *The Return of Mel Powell*) and again in 1988.

Powell had an engaging personality and, as Hank O'Neal recalled, Davern, like many other musicians, often spent time with him on these cruises.

> I remember that he was absolutely in awe of Mel Powell, as was everybody, because Kenny may not have been as interested in classical music as he was in jazz, but it shaped him far more than many other musicians. Mel was so smart in talking about things like that, as was Kenny, that he was able to sit there with Mel and pick his brain. Mel was equally versed on the dramatic literature, which was what he was the most interested in as far as I could tell. They had wonderful conversations together, and I'm sure that Kenny went running back, when he left the ship, to the record store, and buying things that Mel suggested. . . .
>
> It was not unusual for Mel to get up early and go into a room that was sort of secluded. Nobody would be around, and he would be playing Bach all morning. The musicians would sneak in and listen, and sit there and listen quietly as Mel played his non-jazz repertoire. He didn't concertize, he didn't do any of that anymore. The only public performances he probably had since the early 1960s were the three years that he played at the Floating Jazz Festivals, which was a great loss from the standpoint of all the music that wasn't played. Of all the people who were on board the ships in those years, this was the person that Kenny was the most enthusiastic about spending time with. But then you could say that about Dizzy Gillespie or anybody else. They all wanted to spend time with Mel Powell.[24]

Back on land, Davern worked one weekend in Colorado for Dick Gibson followed by another at the end of November in Manassas, Virginia. He closed out the year with dates at Windows on the World at the top of the World Trade Center; at J's, a new club on West 97th Street and Broadway in Manhattan; and at the Cornerstone. Kenny noted in his date book that he had spent 163 days on the road in 1988.[25]

Davern seemed to start 1989 as if he wanted to surpass that figure. After working at the Rainbow Room on New Year's Day, Kenny and Elsa flew to New Mexico to join Ralph and Sunnie Sutton at the Thunderbird Lodge for a week that mixed vacation and work. He was home and worked a weekend at the Cornerstone before heading off, first to play on January 18 in Jackson, Mississippi, for the Bourbon Street Jazz Society, and then at the Pensacola Jazz Party on the following weekend. On three successive weekends, he was in Decatur, Illinois, at the North Carolina Jazz Festival, and at San Diego's Jazz Party. He came home for what turned out to be a badly thought-out recording date.[26]

George Shearing had enjoyed playing in a dixieland format at his 1987 Town Hall concert and decided that he wanted to record an album of that type of music. On February 14 and 15, 1989, he assembled many of the same musicians who had been with him on that date: Warren Vache, Jr., George Masso, and Kenny Davern, plus Ken Peplowski for the tenor saxophone spot, bassist Ian Swainson, and drummer Jerry Fuller. The album was called *George Shearing in Dixieland*.[27]

The result was less than satisfactory. Most of the pieces were far from the dixieland genre—they included *Clap Your Hands*; *Destination Moon*, *Soon*; *Take Five*; *Lullaby of Birdland*; and *Desafinado*, and simply did not lend themselves to this type of treatment. Almost all of the tunes were over-arranged, often in what seemed to be a parody of dixieland, and most of the solos were short and relatively uninspired.

As Davern spent increasing amounts of time leading small groups playing improvised music, he had allowed his sight reading skills to atrophy. The relatively complex charts that Shearing had written were sometimes difficult for Kenny, and his struggles adversely affected his mood and the progress of the session.[28] That problem aside, Davern thought the entire project was a waste of time, a view shared by some of the other musicians. As Ken Peplowski said: "It was just a weird project. Somebody must have thought this would be a fun project to do. But, the arrangements were corny, and the rhythm section was not the right rhythm section for that kind of music."[29] Warren Vache, Jr., echoed that opinion.

> I thought it was ill-conceived. I thought that George could have done better things with his time. I'd heard him play better. Certainly, we could have done better things with our time. But that's what they wanted to make, and that's what we made. I happily cashed the check and went home and forgot all about it.[30]

The liner notes had been written by Leonard Feather and began: "Why a dixieland recording by George Shearing? Well, why not?" Most of the critics savaged the album and, although they gave the soloists good reviews, they answered Feather's question, often in excruciating detail. Floyd Levin said, "After playing it a few times, I realized that I could not deal with the presentation . . . and decided to set it aside and forget it." Another reviewer said: "The arrangements were 'slick,' the album a rather bland pastiche . . . , the rhythm section adequate but unimaginative. . . . However, the album was rescued by the excellent solo contributions from the gifted front-line musicians."[31]

On Sunday, February 19, Davern joined the World's Greatest Jazz Band (WGJB) for a short but leisurely tour through the Southeast. On this trip, Lawson and Haggart were joined by Davern, George Masso, Al Klink on tenor sax, John Bunch, Bucky Pizzarelli, and Jake Hanna. Davern landed in Atlanta that afternoon and, at 7:30 p.m., the band performed for a buffet and dance at the Atlanta Music Club. Recording sessions for George Buck were scheduled for the afternoons of the next two days, then the band had the 22nd off. They traveled to Hilton Head, South Carolina, on Thursday, but did not work until Friday night, when they gave a concert at the Hilton Head Inn. Saturday was an off-day in Savannah.

From Sunday, February 26 through March 2, they ate, slept, and performed at the Cloisters on Sea Island, an exclusive and expensive resort off the coast of Georgia. The schedule was not grueling. Their days were free. From 6:30 to 7:30 p.m., they played for dancing. Then, they had dinner with the guests of the hotel. At 9:30, they went back to work and played until 12:30 a.m. The band returned to Savannah on March 3 and played a private party. They traveled to Atlanta on Saturday and played at a local country club and, on the next day, they flew home.[32]

The recordings made at the two sessions for George Buck's Jazzology label were both released under the name of the Lawson–Haggart Jazz Band. Although the personnel did not change from when they had appeared at the resort as the WGJB, the difference was in the repertoire and the absence of the arrangements that gave the WGJB its distinctive sound. On February 20, they recorded an album of instrumentals that was titled *The Legendary Lawson–Haggart Jazz Band, Jazz at Its Best*. Most of the selections were evergreens—*Yellow Dog Blues, Wolverine Blues, Squeeze Me, and Blue Lou*, among them—and the atmosphere was relaxed as old standards were revisited and revised. Kenny was featured on *Jazz Me Blues*, and had some nice exchanges with the band near the end.

Barbara Lea joined the band on the following day, and the CD was called *Barbara Lea and the Legendary Lawson–Haggart Jazz Band, You're the Cats*. Many of the songs that Lea selected for this date were relatively obscure, including *You're the Cats, Do What You Do, Moonshine Lullaby, Dixie*

Cinderella, and *My Walking Stick*. There are some more recognizable pieces, including *For You, For Me, For Evermore*; *Waiting at the End of the Road*; and *There's a Man in My Life*. Hugh Rainey gave the instrumental album a decent review. The Barbara Lea release was reviewed well by David Badham and Dick Neeld.[33]

Davern played at the Cornerstone before heading off to Arizona for the Paradise Valley Jazz Party. He was in St. Louis on March 18–19, then stopped at home to repack his bags, pick up his passport, and head for the United Kingdom. His tour began in Belfast, Ireland, on March 23. Two days later, he was in London, and then he set off for a series of one-night engagements at his usual places. Kenny flew back to the United States on April 19, spent the next weekend playing in Colorado Springs, and then worked the last week of the month in Bern, Switzerland.

The Jim Cullum Jazz Band made its home at the Riverwalk in San Antonio, and Kenny joined them on the first weekend in May. Later that month, he was in Manassas, Virginia, for a recreation of a typical Eddie Condon Town Hall program. On May 25–30, he played in Santa Fe, came home to play with Ed Polcer, followed by a gig with Howard Alden, Milt Hinton, and Giampaolo Biagi. From there, it was out to the Glenn Ranch Jazz Party in Rialto, California.[34]

Kenny's next recording date was put together by Milt Hinton. Howard Alden, who was also on the date, recalled how it came about. "When Milt's first book of photographs was published, it turned out to be far more of a success than he ever expected. He started getting a lot of royalties. He decided that whenever he wanted to record with someone he really liked, he'd put together a record date and record two or three tunes just to collect an archive."[35]

At various times, beginning in 1989, Hinton rented studio space at the Manhattan Recording Company and invited four different groups of musicians, led by Davern, Warren Vache, Jr., Frank Wess, and Sylvia Sims to record sets of three or four tunes with him. They were not released during Hinton's lifetime: after his death in the year 2000, they were issued on a Chiaroscuro CD, which was given the picturesque title of *The Basement Tapes*.[36]

Davern, Howard Alden, and drummer Jackie Williams joined Milt for the first session that was held on June 23, 1989. Milt not only played, but also sang on their first number—*Old Man Time*, a humorous tune that Hinton adopted as his anthem in his advancing years. The other songs, *Summertime* and *Travelin' All Alone*, were both taken at faster-than-usual tempos and had little of the emotion that Kenny often imparted to them.

Davern always attempted to avoid participating in any tribute to or recreation of the works of Benny Goodman. However, on June 24, he was at

Carnegie Hall to participate in a Salute to Benny Goodman. Kenny played *That's a Plenty* in the style that Benny had when he recorded the tune in 1928. At the end of the month, he was again on the road, performing in North Indianapolis on June 30–July 2, then moving on to Elkart, Indiana, one week later. He spent a week in France at the festival in Nice, came home to play at Windows on the World, and appeared at the 92nd Street Y in its *Jazz in July* series.

The Fifth Annual Minneapolis Jazz Party was held on August 4–6, and Davern was there. He had jobs in New York and Pennsylvania, then it was off to Europe for a round of festivals. He played in Ireland on August 17 at the Belfast Jazz Festival. The next day, he was in Wales at the Brecon Jazz Festival, followed by an appearance at the Edinburgh Jazz Festival with the WGJB.[37]

The fall season began in Colorado with the Gibsons' Labor Day party. He played a Friday night date at the Cornerstone, then flew to Charlotte, North Carolina, for a Sunday engagement. The Fortune Garden was an upscale Chinese restaurant located on the second floor near the corner of 3rd Avenue and East 49th Street in Manhattan. It had a grand piano in the middle of the room and featured pianists such as Sir Roland Hanna, Tommy Flanagan, Dave McKenna, and Dick Wellstood. Kenny was there with Jane Jarvis from September 12 to 17. Then it was off to Aspen for Jerome Jazz, a party at the Jerome Hotel put together by Ralph and Sunnie Sutton and, at the end of the month, he was in Raleigh for the Triangle Jazz Party.

At the beginning of October, he had two jobs in Connecticut and a date at the Juilliard School. During the week of October 14–21, he and Elsa were on a cruise to Bermuda aboard the S.S. *Royal Viking Star* with guitarist James Chirillo, bassist Frank Tate, and Jake Hanna. On October 26, he was at Tavern-on-the Green in Manhattan's Central Park. After dates at the Zimmerli Art Museum on the campus of Rutgers University in New Brunswick, and the Cornerstone, he boarded the S.S. *Seaward* for a week on the Floating Jazz Festival.[38]

On the weekend of November 10, he played at the Cornerstone on Friday and Saturday, and in Sarasota on Sunday. On the following weekend, he played for Dick Gibson in Denver, and at the Church of the Heavenly Rest in Manhattan the next day. There was a party for Zoot Sims at the New School on December 3, and a gala at the Riviera Hotel in Las Vegas on the weekend of December 8. After several dates around Manhattan, Davern flew back to Colorado for a private party. At year end, Davern totaled up his days on the road: they numbered 179.[39]

The statistic only confirmed a disturbing fact: that he had to keep on traveling to earn a living. Almost all of the restaurants in southern New Jersey where he had worked with some regularity had either closed or abandoned their policies of presenting jazz music. There were no more jobs at such as places the Yankee Clipper, Ishkabibble, the Old Mill, and the Union House. The was still some activity in the middle of the state: he worked regularly at the Cornerstone and occasionally at O'Connor's and Gullivers, and he continued to appear at private parties. Although there were jobs in Manhattan, most of them were one-night stands. The real money was out of town—at jazz parties and festivals—or overseas.

So, as 1990 began, Davern was on the road. First was his annual visit to the Thunderbird Lodge in early January. Then, on successive weekends, he was at the Pensacola Jazz Party, the Central Illinois Jazz Festival, and the North Carolina Jazz Festival. He flew to California for a visit to the University of Redlands on February 8, followed by a weekend in San Diego. Dates in New Jersey and Manhattan preceded a return visit to North Carolina. Over the weekend of March 10–11, he was the guest of honor at the Paradise Valley Jazz Party in Scottsdale.[40]

From mid-March to April 15, he was on tour in England and Scotland, playing on several different occasions at London's Pizza Express, then making stops in the smaller towns. For a week, beginning on April 16, he was in Italy, appearing at venues in Milan, Turino, Spezia, Genoa, and Venice. In this same period, he was profiled in an extended article in *Destinations* magazine that was written by Abby Ellis.[41]

He came home; played at the Cornerstone; traveled to Vero Beach, Florida, where he performed for the Treasure Coast Jazz Society; and then left for Europe. From May 7–13, he was at the Bern, Switzerland, Jazz Festival, where he performed as part of the WGJB. While they were there, Davern, Vache, and Hanna recorded some tracks with the Wolverines, a jazz orchestra domiciled in Bern. The CD, which was not released in the United States, was titled *The Wolverines Jazz Band and Their American Friends*.

At the conclusion of the festival, Davern traveled to Rome to participate in making the soundtrack of *Bix: An Interpretation of a Legend*. The movie was produced by Lino Patruno and purported to portray the life of Bix Beiderbecke. Patruno had put together an orchestra composed mainly of local musicians who were augmented by Davern, Tom Pletcher, David Sager, Bob Wilber, and Vince Giordano. In most cases, the tunes on the soundtrack had been recorded by Bix; however, some were in vogue at the time of Bix's life and were included for setting.

Davern appeared on only four titles. On *Singin' the Blues*, he took the role of Jimmy Dorsey and played his part sounding much like the older man. Although Bix never played with the New Orleans Rhythm Kings, he did listen to and sit in with them. There were two pieces from the Kings' repertoire on the soundtrack, *Maple Leaf Rag* and *Tin Roof Blues*. The clarinetist in the New Orleans Rhythm Kings was Leon Roppolo, whom Kenny admired. In what the liner notes described as "symbolic dedication" to Roppolo, Kenny emulated the unusual vibrato and tone that marked older man's playing. The fourth tune was *My Pretty Girl*, which Bix recorded on February 1, 1927, with Jean Goldkette and His Orchestra. Danny Polo was the clarinet player then: on this version, Davern made no effort to recreate Polo's part, and the musical voice that soars above the orchestra was clearly Kenny's.

Although the film was flayed by the critics, they treated the music more kindly. Kenny was very unhappy with this recording and, although he was given a number of copies that he could resell, he never took them with him to parties or other gigs. (A box of them was in his garage when he died.)[42] This was the last recording on which Kenny attempted to replicate the sound of anyone else. From this time forward, he insisted on playing in his own voice, regardless of the nature of the project.

When Kenny came home, he played a few jobs before, at the end of May, he, Bob Wilber, and the musicians who were onstage in Denver in 1972, when Soprano Summit was born, reassembled to make the first recording by Summit Reunion.

Notes

1. Davern, quoted by Steve Voce in "Scratching the Surface," *Jazz Journal International*, 41, no. 6 (June 1988): 12.
2. Shirley Klett, "Flip Phillips, Bjarne Nerem, Kenny Davern, Mood Indigo," *Cadence*, 15, no. 8 (August 1989): 33.
3. Date Book; *Jersey Jazz*, 15, no. 7 (September, 1987): 7; High School event program; Minneapolis party schedule; Thomas P. Hustad, interview by the author.
4. Elsa Davern, interview by the author.
5. Hank O'Neal, Recorded Recollections.
6. Date Book.
7. Peter Clayton interviewer, recorded and broadcast on *The Sounds of Jazz*, on BBC Radio 2, probably 26 March 1989.
8. Quoted in Dan Morgenstern, liner notes to *Kenny Davern, Breezin' Along*, Arbors ARCD 19170, December 1996.
9. Howard Alden, interview by the author.
10. Although the inserts to both CDs say that they were recorded in January 1988, Davern's date books for 1987 and 1988, coupled with interviews with Howard Alden and Leroy "Sam" Parkins, all confirm that both recordings were made on December 7–8, 1987.

11. Leroy "Sam" Parkins, interview by the author.

12. George Kanzler, liner notes to *I'll See You in My Dreams*, Musicmasters CIJD 60212.

13. Shirley Klett, "Kenny Davern, One Hour Tonight," *Cadence*, 15, no. 4 (April 1989): 63–64; *Jazz Journal International*, 42, no. 2 (February 1989): 6; Russ Chase, "Kenny Davern, One Hour Tonight," *IAJRC Journal*, 22, no. 2 (Spring 1989): 63.

14. Jack Sohmer, "Kenny Davern, I'll See You in My Dreams," *Jazz Times*, March 1990, p. 32; Will Friedwald, "Recordings View, A New Swing for the Once-Forgotten Clarinet," *New York Times*, 3 February 1991; *Time*, "Critics Voices," 12 February 1990, Randy Salman, "I'll See You in My Dreams," *The Clarinet*, November–December 1992.

15. Howard Alden, interview by the author.

16. Frank Rubolino, "Kenny Davern, The Last Reunion," *Cadence*, 24, no. 6 (June 1998): 46.

17. *Jazz Journal International*, 41, no. 5 (May 1988): 3; Swissair in-flight brochure. Responsibility for putting Wellstood's recordings on Swissair's flights rested with Johnny Simmen, a jazz fan and writer who worked for Swissair.

18. Les Jeske, "This One Was for Satchmo," *New York Post*, 27 June 1988.

19. Monk Rowe, interview by the author.

20. Elsa Davern, conversation with the author.

21. Dick Hyman, *Thinking of Kenny Davern*, unpublished.

22. Peter Watrous, "Review/Music, The Sound of Martinique," *New York Times*, 28 July 1988.

23. Michael Steinman, "When Sutton Smiles," *Mississippi Rag*, xxxii, no. 10 (October 2004): 31; Eddie Cook, "Revelations," *Jazz Journal International*, 55, no. 11 (November 2002): 44.

24. Hank O'Neal, Recorded Recollections.

25. Date Book; Thomas P. Hustad, interview by the author; *Jersey Jazz*, 16, no. 7 (September 1988): 23, and 16, no. 10 (December 1988): 14; Schacter, Sutton, 289.

26. Date Book; Thunderbird Lodge event program; *Jersey Jazz*, 16, no. 11 (January 1989): 7; Contract for North Carolina Jazz Festival; *Jazz Journal International*, 42, no. 5 (May 1989): 12.

27. Leonard Feather, liner notes to *George Shearing in Dixieland*, Concord CCD 4388. Davern's Date Book furnishes the dates in February on which the recording was made.

28. Ken Peplowski, Warren Vache, Jr., interviews by the author.

29. Ken Peplowski, interview by the author.

30. Warren Vache, interview by the author.

31. Floyd Levin, *Jersey Jazz*, 18, no. 6 (July–August 1990): 20; Hugh Rainey, "George Shearing in Dixieland," *Jazz Journal International*, 43, no. 2 (February 1990): 46.

32. Tour itinerary.

33. Hugh Rainey, "The Legendary Lawson–Haggart Jazz Band, Jazz at Its Best," *Jazz Journal International*, 46, no. 4 (April 1993): 37; David Badham, "Barbara Lea

and the Legendary Lawson–Haggart Jazz Band, You're The Cats," *Jazz Journal International*, 43, no. 6 (June 1990): 36; Dick Neeld, "Views and Reviews," *Jersey Jazz*, 18, no. 11 (January 1991): 16-17.

34. Date Book; *Jazz Journal International*, 42, no. 3 (March 1989): 3.

35. Howard Alden, interview by the author.

36. Bill Crow, liner notes to *Milt Hinton, the Basement Tapes*, Chiaroscuro CR(D) 222.

37. Date Book; contract for north Indianapolis appearance; *Jazz Journal International*, 42, no. 9 (September 1989): 2, 15, and 42, no. 10 (October 1989): 2–3; contract for Jazz in July appearance; *Jersey Jazz*, 17, no. 6 (July–August 1989): 11; contract with Edinburgh International Jazz Festival Limited.

38. Date Book; *Jersey Jazz*, 17, no. 7 (September 1989): 25; Schacter, Sutton, 291–292; contract for Triangle, Jazz Party; *Star Ledger*, 27 (October 1989): 53.

39. Date Book; *Jersey Jazz*, 17, no. 9 (November 1989): 19; contract for the Riviera appearance.

40. Date Book; North Carolina Jazz Festival program; Redlands, *Daily Facts*, 14 January 1990; Paradise Valley Jazz Party program

41. Abby Ellis, "Kenny Davern, Jazz Ambassador," *Destinations* (Air Wisconsin edition), April, 1990, 13.

42. Kenny Davern, conversation with the author; Elsa Davern interview by the author.

CHAPTER THIRTEEN

Summit Reunion

As the events that precipitated the dissolution of Soprano Summit faded in the memories of the principals, Wilber and Davern began to perform together occasionally at jazz parties and festivals. Their appearances were usually punctuated by requests for tunes like *Song of Songs* and the other mainstays of Soprano Summit. However, Davern had given up the soprano saxophone, and both he and Wilber had matured musically over the years. They steadfastly refused to regress musically or attempt to recreate a long-gone group. Nonetheless, they still enjoyed playing together and ultimately decided to record together.[1]

When they met at Rudy Van Gelder's recording studio at the end of May 1990, they were fortunate in that Dick Hyman, Bucky Pizzarelli, Milt Hinton, and Bobby Rosengarden—all of the members of the group that started everything at the Gibsons' Labor Day party almost eighteen years before—were available. They spent two days completing nine acceptable takes, which were released on Hank O'Neal's Chiaroscuro label. Because Davern no longer played soprano saxophone, they called this group Summit Reunion.

The recording starts with a medium-tempo *As Long As I Live*. The opening theme is played in thirds by Wilber on soprano and Davern on clarinet and, from the outset, it is clear that the unplayed third note—the added harmonic that Davern always mentioned—is still present. The next tune is *Lover Come Back to Me*, which features some exciting solos by both leaders.

The song that established Summit Reunion as an exciting and viable group is *St. Louis Blues*, which runs about eleven-and-one-half minutes in length. The theme begins in harmony and continues for two choruses with either Davern or Wilber playing melody while the other plays counterpoint, all propelled by the four-man rhythm section. Solos by Hinton, Pizzarelli, and Hyman follow, and then Wilber launches into a three-minute outing that, spurred along by Hyman's piano, relentlessly builds to an exciting climax. It was an exceptional performance, and Davern remembered it well.

> Wilber is a challenge. He plays things that are incredibly sublime, so magnificently put together that I say, "I wish I'd played that." He did it on *St. Louis Blues*, on the Hank O'Neal date. I couldn't believe what he did. He played his chorus, and I thought, "I gotta follow this? How am I gonna do that?" So I started very, very soft, and I had to build. Thank Christ that I rose to the occasion. But it was a very, very difficult thing to do. He played so great. And he'll do that, and I'll say, "I wish I'd gone first."[2]

Davern's solo is generally regarded as one of his best and, after it is finished, he and Wilber join together to close out the song.

A stately *Black and Blue* brings the temperature down, and then the pair embark on a lively *Should I*. The Original Dixieland Jazz Band had recorded (*Leena Was the Queen of*) *Palesteena*, a minor key Middle-European sounding piece, at the end of 1920. Davern, who was playing it at live appearances throughout this period, had retained much of its klezmer-sounding origins but stripped it of the schmaltzy, bar mitzvah-party effects. He has the leading voice on this version. *Old Fashioned Love* features some interesting inside work among Davern, Wilber, and Hyman. *Sunny Side of the Street*, is next and *Limehouse Blues* ends the music on the CD.

Although Kenny and Bob were pleased with the music, there was always the uncertainty of how the audience would react to their new collaboration. They needn't have worried. When Davern went to the Oslo Jazz Festival in August, he took a cassette of the session with him. He was interviewed on a radio program that had a live audience and, during the show, he played *St. Louis Blues*. When it was finished, the audience stood and cheered, and Davern thought, "These people are cheering a cassette: maybe this band should go on the road."[3]

The release was reviewed favorably by the jazz and non-jazz press alike. Eddie Cook was enthusiastic in *Jazz Journal International*, and the CD was voted one of the magazine's ten best new albums for 1991. Ira Gitler picked it as one of the best Jazz CDs for 1991.[4] The disc got a good review from George Kanzler, and Russ Chase said "If you have to, trade your yacht for it." Writing in the *Wall Street Journal*, John McDonough remarked: "The work of Kenny Davern is so singular among world-class clarinetists. . . . One note from Davern may do the work of twenty from another." *Time* magazine said that the group ". . . scales a new peak."[5]

The CD generated a demand for appearances by Summit Reunion and, over the next sixteen years, Davern and Wilber obliged. However, there were substantial differences from their earlier association. Summit Reunion did not have a library of written arrangements, as did Soprano Summit, and Bob and Kenny did not bring a third musician with them as they had with Marty Grosz. Instead, when they went on tour, they used local musicians to fill out the band, with the result that their live performances contained more tried-and-true songs and less novel ones.

There was one other difference between Soprano Summit and Summit Reunion. When Soprano Summit began to generate public interest, Davern believed that it had a chance to achieve an audience beyond the jazz party–jazz festival community. He was excited by its prospects, and allowed himself to become emotionally involved in the possibilities that popular success offered. But, Soprano Summit fell apart and none of these dreams came to pass.

Davern harbored no such vision with Summit Reunion. It was nothing more than an opportunity for him to perform with someone whose playing sparked and musically challenged him. And thus, there was no written agreement between them as there had been with Soprano Summit. If work came, they would deal with it on an ad hoc basis. If it did not, Davern knew that he would survive.[6]

Less than one week after completing the Summit Reunion CD, Davern was back in the recording studio. Warren Vache, Jr., had met French trumpet player Alain Bouchet when both of them appeared at the *Grande Parade du Jazz* in Nice in 1984. They became friends, and Vache decided to arrange a recording date for Bouchet in the United States. He put together a rhythm section of John Bunch, Howard Alden, Major Holley, and Jackie Williams. Kenny Davern joined them on June 5, and Ken Peplowski performed on the 6th.[7]

Davern appeared on only three tunes. *Sugar*, the first song on the CD, is taken at a leisurely pace with solos by Bouchet, Vache, and Davern. All three again solo on *I Can't Believe That You're in Love with Me*, but the brass have the dominant part. The third song is *Black and Blue*, on which Davern is featured. This was a thoroughly enjoyable album that received good reviews, but it did not create a great demand for Bouchet in the United States. Moreover, he had a wife and children in France. Shortly after the recording date, he returned home to Paris and resumed his career there.[8]

In between these sessions, Elsa Davern had the opportunity to enjoy the spotlight. On June 3, 1990, she was the subject of an article in the *Style Makers* column of the *New York Times*. Written by C. Clairborne Ray, the article was entitled *Elsa Davern, Jewelry Maker*, and related that Elsa's necklaces were in great demand wherever she went. She was quoted as saying: "If I wear a piece I particularly like, I end up selling it."[9]

The summer season took its usual course. There were jobs in Manhattan and at the Cornerstone before the Daverns embarked on a week-long cruise aboard the Royal Viking Lines' S.S. *Royal Star*. Along with Howard Alden, Marshal Wood, and Giampaolo Biagi, they sailed to Bermuda and back, playing on about half of the nights. The ship docked in New York on June 23, and Davern drove directly to Stanhope for the New Jersey Jazz Society's annual picnic at Waterloo Village. He was in Indianapolis on June 29–July 1, worked at the Cornerstone, and spent July 10 at Rudy Van Gelder's studio, helping to mix the Summit Reunion album.[10]

On the following day, he was interviewed by Dan Morgenstern. Born in Munich, Germany, in 1929, Morgenstern spent his youth growing up in Vienna and Copenhagen before immigrating to the United States in 1947. From 1964, he was the New York editor of *DownBeat* magazine until 1967, when he became its chief editor, a post that he held until 1973. He became the director of the Institute of Jazz Studies at Rutgers University in 1976, and continues to hold that position today. A prolific writer, he authored numerous articles, contributed to and helped edit a number of books, won six Grammy Awards for Best Album Notes, and received ASCAP's Deems Taylor Award for *Jazz People* in 1977, and again in 2005 for *Living with Jazz*.[11] He serves as the series editor of the *Studies in Jazz* series, published by Scarecrow Press.

Morgenstern was also the host of an hour-long show on radio station WBGO, titled *Jazz from the Archives*. From time to time, he would interview an artist and, over the course of the hour, intersperse some of that musician's recordings with his comments. The interview with Davern lasted two hours: half of it was broadcast on August 19, 1990, and the remainder was aired one week later.

In the first segment, Morgenstern played a variety of Kenny's recordings including *St. Louis Blues* from the Summit Reunion album, *Day Tripper* from the Jersey Ramblers/Can O' Worms demo tape that Kenny and the ex-Ferryboat musicians had made in 1969, *Misery and the Blues* from his first album with Jack Teagarden in 1954, and *Trio 3* from the 1978 *Unexpected* album. As Morgenstern introduced each cut, Davern supplied some history that surrounded the making of the record.

The second hour opened with *I'll See You in My Dreams* from the CD of the same name. After Davern discussed why he was then playing in a quartet with guitar, bass, and drum, Morgenstern switched subjects and asked Kenny about the differences between the Albert and the Boehm systems. That led up to *I've Been Working on the Railroad* from the *Dixieland Doodlers* album with Dick Cary. Kenny had brought with him the tape that Dave Frishberg had made in 1961 of the band at Nick's, and played *Royal Garden Blues*. Next was *Milton Swing* from *The Very Thought of You* CD, and the last cut was from the *Live and Swinging* album.

Three days after the interview, Kenny and Elsa were off on another Royal Viking line cruise, this time to Alaska, along with Bob and Windy Haggart, Jake and Denisa Hanna, and Johnny Varro. The work wasn't very taxing: they played five nights out of fourteen.[12] Davern was not an adventuresome tourist. He joked that the best way to see Alaska was by sitting in his La-Z-Boy with a *National Geographic* magazine on his lap. He wouldn't shoot the rapids because he had never learned to swim, and he wouldn't take a helicopter ride to view and stand on the glaciers. He preferred to stay on the ship and let Elsa go.

She remembered that Kenny had agreed to meet her for lunch after one of her excursions. He didn't show up and, when she found him on the ship, he explained, "I left the ship, walked down a long dock, and saw three burly men coming toward me wearing t-shirts printed with an American flag and the words 'Burn this, ass-hole.' I turned around and went back to the ship."[13]

When the boat docked at Vancouver, Kenny flew to Toronto, where he recorded five titles on what turned out to be Art Hodes's last recording.[14] The CD was called *Art Hodes, the Final Session*, and it presented him in four different groupings, none of which had a rhythm section. In addition to playing solo, Hodes duetted with either Jim Galloway or Davern, and performed four titles in a trio setting with both of them.

The trio numbers, *Old Grey Bonnet*, *Swanee River*, *In the Shade of the Old Apple Tree*, and *Melancholy Baby*, are interesting for the interplay between the horn players. Galloway has a instantly recognizable sound on the soprano saxophone, and he took an uncommon approach to all of the tunes. The harmonies and counterpoint melodies played by Davern and Galloway brought a fresh sound to these well-played titles. Davern's only duet number was *Summertime*.

Davern went back to New Jersey and, after a few days, flew to Norway for the Oslo Jazz Festival. From there, he went on to the United Kingdom for a tour that had been arranged by Brian Peerless. He appeared in several small towns on the 13th and 14th and, after a day off for travel, performed in Belfast with the Eddie Condon Celebration Band, led by Ed Polcer.[15]

Davern, Scott Hamilton, Howard Alden, bassist Leonard Gaskin, and Giampaolo Biagi appeared for a set at the Brecon Jazz Festival on August 17. Peerless recorded the event and subsequently released it on videotape. Hamilton, Davern, and Alden were in excellent form that day. The set started with *Elsa's Dream*, on which everyone was cooking. Another fast number with extended solos by everyone, *The Man I Love*, followed, and then the tempo slowed down for Hamilton's feature, a lyrical duet with Alden on *How Long Has This Been Going On*.

The pace picked up again for *After You've Gone*, which was fast, but not frantic. Davern's solo feature was *Summertime*, which had a lovely lush sound and an exceptional chorus by Alden. The scheduled closing tune was *Hindustan*, but, when that barnburner left the crowd demanding "more," Hamilton, Davern, and Alden gave them a warm version of *Mood Indigo*.

The Davern–Hamilton Quintet performed again at Brecon on the 18th, then traveled by bus overnight to Scotland for the Twelfth Edinburgh International Jazz Festival. At this point, the pace of his appearances increased. Over the next eight days, Davern performed several times daily in different venues with differing groups, appearing at times with the Condon Band, Ken Peplowski, Mose Allison, Alden, Roy Williams, and Danny Moss. On August 26, he returned home. Martin Gayford, who was at Brecon and Edinburgh, gave him high praise for both events.[16]

At about this time, *Windplayer* magazine published the responses to its interviews of a number of clarinet players who had been asked: "What do you tell sax players who want to take up clarinet?" Davern was one of the interviewees, and he responded "Why bother?"[17]

The Gibson party consumed Davern's Labor Day weekend. He was back in the New Jersey–New York–Pennsylvania area for two weeks before returning to Colorado for the Jerome Jazz Party in Aspen. There were dates in Wilkes Barre, Pennsylvania, and Raleigh, North Carolina, and some appearances at the Cornerstone before Davern left on October 5 for two weeks in Germany. He came home and, after four days, left for a week on the S.S. *Norway* at the Floating Jazz Festival.

For several years, Hank O'Neal had teamed Kenny with Flip Phillips, and they were together on this trip. Writer Stanley Dance was also on the cruise and afterward he wrote: "Davern's fluency and intuitive syncopation, often imbued with passion, accounted for some of the week's high spots. He loves to climb through all his instrument's registers and is surely the most individual of today's clarinetists."[18]

For the rest of the year, Kenny played another party for Dick Gibson, performed at the Rhode Island School of Design in Providence, and worked with Howard Alden and Ed Polcer. He spent Christmas in Sarasota, followed by two days in Naples, Florida. At the end of the year, he played the Cornerstone.[19]

Although Davern had sporadically played with Tony DeNicola since the late 1970s, there seemed to be no exceptional spark between them. About eight years older than Kenny, DeNicola had played with several small bands, until he caught on with the Freddie Martin Orchestra, which was then featuring a young singer named Merv Griffin. DeNicola stayed with them until his grandfather became ill, and he had to quit and return home to help run the family bar in North Trenton. A call from tenor saxophonist Charlie Ventura's manager ended that career for Tony, and he went back to music playing drums in Ventura's trio.

Ventura was stranded in Las Vegas and the group broke up. DeNicola scuffled for a while until Ventura was able to land another booking, this time at the Flamingo Hotel, opposite the big band of Harry James. Harry was having problems with his drummer, and periodically asked Tony to sit in. James liked DeNicola, who was having his own problems with Ventura's manager. Eventually, DeNicola quit the Ventura job, and he was immediately hired by Harry James.

Tony did not enjoy being away from home and, shortly afterward, he left the James organization and went back to Trenton. He took a part-time job teaching music in the school system of Lawrenceville, New Jersey, and went back to school at Trenton State College (now known as the College of New Jersey), where he was awarded a bachelor's degree and then a master's. He began to teach at Trenton State, and, although he formally retired in 1992, he stayed on as a consultant for three more years.[20]

Davern first heard DeNicola when Kenny came to Las Vegas with the Dukes of Dixieland in 1962. He liked the way DeNicola played. Tony must have liked Davern because, when the opportunity came for DeNicola to hire musicians to play at the school for his students, he often picked Kenny. On weekends, DeNicola took jobs playing at parties or at clubs and restaurants around Trenton, and Kenny was one of the musicians that he hired on those gigs.

Davern and DeNicola worked together for more than ten years before Tony became Kenny's first call. During that time, Davern had most frequently used Bobby Rosengarden, Chuck Riggs, and Giampaolo Biagi. In the early 1990s, he reestablished his relationship with DeNicola, and it developed on an extraordinarily sound footing. Tony had an easy smile and appeared to be as unflappable in life as he was behind the drums. His solos were understated and musical; he often seemed to be able to play the melody with his sticks and brushes. Most important, DeNicola had a rock-solid, shuffle rhythm that Davern liked.

Beginning in about 1992, Davern used him whenever he could at clubs, festivals, and parties, and on all of his recordings. Howard Alden recalled: "Kenny was using Giampaolo a lot until he rediscovered Tony. He loved Tony's really big, solid, centered, beat—straight-ahead sound. Giampaolo's a little subtler, quieter. Kenny was always trying to get him to play more solidly."[21]

James Chirillo, who played with Tony and Kenny for over a decade in the Kenny Davern Quartet, appreciated that DeNicola was always paying attention to what the others were doing.

> Tony had an unbelievably big, wide beat that you could sit on. I loved playing with Tony because he was always listening. Even when I was playing the blues—a real straight-ahead, down-home, 1-4-5 kind of chord blues—he had a great shuffle beat. Tiny Grimes said that's the mark of a great drummer—to play a good shuffle, to keep it going without slowing down or getting uneven, or tiring. Any time I did anything, he'd always have a perfect answer. He was always listening.[22]

The ability of DeNicola and the other musicians that he played with to listen and anticipate was critical to Davern. It meant that he could rely on them to hear where he was going and to go there with him. He once described the process of communication as "telepathic." "We're tuned in to each other. He's listening to what I'm doing, and I'm listening to what he's doing. And, he'll vary on me, sometimes. It makes me change gears, which is fine, because I trust him. That's the key word: you've got to trust everybody around you."[23]

In the years to come, they would play together with increasing frequency, each calling the other when he had jobs. As Davern began to assemble a group of players around him who were able to play the music that he wanted to play in the way he wanted it played, Tony DeNicola became the first charter member.

For the ninth consecutive year, Davern celebrated his birthday at the Thunderbird Lodge in Taos, playing with Sutton, Hinton, and Johnson. As in past years, he came home to play Jack Kleinsinger's Highlight in Jazz concert, appeared the Central Illinois Jazz Festival on the weekend of January 25, and was at the North Carolina Jazz Festival one week later.

Bassist Bill Holaday had become the contractor as well as the house bassist at the Cornerstone, and he continued the policy of hiring first-rate musicians including Warren Vache, Jr., Dan Barrett, Jon-Erik Kellso, Randy Sandke, Randy Reinhart, Neville Dickie, and Bobby Gordon. The restaurant presented live music on three days of the week. A drumless trio usually played on Wednesdays, and a quartet appeared on Fridays and Saturdays. Holaday was usually the bassist, and the leader could bring whoever else he chose, subject to the monetary limits set by management. However, Davern did not like playing without a drummer and, when he played on Wednesday nights, it was almost always in a quartet with Tony DeNicola.

One of Davern's admirers was a New Jersey attorney named Joe Buttafuoco. (He was not the gentleman who had been involved with Amy Fisher.) Buttafuoco raised funds for causes such as St. Jude's Hospital, and for candidates for political office, often hosting parties at which he solicited prospective donors. He frequently hired Davern to assemble and lead a band at these events. Sometimes Buttafuoco brought his friends to the Cornerstone when Kenny was playing and put up money to enlarge the band by adding a trumpet and a trombone.

For several years, the Cornerstone had a problem with its piano. It was an old and battered upright: several keys did not work and it was invariably badly out of tune. There was a persistent rumor that a number of pianists had refused to work there, and many of the horn players who were hired to play brought guitarists (or an occasional vibraphone). The issue went unresolved until Frank Nissel, a constant visitor to the Cornerstone, director of the New Jersey Jazz Society, and friend of many musicians, stepped in. He bought a seven-foot grand piano, and donated it to the New Jersey Jazz Society with the understanding that it would be installed in the Cornerstone, where it would be kept tuned and would remain at the Society's discretion.

In mid-February, Davern flew to Redlands, California, for an appearance at the university, followed by a short trip to San Diego for its annual jazz party. From there he flew to Phoenix, then came home to appear at the Pee Wee Russell Memorial Stomp. He left for Raleigh on the 25th, stayed for two days, then traveled to Atlanta to join up with the World's Greatest Jazz Band (WGJB) on March 1.[24] The band had been booked to appear at Hilton Head, South Carolina, where the Hilton Head Island Institute of the Arts had planned a surprise party for television host Garry Moore, who was celebrating his seventy-sixth birthday. After a weekend at the island resort, the band motored to Atlanta, where they recorded ten tunes for George Buck, each of which had some reference to the South in its title. The CD, released in the following year on the Jazzology label, was called *The Legendary Lawson–Haggart Jazz Band, With a Southern Accent*.[25]

The album began with a vigorous rendition of *Sweet Georgia Brown*. Davern and Bucky Pizzarelli took the opening chorus of *Is It True What They Say about Dixie* and imbued the tune with a not-often-found gentility. *Creole Love Call* followed, with Davern taking the Adelaide Hall part, and then came a version of *Beale Street Blues* that featured Kenny in the upper reaches of his horn. *Georgia on My Mind*; *Charleston*; *Carolina in the Morning*; and a surprising and enjoyable *Tennessee Waltz* preceded a warm *Stars Fell on Alabama*. To fill up space on the CD, the two closing tunes, *New Orleans* and *Glory, Glory to Old Georgia* (better known as *The Battle Hymn of the Republic*) were interspersed between alternate takes of *Beale Street Blues* (without Davern's upper register solo) and *Creole Love Call*.

After a few more days in the South, Davern returned home, played one date at the Cornerstone, and another with Tony DeNicola, then left again on March 19 for a four-week tour of the United Kingdom. He visited most of his usual stops, often playing with different groups from night to night. He joined up with Scott Hamilton for a night at London's Pizza in the Park, but, for the rest of the tour he was the headline performer. He came home on April 14 and spent the following weekend playing at an unusual musical birthday celebration.

The Galvanized Jazz Band had made its home at the Milpond Tavern in Northford, Connecticut, for twenty years. They celebrated that birthday on April 20 at the New Haven Theater in New Haven, and invited the WGJB, including Davern, to perform.

The celebration continued on the following day and Davern and George Masso joined the Galvanized Jazz Band and its fans at the Millpond Tavern. The piano at that venue had a tinny, ragtimey sound that blended perfectly with the band's banjo-and-tuba rhythm section. It also furnished a fitting background for Janie Campedelli, a big-voiced, red-hot-mama-style of singer, whose selections included *Melancholy Blues*, *Saloon*, *Ain't Misbehavin'*, and *After You've Gone*. Although Davern did not play on all of the numbers, he played on most, lending his voice to a festive event. His featured number was *Summertime*, on which he was backed only by a bass and drum. The event was recorded, and the band released and marketed it on a cassette that was sold at Galvanized Jazz Band events.

Kenny flew to Phoenix, returned two days later, and, on the last day of the month, traveled to Bern, Switzerland, for a week-long engagement. In the middle of May, he was at the Cornerstone, then was back in the Southwest for a weekend in Santa Fe. On the last two days of the month, he was in a recording studio, making one of his rare appearances with a vocalist.[26]

In all of his recording career, Davern made only six albums on which a singer was the featured artist. Three of them were made with Cynthia Sayer, who, in addition to her vocal talents, was an accomplished banjoist and guitarist and had an ear for unusual voicings and instrumentation.[27] Their first album together was titled *Cynthia Sayer with Kenny Davern, Forward Moves*, and was recorded in two sessions.

Although Sayer wanted to play with Davern, his reputation had preceded him, and she was concerned about how they would work together.

> When I first met him, I was really young and I found him a little scary because he was sort of a crotchety kinda guy. I learned that he had a heart of gold, and he was very supportive and very nice to me. He was really great to me.... My first impression of him was so different from who I ended up thinking he was. He was really golden-hearted, a great guy.[28]

The first part of the album was recorded on May 30, 1991. Sayer sang and played banjo, Davern was on clarinet, and the only other musician on the date was Vince Giordano, who brought his bass saxophone. The trio successfully avoided the thumping rhythm that the banjo often engenders. Instead, Sayer frequently played harmonic lines that complemented what the others were doing and, when she did revert to playing chords, her strokes were soft and flowing. Davern had a significant role on all of the tunes, his effort on Django Reinhardt's *Douce Ambiance* being exceptionally lyrical. Giordano is a superb accompanist: on *Blues in My Heart*, he played stirring counter-melodies to Sayer's single string solo. *Kansas City Kitty* showed the trio at its best: Sayer sang and provided a foundation while Davern and Giordano weaved their own melodic strains at the top and bottom of the musical scale.

When Sayer and Davern returned to the studio to complete the album in October, the personnel and the concept had changed. Peter Ecklund was added on cornet, and Greg Cohen, playing string bass, replaced Giordano on bass saxophone. The result was a more modern and linear sound. Again, the repertoire was varied, including two Sayer compositions, *Forward Moves* and *Crazy Man Blues*, and three songs that were moderately familiar, *Cryin' for the Carolines*, *Melancholy*, and *Moonlight on the Ganges*.

On the following weekend, Kenny and Elsa's son, Mark Lass, married Patti Drazen. Immediately afterwards, Davern flew to Chicago to appear in the city's Jazz in June program. In the last ten days of the month, he was part of the JVC Jazz Festival, appearing first at Waterloo Village for the New Jersey Jazz Society. and then in Manhattan for the Wein Organization.

He and Wilber toured Italy during the week of July 3, appearing as Summit Reunion at venues in Milan, Ascona, Sari, Trieste, and Balzano. There were gigs at the Cornerstone before Davern played the 92nd Street Y on July 17 for its Jazz in July series. The program was titled *Licorice Shticks*, and Kenny was on the program with Giora Feldman, a Klezmer clarinetist. Feldman had his own trio, and Davern played with Dick Hyman, Bob Haggart, and Tony DeNicola. At the close of the program, they appeared together playing *Bei Mir Bist Du Schon*. Both Feldman and Davern were combative that night, each circling the other in an attempt to dominate the stage. Eventually, Feldman climbed up on a chair as he continued to play, thereby winning the unspoken competition.[29]

That weekend saw Davern in Raleigh. For the following week, he appeared with Jane Jarvis at Zinno's, a restaurant that had opened on 24th Street in Manhattan on the site formerly occupied by Reno Sweeney's. Kenny was overseas for almost all of August, playing in Oslo, where he appeared as a solo performer and also with Wilber as part of Summit Reunion. From there, he went on to London, then to Wales for the Brecon Festival, and finally to the Edinburgh Festival with Yank Lawson's All-Stars. Davern was home for a few days at the end of August before flying to Colorado for the Gibson party.[30]

The idea for Davern's next recording came from bassist-composer-arranger Bob Haggart when they were playing with the WGJB several years earlier. Haggart suggested that Kenny make a record with a background of strings. The concept was not a novel one—Charlie Parker had done it successfully years before, and Davern had led his brass choir with strings at the Old Mill in 1983. When Haggart broached the idea, Davern immediately agreed. "It's every horn player's dream to hear himself with a lush bed of strings," he said.[31]

Davern selected the tunes, and Haggart undertook to create the arrangements, a task that took two years to complete. Kenny told Haggart that he wanted about thirty-five to forty strings—as many as they could get.[32] They wound up with seven violins, two violas, and two cellos, supporting a quartet of Davern, Alden, Haggart, and Rosengarden. Although Davern and Alden rehearsed their parts before the session, as did the string section, the entire group did not get together until September 11, 1991. They worked from 1:00 to 11:00 p.m., with a dinner break, and, when they were finished, sixteen tunes had been recorded.[33] Howard Alden remembered the session. "It was very easy, very pleasant. Kenny was very excited about the strings playing behind him. It went very smoothly, and the results came out really nice."[34]

The album was titled *My Inspiration*. Most of the songs were ballads, and Davern's performance was affected by the cushion of sound provided by the strings. On *She's Funny That Way*, *Embraceable You*, *More Than You Know*, and *It Had to Be You*, normally not part of his repertoire, Kenny's sound was unusually full. Three of his choices, *My Inspiration*, *What's New*, and *Dogtown Blues* were written by Haggart. The title tune had been an Irving Fazola feature while he was in the Bob Crosby band, and Davern's solo tipped his hat to one of his early influences.

Davern included several songs from his performance list, including *Georgia on My Mind*, *Brother, Can You Spare a Dime*, *Summertime*, and *Sweet Lorraine*, but his treatment of them differed markedly from his usual performances. Only three selections were taken at a fast pace: *Spreadin' Knowledge Around*—a tune that Fazola had recorded with The Dean and His Kids, a small group from the Ben Pollack orchestra—*Farewell Blues*, and *Should I*.[35] The strings were absent on the first two of these selections and made only a minimal contribution on the last.

Davern was pleased with the final product and with his own performance. He told Clarrie Henley, the jazz critic for the *London Daily Telegraph*, "I tried to imagine some poor guy stuck in his car in a traffic jam on a hot day . . . To play this over the car's music system might take him up on a higher plane and sooth his frustration."[36]

Although there was an occasional mention of whether strings are "properly" part of a jazz performance, the album received good reviews. Jack Sohmer was one of the many writers who praised the CD, saying, "Of all the pure jazz albums Kenny Davern has recorded in his forty-year career, the present undertaking was without doubt the most challenging and, ultimately, the most rewarding." Joe H. Klee thought Davern was excellent and the arrangements faultless. Eddie Cook gave good reviews to Davern and Alden, and said that the music was easy listening but still hot jazz. "GG" writing in *Entertainment Weekly*, thought that the album had an "overall lyricism, a nearly innocent charm rarely found in modern music," and Gary Giddins said it was one of the ten best albums of 1992.[37]

The album was not as widely distributed as Davern had expected, and the sales were disappointing. He blamed it on the company, with whom he was then involved in a contractual dispute, saying: "The company, who shall remain nameless, never pushed the record. It could have been a contender . . . it could have been a contender."[38]

On three successive weekends in September, Davern appeared at the King of France Tavern, then at the Minneapolis Jazz Party, and finally in Denver for Summit Jazz. He finished recording the quartet section of *Forward Moves* with Cynthia Sayer on October 3, played some local jobs, and flew back to Colorado for the Jerome Jazz program in Aspen. He was with the WGJB in for two weeks touring Germany in October–November and appeared in Baden, Switzerland, with Ralph Sutton.

Davern flew home on November 18, and, after a week of playing locally, resumed his whirlwind existence. He was in Los Angeles for the Jazz at the Airport Hilton party until December 1, and spent December 4–8 in Genoa, Italy, with Summit Reunion. The following week saw him in Valencia, Spain, performing at the Cultural Center with Johnny Varro and Jeff Joralemon, a local drummer. The trio played at the Entral Café in Madrid from December 16 to 22.

Kenny returned to the States and, after a break for the Christmas holiday, flew to Florida for a series of appearances. On December 27, he directed a program at the Philharmonic Center for the Arts in Naples titled *Joys of Jazz* with Jon-Erik Kellso, Dan Barrett, Scott Hamilton, Dick Hyman, Dave Frishberg, Howard Alden, Milt Hinton, and Bobby Rosengarden. The same group appeared on the following night at Van Wetzel Hall in Sarasota, and on the 29th, Davern, Frishberg, Haggart, and Rosengarden were in Venice.[39]

In January 1992, after a week in Taos, an appearance at Jack Kleinsinger's *Highlights in Jazz* and a performance at the Church of the Heavenly Rest, Davern flew to Australia for one week of performances. That tour ended on January 28 and, to meet a long-standing commitment, Kenny left from Sidney on the 28th, arrived in Los Angeles on the 29th, laid over for four hours, and caught a flight to Charlotte, North Carolina. Upon his arrival there, he had ninety minutes to connect with another flight to Wilmington, where he performed from January 30 to February 2. He rested at home for a few days, then went back to California to play in Redlands, which was followed by San Diego.[40]

On February 10, 1992, Kenny's second cousin, Martin E. Greene, died. Greene was a dentist who always wanted to be a musician. He had studied clarinet and idolized Kenny, who was well established when Greene was growing up. Although they were not close relatives, Davern liked Greene, befriended him, gave him lessons, and invited him to some of his performances. When Greene died, he named Davern as the executor of his will and his sole beneficiary. The money that he left gave Kenny and Elsa some financial breathing space, and allowed them to enjoy some pleasures and projects that they had long deferred.[41]

One such project was the building of an addition on the back of the house that Kenny could use as his music room. Until that time, his horns, tools, books, cassettes, records, and CDs had been stored on shelves and in furniture throughout the house, as well as in the attic. The addition was a bright room that looked out into the backyard. There were shelves for some of his favorite books and recordings, a stereo system on which to play them, and a desk, two chairs, and a couch on which he could relax. Before the music room was constructed, Kenny's daily practice sessions were conducted at the dining room table. Afterward, he worked in his new den.

He played frequently at the Cornerstone during the rest of February, and had a weekend in Annapolis with Howard Alden. There was a trip to the Mid-America Jazz Festival in St. Louis in March, and an engagement on the last day of the month at the 92nd Street Y with Dick Hyman. He was at the Cornerstone in April, and had a date in Chicago before he left on the 10th for four weeks in England and Scotland. He came home on May 6, played some dates with Tony DeNicola, and flew to Santa Fe for a weekend. More dates at the Cornerstone and gigs with DeNicola and Ed Polcer preceded the beginning of the summer festival season.[42]

From June 19 to 21, Davern was at Waterloo Village where he performed with pianist Dave McKenna and also as leader of a group that consisted of Jon-Erik Kellso, Dan Barrett, Derek Smith, Frank Vignola, Greg Cohen, and Tony DeNicola. There were appearances in Manhattan for the JVC Jazz Festival, and then he was off to Indianapolis at the beginning of July.

From there, he traveled to the Hague for the Northsea Jazz Festival, and then on to Nice, where he and Wilber were joined by Derek Smith, Frank Tate, and Bobby Rosengarden. The quintet also had engagements in Amsterdam and the Hague before Davern flew home on July 19. There was a performance in Denver and a picnic in Connecticut before he was at the 92nd Street Y on July 30 for *Jazz in July*. The program was a salute to Frank Teschmacher: Dick Hyman had transcribed six of his recordings and called upon Davern to help him perform them. Chip Defeaa, previewing the program, called Davern "maybe the greatest active jazz clarinetist."[43]

Kenny was at the Cornerstone at the beginning of August, and then played with Dick Hyman in Minnesota and Wisconsin. From the 12th through the 31st, he and Wilber toured England and Scotland as Summit Reunion, appearing at Eastleigh, Croydon, and in Edinburgh. After several days in Scotland, they arrived in London, playing at Barbican Hall, followed by a week at Pizza on the Park. The last stop was in Clacton-on-the Sea on August 31.

As had been the case for twenty years, Davern was at the Gibsons' annual Labor Day party on September 4–7. A date in Pittsburgh with Bobby Rosengarden was followed by three dates at the Cornerstone. Then, Kenny was off to Germany.[44]

Hans Nagel-Heyer was born in Germany in 1941. As a young man, he learned to play the clarinet, and he wanted to become a jazz musician. He went to school, studied economics, and, when his father died, Hans took over the operation of the family's construction company. He celebrated his twenty-first birthday by marrying his fiancé, Sabine.

He remained interested in jazz, studied its history, and avidly collected records. Sabine, who shared his interest, went on to become the chief executive officer of Jazz Welle Plus, a twenty-four-hour radio station in Hamburg devoted to jazz. In addition to running the construction company, Hans hosted a weekly radio show named My Monday Date.

Manfred and Hans Selchow, who were active in a number of aspects of jazz, annually packaged a tour of Germany by foreign musicians. In the summer of 1992, Manfred contacted Hans Nagel-Heyer and asked for his help. He had assembled a band led by George Masso and was putting a tour together for September. Manfred told him that they needed a venue in Hamburg and someone to act as a promoter for the event. Nagel-Heyer was unable to find anyone in the short time that was available, and so he booked the band into the Musikhalle in Hamburg and became the event promoter.[45]

The concert was called *The Wonderful World of George Gershwin* and was presented on September 26, 1992. In addition to Masso, the band consisted of Randy Sandke, Davern, Danny Moss, Eddie Higgins, Len Skeat, and Jake Hanna. From time to time, Davern would opine that most of Gershwin's tunes weren't really "jazz" songs. That viewpoint did not prevent him from making *Summertime* one of his signature pieces, or from constructing lyrical solos on *Lady Be Good*, a piece that he often called as the opening number for a night's performance. And, as the recording from this performance shows, Davern's opinion of Gershwin's tunes did not interfere with his ability to play them with emotion.

The program began with a driving seven-and-one-half-minute performance of *Strike Up the Band* that ended with Davern soaring high above the closing chorus. The tempo cooled down a for an extended, medium-tempo *But Not for Me*, and then Kenny rose for his feature, *Summertime*. This performance was taken at a slightly faster than usual pace, and Davern displayed more technique in his improvisation than usual. *Soon* was followed by a slow, blues-oriented *Lady Be Good* that was a Danny Moss showpiece. An extended *Somebody Loves Me* preceded Higgins's solo, a medley from *Porgy and Bess*. Masso was spotlighted on *I've Got a Crush on You*. The program ended with the aptly named *S'Wonderful*.

Nagel-Heyer recorded the performance and issued a CD with liner notes in German. Sabine began to play it over the radio, and people began to call, asking where they could buy it. Masso wanted to sell the CD at his gigs, and asked if the liner notes could be translated into English. That was quickly accomplished, and Hans and Sabine launched their new venture, called Nagel-Heyer Records: *The Wonderful World of George Gershwin* was CD 001. It was warmly received by the critics, and the Nagel-Heyer label was off and running.[46] It recorded three other Davern performances and issued more than 200 CDs prior to the death of Hans Nagel-Heyer on March 29, 2007.[47]

When Kenny came back from Germany, he spent little more than a week in Manesquan before going to Aspen to play the Jerome Jazz Party. He flew back to New Jersey, played one night at the Cornerstone, and then spent October 16–18 playing first in Salinas, Kansas, and then in Topeka at the Topeka Jazz Workshop. From October 24 to 31, he was on the S.S. *Norway*.[48]

Hank O'Neal had also booked Wilber, Hyman, Pizzarelli, Hinton, and Rosengarden, intending to make another Summit Reunion CD. The group performed at one of the ship's venues on several nights, in effect rehearsing in front of the passengers, before actually recording the disc. O'Neal released it on his Chiaroscuro label under the title *Summit Reunion, 1992*.

There is a curious lack of drive to some of the tunes, as if the musicians had played them one time too often. But, there are some moments of beauty. *The Theme from Picnic/Moonglow* has a deliciously languorous feeling. *New Orleans* seems especially poignant, and Kenny's opening and closing statements of the melody in the lower register capture the mood perfectly.

Flip Phillips was also on the cruise: he joined in on tenor for the last three selections, and Wilber switched to alto. *Solitude* is a somber piece, the third-part harmony of the tenor lending a brooding air. *My Blue Heaven* is not exciting, but *My Mother's Eyes* is fresh and interesting.

It was far from the best performance that Davern and Wilber ever recorded and, as Hank O'Neal remembered, it was one of the most troubled. Even if the events that caused the demise of Soprano Summit were long buried, Bob and Kenny's basic personalities remained unchanged and the conflicts that had arisen two decades before continued to plague them. O'Neal remembered that

> It was an extraordinarily difficult live recording to make. By this time the tension between Kenny and Bob was sometimes quite profound, and it was just sometimes very difficult to get them to see eye to eye, because Bob liked to have things very carefully structured and Kenny liked to have things very loose and improvised, and you had to find something to work in the middle. . . . But those recordings were very, very hard, and Milt Hinton, who was always the mediator in situations like this, probably had to do extra-special mediating. . . .[49]

Wilber was not happy about this session, Davern wanted to remake the entire recording, and Bucky Pizzarelli thought that the group really "never got started."[50]

When the ship docked, most of the quintet flew together to New Brunswick, New Jersey, to perform on November 1 for the New Jersey Jazz Society. Davern flew to London on November 4 for a short engagement and continued to Vienna on the 10th. He played there for several days, returned home on the 19th and stayed in the New York–New Jersey area until he left for New Mexico on January 7, 1993.

He was at the Thunderbird Lodge through the 16th, then back in the Northeast, where he remained until the end of February. There were jobs at the Cornerstone, a Sunday at the Church of the Heavenly Rest, a week at the Village Corner in Greenwich Village, and a buffet at the Water Club in Manhattan to honor David Weber.[51]

With increasing frequency, Davern had been playing with a crop of younger musicians including Howard Alden, Jon-Erik Kellso, Randy Reinhart, and Joel Helleny. They were only a little older than he had been when he was standing next to Red Allen, Rex Stewart, Buster Bailey, and their contemporaries. Those men had known Armstrong, Morton, Ellington, and the other pioneers. They were the proud bearers of a tradition, and they passed it on to Davern, teaching him the history of the music, how it should be addressed, and how a musician should comport himself. "It was out there for people to share," Davern once said. "Those guys were quite generous in giving tips and teaching."[52]

Now Davern was cast in the role of teacher. He believed that it was his obligation to preserve the tradition and to pass it on to the younger musicians—as it had been given to him. It was something that he had done all of his adult life, beginning as early as 1961 at Nick's. Jack Six, the bassist in Kenny's band, recalled that playing with Davern was a learning experience.

> I learned more from Kenny about jazz and what jazz is in that band at Nick's. It was a concept that I did not have, playing with the bebop bands. I did not understand what jazz was. I learned that from Kenny, and I'll always be thankful to him for it. He opened my mind up to what jazz was in its inner conception. It was an education in a lot of ways; a discipline and a freedom, and that understanding. He never said anything. But, it was his attitude and his approach to playing that taught me that. He never gave me a lecture or said a word about "do that," or "do this." It was just his approach to what jazz is. It was not just executing a piece of music: it was being a piece of music. I had studied at Juilliard. But I learned a lot more on the stage at Nick's. He was a truly remarkable person.[53]

When he joined Davern at Nick's, Dave Frishberg's primary interest was in the more modern styles in jazz. "Kenny changed my life by opening my ears to the past, to the excellence of old jazz. I always had a good feeling about it, but he showed me that it really was excellent, and, in his mind, superior to what followed."[54]

Davern felt that knowing the history of the music was important to being able to play it well. When guitarist Vinnie Corrao started playing with Davern in the mid 1970s, he had little experience with the music that Kenny liked to play. Davern quickly addressed the problem. "Kenny was very serious about his music. He wanted his players to be aware of the history of the music—not that it was a requirement—but when he called some of these obscure tunes, if you knew the history of the music, you would know how to play them."[55]

Part of Davern's education as a young man was learning where he fit within the group in which he was playing. He learned how and what to play, how to act, what the other musicians expected of him, and what he could expect from them. And, as he grew and matured, he taught those things to those who were learning from him. Allan Vache thought that the process never stopped. "[W]hen I was studying with him—and all through my whole career, I never really stopped studying with him—we'd get together and do something, or at a festival, and he'd look at me and say 'Why are you doing that?' Throughout the whole time that we knew each other, he was always my teacher."[56]

Although he occasionally made a tart comment directly to a band member, he often told stories about himself that made his point or asked questions that prompted the recipient to think about what he was playing. Randy Reinhart remembered that he and Davern would often discuss the roles of their instruments within a larger group. Reinhart called it "a free music school."

> He would talk about playing harmony notes with the trombone player. He'd say "When I was growing up, if I played the wrong note, these guys would let me know in spades. These guys would read me the riot act." (I'm cleaning it up.) He said "I went home hurt. But I came back knowing what I was doing the next time, or else!" It was a great learning experience. That's just an example of so many things that Kenny would tell us on the job. It was so educational.[57]

It was never a formal process: in casual conversation, he would talk about his craft with other musicians and they might come away with bits of useful information. As Cynthia Sayer recalled: "Just by being around him, he helped me to go in some musical directions that I needed to go in. It was a wonderful influence: I remember talking about swing and jazz and drive with him. It's hard for me to put my finger on it. But, I just know that I did learn from him."[58]

One of the young musicians who became increasingly important to him was bassist Greg Cohen. For a while, Bob Haggart had been Kenny's bassist of choice. But, Bob was in Florida, approaching eighty years of age, and unwilling to travel north to play on weeknights for relatively small amounts. Cohen, along with Phil Flanagan, Frank Tate, and Murray Wall were the people who Davern usually called. Eventually, he began to turn to Greg with increasing frequency.

Cohen had been born in Los Angeles in 1953, and by the age of six he was playing rock 'n' roll with his brother Danny. Greg enjoyed a wide range of interests: he had been a part of John Zorn's Masada Quartet, and recorded with such diverse artists as Tom Waits, Elvis Costello, David Sanborn, Keith Ingham, Marty Grosz, and Cynthia Sayer. He would go on to play with Ornette Coleman. He listened to a wide range of music, from African tribal drumming to the great European classical composers, and brought what he heard to his playing. Guitarist James Chirillo said:

> Greg does things, rhythmically, conceptually and style-wise—because his knowledge is so vast—that can put you into another direction. Not that you're going to turn it into a Reggae tune. It's simply that rhythmically—or his choice of notes—that can put you into a whole 'nother direction. So, that's Greg. He truly does things that I've never heard any other bass player do.[59]

For several years, Davern had been narrowing the scope of the music that he liked to play, and logic would suggest that he would choose to play with musicians who shared his interests. But Cohen thought that Davern chose him for the opposite reason: because he embraced a wide spectrum of musical interests.

> Obviously, that being the type of personality that he was, he wanted musicians around him that would be supportive of that. Not necessarily the same, because he was an intellectual, and he thought a lot about a lot of things. One of the things that he thought a lot about—because we talked about it—was how music, especially this music we call jazz, or improvisation, doesn't necessarily benefit from everybody being out of the same box. Like four bulbs out of the same box gives you a box of four of the same bulbs.
>
> Besides being a great clarinetist, probably the greatest that ever lived, he was a great bandleader, which is something that's a whole other art. It's not the same as being a composer or an arranger or a conductor: it's a bandleader—

how to get the right people on the bandstand and get it happening from tune to tune, without any down time, without any bullshit, just in a relaxed way. Boom—there it goes.[60]

Cohen would become Davern's first call whenever he needed a bassist and, with Tony DeNicola, became the third member of the Kenny Davern Quartet.

Davern was in Colorado Springs over the weekend of February 26, 1993. In March, he worked for Jack Kleinsinger and, at the end of the month, was in St. Louis for the Mid-American Jazz Festival. He was overseas for the entire month of April, spending the first twenty days of the month in England, Scotland, and Ireland. From April 19 through the 30th, he was in Spain, then came back to England for a week. There was a job in Paris, from May 9 to 19, and a stop at the jazz festival in Breda for a day before he went back to England for three days, and then home.[61]

Tony DeNicola was calling him for jobs with increasing frequency. In addition, Kenny played five dates at the Cornerstone in May and June, and performed at several private parties before appearing at Waterloo Village on June 19–20. He appeared for one night at Jimmy Walker's in Manhattan, and then went out of town for the July 4th hiatus. He was in Boston for a week, played locally upon his return, and was at the 92nd Street Y on July 28. DeNicola called him to play a wedding on July 31, and for three other dates in August. He worked with Jerry Jerome on the 18th of that month, and played for Jack Kleinsinger on the 28th.

He was in Denver at the end of September and, at the beginning of October, flew to Chicago to play with James Dapogny's Chicago Jazz Band and with Butch Thompson in a tribute to Art Hodes, who had died on March 4, 1993. Kenny played some dates near home for a week and then flew to Aspen for the weekend of October 7. He came back to New Jersey on October 10 and, two days later, left for his fall tour of Europe and the United Kingdom.

The tour began in Vienna with a three-day gig. Kenny went on to England for four days, followed by a weekend at the jazz festival in Cork, Ireland, where he and Wilber performed. From there, he went to Paris for an engagement ending on November 9.[62]

The remainder of 1993 passed uneventfully. He played at Monmouth College in West Long Branch with John Bunch, Bucky Pizzarelli, and Tony DeNicola. There was a date for the New Jersey Jazz Society and then, as the holiday season approached, a round of Christmas parties. At the end of the month, he was in North Carolina, then came back to continue the year-end party circuit. He went into New York to help his teacher and friend, David Weber, celebrate his eightieth birthday and ended the year working with DeNicola.

There was a pattern to Davern's life. He started the new year as he had started over a dozen years in the past, playing with Ralph Sutton at the Thunderbird Lodge. There was a date with Ralph in Denver on January 13, some work at the Cornerstone, a job at the Church of the Heavenly Rest and, at the end of the month, his regular appearance at the Central Illinois Jazz Festival. He spent the first weekend in February at the North Carolina Jazz Festival. Amid jobs around town, he made a one-day trip to Chicago and performed at a party held on February 27 to honor the memory of saxophonist Zoot Sims. In early March, he traveled to Scottsdale, Arizona.[63]

There was a new event on Davern's calendar for the weekend of March 11–13, 1994—the *March of Jazz* party in St. Petersburg, Florida. Playing there had a dramatic effect on his life.

Notes

1. Hank O'Neal, producer's notes to *Bob Wilber, Kenny Davern, Summit Reunion*, Chiaroscuro CR(D) 311; *Jazzspeak*, interview with Bob Wilber, Kenny Davern, *Summit Reunion*, Chiaroscuro CR(D) 311. The CD had a tenth track entitled *Jazzspeak*, on which Wilber and Davern chatted informally about their history together. Although some of it is a little stilted, it is an interesting insight into the background of this recording. O'Neal has included a *Jazzspeak* track on several other Chiaroscuro CDs, and they are all worth hearing.

2. Kenny Davern, interview by the author.

3. Hank O'Neal, producer's notes to *Bob Wilber, Kenny Davern, Summit Reunion*, Chiaroscuro CR(D) 311.

4. Eddie Cook, "Summit Reunion, Bob Wilber and Kenny Davern," *Jazz Journal International*, 44, no. 7 (July 1991): 43, and 45, no. 2 (February 1992): 6; Ira Gitler, "Jazz CDs of 1991," *World Monitor*, November 1991: 48; George Kanzler, "N' All That Jazz," *Star Ledger*, 19 May 1991; Russ Chase, "Summit Reunion, Bob Wilber and Kenny Davern," *IAJRC Journal*, 25, no. 1 (Winter 1992): 72.

5. John McDonough, "Jazz; Very Cool, Very Hot," *Wall Street Journal*, 11 January 1993; "Critics Voices," by Time's reviewers, compiled by Andrea Sachs, *Time*, 25 March 1991.

6. Eddie Cook, "Bob Wilber Talks to Eddie Cook," *Jazz Journal International*, 36, no. 10 (October 1993): 14; Kenny Davern, conversation with the author; Elsa Davern, interview by the author.

7. Liner notes to *Introducing Alain Bouchet*, Jazzology JCD 192; Warren Vache, Jr., interview by the author.

8. Warren Vache, Jr., interview by the author.

9. R. Clairborne Ray, "Style Makers, Elsa Davern, Jewelry Maker," *New York Times*, 3 June 1990.

10. Date Book; *Jersey Jazz*, 18, no. 4 (May 1990): 607, and 18, no. 5 (June 1990): 27; Royal Viking Cruise Line newsletters.

11. National Endowment for the Arts, NEA Jazz Masters, *Dan Morgenstern, Jazz Historian, Archivist, Author, Editor, Educator*, available at www.NEA.gov/national/jazz/jmCMS/master.php?id'2007_04.

12. Cruise passenger list and entertainment program.

13. Elsa Davern, interview by the author.

14. The discographical notes on the cover of the CD state that the segments with Hodes and Galloway were recorded at Café Des Copains on 30 July, and 1, 2 August, and that Davern's segment was recorded in a studio on 19 August 1990. This is an error. On 19 August, Davern was at the Brecon Festival in Wales. Elsa Davern recalls that Kenny flew from Vancouver to Toronto directly after they got off the Alaska cruise and that he started recording with Hodes and Galloway immediately. This is borne out by Hodes's liner notes, in which Art describes the part of the recording session with Davern, and then goes on to say "Jim and I spent a good part of the *next* three days filling out the rest of this project (Kenny had dates in N.Y.C. to fulfill)." *Americana with Art Hodes*, p. 3 (emphasis added). It all likelihood, the Davern segment of this CD was recorded in a studio on 30 July 1990, before Hodes and Galloway were at Café des Copains. (Date Book; e-mail from Brian Peerless, Elsa Davern, Kenny Davern, conversations with the author.)

15. E-mail, Brian Peerless to the author.

16. E-mail, Brian Peerless to the author; Martin Gayford, "When Jazzmen Take to the Hills," *The Daily Telegraph*, 22 August 1989: 12; Martin Gayford, "Spontaneous Jazz and a Star from Saturn, *The Daily Telegraph*, 25 August 1989: xvii.

17. "Hot Topics, What Do You Tell Sax Players Who Want to Take Up Clarinet?" *Windplayer*, 8, no. 5 ((September–October 1991): 8.

18. Stanley Dance, "Lightly and Politely," *Jazz Journal International*, 44, no. 6 (June 1991): 16.

19. Date Book; Jerome Jazz event program; *Jersey Jazz*, 18, no. 7 (September 1990): 19, and 18, no. 8 (October 1990): 9, and 18, no. 9 (November 1990): 7, and 18, no. 10 (December 1990): 21.

20. Warren Vache, Sr., "Tony Tells It Like It Was," *Mississippi Rag*, xxvi, no. 2 (February 1998): 25.

21. Howard Alden, interview by the author.

22. James Chirillo, interview by the author.

23. Kenny Davern, interviewed by Mark Weber, 17 January 2006.

24. Date Book; *New York Times*, 9 October 1990; *San Diego Union*, 19 February 1991; *Jersey Jazz*, 18, no. 1 (February 1990): 3.

25. Zach and Dot Cullens, liner notes to *The Legendary Lawson–Haggart Jazz Band, With a Southern Accent*, Jazzology JCD 203, Atlanta, Georgia, 29 February 1992.

26. Date Book; *Jazz Journal International*, 44, no. 3 (March 1991): 3; *New York Times*, *The Guide*, 4 April 1991; *Jersey Jazz*, 19, no. 4 (May 1991): 27.

27. She had also recorded with Wellstood.

28. Cynthia Sayer, interview by the author.

29. Date Book; *Jersey Jazz*, 19, no. 4 (May 1991): 14–15, and 19, no. 6 (July–August 1991): 37; Peter Watrous, "Review/Jazz, Klezmer and Cool at the Y," *New York Times* 27 July 1991; Dick Hyman, *Thinking About Kenny Davern*, unpublished.

30. Date Book; Oslo event program; *Jazz Journal International*, 44, no. 7 (July 1991): 3; Edinburgh event program.

31. Kenny Davern, quoted in Tommy Sancton, liner notes to *My Inspiration*, Musicmasters 61912-65077-2.

32. Kenny Davern, interviewed by Mark Weber, 11 July 2002.

33. Tommy Sancton, liner notes to *My Inspiration*, Musicmasters 61912-65077-2. This was the last of Davern's recordings that was released on long-playing record and a compact disc. Davern's subsequent recordings appeared only on CD.

34. Howard Alden, interview by the author.

35. Harry James and Ben Pollack claimed composer credit for *Spreadin' Knowledge Around*, but they borrowed heavily from Ellington and Johnny Hodges's composition *Rent Party Blues*.

36. Kenny Davern quoted in Clarrie Henley, "Letter from England," *Jersey Jazz*, 20, no. 6 (July–August 1992): 8.

37. Jack Sohmer, "Kenny Davern, My Inspiration," *Jazz Times*, October 1992, 75; Joe H. Klee, "Kenny Davern My Inspiration," *Mississippi Rag*, xxi, no. 8 (August 1993): 30; Eddie Cook, "Kenny Davern My Inspiration," *Jazz Journal International*, 45, no. 11 (November 1992): 28; GG, *Entertainment Weekly*, 4 September 1992: 73; Gary Giddins, "Multitudes of '92," *Village Voice*, 2 February 1993: 78.

38. Kenny Davern, interviewed by Mark Weber, 11 July 2002.

39. Date Book; Colorado events programs; *Jersey Jazz*, 19, no. 9 (November 1991): 23; World's Greatest Jazz Band tour program; Schacter, Sutton, p. 310; advertisement for Italian performances; event programs for Spanish and Florida appearances.

40. Date Book; program from Kleinsinger event; *Village Voice*, 19 January 1992.

41. Kenny Davern, conversations with the author; Elsa Davern, interview by the author.

42. Date Book; *Jersey Jazz*, 20, no. 1 (February 1992): 21; program from Mid-America Jazz Festival; *Jazz Journal International*, 45, no. 4 (April 1992): 3.

43. Date Book; George Kanzler, "Stompin' at Waterloo," *Sunday Star Ledger*, 14 June 1992, Sec. 4, 1; Northsea event program; letter from Festival Productions to Davern, dated 22 June 1992; Chip Deffaa, "The Force of July, Fest of Jazz Like You've Never Heard," *New York Post*, 21 July 1992: 19.

44. Date Book; *Jersey Jazz*, 20, no. 6 (July–August 1992): 21, and 20, no. 7 (September 1992): 7; *Jazz Journal International*, 44, no. 8 (August 1991): 3.

45. E-mails from Sabine Nagel-Heyer to the author.

46. Eddie Cook, "The Wonderful World of George Gershwin," *Jazz Journal International*, 46, no. 5 (May 1993): 36; Shirley Klett, "The Wonderful World of George Gershwin," *IAJRC Journal*, 27, no. 2 (Spring 1994): 70.

47. E-mails from Sabine Nagel-Heyer to the author.

48. Date Book; *Jersey Jazz*, 20, no. 8 (October 1992): 21, and 20, no. 10 (December 1992): 5; *Topeka Capital-Journal*, 23 October 1992, 2-B.

49. Hank O'Neal, recorded recollections.

50. Eddie Cook, "Bob Wilber Talks to Eddie Cook," *Jazz Journal International*, 46, no. 10 (October 1993): 14; Kenny Davern, conversation with the author.; Bucky Pizzarelli, interview with the author.

51. Date Book; *Jersey Jazz*, 20, no. 8 (October 1992); *Star Ledger*, 3 October 1992: 50.

52. Kenny Davern, interviewed by Mark Weber, 15 May 2003.

53. Jack Six, interview by the author.

54. Dave Frishberg, interview by the author.

55. Vinnie Corrao, interview by the author.

56. Allan Vache, interview by the author.

57. Randy Reinhart, interview by the author.

58. Cynthia Sayer, interview by the author.

59. James Chirillo, interview by the author.

60. Greg Cohen, interview by the author.

61. Date Book; *Jazz Journal International*, 46, no. 4 (April 1993): 3; Breda event program.

62. Date Book; *Chicago Tribune*, 23 September 1993, sec. 5, 6; Cork Festival program.

63. Date Book.

CHAPTER FOURTEEN

The Arbors Years

Mat Domber began his career as an attorney in Philadelphia. In the 1970s, he organized the law firm of Domber & Ward, and, over time, became involved as a principal in real estate development projects in Pennsylvania. Domber began building senior citizens' housing and, with his associates, acquired some management companies in Florida. Those operations required increasing amounts of Mat's time and, in 1987, he and his wife Rachel moved to Florida.

Domber's career as a record producer was a result of his friendship with tenor saxophonist Rick Fay. Mat had met Fay when Rick was working in Los Angeles at the hotel where Mat stayed when he traveled to the West Coast. They found that they had a number of musical interests in common and became friends. Fay also worked at Disneyland, and when Disney World opened in Orlando, management at Disney asked him to lead a group in one of the park's venues.

Domber learned that Fay was working in Florida and went to see him. After one particularly enjoyable set, Mat asked if Rick had any records to sell and Rick said that he had never recorded. As Mat remembered the occasion, "I said, 'You mean to say that you've been in the business for 40 years and never recorded? Would you like to?' And that was the start of Arbors Records. We recorded in late 1989, and our first record came out in January 1990."[1]

Over the next several years, Arbors expanded its roster of recording artists as Domber became more involved in producing and perpetuating the music that he loved. One of the people with whom he became friendly was Bob Haggart. Early in 1993, Domber was at breakfast with Haggart and his wife, Windy, and mentioned that he was thinking of putting on a jazz party. Windy said that Bob would be eighty years old in the following year, and the idea of having a party to celebrate that event was born.

> In planning the party, I met with Bob—we had a number of lunches together—and I said: "It's a birthday party and we should invite musicians to the party who are meaningful to you. So, give me a list of names of musicians who you played with and who are meaningful in terms of your musical history." Among the people he gave me were Kenny Davern and Bob Wilber and Ralph Sutton and Yank Lawson. We had twenty-four or twenty-five musicians there.[2]

The party was billed as a celebration of the eightieth birthday of Bob Haggart and titled *The March of Jazz*. Over the weekend of March 11–13, 1994, Davern was featured in a number of different groups including a Summit Reunion set that included Wilber, Derek Smith on piano, guitarist George Van Eps, Milt Hinton, and Jackie Williams on drums. In a variant of that concept, Davern, Wilber, and Ken Peplowski reprised the original Soprano Summit crowd-rousing version of *The Mooche*—also on the last day of the party—which, like the original, brought the audience screaming to its feet. There was an exciting end-of-the-evening blow-out with Ruby Braff, Dan Barrett, Rick Fay, Davern, Peplowski, Dick Hyman, Bucky Pizzarelli, Haggart, and Jake Hanna, and several other interesting match-ups. Domber recorded the proceedings and released a two-CD package titled *The All-Stars at Bob Haggart's Eightieth Birthday Party*.

It was the start of a personal friendship and professional relationship that only ended with Davern's death almost thirteen years later. Over that period, Domber recorded Davern prolifically. He appeared as a leader on six CDs and as a co-leader with Bob Wilber (once), and Ken Peplowski (twice). He was a sideman on three recordings led by Ruby Braff, one by Randy Reinhart, and one by the Statesmen of Jazz. In addition to the CDs from the 1994 *March of Jazz*, Davern appeared on a videotape from the 1995 party that honored Flip Phillips. Domber acquired and Arbors released a CD of a 1971 performance by Kenny with a group led by Eddie Condon and also a CD from the short-lived Kings of Jazz tour in 1974. In 2008, Arbors released a two-CD package of performances by Soprano Summit and the Blue Three in the 1970s and, in the following year, issued a DVD of the appearances of Davern and Wilber together at the first three *March of Jazz* parties. In all, twenty Arbors CDs, videotapes, and DVDs feature or include at least one performance by Davern.

Kenny also appeared at all of the *March of Jazz* parties and was an honoree at the last of them, in 2004.

On March 25, 1994, Kenny's mother, Josephine, died. In the late 1950s, she had taken a job at the Nevele Hotel, a resort facility located in the Catskill Mountains in Ellenville, New York. She worked as a secretary for the Slutsky family, the founders and owners of the hotel, and part of her compensation included the use of a cabin on the property. Living in that rural environment allowed her to indulge her passion for riding horses and for outdoor life in general.

In the 1970s, Josephine moved back to Manhattan and took an apartment on the Upper West Side at 37 West 72nd Street. She supported herself by continuing to perform services for the Nevele organization. However, time was not kind to her. Her health deteriorated over a long period, and the mother who loved, doted on, and sought to protect her son slowly changed into an unhappy soul who alienated the person whom she loved the most.[3]

John Bunch, bassist Murray Wall, and Tony DeNicola joined Davern on a cruise that lasted from April 2 to 10. Three days after that trip ended, Kenny was off to England, appearing at the Pizza Express in London, and the Stables in Waveden, as well as at venues in Cambridge, Eastleigh, Tunbridge Wells, Upton-Upon-Severn, Woking, and Newcastle-Upon-Tyne. He came home on April 27 and appeared in Colorado Springs on the weekend of the 29th.

In May, he worked with Dick Hyman at the 92nd Street Y, flew to Denver to play with Ralph Sutton and Flip Phillips on the 14th and 15th, and played four jobs with Tony DeNicola before the month came to an end. June saw Kenny in Red Bank playing with Chirillo, Wall, and DeNicola, and in Princeton on the next day with Ed Polcer. He had dates at the Cornerstone and with Tony DeNicola, went back to Colorado for two days in Aspen with Ralph Sutton, and returned to New York to make his first studio recording for Mat Domber's Arbors label.[4]

There were some unusual aspects to the group that Davern put together. Most groups larger than a quintet included a piano as part of the rhythm section. The band for *Kenny Davern and His Jazz Band, East Side, West Side*, that consisted of Dan Barrett, Joel Helleny, Bucky Pizzarelli, Bob Haggart, and Tony DeNicola, did not. In addition, although Barrett was better known for his work on trombone, Davern thought that he was even more inventive and exciting on cornet and asked him to play that instrument. Helleny took the trombone part.[5]

Although Domber and Davern discussed the concept of the CD in advance, Mat gave Kenny almost complete freedom in the selection of the musicians, the choice of tunes, and all of the musical decisions that had to be made. Once the musicians assembled in the studio, Domber's only involvement in the process, other than making sure that they had everything that they needed, was to create a videotape diary of the entire session. He unobtrusively stationed himself at posts throughout the studio and filmed the sometime arduous, always fascinating process of creating a polished piece of music from scratch.

Domber's respect for Davern's artistry led to an enduring friendship between them.

> We got to like each other and shared a number of interests. He would grumble sometimes. But, he would never create a real fuss or a problem as he did on some other occasions. Insofar as the recording studio was concerned, yes: he had his own ideas about amplification. He had his own ideas about engineers, most of whom he disliked because he thought that they were trying to control the sound and the music, rather than the musicians. He was a firm believer in playing acoustically and in letting the musicians control the dynamics of the music, rather than having an engineer flipping dials around. He had a favorite microphone, his RCA 44, and he would bring that to most of the recordings. He would be very critical of how the band was set up, and very critical about what the engineer was doing. Sometimes, it took us a while to get things right in the final mastering of the recording because he was very critical about the post-production engineering, on the mix and how the clarinet sounded.
>
> His feeling was—and I think he was perfectly right—that what makes an outstanding musician is the individuality of his playing. And his tone is a large part of that. One of the first things that most people who knew anything about Kenny would say, as they did about Ruby Braff, is that his tone and his playing were instantly identifiable. I think that this was very important to him.[6]

The CD opens with *There'll Be Some Changes Made*, taken at a medium-to-fast tempo. The brass sit out, and Kenny is warm and inventive on *Wrap Your Troubles in Dreams*. *Delta Bound* is a tightly arranged feature that highlights the joint muted efforts of Barrett and Helleny, and hand-played tom-toms by DeNicola. Davern takes a break and Barrett joins Helleny for a humorous plunger-muted trombone duet on *Sidewalks of New York*. *Am I Blue* is another quartet piece, followed by Dan Barrett's tightly crafted arrangement of *There's Yes, Yes in Your Eyes*, on which the full band returns. *Always* is a Helleny feature with a solo by Haggart, followed by *I'm Sorry Dear I Made You Cry*, on which there are no trombones. *Please Be Kind* is a Barrett feature, and the album closes with a refreshing arrangement of *Sugar*.

Jack Sohmer said it was "a great record." Russ Chase called Davern "the best of the active jazz clarinetists," and called the recording it "a marvelous disk." John Chadwick also gave it a good review.[7] The album was voted one of the ten best new issues of 1995 by *Jazz Journal International*.[8]

The summer festival season had opened, and Davern was at Waterloo Village on the weekend following the recording date. He was in Pennsylvania with Ed Polcer on the last day of the month and, immediately after, made his annual appearance in Indianapolis. Then he was in Topeka and, on July 14, he left for Spain, where he had five concerts and two club dates ending on the 24th. He came home to play on July 28 at *Jazz in July* and, less than a week later, was off to England. The International Association of Jazz Record Collectors held its annual convention in London that year, and Davern appeared there with Scott Hamilton and the Colin Purbrook Trio. From August 7, Davern and Warren Vache, Jr., were on tour, billed as the Kenny Davern–Warren Vache Sextet. They played at several venues in England, then journeyed to Scotland for the Edinburgh Jazz Festival, where Scott Hamilton joined them. After appearances on the 10th and 11th and a day off for travel, Vache and Davern performed at the Brecon Jazz Festival.[9]

There were some jobs in New Jersey before the Labor Day weekend arrived. After a run of thirty years, Dick and Maddie Gibson's Labor Day party had finally come to an end. In 1994, Davern spent his Labor Day weekend in California, performing at the LA Classic in Los Angeles. He came home and played a job at the Skyclub atop the Pan Am Building in Manhattan. After a night at the Cornerstone, he was off to play a one-night stand, some 4,000 miles away.

Jazz Im Amerika Haus was the title of a series of concerts featuring American musicians that was produced at the America House in Hamburg, Germany, by Jazz Welle Plus, the radio station owned by Sabine Nagel Heyer. On September 24, Davern and Wilber, backed by an English rhythm section consisting of Dave Cliff, Dave Green, and drummer Bobby Worth, appeared, billed as Summit Reunion. For Kenny, it was little more than an overnight trip. He left his home in Manasquan at 3:00 p.m. on Thursday, arrived in Hamburg on Friday morning, played on Saturday night, and departed Germany for home at 10:30 a.m. on Sunday.[10]

The program was drawn from what had become Wilber and Davern's standard ad-hoc concert fare. There was *Lady Be Good*, *Beale Street Blues*, *Rosetta*, *Comes Love* (a two-clarinet excursion that lasted for more than ten minutes), *Apex Blues*, and *Porter's Love Song to a Chambermaid*. Wilber's feature was Franz Lehar's *Yours Is My Heart Alone*, and Davern treated *Indiana* as a mournful ballad. Cliff and Green were two of Britain's best, and both of them had played frequently with Bob and Kenny. Along with Bobby Worth, they were supportive in their role as members of the rhythm section and engaging as soloists.

The performance was recorded by Hans Nagel Heyer and released on a CD as *Jazz Im Amerika Haus, Vol. 5, Summit Reunion*. The album was well received. Bill Bennett gave it a good review in *Jazz Times*, and George Wilson called Wilber and Davern "incredibly exciting." The CD was voted one of *Jazz Journal International*'s ten best new releases for 1998.[11]

Davern was in Richmond, Virginia, on the weekend of September 30, and in Aspen one week later. He was in New Hampshire playing with Bobby Rosengarden on October 14, in New Jersey playing with Tony DeNicola on the following night, and then he flew back to Europe. He was in Vienna for a week beginning on Monday, October 17. From the 24th through the 26th, he played in London, then went over to Paris until the 29th. He returned to London, where he remained until he returned to the States on November 6th.

From then until the end of the year, he worked every Saturday night with Tony DeNicola—the singular exception being on November 19, when he was at the Cornerstone. There was a job at the Hilton Hotel in Short Hills, a concert at William Paterson College in Wayne, and a private party in Tenafly. Kenny led the band at Joe Buttafuoco's Christmas party on December 16 and at the event that he threw on December 30.[12]

Dick Hyman was the musical director for Woody Allen's film *Mighty Aphrodite*. For the closing scene, he had put together a chorus of nineteen vocalists plus a thirteen-man band to perform his arrangement of *When You're Smiling*. When it came for Kenny to do his part, he was unmistakable. Hyman said:

> I learned that the best way to arrange for Kenny was to set up a background and leave him alone. A great result of that hands-off policy was the ending of Woody Allen's film, *Mighty Aphrodite*, which starts with a chorus singing *When You're Smiling* and then turns into an inspiring instrumental, with Kenny soaring above the band.[13]

Davern celebrated his sixtieth birthday in Taos on January 7, 1995. Jobs in Denver, in Manhattan at the Church of the Heavenly Rest, and at the Cornerstone followed, and then Davern made his annual visit to the North Carolina Jazz Festival on February 3–4. He was at the party in San Diego one week later, where he was joined by Wilber, Peplowski, and Allan Vache. Author Stanley Dance was also at the party. Although he thought that all of them were "expert players," he said that Davern "quickly proved himself to be the boss," and was "undoubtedly the top man on the instrument."[14]

There was a four-night stand at the Village Corner, followed by a private party, and a performance at the Pee Wee Russell Memorial Stomp before Kenny headed out to the Paradise Valley Jazz Party on March 4–5. Ten days later, at the behest of Hank O'Neal, he was at the recording studio of Rudy Van Gelder in Englewood Cliffs, New Jersey, for a recording date with Bob Wilber, Dick Hyman, Bucky Pizzarelli, Milt Hinton, and Bobby Rosengarden. The resultant CD was called *Summit Reunion, Yellow Dog Blues*, and it was the last time that all of them would record together.

Hyman introduces the first number, Irving Berlin's *I'll See You in C-U-B-A*, with a Latin figure that leads into the theme statement. Much of the credit for the tone and feeling of this recording belongs to Dick. His opening statements on *C-U-B-A*, *Frankie and Johnny*, which also has a Latin tinge, and on an up-tempo *Hindustan* all establish the tenor of the pieces immediately. On the final tune on the disc, he begins with an unaccompanied excursion, which only becomes recognizable as *Somebody Stole My Gal* when he gets to his second chorus. Hyman's solos on *Japanese Sandman* and *Wang Wang Blues* are unusually and lyrically constructed, and on *C-U-B-A* he takes two entirely different solos. His backing for Wilber and Davern throughout the CD adds to the tension and provides them with a solid underpinning.

Darktown Strutters Ball required five starts before Bob and Kenny completed a version that they liked. *Frankie and Johnny*, which is not often thought of as a jazz standard, is surprisingly attractive. Both Wilber and Davern play clarinet on *Japanese Sandman*, which is simply outstanding. *Yellow Dog Blues*, the highlight of the disc, is over eleven minutes in length and has Davern soloing directly after Wilber—as they did on *St. Louis Blues* on their first CD. After two choruses of the theme followed by solos from each member of the rhythm section, Wilber, playing straight soprano saxophone, picks up and plays two powerful choruses. It always seemed that when Bob was "on," Kenny would reach dramatic heights and this was no exception. He starts his solo in a very subdued chalumeau manner and drives up the entire range of the clarinet, building over Hyman's figures to a powerful climax.

Hindustan is taken at a fast pace, *Rosetta* is slightly slower, and *Darling Nelly Gray* is delicate. Wilber takes one of his rare chalumeau outings on *Wang Wang Blues* and sounds something like Davern, while Kenny stays in the middle and upper registers on his solo. Wilber plays alto on *Somebody Stole My Gal*, which, after Hyman's introductory choruses, is a barnburner.

Although Davern and Wilber were able to control whatever ill-feelings existed between them whenever they were onstage, the recording studio seemed to bring out the worst in them. Hank O'Neal recalled that they were definitely not on their best behavior that day. "The *Yellow Dog* was really the hard one, that was the hardest. Kenny and Bob *really* weren't getting on. The peacemaker was Milt: he was the one who held it all together. He was a grand guy and, if he said 'Hey, you're being an asshole,' they would tend to notice that."[15]

The CD received excellent reviews. David Badham, writing in *Jazz Journal International*, called it "ageless music in its most uplifting form," and Dick Neeld said that ". . . [S]o what we get is top musicianship, highly reminiscent of the original group, offering new and attractive versions of old jazz staples . . ."[16] *Yellow Dog Blues* was voted one of *Jazz Journal International*'s best new issues for 1996.

After the recording session ended, Kenny was off to St. Louis for a weekend and then went to Florida for the second of Mat Domber's *March of Jazz* parties. In 1995, Flip Phillips turned eighty years of age, and the event was styled as a birthday party for him. The cast of musicians included trumpeters Jack Sheldon and Clark Terry, plus Dan Barrett and Carl Fontana, and George Masso on trombone. The were four clarinet players, Davern, Buddy DeFranco, Peanuts Hucko, and Wilber; three saxophonists, Phil Woods, Scott Hamilton, and Flip Phillips; and an assortment of rhythm section players.

The party ended on March 26, and Davern stayed in Sarasota to work with Bobby Rosengarden, and then to take a few days off. Back in New Jersey, he played at the Princeton Marriott and had an evening at the Cornerstone before flying out to Carleton College in Northfield, Minnesota, on April 14, 1995. He worked for two more weeks near home, then went to the Colorado Jazz Party at the Broadmoor Hotel in Colorado Springs.

Davern spent May overseas, starting with five days in Bern. He was in England for a few days, then opened in Paris on May 14 for a two-week gig. On May 31, he was in Inverness, Scotland. From there, he appeared in Belfast, then went on to England, where he played three dates before going home on June 5. Some jobs near home followed, and then Davern made his second recording for Arbors Records.[17]

When Davern and the musicians assembled to record the CD that was eventually released as *Kenny Davern and the Rhythm Men*, he told them that he wanted them to play with the same informality and professionalism as if they were playing a club date. They were clustered together as they would be on a stage and not separated by partitions or baffles to insulate the sound of the drums. Davern wanted no rehearsals, no stops, and, hopefully, no retakes. Once they started a tune, they would finish.

This could only have been accomplished by a group of professionals who could anticipate and adapt to the playing of their colleagues. The "Rhythm Men" met that requirement. Bucky Pizzarelli had been playing guitar with Davern for over twenty years. He was a premier member of the jazz party–festival circuit and had accompanied Davern on the stage and on record countless times. Pianist John Bunch had first played with Davern in 1975. At the time of this recording, he was a part of Kenny's working, piano-driven quartet, and was also Pizzarelli's partner in a trio (with bassist Jay Leonhart) called *New York Swing*. Tony DeNicola was then also part of Davern's working quartet. The final member of the group had played with almost every musician of significance over a career of more than sixty years: there was no musical challenge that Bob Haggart could not conquer.

When Jimmie Noone recorded *That Rhythm Man* in 1929, it seemed to plod along heavily, encumbered by a Mae Alix vocal. On this release, Bunch introduces it in a light and buoyant vein; then Davern comes in and sails along on top of the crisp four-man rhythm section. Bunch and Haggart give *Out of Nowhere* a relaxed feeling, then increase the pace for *Three Little Words*, one of the two tunes on this disc that Kenny had recorded previously.

In the mid 1990s, *Say It Isn't So* was one of the pieces that Kenny played slowly and with great emotion: his rendition of the Irving Berlin tune here is haunting. *Cherry*, a tune that the late Red Allen liked to play, came next, followed by *You're Lucky to Me*. The final tune was *Lullaby of the Leaves*. Kenny dedicated the CD to the memory of his cousin, Dr. Martin E. Greene.

Although Davern was undoubtedly the leader of this group, a collective spirit bound everyone together, and the result was an hour of uniformly excellent music. Kevin Jones said that Davern played "like a dream." On the other side of the world, a reviewer in *Australian Hi-Fi* said, "There is no better swing combination playing today." However, Russ Chase was the most succinct. His review, in its entirety, read: "Yes! Yes!! Yes!!! Yes!!!!"[18]

Financial difficulties caused Waterloo Village to close, and the New Jersey Jazz Society moved its annual JazzFest picnic, which was held on June 17–18, 1995, to Stevens Institute on the banks of the Hudson River in Hoboken. Davern played there, and also played at Avery Fisher Hall as part of the JVC Jazz Festival before leaving on June 30, for his annual weekend in Indianapolis. The July issue of *Jazz Journal International* had an article about Boehm system clarinets and a picture of Kenny captioned "Kenny Davern, Boehm system exponent."

There were appearances at the Red Blazer Too in New York City, and some dates at the Cornerstone before the *Jazz in July* programs began at the 92nd Street Y. Davern was in two of them: on July 20, he participated in a recreation of the *Salute to Satchmo* program that he had first performed in Carnegie Hall in 1974. One week later, he returned to the Y to perform as part of Summit Reunion. Chip Deffaa was there and wrote: "The greatest clarinet playing I've heard in the past year was Kenny Davern's on *St. Louis Blues* at Thursday's *Jazz in July* at the 92nd Street Y concert."[19]

Davern took a shortened annual summer tour in August, starting in England on the 3rd and moving to Edinburgh on the 9th. He played Oslo from the 10th through the 14th, and then flew home. He played some local jobs, then flew to St. Louis for the weekend of August 25.

The music world was surprised when, in late August, Bob Wilber sent a letter to all of his friends announcing that he would retire from performing at concerts, jazz parties, and recordings at the end of 1996. Davern was somewhat taken aback when he received the letter. He had seen Wilber only a few days earlier, and Bob had never mentioned that he was thinking of quitting. Within a few days, Wilber apparently changed his mind and spread the word that the letter had been the result of a "misunderstanding."[20]

Beginning in 1966, actor-comedian Jerry Lewis had hosted an annual telethon for the fight against muscular dystrophy on the Labor Day weekend. The event ran for over twenty-four hours. Over the years, the program expanded to include hosts, audiences, and live entertainment from several other cities. In New York, Lewis hired jazz musicians to entertain the audience and the volunteers who were manning the telephones and working the cameras, microphones, and other equipment when the network had switched to a remote location. For the 1995 program, Lewis hired Bobby Rosengarden as his contractor and, on September 3–4, Kenny was one of the musicians who played for the audience and crew.[21]

Kenny was in Iowa in September 9, and in Denver on the following day, playing with Ralph Sutton. On the weekend of September 23–24, he was playing at Hamilton College in Clinton, New York.

Milton Filius, Jr., had graduated from Hamilton in 1944. Filius liked big band and classic jazz: he collected a large number of recordings and went to the Gibson parties. Filius wanted to create a library at Hamilton of interviews with musicians, and he provided the funds to do it. He got to know a lot of the musicians and, if they played in San Diego, where he lived, he would have them out to his house. Kenny was one of his favorites. Mark Rowe, the Joe Williams Director of the Hamilton College Jazz Archive remembered: "In addition to the interviewing project, he also started a tradition. Every fall at Hamilton, they have this weekend called *Fallcoming*—and he would fund a jazz band. Because he funded it, he picked the musicians. . . . Kenny, from the start, was almost always part of this."[22]

The day after he returned from Hamilton, Davern left for Germany, playing there from September 26 to October 8. Upon his return, he was part of a program at Carnegie Hall. He played some jobs near home, before traveling to New Orleans to appear with Ralph Sutton on November 1–2. From there, he flew to Florida for a week on the S.S. *Norway*.[23] As usual, Hank O'Neal had booked a cast of stars for the trip and, over three nights, he recorded Kenny and Flip Phillips backed by Derek Smith, Howard Alden, Milt Hinton, and Joe Ascione. The CD was titled *John and Joe Revisited, Spanish Eyes*.

Although Flip and Kenny had worked harmoniously on a number of occasions, this was not one of them. Flip was not a retiring soul; he had strong opinions on how music should be played. Kenny was much the same. Flip had his favorite tunes and so did Kenny. Flip liked to get together to work out lines but Kenny preferred spontaneity. Howard Alden remembered the trip.

> He and Flip weren't getting along all that well that week. Flip was a very strong personality, too. He had a bunch of tunes, and he wanted Kenny to come and learn them. He was putting a lot of pressure on Kenny to learn these things very quickly, and it wasn't a real happy week. . . .
>
> It wasn't Kenny's thing. It wasn't his personality or what he wanted to do. For a while, he had a real close relationship with Flip. Kenny was the one who got me on the gig with Flip. They used to play a lot together. But, they had a standoff that week. We did the gig and I thought there were some nice things on it.[24]

Those problems notwithstanding, the sessions yielded some excellent performances. *Elsa's Dream* was the opener, and featured some unison work by Phillips and Alden and solos from everyone. The mysteriously named *Flip's Dido* is a lazy piece based on a twelve-bar blues with a pretty melodic line played by Phillips and Davern in harmony. Flip liked to test his audiences by jumping into an improvisation on *Spanish Eyes* without ever stating the melody and then challenging them to guess the title. This version was not as inventive as some of his other ones.

Davern was featured on *Please Don't Talk about Me When I'm Gone*, done as a ballad. The group then turned to a rendition of *Royal Garden Blues* that sounded very modern and far from its roots in Chicago. Another Phillips composition (which was named for his wife), *Miki's Dream*, followed by *All of Me* were next, and the CD ended with twelve and one-half minutes of *Lover Come Back to Me*, on which Phil Woods joined on alto.

Kenny played the Cornerstone on November 15. The next night, he took the 7:55 p.m. "red-eye" from JFK International Airport and arrived on Friday morning in Hamburg, Germany. He was onstage on Saturday night before an audience of 1,500 at the Hamburg Congress Centre for a concert of songs associated with Louis Armstrong. The group consisted of Randy Sandke and Byron Stripling on trumpets; Joel Helleny, Davern, Mark Shane on piano; David Ostwald on tuba; Greg Cohen; and drummer Joe Ascione.[25]

Although the instrumentation of the All-Stars closely resembled King Oliver's Creole Jazz Band, the arrangements by Randy Sandke were far from dated. The ensemble portions were sharp, and there was plenty of space for soloing. Everyone had at least one feature; Davern took the spotlight on *Wild Man Blues* and *One Hour Tonight*, and he had solos on *Potato Head Blues*, *Savoy Blues*, and *Struttin' with Some Barbecue*. The program was produced by Hans Nagel-Heyer and was released in 1996, titled *We Love You Louis, The New York All-Stars Play the Music of Louis Armstrong*. The release and Davern's performance received good reviews.

Kenny finished out the year playing locally, but for the first time in over a decade, did not spend the beginning of the year in Taos. Tom and Elizabeth Brownell, owners of the Thunderbird Lodge, had decided that organizing, promoting, and financing their annual get-together had become too burdensome, and so the parties came to an end. Davern had a job in Denver on the weekend of January 5 and celebrated his birthday in the airport when he became stranded there. He came home to play a weekend at the Cornerstone, worked at Red Blazer Too on West 46th Street in Manhattan, and had a job with Bucky Pizzarelli, Greg Cohen, and Tony DeNicola.

Kenny was at the Cornerstone at the beginning of February and in Baltimore on the weekend of February 10–11. On the following day, he performed at a memorial service for baritone saxophonist Gerry Mulligan, who had died one month earlier. He was in Boston on the 23rd and 24th, and at the Sherborn Inn in Dover, Delaware. Davern spent the first weekend in March in Scottdale, then worked in New Jersey before he left for Florida.

Summit Reunion performed in concert at Philharmonic Hall in Naples, Florida, on March 20. They were in Sarasota on the next evening, and then moved on *en masse* to join a larger group at Mat Domber's *March of Jazz* in Clearwater. Davern played with Tony DeNicola on the last Saturday of the month. Summit Reunion made an appearance in Oklahoma City on April 6. Davern flew home and, on the next day, he made his second recording with Cynthia Sayer.[26]

Sayer had been working abroad for some time and when she returned to New York, she decided to make a CD that showed her appreciation to all of the New York musicians with whom she had worked. She assembled two front lines, one of which consisted of Peter Ecklund, Randy Reinhart, and Davern, and another made up of Jon-Erik Kellso, Tom Artin, and Scott Robinson. A rhythm section of Keith Ingham on piano, Sayer, Greg Cohen, and drummer Arnie Kinsella worked with both groups.[27] The tunes that she selected were arranged in ways, or played at tempos, that were different from the way they were usually presented. The resultant recording was released under the title of *Cynthia Sayer, Jazz at Home*.

Although Sayer was clearly the centerpiece of this disc, she gave her sidemen more than ample space. Kenny was featured on *Am I Blue*, a number that he often played in his live appearances, investing it with great emotion. He had solos on *Bougalousa Strut*, *With Plenty of Money and You*, and *You Always Hurt the One You Love*. The closing song was *Seems Like Old Times*, and Kenny approached it with a feeling of calm satisfaction that never veered into schmaltz. The album and the musicians received an excellent review in the *IAJRC Journal*.[28]

Three dates at the Cornerstone were followed by three weeks in England. When he returned to the United States, Kenny had a job for Jack Kleinsinger, three more days at the Cornerstone, and a weekend in Billings, Montana, followed by a weekend in Annapolis. Then it was time to make another recording for the Arbors label.[29]

Over the years, Davern had performed frequently with Bucky Pizzarelli and Howard Alden. Each gave him the rhythmic support that he liked, could construct meaningful solos, and was able to musically joust with and complement him during his solos. He brought both of them, along with Greg Cohen and Tony DeNicola, to the Edison Studios in New York in June 1996, to record *Kenny Davern, Breezin' Along*.

The CD begins with an up-tempo *Since My Best Gal Turned Me Down*. Bix Beiderbecke had recorded it in 1927 and had played part of a chorus in half-time. Davern, who rarely played it, included a short section in half-time in this performance. *Jazz Me Blues* features some fiery exchanges between the guitars. On *Rose Room*, not one of his frequently played tunes, Kenny states the melody in the chalumeau register, then lets Pizzarelli and Alden stretch out. *Dark Eyes* is an old Russian–Jewish melody on which Davern is appropriately mournful. In his liner notes, Dan Morgenstern called it "Davern davening."[30]

Kenny liked to select a song that was usually played at a fast tempo and turn it into a ballad. *Baby Won't You Please Come Home* gets the treatment and comes off as a warm and soulful plea. The same is true of *I Surrender Dear*. Everyone has space on *My Honey's Lovin' Arms* and *Exactly Like You*;

Cohen's outing on the latter tune is especially inventive. *My Mama Socks Me* (in reality *My Daddy Rocks Me*) was a Davern favorite that features both guitarists trading fours with Kenny, who comes up with one of his amazing, long-held high notes. *Breezin' Along with the Breeze* is a feature for Tony DeNicola, whose solid rhythm anchored the session. He took two tasteful solos on this, the closing tune.

The album received rave reviews in the *Mississippi Rag*, *The Star-Ledger*, *Jazz Journal International*, and *Jersey Jazz*. Cam Miller said, "Clarinetist Kenny Davern, who took one over the wall with his last recording on the Arbors label (*Kenny Davern and the Rhythm Men*), changes the cast of characters slightly but again demonstrates why he's among jazz's best and brightest."[31] The album was voted one of the best for 1999 in *Jazz Journal International*.[32]

Although Davern was recording more frequently than before, the other aspects of his segment of the music business were showing signs of decay. The process of contraction that had begun in the 1980s accelerated: audiences aged and, as they grew older, they stopped going out. Younger customers wanted different music, and venues either changed their music policy, abandoned it, or went out of business.

Economics—and age—were taking a toll on the festivals and parties that formed such a large part of Davern's life. Renting a venue for an event cost more, as did airfares and hotels for musicians. There was a limit to how much the public would pay for a day or weekend of music—especially when the prospective attendee was retired and living on a fixed income. Some events had corporate sponsors that made up part of the shortfall, but other events were forced to contract their lineups, or to use fewer "name" musicians and more relatively unknown personnel. Some events came to an end because of finances. Some ended because the people who did the bulk of the work, like their audiences, died, became ill, moved away, or simply became tired.

To some extent, the jazz parties were less affected by rising costs. The price of admission was substantially higher than at jazz festivals, and the promoters did not depend on the general public for attendance and revenue. Most of the attendees had the financial wherewithal to pay for the airfare, plus a hotel room, and an admission ticket to the event. A modest increase in the cost of admission would not deter them from coming. However, they were aging. As Kenny once said: "The people are of a silver-haired vintage. They're very nice, they all have some bread, they're sorta like groupies. They go from party to party because they're the only ones who can afford it."[33] Most of the promoters of these events were like their audiences. They were relatively well off and loved the music. Age took its toll of them, as well as of their audiences.

The one expense that promoters and producers did control was the amount that they paid to musicians. Jazz musicians do not get rich playing music. They do not always work regularly, and they are not well paid when they do. The fees that they earn for parties and festivals remain relatively static over time, even though their basic living expenses have risen through inflation.

Once a party or festival establishes its pay scale, it rarely is increased. Promoters of these events are not ignorant or venal. To the contrary, almost all of them are driven by a genuine love for the music and the men who play it. They devote countless hours of uncompensated time, and often reach into their own pockets when there is no money to cover a bill that must be paid.

But, they are caught between the Scylla of smaller audiences with static or shrinking pocketbooks and the Charybdis of rising costs. So, they try to curb costs by limiting salaries paid to musicians, for whom being underpaid is a chronic condition. Since there rarely is more than one event on a given weekend, the musician has the unpleasant choice of accepting less than he feels is due him, or remaining home and possibly not working at all.

Musicians can make some extra money by teaching, writing arrangements, consulting on a television or movie project, writing liner notes, or being the musical director for some event. However, playing music is not, and never was, the way to financial security.

Although it sometimes rankled, that wasn't why Davern was in the business. He told interviewer Shirley Klett.

> I knew that I had to make a living as a professional musician, and I've never done anything else. There have been some pretty lean years. To a degree, they're *still* lean. But what is rewarding is, I've been places and done things that money can't buy, and I consider myself a very wealthy man in that way.[34]

At another time he said, "That freedom, I love it. I never made a fortune, but that's not why I got into music in the first place."[35] Davern once told an interviewer who asked him if he ever wanted to be a millionaire: "I'm still trying to become a hundred-aire."[36]

Kenny did not tour England in the summer of 1996. Nor did he appear at Breda or any of the other festivals. Instead, he stayed close to home. Waterloo Village in Stanhope had resolved its financial problems and had reopened for the summer of 1996. On June 7–9, Davern appeared there for the New Jersey Jazz Society's annual picnic. He had jobs in Newtown, Pennsylvania, and in Philadelphia, played with Johnny Varro and Tony DeNicola at the Watchung Art Center, and had a date with Howard Alden on June 28. Beginning on June 15, he played the next eight consecutive Saturdays with Tony DeNicola.

There were fewer venues in New York and New Jersey that offered jazz as a weekend attraction, and fewer venues that could afford big bands to play for dancing. Tony DeNicola had a permanent job playing on Saturday nights at the Forrestal Center in Princeton, and, if Davern was not out of town at a jazz party or festival, or playing a private event, he found himself working with increasing frequency with DeNicola on Saturday night. Like the Cornerstone, it did not pay a great deal, but it was steady work.

In July and August, there were dates at the Cornerstone and an appearance in the *Jazz in July* concerts at the 92nd Street Y. He had a job at the Westhampton Country Club on August 10, and a date with Jerry Jerome. On Labor Day weekend, he was invited back to participate in the Jerry Lewis telethon. He had two gigs in Princeton in September. On the 9th, he played with Ed Polcer and, on the 28th, he appeared at the annual *JazzFeast* party, produced by Jack Stine and held at Palmer Square. He was in Clinton, New York, playing for *Fallcoming* at Hamilton College on October 4–6, had a job at the Cornerstone, and then flew to Aspen for a weekend.

David Niu, an attorney, and his wife, Martha Chiang, who was then working on her doctorate at Harvard University, purchased the Four Seas Cuisine of China restaurant in Madison, New Jersey, in 1995. They began serving an upscale Asian-American menu in a subdued atmosphere, changed its name to Shanghai Jazz, and hired first-class musicians to perform there, including Marian McPartland, Bucky and John Pizzarell, and Harry Allen. Kenny made the first of many appearances there on October 25. He had a job in Tenafly before he left for a week on the S.S. *Norway* on November 2.

In November and December, Kenny played five nights at the Cornerstone and eight consecutive Saturdays with Tony DeNicola. On December 8, he played a fortieth anniversary party at the Manor, an upscale venue in West Orange, New Jersey. He appeared with Flip Phillips at Pace University for Jack Kleinsinger, and was back at the Manor for another private party on the 13th. There was one more gig at Shanghai Jazz before the end of the year.[37]

Kenny began 1997 in a new setting. Alto saxophonist Dick Johnson had spent a number of years leading the New Artie Shaw Orchestra, an entity that played the songs that were associated with Shaw. Artie had retired from performing over forty years before and, although he occasionally appeared at the band's performances, he never played with them. On January 3–4, Johnson and Davern appeared at the Regattabar in the Charles Hotel in

Boston, co-leading a group calling itself Reed Summit. Dave McKenna was on piano, Gray Sargent played guitar, Marshall Wood was on bass, and Artie Cabral on drums.

Davern had a Wednesday date at the Red Blazer Too, then traveled to Phoenix on January 10–11 with Howard Alden, Bucky Pizzarelli, and Greg Cohen. The following weekend, he had a job with Randy Reinhart on Friday, played with Tony DeNicola on Saturday, and was at the Church of the Heavenly Rest with Alden, Cohen, and DeNicola on Sunday. One week later, he was in Pittsburgh, played on the 29th at Red Blazer Too, and, on the first weekend in February, he performed at the North Carolina Jazz Party in Wilmington.

From February 3 to 9, he was in Bern. When he returned, there was a job at the Red Blazer Too, followed by one-night engagements at Shanghai Jazz and the Cornerstone before he went off to the San Diego Jazz Party. At the end of February, he was back at the Red Blazer Too, and on March 1, he was one of sixteen musicians who participated in a program at St. Ann's Church in Manhattan to celebrate the documentary film by Jean Bach, *A Great Day in Harlem*. He spent the weekend of March 14 in St. Louis, and was in Clearwater Beach on the following weekend for the *March of Jazz Party*.

Domber scheduled a recording session with Davern and Wilber on the day after the party ended. In an effort to do something different, Wilber suggested that they should use Dave Frishberg on piano and, when the group convened, the rhythm section consisted of Dave, Bucky Pizzarelli, Bob Haggart on bass, and Ed Metz, Jr., on drums.[38]

In the years since Frishberg and Kenny had played together at Nick's, Dave had recorded with Al Cohn, Phil Woods, Zoot Sims, Bobby Hackett, Charlie Shavers, Dick Sudhalter, and Jimmy Rushing, In the early 1970s, he moved to the West Coast and, in the 1980s, he appeared frequently as a singer who accompanied himself on piano and occasionally played an instrumental solo. He was a prolific and award-winning composer, often writing quixotic lyrics to his compositions that included *My Attorney Bernie*, *Van Lingle Mungo*, *Dodger Blue*, *Marilyn Monroe*, *I'm Hip*, and *Saratoga Hunch*.

Frishberg lent an entirely different air to the Wilber–Davern group. His style is unique, with a rollicking, joyous, feeling that he transmits to the band. *Cherry*, the opening number, was exuberant, as was *Who's Sorry Now*. The other up-tempo tunes were *Sheik of Araby*, *Sometimes I'm Happy*, and the closing cut, *Arbors Stomp*, which was a thinly disguised *Bye Bye Blues*. Each of the leaders had a solo outing: Davern essayed a plaintive rendition of *I Want a Little Girl*, and Wilber performed his own composition, *Dear Sidney*. Bob Haggart introduced *Sentimental Journey* by whistling the verse, as well as the closing chorus. Cam Miller wrote, "Wilber and Davern create a magic that not only mystifies the musicians themselves, but also blows audiences away." The disc was voted a Writers Choice for 1998 in *Coda* Magazine.[39]

After playing a private party in Punta Gorda, Kenny returned to New Jersey and a night at the Cornerstone. On March 29, he appeared at the 92nd Street Y, and on the first of April flew to London to begin a three-week tour of England, Scotland, and Ireland, where he played some of his usual places. That part of the tour ended on April 20, and on the 24th he and Swedish reedman Tomas Ornberg began a week-long tour of Germany. They were back in Sweden on May 1, and on the 3rd they recorded together.[40]

In the years following Davern's 1981 recording with Ornberg's Blue 5, the group had changed its name to the Swedish Jazz Kings, toured Europe, the United States, Australia, and Japan, and recorded with artists from several different countries. In addition to Ornberg, who played alto and soprano saxophones, the members of the Kings were Bent Persson, who played cornet or trumpet; Olie Nyman on banjo or guitar; and Bo Juhlin on sousaphone. For this occasion, they were joined by pianist Martin Litton. The CD was issued on the Opus 3 label and titled *The Swedish Jazz Kings Featuring Kenny Davern, Comes Love*.

Unlike the Blue 5 CD, this release is made up of familiar tunes, albeit performed by a lineup that was different from Davern's usual groups. The first tune is *Apex Blues*, which contains a few unusual twists in Davern's solo, but no real surprises. Persson and Litton drop out for *Buddy Bolden's Blues* and return for a brisk version of *Shine*. Davern is the only horn on *Travelin' All Alone*, and he ends the tune playing at the very top of the clarinet's range. Persson returns, but Ornberg drops out for *Nobody Else but You*, another one of Davern's standbys at the time. Although Kenny liked to play *Please Don't Talk about Me When I'm Gone* as a ballad, he, Ornberg, Nyman, and Juhlin take this version at a sprightly tempo. The entire group performs *I Would Do Anything for You*, and then Davern has a feature on *Comes Love*. Interspersed among these selections are tunes on which Davern is not present and two solos by Litton. When the CD was issued, David Badham called the tracks with Kenny "absolutely top notch in their chosen field of updated classic jazz."[41]

Davern was home on May 5. He played every Saturday for the balance of the month with Tony DeNicola, had three nights at the Cornerstone (including one with British pianist Neville Dickie), a concert at the Watchung Art Center, and two Wednesday gigs at Red Blazer Too. On the first weekend in June, he was honored in a ceremony at Waterloo Village.

Notes

1. Mat Domber, President of Arbors Records, interview by the author.
2. Domber interview.
3. Kenny Davern and Elsa Davern, conversations with the author; Marty Grosz, Roswell Rudd, Claire Weintraub, David Weintraub, interviews by the author. Some persons recalled that Josephine worked at the Fallsview Hotel, and others remembered that she lived or worked in Fallsburg, New York. In all likelihood, both recollections are correct. The Slutsky family also operated the Fallsview Hotel, which was located near, and is now part of the Nevele. Ellenville, where both properties are located, is only a few miles from South Fallsburg, New York.
4. Date Book; *Jazz Journal International*, 47, no. 4 (April 1994): 3.
5. Kenny Davern, conversation with the author.
6. Mat Domber, President of Arbors Records, interview by the author.
7. Jack Sohmer, Kenny Davern, "East Side, West Side," *Mississippi Rag*, xxiii, no. 11 (November 1995): 28; Russ Chase, "East Side, West Side: Kenny Davern and His Jazz Band," *IAJRC Journal*, 28, no. 3 (Summer 1995): 76; John Chadwick. "Kenny Davern, East Side, West Side," *Jazz Journal International*, 48, no. 6 (June 1995): 35.
8. *Jazz Journal International*, 49, no. 2 (February 1996): 10.
9. Date Book; *Jazz Journal International*, 47, no. 8 (August 1994): 3.
10. Hans Nagel-Heyer, liner notes to *Jazz Im Amerika Haus, Vol. 5, Summit Reunion*, Nagel-Heyer CD 015, November 1994; Date Book.
11. Bill Bennett, *Jazz Times*, May 1999: 147; George Wilson, "Compact Views," *Jersey Jazz*, 23, no. 1 (February 1995): 21.
12. Date Book.
13. Dick Hyman, *Thinking about Kenny Davern*, unpublished.
14. Stanley Dance, "Lightly & Politely," *Jazz Journal International*, 48, no. 7 (July 1995): 10; Date Book; *Jersey Jazz*, 22, no.11 (January 1995): 5; North Carolina event program.
15. Hank O'Neal, recorded recollections.
16. David Badham, "Summit Reunion: Yellow Dog Blues," *Jazz Journal International*, 49, no. 8 (August 1996): 32; Dick Neeld, "Views and Reviews," *Jersey Jazz*, 24, no. 10 (December 1996): 18.
17. Date Book; *Jersey Jazz*, 23, no. 3 (April 1995): 7; Colorado Springs event program; *Jazz Journal International*, 48, no. 5 (May 1995): 4.
18. Kevin Jones, "Reviews, Jazz," *Soundscape*, April–May, 1997, p. 77; Anonymous, "Kenny Davern, The Rhythm Men," *Australian Hi-Fi*, April 1997; Russ Chase, "Kenny Davern and His Rhythm Men," *IAJRC Journal*, 29, no. 3 (Summer 1996): 66.
19. Chip Deffaa, "Summit at Peak Form"," *New York Post*, 1 August 1995. See also *Jersey Jazz*, 23, no. 7 (September 1995): 8; Date Book; *Jazz Journal International*, 48, no. 7 (July 1995): 2; Chip Deffaa, "Satchmo Recalled with Style," *New York Post*, 24 July 1995: 29.

20. Kenny Davern, conversation with the author.
21. Date Book; Kenny Davern, conversation with the author.
22. Monk Rowe, interview by the author.
23. Date Book; Carnegie Hall event program; *New York Times* 17 October 1995.
24. Howard Alden, interview by the author.
25. Hans Nagel-Heyer, liner notes to *We Love You Louis, The New York All-Stars Play the Music of Louis Armstrong*, Nagel-Heyer CS 029, Hamburg, November 1996. As he had done before, Kenny was on a plane home the next morning.
26. Date Book; *Jersey Jazz*, 23, no. 10 (December 1995): 5, and 23, no. 11 (January 1996): 5; and 24, no. 1 (February 1996): 5, and 24, no. 2 (March 1996): 5; Naples event program.
27. Cynthia Sayer, interview by the author.
28. Ken Crawford, *IAJRC Journal*, 30, no. 3 (Summer 1997): 76.
29. Date Book; *Jersey Jazz*, 24, no. 3 (April 1996): 5, and 24, no. 4 (May 1996): 5; *Jazz Journal International*, 49, no. 4 (April 1996): 3.
30. Dan Morgenstern, liner notes to *Kenny Davern, Breezin Along*, Arbors ARCD 19170, December 1996.
31. Cam Miller, "Breezin' Along," *North County Times*, 9 May 1997.
32. *Jazz Journal International*, 53, no. 2 (February 2000): 8.
33. Kenny Davern, quoted in Peter Vacher, "Straight Talk from Kenny Davern," *Mississippi Rag*, xxv, no. 5 (May 1997): 32.
34. Kenny Davern, quoted in Shirley Klett, "Kenny Davern, Interview," *Cadence*, 4, no. 12 (December 1978): 18, 20.
35. Kenny Davern, quoted in Zan Stewart, "Kenny Davern, Craftsman on Clarinet"," *The Star Ledger*, 15 December 2006.
36. Kenny Davern, interviewed by Peter Clayton, recorded between 4 and 7 November 1984 and broadcast 9 November 1984 on BBC Radio 2.
37. Date Book; *Jersey Jazz*, 24, no. 5 (June 1996): 26, and 24, no. 8 (October 1996): 7, and 24, no. 9 (November 1996): 5, and 24, no. 10 (December 1996): 5.
38. Ross Firestone, notes to *Bob Wilber and Kenny Davern, Reunion at Arbors*, Arbors Records, ARCD 19183, 1998.
39. Cam Miller, "Choice Cuts, Bob Wilber and Kenny Davern, Reunion at Arbors," *The American Rag*, 10, no. 8 (September 1998); *Coda*, issue 283 (January/February 1999).
40. Date Book; Bob Blumenthal, "Davern and Johnson Soar in Reed Summit," *The Boston Globe*, 4 January 1997; *Jersey Jazz*, 24, no. 11 (January 1997): 5, 28; *New York Daily News*, 28 February 1997; *Jazz Journal International*, 50, no. 4 (April 1997): 3.
41. David Badham, "The Swedish Jazz Kings Featuring Kenny Davern, Comes Love," *Jazz Journal International*, 53, no. 7 (July 2000): 44.

CHAPTER FIFTEEN

Recognition

On June 7, 1997, Kenny Davern was inducted into the American Jazz Hall of Fame. Founded by the New Jersey Jazz Society (NJJS) and the Institute of Jazz Studies at Rutgers University, the Hall of Fame selected its first honorees in 1983. In every year thereafter, a group of eleven electors, composed of three representatives of the Institute of Jazz Studies, three from the NJJS, and five generally well-regarded and knowledgeable members of the jazz community selected the persons to be inducted.

By 1997, the members of the Hall of Fame included Louis Armstrong, Henry "Red" Allen, Sidney Bechet, Benny Carter, Bix Beiderbecke, Eddie Condon, Duke Ellington, Dizzy Gillespie, Bobby Hackett, King Oliver, Pee Wee Russell, and Ben Webster. In that year, the electors selected Davern, and he was inducted in a ceremony held at Waterloo Village during the NJJS's annual picnic. Dan Morgenstern, director of the Institute of Jazz Studies at Rutgers University, gave the induction speech.

When Davern was first called and told that he was going to be inducted into the Hall of Fame, his initial reaction was disbelief. Notwithstanding all of the glowing reviews that had been written about his work over the years, the positive audience responses, favorable interactions with other musicians, and the other indicia of success, Davern never quite believed that he was as good as people said he was. He found it difficult to accept the fact that he was going to be enshrined among the musicians who had been, and still were, his heroes. When he finally realized that the call was genuine and the election a reality, he was unable to speak for several minutes.[1]

Some dates at the Cornerstone preceded Davern's appearance at the Danny Kaye Playhouse on June 21 as part of the JVC Jazz Festival. On the next night, he was at Shanghai Jazz. He had a number of local jobs before he made his annual appearance at the 92nd Street Y.

A highlight of the *Jazz in July* program was the annual Dick and Derek Piano Party. Centered about Hyman and Derek Smith, the party always included several horn players. On July 29, Davern was one of the musicians whom Hyman invited to participate. Two days later, he was back at Shanghai Jazz and, on the following day, he was off to the United Kingdom. He appeared at the Edinburgh Jazz Festival for three days beginning on August 4 and then went on to Brecon, where he was grouped with Scott Hamilton, Brian Lemon, and Dave Green.[2]

Kenny returned to Shanghai Jazz on August 20 and, over the next month, played a private party and some dates at the Cornerstone, and performed at the Jerry Lewis telethon. He worked in Philadelphia and Pittsburgh before attending the annual *Fallcoming* weekend at Hamilton College that began on September 19.

There were aspects of Kenny's appearances that were somewhat stressful to the college personnel who were involved in the program. Monk Rowe, the director of the Joe Williams Jazz Archive at Hamilton, recalled:

> We would be on pins and needles. What's he going to say? These concerts were not in a concert hall. It was more like a club. It was a beautiful round building. Students would tend to come and go. I remember one incident where some of the students got up to leave after the third or fourth song, and he said something like "I see. You're going to go out and do some drugs now." Or, even worse. Sometimes these people who got up to go were VIPs, or life trustees, and he would say things like, "Oh, is it past your bedtime now? You gotta go watch Letterman?" . . . But, we got used to it. God, he was so funny, once you got used to his acerbic wit.[3]

Romy Britell, Monk's wife, who was also involved in these weekends, said:

> At first, I was very put off by this. But, year after year, when I'd go back and I got to have dinner with him and talk to him offstage, I realized that he was *never* rude offstage. It was just the opposite. It was that he didn't seem to be very happy when he felt that people were not paying him the respect that he deserved to have. . . . Over the about ten years that he used to come here, I went from being annoyed, to not being able to wait until he came. Because I felt that I was in on knowing that the real Kenny was not at all what he said

on stage. . . . I think he was very charming—at least to me. He always treated the women very carefully and with a great deal of respect.[4]

Davern had a date at Shanghai Jazz before joining Hank O'Neal's weeklong *Dixieland at Sea* cruise aboard the S.S. *Norway* on September 27, where he appeared with Reinhart, Helleny, Bunch, Haggart, and DeNicola.[5] During the last quarter of 1997, Davern was often at his usual venues, playing with his usual colleagues. In October, there was a job in Aspen and a date at Windows on the World. He spent a weekend in Phoenix during November, played for Jack Kleinsinger, and had a date with Dick Hyman during December. In addition, he made the first of three recordings with Ken Peplowski.[6]

Peplowski had assembled a rhythm section of Ben Aranov on piano, along with Greg Cohen and drummer Chuck Redd, for a recording session for Concord Records that was released under the title of *Grenadilla*. He was seeking to expand his musical horizons, and chose to play some original compositions by Aranov, Marty Ehrlich, and Greg Cohen. Howard Alden was there for several numbers, and Davern joined Peplowski, Alden, and the rhythm section for one tune.

Peplowski wanted Davern to try something outside of his normal range of tunes, but Kenny was adamant in refusing to venture beyond what had become his comfort zone. Eventually, they settled on *Farewell Blues*, a song from the repertoire of the New Orleans Rhythm Kings. Peplowski was disappointed.

> To be honest, I wanted him to stretch a bit and do something else. Here we are, talking about what a great player he was. He was very insecure about his own playing and his own self. It's like a security blanket; he always fell back on the same tunes that he'd do over and over. He was so much more than that, and I don't think he needed to do that. But, when you tried to get him to stretch, he was so resistant. He'd give you twenty reasons why "that's not a good idea for two clarinets." He'd say that. We wound up playing *Farewell Blues*, which we'd played together on some jazz parties. We'd already been doing that piece.[7]

In January 1998, Davern made a winter tour of England, leaving on the 6th and returning two weeks later. He played at the 92nd Street Y on the 24th, and was at the Church of the Heavenly Rest with Howard Alden, Greg Cohen, and Tony DeNicola on the following day. There were dates at the Cornerstone and at Shanghai Jazz before he traveled to Little Rock, Arkansas, to help photographer and promoter Al White celebrate his birthday. In mid-March, he was in Clearwater, Florida, for the annual *March of Jazz* and, from March 30 to April 4, he played at Zinnos in Manhattan.

The Red Blazer Too on West 46th Street had closed, but the Red Blazer, located at 32 West 37th Street was open for business, and Davern was there for three consecutive Tuesdays starting on April 7. He played the Cornerstone and Shanghai Jazz before he joined Ruby Braff in a recording studio for Arbors Records.[8]

Braff had a unique musical voice: like Davern he was instantly recognizable, and took his instrument to places that were beyond the abilities of most others. Mat Domber liked the way that Ruby played and made the decision to create a musical record of Braff's performances. From his first recording for Arbors in 1996, Braff was on more than fifteen CDs, the last of which was released posthumously in the fall of 2008.

Although Braff and Davern had known each other for nearly forty years, and played together at numerous parties and festivals, *Born to Play* was their first studio collaboration. Ruby was an argumentative person whose unkind remarks and feuds with other musicians were legendary. From time to time, he and Davern would stop speaking to each other, although they would continue to work together. When Braff was planning the session, he called Davern to ask him to play one number, and Kenny agreed to come.

Braff had written the arrangements for the songs and assembled an unusual complement of musicians to work with: Howard Alden, Bucky Pizzarelli, and Jon Wheatly all played guitar, plus Michael Moore and Marshal Wood on bass—the former bowing his instrument and the latter plucking his—and Jim Gwin on drums. Equally eclectic was Braff's selection of tunes.

When Braff called Davern to do the date, he only intended that Kenny play with him on *Born to Lose*, a tune written by Frankie Brown that became associated with Willie Nelson. Although this was far from Kenny's normal repertoire, he was clearly comfortable with the tune, accompanying Braff during his vocal, as well as on cornet, and taking an imaginative solo.

Davern had arrived when the group was preparing to record *Avalon* and, although Ruby had not planned to use Kenny on the tune, he asked him to sit in.[9] Davern obliged, turning in a performance that was restrained and musical. He also performed on two other numbers: *The Doodle King*, which is a Braff composition, and *I Want a Little Girl*.

Kenny was usually ill at ease working with Ruby. Mat Domber observed:

> Kenny was never really comfortable with his playing on his records with Ruby. Kenny always felt that he was sort of intimidated by Ruby. Ruby had a manner—certainly dictatorial is the word. Ruby had what he called Instant

Conducting. What he loved to do is to be surrounded by the musicians as best you could be in a studio. He would have a swivel chair and, in his mind, spell out the music. When it was time in the tune to take a chorus, Ruby would point to someone, and after that he would suddenly point to somebody else to take the next chorus, and then somebody else. It was never arranged in advance: there was always that spontaneity that Ruby liked. It meant that musicians had to be on their toes. Because when Ruby looked at you, you had to be ready to perform then and there. . . . But, Kenny didn't like that because that was not the way he felt comfortable in playing.[10]

Kenny told interviewer Bob Rusch:

I never feel as comfortable as I would like to on the bandstand with him, even though I admire the man's playing and his wit and his intelligence and his intuitiveness. . . . I always feel like I'm auditioning. . . . I don't feel that I can really just sit down—settle down and get into playing, 'cause too much is going on as far as watching the cues.[11]

At the end of April, Davern took a week-long tour of Japan, his first visit to that country. He returned on May 4, played the Watchung Art Center on the 8th and, before the end of the month, he was in Wisconsin for the First Milwaukee Hot Jazz Party. After dates at the Cornerstone and Shanghai Jazz, Davern was at the Danny Kaye Playhouse on June 15, for the JVC Jazz Festival: Ralph Sutton and Clark Terry were also on the bill. The NJJS had moved its annual JazzFest picnic to Fairleigh Dickenson University in Madison, and Davern played there at the end of June.

Kenny traveled to the North Fork of Long Island to appear on July 4 at the Paumanok Vineyards in Aquebogue, in a program labeled *Sunset at the Vineyard*.[12] Then, on the 10th, he was off to Italy to perform with Bob Wilber. For about a week, Davern and Wilber toured with a local rhythm section consisting of a guitar, bass, and drums. Their performances in Sori and San Marino were recorded and released on an Italian-label CD entitled *Bob Wilber—Kenny Davern, Travelin'*. The disc illustrates some of the difficulties that Kenny and Bob faced on tours such as this.

The rhythm section was wooden and over amplified; the plodding and unvarying four-notes-to-the-bar bass, coupled with the clanging guitar, was intrusive; and the drummer dropped far too many bombs that were out of place. The repertoire consisted entirely of tunes that Wilber and Davern had played countless times together.

Davern appeared in two concerts in the *Jazz in July* series in 1998. The program on July 28 featured Davern, along with Ken Peplowski, Allan

Vache, Dan Block, and Walt Levinsky. Performing with Hyman, Michael Moore, and drummer Joe Ascione, Kenny played *Yellow Dog Blues*. Veteran jazz writer Chip Deffaa said: "Kenny Davern's inspired performance of W.C. Handy's *Yellow Dog Blues* . . . was not only the peak moment of that concert, it was one of the peak moments I've witnessed in the fifteen-year history of the concert series."[13]

Kenny played a date at Shanghai Jazz before he left on July 31 for a two-week tour of England and Scotland that included an appearance at the Edinburgh Jazz Festival. He spent two days in Norway, then came home and, after a few local appearances, made his third CD as a leader for Arbors Records.[14]

Smiles was Davern's second recording with the two-guitar team of Howard Alden and Bucky Pizzarelli, plus Greg Cohen and Tony DiNicola. As was the case with their earlier outing, Davern was plainly at ease in this setting, where he was supported by four musicians who knew him intimately. Throughout the set, Alden and Pizzarelli effortlessly trade off the roles of soloist and accompanist, and Cohen and DiNicola provide rhythm and a solid bottom to the music.

Even before he recorded *Palesteena* with Summit Reunion in 1990, it had been a staple of Davern's club act. Like *Dark Eyes* on the *Breezin' Along* CD, *Palesteena* has overtones of a Jewish setting and Davern, as good as anyone in that idiom, combines a touch of klezmer with a heavy dose of jazz. *Sweet Lorraine* had also been a part of Kenny's performance repertoire for several years, and the group takes it at a lazy, medium tempo that keeps building in tension until Davern's final chorus. *Bernie's Tune*, written in the 1950s, was not from the era of songs that Kenny favored: Howard and Bucky have the lion's share of space here. The next tune is *Summertime*, a work in progress for Davern that he kept honing and refining for years. On this recording, the pace is slow, and Kenny vests his performance with an emotional and meditative quality.

That Da Da Strain and *Apex Blues* were both tunes that Davern played frequently: on the former, Cohen provides driving support and a lyrical solo and, on the latter, Pizzarelli takes the Joe Poston role and provides harmonic support while Kenny essays this Jimmie Noone favorite. Another ballad, *I Must Have That Man*, is next, with Kenny delivering a warm and woody chalumeau-range chorus, followed by the title tune played at a medium tempo.

Eddie Cook gave the release an excellent review in *Jazz Journal International*. It got four stars from Paul de Barros in *DownBeat*, who generally liked the disc but was less than pleased with *Summertime* and *I Must Have That Man*. Readers of *Jazz Journal International* voted it one of 1999's ten best CDs.[15]

Playing for the Jerry Lewis Muscular Dystrophy telethon occupied Kenny on the Labor Day weekend. For the rest of the year, he worked frequently at the Cornerstone and with Tony DeNicola in Princeton, plus an occasional appearance at Shanghai Jazz. He cruised on the S. S. *Norway*, flew to San Francisco for "Swingin' on Nob Hill" at the Mark Hopkins Hotel, spent the weekend of November 13 in Denver, and played at Zinnos during the first week of December.

The highlights of January 1999 were two concerts at the Museum of Modern Art on the 21st and 29th, with John Bunch, John Beal, and Tony DeNicola. He had several festivals and parties scheduled for February and March, as well as a tour of England. But, at the beginning of February, Davern was stricken with an attack of what manifested itself as vertigo. He suffered from double vision, was dizzy and unsteady on his feet, and was sometimes even unable to stand. He was forced to cancel all of his appearances for February and to curtail his activities in March, before the illness faded away as mysteriously as it arrived.[16]

He was well enough to record with Ruby Braff on March 26. Braff chose Tommy Newsom on tenor, John Bunch, Howard Alden, Michael Moore on bass, and drummer Kenny Washington, to record six titles for a CD that was titled *The Cape Codfather*. The longest song was a fifteen-plus minute recording of *Love Is Just Around the Corner* that began as a ballad and then, after about four and one-half minutes, was transformed into a medium-tempo piece. Kenny had a nice outing in the faster section. On first hearing, Kenny was not pleased with the CD, saying that "It had no reason to exist."[17] Critics disagreed: David Badham gave the album a good review and said that Kenny's best work was on *Melancholy Baby* and *If Dreams Come True*.[18]

By the beginning of April, Davern was able to travel to Pittsburgh with Bobby Rosengarden. He spent a weekend in Dallas, returned to play an evening at Shanghai Jazz and, on April 23–25, was in Atlanta for Phil Carroll's annual jazz party. As was customary, George Buck had set up a recording date to follow the party: this year he made arrangements for Davern and Bob Wilber to record as Summit Reunion, with Mark Shane on piano, Bucky Pizzarelli on guitar, Frank Tate on bass, and Hal Smith on drums. The album was called *You Ain't Heard Nothin' Yet! Summit Reunion Plays Some Al Jolson Songs*, and it was less than might have been expected.

There were several causes. This recording was made on a Sunday evening after three days of performing, and the musicians were tired.[19] But, the most significant problem was Wilber's choice of songs. Davern felt that most of Al Jolson's music was not a suitable jazz vehicle. He and Wilber had some telephonic arguments before they arrived in Atlanta, but Wilber insisted that the concept was workable.[20] The dispute continued at the studio, and the result seemed to validate Davern's concern. With the exception of *Anniversary Song* and *Avalon*, no song lasted more than five minutes. Solos rarely exceeded one chorus, and there was little extended improvisation and even less excitement. Bucky Pizzarelli thought that the Jolson repertoire was "terrible" and said that it was the worst album they had ever made.[21] Afterward, Davern and Wilber did not speak to each other for several months.[22]

At the end of April, Davern was off to Japan for a week with Ralph Sutton, Greg Cohen, and Jake Hanna. He came back to play at the Cornerstone; had a week at Zinnos; a date in Plainsboro, New Jersey; and three dates with Tony DeNicola at Scanticon, a hotel and conference center in Princeton, where DeNicola had a steady, Saturday-night job. On June 13, he appeared in the Jazz at Ravinia festival held in Ravinia Park, Chicago, for a Fats Waller tribute. Five days later, he was at the Danny Kaye Playhouse as part of the JVC Jazz Festival. He spent the weekend of June 25–26 at the Elkhart Jazz Festival, then traveled to Chicago to play a week at the Jazz Showcase on West Grand with the Eddie Higgins trio.

Kenny appeared in Newport, Rhode Island, on July 9, and was at Scanticon with Tony DeNicola on the following night. He played twice at Lincoln Center, once as part of its Midsummer Night Swing program and again on July 17 as a participant in *Black Stick Summit*. The musicians were billed as Ken Peplowski and His All-Star Clarinets, featuring Davern, Peplowski, Evan Christopher, and Matt Dariau. They played for an evening of dancing to a program of beguine, swing music, and klezmer.[23]

Kenny was one of the featured players at a tribute to Bob Haggart, presented on July 21, 1999, as part of the *Jazz in July* program. He at the Watchung Arts Center with Alden, Murray Wall, and DeNicola on the 23rd and, in August, had several dates at the Cornerstone, three Saturday nights in Princeton with DeNicola, and a weekend in Eugene, Oregon. He was in the recording studio on the first day of September, working on a CD for Hans Nagel-Heyer.

In addition to producing excellent recordings of jazz for over fifty years, many of them for Columbia Records, George Avakian was a jazz historian. He had begun looking for compositions that Louis Armstrong had written, but never recorded, and, in the course of his research had learned that Randy Sandke, Brian Nalepka, and Scott Robinson had lead sheets for some otherwise-unknown Armstrong compositions. Using a pool of musicians that changed from song to song, they recorded seven tunes written by Armstrong, plus some songs that Bix Beiderbecke had recorded, but that had not been released. The album was called *The Re-Discovered Louis and Bix, Lost Musical Treasures of Louis Armstrong and Bix Beiderbecke*.[24]

Davern appears on four cuts in the Armstrong segment, and solos on three of them: *Papa, What Are You Trying to Do to Me*; *I've Been Doing It for Years*; *When You Leave Me Alone to Pine*; and *Drop That Sack*. These are period pieces, and Kenny's solos evoke images of Johnny Dodds and the other clarinetists of the time. The album was voted one of *Jazz Journal International*'s best new issues for 2000.

Directly after the recording session, Davern played the Jerry Lewis telethon. He had a private party in Philadelphia, a date at the Cornerstone, and on September 18 was in Minneapolis with Ralph Sutton. The following weekend saw him in Clinton, New York, playing for the *Fallcoming* weekend at Hamilton College. In October, he was at the New York Hilton, played at date at the United Nations Building, and finished out the month aboard the S.S. *Norway*. Almost every Saturday night in November and December was spent playing with DeNicola. As the holiday season approached, Kenny had some private parties and some dates at the Cornerstone and Shanghai Jazz. He spent New Year's Eve playing a party in Manhattan.

During this period, he was working around the New York–New Jersey area with several pianists, most frequently with John Bunch, but occasionally with Marty Napoleon and Mark Shane. Bunch was born in Indiana in 1921, and had been inspired by Teddy Wilson, as well as by Fats Waller. His musical career was interrupted by World War II: while flying in a bomber he was shot down over Europe and spent several years as a prisoner of war. In the late 1950s, he worked in the big bands of Woody Herman and Benny Goodman and, over time, became associated with the bop and swing schools of music. He spent six years as musical director for Tony Bennett, worked with Goodman on his tours of the USSR and Mexico, and recorded with Scott Hamilton in the 1980s. Beginning in 1991, and continuing through 2009, he teamed up with guitarist Bucky Pizzarelli and bassist Jay Leonhart to perform in concert and on recordings, usually billed as New York Swing.

Playing with Davern required Bunch to revisit his early years, when he had worked at Condon's with musicians like Bud Freeman. Although a dynamic pianist, Bunch was not an intrusive one. He gave Davern the harmonic support that he needed without ever forcing him down musical paths that he didn't want to tread. Bunch thought that Kenny was unique.

> He was his own man. He didn't go the Benny Goodman or Artie Shaw route. Others did: Peanuts Hucko did and Johnny Mince played in sort of that style.

But, not Kenny. I'm sure he had the technique and ability to play in that style. But, he didn't want to do it. He was an individual, and there are not many like that. Nowadays, there are some brilliant piano players on the West Coast and in New York, and they mostly play in the style of Bill Evans; even players like Herbie Hancock. And along came Erroll Garner: completely different. That's what Kenny is on a clarinet. You hear a record, and you say "That's Kenny." Even my wife, who's not a musician and claims not to know anything about jazz, says "That's Kenny." That's terrific.[25]

However, Davern's first choice of accompanying instrument had become the guitar, usually played by Howard Alden. Davern was not the only musician who liked to play with him and, as Alden became more popular and in demand for personal appearances and recording dates, he became less available to play with Davern. Howard also contracted sarcoidosis, a little known viral disease that inflamed the lining of his brain and limited his ability to work. (He has since made a complete recovery.) Howard had once recommended James Chirillo to Davern and, in the middle years of the 1990s, Kenny began to call on James with increasing frequency.

Chirillo was born in Belleville, Washington, in 1953. He had studied at North Texas State University and had recorded with the school's prestigious 1:00 O'Clock Lab Band. In the years that followed, he performed with several singers, including Vic Damone and Marilyn Maye, and had spent three years in the U.S. Military Academy Band at West Point. He came to New York in 1982, where he played with Tiny Grimes, Remo Palmier, Joe Newman, Eddie Heywood, Dick Sudhalter, and Randy Sandke. He became a member of the Smithsonian Jazz Masterworks Orchestra, and played with big bands led by Benny Goodman, Buck Clayton, and Loren Schoenberg. In addition to his talents as a guitarist, he is also a gifted composer and arranger.

Chirillo recalled that his first date with Davern had been arranged by Alden.

You hear stories about him being a tough cookie to deal with. So, I was a little apprehensive at the time. But, he was a complete gentleman: he's very direct. He tells you what he wants. He wanted four-to-the-bar rhythm. He didn't want a lot of loose comping kind of things that would get in his way. Rhythm's one thing I can do really well. So, that was no problem.[26]

It took Davern and Chirillo several years before they began to understand and musically complement each other. Chirillo said:

In the couple of years leading up to the *Mill Hill* record, we really started to hit it off, and I became his mainstay guy. Even though I'd just be playing that four-four rhythm a lot of the time, sometimes I'd throw something extra rhythmically in there or I'd throw one little thing in there or in my solos. He would hear things that would put him in a direction musically that was different from where he normally would have gone.²⁷

Davern, James Chirillo, Greg Cohen, and Tony DeNicola became the Kenny Davern Quartet—the culmination of Kenny's search for a group of band mates who shared his musical values and with whom he could express himself. Greg Cohen had a view of the dynamics of the band.

> Eventually, he found a group of people who were really nothing alike. There was James Chirillo, who was a graduate from West Point. There was Tony DiNicola, who looked like a farmer who had just come from the Abruzzo hills, who had just finished making half-a-gallon of moonshine and who wanted to go out in the back and shoot a few rabbits. He was very conservative, a very old-fashioned, Old-World guy. And then there's me, a gangling kind of weirdo guy who did all of these strange musics that none of them understood.
>
> We got together and we played music, and it worked. Because we all had this same respect for the elements of the music that were important to Kenny Davern. And those elements were tempo, timbre, knowledge of harmony, and the ability to make people want to dance.
>
> But, Kenny wasn't so simple as to have that be the criteria as to why he wanted to play with one musician or another. I think that, with Kenny, it was the craft and humor and groove, and the ability for all of those things to exist simultaneously. Sometimes, music doesn't make sense.²⁸

As the quartet grew more cohesive and comfortable together, Davern wanted to play with it whenever he could. He tried to avoid situations in which he was thrown into a large group with players of different backgrounds, interests, values, and talents, and would importune the people who scheduled events to let him play with his quartet. Clarinetist Evan Christopher understood Kenny's reasoning.

> He loved Chirillo's use of counterpoint. The clarinet is playing the lead because there is no other horn. But, what Chirillo is doing with his guitar voicings is: he's got a moving line in his guitar voicings that is essentially providing the same counterpoint that a clarinet or a trombone would provide to a trumpet. It's very subtle. Sometimes it's actually counterpoint, sometimes he's playing lines that are in counterpoint. But even when it's just in the chords he's making, he's choosing his chords in a certain way so that those pivotal harmonic

relationships are inside the voicings. Kenny loved that. And he loved Tony D's kind-of shuffle, those shuffle things that he'd get going. And then Greg, how can you say anything about Greg? Greg's got elephant ears. So, Kenny only wanted to work with them.[29]

However, as collegial and friendly as the Kenny Davern Quartet may have been, there was one unmistakable fact. As Greg Cohen put it, "He needed to get people in his band who understood a few different things, one of which was that Kenny was the boss. This was the unquestionable hierarchy of the event. Kenny was the boss. He didn't like to act like the boss when he was having a good time because he wanted it to grow. He wanted it to be natural."[30]

Aside from the Cornerstone and the Saturday night dates with Tony DeNicola, there wasn't much work in the first month of the new century. As usual, things began to pick up as the year progressed. *Cynthia Sayer, String Swing*, recorded early in February 2000, was Davern's third recording with Sayer, who also invited Jay Leonhart on bass and Joe Ascione on drums to join her. As with her prior recordings, she chose a variety of song types and arranged them with uncommon taste. And, as before, some of her selections were far from Davern's usual playlist.

Yet, on *Tumblin' Tumbleweeds* he is obviously comfortable, soloing effortlessly throughout. He dances along on the Latin beat that Ascione supplies to *South of the Border*, sharing the lead with violinist Bob Mastro, who joined the group for this tune, and he softly accompanies Sayer on *Someday (You'll Want Me to Want You)*. When Pha Terrell recorded *Until the Real Thing Comes Along* with the Andy Kirk band in 1936, he treated it as a ballad. In Sayer's hands it becomes a light, swinging vehicle. The two other tunes are *You*, with Mastro added, and *More Than You Know*. Although he was not enthused about all of the aspects of the album, Hugh Rainey called Davern "pure class."[31]

Two dates at the Cornerstone preceded three months of parties and festivals. He was in San Diego in February, Clearwater in the next month for the *March of Jazz* program, followed by the Atlanta Jazz Party in the middle of April, and the first United Kingdom Swinging Jazz Party in Blackpool, England at the end of the month. When May began, Davern, Wilber, and Pizzarelli were at the New Orleans Jazz and Heritage Festival, performing as Summit Reunion.[32]

At the urging of Milt Filius, Hamilton College had conferred the degree of Doctor of Music (D.Mus) upon singer Joe Williams in 1989. In subsequent years, Milt Hinton was similarly honored, as were George Shearing, Clark

Terry, Harry "Sweets" Edison, Bob Wilber, and Bobby Rosengarden. In 2000, the College decided to honor Kenny Davern.

The lack of confidence that prompted his skeptical reaction when told of his election to the American Jazz Hall of Fame caused a similar reaction when Filius called to say that Hamilton intended to honor him. Davern's first reaction was disbelief, but when that emotion passed, another took its place. Elsa saw it happen. "He was absolutely thrilled, absolutely thrilled. He just couldn't believe it. He was absolutely mind boggled over the whole thing. He was genuinely touched that they would do this for him."[33]

Hamilton held a dinner for the recipients of honorary degrees on the Saturday before commencement and Davern spoke. Monk Rowe was there and recalled that Kenny was "thoughtful, gracious and not at all sarcastic, etc." Afterward, he played a few numbers. At the ceremony, held on May 21, 2000, Eugene Tobin, president of the college, presented the award; Milt Filius placed the academic hood over Davern's head.[34]

In June, he was at the Danny Kaye Playhouse at Hunter College as part of the JVC Jazz Festival, and was at Fairleigh-Dickenson University in Madison, New Jersey, for the NJJS's *JazzFest*. At the end of the month, he left for Ascona, a holiday resort located on Lake Maggiore and surrounded by the Alps in the Italian-speaking Ticino region in the south of Switzerland. The town has picturesque, narrow streets and a lakeside promenade that is lined with hotels. It holds an annual jazz festival and, in 2000, Davern appeared with Bob Wilber. Then it was back to New York to perform at the 92nd Street Y on July 20, in its *Jazz in July* Program.[35]

In late July, Ruby Braff assembled a large and diverse group of musicians to record with him in several different settings. The CD was called *Variety Is the Spice of Braff*, and there were several cuts with strings, two others in front of a piano, two guitars and a bass, and five songs recorded with a large orchestra. Braff asked Davern to join him on the big-band recordings.

The territory was not unfamiliar to Kenny. He had started his career in the 1950s with Ralph Flanagan's orchestra. But then, he was an unknown, playing an unheard alto in a five-man reed section: here he was a featured artist. Two songs were recorded with a band of fourteen musicians consisting of five brass, five reeds, and four rhythm. On Braff's arrangement of *Crazy Rhythm*, Davern appears toward the end, beginning his solo softly in the chalumeau range and building the tension until Braff comes in. George Gershwin's *Liza* comes next, on which Kenny is audible, but doesn't solo.

The group slimmed down to eleven, shedding all of the brass except Braff and George Masso, for three more songs. A twelve-and-a-half-minute *Jumpin' at the Woodside* came first, with Kenny playing counterpoint over the opening statement and then taking a laid-back chalumeau solo in the middle of the piece. Kenny took an easygoing solo to open a medium-tempo *I Ain't Got Nobody*. The instrumentation changed slightly for *Somebody Stole My Gal*, featuring Howard Alden at the outset. Davern soloed in the middle.

When the album was released, it and Braff got high praise for the effort that he had made, as well as his interpretations. No one knew that Braff had been so ill from asthma and emphysema at the time of the session that he had to be wheeled into the studio. He had grouped the musicians in a circle facing him, so that he could maintain eye contact and, if he felt his breath was failing, he could signal one of them to jump in.[36]

The session almost marked the end of the relationship between Braff and Davern. Mat Domber recalled the event.

> I'm not sure that whether it was at that session or at the Spice of Braff session where Ruby made a famous remark. Kenny came in and was tuning up his clarinet before the recording session started, and Ruby came over and said: "Stop all that noise. You tune up at home. When you come to the session, you come to play." That was the kind of relationship that they had. I don't think anyone else would have dared to tell that to Kenny.[37]

In August, it was back to the United Kingdom for the Nairn Festival, then on to Breda in Holland. After a week, he was back home to finish out the summer at the Cornerstone and playing Saturdays with Tony DeNicola. There was a break at Labor Day to play the Muscular Dystrophy telethon, then Davern returned to the Cornerstone plus Saturdays-with-Tony pattern through early October. On October 12, he made his second CD with Ken Peplowski.

Although Peplowski was best known for his work on clarinet and tenor saxophone, Davern had heard him playing alto saxophone and thought he was excellent and original. He wanted to record with Peplowski playing alto, and invited John Bunch, Howard Alden, Greg Cohen, and Tony DeNicola to join him. The CD was called *Kenny Davern, Ken Peplowski, The Jazz KENNection*.

This is a startling album, different in tone, texture, and concept from Davern's collaborations with Bob Wilber. There is a sense of excitement that pervades every number on this disc and clearly inspires the leaders, as well as the rest of the group. Peplowski and Davern often play counterpoint phrases and melodies under the other's leads, which seems to propel both of them to musical places that neither had visited before.

The CD opens with *I'm Satisfied with My Gal*, a little-played tune written by Sharkey Bonano, which he first recorded in 1936 with Irving Fazola. On

Mama's Gone, Goodbye, Bunch leads off with a beautiful ballad introduction before the group comes in at a medium tempo. Howard Alden excels on *I'll See You in My Dreams*, and the two leaders trade chase choruses near the end. *Georgia on My Mind*, a Davern feature, is usually taken at a slow tempo. Here, he plays it slightly faster, rolling off a four-minute inventive statement at the beginning. *Careless Love*, also done faster than usual, has solos by Davern, Peplowski, and Alden.

The only tune on which Davern and Peplowski play any harmonic passages together is *Creole Love Call*, which is also the only ballad on the disc. Peplowski states the melody, while Davern does the obligato. Although the combination of alto saxophone and clarinet was the front line used by Jimmie Noone at the Apex Club, *Chicago Rhythm* (described in the liner notes as a "transvestite dance from the Apex Club") is the only tune on this CD that Noone had recorded using an alto clarinet front-line.[38] Although less than three minutes long, this version is punchy and playful. Everyone stretches out on *All of Me*. Peplowski switches to clarinet on *Porter's Love Song to a Chambermaid*, and he and Davern have an exciting chase chorus at the end.

The album was not what Peplowski had envisioned, and he was disappointed with the result. He had expected that they would play several two-clarinet pieces, and Davern did not want to play any. Peplowski spoke about the session.

> When we did *The Jazz KENNection*, the first thing he said to me was "you should play saxophone." He didn't want to do a two-clarinet record. . . . So, grudgingly, I wound up playing saxophone on most of those tunes. And again, it was a little difficult finding new material for him. And frustrating for me because I thought that he could have played anything. And I wish that he would have.
>
> He was obviously happier when I played saxophone. I think it's a shame. To me, it's not a competition, and you try to make music together and everybody learns from everybody else. He had a tough hide, but he never quite got that he was as respected as he was among musicians. He was always cautious around everybody because of this. . . . So, it wasn't an ideal record date.[39]

The tension between Davern and Peplowski was obvious to those who were present at the recording session.[40] However, there was no evidence of any discord on the CD, and Davern was pleased with the result. George Kanzler said that Davern was "masterly in shaping and billowing notes, using timbre and pitch with elastic flexibility." Thomas Jacobsen, reviewer for *The Clarinet*, praised the contributions of both leaders, calling the performance "ensemble playing at its very best."[41]

Several factors shaped Davern's attitude at the recording session. He did not like to play in a two-clarinet setting, especially when the other musician could play another instrument. He was aggravated when Wilber picked up a clarinet in any of their sessions, and he was equally unhappy when Peplowski wanted to play in that format. In Davern's view, they should have performed on their other instruments and left the clarinet playing to him.[42] Although he never expressed the view aloud, he may well have believed that he was simply better than anyone else on his chosen instrument.

Like Peplowski, many of his friends urged Kenny to reach out for new songs, suggesting that, along with the old favorites, he should introduce some new material. For the most part, Davern refused to do so. Part of his attitude stemmed from sheer stubbornness—he shouldn't *have* to play the songs that he didn't *want* to play. Part was from a reluctance to experiment in public, where he might not be able to give the audience his best effort on a song that he had not played often.[43]

Still another factor was that Davern had refined the list of tunes that he believed to be suitable vehicles through which he could express himself. He played them differently each time, discovering new facets to explore and polish, and he became increasingly reluctant to go outside of that group of songs. For the most part, they were blues and other pieces that came from the New Orleans–Chicago tradition, with some exceptions—*Summertime* being the most notable. Finally, there was a very practical aspect to Davern's attitude. As Marty Grosz put it,

> Kenny understood, before any of us, that you have to get the asses into those seats. Kenny understood what his strengths were. When you went to see Kenny, it was not to hear some startling new innovations. It was like going to see John Barrymore in his third year as Hamlet. You go to see if he can still keep the intensity up. How Kenny would throw himself into playing *I'm Sorry I Made You Cry* and make it work after the six hundredth time. Yes, he could have expanded within that concept. But, Louis Armstrong could have expanded too.... You have to put this over. And, if you don't put this over, you're driving a cab.[44]

The S.S. *Norway* was being refurbished, so Hank O'Neal moved the Floating Jazz Festival to the *Queen Elizabeth 2*, which sailed at the end of October. O'Neal, who had never been able to record Davern with baritone saxophonist Gerry Mulligan, paired Kenny with Scottish-born Joe Temperley, whose baritone saxophone had been heard in appearances with Woody Herman and Buddy Rich and on recordings with Clark Terry and the Thad Jones–Mel Lewis Orchestra. John Bunch, Joe Cohn, Michael Moore, and Joe

Ascione rounded out the rest of the group. Their performances were recorded and released under the title of *Live at the Floating Jazz Festival, Kenny Davern and Joe Temperley*.

Everyone stretches out on the up-tempo tunes, *Bernie's Tune, Blue Lou, Undecided*, and *Three Little Words*, the last of which features Temperley on baritone. The slower tunes are the delightful surprises here, with Temperley switching to bass clarinet. On *Mood Indigo, Blue Monk*, and *Creole Love Call*, the two reeds combine to state the opening and closing themes, either playing harmonically in thirds or weaving counterpoint melodies. Davern and Michael Moore have some nice interplay near the end of *Indigo*, and Kenny takes a solo on *Creole Love Call*, with only bass and drum.

Temperley's musical orientation stemmed from a more modern background, and there were some issues over tune selection. As was always the case with live shipboard recordings, the sound was less than ideal, and several of the tunes had to be played more than once in order to get an acceptable take.[45] However, there is a sense that the musicians enjoyed themselves, and this is reflected in the music.

Writing in *DownBeat*, author John McDonough said that on *Mood Indigo, Blue Monk*, and *Creole Love Call*, Davern moved "from subdued diffusion to a swashbuckling melodrama that is almost Churchillian in its expansiveness." He awarded four stars to the CD. David Franklin, in *Jazz Times*, also gave the release a favorable review.[46]

The *QE2* docked at Southampton at 5:30 a.m. on November 6. Davern caught a 9:30 train to London and hurried across the city to begin the first set at the Pizza Express. He was in Glasgow on the 9th, moved on to Nairn, and then performed at venues in England before returning home on November 20. For the remainder of the year, he worked locally.[47]

There wasn't much work in January 2001, outside of dates at the Cornerstone and with Tony DeNicola. He appeared at the North Carolina Jazz Party on the first weekend in February, and stopped in Raleigh before going home. After some more local dates, he flew to San Francisco for an appearance on the 15th, followed by a weekend in San Diego, at its annual jazz party.

Kenny appeared in concert in Bridgewater, New Jersey, on March 10, with a group led by Randy Reinhart, in a program titled *Bix Bash*. He performed with Tony DeNicola on three of the four Saturdays in March. On the other weekend, he was in Clearwater Beach, performing at Mat Domber's annual *March of Jazz*, which celebrated the birthday of Ruby Braff. While in Florida, Davern joined Braff in performing for the Treasure Coast Jazz Society in Vero Beach. At the end of the month, he played two dates at the Cornerstone and a night at Shanghai Jazz. The routine was much the same until mid-April, when he left to play the Atlanta Jazz Party.[48]

Phil Carroll's annual gathering was scheduled for the weekend of April 20–21 and, as he had done before, Wendell Echols, George Buck's associate, had arranged for several of the artists who were performing at the party to record for him. Davern was scheduled to be part of two sessions, a CD with Daryl Sherman and another with Wilber, as Summit Reunion.

More often than not, these record sessions were held at the conclusion of the weekend, and the musicians had an opportunity to perform together at the party before they got to the studio. These informal rehearsals were especially important when a singer was involved, since vocalists often want to record obscure tunes and have written arrangements in unusual keys. That was not possible on the date with Daryl Sherman. Echols had arranged to record on Friday, the day before the party. Most of the musicians flew into Atlanta that morning, dropped their bags at the hotel, and went directly to the studio. No one was happy with the scheduling, everyone grew increasingly hungry, and, in Sherman's words, the mood grew increasingly "crabby" as the day progressed.[49]

Davern and Sherman had spoken about the date before they arrived in Georgia. "I'm looking forward to playing with you," Kenny told her. "But, none of this Cole Porter shit. Okay?" She agreed.[50] There were no Porter songs among the fourteen titles that she chose. The CD was called *Born to Swing*, and the band included Ed Polcer, Bob Havens, Davern, John Sheridan, James Chirillo, Frank Tate, and Joe Ascione. Sherman also played piano on some of the tunes.

Davern only appeared on six songs. Sherman said that the opening number, *Breezin' Along*, was her gift to Kenny.[51] It was one of his favorites, and his warm clarinet and her soft voice caressed the melody of this standard from 1926. Although Kenny was audible on *Just a Lucky So-and-So*, *Pretty-Eyed Baby*, *I Double Dare You*, and *Born to Swing*, his other noteworthy performance came on *Travelin' All Alone*.

Several years earlier, Sherman had recorded *Travelin'* as part of a salute to Mildred Bailey. George Wein had heard it, and asked her to perform at the 1998 JVC Jazz Festival. The song was also a favorite of Davern's, and he was onstage with Sherman at JVC. She decided to reprise it on this recording, and the two of them excelled. After Sherman's opening statement, Davern and Sheridan sparred with each other, trading short statements back and forth. Then when Sherman entered to finish up the tune, Davern complemented her by filling in the open spaces in the lyrics with counter-melodic phrases, ending with his signature high C closing note.

When the party ended, Davern and Wilber, together with Johnny Varro, James Chirillo, Frank Tate, and Joe Ascione, cut *Summit Reunion in Atlanta*.

Although this group, like the one that cut the *Al Jolson* CD two years earlier, was an ad hoc assemblage, the process was far less ridden with strife. All of the selections were familiar standards, including *Love Me or Leave Me, Loveless Love, Diga Diga Doo, If I Had You, Wabash Blues*, and *Song of the Wanderer*. The album did not overwhelm the critics. ". . . [C]ompletists will no doubt wish to add this to their collections," said one.[52]

Kenny was in Colorado Springs at the end of April, and in Odessa in mid-May. In between, he played a benefit concert, did several gigs with DeNicola, and appeared at the Cornerstone with John Bunch. Near the end of the month, he recorded two cuts on a CD featuring Dennis Gruenling.[53]

Davern first met Gruenling in the mid 1990s. Dennis, who was then in his early twenties, was interested in the blues, which he played professionally on the harmonica. He had been impressed by Davern's playing on a Soprano Summit album and, when he read that Kenny was influenced by Pee Wee Russell, he began listening to the older man's recordings as well. Gruenling lived within driving distance of the Cornerstone and, when Davern was appearing there, Dennis went to see him. At the end of the evening's performance, the lanky, long-haired youngster approached Davern and piqued his interest by asking him about Pee Wee.

Davern took a liking to Dennis and, over time, they developed a friendship. On several occasions, Davern invited Gruenling to his home in Manasquan to have dinner, talk, and listen to music. There were times when, at the end of an evening at the Cornerstone, Davern asked Dennis to join him on the bandstand.

Gruenling was then leading a group called *Jump Time* that combined rhythm and blues and a Kansas City boogie-woogie, stomping, style into what Gruenling called "jump blues." In the spring of 2001, he asked if Davern would join them in recording several cuts on a CD that Grueling was planning. "I told him what songs we were doing, and he agreed. I told him I can't pay all that much, I could only afford so-and-so. He didn't seem to be too concerned about it. I said 'I'd be honored to have you—just on a couple songs' and he said 'Sure.'"[54]

The recording studio was about 100 miles from Kenny's home. But, on the morning of Sunday, May 27, Davern made the trip. He cut two songs with Gruenling's group, *I Can't Believe That You're in Love with Me* and *More of What You've Got*. The CD was released on the Backbender label, titled *Dennis Gruenling, Jump Time, That's Right*.[55]

Davern did not travel much during the last half of 2001. On June 1, he played in Red Bank for the Riverfest festival. The Kenny Davern Quartet (Davern, Chirillo, Cohen, and DeNicola) appeared at the Watchung Art

Center on June 15, and at the NJJS *JazzFest* on the 23rd. He played the Madison Hotel in Morristown, and appeared at the 92nd Street Y on the 25th and 26th. For the balance of the summer, he appeared sporadically at the Cornerstone, usually with Chirillo, DeNicola, and Bill Holaday, the contractor and resident bassist, and performed regularly with Tony DeNicola. He did not play the Jerry Lewis telethon that year, but was in Denver on August 30–September 1.

Davern was invited to participate in Hamilton College's annual *Fallcoming* celebration. But the events of September 11, 2001, caused the event to be canceled. Kenny was in San Francisco in early November and spent November 10–11 in Topeka, followed by appearances in Kansas City and St. Joseph, Missouri. On the following weekend, he was in Greenville, Alabama. For the rest of 2001, he played his Saturday gigs with DeNicola and at the Cornerstone, and also had an engagement on December 28 at the Museum of Modern Art.[56]

On December 30, 2001, Ralph Sutton suffered a stroke and died at the age of seventy-nine. In 1992, he had a stroke that affected his left hand. He recovered from that and continued playing and touring, although his stamina was less than it had been. In recent years, he had been afflicted with several serious illnesses, but his death was unexpected.

Theirs was an unusual relationship. Sutton was enigmatic and quiet: Davern was garrulous and voluble. Sometimes, they took extended walks in silence. There were stretches when they did not see each other. Yet they loved each other as men sometimes do. It took Davern a long time to adjust to his loss.

Notes

1. The author was the person who made the first call to Davern. For more than ten minutes, Kenny refused to believe that it was not a joke and insisted that I was pulling his leg.

2. Edinburgh event program; Brecon event program.

3. Monk Rowe, interview by the author.

4. Romy Britell, interview by the author.

5. Date Book; *Jersey Jazz*, 25, no. 6 (July–August 1997): 5, 7; S.S. *Norway* event program.

6. Date Book; *Jersey Jazz* 25, no. 9 (November 1997): 7, and 25, no. 10 (December 1997): 5, 7.

7. Ken Peplowski, interview by the author.

8. Date Book; *Jazz Journal International*, 51, no. 1 (January 1998): 3; *Jersey Jazz*, 25, no.11 (January 1998): 5, and 26, no. 2 (February 1998): 5; Chip Deffaa, "Savor It: Davern on for Not Much Green," *New York Post*, 17 April 1998.

9. Charles Champlin, liner notes to *Born to Play*, Arbors ARCD 19203, October 1998; Kenny Davern, quoted in Ken Gallacher, "Musicians Born to Play Together," *The Herald*, 31 March 1999.

10. Mat Domber, president, Arbors Records, interview by the author. See also Howard Alden, interview by the author.

11. Kenny Davern, quoted in Rusch interview part 2, p. 11.

12. Date Book.

13. Chip Deffaa, "This Man Is Dog's Best Friend," *New York Post*, 30 July 1998. After the concert, Davern told Dan Morgenstern that Peplowski was "the best of us out there." E-mail from Dan Morgenstern to the author.

14. Date Book; *Jersey Jazz*, 26, no. 6 (July–August, 1998): 5, 7, and 26, no. 7 (September 1998), 30; *Jazz Journal International*, 51, no. 7 (July 1998): 2.

15. Eddie Cook, "Kenny Davern, Smiles," *Jazz Journal International*, 52, no. 9 (September 1999): 28; Paul De Barros, "Kenny Davern, Smiles," *DownBeat*, 67, no. 3 (March 2000): 78; *Jazz Journal International*, 53, no. 2 (February 2000): 8.

16. Date Book; *Jersey Jazz*, 26, no. 7 (September 1998): 5, 7; *Mississippi Rag*, xxvi, no. 10 (October 1998): 13, and xxvi, no. 12 (December 1998): 22.

17. Kenny Davern, conversation with the author.

18. David Badham, "Ruby Braff, the Cape Codfather," *Jazz Journal International*, 53, no. 12 (December 2000): 22–23.

19. Bucky Pizzarelli, interview with the author.

20. Kenny Davern, conversation with the author.

21. Bucky Pizzarelli, interview by the author.

22. Elsa Davern, conversation with the author.

23. Date Book: *Chicago Reader*, 25 June 1999; *Star Ledger*, 4 July 1999.

24. George Avakian, liner notes to *The Re-Discovered Louis and Bix, Lost Musical Treasures of Louis Armstrong and Bix Beiderbecke, How This CD Was Born*, Nagel Heyer CD 058. The liner notes say that the recording was made over a two-day period: according to Kenny's date book, he was only in the studio on September 1.

25. John Bunch, interview by the author.

26. James Chirillo, interview by the author.

27. Chirillo interview.

28. Greg Cohen, interview by the author.

29. Evan Christopher, interview by the author.

30. Greg Cohen, interview by the author.

31. Hugh Rainey, "Cynthia Sayer, Swing String," *Jazz Journal International*, 53, no. 12 (December 2000): 50.

32. *Jersey Jazz*, 27, no. 10 (December 1999): 9, and 26, no. 1 (February 2000): 5, 15, and 26, no. 2 (March 2000): 5, and 26, no. 3 (April 2000): 5.

33. Elsa Davern, interview by the author, e-mails from Monk Rowe to the author.

34. Monk Rowe, e-mail to the author.

35. JVC program; Date Book; Ascona event program; *New York Times*, 16 July 2000.

36. Thomas P. Hustad, interview by the author.

37. Mat Domber, president, Arbors Records, interview by the author. At some later time, Kenny took offense at a comment made by Ruby, and the two stopped speaking. In describing their relationship, someone said that "Ruby Braff was Kenny Davern's Kenny Davern."

38. Noone recorded *Porter's Love Song to a Chambermaid* in 1934, with Jimmy Cobb on trumpet and Eddie Pollack playing alto saxophone.

39. Ken Peplowski, interview by the author.

40. Mat Domber, president, Arbors Records, interview by the author.

41. George Kanzler, "Six That Make the Mainstream Swing," *The Sunday Star Ledger*, 13 January 2002, Section 4, 4; Thomas Jacobsen, "Kenny Davern and Ken Peplowski, The Jazz KENNection," *The Clarinet*, June 2002.

42. Kenny Davern, conversation with the author.

43. When portable cassette recorders that allowed members of the audience to record live performances in clubs or concerts became available, Davern usually refused to allow people to record him. He didn't want anyone to preserve, and possibly circulate, a performance that might not have been as good as he would have liked.

44. Marty Grosz, interview by the author.

45. Hank O'Neal, interview by the author; Hank O'Neal, recorded recollections.

46. John McDonough, "Kenny Davern and Joe Temperley, Live at the Floating Jazz Festival," *DownBeat*, 70, no. 4 (April 2003): 64; David Franklin, "Kenny Davern, Joe Temperley, Live at the Floating Jazz Festival," *Jazz Times*, May 2003, 118–119.

47. Jack Massarik, "He's Got Rhythm, But No Drummer," *Evening Standard*, 7 November 2000: 57; *Jazz Journal International*, 53, no. 11 (November 2000): 3; *Jersey Jazz*, 28, no. 9 (November 2000): 5, and 28, no. 10 (December 2000): 5.

48. Date Book; Thomas P. Hustad, interview by the author.

49. Daryl Sherman, interview by the author.

50. Sherman interview.

51. John McDonough, liner notes to *Daryl Sherman, Born to Swing*, Audiophile ACD 316.

52. Eddie Cook, "Summit Reunion, Summit Reunion in Atlanta," *Jazz Journal International*, 55, no. 9 (September 2002): 47.

53. Date Book; *Jersey Jazz*, 29, no. 3 (April 2001): 5, and 26, no. 4 (May 2001): 5; High School event program.

54. Dennis Gruenling, interview by the author.

55. The date on which Davern made the recording comes from his date book.

56. Date Book; *Jersey Jazz*, 29, no. 4 (May 2001): 5; *Star Ledger*, 1 June 2001: 42; *Jersey Jazz*, 28, no. 5 (June 2001): 5, 8; event program; *Jersey Jazz*, 28, no. 10 (December 2001): 5.

CHAPTER SIXTEEN

Change of Place, Change of Pace

By this time, Kenny and Elsa's family included four grandchildren: Hayleigh and Tyler, born to Debbie and Rob, and Rebecca and Lauren, the children of Mark and Debbie. Both families were then living on the West Coast and, although Elsa was able to fly across the country to visit them, the only opportunities that Kenny had to see his grandchildren were when their parents came east, which was relatively infrequently, or on those rare occasions when he was playing near enough to one of them to visit.

Nonetheless, he was able to establish relationships with them. When Hayleigh decided to take up playing the clarinet, Kenny was pleased and proud to give one of his horns to her.[1] The parent who raised Debbie and Mark was virtually unrecognizable as a grandparent. Relieved of the burden of parenting, Kenny was more tolerant and relaxed when he was around the grandchildren, laughing and joking with them. As they got older, he began to teach them some of the skills that they would need later in life—like playing gin rummy.

Elsa periodically visited her sister, Elaine Corbalis, who had settled with her husband Fred in Albuquerque. One day, the sisters went to lunch at the home of a friend in Sandia Park, a rural community about thirty miles east of Albuquerque. As she stood on the balcony of the friend's home, Elsa said "I felt as if I'd come home. . . . There was something that spoke to me here."[2]

When she returned to New Jersey, she mentioned the experience to Kenny. At first, he had no interest in relocating. However, Elsa kept insisting that there was something unique about the area, and he came to realize that it was important to her. He ultimately agreed to go and look and, when he did, he was also drawn to the location. Their son, Mark, told Kenny and Elsa that if they wanted to move, he would help.

The decision did not seem to be a drastic one. Life in the Northeast had lost its charm. The beauty of the great green pine trees and white sandy beaches on the Jersey Shore was being eclipsed by deteriorating downtown areas and increasingly dirty streets and highways. It was overcrowded: there were too many people in a region that did not have the homes, roads, and infrastructure to serve them. Winters seemed to be colder, darker, and longer.

The amounts that Kenny was able to earn had steadily diminished. With each passing year, the number of festivals and parties decreased. He was making fewer trips abroad—there were none in 2001—which were the sources of a substantial part of his income. In the Northeast, almost all of the bars and restaurants that featured jazz had closed or abandoned that style of music: his only regular jobs were with Tony DeNicola on Saturday night and a few days a month at the Cornerstone. Neither job paid enough to put a meaningful dent in the expenses of the Davern household. The only drawback that they envisioned was that Albuquerque was not a major airline hub and that it would take longer for Kenny to travel to and from jobs.

There was another factor that impacted Kenny's decision. Over the years, Elsa had suffered from several debilitating and serious illnesses. Kenny was always concerned that she had no one to turn to while he was working or away. He felt that living near her sister, with whom she had always been very close, would ease the loneliness when he was on the road and give her someone to turn to in case of emergency.[3]

While Kenny and Elsa were in Sandia Park, they picked out the parcel of land on which they would build: a six-acre plot at the top of a hill, with unobstructed views in all directions. Mark purchased the land for them and provided financing for the construction of their home, which they repaid when the house in New Jersey was sold. He also helped with the permanent financing. Having participated in the selection of the site, Kenny's involvement in the project ended: he left the task of designing and planning their new home to Elsa. "I went through probably five hundred house plans and took some from here, and some from there, and some from there—based on our lifestyle. He knew he was going to get a studio. All he asked for was air-conditioning in the house."[4]

It was Elsa who drew the plans, hired an architect and a builder, flew to New Mexico from time to time to review the progress of construction, and argued with workmen and tradespeople. Kenny, who professed to be unable to understand drawings and plans, had no input in the process and no understanding of how his new place would look. That came, for the first time, when he and Elsa drove up the driveway to move into their new home.

Construction had begun in 2001 and was finished early in the New Year. While the house was nearing completion, Davern was away on tour. On the 2nd and 3rd of January, he was in Colorado Springs. After an evening at the Cornerstone, he flew to the United Kingdom for a four-week tour that ended at Henry's Cellar Bar in Edinburgh. After he returned to Manasquan, there were some dates near home and, at the beginning of March, the move to New Mexico was on.[5]

The house that Elsa had designed for them had four bedrooms, a large living and dining area, and was constructed on two levels. Kenny and Elsa each had their own study: hers held her paints, brushes, and jewelry supplies. Kenny's office contained all of his books, and the thousands of LPs, CDs, audio- and videotapes, and DVDs that he had collected. There was recording and playing equipment, a television, and a comfortable chair for Kenny to lounge in. Outside of the window in Davern's study was a small hill. Although Elsa had designed Kenny's study as a room in which he could practice, he never used it for that purpose. Instead, he practiced at the kitchen table, where he could look to the east out of the large picture window where, on the other side of a deep valley, were lush green mountains less than five miles away.

Davern had deliberately left some open space in his schedule so that he could settle into his new surroundings. There were no dates in the last week of February and only one in March—the *March of Jazz* in Clearwater. The program had originally been intended as a celebration of the eighty-fifth birthday of Ralph Sutton. His death caused the event to be turned into a memorial to him.

Although Kenny understood that it would take time for him to learn about the music scene in New Mexico and begin to get work in Albuquerque and Santa Fe, he was not prepared for the extended period of enforced idleness that followed the move. He had only one job in April, a date in Denver, and the only work that he had in May was out of town. He was in Japan for May 1–5, and traveled to Switzerland to play at Marian's Jazz Room in Bern. On the last three days of the month, he played at the Cornerstone and Shanghai Jazz, and a party in Princeton. On June 1, Davern was at the Watchung Arts Center with Chirillo, Cohen, and DeNicola. After that, he was idle until the 23rd, when he performed at *JazzFest*. He went home on June 29, after playing two nights at the Cornerstone and one at Shanghai Jazz.[6]

Davern made his first inroads into the Albuquerque jazz community when Mark Weber called him. Weber had grown up in California and moved to Albuquerque in 1991, when he was forty years old. He was interested in jazz, and he had written columns for *Coda* magazine. He had also produced several record dates. That experience stood him in good stead when he began a weekly jazz-oriented show on KUNM, the local public radio station.

Weber learned that Davern had moved to Sandia Park and asked him to be a guest on his show. Davern made his first appearance on July 11. Over the course of an hour, Weber played a number of Kenny's recordings, beginning with *Mis'ry and the Blues* with Jack Teagarden, and continuing through the *Jazz KENNection* CD. Between the music, Kenny reminisced about some of the musicians he had known, including Teagarden, Condon, and Wild Bill Davison.

In the next four years, Davern appeared on eight of Weber's shows. In addition, Weber interviewed him for an uninterrupted hour for the *Jazz of Enchantment* radio series. Kenny was an entertaining guest. He had an encyclopedic knowledge about music and musicians, along with a wealth of stories about the people with whom he had worked. His sharp sense of humor enlivened the discussions between him and Weber, as did the long anecdotes that he liked to tell. As might be expected, Davern was unusually candid in his opinions for a radio-show guest, and Weber found that his ratings rose substantially whenever he had Davern on the program.[7]

Weber was not only the host of his show, he was also the engineer and the programmer. While the music was playing, he had other things to do. But, the appeal of a microphone and a potentially limitless audience was irresistible for Davern. And, just because the microphone was off didn't mean that Kenny would turn mute.

> While I was engineering a show, Kenny would just talk all the time. That was how he kept himself up. But, meanwhile, it was my show, and my *shtick* was suffering. I had to look at my notes. . . . I had to think of all this stuff in advance. I had to keep familiarized with what's on the records. And, Kenny just wants to talk the whole damn time. There were times that I would tell him "Kenny, you have to be quiet a minute and let me think here." He would just get mad, and when we got on mike the madness would carry over and then I'd have double problems on my hands. Not only would he not shut up but he was mad. The audience loved it, but my health was suffering.[8]

They became good friends. Davern occasionally had Weber to his home, where they would talk and listen to music. Weber helped familiarize Davern with the local musical scene.

But, there still were no jobs near home. In August, Kenny went overseas, appearing at the Edinburgh International Jazz Festival on the 4th, and at the Nairn International Jazz Festival for the next two days. He was at the Pizza

Express in London on the 7th, played a date in Middlesex, and then went on to the Brecon Jazz Festival in Wales. After playing dates in Woking and Eastleigh, he performed at the Pizza Express in London for two nights before flying home.[9]

Except for playing Sunnie Sutton's Rocky Mountain Jazz Party over Labor Day, Kenny did not work at all during September. At the beginning of October, he flew up to Hamilton College to perform at *Fallcoming*, and tacked on several dates at the Cornerstone. He was in Los Angeles and San Diego on the 19th and 20th; these were his only jobs that month.

Having a great deal of free time allowed Kenny to go shooting. He was fascinated by guns: he had a World War II–vintage German Mauser with a swastika embossed on it, as well as a Colt .45, a .38, and a .22 caliber pistol. He had two shotguns, plus one that he had the barrels sawn off for home protection. Sometimes he dressed in camouflage clothing; on other occasions, he wore a short-sleeved shirt, pressed khaki pants, boots, a baseball cap, and sunglasses, looking every inch like Deputy Sheriff Davern. He would go shooting with Mark Weber or Fred Corbalis at the police academy south of town or near the private airport to the west of Albuquerque. There was a target range in the basement of a gun shop: Davern liked to forgo the traditional concentric-ringed target for one that had a picture of a mugger on it.[10]

A break in the work-drought finally occurred when Davern and Howard Alden appeared in Santa Fe on November 30, as co-leaders of a quartet that included David Parlato on bass and John Trentacosta on drums. On December 2, the same group appeared in Albuquerque at the Outpost Performance Space.[11]

The Outpost was, and remains, the premier venue for live music in Albuquerque. Founded in 1988, it opened its doors as a one-hundred-seat room located in a building that formerly housed a printing shop. Under the guidance of Tom Guralnick, its founder and presently its executive director, it prospered and, in 2000, it moved to its present site, a 175-seat performance center in Albuquerque's University district. Over the years, the Outpost has hosted more than 1,000 concerts by artists that covered the musical spectrum, ranging from Dave Brubeck and Wayne Shorter to Rosalie Sorrels.[12] Kenny appeared there several times.

Davern played a gig in Venice, Florida, with Dick Hyman on January 16, 2003, and, two days later, returned to the Thunderbird Lodge in Taos for a date with Michael Anthony, David Parlato, and Trentacosta. He had no other appearances in that month except for an interview on Mark Weber's radio show.

On February 9, 2003, Ruby Braff died. The combination of emphysema and asthma had wreaked havoc on Braff, who gave his last public performance at the Nairn festival in Scotland in July 2002. A few days later, he cut his trip short and flew home to Boston, where he entered a hospital and then a convalescent center. The relationship between Braff and Davern, never on the most solid of footings, had deteriorated to the point where Davern simply stopped speaking to him. Personalities aside, Braff's death meant the loss of another unique musical voice.[13]

In February, Kenny played the San Diego Jazz Party and in March, he traveled to Clearwater for the *March of Jazz*. At the end of the month, he left for a two-week tour of England, Cork, and Dublin. His first trip in May was to Kobe, Japan. He returned to New Mexico for about ten days, and then flew to New Jersey for a recording date and several local gigs.[14]

Although the quartet of Davern, Chirillo, Cohen, and DeNicola had been working together as a functioning unit since about 1997, they did not record until May 2003. The group appeared at a concert in Bridgewater on May 17, which served as a reunion and an unofficial rehearsal and, two days later, they traveled to Trenton to make a CD titled *The Kenny Davern Quartet at the Mill Hill Playhouse, Celebrating Fifty Years of Recording*.[15]

The opening tune is *I Want to Be Happy*, which has a light and fleeting feel to it. Jelly Roll Morton's *Someday Sweetheart* follows at medium tempo. Phil Schaap's liner notes say that Tony DiNicola thought that the next tune, *Tight Like That*, was the high point of the session. At the beginning, Cohen plays counterpoint to Davern's improvisations, and then the quartet takes off, building the tension until the song reaches its dramatic climax. Davern was especially pleased with *Wabash Blues*, the longest tune on the disc at just over nine minutes. His emotional solo is filled with bent notes and half-tones, and he closes the tune with three high notes that are far beyond the usual range of the clarinet. Schaap thought it was the best tune of the day.[16]

Kenny had played *My Gal Sal* many times before, but this was his first recording of it. By way of contrast, Davern had recorded *Wild Man Blues* twice before (playing soprano both times). This version was far more introspective than his earlier renditions. The mood changes with a crisp *My Blue Heaven*, followed by a medium-tempo, meandering version of *Up a Lazy River*. The last tune is a rousing *Diga, Diga, Doo* and features what the liner notes describe as Tony DiNicola's "hand job" on the drums.

For the most part, the CD received excellent reviews. Martin Gayford, writing in the London *Daily Telegraph*, said that Davern's work was "lithe, light, sinuous, supple, sensuous, and joyous, his imagination audacious, his technique superb." Gayford went on to say "He is evidently among the finest clarinetists in the jazz tradition—or any other, for that matter." Will Friedwald said it was one of "the finest albums of his career." John Postgate called it "an excellent issue," and said that the rhythm section "jells gloriously." He described *It's Tight Like That* as "One of the great moments of jazz!"[17] The CD was voted one of *Jazz Journal International*'s top 20 albums for 2005.[18]

Davern stayed in New Jersey for the remainder of the week, playing dates at the Cornerstone on May 21, 23, and 24, with an appearance at Shanghai Jazz on the intervening evening. He flew home on the next day and remained there until he returned to New York for the festival season. Tony Scott and Buddy DeFranco were the only two clarinetists who were able to play coherently in the bop idiom. They and Davern were featured on June 19–20 in a program titled *Legends of the Clarinet*, which was produced at the Iridium nightclub as part of the JVC Jazz Festival. Kenny was at the New Jersey Jazz Society *JazzFest*, leading a quartet on June 21 and returning on the following day as a sideman in Randy Reinhart's group. On the last day of the month, he left for the annual festival at Ascona, Switzerland, where he appeared with, among others, pianist David Boeddinghaus and drummer Trevor Richards.[19]

Had he lived, Bix Beiderbecke would have been one hundred years old at the time of the festival. The event was dedicated to Beiderbecke, and was organized by Lino Patruno who, in 1990, had produced the music for the soundtrack of the film *Bix, An Interpretation of a Legend*. Although several of the musicians who played on the soundtrack performed at Ascona, there was more of a spontaneous atmosphere to these proceedings, and some of the arrangements were clearly "heads" that had been agreed upon shortly before the musicians performed them.

The programs were recorded and later released on a CD titled *Lino Patruno Presents a Tribute to Bix Beiderbecke*. Davern appeared on three tracks. On *Royal Garden Blues*, he performed with a thirteen-man orchestra. He was part of smaller groups on *China Boy* and *Way Down Yonder in New Orleans*. On all of his performances, Davern was clearly himself, and made no effort to evoke the images of the clarinet players who performed with Bix.

Davern came home to play the Outpost Performance Space on July 18 with Michael Anthony on guitar, David Parlato on bass, and drummer John Trentacosta. He left to perform in Manhattan at the 92nd Street Y in its *Jazz in July* program on the 31st. He continued eastward, landing in Frankfurt, Germany, for a concert with Randy Sandke on August 2. Then he was off to London and its outskirts for several nights. From August 12 to 17, he was in Norway for the Oslo Jazz Festival, performing at the Concorde Jazz Club, then he flew home on August 21. He had no work for the rest of the month and for all of September. In October, he appeared at Sunnie Sutton's Rocky

Mountain Jazz Party and also at *Fallcoming* at Hamilton College. Those were his only live performance engagements until 2003 came to an end.

Davern had been reading a biography of clarinetist Buddy DeFranco and, although he had previously rejected the notion of writing, or participating in the writing, of his biography, the idea suddenly began to intrigue him. He approached Mark Weber with the idea of a book, and Weber came to his house one afternoon in September 2003. They talked, filling a ninety-minute tape with seemingly random discussions of mouthpieces, Mel Powell, and Kenny's band at Nick's. After the tape had run out, Weber and Davern continued to talk. When they were finished, Mark left the cassette with Kenny. There was never a second session, and the project died.[20]

On December 9, 2003, Davern flew to New York, and on the next day recorded four tracks as part of a unit of the Statesmen of Jazz. The Statesmen was the idea of Maurice Lawrence and was brought to fruition by the American Federation of Jazz Societies, with the assistance, financial and otherwise, of Mat Domber and Arbors Records. The idea was to enlist the outstanding senior members of the jazz community, who would perform at venues around the country, hold seminars and instructional sessions for young audiences, and raise public awareness of jazz. The Statesman worked from a pool of talent that began with Clark Terry, Joe Wilder, Al Grey, Benny Waters, Buddy Tate, Jane Jarvis, Claude "Fiddler" Williams, Milt Hinton, and Panama Francis, and changed as the years went on. Everyone involved in the project donated their time, and the proceeds from the group's appearances went to a fund to make the Statesmen a permanent part of the jazz scene.

The Statesmen made their first recording in 1994, and had been on tour since May of the following year. In December 2003, Domber and Clark Terry, acting as musical director, assembled over twenty-five of the current—and soon to be—Statesmen to record a double-CD package entitled *Statesmen of Jazz, A Multitude of Stars*. The musicians separated into bands of seven or less, and each group recorded three or four songs. Davern was teamed with Buddy DeFranco, Johnny Varro, Bucky Pizzarelli, Earl May, and Louie Bellson. DeFranco and Davern played one song together, each had his own feature, and they played a medley of four songs. On the day after the recording, Davern flew back to Albuquerque.

With the wisdom of hindsight, it is now clear that there were unforeseen benefits and drawbacks to the decision to relocate to New Mexico. The venues and musicians that had created the magic and excitement of playing jazz—as Davern knew it—were gone, and there was nothing to tie him to Manhattan anymore. The music scene had changed, and Kenny lamented the passing of the people and places that had given life to the music he loved.

Thus, when Christian Plattner, one of his younger friends, decided to give up playing music for a living, Davern applauded his decision and wrote:

> The choice you made was the right one and I'm happy for you because the business is not, and will not get better. How can it? When I was coming up in the late '40s, early '50s, there were clubs where you could work six nights a week with the same band. There were also big bands, as unrewarding as they were, they still had merit as a training ground. I mean, you traveled hundreds of miles a night to do the next gig, played for hundreds of dancers all across the country, and literally lived with your fellow side-men in shabby hotels, night after night after night. But, you either fell in or were out.
>
> This kind of discipline is sadly lacking today where the traveling "star soloist" talks over the tunes before the first set and "Bang!" instant arrangements, energy, etc. etc. In short, even if you're good, even great, there's no real solid career-belief to follow. Maybe it was an optical illusion, or delusion, then. But, I believe there was a common bond, a sensibility in the style and sentiment in the music, a focal point out of which the musicians performed collectively.
>
> That was worth starving for. There's not much out there worth starving for today unless you join a commune, form your own group, and work out together daily for the ultimate reward—working one, two, or three gigs a month in a place acoustically unsuitable for creating a mood for that which you truly believe in. And no pay!!
>
> These are different times from then. Your points of reference when you play are lost on a crowd who would prefer a disco, a DJ, a synthesizer, an animated frenzied dance. Oblique, styleless, and totally meaningless gestures constitute what's out front these days responding to your output. In short, they haven't a clue as to what you're doing and sadly, they don't really care. I mean, you're thinking Sidney Bechet—they're thinking Kenny G. It's difficult to go on knowing this.[21]

More than just the nature of the music business had changed. There was a glamour attached to playing jazz when Kenny was growing up. Davern not only admired Red Allen, Eddie Condon, and all of their contemporaries because of the way in which they played music, he was drawn to their lifestyle as well.

> There are no clubs and there are no places for young kids to really work out in a professional place that's conducive to making jazz music. I bought that when I was a kid. That meant the smoke-filled whiskey-drinking nightclub. And that was my great ambition; to be like one of those guys that I admired. They were the social miscreants: they had the attitude of "we do what we do, you do what you do, and the twain won't meet." There's a definite nine-to-five separation

there. There were those who went to work at nine in the morning and went home at five at night, and those who began work at nine o'clock at night and went home at five in the morning. That's the aspect of it that attracted me to the music.[22]

Although Kenny was prepared—even eager—to give up working long hours before apathetic audiences in local restaurants for little pay, he still wanted to play. He was unprepared for the emotional toll that not being called for work would take. The fact that there were no jobs in New Mexico was of no consequence: more important to Davern was that no one was calling him, and he was sitting at home.

The inescapable fact was that work was dwindling everywhere. Death, old age, and economics had finally caught up with the audiences in Great Britain and Europe, just as they had impacted upon the audiences in the United States. Venues closed, or stopped featuring jazz. Tours became shorter, festivals became smaller or just disappeared. There was less work and, although Davern would have been affected by it if he had stayed in New Jersey, it was having a greater impact on him while he was in New Mexico, where there was almost no work at all.

Kenny may not have considered that moving to New Mexico would increase the amount that promoters would have to pay in order to hire him. Round-trip airfare from Albuquerque to the East Coast approximated $500 and, while it was not money in Kenny's pocket, it was an additional expense for a festival or jazz party. There were musicians living on the East and West Coasts who did not bring that expense with them, and they got jobs that might have gone to him.

Finally, Davern was a social animal. He liked to talk, and work was a place where he could talk, kibbitz, or argue with fellow musicians. Many of the people who came to see him at the Cornerstone and similar venues were friends. If nothing else, they were fans who buoyed him up, even though he often dismissed their impact. But, they were in New Jersey, not New Mexico, and the telephone was not always an adequate substitute for personal contact.

The sum of all these facts is that there were times when Kenny was lonely, depressed, and sometimes angry. He could easily persuade himself that the music that he loved was being cast aside and, now that he had moved away, that he had been forgotten or abandoned by his audiences and his friends.[23]

There were several offsets for him. Of all of the things that Kenny Davern cherished in this world, beauty, whether in music, art, literature, or nature, was among the foremost. Inside his home in New Mexico or outside it, he was surrounded by beauty. He could sit in his study, listening to the music that he loved or reading his books, and be at peace. As Greg Cohen said:

> He was ... somebody searching for the truth all of his life.... He surrounded himself with things that he knew could be buffers or protections against a world that he saw that was crumbling around him.... He surrounded himself with the greatest of music, the instruments that he loved, pictures of the great people that he had a chance to work with and befriend. He went into that world, with the books and the music and the talismanic objects, everyday, for solace; to somehow find peace and an explanation for the world that he had entered as that nineteen-year-old who started to get recognized, not as a nineteen-year-old, but as one of the cats....
> To see how the world has changed in the arc of one's lifetime—and toward the end of his life, some fifty years—he felt the need to connect himself: to have these talismanic objects around him and ... to be swept away into a world that made sense for him.[24]

There was more to appeal to Kenny's aesthetic sense. In New Jersey, he lived cheek-by-jowl with his neighbors. In New Mexico, his home sat atop a hill. He could stand in his kitchen, or out on the patio, and look out across a valley upon the majestic Sandia Mountains. There was peace: it was restful, and it revived him.

The lack of work had certain benefits. Playing three or four nights each week, always trying to be original and musical, is difficult and stressful. Sometimes, invention becomes impossible and stagnation sets in. A tendency to play the same songs in the same way develops. It becomes easier to string together a group of well-worn phrases—musical cliches—because the creative juices have ceased to flow.

Freed of the burden of performing all the time, and transplanted to an environment where everything was new to him, Kenny could elect not to play at all, or to experiment with new approaches to his favorite pieces. He was performing with musicians who had never played with him and who played things that were different from what he expected. Sometimes that was beneficial, sometimes it was not. Dan Morgenstern noticed a change. "I think he was more relaxed. He seemed to be more at ease with himself."[25]

As work picked up in the Albuquerque area, and he began to play again with some regularity, he would tell Elsa that he was doing things that he had never done on songs that he had played hundreds of times before. James Chirillo also noticed the difference. "So, in terms of whether I noticed any change in his playing, not so much sound-wise or in command of the instrument. But, in choice of notes he was getting more and more adventurous."[26]

The CDs that Davern made after a few years away from New Jersey sometimes displayed a different approach to the music that he loved. Clearly, it was the voice of Kenny Davern, but he was polishing the facets of the songs that he liked to play in a way that he had never explored before.

Notes

1. Like most children, she gave it up after a while and returned the horn to Kenny. After his death, she asked to have it back, and Elsa gave it to her.
2. Elsa Davern, interview by the author.
3. Kenny Davern, conversation with the author.
4. Davern conversation. Only Kenny's study had air-conditioning, and he froze in there.
5. Date Book; *Jazz Journal International*, 55, no. 1 (January 2002); Elsa Davern, interview by the author.
6. Date Book, event program from Bern.
7. Mark Weber, interview by the author.
8. Weber interview. Mark was kind enough to allow me to use his interviews of Kenny, and excerpts from those conversations appear throughout this book.
9. *Jazz Journal International*, 55, no. 8 (August 2002): 9; event program.
10. Conversation with Elsa Davern; e-mail from Mark Weber to the author.
11. On 28 November, Kenny had appeared on Mark Weber's show to publicize the event.
12. At http://www.outpostspace.org/outpost_story; *Venue*, 29 November 2002: 15; Kenny Davern, interviewed by Mark Weber on 28 November 2002.
13. Kenny Davern, conversation with the author.
14. Date Book; Kobe event program.
15. Phil Schaap, liner notes to *The Kenny Davern Quartet at the Mill Hill Playhouse Celebrating Fifty Years of Records*, Arbors ARCD 19296, September 2003.
16. Ibid. Kenny Davern, conversation with the author.
17. Martin Gayford, "Kenny Davern Quartet," *The Daily Telegraph*, 24 January 2004; Will Friedwald, "The Year in Jazz, Last Year in Jazz," *New York Sun*, 24 January 2004; John Postgate, *Jazz Journal International*, 58, no. 3 (March 2005): 22.
18. *Jazz Journal International*, 59, no. 2 (February 2006): 8.
19. Date Book; press release; John Norris, *Coda*, issue 313 (January–February 2004): 16.
20. Mark Weber, Elsa Davern, conversations with the author; Mark Weber, e-mail to the author.
21. Letter from Kenny Davern to Christian Plattner dated May 1996. Davern was not alone in voicing these concerns. In my interviews for this book, many musicians expressed similar opinions. Of all of them, Ed Polcer was the most vociferous in lamenting the loss of the camaraderie and sense of collegiality that existed when

he began to play professionally. Ed Polcer, interview by the author. And almost everyone, regardless of age, wondered whether, in twenty years, there would be any audience for the music they loved.

22. Kenny Davern, interviewed by Martin Gayford on Meridian, *The Jazz Clarinet*, recorded 14 August 1990 and broadcast on BBC World Service on 4 September 1990.

23. Kenny Davern, conversation with the author; Elsa Davern, Warren Vache, Jr., Allan Vache, interviews by the author.

24. Greg Cohen, interview by the author.

25. Dan Morgenstern, interview by the author.

26. James Chirillo, interview by the author; Kenny Davern, conversation with the author; Elsa Davern, conversation with the author.

CHAPTER SEVENTEEN

Journey's End

In the first quarter of 2004, Kenny played a benefit concert in Tucson, performed at the North Carolina Jazz Party in Wilmington, appeared at Shanghai Jazz, played a date with Dick Hyman and, on the weekend of March 19–21, appeared at Mat Domber's last *March of Jazz*.

Kenny was one of three persons whose birthday was to be celebrated that year; the others were conductor-arranger-pianist Skitch Henderson and Stanley Kay, who had been a drummer, the entertainment director of the New York Yankees, and the creator of Diva, the dynamic and well-regarded orchestra composed solely of female musicians. For the occasion, Domber had produced a 120-page polished, printed program that included a sixty-one-page biography of Kenny, written by Brian Peerless, that was filled with photographs beginning in Kenny's early childhood. On the morning of Sunday, March 21, Don Wolff presented a biographical video that he had prepared, running nearly two hours in length. It contained a number of scarce movie and video clips of Davern's appearances on several television shows, a number of different performances of Soprano Summit and Summit Reunion, and ended with a procession of still pictures of Kenny, Elsa, their children, and grandchildren. Elsa was there, as were as their children, Debbie and Mark, and their spouses Rob Wuensch and Patti Lass. Elsa's sister, Elaine, and her husband, Fred, attended, as did their Brian and Valerie Peerless.

The prospect of having his biography written—and of having to assist in the process—was traumatic for Davern. Aside from the abortive foray with Mark Weber, he never wanted to reflect on or examine his past. There were subjects that he would never discuss, particularly the details of his early childhood. He was unwilling—and probably unable—either to write down a brief history of his life or dictate it into a recorder.

He preferred to be interviewed in person, rather than on the telephone, which was difficult for Peerless, who lived in England. Fortunately, Davern came to Great Britain in August 2003, and Peerless was able to speak with him at length as they traveled to and from jobs. Afterward, Peerless would put together the facts that he knew, and then compile a list of questions about the information he lacked. When the list got long enough, he would call Kenny for answers. Then the process would start again.[1]

Mat and Rachel Domber came to New Mexico so that Mat could select the pictures for the written program. Don and Heide Wolff also visited the Daverns so that Don could work on the video.[2] Wolff is a multitalented person. A successful attorney in the St. Louis area, he also had a long-running radio show on station KMOX, on Saturday evenings, on which he interviewed many musicians, played music, and commented knowledgeably on both. Don now hosts a Friday night radio show on Classic 99 (KFUO-FM 99.1), a television show on HECTV.org, and an Internet show on Live 366.com—all of which are titled *I Love Jazz*. He has amassed a huge collection of commercially released and privately made recordings and is accomplished in audiotaping and videotaping jazz programs and concerts.

Wolff was one of Davern's closest friends, and they had talked intimately many times over the years. But, as Don remembered, Kenny wanted no part of the process of memorializing his life.

> He didn't want to go through this stuff himself. It brought back memories, bad and good, and he didn't want to go through it. "You come out here and take a look at this stuff and see what you want."
> . . . But, as we worked on the project, he mellowed more and more each time. When the film was complete and he saw it (he saw at least part of it before I put it on at the party), his whole attitude about yesteryear changed. And, he went from not wanting to hear anything or see anything—he was so impressed by the project, he was so turned on in seeing the development of his career, musically speaking and family speaking—that it just changed him forever. Then he wanted all kinds of things from the past, wanted to listen to them and determine which was good, which was bad. . . . And he mellowed out and became more of a sentimentalist than he was prior to the project.[3]

Before Kenny returned to New Mexico, he played a private party in Punta Gorda. There wasn't much work before he went back to New Jersey, to appear at the First New Jersey Jazz Society Edison Jazz Party, an event that was put together and underwritten by Davern's old friends, Joe Buttafuoco and Frank Nissel. The party was held on the weekend of May 7–9 and, on the night before, Davern and Howard Alden were at Shanghai Jazz.[4]

From there, Kenny traveled to San Antonio to appear with the Jim Cullum band at *The Landing*, Cullum's home club located on the Riverwalk. Cullum hosted a weekly one-hour broadcast on National Public Radio called *Jazz from the Landing*, and the program on May 13 was entitled *Memories with Kenny Davern*. Kenny played a number of tunes with the band and, during the breaks, he was interviewed by David Holt. One cut, a lively rendition of *Diga Diga Doo*, has been released on an anthology entitled *The Jim Cullum Jazz Band, Chasin' the Blues*.

Davern played at the New Jersey Jazz Society's (NJJS) annual *JazzFest*, which was held at Fairleigh Dickenson University in Madison on June 12–13, 2004. In August, he made a one-week tour of the United Kingdom, appearing at the Edinburgh International Jazz Festival on the 8th and the Nairn International Jazz Festival on the 9th and 10th. He played at the Concorde Club, performed for the Dublin Jazz Society, and appeared at the Brecon Jazz Festival in Wales. There was one final date in Woking on August 16 before he flew home.[5]

Bob Weil, universally known as Bumble Bee Bob, had an abiding interest in jazz and was active in promoting it throughout New Mexico. He was a founder and director of the Santa Fe Jazz Foundation and had been involved in presenting programs at the Outpost Performance Space. Weil also owned the Baja Grille, a fast food Mexican restaurant in Santa Fe where, once a week, a jazz-playing trio led by drummer John Trentacosta performed.

John Trentacosta may have been the most important local musician that Davern met during his years in New Mexico. Born in Staten Island, New York, of Italian parentage, Trentacosta moved to Albuquerque in 1991. He had played with most of the jazz greats who traveled through the area, including James Moody, Lee Konitz, Roger Kellaway, and Bud Shank and, when Kenny mentioned to Howard Alden that he was moving to Albuquerque, Alden suggested that he contact Trentacosta. "I had been leading a trio since 2003 and when Kenny moved here, we got together, and Kenny said that he would like to come up and do it. I was surprised. But, for Kenny, it was just about playing. He wanted to play. And that was all he cared about—it was an opportunity for him to play."[6]

The Grille was a relatively small, narrow place, with the kitchen and cash register on one long wall and tables along the other. A space had been cleared in the center of the tables for the musicians. The staff continued to serve food while the musicians played, but the plastic dishes and cutlery used by the Grille helped to minimize the noise.[7]

Davern, Trentacosta, and Weill agreed that Kenny would play at the Baja Grille once each month. He made his first appearance there on August 28, 2004.[8]

> All of the people were not necessarily there to hear the music. But, Kenny would capture the audience all the time. The people started coming to hear him, and that crowd would overtake the place. The people who were not there for the music would get the hint and eat outside if it was warm out or, if they could find a place, sit on the periphery. They would realize that people are here for the music.
>
> We cultivated an audience who would come in to hear the music. It became like a family; people loved Kenny. When Kenny was there, the place was mobbed, all the time. Kenny captured the audience, and the people hung on him. It was a jazz concert in this little grille. People loved his music. Why? Kenny was great. Kenny's music *swung*.[9]

One of the hallmarks of life outside of the Northeast is that there is a noticeable relaxation in dress codes. Informality and comfort are the order of the day. But Davern believed that a musician had to meet certain standards, regardless of where he was playing. Trentacosta remembered: "One thing I loved was that he would show up to this gig with a jacket and tie—to this little fast food grille in New Mexico, where the governor doesn't even go with a jacket and tie. . . . You look at that picture, *A Great Day in Harlem*: everybody's got a jacket and tie. Kenny comes out of that—pride in the music.[10]

Kenny played the Trenton Jazz Festival on September 18 and, one week later, he was back at the Baja Grille. In the middle of October, Davern returned to New Jersey for a concert in Morristown. Randy Reinhart, Dan Barrett, pianist John Sheridan, James Chirillo, Frank Tate, and Tony DeNicola were onstage that night and, on the next day, they were with him in a recording studio.[11]

Kenny and Mat Domber had been speaking for some time about recording a modern dixieland session. Randy Reinhart had been speaking with Domber during the same period about making a CD using most of the members of the band that Randy and Kenny had performed with at the recent NJJS picnic. The result was *Randy Reinhart at the Mill Hill Playhouse, As Long As I Live*.[12] Reinhart recalled how the gig came about.

Mat wanted to record the band, but with Kenny as the leader. And Kenny said, "Look, I'd rather stick to quartets and trios and do what I'm doing now. Why don't you record it and use Randy as the leader? That way, he'll have a CD out." That's the way it happened. It was terrific. I cherish it.[13]

Barrett, Reinhart, and Davern did the arrangements. At the Jazz Band Ball, the opening number, set the tone of the disc, bringing a twenty-first-century approach to this composition by the members of the Original Dixieland Jazz Band (ODJB). Kenny had two solos on As Long As I Live, both of which differed markedly from his previous approaches to the song. Davern and Barrett sat out for the next tune, Too Late Now, but returned for Nobody's Sweetheart.

For most of the album, Reinhart played cornet and Barrett was on trombone. They switched horns on I Guess I'll Have to Change My Plan. Back on cornet, Reinhart and pianist Sheridan duetted on the Armstrong–Hines specialty, Weatherbird Rag, while the rest of the band laid out. The arrangement of Mood Indigo deferred the traditional trumpet-trombone-clarinet chorus until the end. Reinhart stated the first half of the theme, and Davern finished it off.

The full band attacked Naughty Sweetie Blues in a powerhouse arrangement. A rollicking bass started Yellow Dog Blues and, over the next eleven minutes, Reinhart and Davern showed how time had not taken the edge from their renditions of this piece. Davern was out for More Than You Know and returned for another of the ODJB stalwarts, Clarinet Marmalade, that closed the CD.

The album received excellent reviews. John Postgate called Davern's solo on Naughty Sweetie Blues "one of the finest I have heard from him in recent years. . . . " and this release, as well as the Kenny Davern at Mill Hill CD, were both voted one of Jazz Journal International's top 20 albums for 2005.[14]

At the end of October, Kenny appeared at the Baja Grille. He sailed on a one-week cruise to Alaska on November 10. In mid-December, Chirillo, Greg Cohen, and DiNicola traveled to New Mexico, to appear with Davern in two concerts.[15] The programs were recorded, and the best selections were issued on an Arbors compact disc titled The Kenny Davern Quartet: In Concert at the Outpost Performance Space, Albuquerque, 2004.

Davern had played some of the songs on this recording countless times before; a few were relatively new. But the understanding among Davern and his colleagues ensured that none of the performances were stale or hackneyed. Thus, on the opening title, Ole Miss, Davern rolled along ahead of his driving three-piece rhythm section. There was a jaunty feel to Careless Love, which was taken at a medium pace. An exciting *Somebody Stole My Gal* followed, on which Kenny had a rollicking solo.

Summertime had become Davern's signature ballad and, over more than two decades, he had been honing his interpretation of the tune. His approach on this version was somewhat different from the earlier recordings. James Chirillo had noticed that Kenny had become more adventurous in his choice of notes since he had moved to New Mexico and thought "That version of *Summertime* that was a killer—the emotion."[16]

Davern had heard the recording that Irving Fazola had made of *Spreadin' Knowledge Around*, and thought that Fazola's performance was "just absolutely splendid."[17] Kenny had recorded the tune one time before—in 1991, on the *My Inspiration* album. This version took a different approach. *C.C. Rider* slowed the pace down and had a rhythm 'n' blues feeling to it. The only tune that was new to the Davern recorded library came next, a lush version of *These Foolish Things*. The closer was *Royal Garden Blues*, which ran over ten minutes in length.

The reviews for this release were consistently favorable. "If they were still giving stars," said Art Hilgart, "this album would get the full five." Joe Lang wrote:

> I have seen clarinet master Kenny Davern countless times and have heard most of the recordings that he has made, and I never cease to wonder at how consistent he is. I mean this in the best sense of the word. His playing, both technically and conceptually, never wanders far from excellent. He obviously loves and enjoys the music that he plays, and treats each song that he chooses like a valued friend.[18]

On February 19, 2005, Davern was at the Baja Grille, backed by Jim Fox, a guitarist who made his home in the Los Angeles area, but periodically visited his sister in Albuquerque, along with Jon Gegan and John Trentacosta. In March, Kenny appeared at the 92nd Street Y on the 12th. Two days later, he and Hyman were in Naples, Florida, at the Philharmonic Center for the Performing Arts. Kenny was in Switzerland at the Bern International Jazz Festival at the end of April and returned to the Baja Grille in early June.[19]

Davern flew to New York and, on June 10, he and Ken Peplowski, along with Howard Alden, James Chirillo, Nicki Parrott, and Tony DeNicola, visited the Clinton Studios in New York to cut their second full-length CD together. Titled *Dialogues*, it was a recording that displeased both of them.

Peplowski played tenor sax for the first three songs. The excitement and contrapuntal exchanges of ideas that permeated their *Jazz KENNections* outing was missing from these tunes. *If Dreams Come True* was marked by Davern's solo, which began in the chalumeau range accompanied only by bass and drums. *The Diner*, Peplowski's slow variation of *Dinah*, was his feature. Then Davern, backed only by Alden, wistfully stated the melody on *I Can't Believe That You're in Love with Me*, before Peplowski and the rest of the group joined in at medium tempo.

Peplowski switched to clarinet for the balance of the session, which pleased him, but upset Davern who, as mentioned previously, did not like to play clarinet duets. *Comes Love*, *Should I*, and *Sometimes I'm Happy*, all featured some harmonic statements and interesting exchanges between the two clarinets. *High Society* was probably the most exciting piece on the disc, featuring Alden and Chirillo on banjos and the two Kens on clarinet. *Crazy Rhythm* was followed by *Nobody Else but Me*, a feature for the two guitars, accompanied by Parrott and DiNicola. The final selection was *Muskrat Samba* (in reality, *Muskrat Ramble* with a Latin beat).

The session was not what either Peplowski or Davern had envisioned, and the tension in the studio was obvious. Davern was not only unhappy with his own work, but also thought that Peplowski was not as involved in the session as he would have wished. Peplowski was frustrated that the session had not been as productive as he had expected.

When Davern first heard the tapes of the session, he was still upset about it. However, he came to like it more as time passed.[20] Peplowski was displeased with the results of the session when it was finished and did not change his opinion as time passed.

> I didn't even want that record to come out. Kenny was in a very bad mood during the day; he seemed to be very uncomfortable and wanted to rush through the set. We did one or two takes on everything; I didn't think they were that good. Dan Morgenstern called me when he was writing the liner notes, and I said, "Dan, I don't have anything good to say about this date. I really can't help you, unless you want to write that." It wasn't a good session at all.[21]

None of the conduct of the principals or their concerns was known to the public or reflected in the finished product. It received an excellent review from Harvey Siders in *Jazz Times* who said: "This is what jazz is all about: inventive musicians getting together and having a swinging conversation."[22]

On the day after the recording session, Kenny returned to the campus of Fairleigh Dickinson University for the NJJS's *JazzFest*. On the 14th, he was in Morristown, performing with the Arbors All-Stars, a group that included Pizzarelli, Chirillo, Parrott, and DeNicola. He spent the 17th and 18th at

Shanghai Jazz and, from the 24th to the 26th he was in Indiana, at the Elkhart Jazz Festival. In July and August, he was at the Baja Grille. *Mississippi Rag* featured him on the cover of its September 2005, issue. On the weekend of October 9, he appeared at Sunnie Sutton's Jazz Party in Denver and, on November 16, he was back at the Baja Grille.[23]

Kenny and the Arbors All-Stars returned to Morristown on November 29th and, on the first day of December, the Statesmen of Jazz saluted Davern as part of Jack Kleinsinger's *Highlights in Jazz* series at the Tribeca Performing Arts Theater in New York City. Writing in the New York Sun, columnist Will Friedwald said:

> The clarinetist, Kenny Davern, who is being saluted this Thursday at the TriBeCa Performing Arts Center, is one of those rare musicians for whom every solo is a statement. He doesn't just play for the sake of filling space, but because he has something important to say. . . . When Mr. Davern plays a four-minute solo, you know every note has a clear point of departure and an equally clear point of arrival.[24]

For several decades, Billy Crystal's father, Jack, had been a manager at the Commodore Record Shop and had produced the weekend sessions at the Central Plaza. Billy only saw him one day every week. Years later, he wrote a one-man show about his relationship with his father; *700 Sundays*, which opened on Broadway on December 5, 2005. Afterward, there was a party at Tavern on the Green in Central Park where Kenny, who had known both father and son and had played at some of Billy's birthday parties, was invited to perform. Davern spoke of Crystal's father a few weeks later with Mark Weber.

> I used to do some work for him, outside work, not only the Central Plaza but also the Lighthouse for the Blind. I played some freebie concerts. We went to Sing Sing one time and played for the prisoners. Jack was very philanthropic, except with his family. Billy's play, *700 Sundays*, was the result: the only time that he was able to see his father was Sunday. And, he spent 700 Sundays with his father before he died. Billy was fifteen when it happened.
>
> I played at the Tavern on the Green when he brought the producers in after the opening night. . . . Billy jumped up on the stand. He remembered that I had given him a clarinet lesson when I was out at the house. He was about seven years old, just a precocious little kid who tap danced with only one foot. Can you imagine that?[25]

On January 7, 2006, Kenny turned seventy-one years of age. He still loved to play: it was the essence of his life. He enjoyed performing and, more often than not, he liked to play with the musicians with whom he performed. But, as noted previously, the contraction of the music world that he inhabited, the decrease in venues, the diminishing numbers of young musicians, and the loss of the tradition that he had tried to preserve and pass on, all upset him.

Of equal concern to him was the change in musical tastes.

> I just think that there's good music and bad music, and you're living in a world of bad music. I think that the majority of music that's being perpetrated, foisted upon the American public, especially with children, is a disgrace and it's disgusting. I think that it's doing a lot of damage that's irreparable. They will never know what real music sounded like. . . . I can't explain it. I'd rather not explain it.
>
> I prefer song forms. I prefer tunes that were written in the teens—from 1900, the '20s, the '30s, and the '40s. And those are the tunes that I use for my points of reference and departure, Gershwin, Berlin, and people like that—Harold Arlen, Jimmy McHugh, and Dorothy Fields are the people that wrote songs that people were able to sing, whistle: they knew the words and could dance to.[26]

Nonetheless, life still provided moments of surprise and enjoyment to Kenny. The Instant Composers Pool (ICP) is an eleven-person orchestra founded in the Netherlands in 1967, by pianist and composer Misha Mengelberg, drummer Han Bennick, and saxophonist and composer Willem Breuker. ICP's repertoire consists of a large number of original compositions, plus tunes by Ellington, Monk, and Carmichael. Some of the material is arranged, other parts are improvised freely, and there is some free improvisation in the midst of heavily arranged sections.

The orchestra had performed in Albuquerque on October 25, 2004. Mark Weber, who liked ICP's music, suggested that Kenny should come to listen. Nonetheless, Weber was startled when Davern showed up—and was even more amazed to hear that he liked the band. During the intermission, Davern went backstage to meet the musicians. They were as excited to meet him as he was about their music and, for their second set, they played some of their arrangements of Ellington and Carmichael tunes. At the end of the evening, Davern said that he wanted to play with the band when they returned.[27]

On March 13, 2006, ICP, consisting of Mengelberg, Bennick, and Brueker, together with Michael Moore, Tobias Delius, and Ab Baars (woodwinds and reeds), Thomas Herberer (trumpet), Walter Werbos (trombone), Mary Oliver (violin and viola), Tristan Honsinger (cello), and Ernest Glerum (bass), were booked at the Outpost for a concert. Davern had kept in touch with the band and, on this occasion, he was billed as their Special Guest. He rehearsed with the band for a short time in the afternoon, but most of his performance that evening was completely spontaneous.

For those who brushed Davern aside as a seventy-one-year-old dixieland musician who was mired in the music of a time long ago and past his prime, this concert must have come as a shock. Some of the music played that night was familiar. But the only tune on which the music sounded conventional was Melancholy Baby, and that lasted only until Davern finished his solo. The melodies of Caravan and I Surrender Dear were recognizable. But the harmonies and the improvisations were not, and Davern's solos that night would never be confused with his treatment of these tunes in his usual milieu. There were original compositions that had elements of big-band arrangements, but then sailed off into freely created sound and feeling. Davern was a part of every tune, completely at ease in the avant-garde idiom.

At the beginning of the second set, Davern appeared on stage with Michael Moore, Tobias Delius, and Ab Baars. Performing without a rhythm section, the four reedmen had a musical conversation filled with long tones and short notes, squawks, yells, calls, and responses—all in a free and unstructured setting. The musical intelligence that played so spontaneously on the Unexpected album almost thirty years before was in evidence that night, neither atrophied nor diminished by time.

Four days later, he was in Toronto for a concert and a recording date. Writer and producer John Norris had been in the audience at the Ascona festival in 2003, when Kenny had been teamed with pianist David Boeddinghaus and drummer Trevor Richards. Norris immediately thought to record them, but it took almost three years to arrange to reunite the trio. They appeared at the Estonian Hall on March 17 and, on the following day, were in the studio for Sackville Records. The result was The Kenny Davern Trio, Nobody Else but Kenny, the last recording that Davern made.[28]

All of the songs on this release had been part of Davern's book for many years, and he had recorded some of them in other trios. My Honey's Lovin' Arms and Tain't Nobody's Business were on the two recordings with Ralph Sutton and Gus Johnson, and Kenny had done Sugar with Sutton and drummer Bill Polain for the Revelations release. Dick Wellstood and Bobby Rosengarden had accompanied Davern on Joshua Fit the Battle of Jericho on The Blue Three at Hanratty's.

But, as with much of the music that he played after moving to New Mexico, there was a difference. The feel of the slower tunes was more contemplative, and the improvisations were more complex. As reviewer Herb Young noted: "Kenny is consistent, but on this outing he just seems to be pouring out his feelings to a degree that is almost like he wants you to know that this is his story told in music."[29] Joe Lang, writing in *Jersey Jazz*, called Davern "a jazz institution, a singular voice on clarinet. No matter how many times you hear him, you always find yourself marveling at how he is always exciting to hear. . . ."[30]

There was a gig at the Baja Grille in Santa Fe on May 13, followed by a weekend in Midland, Texas, starting on May 19. He had a one-night stand at the Pranzo Italian Grill in Santa Fe on June 3, billed as Kenny Davern and the Straight Up trio, Trentacosta's standing group.

He was back in the Northeast on the weekend of June 10, at the NJJS *JazzFest*. In the next week, he performed with Chirillo, Cohen, and DeNicola at the Kaye Playhouse as part of the JVC Jazz Festival. He also appeared with Peplowski, Evan Christopher, and Don Byron as part of a program titled *Clarinet Marmalade*. July 21 saw Davern at New Mexico's First Annual Jazz Festival in Santa Fe, where he appeared in a tribute to George Wein. Then he was off to the United Kingdom for the Brecon Jazz Festival in the middle of August.[31]

Tony DeNicola died on September 1, 2006, the day on which he should have celebrated his seventy-ninth birthday. He never told any of his friends that he had been diagnosed with cancer several years before, that he had undergone treatment, that his cancer had recurred, and that he was undergoing chemotherapy. Occasionally, he looked pale or tired, but, if anyone mentioned it, he brushed the comments aside, saying that he was tired or that it was due to jet lag. Davern had no inkling that DeNicola was ill, and his death was devastating.

For over fifteen years, they had been the closest of personal friends. Until the Daverns moved to New Mexico in 2002, Kenny and Tony had played together almost every Saturday night and on many nights in between. Davern had brought DeNicola to jazz parties and festivals, introducing him to dozens of musicians, promoters, and reporters he would not have otherwise met, and they in turn had come to appreciate his talents.

In many ways, Tony embodied the values and lifestyle of the Italian families that Kenny had known in his youth. He was soft-spoken but firm: he said what he believed and brooked no nonsense. Although he was conservative in his outlook, and Davern was far more liberal, they could talk at length without rancor or ill will.

Their relationship did not deteriorate when Kenny moved away.

> He and Tony talked on the phone a lot. When we moved here and he went east, he stayed at Tony's house. He respected Tony a lot. Tony's father was in his '90s when we had a party at Tony's house, and his father taught us all how

to make pasta from scratch—starting without the machine. Tony had cooked the sauce for two days. Kenny loved that stuff. That was like family-home for him. It was a piece of childhood.[32]

Davern was hard pressed to come to grips with the fact that his friend was dead. "He walked around saying 'I'll never find a friend or a drummer like this again in my life,'" Elsa recalled. "'Why didn't he allow me to say goodbye to him.'"[33] The other members of his quartet understood that DeNicola's death meant the end of something for Davern that could never be resurrected. Greg Cohen saw the loss as something from which Davern could not rebound.

He thought so much of Tony. After Tony died, you could see it in his eyes. Kenny had the wind knocked out of him. It was like someone punched him in the stomach, and he fell backwards and he never got the inertia to come forward again.[34]

On September 14, Davern was scheduled to sail aboard the cruise ship S.S. *Crystal Symphony* along with Chirillo, Howard Alden, Dick Hyman, Warren Vache, Jr., Randy Reinhart, and Harry Allen. Someone had to be chosen to replace DeNicola who had been booked on the cruise. A number of possibilities were considered until, eventually, Kenny settled on Chuck Riggs, who had worked with him throughout the 1980s.

At the end of the month he was at the Baja Grille and, in October, he played in Denver at Sunnie Sutton's party. In early November, he appeared on Mark Weber's radio show, along with clarinetist Eddie Daniels, who lived in Santa Fe. Although Daniels' interests were far more modern than Davern's, the two of them developed a rapport, and they began to discuss the possibility of recording a CD together. He was also planning to make a recording in April of the following year with Bob Wilber. But it was not to be.

As far back as the summer of 2006, Kenny began to suffer from shortness of breath and a lack of energy. He stopped practicing the clarinet every day, as he had done all his life, because there were times when he did not have the stamina. In late October, he began to experience episodes where his blood pressure would become erratic, his systolic pressure would skyrocket to over 200 mm Hg, and his pulse would race uncontrollably.

He saw his primary physician, Mary Ellen Lawrence, M.D., on November 6. He had also been suffering from kidney problems and saw his specialist in internal medicine, Lucy Fox, M.D., on the 16th. (She was, coincidentally, the sister of guitarist Jim Fox.) Dr. Fox said that he should return in six months and take a stress test at that time. But Kenny's symptoms were of such concern that he promised Elsa that he would take a stress test after

Christmas, although he believed that he would "fail it," and said that he would also see a cardiologist.

On December 12, Kenny took their daughter Debbie, who had come to visit, to the airport. He returned home, did some errands, ate lunch, and then stayed around the house. At dinnertime, he said he didn't feel well. Elsa was watching television when, at about 8:00 p.m., he came to her and said that he felt "like an elephant was sitting on his chest." He was extremely agitated and restless, but refused to allow Elsa to call 911. She telephoned her sister Elaine, who came over with her husband, Fred, to try to take Kenny to the hospital. He refused to go. Kenny was standing by the fireplace when he looked at Elsa and said "Oh boy," the same words that he said when he first saw her. And then he collapsed. Fred's efforts to revive him were for naught: he was gone.[35]

Kenny had planned for his death as carefully as he lived his life. He had written three detailed letters to Elsa and, in accordance with his wishes, there was no funeral or memorial service. He was cremated on the following day: some of his ashes were spread outside the window of his study, and some were strewn at places in New Jersey that had brought him happiness.

In the weeks and months that followed, condolences poured into the house in Sandia Park, articles were written about Davern's life and music, and tributes to him were held at festivals and jazz parties here and abroad. In 2008, a CD was released of some appearances with Soprano Summit and The Blue Three and subsequently, a DVD of some Summit Reunion performances came on the market, as did a video of Kenny appearance on Art Hodes television show. They are part, but not all, of his legacy.

The legacy of Kenny Davern is manifold. There is the memory of the man, who loved his wife and children without reservation: who was generous, caring, and loyal to those that he trusted with his friendship and respect. Those who were fortunate enough have had that man in their lives saw the joy, the intellect, and the warmth that lay within him. For them, his memory will remain bright and shining, undimmed by the passage of time.

There is the memory of the musician, who had a clear vision of the music that he wanted to create and never deviated from the path that he chose. He had choices: there were other styles of music and performance that offered the prospect of more money and popular recognition. But then, he would not have been able to play the music that he loved in the way that he wanted to play it. For Kenny, that was not a choice at all. There was no compromise in the musical soul of Kenny Davern.

Finally, there is his music. Tastes will change, other artists will become popular, and other styles will catch the public's fancy. But, beauty never goes out of style. And that is the part of Kenny's legacy that will never fade: thousands of hours of beautiful music—sometimes exciting, sometimes challenging, sometimes saddening—but always beautiful. Created by a man who used a clarinet to bring emotion and feeling to music, it speaks in a unique voice that says, in just four bars, "I am Kenny Davern."

Notes

1. Brian Peerless, Elsa Davern, interviews by the author.

2. While Don Wolff and his wife Heide were in Sandia Park working on the video tribute to be shown at the Arbors celebration; Kenny gave Don all of the audio cassette tapes that people had sent him over the years. Wolff already had the largest collection of commercial and privately made recordings of Davern's performances. He had recorded many of them himself, and had thousands that were either given to him by other enthusiasts or came from copies that he made from the collections of Dick Wellstood, Ralph Sutton, Bobby Rosengarden, Bob Wilber, and others. Kenny and Don packed as many cassettes as they could fit into Kenny's largest suitcase, and Don flew home with it to St. Louis. Over time, Kenny and Elsa sent more boxes of materials to Don, which Wolff is organizing and transferring onto CD. They will eventually become part of the Heide and Don Wolff Jazz Institute that they have established at Harris-Stowe State University in St. Louis, Missouri.

3. Don Wolff, interview by the author.

4. Kenny Davern, interview by Mark Weber, 15 January 2004; Date Book; letter from Carl Sturgis to Kenny Davern dated 5 July 2003; Edison Jazz Party event program.

5. *Jersey Jazz*, 32, no. 3 (April 2004): 3; *Jazz Journal International*, 57, no. 8 (August 2004): 3; Brecon event program; Edinburgh event program.

6. John Trentacosta, interview by the author.

7. Trentacosta interview.

8. Trentacosta interview; advertisement for the Baja Grill.

9. Trentacosta interview.

10. Trentacosta interview.

11. Trenton Jazz Festival event program; Baja Grille advertisement; *Jersey Jazz*, 32, no. 7 (September 2004): 9.

12. Mat Domber, president, Arbors Records, Randy Reinhart, interviews by the author.

13. Randy Reinhart, interview by the author.

14. John Postagate, *Jazz Journal International*, 58, no. 11 (November 2005): 34, and 59, no. 2 (February 2006): 8.

15. DeNicola did not bring his drum kit with him. John Trentacosta got a set that Butch Miles had left in Santa Fe and lent them to Tony for the job. Kenny Davern, interview by Mark Weber, 13 January 2005.

16. James Chirillo, interview by the author.

17. Kenny Davern, interview by Mark Weber, 17 January 2006.

18. Art Hilgart, "At the Outpost Performance Space, Kenny Davern Quartet," *IAJRC Journal*, 36, no. 2 (May 2006): 78; Joe Lang, "Compact Views," *Jersey Jazz*, 33, no. 8 (October 2005): 8.

19. Advertisements for the Baja Grille performances; event programs for the remaining appearances.

20. Elsa Davern; conversation with the author; Howard Alden, James Chirillo, Dan Morgenstern, interviews by the author.

21. Ken Peplowski, interview by the author.

22. Harvey Siders, "Kenny Davern and Ken Peplowski, Dialogues," *Jazz Times*, December 2007.

23. *Jersey Jazz*, 33, no. 4 (May 2005): 3, and 33, no. 5 (June 2005): 5, and 33, no. 9 (November 2005): 15; Elkhart event program; *Mississippi Rag*, xxxiii, no. 9 (September 2005); advertisements for the Baja Grille; *Jazz Journal International*, 59, no. 12 (December 2006): 4.

24. Will Friedwald, "A Chat with the Clarinetist, A Traditionalist Who Makes Every Note Count," *New York Sun*, 29 November 2005.

25. Kenny Davern, interview by Mark Weber, 17 January 2006.

26. Davern-Weber interview.

27. Mark Weber, interview by the author.

28. John Norris, liner notes to *The Kenny Davern Trio, Nobody Else but Kenny*, Sackville SKCD 2-3069, August 2006.

29. Herb Young, "The Kenny Davern Trio, Nobody Else but Kenny," *IAJRC Journal*, 37, no. 1 (February 2007): 76.

30. Joe Lang, "Compact Views," *Jersey Jazz*, 34, no. 10 (December 2006): 18.

31. *Jazz Journal International*, 59, no. 10 (October 2006): 17.

32. Elsa Davern, interview by the author.

33. Elsa Davern, interview by the author.

34. Greg Cohen, interview by the author

35. Elsa Davern, interviews by and conversations with the author.

The Issued Recordings of Kenny Davern

Key to Abbreviations

as	alto saxophone	g	guitar
b	string bass	harm	harmonica
bar	baritone saxophone	org	organ
bgo	bongo	p	piano
bj	banjo	perc	percussion
bassax	bass saxophone	ss	soprano saxophone
c	cornet	tb	trombone
c-mel	c-melody saxophone	tp	trumpet
cl	clarinet	ts	tenor saxophone
d	drums	tu	tuba
ele-b	electric bass	v	violin
ele-p	electric piano	vib	vibraphone
flug	flugelhorn	vo	vocal
frh	French horn	xyl	xylophone

Alfredito's Mambo Orchestra

New York, 1952

Kenny Davern (bar), other personnel unknown

Round the World Mambo   Rainbow Records
  (parts 1 & 2)   (number unknown)

Ralph Flanagan and His Orchestra

New York, June 28, 1954

John McCormick, Phil Pratico, Ray Stone (tp), John Mildner, Don Muller, Ogelsby Lowe, Harry Street (tb), Joe Lenza, Kenny Davern (as), Pete Fusco, Boomie Richman (ts), Marty Marks (bar), Ralph Flanagan (p), Tom Kay (g), Jack Keys (b), Bill Smith (d), Kee Largo (vo).

Out of the Bushes	Victor 20/47-5803
In the Chapel in the Moonlight*	" LPM 3237
Winter Wonderland	Victor EPC LPM 1037
What's New	Victor 20/47-6596

*Also issued on Ajazz C-939 and Victor 547-0463.

Ralph Flanagan and His Orchestra

New York, October 13, 1954

Rusty Dedrick, Al Derusa, Ralph LaSala (tp), Jimmy Hemming, Don Muller, Jack Satterfield, Billy VerPlanck (tb), Joe Lanza, Kenny Davern (as), Billy Maynard, Joe Palmer (ts), Marty Marks (bar), Ralph Flanagan (p), Tom Kay (g), George Roumaris (b), Bill Smith (d), George Laguna, Raymond Rodriguez (bgo)

Skokiaan*	Victor 547-0463	Victor LPM 3237
Sh'Boom*	"	"
Little Brown Jug Mambo	Victor 20/47-5908	
American Patrol Mambo	"	
Hold My Hand*	Victor 547-0462	"

*Also issued on Ajazz C-939.

Ralph Flanagan and His Orchestra

New York, October 15, 1954

Rusty Dedrick, Al Derusa, Ralph LaSala (tp), Jimmy Hemming, Don Muller, Lou McGarity, Billy VerPlanck (tb), Joe Lanza, Kenny Davern (as), Billy Maynard, Joe Palmer (ts), Marty Marks (bar), Ralph Flanagan (p), Tom Kay (g), George Roumaris (b), Bill Smith (d), George Laguna, Raymond Rodriguez (bgo)

Hey There	Victor 547-0462	Victor LPM 3237
This Old House	"	
If I Give My Heart to You	Victor 547-0463	"
Smile	"	"

All also issued on Ajazz C-939.

Jack Teagarden, *Meet Me Where They Play the Blues*
New York, November, 1954

Fred Greenleaf (tp), Jack Teagarden (tb, vo), Kenny Davern (cl), Norma Teagarden (p), Kass Malone (b), Ray Bauduc (d)

Riverboat Shuffle	Period SPL 1106	Beth BCP 32
King Porter Stomp	"	"
Milenberg Joys	"	BCP 6042
Mis'ry and the Blues	"	"

All cuts also on Good Time Jazz GTJ CD 12063-2, Jazztone J1022 and J1033, London LTZ-N 15077, Affinity AFF 141, Polydor Special 545 104, and in Japan on London JLC 1010, all of which are entitled "Jazz Great" except the Polydor issue, which is titled "Jack Teagarden, Meet Me Where They Play the Blues: Jazz Masters, Vol. 4." "Milenberg Joys" and "Mis'ry and the Blues" are on Ember (UK) EMB 3340 entitled "Jazz Great." All except "Milenberg Joys" are on "Jack Teagarden, Jazz Great," Bethlehem CD R2 75784.

Empire City Six *Salutes the Colleges*
New York, September 19, 1957

Tony Spair (tp), Harry DeVito (tb), Kenny Davern (cl), Johnny Varro (p), Pete Rodgers (b), Phil Failla (d)

Roar Lion Roar*	ABC Para ABC 210
Washington & Lee Swing*	
Ramblin' Wreck from Georgia Tech*	
The Victors*	
Wiffenpoof Song/Boola Boola	
Notre Dame Victory March	
On Wisconsin	
The Eyes of Texas Are Upon You	

Trojan War Song
Harvardiana
Anchors Aweigh
On Brave Old Army Team

*Also on HMV 7EG 8380.
Kenny Davern's name misspelled on ABC 210 as Kenny LaVerne: Tony Spair's name is misspelled as Tony Spars.

Empire City Six *Plays Dixie*

New York, @1957–1958

Tony Spair (tp), Harry DeVito (tb), Kenny Davern (cl), Johnny Varro (p), Pete Rodgers (b), Phil Failla (d)

Limehouse Blues	Stardust SD 101
That's a Plenty	
Wolverine Blues	
Medley—Indiana/Chicago/ Charleston/Darktown Strutters Ball	
Tin Roof Blues	
Black and Blue	
Muskrat Ramble	
Battle Hymn of the Republic	

First released on Stardust SD 101 as the Empire City Six. Also released on Hallmark HLP 312 as "The Empire City Six, Dixieland in Stereo," on Hollywood Records LPH 149 as the "Barons of Basin Street," on Manhattan MANS 537 as the Barrone Street Five titled "Dixieland—Barrone Street Five."

Ken Davern and His Salty Dogs, *In the Gloryland*

New York, June, 1958

Frank Laidlaw (c), Steve Knight (tb), Kenny Davern (cl), Carl Lunsford (bj), Arnold Hyman (b), Bob Thompson (d)

Tiger Rag	Elektra EKL 7099	Aves (G) 156.511
The Streets of the City	"	
In the Gloryland	"	Aves (G) 156.511
Shake It and Break It	"	
Just a Closer Walk with Thee	"	Aves (G) 156.511

Willie the Weeper	"
Precious Lord	"
The Old Rugged Cross	"

All titles also on Elektra EKL 201 and Columbia (E) 33SX1410: Released on Philips (UK) 838 347-2 as "More of the Best of Dixieland."

Oh Play That Thing, Pee Wee Erwin's Dixieland Eight
New York, October 24, 1958

Pee Wee Erwin (tp), Lou McGarity (tb), Kenny Davern (cl), Dick Hyman (p, org), Tony Gattuso (g, bj), Harvey Phillips (tuba), Jack Lesberg (b), Cliff Leeman (d)

Kansas City Stomps	United Artists UAL 4010	London LTZ 15153
The Chant		
Yaka Hula Hicky Dula		
Temptation Rag		
Black Bottom Stomp		
Dippermouth Blues		
Grandpa's Spells		
Dill Pickles		
Sensation Rag		
Big Pond Rag		
Jazz Frappe Rag		
Georgia Swing		

Also issued on Qualtro 103 and as a stereo album on UAS 5010, London SAH T6011 and London LTZ 15153.

Hans Conreid Narrates Peter Meets the Wolf in Dixieland
New York, 1959

Hans Conreid (narration), Pee Wee Erwin (tp), Lou McGarity (tb), Kenny Davern (cl), Boomie Richman (ts), Billy Maxted (p), George Barnes (g) or Tony Gattuso (bj), Harvey Phillips (b), Cliff Leeman (d)

Peter Meets the Wolf in Dixieland:	Strand SL 1001
Grumpy Grandpa	

Wild Wolf Wailing
Requiem for a Blue Duck
The Cat-Like Cat
In Defense of the Wolf
Pete's Theme

Pee Wee Erwin and the Dixie Strutters, *Down by the Riverside*
New York, Early 1959

Pee Wee Erwin (tp), Lou McGarity (tb), Kenny Davern (cl), Dick Hyman (p, org), Lee Blair (bj), Milt Hinton (b), Osie Johnson (d)

Walking with the King	United Artists UAL 3010	UAS-6071
Swing Low, Sweet Chariot		
When the Saints Go Marching In		
Just a Little While to Stay Here		
Lead Me On		
Down by the Riverside		
Marching into Glory Land		
Careless Love		
Everybody Needs a Helping Hand		
Lord, Lord, You Sure Been Good To Me		
Give Me the Good Word		
Just a Closer Walk with Thee		

All titles on London LTZ T15189 and SAH T6071.

The Dixie Rebels *Strike Back with a True Dixieland Sound*
New York, Mid-1959

Pee Wee Erwin (tp), Lou McGarity (tb), Kenny Davern (cl), Gene Schroder (p), Milt Hinton (b), Cliff Leeman or Panama Francis (d)

When the Saints Go Marching In*	Command RS 801 SD
St. James Infirmary*	

Original Dixieland One Step*
Royal Garden Blues*
Tin Roof Blues
Clarinet Marmalade
Hindustan
Basin Street Blues**
Panama
That's a Plenty
Fidgety Feet
South Rampart Street Parade*

On this album, Pee Wee Erwin recorded under the name of Big Jeb Dooley. Also issued on a double album on Command RSSD 983-2.
*Also on ABCX 821-2, a double album entitled "The Era of F. Scott Fitzgerald," on which "St. James Infirmary" and "Royal Garden Blues" are spliced, edited, and mislabeled as "Wolverine Blues."
**Also issued on Verve 549-364-2 entitled "Pete Fountain Presents the Best of Dixieland."

Phil Napoleon and His Memphis Five

New York, October 1959

Phil Napoleon (tp), Harry DeVito (tb), Kenny Davern (cl), Johnny Varro (p), Pete Rogers (b), Sonny Igoe (d)

Milenberg Joys	Capitol T 1344	Capitol ST 1344
South		
Limehouse Blues		
Black and Blue		
Creole Rag		
After You've Gone		
Wolverine Blues		
Come Back to Sorrento		
Satanic Blues		
Wang Wang Blues		
St. Louis Blues		
Shake It and Break It		

Also issued on Capitol (Eu) CO54-81846.

Dick Cary and the Dixieland Doodlers

New York, October 20, 1959

Dick Cary (tp); Harry DeVito (tb); Kenny Davern (cl); Leroy "Sam" Parkins (ts, bs, cl); Phil Cadway, Harvey Philips (tu); Lee Blair (bj); Dick Wellstood (p); Tommy Potter (b); Cliff Leeman (d)

Billy Boy   Columbia CL 1425   CS 8222
Nobody Knows the Trouble I've Seen
Swanee River

October 23, 1959

Camptown Races
In the Good Old Summertime
I've Been Working on the Railroad
Waltzing Matilda

October 25, 1959

There Is a Tavern in the Town
Swing Low, Sweet Chariot
Mack the Knife
Wait Till the Sun Shines Nellie
Jeannie with the Light Brown Hair

Also on Mosaic MD8-206, an eight-CD set entitled "Classic Columbia Condon Mob Sessions."

The Dixie Rebels, *True Dixieland Sound*

New York, December 7, 1959

Pee Wee Erwin (tp), Lou McGarity (tb), Kenny Davern (cl), John Mortillero (p), Milt Hinton (b), Cliff Leeman (d)

Tiger Rag   Command RS 825SD
Milenberg Joys
Limehouse Blues*
Jada
At the Jazz Band Ball
Indiana

Nobody's Sweetheart Now
Wang Wang Blues*
Avalon
Livery Stable Blues
Jazz Me Blues*
Creole Rag

On this album, Pee Wee Erwin recorded under the name of Big Jeb Dooley. Also issued on UAL 3021 and UAS 6071. All items except "Livery Stable Blues" and "Avalon" were issued on Command RSSD983-2.
*Also issued on ABCX 821-2, entitled "The Era of F. Scott Fitzgerald."

Mardi Gras

New York, 1960

Pee Wee Erwin (tp), Lou McGarity (tb), Kenny Davern (cl), Milt Hinton (b), Panama Francis (d), unknown (p) & (g)

When the Saints Go Marching In   Waldorf Music Hall MHK SD 1405

Phil Napoleon *In the Land of Dixie*

New York, January, 26–27, 1960

Phil Napoleon (tp), Harry DeVito (tb), Kenny Davern (cl), Johnny Varro (p), Pete Rogers (b), Sonny Igoe (d)

Fidgety Feet   Capitol T 1428
Dardanella
Ciri-Biri-Bin
Tin Roof Blues
Just Hot
Shim-Me-Sha-Wabble
Runnin' Wild
Memphis Blues
Southern Comfort
Ballin' the Jack
Anything
Sensation Rag

Phil Napoleon and His Memphis Five, *Tenderloin in Dixieland*

New York, July, 1960

Phil Napoleon (tp), Harry DeVito (tb), Kenny Davern (cl), Johnny Varro (p), Pete Rogers (b), Sonny Igoe (d)

Artificial Flowers	Capitol T 1535	Capitol ST 1535
Tommy, Tommy		
The Picture of Happiness		
Dr. Brock		
Dear Friends		
My Miss Mary		
The Army of the Just		
Reform		
Little Old New York		
Good Clean Fun		
My Gentle Young Johnny		
How the Money Changes Hands		

"Good Clean Fun" and "Artificial Flowers" were issued on a 45-rpm single, Capitol 4485.

Davern and Varro quit after two tunes on the session. Davern thought that he was on "Good Clean Fun" and another title that neither he nor Varro could remember. They were not on "Artificial Flowers." Peanuts Hucko and Buddy Weed finished the date.

The Hustler (Movie)

New York, circa 1961

Dan Terry (tp), Roswell Rudd (tb), Kenny Davern (cl), Phil Woods (as), Billy Bauer (g), Bunny Shawker (d)

Louisville (Incomplete segment)	20th Century Fox Video

The Charleston City All Stars *Go Dixieland*

New York, circa 1961

Pee Wee Erwin (tp), Lou McGarity (tb), Kenny Davern (cl), Johnny Varro (p), Lee Blair (bj), Harvey Phillips (tu), Jack Lesberg (b), Mousie Alexander (d)

Some of These Days	Grand Award 33-411
Baby Won't You Please Come Home	
Sweet Georgia Brown	
When You're Smiling	
Sweet Sue	
Chicago	
Somebody Stole My Gal	
Ballin' the Jack	
Alexander's Ragtime Band	
The Sheik of Araby	
Shine	

The entire album, except for "Shine" was issued on Grand Award GA 243 SD. "Alexander's Ragtime Band" was issued on ABCX 821-2, a double album entitled "The Era of F. Scott Fitzgerald."

Sidney DeParis, *Dixieland Hits, Country and Western*

Englewood Cliffs, New Jersey, August 28, 1962

Sidney DeParis (tp), Benny Morton (tb), Kenny Davern (cl), Charlie Queener (p), Lee Blair (bj), Leonard Gaskin (b), Herb Lovelle (d)

Pistol Packin' Mama*	Swingville SVLP 2040
You Call Everyone Darling	
You Always Hurt the One You Love	
Yellow Rose of Texas*	
It Is No Secret (What God Can Do)*	
Just Because*	
Someday	
Ghost Riders in the Sky	

Also issued as Swingville SV(S) 2040 under Leonard Gaskin's name entitled "Dixieland Hits—Country and Western."

*These items are on Good Time Jazz GTJCD 10060-2 entitled "At The Jazz Band Ball." The non-asterisked items are on GTJCD 10061-2, which is entitled "Memphis Blues, The Swingville All-Stars." Davern is not on other titles on these CDs.

We Gotta Shout: The Dukes of Dixieland with the Clara Ward Singers

New York, April 7, 14, 1963

Frank Assunto (tp), Fred Assunto (tb), Jac Assunto (tb, bj), Kenny Davern (cl), Gene Schroeder (p), Alton Williams (org), Jack Six (b), Buzzy Drootin (d), Clara Ward, Voyla Crowley, Mildred Means, Thelma Bumpess, Gerasldine Jones, Malvilyn Simpson, Vermettya Royster (vo)

Move Along	Columbia CL 2042
Lord, Let the Train Run Easy	
I'm Too Close to Heaven	
In the Morning	
Travelin' Shoes	
Just a Closer Walk with Thee	
Just a Little While to Stay Here	
Go Where I Send Thee	
Michael Row the Boat Ashore	
Will You Be There	
Marchin' In	

Also issued in mono on Harmony HL 7434 and CBS (UK) BPG 62176. Issued in stereo on Columbia CS 8842, Harmony HS 11234, and CBS S 62176. The Harmony Issues are titled "A Little Traveling Music—Clara Ward Singers with the Dukes of Dixieland."

After Hours

Columbus, Ohio, April 6–10, 1966

Wild Bill Davison (c), Kenny Davern (cl), Charlie Queener (p), George Wettling (d)

I Never Knew	Jazzology J 22	Jazzology JCD 22
Tin Roof Blues		
Easter Parade		
Big Butter and Egg Man		
Song of the Wanderer		
Ballin' the Jack		
Beale Street Blues		

Naughty Sweetie Blues
I Can't Believe That You're
   in Love with Me
Wolverine Blues
High Society
You're Lucky to Me
Exactly Like You
   (add unknown [g] and[b])

A Night at the Ferry with George Mauro's Original Ferryboat Dixieland Band
Brielle, New Jersey, 1966

George Mauro (tp, vo), Tim Jordan (tb), Kenny Davern (cl), Dick Wellstood (p), Jack Six (b), Al McManus (d)

Ferryboat Theme   Gamco 1
Birth of the Blues
Nobody's Sweetheart
You Do Something to Me/At Sundown/Whispering/Boo Hoo/ I Can't Get
   Started/Spring in Manhattan
Mood Indigo/More
The Battle Hymn of the Republic

The Ferryboat Dixieland Band
Philadelphia—Early 1967

George Mauro (tp, vo), Ed Hubble (tb), Kenny Davern (cl), Dick Wellstood (p), Jack Six (b), Al McManus (d)

I Found a New Baby   Gamco 2
St. James Infirmary
Russian Rag (Wellstood solo)
Aggravatin' Papa
When the Saints Go Marchin' In
Pink Elephants
Apple Blossom Time/Georgia on My Mind/Danny Boy/ The Days of Wine
   and Roses/I Don't Know Why I Love You Like I Do

Wonderland by Night
Secret Love/I Can't Give You Anything but Love/Bei Mir Bist Du Schon/
  Puttin' on the Ritz/Crazy Rhythm (Davern [vo])

Little Jazz Duets

New York, circa 1970
Kenny Davern (cl), George Duvivier (b), Bobby Donaldson (d)

Cool Waltz   Music Minus One MMO 4050
The Green Danube*
Tone Colours*
Reading Up*
Uptown—Downtown*
Main Street*
Ski Slope*
Doin' Your Chords*
Stop and Go*
Glider*
Jumper*
Da Dit*

The asterisked items on this release were combined with the asterisked items on "Jazz Duets in the Round," to which was added one more tune, "Swing Easy," and released on a Music Minus One CD titled "Easy Jazz Duets, Two Clarinets and Rhythm Section," MMO CD 3213.

Jazz Duets in the Round

New York, circa 1970
Kenny Davern (cl), George Duvivier (b), Bobby Donaldson or John Cresci (d)

Candlelight   Music Minus One MMO 4055
Hot Fudge*
Tiajuana*
La De Da De*
Switcheroo*
Hop Scotch*

Swingin' in the Rain*
4/4 Waltz*
One Note Break*
Lazy*
Bits and Pieces*

The asterisked items on this release were combined with the asterisked items on "Little Jazz Duets," to which was added one more tune, "Swing Easy," and released on a Music Minus One CD titled "Easy Jazz Duets, Two Clarinets and Rhythm Section," MMO CD 3213.

Balaban and Cats, *Bits & Pieces of Balaban and Cats*

Rutherford, New Jersey, October, 1970
Ed Polcer (tp), Ed Hubble (tb), Kenny Davern (cl), Red Balaban (bj), Howard Johnson (tu), Marquis Foster (d)

Girl of My Dreams   GFL 1015
Limehouse Blues

Ed Polcer (tp), Dick Rath (tb), Kenny Davern (cl), Gim Burton (bj), Red Balaban (b), Marquis Foster (d)

January, 1971
Linger Awhile   GFL 1015
The Song Is Ended
Beale Street Blues
Alabama Jubilee
Sultry Serenade
Ballin' the Jack

Davern not on other titles.

Balaban and Cats, *A Night at the Town House*

Rutherford, New Jersey, 1970–1971
Ed Polcer (tp), Dick Rath (tb), Kenny Davern (cl), John Bunch (p), Red Balaban (b), unknown (bj) and (d)

Your Father's Moustache   Unknown issue

Davern not on other titles.

Kenny Davern, A Night with Eddie Condon
Fayetteville, New York, April 30, 1971

Bernie Privin (tp), Lou McGarity (tb), Kenny Davern (cl), Dill Jones (p), Eddie Condon (g), Jack Lesberg (b), Cliff Leeman (d)

At the Jazz Band Ball	Arbors ARCD 19238
Rosetta	
Royal Garden Blues	
Ain't Misbehavin'	
Jazz Me Blues	
Rose of Washington Square	
Muskrat Ramble	
I Can't Get Started	
China Boy	
Rose Room	
That's a Plenty	
St. Louis Blues	

Jazz at the New School
New York, April 3, 1972

Wild Bill Davison (c), Kenny Davern (ss), Dick Wellstood (p), Eddie Condon (g), Gene Krupa (d)

Introduction*	Chiaroscuro CR 110	CR(D) 110
I Want to Be Happy		
Sugar		
Shim-Me-Sha-Wabble		
Avalon		
That Da Da Strain		
Blues in C		
The Mooche		
I Can't Believe That You're in Love with Me		

Struttin' with Some Barbecue*
China Boy*
Closing Remarks*

*Titles on CD only. All titles on CR 110 also issued on Storyville SLP 515. "Blues in C" issued on Chiaroscuro CR 204 entitled "Jazz Greats."

Dick Wellstood and His Hot Potatoes
New York, May 1, 1972
Kenny Davern (ss), Dick Wellstood (p), Gene Ramey (b), Al McManus (d)

Blues My Naughty Sweetie Gives to Me	Seeds 3	Black Eagle 1
George Sanders		
Shout 'Em Aunt Tillie*		
In a Mello Roll		
Atlanta Blues		
That Shakespearian Rag		
Suppertime		

*Franklin Skeete replaces Ramey on this title.

From Dixie to Swing
New York, July 10, 1972
Doc Cheatham (tp), Vic Dickenson (tb), Kenny Davern (ss, cl), Dick Wellstood (p), George Duvivier (b), Gus Johnson, Jr. (d)

Way Down Yonder in New Orleans	Classic Jazz CJ 10	MMO 4091
Red Sails in the Sunset		
Second-Hand Rose		
Royal Garden Blues		
Rose of Washington Square		MMO 4092
The Sunny Side of the Street		
I Want a Little Girl		
Exactly Like You		

All titles also issued on MMO 4095.

This Is Marva Josie

New York, August 6, 1973

Kenny Davern (ss); Earl Hines or Lois Miller or Weldon Irvine (p); Joe Parrino or David Barron (g); Ray Brooks or Roland Wilson (el. b); John Reilly or Napoleon Revels (d); Eric Kress, Manny Senerchia (v); Joe Furia (cello); Marva Josie, Lois Miller, Dante Lemos (vo)

Love, Love, Love	Thimble Rec TLP4
Why Was I Born?	
Scarborough Fair	
You're Not Mine Anymore	
Jelly, Jelly, Jelly	

Davern not on other titles.

Dick Wellstood and His Famous Orchestra, Featuring Kenny Davern

New York, November–December, 1973

Dick Wellstood (p), Kenny Davern (ss)

Fast as a Bastard	Chiaroscuro CR 129
Winin' Boy	
Wild Man Blues	
Georgia on My Mind	
Cashmir and Togas	(*Wellstood out*)*
Smiles	
Sweet Substitute	
Once in Awhile	
Liza	
So in Love (Davern out)*	

**Not on Chiaroscuro CR(D) 129 which was titled "Dick Wellstood and His All Star Orchestra Featuring Kenny Davern."*

1973 Eighth Annual Manassas All Star Jazz Festival

Manassas, Virginia, November 30, 1973

Kenny Fulcher (tp), Billy Allred (tb), Kenny Davern (ss), Dick Wellstood (p), Red Balaban (b), Skip Tomlinson (d)

Beale Street Blues   Fat Cat's Jazz FCJ 172

Davern not on other titles.

Swinging the Soprano

Manassas, Virginia, November 30—December 1, 1973
Kenny Davern, George Probert (ss); Dick Wellstood (p); George "Butch" Hall (g); Billy Goodall (b); Cliff Leeman (d)

Lady Be Good   Fat Cat's Jazz FCJ 155
Apex Blues
I Would Do Most Anything for You

Kenny Davern (ss), Dick Wellstood (p)

Liza

Kenny Fulcher (tp), Bill Allred (tb), Kenny Davern (ss), Dick Wellstood (p), Red Balaban (b), Skip Tomlinson (d)

I Found a New Baby

Davern not on other titles.

The Mighty Driving Horn at Manassas

Manassas, Virginia, November 30—December 2, 1973
Ernie Carson (c); Bill Allred, Bill Rank, Al Winters (tb); Jack Maheu, Herb Hall (cl); Kenny Davern, George Probert (ss); Spencer Clark (bassax), Claude Hopkins, Bob Hirsch, Art Hodes (p); George Hall (g); Van Perry, Stan Booth (b); Bill Goodall (ele-b); Cliff Leeman, Roger Davidson (d) (collective personnel)

Battle Hymn of the Republic   Fat Cat Jazz FCJ 164
Jelly Roll
Clarinet Marmalade

Davern not on other titles.

Doc Evans Is Back: Manassas Memories 1973

Manassas, Virginia, December 2, 1973

Danny Williams (tb), Tommy Gwaltney (cl), Kenny Davern (ss), Dick Wellstood (p), Van Perry (b), George Hall (g), Cliff Leeman (d)

Song of the Wanderer   Fat Cat's Jazz FCJ 163
I Found a New Baby

Davern not on other titles.

Natalie Lamb Wails the Blues

Manassas, Virginia, December 2, 1973

Kenny Davern (ss), Art Hodes (p), Jerry Addicott (bj), Van Perry (b), Bob Thompson (d), Natalie Lamb (vo)

If You Lose Your Money Blues   Fat Cat Jazz FCJ 152
Got Me Goin' and Close

Davern not on other titles.

The Golden Horn Speaks: Jazz in Memoriam

Manassas, Virginia, December 2, 1973

Doc Evans (tp), Danny Williams (tb), Tommy Gwaltney (cl), Kenny Davern (ss), Dick Wellstood (p), George "Butch" Hall (g), Van Perry (b), Cliff Leeman (d)

Louisiana   Fat Cat Jazz FCJ 178
Tishomongo Blues

Davern not on other titles.

Dick Hyman, *Some Rags, Some Stomps, and a Little Blues;* Ferdinand "Jelly Roll" Morton

New York, December 3, 1973

Mel Davis, Joe Wilder, Pee Wee Erwin (tp); Vic Dickenson, Paul Falise (tb); Phil Bodner (pic, fl, cl); Kenny Davern (cl, ss); Jim Buffington, Ray

Alonge (frh); Don Hammond or Harvey Estrin (fl); Dick Hyman (p); Tony Mottola (g, bj); Don Butterfield (tu); Milt Hinton (b); Panama Francis (d); Phil Krause (perc)

Grandpa's Spells   Columbia M 32587   CBS (UK) 61666
Black Bottom Stomp
Buddy Bolden's Blues

Mel Davis, Joe Wilder, Pee Wee Erwin (tp); Urbie Green, Mickey Gravine (tb); Phil Bodner (pic, fl, as); Kenny Davern (cl); Jim Buffington (frh); Don Hammond or Harvey Estrin (fl); Dick Hyman (p); Art Ryerson (g, bj); Don Butterfield (tu); Milt Hinton (b); Panama Francis (d); Phil Krause (perc)

The Crave
Pep
The Pearls

December 11, 1973

Mel Davis, Pee Wee Erwin (tp); Urbie Green (tb); Phil Bodner (pic, fl, cl); Kenny Davern (cl, ss); Dick Hyman (p); Tony Mottola (g, bj); Don Butterfield (tu); Milt Hinton (b); Panama Francis (d)

Fickle Fay Creep
Mr. Jelly Lord
King Porter Stomp

Davern not on other cuts. Also on Sony CD, MDK 52552, titled "The Music of Jelly Roll Morton and James P. Johnson." Davern is not on the James P. Johnson cuts.

Soprano Summit

New York, December 17, 21, 22, 1973

Kenny Davern (cl, ss), Bob Wilber (cl, ss), Dick Hyman (p), Bucky Pizzarelli (g, bj), Milt Hinton or George Duvivier (b), Bobby Rosengarden (d)

Swing Parade   World Jazz WJLP S-5
Egyptian Fantasy
Johnny Was There
Penny Rag
The Mooche

Where Are We
Please Clarify
Song of Songs
Oh Sister, Ain't That Hot*
Stealin' Away*
The Fish Vendor*
Meet Me Tonight in Dreamland*

Milt Hinton on asterisked titles.
*Also issued on World Jazz WJCD-5/13, which also includes the sessions from May 5, 1974 and December 9, 1977.

Soprano Summit II

New York, May 5, 1974

Kenny Davern (cl, ss), Bob Wilber (cl, ss), Dick Hyman (p), Bucky Pizzarelli (g, bj), Milt Hinton (b), Bobby Rosengarden (d)

Solace I   World Jazz WJLP S-13
Solace II
Tango a la Caprice
Sun Flower Slow Drag

Balance of this album recorded on December 9, 1977. This album and the Soprano Summit sessions of December, 1973, were released on World Jazz WJCD 5/13. Both cuts of "Solace" were released on WJS-S-12, a 45-rpm single.

Satchmo Remembered, The Music of Louis Armstrong at Carnegie Hall

New York, November 8, 1974

Ruby Braff (c); Mel Davis, Pee Wee Erwin, Joe Newman, Ray Nance (tp); Vic Dickenson, Eph Resnick (tb); Kenny Davern (cl, ss); Dick Hyman (p); Carmen Mastren (bj); Milt Hinton (b); Bobby Rosengarden (d); William Russell (v); Carrie Smith (vo)

St. Louis Tickle   Atlantic SD 1671
Creole Belles

Pee Wee Erwin, Mel Davis, Ray Nance, Joe Newman (tp); Eph Resnick, Vic Dickenson (tb); Kenny Davern (cl); Dick Hyman (p); Milt Hinton (b); Bobby Rosengarden (d); Carmen Mastren (bass drum)

Flee as a Bird/Oh Didn't He Ramble

Pee Wee Erwin, Mel Davis, Joe Newman (tp); Eph Resnick (tb); Kenny Davern (cl); Dick Hyman (p); Milt Hinton (b); Bobby Rosengarden (d)

Chimes Blues

Pee Wee Erwin, Mel Davis, Joe Newman (tp); Vic Dickenson (tb); Kenny Davern (ss); Dick Hyman (p); Carmen Mastren (bj); Milt Hinton (b); Bobby Rosengarden (d); Carrie Smith (vo)

Cake Walking Babies from Home

Pee Wee Erwin, Mel Davis, Joe Newman (tp); Vic Dickenson (tb); Kenny Davern (cl); Dick Hyman (p); Carmen Mastren (bj); Milt Hinton (b); Bobby Rosengarden (d); Carrie Smith (vo)

Potato Head Blues

Pee Wee Erwin, Mel Davis, Joe Newman (tp); Vic Dickenson (tb); Kenny Davern (cl); Dick Hyman (p); Carmen Mastren (g); Milt Hinton (b); Bobby Rosengarden (d); Carrie Smith (vo)

Willie the Weeper

Ruby Braff (c), Vic Dickenson (tb), Kenny Davern (ss), Dick Hyman (p), Carmen Mastren (g), Milt Hinton (b), Bobby Rosengarden (d)

Big Butter and Egg Man

Pee Wee Erwin, Mel Davis, Joe Newman (tp); Vic Dickenson (tb); Kenny Davern (cl); Dick Hyman (p); Carmen Mastren (bj); Milt Hinton (b); Bobby Rosengarden (d)

S.O.L. Blues

Davern not on other titles.

The Kings of Jazz
Stockholm, Sweden, December 8–9, 1974

Pee Wee Erwin, Bernie Privin (tp); Ed Hubble (tb); Kenny Davern (ss); Johnny Mince (cl); Dick Hyman (p); Major Holley (b); Cliff Leeman (d)

Royal Garden Blues   Arbors ARCD 19267
Rosetta
Someday You'll Be Sorry/
    When Did You Leave Heaven
Sweet Georgia Brown
Black and Tan Fantasy
Indiana
Dear Old Southland
Savoy Blues
Fingerbuster
Buddy Bolden's Blues
Oh Sister, Ain't That Hot (Davern [cl], Mince [as])
Love Is Just Around the Corner

Hanover, West Germany, December 13, 1974

Wild Man Blues

Davern not on other title. "Wild Man Blues" also on Previews 2003, a sampler CD entitled "Arbors Records Previews 2003."

The Soprano Summit in 1975 and More
Martinsville Inn, Bridgewater, New Jersey, April 20, 1975

Kenny Davern (cl, ss), Bob Wilber (cl, ss), Marty Grosz (g, bj, vo), George Duvivier (b), Connie Kay (d)

Swing Parade   Arbors ARCD 19328
The Mooche
Oh Sister, Ain't That Hot
Steal Away
Linger Awhile
Panama

Song of Songs
Swing 39
Egyptian Fantasy
The Fish Vendor

Add Dick Hyman (p)

Kansas City Stomps
Original Jelly Roll Blues
Froggie Moore Rag
Shreveport Stomp
Sidewalk Blues

Soprano Summit III

New York, April 23–25, 1975

Kenny Davern (cl, ss), Bob Wilber (cl, ss), Marty Grosz (g, bj, vo), George Duvivier (b), Connie Kay (d)

Frog-I-More Rag	World Jazz WJLP S25C (cassette only)

Japansy
Swing 39
Once in a While
Milenberg Joys
Rose of the Rio Grande
Oriental Strut
How Can You Face Me
I Had It But It's All Gone Now
Panama

The Second Time Around, The Red Norvo Combo

New York, June 23, 1975

Red Norvo (vib), Kenny Davern (ss), Dave McKenna (p), Milt Hinton (b), Mousey Alexander (d)

Lover Come Back to Me	Famous Door 108	Progressive PCD 7121

Santa Monica Blues*
When You're Smiling
Exactly Like You
Lover Come Back to Me
   (alternate take)*

Lover Come Back to Me (additional alternate take)*
Santa Monica Blues (alternate take)*
Santa Monica Blues (additional alternate take)*

*Alternate takes are on CD only. Titled "A Long One for Santa Monica" on the LP issue. Davern not on other titles.

Jersey Jazz at Midnight

Chester, New Jersey, December 31, 1975

Warren Vache, Jr. (c), Ed Hubble (tb), Kenny Davern (cl), John Bunch (p), Marty Grosz (g), Warren Vache, Sr. (b), Jackie Williams (d)

Auld Lang Syne/The World Is Waiting for the Sunrise   Jersey Jazz JJ 1002
If I Could Be with You
Apex Blues
Fidgety Feet
I'll Be a Friend with Pleasure/Ain't Misbehavin'/
Song of the Wanderer/Honeysuckle Rose
South

Soprano Summit

New York, February 29, 1976

Kenny Davern (cl, ss), Bob Wilber (cl, ss), Marty Grosz (g, bj, vo), George Duvivier (b), Fred Stoll (d)

Lover Come Back to Me   Chiaroscuro CR(D) 148
Nagasaki
Everybody Loves My Baby
Georgia Cabin
Song of the Wanderer

Balance of this CD includes sessions of March 30, 1976 and September 12, 1977.

Blown Bone

New York, March 27, 1976

Roswell Rudd (tb, marimba, percussion), Steve Lacy (ss, percussion), Kenny Davern (cl, ss), Tyrone Washington (ts), Patti Bown (el, p), Wilbur Little (b), Paul Motian (d)

Blown Bone   Philips (Jpn) RJ 7490   Emanem 4131
Cement Blues (add
  Louisiana Red [g, vo])
Street Walking
Bethesda Fountain (add
  Jordan Stecket [batra d])

Davern not on other titles.

Soprano Summit, Chalumeau Blue

New York, March 30, 1976

Kenny Davern (cl, ss), Bob Wilber (cl, ss), Marty Grosz (g, bj, vo), George Duvivier (b), Fred Stoll (d)

Nagasaki   Chiaroscuro CR 148   CR(D) 148
Chalumeau Blue
Black and Tan Fantasy
Granadilla Stomp
Danny Boy
Everybody Loves My Baby
Linger Awhile
Slightly Under the Weather
Wake Up, Chillen
Ole Miss
Debut
Some of These Days

Also issued on Pye NSPL 28226. Chiaroscuro CRD 148 includes sessions of February 29, 1976 and September 12, 1977.

Soprano Summit, Live at the Big Horn Jazzfest

Mundelein, Illinois, May 30, 1976

Kenny Davern (cl, ss), Bob Wilber (cl, ss), Marty Grosz (g), Milt Hinton (b), Fred Stoll (d)

Swing Parade   Jazzology J 56
Black and Tan Fantasy
A Porter's Love Song to a Chambermaid

Ole Miss
Granadilla Stomp
Song of Songs

May 31, 1976

I Had It But Its All Gone Now
Swing That Music

Soprano Summit, In Concert

Concord, California, July 30, 1976

Kenny Davern (cl, ss), Bob Wilber (cl, ss), Marty Grosz (g), Ray Brown (b), Jake Hanna (d)

Stompy Jones   Concord CCD 4019
The Grapes Are Ready
Sequin Gown (Spoken intro by Davern)
Doin' the New Lowdown
The Golden Rooster
Moxie
Brother, Can You Spare a Dime
All by Myself
Swing That Music

Soprano Summit at Thatchers

Surrey, England, October 26, 1976

Kenny Davern (cl, ss), Bob Wilber (cl, ss), Dave Cliff (g), Peter Ind (b), Lennie Hastings (d)

Meet Me Tonight in Dreamland   J&MCD 501   Jazzology JCD 295
The Mooche
Ole Miss
Oriental Strut
Stealin' Away
Oh Sister, Ain't That Hot
Old Stack O'Lee Blues
Swing 39
I Had It But Its All Gone Now
Grenadilla Stomp

The Jazzology CD is titled "Soprano Summit—Live in England."

Soprano Summit at the Illiana Jazz Club
Chicago, November 7, 1976

Kenny Davern (cl, ss), Bob Wilber (cl, ss), Marty Grosz (g), Eddie DeHaas (b), Bob Cousins (d)

Song of Songs	Storyville STCD 8254
Stompy Jones	
Black and Tan Fantasy	
How Can You Face Me	
Egyptian Fantasy	
I Wish I Were Twins	
I Had It, But Its All Gone Now	
Grenadilla Stomp	
Meet Me Tonight in Dreamland	
The Mooche	
Chalumeau Blues	

Cathy Chamberlain: *Rag 'N Roll Revue*
New York, November 19, 1976

Warren Vache, Jr. (c), Kenny Davern (ss), Rich Look (p), Elliott Randall (g), Bob Stewart (tu), Kash Monet (d), Cathy Chamberlain (vo), Rich Look, Linda November, Vivian Cherry, Gwen Guthrie, Arlene Marshall (background vo)

Debbie's Song   Warner Bros. BS 3032

Warren Vache, Jr. (c), Kenny Davern (ss), Rich Look (p), Elliott Randall (g), Howard Johnson (tu), Freddie Moore (d), Cathy Chamberlain (vo), Rich Look, Freddie Moore (background vo)

Rag 'n Roll

Warren Vache, Jr. (c), Kenny Davern (ss), Rich Look (p), Howard Johnson (tu), Freddie Moore (d, vo)

Ol' Rockin' Chair

Warren Vache, Jr. (c), Kenny Davern (cl), Rich Look (p), Bob Stewart (tu). Kash Monet(d), Cathy Chamberlain (vo, concertina)

See Her Run

Warren Vache, Jr. (c), Kenny Davern (ss), Rich Look (p), Elliott Randall (g), Bob Stewart (tu), Cathy Chamberlain (vo)

Mack the Knife

Warren Vache, Jr. (c), Kenny Davern (ss), Rich Look (p), Elliott Randall (g), Neil Jason (b), Kash Monet (d), Cathy Chamberlain (vo), Rich Look, Linda November, Vivian Cherry, Gwen Guthrie, Arlene Marshall (background vo)

Epigrams

Warren Vache, Jr. (c), Kenny Davern (ss), Rich Look (p), David Bromberg (g), Milt Hinton (b), Freddie Moore (d), Cathy Chamberlain (vo), Rich Look (background vo)

Cement Dry

Warren Vache, Jr. (c), Jack Gale (tb), Kenny Davern (ss), Rich Look (p), Howard Johnson (tu), Freddie Moore (d), Cathy Chamberlain (vo)

He May Be Your Man (But He Comes to See Me Sometime)

Warren Vache, Jr. (c), Kenny Davern (ss), Rich Look (p), Elliott Randall (g), Neil Jason (b), Kash Monet (d), Cathy Chamberlain (vo), Rich Look, Cathy Chamberlain (background vo)

Backseat Baby

Davern not on other title.

First Time Out

New York, November 22, 1976

Warren Vache (c), Kenny Davern (ss), Bucky Pizzarelli (g), Wayne Wright (g), Michael Moore (b), Connie Kay (d)

Oh Baby	Monmouth Evergreen MES 7081
I Surrender Dear	

Song of the Wanderer
All of Me

Davern not on other titles. Also issued on Audiophile AP 196 and Audiophile ACD 196 entitled "First Time Out and Encore A93."

Odessa, Sound of Jazz, Vol. 1

Odessa Texas, May 17, 1977

Bob Wilber (cl, ss), Kenny Davern (cl, ss), Bucky Pizzarelli (g), Milt Hinton (b), Jake Hanna (d)

Black and Tan Fantasy   Odessa Jazz OS 1001

Davern not on other titles.

Soprano Summit, Live at Concord '77

Concord, California, August 5, 1977

Kenny Davern (cl, ss), Bob Wilber (cl, ss), Marty Grosz (g), Monty Budwig (b), Jake Hanna (d)

Strike up the Band   Concord CJ 52   CCD 4052
Puggles
Elsa's Dream
How Can You Face Me
Dreaming Butterfly
Tracks in the Snow
Lament
The Panic Is On
Panama Rag

Soprano Summit, Crazy Rhythm

New York, September 12, 1977

Kenny Davern (cl, ss, c-mel), Bob Wilber (cl, ss, as), Marty Grosz (g), George Duvivier (b), Bobby Rosengarden (d)

Prince of Wails   Chiaroscuro CR 178   CRD 148
Netcha's Dream
Oh Daddy

When Day Is Done
When My Dreamboat Comes Home
There'll Be Some Changes Made
I'd Climb the Highest Mountain
Wequasset Wail
Arkansas Lullaby
Crazy Rhythm

CRD 148 includes the sessions from February 29, 1976, and March 30, 1976.

John and Joe: The Kenny Davern–Flip Phillips Quartet
New York, October 23, 1977
Kenny Davern (cl, ss, c-mel), Flip Phillips (ts, ss, bass cl), Dave McKenna (p), George Duvivier (b), Bobby Rosengarden (d)

Elsa's Dream	Chiaroscuro CR 199
Sweet Lorraine	
Mood Indigo	
If Dreams Come True	
Just Squeeze Me	
Candy	
Cottontail	

Soprano Summit
Manassas, Virginia, December 3, 1977
Kenny Davern (cl, ss), Bob Wilber (cl, ss), Marty Grosz (g, vo), Steve Novosel (b), Tommy Benford (d)

Meet Me Tonight in Dreamland	Fat Cat Jazz FCJ 208
I Had It But Its all Gone Now	Fat Cat Jazz FCJ 184
I Wish I Were Twins	"
Old Stack-O-Lee Blues	"
I Want to Be Happy	"

Soprano Summit
Manassas, Virginia, December 4, 1977
Kenny Davern (cl, ss), Bob Wilber (cl, ss), Marty Grosz (g, vo), Steve Novosel (b), Tommy Benford (d)

The Mooche	Fat Cat's Jazz FCJ 184
Oh Sister, Ain't That Hot	Fat Cat's Jazz FCJ 221
Song of Songs	Fat Cat's Jazz FCJ 208

Soprano Summit

Manassas, Virginia, December 4, 1977

Kenny Davern (ss), Bob Wilber (ss), Jacques Kerrien (ss), Mason Thomas (cl), Dick Wellstood (p), Marty Grosz (g), Van Perry (b), Skip Tomlinson (d)

Buddy Bolden's Blues	Fat Cat's Jazz FCJ 184
Sweet Georgia Brown	"

FCJ 184 is entitled "The Meridian," FCJ 208 is "Song of Songs," and FCJ 221 is "Oh Sister, Ain't That Hot." FCJ 221 issued as a cassette only.

Soprano Summit II

New York, December 9, 1977

Kenny Davern (cl, ss), Bob Wilber (cl, ss), Dick Hyman (p), Bucky Pizzarelli (g, bj), George Duvivier (b), Tommy Benford (d)

Frog-I-More Rag	World Jazz WJLP S-13
If You Went Away	
Lincoln Garden Stomp	
Sidewalk Blues	
Creole Nights	
Rialto Ripples	

WJLP S-13 includes the session of May 5, 1974. This session, together with the sessions of December 12, 1973, and May 5, 1974, were issued on WJCD 5/13.

Bacharach Revisited

New York, circa 1978

Ed Hubble (tb), Kenny Davern (ss, cl), Dick Wellstood (p), Jack Six (b), Joe Cocuzzo (d), Manny Senerchia (v), Karl Savran (viola), Winston Brown (viola), Ruth Linsley (cello)

Blue on Blue	Music Minus One MMO 1056
Walk on By	

Magic Moments
The Windows of the World (Wellstood)
Do You Know the Way to Go to San Jose

Davern does not appear on the balance of the recording. Released on a Pocket Songs label CD as "Sing the Songs of Bacharach and David" PS CDG 1266.

Unexpected

New York, May 30, 1978
Kenny Davern (cl, ss), Steve Lacy (ss), Steve Swallow (b, g), Paul Motian (percussion)

Swirls   Kharma FR7
Trio 3
The Sunflower
Predicament in Three Parts
Synonym
Statement
Loops
Unexpected

Wild Bill Davison and Kenny Davern at the King of France Tavern

Annapolis, Maryland, August 20, 1978
Wild Bill Davison (c), Kenny Davern (cl, ss), Larry Eanet (p), Carlos Laguana (b), Eddie Phyfe (d)

On the Alamo   Fat Cat's Jazz FCJ 187
Song of the Wanderer
Our Love Is Here to Stay
I Never Knew
If I Had You
My Monday Date
On the Sunny Side of the Street
Rosetta

Swinging at the Elks': Billy Butterfield and His World Class Jazz Band

Manassas, Virginia, December 1, 1978

Billy Butterfield (tp), Spiegel Willcox (tb), Kenny Davern (cl), Spencer Clark (bassax), Dick Wellstood (p), Marty Grosz (g), Van Perry (b), Tony DeNicola (d)

I Want to Be Happy	Fat Cat's Jazz FCJ 209
Sweet Sue	
I Cried for You	
I Can't Get Started	
China Boy	
Someday Sweetheart	

Soprano Summit

Manassas, Virginia, December 1, 1978

Kenny Davern (cl, ss), Bob Wilber (cl, ss, as), Marty Grosz (g, vo), Van Perry (b), Tony De Nicola (d)

Changes	Fat Cat's Jazz FCJ 221
Everybody Loves My Baby	
Apex Blues	
Jazz Me Blues	
Oh Sister, Ain't That Hot	
Lady Be Good	
Black and Blue	Fat Cat's Jazz FCJ 208
Two Sleepy People	
You're Not the Only Oyster in the Stew	
Ain't Misbehavin'	

FCJ 208 is titled "Song of Songs" and FCJ 221 is titled "Oh, Sister, Ain't That Hot." FCJ 221 issued as a cassette only. These issues contain other titles on which Davern is not present.

The Free-Swinging Trio in the Jazz Tradition

Manassas, Virginia, December 2, 1978

Kenny Davern (cl), Dick Wellstood (p), Cliff Leeman (d)

Maple Leaf Rag	Fat Cat's Jazz FCJ 207
Fidgety Feet	
Yellow Dog Blues	
That's a Plenty	
Sweet Substitute	

The balance of FCJ 207 was recorded on December 2, 1979.

Soprano Summit

Manassas, Virginia, December 3, 1978

Kenny Davern (cl, ss), Bob Wilber (cl, ss, as), Marty Grosz (g, vo), Van Perry (b), Tony De Nicola (d)

Stompy Jones	Fat Cat's Jazz FCJ 208
Caravan	

After Hours at Art's Place, Vol. 2

Minneapolis, March 2–6, 1979

Kenny Davern (cl), Art Hodes (p), Truck Parham (b), George "Red" Maddock (d)

C. C. Rider	Jazzology BVD 4 (DVD)
My Blue Heaven	(Spoken segment with Davern and Hodes)
Apex Blues	(Spoken segment with Davern and Hodes)
Wild Man Blues	
That's a Plenty	
Hodes' closing remarks	

The Soprano Summit in 1975 and More

Somerset-Marriott Hotel, Somerset, New Jersey, March 23, 1979

The Blue Three: Kenny Davern (cl), Dick Wellstood (p), Bobby Rosengarden (d)

C. C. Rider   Arbors ARCD 19328
Fidgety Feet
Sweet Substitute
Shim-Me-Sha-Wabble

Dick Wellstood and His Famous Orchestra

King of France Tavern, Maryland Inn,
Annapolis, Maryland, March 30–April 1, 1979
Kenny Davern (cl), Dick Wellstood (p), Freddie Kohlman (d, vo)

My Daddy Rocks Me   Fat Cat's Jazz FCJ 240
Wellstood Wanderings
Tin Roof Blues
Three Little Words
That Da Da Strain
See See Rider
My Blue Heaven
Handful of Keys
I Would Do Most Anything for You

Kenny Davern and His Famous Orchestra

King of France Tavern, Maryland Inn,
Annapolis, Maryland, March 30–April 1, 1979
Kenny Davern (cl), Dick Wellstood (p), Freddie Kohlman (d, vo)

Shake It and Break It   Fat Cat's Jazz FCJ 239
Black and Blue
Shout 'em Aunt Tillie
Mood Indigo
Lullaby of the Leaves
Birth of the Blues
Ellington Medley
Beale Street Blues

Lino Patruno TV Jazz Show Featuring Kenny Davern

Milan, May 8, 1979
Kenny Davern (cl), Sante Palumbo (p), Lino Patruno (g), Marco Rath (b), Carlo Sola (d)

C. C. Rider					Know How Int. 505
Some of These Days			Know How Int. 586

Kenny Davern (cl), Carlo Bagnoli (ss), Lino Patruno (g), Marco Rath (b), Carlo Sola (d)

Cakewalking Babies from Home		Know How Int. 504

Gianni Acocella (tb), Kenny Davern (cl), Carlo Bagnoli (ss), Sante Palumbo (p), Marco Rath (b), Carlo Sola (d)

Mood Indigo

Georgio Alberti (c), Gianni Acocella (tb), Kenny Davern (cl), Bruno Longhi (cl), Carlo Bagnoli (bar), Sante Palumbo (p), Marco Rath (b), Carlo Sola (d)

Sweet Georgia Brown

Kenny Davern (cl), Bruno Longhi (cl), Sante Palumbo (p), Marco Rather (b), Carlo Sola (d)

Lullaby of the Leaves

Davern not on other titles.

Live at the Louisiana Club
Genoa, Italy, May 10, 1979
Kenny Davern (cl), Riccardo Zegna (p), Luciano Milanese (b), Roberto Gargani (d)

Sweet Georgia Brown			FDC Records, FDC 3002

Kenny Davern, The Hot Three
Annapolis, Maryland, July 1, 1979
Kenny Davern (cl), Art Hodes (p), Don DeMicheal (d)

Fidgety Feet				Monmouth-Evergreen MES 7091
Chimes Blues
Shim-Me-Sha-Wabble

Liberty Inn
Some of These Days
Ballin' the Jack
See See Rider
It Don't Mean a Thing (If It Ain't Got That Swing)
Tennessee Waltz
My Blue Heaven

Lou Stein and Friends

New York, July 26, 1979

Kenny Davern (cl), Lou Stein (p), Bucky Pizzarelli (g), Milt Hinton (b), Connie Kay (d)

The Sweetest Sounds   World Jazz WJLP S 17
A Fine Romance
What Is This Thing Called Love
Let's Face the Music and Dance

Davern not on other titles.

The Free-Swinging Trio in the Jazz Tradition

Manassas, Virginia, December 2, 1979

Kenny Davern (cl), Dick Wellstood (p), Cliff Leeman (d)

Wild Man Blues   Fat Cat's Jazz FCJ 207
Eccentric Rag

The balance of FCJ 207 was recorded on December 1, 1978.

Ralph Sutton and Kenny Davern, Vol. I

Northampton, New Hampshire, December 12–13, 1979

Kenny Davern (cl), Ralph Sutton (p), Gus Johnson (d)

That's a Plenty   Chaz Jazz CJ 105
Jazz Me Blues
Gus Que Raf*
Black and Blue
Take Me to the Land of Jazz

My Honey's Lovin' Arms
Sweet Lorraine
Memphis Blues
I Would Do Anything for You

This album and Volume II (next entry) combined and issued on Chiaroscuro CR(D) 208.
*Title was omitted from the CD.

Ralph Sutton and Kenny Davern, Vol. II

St. Louis Blues   Chaz Jazz CJ 106
Am I Blue
All by Myself
A Porter's Love Song to a Chambermaid
Old Fashioned Love
Tain't Nobody's Business
My Daddy Rocks Me

World's Greatest Jazz Band

Freemantle, Australia, December 28, 1979

Yank Lawson (tp), George Masso (tb), Kenny Davern (cl), Eddie Miller (ts), Lou Stein (p), Bob Haggart (b), Bobby Rosengarden (d)

When the Saints Go Marchin' In   Synapse (Aus) 3 (cassette)
Mandy Make Up Your Mind
Hindustan
Basin Street Blues
St. Louis Blues
My Daddy Rocks Me

December 29, 1979

Do You Know What It Means   Synapse (Aus) 5 (cassette)
  to Miss New Orleans
Can't We Be Friends
Unidentified tune
What's New
There'll Never Be Another You
At the Jazz Band Ball
Everybody Loves My Baby

Oh Baby
I Found a New Baby
Hindustan
Tea for Two

December 30, 1979

Caravan Synapse (Aus) 8 (Cassette)
When the Saints Go Marchin' In
Tin Roof Blues
Stumblin'
South Rampart Street Parade
Sophisticated Lady
Sometimes I'm Happy
Lover Man

Davern not on other titles.

Pee Wee Erwin, Classic Jazz in Hollywood

Hollywood, California, May 26–27, 1980
Pee Wee Erwin (tp), Bob Havens (tb), Kenny Davern (cl), Eddie Miller (ts), Dick Cary (p), Ray Leatherwood (b), Nick Fatool (d)

Farewell Blues Quatro QM 101
Naughty Sweetie Blues
There'll Be Some Changes Made
Hindustan
Bye Bye Blues
Old Fashioned Love
Rose Room
It Don't Mean a Thing (If It Ain't
  Got That Swing)

Davern not on other titles.

El Rado Scuffle: A Tribute to Jimmie Noone

Jarfalia, Sweden June 7, 1980
Kenny Davern (cl), Bent Persson (tp), Tomas Ornberg (as), Ulf Lindberg (p), Holger Gross (bj), Bo Juhlin (tu)

El Rado Scuffle Kenneth KS 2050
Apex Blues
You Rascal You
Tight Like That
My Monday Date
My Daddy Rocks Me
Shine
Oh Sister, Ain't That Hot
Trouble in Mind
A Porter's Love Song to a Chambermaid
Naughty Sweetie Blues

Ralph Sutton and the Jazzband

Minneapolis, February, 1981
Ruby Braff (c), George Masso (tb), Kenny Davern (cl), Bud Freeman (ts), Ralph Sutton (p), Milt Hinton (b), Gus Johnson, Jr. (d)

Struttin with Some Barbecue Chaz Jazz CJ 114
Keepin' Out of Mischief Now
Ain't Misbehavin'
Muskrat Ramble

The Blue Three at Hanratty's

New York, April 14–16, 1981
Kenny Davern (cl), Dick Wellstood (p), Bobby Rosengarden (d)

Original Dixieland One Step Chaz Jazz CJ 109
Don't You Leave Me Here
Tiger Rag
Indiana
Sweet Georgia Brown
Blue Monk
Joshua
Please Don't Talk about Me When I'm Gone
Oh Peter

Also on Chiaroscuro CR(D) 129, which is entitled "Kenny Davern and His All Star Orchestra" and includes all but two titles from the "Kenny Davern and His Famous Orchestra" album of November–December, 1973.

Tomas Ornberg's Blue Five Featuring Kenny Davern

Stockholm, Sweden, April 25, 1981
Tomas Ornberg (ss), Kenny Davern (cl), Hilger Gross (bj), Bo Juhlin (tu)

New Orleans Stomp	Opus 3 8003	Opus CD 8003
Too Busy (take 1)		
Tain't Nobody's Business		
Too Busy (take 2)		
Bienville Blues		
Hot Tamale Man		

Davern not on other titles.

Pee Wee Erwin, A Giant Among Giants

"Turfschip," Breda, Holland, May 28, 1981
Pee Wee Erwin (tp), Ed Hubble (tb), Kenny Davern (cl), Jimmy Andrews (p), Warren Vache, Sr. (b), Johnny Blowers (d)

Savoy Blues	Jazz Crooner (Du)	JC2829581
I Want to Be Happy		
Indiana	" "	JC283581

"Graanpijp," Breda, Holland, May 29, 1981
Nobody's Sweetheart   Jazz Crooner (Du) JC2829581
Rosetta
I Can't Believe That You're in
   Love with Me

Davern not on other titles.

Recovered Treasures: Ruby Braff and His Musical Friends

Wee Burn Country Club, Darien, Connecticut, July 8, 1981
Ruby Braff and the Changing Times All Stars: Ruby Braff (c), Vic Dickenson (tb), Kenny Davern (cl), Al Klink (ts), Ralph Sutton (p), Marty Grosz (g), Jack Lesberg (b), Buzzy Drootin (d)

When You're Smiling   Jump JCD 12-29

Davern not on other titles.

The Great Freddie Moore

Emerson, New Jersey, December 10, 1981

The New York Jazz Repertory Orchestra: Warren Vache, Jr. (tp), Joel Helleny (tb), Kenny Davern (cl), Joe Muranyi (cl, ss), Dill Jones (p), Lew McCallef (g), Eddy Davis (bj), Milt Hinton (b), Freddie Moore (d, vo)

I Got It Bad and That Ain't Good   New York Jazz J-001
Rockin' Chair
Save It Pretty Mama
Rag Alley Blues
Blue Turning Grey over You
Snowball

Davern not on other titles.

Lino Patruno TV Jazz Show,
The ODJB Show Featuring Kenny Davern

Lugano, Italy, October 11–12, 1983

Oscar Klein (c), Roy Crimmins (tb), Kenny Davern (cl), Lino Patruno (g), Isla Eckinger (b), Gregor Beck (d)

Indiana   Domovideo 57851 (videocassette)
At the Jazz Band Ball
Tiger Rag
Satanic Blues
Jazz Me Blues
Original Dixieland One-Step
Singin' the Blues (Crimmins, vo)

Kenny Davern (cl), Isla Eckinger (tb), Oscar Klein (g), Lino Patruno (b), Gregor Beck (d)

Bluin' the Blues/Some of These Days

Davern not on other titles.

Live Hot Jazz

King of France Tavern, Maryland Inn, Annapolis, Maryland, December 18, 1983

Kenny Davern (cl), Dick Wellstood (p), Chuck Riggs (d)

Rose Room	Statiras SLP 8077	Jazzology JCD-177
Travelin' All Alone		
Then You've Never Been Blue		
Oh! Lady Be Good		
Who's Sorry Now		
Wrap Your Troubles in Dreams		
Rosetta		
Beale Street Blues		

Stretchin' Out

The Man I Love	Jazzology JCD-187
Summertime	
Lover, Come Back to Me	
Love Me or Leave Me	
(There Is) No Greater Love	
Chicago Rhythm	

The Gig (Movie)

New York, 1984

Warren Vache (c), Bob Bernard (tp), George Masso (tb), Kenny Davern (cl), Dick Wellstood (p), John Bunch (p), Milt Hinton (b), Reggie Johnson (b), Herb Harris (d)

Got a Lot of Livin' to Do	Castle Hill Productions (videotape)
Gig Blues	
They Blame You	
When the Saints Go Marching In	
My Gal Sal	
La Cucharacha	
My Wild Irish Rose	
Hava Nagila	
After the Ball Is Over	

In the Good Old Summertime
When the Saints Go Marchin' In
Maple Leaf Rag
Somebody Stole My Gal

These are all incomplete segments of songs.

Ralph Sutton and Kenny Davern, *Live at the Thunderbird Lodge; To Elsa and Sunnie with Love*: Thunderbird Lodge, Taos Ski Valley, New Mexico

January 7–9, 1984 and January 7–12, 1985

Kenny Davern (cl), Ralph Sutton (p), Milt Hinton (b), Gus Johnson, Jr. (d)

Lullaby of the Leaves   Victoria VC 4377
Perdido
If I Could Be with You (Sutton Out)
I'm Gonna Sit Right Down and Write Myself a Letter
How Come You Do Me Like You Do
Cherry (Davern Out)*
Beale Street Blues
Exactly Like You
Ain't Misbehavin'
Honeysuckle Rose
Sweet Lorraine
Everybody Loves My Baby
I Got Rhythm
Love Me or Leave Me
My Honey's Lovin' Arms
Please Don't Talk about Me When I'm Gone
Echo of Spring (Sutton solo)
Lover Come Back to Me
Keepin' Out of Mischief Now
New Orleans

The cuts on which Davern does not appear may have been made in January, 1983.
*The pianist on Cherry is definitely not Ralph Sutton. It probably is Tom Brownell, who owned the Thunderbird Lodge.

Never in a Million Years: Jazz from the Vineyard Radio Program

National Public Radio, New York, January 15, 1984

Kenny Davern (cl), Dick Wellstood (p), Dick Sudhalter (moderator)

Oh, Lady Be Good   Challenge 70019
Please Don't Talk
If Dreams Come True (DW solo)
Wellstood Interview
Ellington Medley
The Mooche & Birmingham Breakdown (DW solo)
Summertime
Davern Interview
Mood Indigo (KD solo)
Rosetta

Kenny Davern and the Brian Lemon Trio, *The Very Thought of You*

Wavedon, England, May 7, 1984

Kenny Davern (cl), Brian Lemon (p), Len Skeat (b), Allan Ganley (d)

The Very Thought of You   Milton Keynes Music MKM 841
Don't Get Around Much Anymore
Melancholy Baby
Cherry
Milton Swing
Love Me or Leave Me
What's New
There Is No Greater Love
I Surrender Dear
Keyne on You

Flat Foot Stompers and Friends, Vol. 2

Ludwigsburg, West Germany, October 21, 1984

Ernst Eckstein (c), Roland Muller (tb), Kenny Davern (cl), George Kelly (ts), Peter Buhr (bar), Ralph Sutton (p), Werner Neidhart (bj), Wolfram Grotz (cel), Uli Reichle (sousa), Milt Hinton (b), Uli Fussenhauser (d)

Eccentric Rag   Timeless (Du) TTD 529

Ernst Eckstein (c), Kenny Davern (cl), George Kelly (ts), Peter Buhr (bar), Ralph Sutton (p), Uli Reichle (sousa), Milt Hinton (b), Gus Johnson (d)

Wolverine Blues

Davern not on other titles.

The Humphrey Lyttleton Rhythmakers: *Scatterbrains*
London, December 2, 1984

Humphrey Lyttleton (tp), Kenny Davern (cl), Stan Greig (p), Al Casey (g), Paul Sealey (bj), Paul Bridge (b), Adrian McIntosh (d)

Scatterbrain (Davern out)   Stomp Off SOS 1111
Oh Baby
Yellow Dog Blues
Bugle Call Rag
I Would Do Anything for You
Old Fashioned Love
Fidgety Feet
Shim-Me-Sha-Wabble

The Climax Jazz Band with Kenny Davern
Toronto, April 21, 1985

Bob Erwig (tp), Len Gosling (tb), Mick Lewis, Kenny Davern (cl), Jack Vincken (bj), Chris Daniels (b), Pete McCormick (d)

Ole Miss   Tormax CCO 13 (cassette)
Oh Baby
Jeep's Blues
Bobby Shaftoe
Muskrat Ramble
Mood Indigo
I Want a Girl Just Like the Girl
    That Married Dear Old Dad
Big House Blues
Get Out of Here

Also on CD on Tormax CD032.

Live and Swinging, Kenny Davern and John Petters Swing Band

Essex, England, November 10, 1985

Kenny Davern (cl), Martin Litton (p), Roger Nobes (vib), Keith Donald (b), John Petters (d)

That's a Plenty	CMJ (E) CD001
Love Me or Leave Me	
Blue Monk	
The Man I Love	
Royal Garden Blues	

Makin' Whoopee

It Don't Mean a Thing	Rose Records RRCD 1008
Deed I Do	
Georgia	
Jazz Me Blues	

Davern not on other titles.

Kenny Davern Big Three: *Playing for Kicks*

London, November 24, 1985

Kenny Davern (cl), Martin Litton (p), John Petters (d)

You're Lucky to Me	Jazzology JCD 197	JC 001 (cassette)
Black and Blue		
Willie the Weeper		
Bye Bye Blues		
Sometime's I'm Happy		
New Orleans		
Lullaby of the Leaves		
Dinah		

Davern not on other titles. "You're Lucky to Me" was issued on Jazzology JS-2, a sampler. "Willie the Weeper" was issued on RRMC 1004 as a limited edition cassette entitled "John Petters Meets the International Legends of Traditional Jazz."

This Old Gang of Ours

London, December 10, 1985

Humphrey Lytleton (tp), Kenny Davern (cl), John Barnes (reeds), Martin Litton (p), Mick Hutton (b), Colin Bowden (d)

Mood Hollywood Calligraph CLG LP 012
Jackass Blues
That Old Gang of Mine
Of All the Wrongs You Done to Me
Who's Sorry Now
A Porter's Love Song to a Chambermaid

Also on Upbeat Jazz URCD 138. "My Mama Socks Me" was issued on Calligraph CLGD 031 entitled "A Decade of Calligraph," and in an edited version, called "Sin and Corruption" on an album entitled "Hot Dixieland and Traditional Jazz" on Music Factor TMFCD 1.

Chicago Jazz Summit

New York, June 22, 1986

Randy Sandke, David Brown, Yank Lawson (tp); Joel Helleny (tb); Kenny Davern (cl); Ken Peplowski, Mark Lopeman (ts); Herb Gardner (p); Jim Lawyer (g); Vince Giordano (b, tu, bassax); Arnie Kinsella (d)

Potato Head Blues Atlantic 81844-1 81844-2

Wild Bill Davison (c, vo), George Masso (tb), Kenny Davern (cl), Franz Jackson (ts), Art Hodes (p), Vince Giordano (g), Milt Hinton (b), Barrett Deems (d)

Blue Turning Grey over You
When You're Smiling

Davern not on other titles. 81844-2 is the CD version.

The 1986 Floating Jazz Cruise

Aboard the S.S. Norway, October 19, 1986

Warren Vache (c), George Masso (tb), Kenny Davern (cl), Eddie Higgins (p), Chris Flory (g), Jack Lesberg (b), Mel Lewis (d)

Jazz Me Blues   Chiaroscuro CRD 300

Kenny Davern (cl), Bob Wilber (cl, ss), Howard Alden (g), Phil Flanagan (b), Chuck Riggs (d)

Moonglow

Davern not on other titles.

Mood Indigo

Oslo, Norway, August 9, 1987

Kenny Davern (cl), Flip Phillips (ts), Bjarne Nerem (ts), Egil Kapstad (p), Kare Garnes (b), Jacob Hansen (d)

Mood Indigo   Gemeni GMCD 59
Crazy Rhythm
Squeeze Me
Tin Roof Blues
Jeff's Blues
Embraceable You
Great Scott
If I Had You

One Hour Tonight

New York, December 7–8, 1987

Kenny Davern (cl), Howard Alden (g), Phil Flanigan (b), Giampaolo Biagi (d)

Elsa's Dream   Musicmasters 5003-2-C
Pretty Baby
Comes Love
Love Is the Thing
No One Else but You
Pee Wee's Blues
On with the Dance
Old Folks
Oh Baby
If I Could Be with You

Also on Musicmasters MMD 20148A and CIJD 60148Y. "Love Is the Thing" was issued in the UK on Limelight 820811-2 entitled "Musicmasters Jazz Sampler."

I'll See You in My Dreams

Blue Lou	Musicmasters CIJD 60212L

Sweet and Lovely
Liza
Pee Wee's Blues II
Riverboat Shuffle
Oh Miss Hannah
Melancholy Baby
Royal Garden Blues
Solitude
I'll See You in My Dreams

Also issued in the United Kingdom on Limelight 802839-2.

Kenny Davern Trio Featuring Art Hodes, *The Last Reunion*
London, May 14, 1988
Kenny Davern (cl), Art Hodes (p), Colin Bowden (d)

I Never Knew	Upbeat Jazz URCD 135

There'll Be Some Changes Made
Buddy Bolden's Blues
I Would Do Anything for You
New Orleans
Love Me or Leave Me
After You've Gone
Sometimes I'm Happy
All of Me

Davern not on other titles.

Revelations, Ralph Sutton and Kenny Davern
Adelaide, Australia, August 22, 1988
Kenny Davern (cl), Ralph Sutton (p)

Shine* ** Nif Nuf 43/012
Indiana*
In a Sentimental Mood/Sophisticated Lady/
    Ring Dem Bells (Sutton solo) (Take 1)*
New Orleans (Take 1)*
Three Little Words*
Sugar* **
Should I* **
In a Sentimental Mood/Sophisticated Lady/
    Ring Dem Bells (Sutton solo) (Take 2)
New Orleans (Take 2)
Dinah **

*Also on "Jazz in the Hills" (Aus) A8801 (cassette).
Bill Polain (d) added on entries with two asterisks.

George Shearing in Dixieland
New York, February 14–15, 1989
Warren Vache (c), George Masso (tb), Kenny Davern (cl), Ken Peplowski (ts), George Shearing (p), Neil Swainson (b), Jerry Fuller (d)

Clap Your Hands   Concord CJ 338   Concord CCD 4388
Mighty Like the Blues
Truckin'
Destination Moon
New Orleans
Soon
Take Five
Lullaby of Birdland
Jazz Me Blues
Blue Monk
Desafinado
Alice in Dixieland

Davern not on other titles.

The Legendary Lawson-Haggart Jazz Band, *Jazz at Its Best*
Atlanta, Georgia, February 20, 1989
Yank Lawson (tp), George Masso (tb), Kenny Davern (cl), Al Klink (ts), John Bunch (p), Bucky Pizzarelli (g), Bob Haggart (b), Jake Hanna (d)

Yellow Dog Blues   Jazzology JCD 183
Wolverine Blues
Squeeze Me
Blue Lou
Willow Weep for Me
Bourbon Street Parade
Jazz Me Blues
Lonesome Yank
Mandy Make Up Your Mind
Yellow Dog Blues (alternate take)
Wolverine Blues (alternate take)
Blue Lou (alternate take)

"Jazz Me Blues" was also issued on Jazzology JS-2, a sampler.

Barbara Lea and the Legendary Lawson-Haggart Jazz Band, *You're the Cats*

Atlanta, Georgia, February 21, 1989

Yank Lawson (tp), George Masso (tb), Kenny Davern (cl), Al Klink (ts), John Bunch (p), Bucky Pizzarelli (g), Bob Haggart (b), Jake Hanna (d), Barbara Lea (vo)

You're the Cats   Audiophile ACD 252
True Blue Lou
For You, for Me, for Evermore
Waiting at the End of the Road
Dixie Cinderella
I'm Building Up to an Awful Letdown
I Was Doing All Right
My Walking Stick

Davern not on other titles.

Milt Hinton, *The Basement Tapes*

New York, June 23, 1989

Kenny Davern (cl), Howard Alden (g), Milt Hinton (b), Jackie Williams (d)

Old Man Time   Chiaroscuro CR(D) 222
Summertime
Travelin' All Alone

Davern not on other titles.

Wolverines Jazz Band and Their American Friends
Bern, Switzerland, May 11, 1990
Hans Zurbrugg (tp), Rudolf Knopfel (tb), Kenny Davern (cl), Bert Uhlmann (cl, ss, ts), Heinz Geissbuhler (p), Walter Sterchi (bj, g), Fred Luthi (b), Christian Ott (d)

Mood Indigo   WJB (Swiss) CD P19.193
Panama Rag
As Long as I Live
C. C. Rider
Blue Monk
Please Don't Talk about Me When I'm Gone

Warren Vache (c), Kenny Davern (cl), Heinz Geissbuhler (p), Fred Luthi (b), Jake Hanna (d)

Comes Love
Pretty Baby

Davern not on other titles.

Soundtrack of Bix: An Interpretation of a Legend
Rome, May 14, 1990
Fabrizio Cattaneo (c), David Sager (tb), Kenny Davern (cl), Fabiano Pellini (ts), Keith Nichols (p), Lino Patruno (bj), Vince Giordano (b), Walter Ganda (d)

Maple Leaf Rag   RCA PL 74766 (LP)
Tin Roof Blues

May 15, 1990
Tom Pletcher (c), David Sager (tb), Kenny Davern (cl), Eric Daniel (as), Bob Wilber (c-mel), Keith Nichols (p), Lino Patruno (bj), Vince Giordano (b), Walter Ganda (d)

Singin the Blues I

Patruno's guitar was dubbed in on June 18.

May 15, 17, 1990
Tom Pletcher (c), Al Covini, Claudio Covini (tp), David Sager (tb), Kenny Davern (cl), Eric Daniel (as), Bob Wilber (c-mel), Fabiano Pellini (ts), Keith Nichols (p), Lino Patruno (bj), Vince Giordano (b), Walter Ganda (d), Andy Stein (v)

My Pretty Girl

Also on CD on RCA PD 74766 (CD).

Summit Reunion
Englewood Cliffs, New Jersey, May 30–31, 1990
Kenny Davern (cl), Bob Wilber (ss), Dick Hyman (p), Bucky Pizzarelli (g), Milt Hinton (b), Bobby Rosengarden (d)

As Long as I Live	Chiaroscuro CRD 311
Lover Come Back to Me	
St. Louis Blues	
Black and Blue	
Should I	
(Leena Was the Queen of) Palesteena	
Old Fashioned Love	
On the Sunny Side of the Street	
Limehouse Blues	
Jazzspeak	

A Chiaroscuro Christmas

It Came Upon a Midnight Clear	Chiaroscuro CR(D) 332

Davern not on other titles on Christmas CD.

Introducing Alain Bouchet

New York, June 5, 1990
Alain Bouchet (tp), Kenny Davern (cl), John Bunch (p), Howard Alden (g), Major Holley (b), Jackie Williams (d)

Sugar   Audiophile JCD 192
Black and Blue
I Can't Believe That You're in Love
  with Me (add Warren Vache, Jr. [c])

Davern not on other titles.

Art Hodes, The Final Sessions

Toronto, July 30, 1990
Kenny Davern (cl), Jim Galloway (ss), Art Hodes (p)

Old Grey Bonnet   Music and Arts CD 782
Melancholy Baby
In the Shade of the Old Apple Tree
Swanee River
Summertime (Galloway out)

Davern not on other titles.

Scott Hamilton—Kenny Davern Quintet

Brecon, Wales, U.K., August 17, 1990
Scott Hamilton (ts), Kenny Davern (cl), Howard Alden (g), Leonard Gaskin (b), Giampaolo Biagi (d)

Elsa's Dream   Peerless Productions BPVC 001 (videotape)
The Man I Love
How Long Has This Been
  Going On
After You've Gone
Summertime
Hindustan
Mood Indigo

The Legendary Lawson–Haggart Jazz Band: With a Southern Accent

Atlanta, Georgia, March 5, 1991
Yank Lawson (tp), George Masso (tb), Kenny Davern (cl), John Bunch (p), Bucky Pizzarelli (g), Bob Haggart (b), Jake Hanna (d)

Sweet Georgia Brown	Jazzology JCD 203
Is It True What They Say about Dixie	
Creole Love Call	
Beale Street Blues	
Georgia on My Mind	
Charleston	
Carolina in the Morning	
Tennessee Waltz	
Stars Fell on Alabama	
New Orleans	
Glory Glory to Old Georgia	

Galvanized Jazz Band, GJB 20th Anniversary

Millpond Taverne, Northford, Connecticut, April 21, 1991
Fred Vigorito (c), George Masso (tb), Kenny Davern (cl), Noel Kaletsky (cl, saxes), Bill Whitcraft (p), Joel Schiavone (bj), Art Hovey (b, tu), Bob Bequillard (d), Janie Campedelli (vo)

Ain't Misbehavin'*	GJB 20
Melancholy Blues*	
Saloon*	
After You've Gone*	
One Hundred Years from Today*	
When the Saints Go Marchin' In*	
Fidgety Feet	
Basin Street Blues	
Avalon	
Summertime	
Oh Baby	
Keepin' Out of Mischief Now	
Naughty Sweetie Blues	
Lassus Trombone	

Davern not on other titles. "Melancholy Blues" *was issued on a CD entitled "A June Night, June Campedelli with the Galvanized Jazz Band," number GJB 6/28/03.*
*Janie Campedelli (vo) on these titles only

Cynthia Sayer with Kenny Davern, Forward Moves
New York, May 30, 1991
Kenny Davern (cl), Cynthia Sayer (bj, vo), Vince Giordano (bassax)

Kiss Me Sweet	Yerba Buena Jazz YBJ 401
My Honey's Lovin' Arms	
Douce Ambiance	
Blues in My Heart	
Kansas City Kitty	
Them There Eyes	
Is You Is or Is You Ain't My Baby	

Session continued on October 3, 1991.

My Inspiration
New York, September 11, 1991
Kenny Davern (cl); Howard Alden (g); Bob Haggart (b); Bobby Rosengarden (d); Lamar Alsop, Raymond Kunicki, Sanford Allen, Elliott Rosoff (v 1); Yuri Vodovoz, Byung Kook Kwak, Eric DeGiola (v 2); Manny Vardi, Alfred Brown (violas); Kermit Moore, Ann Callahan (cello)

My Inspiration	Musicmasters 01612-65077-2
It Had to Be You	
Then You've Never Been Blue	
Dogtown Blues	
Georgia on My Mind	
Brother Can You Spare a Dime	
What's New	
She's Funny That Way	
Should I	
Summertime	
I'm Confessin'	
Sweet Lorraine	
Embraceable You	

Kenny Davern (cl), Howard Alden (g), Bob Haggart (b), Bobby Rosengarden (d)

Farewell Blues
Spreadin' Knowledge Around
Travelin' All Alone

All titles on Limelight 842288-2.

Cynthia Sayer with Kenny Davern, *Forward Moves*
New York, October 3, 1991

Peter Ecklund (c), Kenny Davern (cl), Cynthia Sayer (bj, vo), Greg Cohen (b)

Moonlight on the Ganges	Yerba Buena Jazz YBJ 401
Melancholy	
Cryin' for the Carolines	
Forward Moves	
Crazy Man Blues	

Session continued from May 30, 1991.

A Jazz Christmas, *Hot Jazz for a Cool Night*
New York, June 15, 1992

Kenny Davern (cl), Howard Alden (g)

Jingle Bells	Musicmasters 01612-65089-2

Davern not on other titles on this Christmas sampler.

George Masso All Stars: *The Wonderful World of George Gershwin*
Hamburg, Germany, September 26, 1992

Randy Sandke (tp), George Masso (tb), Kenny Davern (cl), Danny Moss (ts), Eddie Higgins (p), Len Skeat (b), Jake Hanna (d)

Strike Up the Band   Nagel Heyer CD 001
But Not for Me
Summertime
Soon
Somebody Loves Me
I've Got a Crush on You
S'Wonderful

The First Three Concerts

Fascinating Rhythm   Nagel Heyer CD 008

Davern not on other titles.

Summit Reunion, 1992

Aboard the S.S. *Norway*, October 30–31, 1992
Kenny Davern (cl), Bob Wilber (cl, ss. as), Dick Hyman (p), Bucky Pizzarelli (g), Milt Hinton (b), Bobby Rosengarden (d)

Lady Be Good   Chiaroscuro CR(D) 324
Apex Blues
Love Theme from Picnic/Moonglow
I'm Sorry Dear (I Made You Cry)
Love Me or Leave Me
New Orleans
Chinatown*
Solitude*
My Blue Heaven*
My Mother's Eyes*

Flip Phillips (ts) on asterisked titles.

The All Stars at Bob Haggart's 80th Birthday Party

St. Petersburg, Florida, March 11–13, 1994
Kenny Davern (cl), Bob Wilber (cl, ss), Derek Smith (p), George Van Eps (g), Milt Hinton (b), Jackie Williams (d)

Nobody's Sweetheart Now   Arbors ARCD 19265

Randy Sandke (tp), George Masso (tb), Kenny Davern (cl), Rick Fay (ts, vo), Derek Smith (p), Bucky Pizzarelli (g), Jack Lesberg (b), Jake Hanna (d)

Blue Turning Grey over You

Ruby Braff (c), Dan Barrett (tb), Kenny Davern (cl), Rick Fay (ss, vo), Ken Peplowski (ts), Dick Hyman (p), Bucky Pizzarelli (g), Bob Haggart (b), Jake Hanna (d)

Muskrat Ramble

Kenny Davern (cl), Bob Wilber, Ken Peplowski (reeds), Ralph Sutton (p), Howard Alden (g), Bob Haggart (b), Bobby Rosengarden (d)

The Mooche

Joe Wilder (tp), George Masso (tb), Kenny Davern (cl), Jerry Jerome (ts), Derek Smith (p), George Van Eps (g), Jack Lesberg (b), Jackie Williams (d)

Bill Bailey Won't You Please Come Home

Davern not on other titles.

The Kenny Davern and Bob Wilber Summit at the March of Jazz, 1994, 1995, and 1996

St. Petersburg, Florida, March 12, 1994
Kenny Davern (cl), Bob Wilber (ss), Derek Smith (p), George Van Eps (g), Milt Hinton (b), Jackie Williams (d)

Beale Street Blues	Arbors ARDVD-3 (DVD)
Love Me or Leave Me	
Nobody's Sweetheart Now	

Kenny Davern (cl), Bob Wilber (as), Flip Phillips (ts), Dick Hyman (p), Howard Alden (g), Jack Lesberg (b), Bobby Rosengarden (d)

Cottontail

This DVD contains material from sessions on March 22, 1995, March 22, and March 24, 1996.

Kenny Davern and His Jazz Band, *East Side, West Side*
New York, June 24, 1994
Kenny Davern (cl), Dan Barrett (c, tb), Joel Helleny (tb), Bucky Pizzarelli (g), Bob Haggart (b), Tony DeNicola (d)

There'll Be Some Changes Made	Arbors ARCD 19137
Wrap Your Troubles in Dreams	
Delta Bound	
Sidewalks of New York	(*Davern out, Barrett on cornet*)
Am I Blue	
There's Yes! Yes! in Your Eyes	
Always	
I'm Sorry Dear I Made You Cry	
Please Be Kind	
Sugar	

Jazz Im Amerika Haus, Vol. 5, Summit Reunion
Hamburg, Germany, September 24, 1994
Kenny Davern (cl), Bob Wilber (cl, ss), Dave Cliff (g), Dave Green (b), Bobby Worth (d)

Lady Be Good	Nagel Heyer CD 015
Beale Street Blues	
If Dreams Come True	
Indiana	
Comes Love	
Rosetta	
Yours Is My Heart Alone	
Apex Blues	
Porter's Love Song to a Chambermaid	

"Indiana" *was issued on NHR SP5, a sampler.*

Soundtrack from the Movie Mighty Aphrodite:
New York, 1995

Randy Sandke, Joe Wilder, John Frosk (tp); Joel Helleny, George Masso (tb); Kenny Davern (cl); Frank Wess, Chuck Wilson, Sid Cooper (reeds); Dick Hyman (p); Bucky Pizzarelli (g); Vince Giordano (bassax); Ted Sommer (d); and chorus consisting of Mary Sue Berry, Al Dana, Kevin De Simone, Paul Evans, Chrissy Faith, Milt Grayson, Kenny Karen, Randy Lawrence, Jeff Lyons, Charles Macgruder, June Macgruder, Michael Mark, Arlene Martell, Helen Miles, Jenna Miles, Robert Ragini, Lenny Roberts, Annette Sanders, Vanette Thomas (vo)

When You're Smiling   Sony SK 62253 (DVD)

Davern not on other titles. Also on Miramax 7173 (videotape).

Summit Reunion, Yellow Dog Blues
Englewood Cliffs, New Jersey, March 14–15, 1995

Kenny Davern (cl), Bob Wilber (cl, ss, as), Dick Hyman (p), Bucky Pizzarelli (g), Milt Hinton (b), Bobby Rosengarden (d)

I'll See You in C-U-B-A   Chiaroscuro CR(D) 339
Darktown Strutters Ball
Frankie and Johnny
Japanese Sandman
Yellow Dog Blues
Hindustan
Rosetta
Darling Nelly Gray
Wang Wang Blues
Somebody Stole My Gal

Flip Phillips 80th Birthday Party
Deerfield Beach, Florida, March 22, 1995

Kenny Davern (cl), Bob Wilber (ss), Dick Hyman (p), Milt Hinton (b), Tony DeNicola (d)

Rosetta   Arbors ARVHS-2 (videotape)

Hindustan

Randy Sandke, Jack Sheldon, Clark Terry, Joe Wilder (tp, flug); Dan Barrett, Carl Fontana, George Masso (tb); Kenny Davern, Buddy DeFranco, Peanuts Hucko (cl); Bob Wilber (ss); Phil Woods (as); Scott Hamilton, Flip Phillips (ts); Howard Alden, Herb Ellis (g); Dick Hyman, Derek Smith (p); Milt Hinton, Sean Smith (b); Joe Ascione, Butch Miles (d)

Jumpin' at the Woodside

Davern not on other titles.

The Kenny Davern and Bob Wilber Summit at the March of Jazz, 1994, 1995, and 1996

Deerfield Beach, Florida, March 22, 1995
Kenny Davern (cl), Bob Wilber (ss), Dick Hyman (p), Bucky Pizzarelli (g), Milt Hinton (b), Tony DeNicola (d)

Rosetta	Arbors ARDVD-3 (DVD)
Yellow Dog Blues	
Hindustan	

This DVD also contains material from sessions on March 12, 1994, March 22, and March 24, 1996.

Kenny Davern and the Rhythm Men

New York, June 15, 1995
Kenny Davern (cl), John Bunch (p), Bucky Pizzarelli (g), Bob Haggart (b), Tony DeNicola (d)

That Rhythm Man	Arbors ARCD 19147
Out of Nowhere	
Three Little Words	
Say It Isn't So	
Cherry	
How Come You Do Me Like You Do	
You're Lucky to Me	
Lullaby of the Leaves	

"You're Lucky to Me" was issued on ARCD 19192, entitled "Arbors Record Sampler, Vol. 1."

Joe and John Revisited, *Spanish Eyes*

Aboard the S.S. Norway, Nov. 5, 7, 9, 1995

Kenny Davern (cl), Flip Phillips (ts), Derek Smith (p), Howard Alden (g), Milt Hinton (b), Joe Ascione (d)

Opening Remarks	Chiaroscuro CRD 344
Elsa's Dream	
Flip's Dido	
Spanish Eyes	
Please Don't Talk about Me When I'm Gone	
Royal Garden Blues	
Miki's Dream	
All of Me	
Lover Come Back to Me	(Add Phil Woods [as])

We Love You Louis, The New York Allstars
Play the Music of Louis Armstrong

Hamburg, Germany, November 18, 1995

Randy Sandke (tp), Byron Stripling (tp, vo), Joel Helleny (tb), Kenny Davern (cl), Mark Shane (p), David Ostwald (tu), Greg Cohen (b), Joe Ascione (d)

When Its Sleepy Time Down South*	Nagel Heyer CD 029
Mabel's Dream	
Sugarfoot Stomp	
Cornet Chop Suey	
Wild Man Blues	
Potato Head Blues	
Muskrat Ramble	
Savoy Blues	
Struttin' with Some Barbecue*	
Basin Street Blues	
Swing That Music	
If I Could Be with You*	
Mack the Knife/The Faithful Hussar*	

Ole Miss/Mabel's Dream
When Its Sleepy Time Down South

*Davern not on other titles. **
**Also on Nagel-Heyer 1010 entitled "Byron Stripling and Friends."*

The Kenny Davern and Bob Wilber Summit at the March of Jazz, 1994, 1995, and 1996

Clearwater Beach, Florida, March 22, 1996
Kenny Davern (cl), Bob Wilber (cl, ss), Ralph Sutton (p), Bucky Pizzarelli (g), Phil Flanigan (b), Jake Hanna (d)

I'm Sorry I Made You Cry   Arbors ARDVD-3 (DVD)
All by Myself
Somebody Stole My Gal
Budy Bolden's Blues

Kenny Davern (cl), Bob Wilber (cl, ss), Derek Smith (p), Bucky Pizzarelli (g), Jack Lesberg (d), Joe Ascione (d)

March 24, 1996

As Long As I Live
Should I
Comes Love

This DVD also contains material from sessions on March 12, 1994, and March 22, 1995.

Cynthia Sayer, Jazz at Home

New York, April 9 or 17, 1996
Peter Ecklund (c, tp), Randy Reinhart (tb), Kenny Davern (cl), Keith Ingham (p), Cynthia Sayer (bj, g, vo), Greg Cohen (b), Arnie Kinsella (d and washboard)

Bogalousa Strut   Jazzology JCD 270
With Plenty of Money and You
Seems Like Old Times

Peter Ecklund (c), Kenny Davern (cl), Cynthia Sayer (bj, g, vo), Greg Cohen (b), Arnie Kinsella (d)

The Glory of Love   (*Ecklund and Davern chorus*)
You Always Hurt the One You Love

Kenny Davern (cl), Keith Ingham (p), Cynthia Sayer (g), Greg Cohen (b), Arnie Kinsella (d)

Am I Blue

Davern not on other titles.

Kenny Davern, *Breezin' Along*
New York, June 13, 1996
Kenny Davern (cl), Bucky Pizzarelli (g), Howard Alden (g), Greg Cohen (b), Tony DeNicola (d)

Since My Best Gal Turned Me Down   Arbors ARCD 19170
Jazz Me Blues
Rose Room
Dark Eyes
Baby Won't You Please Come Home
My Honey's Lovin' Arms
I Surrender Dear
Exactly Like You
My Mama Socks Me
Breezin' Along with the Breeze

Bob Wilber and Kenny Davern, *Reunion at Arbors*
Bradenton, Florida, March 24, 1997
Bob Wilber (ss, cl), Kenny Davern (cl), Dave Frishberg (p), Bucky Pizzarelli (g), Bob Haggart (b), Ed Metz, Jr. (d)

Cherry   Arbors ARCD 19183
Sentimental Journey
Who's Sorry Now

I Want a Little Girl   (*Wilber out*)
The Sheik of Araby
Dear Sidney   (*Davern out*)
Sometimes I'm Happy
I'm Confessin'
Arbors Stomp

The Swedish Jazz Kings Featuring Kenny Davern with Martin Litton

Jarfalla, Sweden, May 3–4, 1997

Bent Persson (tp, c), Kenny Davern (cl), Tomas Ornberg (ss, as), Martin Litton (p), Ole Nyman (bj, g), Bo Juhlin (sou)

Apex Blues   Opus 3 CD 19703
Shine
I Would Do Anything for You
Nobody Else but You
Travelin' All Alone   (*Persson, Ornberg out*)
Comes Love   (*Persson, Ornberg out*)

Kenny Davern (cl), Tomas Ornberg (ss), Ole Nyman (bj), Bo Juhlin (sou)

Buddy Bolden's Blues
Please Don't Talk about Me When I'm Gone

Davern not on other titles.

Ken Peplowski, *Grenadilla*

New York, December 8 or 10, 1997

Kenny Davern, Ken Peplowski (cl); Ben Aranov (p); Howard Alden (g); Greg Cohen (b); Chuck Redd (d)

Farewell Blues   Concord CCD 4809 2

Davern not on other titles.

Ruby Braff, *Born to Play*

New York April 20, 21, 1998

Ruby Braff (c), Kenny Davern (cl), Howard Alden (g), Bucky Pizzarelli (g), Jon Wheatley (g), Michael Moore (b), Marshall Wood (b), Jim Gwin (d)

Avalon	Arbors ARCD 19203
The Doodle King	
I Want a Little Girl	
Born to Lose	

Davern not on other titles.

Bob Wilber, Kenny Davern, *Travelin'*

Sori, Italy, July 16, 1998

Bob Wilber (cl, ss), Kenny Davern (cl), Roberto Columbo (g), Aldo Zunino (b), Stefano Bagnoli (d)

There'll Be Some Changes Made	Musica Jazz MJCD 1126
Limehouse Blues	
Travelin' All Alone	
Rosetta	

San Marino, Italy, July 17, 1998

Cherry
Yellow Dog Blues
Dear Sidney
Mood Indigo

Kenny Davern, *Smiles*

New York, August 24, 1998

Kenny Davern (cl), Bucky Pizzarelli (g), Howard Alden (g), Greg Cohen (b), Tony DeNicola (d)

(Leena Was the Queen of) Palesteena	Arbors ARCD 19207
Sweet Lorraine	
Bernie's Tune	
Summertime	

That Da Da Strain
Apex Blues
I Must Have That Man
Smiles

Ruby Braff, *The Cape Codfather*
New York, March 26, 1999
Ruby Braff (c), Kenny Davern (cl), Tommy Newsom (ts), John Bunch (p), Howard Alden (g), Michael Moore (b), Kenny Washington (d)

My Melancholy Baby   Arbors ARCD 19222
Love Is Just Around the Corner
Orange
If Dreams Come True
Tain't So, Honey, Tain't So
As Time Goes By

Summit Reunion, You Ain't Heard Nothin' Yet
Atlanta, Georgia, April 25–26, 1999
Kenny Davern (cl), Bob Wilber (cl, ss), Mark Shane (p), Bucky Pizzarelli (g), Frank Tate (b), Hal Smith (d)

Baby Face   Jazzology JCD 328
Carolina in the Morning
Chinatown, My Chinatown
Rock-a-Bye Your Baby with a Dixie Melody
Swanee
After You've Gone
The Anniversary Song
When the Red Red Robin Comes Bob Bob
   Bobbin' Along
You Made Me Love You
April Showers
Rose of Washington Square
Avalon
Indiana
California, Here I Come

The Re-Discovered Louis and Bix: Randy Sandke and the New York All Stars

New York, August 31–September 1, 1999

Randy Sandke, Jon-Erik Kellso (tp); Wycliffe Gordon (tb); Kenny Davern (cl); Dick Hyman (p); James Chirillo (bj); David Ostwald (tu); Greg Cohen (b); Joe Ascione (d)

Papa What Are You Trying   Nagel Heyer CD 058
   to Do to Me, I've
   Been Doing It For Years
When You Leave Me Alone to Pine

Nicholas Payton (tp), Wycliffe Gordon (tb), Kenny Davern (cl), Dick Hyman (p), James Chirillo (bj), David Ostwald (tu), Greg Cohen (b), Joe Ascione (d)

Drop That Sack

Randy Sandke (tp), Wycliffe Gordon (tb), Kenny Davern (cl), Dick Hyman (p), James Chirillo (g), Peter Washington (b), Joe Ascione (d)

Got What It Takes/I Need Your Kind of Lovin'

Davern not on other titles.

Cynthia Sayer, *String Swing*

New York, February 8 or 9, 2000

Kenny Davern (cl), Cynthia Sayer (bj, g, vo), Jay Leonhart (b), Joe Ascione (d)

You*   Jazzology JCD 370
More Than You Know
Tumbling Tumbleweeds
Until the Real Thing Comes Along*
South of the Border*
Someday (You'll Want Me to Want You)

Davern not on other titles. Bob Mastro (v) on asterisked titles.

Variety Is the Spice of Braff

New York, July 24-25, 2000

Ruby Braff (c), Randy Reinhart (c), Joe Wilder (tp), Jon-Erik Kellso (Puje), George Masso (tb), Kenny Davern (cl), Chuck Wilson (cl, as), Jack Stuckey (as), Tommy Newsom (ts), Scott Robinson (bar), Bill Charlap (p), Bucky Pizzarelli (g), John Beal (b), Sherri Maricle (d)

Crazy Rhythm   Arbors ARCD 19194
Liza

Ruby Braff (c), George Masso (tb), Kenny Davern (cl), Chuck Wilson (cl, as), Tommy Newsom (ts), Bill Charlap (p), Bucky Pizzarelli (g), John Beal (b), Joe Ascione (d)

Jumpin' at the Woodside
I Ain't Got Nobody

Ruby Braff (c); George Masso (tb); Kenny Davern (cl); Chuck Wilson (cl, as); Tommy Newsom (ts); Bill Charlap (p); Bucky Pizzarelli, Howard Alden (g); John Beal (b); Joe Ascione (d)

Somebody Stole My Gal

Davern not on other titles.

Kenny Davern and Ken Peplowski, *The Jazz KENNection*

New York, October 12, 2000

Kenny Davern (cl), Ken Peplowski (as), John Bunch (p), Howard Alden (g), Greg Cohen (b), Tony DiNicola (d)

I'm Satisfied with My Gal   Arbors ARCD 19246
Mama's Gone, Goodbye
I'll See You in My Dreams
Georgia on My Mind   *(Peplowski out)*
Careless Love
Creole Love Call
Chicago Rhythm
All of Me
A Porter's Love Song to a Chambermaid   *(Peplowski [cl])*

Kenny Davern and Joe Temperley, *Live at the Floating Jazz Festival*

Aboard the *Queen Elizabeth 2*, October 30, November 1, 3, & 4, 2000
Kenny Davern (cl), Joe Temperley (bass cl, bar), John Bunch (p), Joe Cohn (g), Michael Moore (b), Joe Ascione (d)

Bernie's Tune	Chiaroscuro CR(D) 369
Mood Indigo	
Three Little Words	
Blue Monk	
Blue Lou	
Creole Love Call	
I Can't Believe That You're in Love with Me	
Undecided	

Daryl Sherman, *Born to Swing*

Atlanta, Georgia, April 19, 2001
Ed Polcer (c), Bob Havens (tb), Kenny Davern (cl), John Sheridan (p), James Chirillo (g), Frank Tate (b), Joe Ascione (d), Daryl Sherman (p, vo)

Breezin' Along with the Breeze	Audiophile ACD 316
Travelin' All Alone	
I'm Just a Lucky So and So	
Pretty Eyed Baby	
I Double Dare You	
Born to Swing	

Davern not on other titles.

Summit Reunion in Atlanta

Atlanta, Georgia, April 23, 2001
Kenny Davern (cl), Bob Wilber (cl, ss), Johnny Varro (p), James Chirillo (g), Frank Tate (b), Joe Ascione (d)

I Found a New Baby	Jazzology JCD 365
If I Had You	
Mama's Gone, Goodbye	
Wabash Blues	

Love Me or Leave Me
Loveless Love
Song of the Wanderer
Naughty Sweetie Blues
Someday Sweetheart
Diga Diga Doo

Dennis Gruenling and Jump Time, *That's Right*

Lafayette, New Jersey, May 27, 2001

Dennis Gruenling (harm), Kenny Davern (cl), Doug Sasfai (ts), Scott Monetti (p), Andy Riedel (g), Dave Rodriguez (b), Eric Addeo (d), Gina Fox (vo)

I Can't Believe That You're in Love with Me   Backbender BBR 703
More of What You've Got

Davern not on other titles.

The Kenny Davern Quartet at the Mill Hill Playhouse, *Celebrating 50 Years of Recording*

Trenton, New Jersey, May 19, 2003

Kenny Davern (cl), James Chirillo (g), Greg Cohen (b), Tony DeNicola (d)

I Want to Be Happy   Arbors ARCD 19296
Someday Sweetheart
It's Tight Like That
Wabash Blues
My Gal Sal
Wild Man Blues
My Blue Heaven
Lazy River
Diga Diga Doo

Lino Patruno Presents a Tribute to Bix Beiderbecke

Ascona, Italy, Summer, 2003

Tom Pletcher, Randy Reinhart, Randy Sandke, Jon-Erik Kellso (tp); David Sager (tb); Kenny Davern (cl); Bob Wilber (ss); Andy Stein (v); Keith Nichols (p); Lino Patruno, Howard Alden (g); Joel Forbes (b); Ed Metz, Jr. (d)

Royal Garden Blues   Jazzology JCD 343

Tom Pletcher (c), David Sager (tb), Kenny Davern (cl), Bob Wilber (ss), Frank Sjostrom (bassax), Andy Stein (v), Keith Nichols (p), Lino Patruno (g), Joel Forbes (b), Walter Ganda (d)

China Boy

Kenny Davern (cl), Bob Wilber (ss), Keith Nichols (p), Lino Patruno (g), Joel Forbes (b), Ed Metz, Jr. (d)

Way Down Yonder in New Orleans

Davern not on other titles.

The Statesmen of Jazz, *A Multitude of Stars*
New York, December 8–10, 2003

Buddy DeFranco, Kenny Davern (cl); Johnny Varro (p); Bucky Pizzarelli (g); Earl May (b); Louie Bellson (d)

If I Had You	Arbors, SOJCD 202
Love Me or Leave Me	(*DeFranco out*)
New Orleans/These Foolish Things/	
Poor Butterfly/Street of Dreams	

Davern not on other titles.

The Jim Cullum Jazz Band, *Chasin' the Blues*
San Antonio, Texas, May 13, 2004

Jim Cullum (c), Kenny Rupp (tb), Kenny Davern (cl), Jim Turner (p), Howard Elkins (g), Don Mopsick (b), Michael Waskiewicz (d)

Diga Diga Do   Riverwalk RWCD 9

Davern not on other titles.

Randy Reinhart at the Mill Hill Playhouse, *As Long As I Live*

Trenton, New Jersey, October 19, 2004

Randy Reimhart (c, tb), Dan Barrett (tb, c), Kenny Davern (cl), John Sheridan (p), James Chirillo (g), Frank Tate (b), Tony DeNicola (d)

At the Jazz Band Ball	Arbors ARCD 19313
As Long as I Live	
Nobody's Sweetheart	
I Guess I'll Have to Change My Plan	
Mood Indigo	
The Blues My Naughty Sweetie Gave to Me	
Yellow Dog Blues	
Clarinet Marmalade	

Davern not on other titles.

The Kenny Davern Quartet: *In Concert at the Outpost Performance Space*

Albuquerque, New Mexico, December 12–13, 2004

Kenny Davern (cl), James Chirillo (g), Greg Cohen (b), Tony DeNicola (d)

Ole Miss	Arbors ARCD 19315
Careless Love	
Somebody Stole My Gal	
Summertime	
Spreadin' Knowledge Around	
C. C. Rider	
These Foolish Things	
Royal Garden Blues	

Kenny Davern and Ken Peplowski *Dialogues*

New York, June 10, 2005

Kenny Davern (cl); Ken Peplowski (cl, ts); Howard Alden, James Chirillo (g, bj); Nicki Parrrott (b); Tony DiNicola (d)

If Dreams Come True   Arbors ARCD 19317
The Diner
I Can't Believe That You're in Love with Me
Comes Love
Should I
Sometimes I'm Happy
High Society
Crazy Rhythm
Nobody Else but Me
Muskrat Samba

"If Dreams Comes True" appears on *Arbors Records Previews 2007*, an unnumbered sampler.

Kenny Davern Trio, *Nobody Else but Kenny*
Toronto, March 19, 2006
Kenny Davern (cl), David Boeddinghaus (p), Trevor Richards (d)

Sugar   Sackville SACD 2 3069
Moonglow
Nobody Else but You
DBR Drag
You're Lucky to Me
Joshua Fit the Battle of Jericho
Tishomongo Blues
All by Myself
Pretty Baby
There Is No Greater Love
Beale Street Blues
My Honey's Lovin' Arms

Selected Bibliography

Books, Magazines, and Newspapers

Anonymous, "Top Clarinet Player Blows in for Season," *Daily News* (Durban), 15 November 1972.

Anonymous (Daily News Woman Reporter), "Fascinated by Her Husband's Jazz," *Daily News* (Durban), 26 November 1972.

Anonymous, "Jazz Trio Shares Bill with Wall Students," *Asbury Park Press*, 9 February 1982.

Balliett, Whitney, *Such Sweet Thunder, Forty-nine Pieces on Jazz*, New York, Bobbs-Merrill, 1966.

———, "Ecstasy at the Onion," reprinted in *Ecstasy at the Onion, Thirty-one Pieces on Jazz*, New York, Bobbs-Merrill, 1971.

Bennett, Dave, "Memories of Albert Burbank by Kenny Davern," *Footnote*, 19, no. 1 (October–November 1977).

Bernstein, Adam, "Jazz, Swing Clarinetist, Kenny Davern, 71," *Washington Post*, 15 December 2006.

Brown, Allan, "Davern Returns and This Time He Really Is Tops," *Mercury* (Hobart), Wednesday, 6 August 1986.

Chilton, John, *Who's Who in Jazz*, Philadelphia, Chilton Book Company, 1972.

———, *Ride Red Ride, The Life of Henry "Red" Allen*, London, Cassell, 1999.

Coller, Derek, and Bert Whyatt, "Soprano Summit Discography, Part One, 1973–May 1977," *Jazz Journal International*, 30, no. 4 (April 1982): 22–23, and "Part Two, August 1977–December 1978," *Jazz Journal International*, 30, no. 5 (May 1982): 43.

Cook, Eddie, "Bob Wilber Talks to Eddie Cook," *Jazz Journal International*, 46, no. 10 (October 1993): 14.
Davern, Kenny, "Davern's Tavern," *Off Beat Jazz*, 1, no. 1 through 2, no. 2.
Deffaa, Chip, "Ken Peplowski, Keep It Fresh, " printed in *In The Mainstream*, Metuchen, N.J., Scarecrow Press and the Institute of Jazz Studies, 1992: 289–326.
———, "Marty Grosz, Listen to the Rhythm King," printed in *Traditionalists and Revivalists in Jazz*, Metuchen, N.J., Scarecrow Press and the Institute of Jazz Studies, 1993: 126–154.
———, "Satchmo Recalled with Style," *New York Post*, 24 July 1995.
———, "Summit at Peak Form," *New York Post*, 1 August 1995.
———, "This Man Is Dog's Best Friend," *New York Post*, 30 July 1998.
Dirk, Leroy, "Kenny Davern Interviewed," transcribed and edited by Richard Cowie, *Jazz Journal International*, 33, no. 9 (September 1980): 6–7.
Elliott, Grant, *Swingin' Americans, No. 3, Kenny Davern Discography*, Zwolle, Netherlands, Gerard Bieldeman, 2001.
Feather, Leonard, *The Encyclopedia of Jazz*, New York, Horizon Press, 1960.
Feather, Leonard, and Ira Gitler, *The Biographical Encyclopedia of Jazz*, New York, Oxford University Press, 1999.
Foster, Pops, as told to Tom Stoddard, *The Autobiography of Pops Foster, New Orleans Jazzman*, Berkeley, University of California Press, 1971.
Friedwald, Will, "A Chat with the Clarinetist, a Traditionalist Who Makes Every Note Count," *New York Sun*, 29 November 2005.
Gallacher, Ken, "Musicians Born to Play Together," *The Herald* (Glasgow), 31 March 1999.
Gelly, Dave, "Dixie Dean," *Observer*, 23 June 1985.
———, "Long Breathy Sighs from the Reeds," *Observer*, 31 March 1991.
Giddins, Gary, "Kenny Davern/Colorado Jazz Party, Minding the Mainstream," *Village Voice*, 16 October 1988.
Grosz, Marty, "The View from the Stand, Plug Me Out," *Jersey Jazz*, 15, no. 9 (September 1987): 23.
Hatfield, Neville, "Woodwind Whiz," *Star* (Columbus, Ohio), 19 March 1966.
Hentoff, Nat, "Riffs," *Village Voice*, 25 October 1973.
Hevesi, Dennis, "Kenny Davern, 71, Clarinetist Who Loved Traditional Jazz," *New York Times*, 14 December 2006.
Hilbert, Robert, *Pee Wee Russell, The Life of a Jazzman*, New York, Oxford, 1993.
Hodes, Art, and Chadwick Hansen, *Hot Man, The Life of Art Hodes*, Urbana, University of Illinois Press, 1992.
Hovey, Art, "Early History of the Galvanized Jazz Band," www.GalvanizedJazzband.com.
Jackson, Andra, "New York Clarinetist Melbourne Bound," *Melbourne Sun*, 7 August 1986.
Jeske, Les, "This One Was for Satchmo," *New York Post*, 27 June 1988.
Johnson, Ron D., "Goodbye Soprano, Hello Clarinet," *Mississippi Rag*, vii, no. 4 (April 1979): 1.

Kaminsky, Max, and V. E. Hughes, *Jazz Band, My Life in Jazz*, New York, Da Capo, 1963.
Kanzler, George, "Two Men Bring a Sound, Floating, Tinkling, Back," *Star Ledger*, 17 April 1974.
Kelly, Lynne, "Jazzman at Home with the Classic," *Natal Mercury* (Durban), 20 August 1975.
Klett, Shirley, "Kenny Davern, Interview," *Cadence*, 14, no. 12 (December 1978): 18.
Kroll, Oskar, *The Clarinet*, New York, Taplinger, 1968.
Lord, Tom, *The Jazz Discography*, Version 9.0, West Vancouver, B.C., 2008.
M. M., "Exquisite Jazz from a Young Performer," *Daily News* (Durban), 17 November 1972.
Massarik, Jack, "He's Got Rhythm, But No Drummer," *Evening Standard* (London), 7 November 2000.
McRae, Barry, "Steve Lacy," *Jazz Journal International*, 57, no. 8 (August 2004): 16–17.
McDonough John, Jazz; "Very Cool, Very Hot," *Wall Street Journal*, 11 January 1993.
———, *Pee Wee Russell, Biography and Notes on the Music*, Time Life Records, TL-J17.
Meeker, David, *Jazz in the Movies*, New York, Da Capo Press Inc., 1981.
Meyer, Edward N., *Giant Strides, The Legacy of Dick Wellstood*, Lanham, Md., Scarecrow, 1999.
Meyers, Neville, "More Than a Traditionalist," *The Courier Mail* (Brisbane), 6 August 1986.
Morgenstern, Dan, "Kenny Davern, Overdue," *Down Beat*, 35, no. 10 (16 May 1968): 23.
———, "Kenny Davern, Unexpected," *Jazz* [U.S.A.] Winter 1979: 74–75.
O'Haire, Patricia, "Night Owl Reporter, Rambling Along," *Daily News*, 5 April 1972: 6.
———, "Inspired Jazz Combo," *Daily News*, 16 October 1973: 52.
Peerless, Brian, *Kenny Davern*, "My Personal Observations on His Life in Jazz," printed in the program for *Arbors Records, The Final March of Jazz Celebrates the Birthdays of Kenny Davern, 69; Skitch Henderson, 86; Stanley Kay, 80*; Clearwater Beach, FL, 19–21 March 2004.
Porter, Bob, "Before and After, Kenny Davern," *Jazz Times*, December 1997: 119–120.
Ray, Clairborne R., "Style Makers, Elsa Davern, Jewelry Maker," *New York Times*, 3 June 1990.
Roach, Willo, "800 Pay Honor to Pee Wee's Memory," *Somerset Messenger Gazette*, 19 February 1970: 33.
Rusch, Bob, "Kenny Davern" interviewed on 15 October 1987, published in part in *Cadence* 15, no. 5 (May 1989): 11, and in *Cadence* 15, no. 6 (June 1989): 9.
Rust, Brian, *Jazz Records, 1897-1942*, New Rochelle, N.Y., Arlington House, 1978.
R.S. "Sax-Man Blows a Treat for Jazz Fans," *Daily News* (Durban), 15 November 1972.

Schacter, James D., *Loose Shoes, the Story of Ralph Sutton*, Chicago, Jaynar Press, 1994.
Schafer, William J., "Learning from the Gig," *Mississippi Rag*, xxxv, no. 11 (November 2007): 33.
Schuller, Gunther, *The Swing Era, The Development of Jazz, 1930–1945*, New York, Oxford, 1999.
Skelly, Richard, "Traditional Jazzman Paints Music with His Clarinet," *Home News*, 7 April 1991: F 1.
Stewart, Zan, "Clarinet's Range Lets Davern Express His Feelings," *Star Ledger*, 16 May 2003: Ticket Section, p. 17.
———, "Kenny Davern, Craftsman on Clarinet," *Star Ledger*, 15 December 2006.
Stine, Jack, "Classic Stine," *Jersey Jazz*, 33, no. 5 (June, 2005): 4.
Sudhalter, Richard M., *Lost Chords, White Musicians and Their Contribution to Jazz, 1915–1945*, New York, Oxford, 1999.
Sylvester, Robert, "Dream Street," *News*, 27 May 1961.
———, "Dream Street," *News*, 29 July 1961.
———, "Dream Street," *Music Notes, Daily News*, 23 December 1963.
Terry, Sue, "Personal Sound, a Portrait of David Weber at 90," *Allegro*, April 2004: 14.
Traill, Sinclair, "Two of a Kind," *Jazz Journal*, 27, no. 10 (October 1974): 8–9.
———, "Editorial," *Jazz Journal International*, 33, no. 11 (November 1980): 3.
Vache, Allan, "Jersey Jazzmen of Note, Kenny Davern," *Jersey Jazz*, 1, no. 1 (February 1974): 7.
Vache, Warren Sr., *This Horn for Hire, The Life and Career of Pee Wee Erwin*, Metuchen, N.J. Scarecrow Press and the Institute of Jazz Studies, Rutgers, University, 1987.
———, "A Visit with Johnny Varro," *Mississippi Rag*, xxii, no. 9 (September 1994): 1.
———, "Tony Tells It Like It Was," *Mississippi Rag*, xxvi, no. 2 (February 1998): 25.
Vacher, Peter, "Straight Talk from Kenny Davern," *Mississippi Rag*, xxv, no. 5 (May 1997): 32.
Voce, Steve, "Kenny Davern, 'Hot' Jazz Clarinetist," *Independent*, 14 December 2006.
Waters, John, "The Man Who Said 'No' to Armstrong," *Tribune Insight (Durban)*, 26 November 1972.
Wein, George, with Nate Chinen, *Myself Among Others, a Life in Music*, New York, DaCapo, 2003.
Weintraub, Boris, "Lively Dead Music, Deadly Live Music," *Washington Star News*, 4 November 1974.
White, Al, *Jazz Party, a Photo Gallery of Great Jazz Musicians*, Little Rock, August House, 2000.
Willard, Hal, *The Wildest One, The Life of Wild Bill Davison*, Monkton, Md., Avondale Press, 1996.

Wilber, Bob, assisted by Webster, Derek, *Music Was Not Enough*, New York, MacMillan, 1987.
Wilson, John S., "Jazz Group Finds a Home in New Jersey," *New York Times*, 4 March 1973.
———, "A First for Two Clarinetists at Heavenly Jazz Session," *New York Times*, 11 December 1981.
———, "A Night to Benefit Colleagues," *New York Times*, 1 July 1981.

Liner Notes

Anonymous, Liner notes to *Ken Davern and His Salty Dogs, in The Gloryland*, Electra 201-X.
Avakian, George, Liner notes to *The Re-Discovered Louis and Bix, Lost Musical Treasures of Louis Armstrong and Bix Beiderbecke, How This CD Was Born*, Nagel Heyer CD 058.
Baron, Charlie, Liner notes to *Ralph Sutton and the Jazz Band*, Chaz Jazz CJ 113.
Byers, Lou, Liner notes to *Wild Bill Davison and Kenny Davern at the King of France Tavern, Annapolis*, Fat Cat Jazz FCJ 187, 7 November 1978.
Champlin, Charles, Liner notes to *Ruby Braff, Born to Play*, Arbors, Arbors ARCD 19203, October 1998.
Crow, Bill, Liner notes to *Milt Hinton, the Basement Tapes*, Chiaroscuro CR(D) 222.
Cullens, Zach and Dot Cullens, Liner notes to *The Legendary Lawson–Haggart Jazz Band, With a Southern Accent*, Jazzology JCD 203, Atlanta, GA, 29 February 1992.
Daniels, Chris, Liner notes to *The Climax Jazz Band with Kenny Davern*, Tormax CD032.
Feather, Leonard, Liner notes to *George Shearing in Dixieland*, Concord CCD 4388.
Firestone, Ross, Liner notes to *Bob Wilber and Kenny Davern, Reunion at Arbors*, Arbors Records, ARCD 19183, 1998.
Grosz, Marty, *The Tweetie Birds, Liner Notes to Soprano Summit, 1975 and More*, Arbors ARCD 19328, December 2007.
Hagglof, Gusta, Liner notes to *Kenny Davern, El Rado Scuffle, a Tribute to Jummie Noone*, Kenneth KS 2050, October 1980.
Jones, Wayne, Liner notes to *Soprano Summit Live at The Big Horn Jazzfest*, Jazzology J-56.
Kanzler, George, Liner notes to *I'll See You in My Dreams*, Musicmasters CIJD 60212L.
Lass, Don, Liner notes to *Soprano Summit: Chalumeau Blue*, Chiaroscuro, CR 148.
Levin, Floyd, Notes to *Kenny Davern and His Jazz Band, East Side, West Side*, Arbors ARCD 19137.
Lim, Harry, Liner notes to *The Second Time Around, The Red Norvo Combo*, Progressive PCD 7121 (1976).

McDonough, John, Liner notes to *Daryl Sherman, Born to Swing*, Audiophile ACD 316.
Morgan, Alun, Liner notes to *Flip Phillips, Kenny Davern, Bjarne Nerem, Mood Indigo*, Gemeni GMCD 59.
———, Liner notes to *Soprano Summit, Live at Thatchers*, J&M CD 501, July 1992.
Morgenstern, Dan, Liner notes to *Soprano Summit*, World Jazz WJLP-S-5.
———, Liner notes to *Kenny Davern, Breezin Along*, Arbors ARCD 19170, December 1996.
Nagel-Heyer, Hans, Liner notes to *Jazz Im Amerika Haus, Vol. 5, Summit Reunion*, Nagel-Heyer CD 015, November 1994.
———, Liner notes to *We Love You Louis, the New York Allstars Play the Music of Louis Armstrong*, Nagel-Heyer CS 029, Hamburg, November 1996.
Norris, John, Liner notes to *The Kenny Davern Trio, Nobody Else But Kenny*, Sackville SKCD 2-3069, August 2006.
O'Neal, Hank, Producer's notes to *Soprano Summit*, Chiaroscuro CR (D) 148.
———, Producer's notes to *Bob Wilber, Kenny Davern, Summit Reunion*, Chiaroscuro CR(D) 311.
Peerless, Brian, Liner notes to *One Hour Tonight*, Musicmasters CIJD 60148Y, London, March 1988.
———, Liner notes to *Kenny Davern, A Night with Eddie Condon*, Arbors ARCD 19238, December, 2000.
———, Liner notes to *The Kings of Jazz Featuring Kenny Davern*, Arbors ARCD 19267, April 2003.
———, *Kenny Davern, My Personal Observations on His Life in Jazz*, printed in the program for *Arbors Records, The Final March of Jazz Celebrates the Birthdays of Kenny Davern, 69; Skitch Henderson, 86; Stanley Kay, 80*; Clearwater Beach, FL, 19–21 March 2004.
Rudd, Roswell, Liner notes to *Blown Bone*, Emanem 4131, 2006.
Sancton, Tommy, Liner notes to *My Inspiration*, Musicmasters 61912-65077-2.
Schaap, Phil, Liner notes to *The Kenny Davern Quartet at the Mill Hill Playhouse Celebrating Fifty Years of Records*, Arbors ARCD 19296, September 2003.
Sohmer, Jack, Liner notes to *Soprano Summit, Recorded Live at the Iliana Club*, Storyville STCD 8254.
Stine, Jack, Liner notes to *Soprano Summit, 1975, and More*, Arbors ARCD 19328, October 2007.
Sudhalter, Richard M., Liner notes to *Never in a Million Years*, Challenge CHR 70019.
Traill, Sinclair, Liner notes to *Soprano Summit II*, World Jazz WJLP, S-13.
Trudinger, John, Liner notes to *Revelations*, Nif Nuf 43/012, August 2002.
Vache, Warren, Jr., Liner notes to *Introducing Alain Bouchet*, Jazzology JCD 192.
Voce, Steve, Liner notes to *Scatterbrains, the Humphrey Lyttelton Rhythmakers Featuring Kenny Davern and Al Casey*, Stomp Off, S.O.S. 1111.

Wirz, Alfred, Original liner notes to *The Wolverines of Bern at 35*, 1996 adapted upon release by Arbors Records in 1998, Arbors ARCD 19196.

Yanow, Scott, Liner notes to *The Clarinet Virtuosity of Phil Bodner, Once More with Feeling*, Arbors ARCD 19347, September 2006.

Interviews by the Author

Howard Alden, 20 December 2007, by telephone.
Red Balaban, 23 June 2007, by telephone.
Ron Brady, 28 November 2007, by telephone.
Romy Britel, 18 September 2007, by telephone.
John Bunch, 6 October 2007, Denver, CO.
James Chirillo, 6 October 2007, Denver, CO.
Evan Christopher, 13 September 2007, and 16 January 2008, by telephone.
Greg Cohen, 6 October 2007, Denver, CO.
Vincent Corrao, 16 August 2008, by telephone.
Elsa Davern, 9, 10 November 2007, Sandia Park, New Mexico; 7, 14 May, 17 July, 6, 30 August, 17 September, 5 October, 10 November 2008; 10, 12, 21 January 2009, by telephone.
Kenny Davern, Manasquan, NJ, 4 June 1993.
Mat Domber, 6 August and 20 September 2007, by telephone.
Sylvia Fogarty, 27 October and 5 November 2008, by telephone.
Dave Frishberg, 21 July 2007, by telephone.
Nat Garratano, 24 September 2008, by telephone.
Marty Grosz, 7, 17 October 1992, Metuchen, NJ, and 9, 18 July 2007, by telephone.
Dennis Gruenling, 8 October 2007, by telephone.
Tom Guralnick, 28 April 2008, by telephone.
Ed Hubble, 13 July 1995, Canajoharie, NY, and 7 August 2007, by telephone.
Nancy Hubble, 16 August 2007, by telephone.
Thomas P. Hustad, 21 December 2007, by telephone.
Dick Hyman, 6 October 2007, Denver, Colorado.
Conrad Janis, 12 July, 5 August 2007, by telephone.
Jon-Erik Kellso, 21 June 2007, by telephone.
Frank Laidlaw, 27 June, 13 July, 16 November 2007; 23 January 2009, by telephone.
Mark Lass, 5 March 2008, by telephone.
John Luckenbill, 3 September 2008, by telephone.
Jon Manasse, 21 May 2008, by telephone.
Dan Morgenstern, 8 October 1995, Newark, NJ, and 16 May and 12 June 2007, by telephone.
John Norris, 18 April 2008, by telephone.

Hank O'Neal, New York City, 13 May 1993; 11 September and 11 December 2007, by telephone; recorded recollections on audio files, forwarded to the author on 19 February 2008.
Leroy "Sam" Parkins, 2 November 1994, New York City, and 16 January 2008, by telephone.
Brian Peerless, 31 July 2007, by telephone.
Ken Peplowski, Midland, Texas, 19 May 2007.
Jimmy Pirone, 26 June 2007, by telephone.
Bucky Pizzarelli, 8 May 2007, by telephone.
Ed Polcer, Midland, Texas, 19 May 2007.
Randy Reinhart, 19 January 2008, by telephone.
Monk Rowe, 4 September 2007, by telephone.
Roswell Rudd, 22 August and 24 September 2007, by telephone.
Cynthia Sayer, 25 February 2008, by telephone
Daryl Sherman, 30 August 2008, by telephone.
Jack Six, 4 December 2007, by telephone.
Jack Stine, 29 May 2007, by telephone.
John Trentacosta, 13 April and 9 November 2008, by telephone.
Allan Vache, 23 January and 11 February 2008, by telephone.
Warren Vache, Jr., 27, 28 February 2008, by telephone.
Johnny Varro, Midland, Texas, 19, 20 May 2007.
Al Vogl, 25 June 2007, by telephone.
Mark Weber, 21 June 2008, by telephone.
George Wein, 28 January 2008, by telephone.
Claire Weintraub, 12 September 2007, by telephone
David M. Weintraub, 2 October 2007, by telephone.
Don Wolff, 30 May and 21 June 2007, by telephone.
Deborah Wuensch, 20 September 2007, by telephone.

Interviews of Kenny Davern Not Published in Written Form

Peter Clayton, interviewer, recorded and broadcast on *The Sounds of Jazz* on BBC Radio 2 on 22 April 1984.
Peter Clayton, interviewer, recorded 4–7 November 1984 and broadcast 9 November 1984 on BBC Radio 2 (Clayton interview).
Peter Clayton, interviewer, recorded and broadcast on *The Sounds of Jazz*, on BBC Radio 2 prob. 26 March 1989.
Roger Dallywater, interviewer, at the Tunbridge Wells Jazz Club on 17 April 1992, subsequently broadcast on BBC Radio Kent.
Martin Gayford, interviewer, *Meridian, The Jazz Clarinet*, recorded 14 August 1990 and broadcast on BBC World Service on 4 September 1990.
Terry Gross, interviewer, on *Fresh Air*, a program broadcast on WHYY, the National Public Radio Station in Philadelphia (date unknown).

———, on *Fresh Air*, a program broadcast on WHYY, the National Public Radio Station in Philadelphia on 18 February 1988 and rebroadcast on 15 December 2006.

David Holt, interviewer, Broadcast on Jim Cullum's NPR radio show, *Jazz from the Landing*, about 1990.

———, interviewer, Broadcast on Jim Cullum's NPR radio show, *Jazz from the Landing* on 13 May 2004: program entitled *Jazz Memories with Kenny Davern*.

Dan Morgenstern, interviewer: recorded in July 1990, the first hour broadcast on *Jazz from the Archives*, hosted by Dan Morgenstern on radio station WBGO on 11 August 1990, and the second on 26 August 1990.

Monk Rowe, Director of Hamilton College Jazz Archive, interviewer, 16 March 2001.

Mark Weber, interviewer, recorded and broadcast on KUNM, Albuquerque, New Mexico, on the following dates: 11 July 2002; 5 September 2002; 28 November 2002; 15 May 2003; 15 January 2004; 13 January 2005; 28 July 2005; 9 November 2006.

———, recorded conversation in about September 2003. Cassette entitled "Penultimate Link."

———, interviewer, recorded for the *Jazz of Enchantment* radio series in the studios of KUNM, Albuquerque, New Mexico on 17 January 2006; Paul Ingles, producer.

Dr. Michael Woods, interviewer, at Hamilton College, 23 September 1995.

Interviewer unknown, interviewed on 10 May 1984 at Hereford, UK, broadcast on *All That Jazz*, probably on BBC Radio Hereford on same date.

Interviewer unknown, interviewed on 14 November 1985 at Heresford, UK, broadcast on an unknown date on the BBC Radio Hereford.

Miscellaneous Sources

Davern, Kenny, recorded on *Jazzspeak* on *Summit Reunion*, Chiaroscuro CRD 311.

Davern, Kenny, Questionnaire Completed for Leonard Feather's Jazz Encyclopedia in about November 1954.

Grosz, Marty, recorded on Jazzspeak on *Soprano Summit*, Chiaroscuro CRD 148.

Hyman, Dick, *Remembering Kenny Davern*, Unpublished, Venice, Florida, 2008.

Plattner, Christian, *Kenny Davern and the Clarinet*, Unpublished, Altenmarkt, Austria, 15 September 2008.

———, *Kenny Davern and Wilhelm Furtwangler*, Unpublished, Altenmarkt, Austria, 9 November 2008.

Index

After Hours with Wild Bill Davison, 65
Albert system clarinet, 40
Alden, Howard, 229–31, 239, 256–57, 281, 296, 300
Alfredito's Mambo Orchestra, 15, 19n53
Allaire Hotel, 86
Allen, Henry "Red," 13–14, 25, 31, 56
All-Stars, 88–89
The All-Stars at Bob Haggart's Eightieth Birthday Party, 272
alto saxophones, 137
American Federation of Musicians, 11–12
American Jazz Hall of Fame, 291
Amiel, Joe, 201–2
Anthony, Ray, 21
Arbors Records: beginnings, 271–72; *Bob Wilber and Kenny Davern, Reunion at Arbors*, 287–88, 290n38; *Born to Play*, 294–95; *Kenny Davern and His Jazz Band, East Side, West Side*, 273–75; *Kenny Davern and the Rhythm Men*, 278–79; *Kenny Davern, Breezin' Along*, 283–84; *The Kenny Davern Quartet: In Concert at the Outpost Performance Space, Albuquerque, 2004*, 331–32; *Smiles*, 296
Armstrong, Louis: influence of, 13; Louis Armstrong's All-Stars, 76–77; *The Re-Discovered Louis and Bix, Lost Musical Treasures of Louis Armstrong and Bix Beiderbecke*, 299; *Satchmo Remembered, A Salute to Louis Armstrong*, 115, 122–23; *We Love You Louis, The New York All-Stars Play the Music of Louis Armstrong*, 282
Art Hodes, the Final Session, 249
Assunto family, 59–61
audiences, 185–86, 194–95
awards. *See* honors

Bacharach Revisited, 93–94
Baja Grille, 329–32, 338
Balahan, Leonard "Red," 87, 102n6
ballads, 173
Barbara Lea and the Legendary Lawson–Haggart Jazz Band, You're the Cats, 238–39

baritone saxophone, 8, 12–13, 15
Baron, Charlie, 160
Barrett, Dan, 330–31
The Basement Tapes, 239
bass saxophone, 12–13
Bauduc, Ray, 26
B♭ clarinet, 72–73
Beatles, 71, 80
Beiderbecke, Bix, 117, 241–42, 298–99, 319
benefits for needy musicians, 175
Biagi, Giampaolo, 229–30
big band era, 6–7
Big Pond Rag, 36–37
biography project, 327–28
Bits and Pieces, 87
Bix: An Interpretation of a Legend, 241–42
Blown Bone, 128–29
Blues Is a Woman, 168
Blue Three, 155–56, 172–74, 177, 180–82, 202–3
The Blue Three Live at Hanrattys, 172–74
Bob Wilber and Kenny Davern, Reunion at Arbors, 287–88, 290n38
Bob Wilber—Kenny Davern, Travelin', 295
Boehm system clarinets, 40, 279
book collections, 189–90, 191–92
Born to Play, 294–95
Born to Swing, 308
Bouchet, Alain, 247
Braff, Rudy, 44, 294–95, 297, 303–4, 318
Brownell, Tom and Elizabeth, 203
Buck Clayton, 31
Bunch, John, 279, 299–300
Burbank, Albert, 33–34
bus driver, 81
Buttafuoco, Joe, 253
Butterfield, Billy, 29, 154

Can O' Worms, 79–80, 86, 248
The Cape Codfather, 297
Cary, Dick, 39
Central Plaza, 31–32
Chalumeau Blue, 129
Chamberlain, Cathy, 130, 132, 134
The Charleston City All-Stars Go Dixieland, 55
Chicago Jazz Summit, 217
Chirillo, James, 73, 252, 264, 300–301, 323
Christopher, Evan, 301–2
Church of the Heavenly Rest, 154–55
Cinderella Club, 28–29
Clara Ward Singers, 60
clarinets: Albert system, 40; B♭, 72–73; Boehm system, 40, 279; challenges, 147–48; emotions when playing, 186–89; knowledge of, 132–33; learning to play, 7–8, 11–12; Van Doren mouthpieces, 133, 142n16
classical music, 6
Clayton, Buck, 24, 32
Cliff, Dave, 133
The Climax Jazz Band with Kenny Davern, 212
club owners' relationships with KD, 188–89
C-melody saxophones, 137
Cohen, Greg, 264–65, 296, 323
Coleman, Ornette, 42
college songs, 30
columns in *Off Beat Jazz*, 179
Condon, Eddie: All-Stars, 88–89; club of, 27, 50–51, 56; death and memorial service, 101–2; Eddie Condon Memorial Band, 212–13; *Jazz at the New School*, 91; KD on, 8–9
Condon Gang First Anniversary Reunion, 216–17
Conreid, Hans, 37

Corrao, Vinnie, 179, 263
Crazy Rhythm, 136–37
cruise ship appearances, 209–10, 228
Crystal, Jack, 31, 334
Cullum, Jim, 329
Cutshall, Cutty, 51
Cynthia Sayer, Jazz at Home, 282–83
Cynthia Sayer, String Swing, 302
Cynthia Sayer with Kenny Davern, Forward Moves, 255

Date Books, 103n10
Davern, Elsa: graduation, 166; Hungarian family festivities, 176; jewelry business, 170, 219–20, 248; on KD's career, 135; KD's courtship of, 77–78; on KD's health, 200; on KD's music store idea, 122; on life with KD, 169–70; marrying KD, 87–88; New Mexico move, 313–15; traveling with KD, 96–97, 170, 228
Davern–Hamilton Quintet, 250
Davern, John Joseph "Buster," 2, 10–11, 18n41
Davern, John Joseph "John Joseph," 2
Davern, Josephine. *See* Roth, Josephine
Davern, Kenny: adventurous choices, 323–24; birthday celebration, 327–28; on changes in music business, 321–22, 335; death of, 339; drinking, 50, 233–34; early life, 4–8; emotional anguish of, 44; enthusiasm for music, 43, 192–94; first recorded solos, 26; as grandfather, 313; health issues, 199–200, 338–39; high school years, 8–16; high standards, 53–54, 188–89, 274; identifiable sound of, 1–2, 72–75, 274; influences, 75; insecurities, 291, 293, 303; interests, non-musical, 189–90, 190–91, 317; legacy, 339–40; marriage to Elsa. *See* Davern, Elsa; marriage to Sylvia, 58–60, 65, 69, 88; name change, 10; name misspelling, 30; New Mexico move, 313–15, 320, 322–24; personality, 33, 53–55, 58–59, 147, 169, 188–89, 192–96, 292–93; relationship with father's family, 10–11; reluctance to play new songs, 306; as step-parent, 97–100; teaching role, 262–64; young adult years, 32–33. *See also* honors
Davern, Stanley, 10–11
Davern, Sylvia, 58–60, 65
Davison, Wild Bill: *After Hours with Wild Bill Davison*, 64–65; appearing with KD, 61–62, 81, 153; *Wild Bill Davison and Kenny Davern at the King of France Tavern*, 153
A Day in New Orleans, A Night in Martinique, 234
DeFranco, Buddy, 320
DeMichael, Don, 178
DeNicola, Tony, 251–52, 253, 254, 296, 337–38
Dennis Gruenling, Jump Time, That's Right, 309
DeVito, Harry, 29–30
Dialogues, 332–33
Dick Cary and His Dixieland Doodlers, 39–40
Dick Wellstood and His Famous Orchestra, 156–57
Dick Wellstood and His Famous Orchestra Featuring Kenny Davern, 105–6
Dick Wellstood and His Hot Potatoes, Featuring Kenny Davern, 92
Di Minno, Danny, 3
Dippermouth Blues, 36
Disney World appearance, 176
The Dixie Rebels Starring "Big Jeb Dooley," True Dixieland Sound, 40
The Dixie Rebels Strike Back with True Dixieland Sound, 38–39

Domber, Mat, 54, 271–72, 274, 294–95, 304, 330–31
Drootin, Buzzy, 51
Dukes of Dixieland, 59–61

early recordings of KD, 14
E♭ clarinet, 60–61
Eddie Condon Memorial Band, 212–13
Eldridge, Roy, 24
Elgart brothers, 21
emotions and clarinet, 186–89
Empire City Six, 30, 50
Empire City Six Plays Dixie, 30
Empire City Six Salutes the Colleges, 30
Empire State Six. *See* Empire City Six
Erwin, Pee Wee: *The Charleston City All-Stars Go Dixieland*, 55; *The Dixie Rebels Strike Back with True Dixieland Sound*, 38–39; early appearances with, 29; friendship with, 33; *Hans Conreid Narrates Peter Meets the Wolf in Dixieland*, 37; in Kings of Jazz, 115–16; *Pee Wee Erwin and the Dixie Strutters, Down by the Riverside*, 37–38; *Pee Wee Erwin – Memorial, A Giant among Giants*, 175; *Pee Wee Erwin's Dixieland Eight, Oh Play That Thing*, 36–37, 44; playing at Nick's, 35, 38, 50
Evans, Tony, 14

Failla, Phil, 29
Fay, Rick, 271
Ferryboat band, 70–72, 74–75, 78–79
The Ferryboat Dixieland Band, 71–72
Fields, Shep, 15
Filius, Milton, Jr., 280–81
financial issues for musicians, 285
First Annual Pee Wee Russell Memorial Concert, 85–86
Flanagan, Ralph, 21–24, 25
Flanigan, Phil, 229
foster homes, 5, 17n21

Free Jazz, 42–43, 128, 149–51
The Free Swinging Trio in the Jazz Tradition, 154
Frishberg, Dave: on KD, 117, 193, 263; in Kenny Davern and the Washington Squares, 51–53; later career, 287; recording project not pursued, 136
Furtwangler, Wilhelm, 190–91

Galvanized Jazz Band, 254
Garratano, Nat, 202
Gaslight Club, 91
Gene Shannon's Dixieland All-Stars, 15
George Schoette, 8
George Shearing in Dixieland, 237–38
Gershwin, George, 260–61
Gibson, Dick, 94–96, 104n33
The Gig, 208–9
Gleason, Jackie, 28, 37, 63
Goodall, Bill, 24
Goodman, Benny, 6–7, 214, 239–41
Goodman, Lee, 85
gospel genre, 37–38, 60–61
Grauso, Bobby, 8–10
Greene, Martin E., 258–59, 279
Greenleaf, Fred, 26
Grenadilla, 293
Grosz, Marty: on KD's attitude toward song selection, 306; on pranks, 122; in Soprano Summit, 110–11, 112, 116, 120–21; strengths of, 147; on Swing 39, 119
Gruenling, Dennis, 309
gun fascination, 317

Haggart, Bob, 137–38, 256–57, 272. *See also* Lawson-Haggart Jazz Band
half-bills, 222, 225n69
Hamilton College, 302–3
Hamilton, Scott, 250
Hanratty's, 172–74

Hans Conreid Narrates Peter Meets the Wolf in Dixieland, 37
Harlem River rafting, 52
Henderson, Fletcher, 13
Hickey, Vince, 34
Hilton, Milt, 239
Hodes, Art, 157–59, 232–33, 249
Holaday, Bill, 253
honors: American Jazz Hall of Fame, 291; Hamilton College Doctor of Music degree, 302–3; high school award, 16; *Jazz Journal International* awards, 180, 216; KD memorial, 327–28; Music Trades Association Records Awards, 207; NJJS Outstanding Musician award, 172; Svenska Grammophon Priset, 175
Hot Three, 157–59, 170–71, 178
Hubble, Ed, 62, 70, 76, 79, 80
Hungarian family festivities, 176
Husing, Ted, 7
The Hustler, 49–50
Hyman, Arnold, 34–35
Hyman, Dick, 43–44, 107–8, 108, 277

ICP (Instant Composers Pool), 335–36
identifiable sound of KD, 1–2, 72–75, 274
I Found a New Baby, 23
I'll See You in My Dreams, 230–31
inheritance, 258–59
Instant Composers Pool (ICP), 335–36
In the Gloryland, 35

Janis, Conrad, 31, 33, 61, 62
Jazz at the New School, 91–92
jazz clubs, closing of, 166–67
jazz festivals: aging of, 284; *Live at the Floating Jazz Festival, Kenny Davern and Joe Temperley*, 306–7; Manassas Jazz Festival, 106–7, 160, 218; Newport Jazz Festival, 40, 131
Jazz Im Amerika Haus, 275–76

Jazz Journal International awards, 180, 216
jazz parties, importance of, 284–85
jazz tours, pattern of, 220
Jersey Jazz at Midnight, 123
The Jersey Ramblers. See Can O'Worms
jobs, odd, 32, 81
John and Joe, 138–39
John and Joe Revisited, Spanish Eyes, 281
Johnson, Dick, 286–87
Jolson, Al, 297–98
Josie, Marva, 101

Kaminsky, Maxie, 31
Ken Davern and His Salty Dogs, 35
Kennedy, Wilbur, 3–4
Kenny Davern and His Clamdiggers, 86
Kenny Davern and His Famous Orchestra, 156
Kenny Davern and His Jazz Band, East Side, West Side, 273–75
Kenny Davern and His Washington Squares, 50–53
Kenny Davern and The Brian Lemon Trio, The Very Thought of You, 207
Kenny Davern and the Rhythm Men, 278–79
Kenny Davern, A Night with Eddie Condon, 88–89
Kenny Davern, Breezin' Along, 283–84
Kenny Davern, El Rado Scuffle, a Tribute to Jimmie Noone, 167–68
Kenny Davern, Ken Peplowski, The Jazz KENNection, 304–6
Kenny Davern Quartet, 301–2, 318–19, 331–32
The Kenny Davern Quartet at the Mill Hill Playhouse, Celebrating Fifty Years of Recording, 318–19
The Kenny Davern Quartet: In Concert at the Outpost Performance Space, Albuquerque, 2004, 331–32
Kenny Davern's Dixiecats, 14

Kenny Davern, The Hot Three, 157–59
Kenny Davern Trio, 81, 114, 215, 232–33, 336–37
The Kenny Davern Trio Featuring Art Hodes, The Last Reunion, 232–33
The Kenny Davern Trio, Nobody Else but Kenny, 336–37
King Porter Stomp, 26
Kings of Jazz, 115–16
The Kings of Jazz Featuring Kenny Davern in Concert, 1974, 116
Knight, Steve, 34–35
Kratka, Irving, 93–94
Kwas, Tone, 14

Lackritz, Steve. See Lacy, Steve
Lacy, Steve, 24–25, 42, 150
Laidlaw, Frank, 34–35, 74
Lanza, Joe, 25
Lass, Ernest Donald "Don," 77
Latin music, 15
Lawson–Haggart Jazz Band, 238–39, 254
Lawson, Yank, 137–38, 238–39, 254
Lea, Barbara, 238–39
leadership role, 152–53
The Legendary Lawson–Haggart Jazz Band, Jazz at Its Best, 238
The Legendary Lawson–Haggart Jazz Band, With a Southern Accent, 254
Let's Dance radio program, 11
Lewis, George, 33–34
library of recordings, 190–92
Lino Patruno Presents a Tribute to Bix Beiderbecke, 319
Little Jazz Duets, 86–87
Little Jazz Duets in the Round, 86–87
Live and Swinging, Kenny Davern and John Petters Swing Band, 214–15
Live at the Floating Jazz Festival, Kenny Davern and Joe Temperley, 306–7
Live Hot Jazz, 202–3
Long, Johnny, 24, 29
Lopez, Juanucho, 15

Louisiana Rhythm Kings, 56
Lovett, Robert, 14
Lunsford, Carl, 34–35
Lyttelton, Humphrey, 210–11, 215–16

Malone, Kass, 26
Manassas Jazz Festival, 106–7, 160, 218
Manhattan jazz clubs, 9
Manhattan Trio, 64–65
Marathon 33, 61
The March of Jazz, 272–73
Marterie, Ralph, 21
Mauro, George, 62–63, 70–72, 75–76, 79
McCree, Johnson "Fat Cat," 106–7, 153
McGarity, Lou, 38, 55
McManus, Al, 79
Meet Me Where They Play the Blues, 26
Memphis Five, 40–41
Metcalf, Louis, 31–32
microphone, performing without, 74
Mighty Aphrodite soundtrack, 276
Milenberg Joys, 26
Mills Blue Rhythm Band, 13
Mis'ry and the Blues, 26
Mood Indigo, 227
Moore, Freddie, 177–78
Morgenstern, Dan, 248–49
Morton, Jelly Roll, 107–8, 116, 118
movies: *The Gig*, 208–9; *The Hustler*, 49–50; *Mighty Aphrodite*, 276; *The Next Man*, 127
MPTF (Music Performance Trust Fund), 179
Music Minus One label, 93–94
Music Performance Trust Fund (MPTF), 179
Music Trades Association Records Awards, 207

Nagel-Heyer, Hans, 260–61
Napoleon, Phil: influence on Empire City Six, 29–30; leading Original Memphis Five, 27–28; at Napoleon's

Retreat, 63–64; recording with, 39, 40–42; relationship with KD, 33
Nardossa, John, 14
New Jersey Jazz Society (NJJS), 118, 123, 172
New Orleans-style bands, 34–35, 119
Newport Jazz Festival, 40
New York Jazz Repertory Company (NYJO), 114–15, 116
The Next Man, 127
Nick's, 30, 35–36, 44, 50
"Nicksieland," 27, 33
A Night at the Ferryboat, 71–72
Noone, Jimmie, 167–68
Norvo, Red, 119–20
Novo, Tony, 15

O'Brien, Larry, 14, 15
O'Connell, Elizabet "Bessie," 2
O'Connor's Steak House, 121–22
odd jobs, 32, 81
Off Beat Jazz columns, 179
Oh Sister, Ain't That Hot, 154
O'Neal, Hank, 53–54, 91–92
One Hour Tonight, 230–31
One Mo' Time, 168–69
Original Memphis Five, 27
Ornberg, Tomas, 157, 174–75, 288
Outpost Performance Space, 317
Over the Waves, 36

Page, Hot Lips, 25
Parkins, Leroy "Sam," 28–29, 33, 230
Pastor, Tony, 21
Patruno, Lino, 157, 319
pay scales, 285
Peerless, Brian, 194, 205–7, 327–28
Pee Wee Erwin and the Dixie Strutters, Down by the Riverside, 37–38
Pee Wee Erwin – Memorial, A Giant among Giants, 175
Pee Wee Erwin's Dixieland Eight, Oh Play That Thing, 36–37, 44

Peplowski, Ken: *Dialogues*, 332–33; *Grenadilla*, 293; on KD's insecurities, 293; on KD's personality, 193–94; on KD's sound, 2, 74, 75; *Kenny Davern, Ken Peplowski, The Jazz KENNection*, 304–6
Petters, John, 214–15
Phillips, Flip, 138–39, 281
Phil Napoleon in the Land of Dixie, 40–41
Phyfe, Eddie, 24
Pizzarelli, Bucky, 279, 296
Plattner, Christian, 75
"play along" disks, 86–87
Playing for Kicks, The Kenny Davern Trio, 215
Powell, Mel, 235–36
President, playing for, 165
Prima, Louis, 56
Probeck, George, 3–4

Quinichette, Paul, 25

Rag 'N Roll Revue, 130, 134
Ralph Flanagan Orchestra, 21–24, 25
Ralph Sutton and Kenny Davern, Trio, Volumes 1 and 2, 161
Randy Reinhart at the Mill Hill Playhouse, As Long As I Live, 330–31
Rappolo, Leon, 14
Rayburn, Boyd, 21
Record Hunter, 32
The Re-Discovered Louis and Bix, Lost Musical Treasures of Louis Armstrong and Bix Beiderbecke, 299
Red Onion Jazz Band, 34
Reed Summit, 287
Reinhart, Randy, 263, 330–31
Revelations, 234–35
Rhythmakers, 56
Riverboat Shuffle, 26
Rodgers, Pete, 29
Rollini, Adrian, 12–13
Romo, Jimmy, 15, 24

Rongetti, Grace, 30, 52
Rongetti, Nick, 27–28. *See also* Nick's
Rooth, Fritz Alfred. *See* Roth, Fred
Rosengarden, Bobby, 111, 155. *See also* Blue Three
Roth, Charlotte "Lottie," 2–3, 4–6
Roth, Fred, 2–3, 5–6
Roth, Josephine, 3–7, 10–11, 58, 273
Roy Eldridge, 31
Rudd, Roswell, 42–43, 128–29
Russell, Charles Ellsworth. *See* Russell, Pee Wee
Russell, Jack, 53
Russell, Luis, 13–14
Russell, Mary, 57–58, 58–59, 80
Russell, Pee Wee, 7, 33, 55–59, 80–81, 85–86
Rustic Lodge, 32

Satchmo Remembered, A Salute to Louis Armstrong, 115, 122–23
saxophones: alto, 137; baritone, 8, 12–13, 15; bass, 12–13; C-melody, 137; soprano, 75–76, 94, 147–49
Sayer, Cynthia, 255, 263–64, 282–83, 302
Scalza, Anthony, 3–4
Scarsdale High Gang, 70
Schoebel, Elmer, 24
Schroeder, Gene, 38
Schwartz, Dick, 24, 52
The Second Time Around, The Red Norvo Combo, 120
Shanghai Jazz, 286
Shannon, Gene, 15
Shaw, Artie, 7
Shearing, George, 237–38
Sherman, Daryl, 308
sight reading, 155, 237
Six, Jack, 51, 70–71, 79–80, 194, 262
Smiles, 296
soloist work, 152–53

Some Rags, Some Stomps, and a Little Blues, Ferdinand Jelly Roll Morton, 107–8
Song of Songs, 154
soprano saxophone, 75–76, 94, 147–49
Soprano Summit: breaking up, 136–37, 145–47, 154; forming, 96, 108, 110–11, 113; personalities of members, 145; reuniting, 219; touring, 116–18, 120–21, 130; uniqueness of, 111–13
Soprano Summit recordings: *Chalumeu Blue*, 129; at Condon's, 127; *Soprano Summit*, 108–9; *Soprano Summit, 1975, and More*, 156; *Soprano Summit, Concord '77*, 136; *Soprano Summit II*, 109–10, 114, 140–41, 171; *Soprano Summit III*, 119; *Soprano Summit, In Concert*, 131–32; *Soprano Summit, Live at Thatchers*, 133–34; *Soprano Summit, Live in England*, 133–34; *Soprano Summit: The Meridian*, 140
Spair, Tony, 29
Spargo, Tony (Sbabaro), 29, 35
speakeasies, 27
Spring Lake Lodge, 100–102
Statesmen of Jazz, 320
Statesmen of Jazz, A Multitude of Stars, 320
Stein, Lou, 159–60
Stellio, Alexandre, 234
stereophonic sound, 39
Stine, Jack, 121–22, 172
St. Pierre Six, 234
Stretchin' Out, 202–3
Studio One television program, 11
Stuyvesant Casino, 31–32
style, transitioning, 55
Sudhalter, Dick, 203–4
Summit Reunion: appearances, 282; *Bob Wilber and Kenny Davern, Reunion at Arbors*, 287–88, 290n38; first

recording, 245–47; *Jazz Im Amerika Haus, Vol. 5, Summit Reunion,* 275–76; *Summit Reunion, 1992,* 261–62; *Summit Reunion in Atlanta,* 308–9; *Summit Reunion, Yellow Dog Blues,* 277–78; *You Ain't Heard Nothin' Yet! Summit Reunion Plays Some Al Jolson Songs,* 297–98
Sutton, Dick, 14
Sutton, Ralph, 160–61, 171, 234–35, 310
Svenska Grammophon Priset, 175
The Swedish Jazz Kings Featuring Kenny Davern, Comes Love, 288
Swing 39, 119
Swinging At The Elks'—Billy Butterfield and His World Class Jazz Band, 154

teaching role, 262–64
Teagarden, Jack, 25–27
Teagarden, Norma, 26
television, 11, 37, 171
Temperley, Joe, 306–7
Tenderloin in Dixieland, 40, 41–42
That's a Plenty, 23
This Is Marva Josie, 101
This Old Gang of Mine, 215–16
Thomas, Joe, 31
Thompson, Bob, 34–35
torn dollar bills, 222, 225n69
touring, need for, 240–41
travelling, hardships of, 122, 174
Trentacosta, John, 329–30

Unexpected, 149–51

Vache, Allan, 54, 73, 263
Vache, Warren, Jr.: on Disney World appearance, 176; on dixieland recording, 237; in film, 208–9; on KD's control of programs, 153; on KD's enthusiam for music, 192; on KD's personality, 196; on KD's unique sound, 2; recordings, 134–35
Van Doren mouthpiece for clarinet, 133, 142n16
Variety Is the Spice of Braff, 303–4
Varro, Johnny, 28, 29–30, 33, 35, 38, 42, 47n73, 63
Vitale, Ray, 14, 15
vocal recordings, 72

Weber, David, 89–90
Weber, Mark, 315–17, 320
We Gotta Shout—The Dukes of Dixieland, 60–61
Weil, Bob "Bumble Bee Bob," 329–30
Wein, George, 114, 122–23, 131, 217
Weintraub, Celia, 10
Wellstood, Dick: Can O' Worms, 79–80, 86, 248; death of, 221–22, 229; *Dick Wellstood and His Famous Orchestra,* 156–57; *Dick Wellstood and His Famous Orchestra Featuring Kenny Davern,* 105–6; *Dick Wellstood and His Hot Potatoes, Featuring Kenny Davern,* 92; early life, 69–70; Ferryboat band, 70–72; *The Free Swinging Trio in the Jazz Tradition,* 154; *Never in a Million Years,* 204; not invited to be Soprano Summit member, 108, 124n9; relationship with KD, 79; unissued recording, 14. *See also* Blue Three
We Love You Louis, The New York All-Stars Play the Music of Louis Armstrong, 282
Wettling, George, 64–65
Wilber, Bob: background, 95–96; *Bob Wilber—Kenny Davern, Travelin',* 295; conflicts with, 261–62; on KD's saxophone playing, 148–49; relationship with KD, 113, 277–78; retirement misunderstanding, 280;

touring with, 256, 295; Wilber's Wildcats, 70. *See also* Soprano Summit; Summit Reunion
Wilber's Wildcats, 70
Wild Bill Davison and Kenny Davern at the King of France Tavern, 153
Wiley, Lee, 101–2
Williams, Martin, 132
Windhurst, Johnny, 50

Wolff, Don, 195–96, 328
World's Greatest Jazz Band (WGJB), 137–38, 166, 238, 253–54
writing projects, 179, 320

You Ain't Heard Nothin' Yet! Summit Reunion Plays Some Al Jolson Songs, 297–98
Your Father's Moustache, 87, 102n6

About the Author

Edward N. Meyer is the author of the critically acclaimed biography, *Giant Strides, the Legacy of Dick Wellstood* (Lanham, Md., Scarecrow, 1999). He lives in Austin, Texas, with his wife Sharon, where he teaches a course in the history of jazz at St. Edwards University. Ed has donated his collections of long-playing records, magazines, and reference materials to St. Edwards to establish the Edward N. Meyer Jazz Archive.

For more than thirty years, prior to moving to Austin in 1998, Ed practiced commercial trial law in New York City. Presently, he and Sharon spend their spare time traveling around the country to see their four children, eight grandchildren, and one granddog.

Lightning Source UK Ltd.
Milton Keynes UK
UKOW05n0912291116

288791UK00014B/301/P